Joint Commitment

Joint Commitment

How We Make the Social World

MARGARET GILBERT

OXFORD
UNIVERSITY PRESS

OXFORD
UNIVERSITY PRESS

Oxford University Press is a department of the University of Oxford.
It furthers the University's objective of excellence in research, scholarship,
and education by publishing worldwide.

Oxford   New York
Auckland   Cape Town   Dar es Salaam   Hong Kong   Karachi
Kuala Lumpur   Madrid   Melbourne   Mexico City   Nairobi
New Delhi   Shanghai   Taipei   Toronto

With offices in
Argentina   Austria   Brazil   Chile   Czech Republic   France   Greece
Guatemala   Hungary   Italy   Japan   Poland   Portugal   Singapore
South Korea   Switzerland   Thailand   Turkey   Ukraine   Vietnam

Oxford is a registered trademark of Oxford University Press
in the UK and certain other countries.

Published in the United States of America by
Oxford University Press
198 Madison Avenue, New York, NY 10016

Library of Congress Cataloging-in-Publication Data
Gilbert, Margaret.
Joint commitment : how we make the social world / Margaret Gilbert.
pages cm
Includes bibliographical references and index.
ISBN 978-0-19-997014-8 (alk. paper)
1. Social sciences—Philosophy. 2. Sociology—Philosophy.   I. Title.
H61.15.G55 2013
300.1—dc23
2013007587

1 3 5 7 9 8 6 4 2
Printed in the United States of America
on acid-free paper

For Martin

CONTENTS

Preface   ix
Acknowledgements   xi
Sources   xiii
Introduction   1

PART ONE   SHARED AGENCY

1. Acting Together   23

2. Considerations on Joint Commitment   37

3. Who's to Blame?   58

4. Rationality in Collective Action   81

5. Two Approaches to Shared Intention   94

PART TWO   COLLECTIVE ATTITUDES

6. Belief and Acceptance as Features of Groups   131

7. Collective Epistemology   163

8. Shared Values, Social Unity, and Liberty   181

9. Social Convention Revisited   207

10. Collective Guilt and Collective Guilt Feelings   229

PART THREE   MUTUAL RECOGNITION, PROMISES, AND LOVE

11. Fusion: Sketch of a "Contractual" Model   259

12. Scanlon on Promissory Obligation: The Problem of Promisees'
       Rights   271

13. Three Dogmas About Promising   296

14. Mutual Recognition and Some Related Phenomena   324

PART FOUR   POLITICAL LIFE

15. A Real Unity of Them All   341

16. *Pro Patria*: An Essay on Patriotism   357

17. De-Moralizing Political Obligation   389

18. Commands and Their Practical Import   409

*Bibliography of the Author's Publications in the Philosophy
  of Social Phenomena*   427
Subject Index   433
Name Index   447

PREFACE

This book comprises eighteen essays that argue for the importance of *joint commitment* in the lives of human beings. The essays argue this individually and, even more forcefully, collectively. Together they address a wide range of topics: from the "mutual recognition" of two people to large-scale features of whole societies, from marital love to the unity of the European union. If we need to invoke joint commitment in order fully to understand all these things, it must indeed be central to human life in both public and private contexts.

The central role of joint commitment has been an implication of much of my work over the past several decades, including two monographs—*On Social Facts* (1989) and *A Theory of Political Obligation* (2006)—and three previous essay collections—*Living Together* (1996), *Sociality and Responsibility* (2000), and (in French) *Marcher Ensemble* (2003). My current projects continue in this vein.

The essays in this book were written since 2000, with one exception. Some of them amplify or refine previous work, emphasize a thread in a broader discussion, or approach a topic from a different angle; others bring joint commitment to bear on new lines of inquiry.

They were relatively self-contained when they were written, and they retain this feature here. At the same time, many find amplification in one or more of the other essays in the collection. Given the opportunity I have corrected typological errors in the previously published essays. I have also made a few minor changes in some of them to clarify my meaning. Each chapter retains its original citation style and is bibliographically complete.

It has not always been easy to select one essay over another for this collection. At the end there is a comprehensive bibliography of my publications relating in one way or another to joint commitment, including those that are currently in press.

ACKNOWLEDGMENTS

Each chapter thanks those particular people whose comments on a draft or on related material were helpful. I shall not attempt to make up a cumulative list here, but will repeat those thanks.

Special thanks in relation to this book go to Peter Ohlin of Oxford University Press, whose idea it was, and to Maura Priest and Philip Walsh for assistance in relation to its preparation. Thanks also to Lucy Randall, Emily Sacharin, Stacey Victor, and their colleagues for help in the production process, and to Aaron James and Nicholas Jolley for comments and advice.

I am also happy to thank for their support the two philosophy departments of which I have been a member while writing the essays in this book. The Department of Philosophy at University of Connecticut, Storrs, was my academic home from 1983 until 2006. In 2006 I took up the Melden Chair in Moral Philosophy in the Department of Philosophy at the University of California, Irvine, where the present work was completed. I am grateful, in addition, for the support I have received from the University of Connecticut Humanities Institute, where I was an inaugural Fellow in 2002–3, to the NEH, for a Fellowship for Research for fall 2003, and to the Swedish Collegium for Advanced Study in the Social Sciences, in Uppsala, where I spent a congenial six months of research and writing as a resident Fellow in the spring of 2004.

SOURCES

The following articles are reprinted with permission.

"Acting Together," *Social Facts and Collective Intentionality*, ed. Georg Meggle, *German Library of Sciences*, Frankfurt: Hansel-Hohenhausen, 2002, pp. 53–72.

"Considerations on Joint Commitment: Responses to Various Comments," in *Social Facts and Collective Intentionality*, ed. Georg Meggle, *German Library of Sciences*, Frankfurt: Hansel-Hohenhausen, 2002, pp. 73–102.

"Who's to Blame? Collective Moral Responsibility and Its Implications for Group Members," in *Midwest Studies in Philosophy*, ed. Peter French, vol. 30, 2006, pp. 94–114

"Rationality in Collective Action," *Philosophy of the Social Sciences*, vol. 36, no. 1, 2006, pp. 3–17.

"Two Approaches to Shared Intention: An Essay in the Philosophy of Social Phenomena," *Analyse u. Kritik*, vol. 30, 2009, pp. 483–514.

"Belief and Acceptance as Features of Groups," *Protosociology*, vol. 16, 2002, pp. 35–69 (online journal: www.protosociology.de).

"Collective Epistemology," *Episteme* vol. 1, 2004, pp. 95–107.

"Shared Values, Social Unity and Liberty," *Public Affairs Quarterly*, vol. 19, 2005, pp. 25–49.

"Social Convention Revisited," *Topoi*, vol. 27, 2008, pp. 5–16.

"Collective Guilt and Collective Guilt Feelings," *Journal of Ethics*, vol. 6, 2002, pp. 115–130. © 2002 Kluwer Academic Publishers.

"'Fusion': sketch of a contractual model," in *Perspectives on the Family*, eds. R.C. L. Moffat, J. Grcic, and M. Bayles, Lewiston: Edwin Mellen Press, 1990, pp. 65–78.

"Scanlon on Promissory Obligation: the Problem of Promisees' Rights," *Journal of Philosophy*, 2004, vol. 101, pp. 83–109.

"Three Dogmas about Promising," in *Understanding Promises and Agreements* ed. H. Sheinman, New York: Oxford University Press, 2011, pp. 80–108.

"Mutual Recognition and Some Related Phenomena," in *Recognition and Social Ontology* eds. H. Ikaheimo and A. Laitinen, Leiden: Brill, 2011, pp. 270–286.

"A Real Unity of them All?" *The Monist*, vol. 92, 2009, pp. 268–285.

"*Pro Patria*: An Essay on Patriotism," *Journal of Ethics*, special issue ed. I. Primoratz, vol. 13, 2009, pp. 319–346.

Introduction

Philosophers often appeal to *Ockham's razor*: "entities are not to be multiplied beyond necessity." Many would also say the same about ideas: if you are trying to explain something, do so in familiar terms, stick with the tried and true. Only when the familiar fails us should we invoke something new.

The new idea of one age may bear some resemblance to an idea that held sway at some point in the past. Still, if it is new now, any reign it, or its likeness, once had came to an end. If it is to be raised to eminence again, it must merit such elevation.

Over the course of the past twenty years or so I have come ever more firmly to believe that a number of branches of contemporary philosophy, as well as other disciplines, stand to benefit from the introduction of a particular new idea. One way to characterize these diverse fields is by reference to a very general concern: to understand how human lives are lived, both publicly and in private.

The idea in question is what I have labeled *joint commitment*. It plays a large part in this book: though the chapters cover a wide range of topics, all of them appeal to joint commitment in one way or another.

These topics all fall within the multifaceted domain of the philosophy of social phenomena.[1] In so doing they address matters of great significance to several other philosophical specialties—including ethics, epistemology, political philosophy, philosophy of science, and philosophy of law—and outside philosophy as well. I say something about joint commitment later in this introduction. For now I simply mark what I take to be its importance.

I first invoked joint commitment in my book *On Social Facts*, published in 1989.[2] Since then I have further developed my understanding of its nature,

---

[1] Other labels often used for roughly the same domain as "the philosophy of social phenomena" are "collective intentionality theory," and "social ontology." For some discussion of the contemporary development of this field, and its impact on other fields, see chapter 5, this volume.

[2] Margaret Gilbert, *On Social Facts* (London: Routledge and Kegan Paul, 1989) (reprinted Princeton, NJ: Princeton University Press, 1992), especially 198f. I discuss some potentially misleading aspects of the discussion there in chapter 2, this volume. My routine use of the phrase "joint commitment" followed the publication of *On Social Facts*. Margaret Gilbert, *Living Together: Rationality, Sociality, and Obligation* (Lanham, MD: Rowman and Littlefield, 1996), Introduction, discusses my trajectory in this respect with special reference to the topic of collective belief.

implications and relevance to a wide range of topics. Each of the chapters in this book exemplifies this development in one way or another.

This introduction aims to provide some context for the chapters that follow. First, it says something about the general project of understanding the terms in which human lives are lived. Next, it comments briefly on the kinds of explanatory tools that have commonly been appealed to in pursuit of this project. Joint commitment and some related ideas are then introduced. Finally, there is a review of the concerns approached in the different parts of the book and in the individual chapters.

The terms of human life

In 1969 the philosopher David Lewis's published his now famous book *Convention: A Philosophical Study*. As Lewis explained, he was interested in analyzing the everyday concept of a social convention.[3] In other terms, he wanted to characterize social conventions as conceived in everyday thought and talk. His aim, then, was not to stipulate a definition for the phrase "social convention" or, more briefly, "convention." His aim was to discover how these terms were implicitly defined in everyday life.

Such an aim is consonant with the sociological approach emphasized by Max Weber, one of the founders of contemporary social science. Weber urged that an important part of the study of human society, in the small and in the large, was to understand the ideas that informed the actions of the individuals involved.[4] These were the ideas in terms of which these individuals would couch their goals and their reasons. Without an idea of democracy, say, one's goal could not be the establishment of a democratic polity.

Weber did not assume that all of the ideas in question would be realistic. Though needed for interpretive purposes, some at least may not be otherwise useful for social scientists aiming at a realistic description of the world.[5]

Given that caveat, one would presumably do well not to go too far in the other direction, and assume that everyday concepts are of little utility for the purposes of realistic description. Quite possibly the idea of democracy, say, is such that the goal of establishing a democratic policy is achievable and has, indeed, sometimes been achieved. Quite possibly the everyday concept of a social convention

---

[3] David Lewis, *Convention: A Philosophical Study* (Cambridge, MA: Harvard University Press, 1969). This is discussed in chapter 9 here. Lewis does not tend to use the qualifier "social" of the conventions he studies but his examples suggest that it is reasonable to label his target in this way.

[4] Max Weber, *The Theory of Social and Economic Organization*, trans. T. Parsons and A. M. Henderson (Glencoe, IL: Free Press, 1964).

[5] Cf. Gilbert, *Social Facts*, 4–5.

and other such concepts apply to the world—there are social conventions, and so on, as ordinarily conceived.

As is well-known to anthropologists in particular, different societies and different sub-groups within societies may and often do operate in terms of different sets of ideas. Sometimes the differences in question are thought of as cultural differences. Some societies think in terms of witchcraft, for instance, others do not. Meanwhile, one may expect some ideas to be common to many different cultures, if not all.

Consider, for instance, the idea of doing something together with another person. Doing something together with another person, and understanding that this is what one is doing, is the kind of thing one would expect to be common to many different societies, at least, whatever their differences. There is reason to suppose, then, that they are central determinants of the human condition. The ideas explored in this book are of that nature.

The way in which these ideas are explored here will be clear enough from the individual articles. Suffice it to say that if one talks of "conceptual analysis" in this regard one must understand that phrase broadly. The aim is roughly this: perspicuously to describe the phenomenon to which the relevant everyday statements refer. For instance, when people say "They have this convention...." what phenomenon, in general terms, is at issue?

Some familiar tools of analysis: singularism

In developing his account of social convention David Lewis drew heavily on the mathematical theory of games. He was inspired by economist Thomas Schelling's proposal that underlying the stability of customs and traditions were situations he referred to as "coordination games."[6] Lewis referred rather to "coordination problems" and defined these in his own way.

For present purposes what is significant is that the basic elements of Lewis's account are sets of personal preferences and personal beliefs about the future actions of others. According to Lewis, there is a convention in a given population when, roughly, the people in question conform to a particular pattern of behavior—driving on the right side of the road, say—because each of them expects the others to do so and prefers to conform if the others do; there is another regularity that each would prefer to conform to if the others conformed to it; and it is entirely out in the open among the people in question that all these things are so.

I have elsewhere referred to such accounts of social phenomena as *singularist*: they understand the social phenomenon in question in terms of the

---

[6] Thomas Schelling, *The Strategy of Conflict* (Oxford: Oxford University Press, 1960).

personal preferences, expectations, and so on of the relevant individuals.[7] To cite another example, Michael Bratman's singularist account of shared intention, focuses on personal intentions as opposed to personal preferences or expectations.

No one would dispute that people have their own personal preferences, expectations, intentions, and so on. It may seem, then, that we should attempt to understand the social world in such terms: that is what Ockham's razor suggests. How, though, do we—the participants—understand the social world? Can one give an account of that understanding in singularist terms? If not, there is a case for thinking that descriptive social science will need to go beyond singularism. In any case the question stands: as we approach one another in our daily lives, are we dyed-in-the-wool singularists?

The answer for which I have been arguing is that we are not. The social world, the world of conversations, friendships, marriages, sports teams, discussion groups, religious orders, partisans, citizens, and so on, is not conceived of in singularist terms. The frame of mind exemplified in game-theory, which one might describe as a matter of "me watching you watching me" does not approach the heart of the matter. In particular, there is no basis there for the ever-present use of the collective "we." When we talk of *our* convention, then, we are not expressing a singularist conception.

Familiar ways of thinking about human sociality indicate as much. It is common to use such terms as "unity" and "union" when thinking about social relationships on both a small and a large scale. It is hard to speak appropriately of *unity* or *union* in a world perceived through the lens of singularism. This is so even when people are effectively coordinating their behavior in the context of a Lewisian convention Indeed, if even one person's personal preferences change, the beautiful "self-perpetuating system" that constitutes a Lewisian convention collapses.[8] Again, even when you and I think the same thing, we are still as "loose and separate" from each other—to use Hume's phrase—as when we thought differently: there are two separate "I thinks" but no "we think," no *cogitamus*— whatever that might amount to.[9]

---

[7] Gilbert, *Social Facts*, 12.

[8] Lewis, *Convention*, 42, refers to the situation when a convention in his sense is up and running as a "metastable, self-perpetuating system." Michael Robins, *Promising, Intending, and Moral Autonomy* (Cambridge: Cambridge University Press, 1984), 137, aptly refers, in connection with this situation, to the "shifting sands" of preference.

[9] Several chapters in this volume have more to say on the topic of social unity. See e.g., chapters 8, 11, and 15.

Some familiar tools of analysis: moralism

As will emerge in the following chapters, many central social phenomena—as conceived of in everyday life—involve obligations. More precisely, they involve obligations of one person *to another*. To take a familiar example, suppose we have agreed to meet at a certain café at six. There is nothing suspect about this agreement, it has not been rescinded, and there are no further facts that bear on the case. In that case, at least, I am obligated to you to go to the café at six. If one wishes to ignore the relational aspect of the situation, one can drop the words "to you" and say simply that I am obligated to go to the café at six—as are you.

Obligation has largely been studied by moral philosophers, and they are the theorists who have most attended to agreements and—more often—promises. In doing so they generally conceive of the obligation in question as a matter of a moral requirement. In the above case, each of the parties to the agreement would be characterized as morally required to go to the café at six. It is of course reasonable to consider whether the obligations most closely associated with agreements, and many other social conditions, are moral requirements. That they are, however, is not obvious.

One aspect of the matter is emphasized in several places in this volume. Consider the agreement described above. I take it to be part and parcel of one party's obligation to the other that each has the standing or authority to demand of the other that he—or she—act as required by the agreement.[10] It is by no means obvious that by virtue of one party's being morally required to conform to the agreement—if he is—the other accrues the standing to demand of him that he does so. Nor do such considerations as the fact that the moral requirement is grounded in the interests of the promisee seem to change this.[11]

When I speak of *moralism,* in the present context, I mean in particular the assumption that the obligations most closely associated with the social phenomena in question are a matter of moral requirement. Moralism, like singularism, faces significant challenges with respect to the characterization of these obligations.

Joint commitment: neither singularism nor moralism

How is one to understand the sense of unity, of connection, the sense of the collective "we"? Given disparate human beings with their own personal beliefs,

---

[10] In what follows I take the "or she" to be understood in relevant contexts.

[11] See chapter 12, this volume.

strivings, and so on, what kind of unity is possible? When we talk about *our* goals, beliefs, values, and so on—what are we talking about?

In most of the chapters that follow, I argue on behalf of a joint commitment account of a given social phenomenon as it is understood in everyday life. This involves going beyond singularism, on the one hand, and moralism on the other. Not only do I argue that there is a viable alternative to singularism or moralism with respect to the phenomenon in question. I argue, further, that the alternative is to be preferred to one or more singularist and/or moralist alternative.

Though these chapters contain a more or less extensive discussion of joint commitment, some pertinent remarks may be helpful here.[12]

First, in writing of *commitments*, personal or joint, my focus is exclusively on what I sometimes refer to as commitments *of the will*.[13] This should be understood in the exposition that follows here.

Commitments are either *personal* or *joint*. The commitment engendered by a personal decision is an example of a personal commitment. All a given person has to do is decide—an exercise of that person's will—and he (or she) is committed in the relevant way.

One's making the decision is in a broad sense a psychological matter. One's being committed is a normative matter. Rephrasing the latter point: if, for example, Jack decides to go swimming tomorrow, and does not change his mind, then, all else being equal, he will act in error if he fails to go swimming tomorrow. This could happen if, for example, when tomorrow comes, he forgets his decision until it is too late.

As one can see, there is both a process and a product of personal commitment. The process is psychological, the product is normative. As we shall see, this is true in the joint case also.

Commitments are susceptible to rescission. Here too there is both a process and a product. In the case of a personal decision, I am in a position unilaterally to rescind my decision: I can simply change my mind. The product of this psychological process is a change in the normative situation of the person involved. More precisely, an existing normative constraint has been removed.

The idea of a personal commitment is a singularist concept. The idea of a *joint* commitment is not.

---

[12] In addition to several extended discussions in the present work, there is a detailed treatment in Margaret Gilbert, *A Theory of Political Obligation: Membership, Commitment, and the Bonds of Society* (Oxford: Oxford University Press, 2006), ch. 7. Some of my various discussions of joint commitment emphasize points that others touch on lightly, if at all. The same is true of the discussion in this introduction.

[13] For a more general discussion of commitment see Margaret Gilbert, "Commitment," *The Encyclopedia of Ethics*, ed. Hugh Lafollette (Hoboken, NJ: Wiley-Blackwell, 2013).

It is important to be clear that a joint commitment is not a concatenation of personal commitments of the parties. It is not the case that you and I are jointly committed if and only if I am personally committed in some way and you are also. This is so however complex the content of the personal commitments, however well they mesh, and however well known the personal commitment of any one party is known to the other.

As I sometimes put it, a joint commitment is a commitment *of* the two or more people involved. It is, more fully, a commitment *by* two or more people *of* the same two or more people. This can be expanded as follows.

Just as a personal commitment of the will is engendered by a process involving one person—the making of a decision being one example—a joint commitment of the will is engendered by a process involving two or more persons. More precisely, in the process of joint commitment, two or more people *jointly commit the same two or more people.*

In the basic case, it is necessary and sufficient to conclude this process that, roughly, each makes clear to each his personal readiness to contribute to it, in a way that is entirely out in the open to all. Each understands that once this has happened, the process will have been concluded. [14]

Once it is concluded, the parties are *jointly committed.* Their being jointly committed—the product of the process described—is a normative matter. In order to say more about this aspect of the matter I first refer to the general form of a joint commitment.

For any joint commitment, the parties are jointly committed *to phi as a body,* where "phi" stands for the relevant verb. Roughly to spell this out: they are jointly committed to emulate, *by virtue of the actions of all,* a single phi-er. For example: they are jointly committed to emulate, by virtue of the actions of each, a single believer of the proposition that justice is the first virtue of institutions.

This commitment is a commitment *of them all.* In other terms, *they* are the subject of this commitment. It is theirs. As a result, if any one party acts in a way that does not conform to the commitment, they, qua subject of the commitment, will have acted in error. Referring to any one party's lack of conformity, then, any one of them might say "We slipped up."

This does not mean that the party in question has not himself slipped up—in his capacity as a party to the commitment. In other terms, *given their* commitment jointly to emulate, by virtue of the actions of all, a single phi-er, *each one* is committed to act in ways appropriate to that joint commitment. The derivative or individual commitment in this case is not a personal one—it is not imposed unilaterally by the committed person. What precisely one is derivatively committed to doing may only emerge as things develop, since what one person

---

[14] See chapter 2, this volume, for related discussion.

must do in order that they together conform to the joint commitment will often depend on what the other or others do.

These points continue to hold as long as the parties do not concur in rescinding the joint commitment. Such rescission is another jointly engendered process, with a normative result for each of the parties.

Beyond these points, I argue that any joint commitment *obligates the parties one to the other* to act in accordance with the commitment. In other terms—though ambiguous ones—each *owes* such action to the others. Correlated with these obligations of the parties are rights in the parties against one another: rights to actions that conform to the joint commitment. Correlated, again, with these obligations and rights is an important kind of standing or authority: the standing to demand conforming action and rebuke for non-conformity.[15]

This is argued more or less elaborately in several of the chapters.[16] None of these arguments appeal to moral requirements or engage in any specifically moral judgements or arguments.

To argue that there are obligations of joint commitment, then, does not commit one to moralism. In particular, it is not to say that one is morally required to conform to one's joint commitments—though one may be, all else being equal. Nor is it to say anything that implies that one is subject to such a moral requirement. Rather, *it is to emphasize important aspects of the relationship* between the parties to any joint commitment.

This is a point of great significance. Among other things, it offers a plausible way of understanding a number of otherwise problematic phenomena. These involve contexts in which the participants take themselves to be *obligated* to act in a certain way, or have certain normatively forceful *duties,* yet to talk of their being *morally* bound so to act in such circumstances appears absurd.[17]

If our acting together, our conventions, and other central aspects of our lives together involve our jointly committing ourselves in one way or another, then our lives together are run through with obligations to one another and rights against each other, with the correlative standing to insist on various actions and

---

[15] I understand the correlation in these cases to be associated with an important kind of equivalence between the correlated items. See e.g. chapter 13, this volume; also Margaret Gilbert "Giving Claim-Rights Their Due," in *Rights: Concepts and Contexts*, eds. B Bix and H. Spector, (Farnham, Surrey: Ashgate, 2012).

[16] In several chapters I take up the idea that one's demanding an action with standing is, more fully, his demanding what he *owns*, what is *his own*, or what is *his*, where the precise sense of the term in question remains to be determined. Discussion of this idea is not strictly necessary in these chapters, where the point is to argue that the parties to a joint commitment owe each other conformity to it. The intuitive judgment that they have the standing to demand conformity of one another, for instance, would suffice. I say this not to disclaim the idea. I take it up again in a monograph on rights, in preparation, that will be published by Oxford University Press.

[17] See in particular chapters 13, 17, and 18, this volume.

rebuke for non-performance. This does indeed seem to be so. Notably, the social scientist can acknowledge the existence of rights and obligations of joint commitment while respecting the point that social scientific description should be free of the imposition of the observer's moral values and in that sense value-free.

Some further notes on joint commitment

In arguing for joint commitment accounts of the phenomena in question I imply that at some level those with the applicable concepts have the concept of a joint commitment. I take it that one can possess a concept without having the ability explicitly to give an account of it—just as one can know how to move one's body in riding a bicycle without having the ability to describe precisely what is going on.

In much of what I have written I use the technical term "plural subject" to refer, by definition, to any set of jointly committed persons. It is useful to have such a term, if only on account of its compactness. Recently I have tended to avoid it, because it has led some to misunderstand my position. One of the problems is that the noun substantive "subject" is often associated with subjectivity or consciousness.

It is worth emphasizing, then, that I have never intended to suggest that there is any collective or group consciousness that is somehow independent of the consciousness of any individual group member. Rather, I see joint commitment as a precondition of the correct ascription of, say, a particular attitude, to a given population of persons. Then we—a plurality of persons—are the *subject* of that attitude. In other terms, it is *ours*.

A related worry that is now, I think, less common is that describing our social world in terms of plural subjects as I understand these somehow introduces a pernicious kind of "holism," "supra-individualism," or "reification" into our theorizing. One problem with such charges is that the meanings of the quoted terms are rarely spelled out.

My proposal is that human beings routinely if inexplicitly understand themselves together to be creating joint commitments throughout their lives. The conditions for such creation are relatively simple to state and easily satisfiable—really not much less so than the making of a personal decision or forming of a personal intention.

I do argue that, for instance, when we believe something no one of us needs to believe that thing.[18] I do *not* argue that what does believe it is something that

---

[18] See e.g. chapter 7, this volume.

exists "over and above" the individuals involved *in the sense that its existence is not a function of a way these individuals have been, and are.*

It might be good if, as theorists, we could fully describe our social world—the world we inhabit together as we understand it—in terms of singularist concepts which suffice for describing many aspects of our personal lives and, indeed, our relations to others. However, if singularism fails, we should not be afraid to introduce a non-singularist concept of joint commitment. In the end, theoretical adequacy has to trump theoretical parsimony.

Preview

This book is divided into four parts that put together essays on related themes. There follows a review of the themes of these different parts of the book and some indication of the contents of the individual chapters and the relationship between them. As I explain below, several of the chapters would fit well into more than one of the four parts, so their placement is somewhat arbitrary.

Part I: Shared Agency

Anyone wishing to understand the human condition needs to understand not only what it is to act on one's own, but what it is to do something together with another person. Part I brings together a number of essays relating in one way or another to our acting together or, as that is sometimes labeled, joint or shared action.

This is a topic that has been the focus of increasing attention by philosophers since the early 1990s when a number of different theorists were offering distinct accounts of acting together and related phenomena.[19] My own contributions to the initial literature are to be found, in particular, in chapter four of *On Social Facts* and in the essay "Walking Together", which offers an overview of the themes and theses of that book.[20]

The first chapter in the present work, "Acting Together" is a compact discussion of its central topic that opens up several important lines of argument that are more fully developed in later chapters. Starting with the observation that a package of rights is associated with acting together, it observes, further, that an agreement often precedes a case of acting together, and would guarantee the noted rights. A prior agreement, however, is not necessary for a case of acting

[19] See chapter 5, this volume, for an overview of the literature in question.

[20] Margaret Gilbert, "Walking Together: A Paradigmatic Social Phenomenon," in *Midwest Studies in Philosophy*, vol. xv, *The Philosophy of the Human Sciences*, ed. P. A. French, T. E. Uehling, Jr., and H. K. Wettstein, Notre Dame: University of Notre Dame Press (1990).

together. Assuming that acting together involves a collective goal, a joint commitment account of such a goal is offered, and it is argued that an account of acting together that incorporates a collective goal so conceived responds well to the initial observations.[21]

A number of the chapters in this volume have more to say of the association of joint commitment and rights, on the one hand, and agreements, on the other.[22]

The second chapter, "Considerations on Joint Commitment", clarifies important aspects of joint commitment and addresses some concerns raised in connection with my discussion of it in *On Social Facts* in particular. Among other things it also responds to criticism of the idea that acting together involves rights and obligations.[23] In the course of this discussion I observe that if acting together with another person involves a diminution of one's own freedom, it also involves a diminution of his freedom, and both may be preferable to a lack of joint engagement.

The third chapter, "Who's to Blame?" concerns collective moral responsibility, a topic often associated not simply with our acting together but with our doing something morally bad together. Supposing that we are blameworthy in connection with something we did together, what, if anything, does that say about your personal blameworthiness or mine? In addressing this question one needs an account of collective blameworthiness. I start, therefore, by offering such an account. At its core are joint commitment accounts of a collective's action and a collective's belief.

This chapter discusses several important aspects of plural subjects and joint commitment, including the way in which a given plural subject can endure from one generation to the next. Relatedly, the discussion of what follows from a collective's blameworthiness for members of the collective includes consideration of one's relation to collective wrongdoing that occurred before one was even born.[24]

Collective blameworthiness also figures in Part II: Collective Attitudes, in a chapter that focuses on the emotional aftermath of collective wrongdoing. Both of these chapters would also have fitted in Part IV: Political Life.

That said, it is worth emphasizing that collective moral responsibility is not restricted to groups of the size of a paradigmatic political society. The issue arises

---

[21] As discussed later in this introduction, and exemplified in several of the chapters here, some of my discussions of acting together have invoked a collective intention as opposed to a collective goal. My main concern has always been to argue that the core of acting together is a joint commitment.

[22] See e.g., chs. 5 and 13.

[23] I respond to some more recent criticisms along these lines in Margaret Gilbert, "A Theory of Political Obligation: Responses to Horton, Jeske, Narveson, and Stoutland," *Jurisprudence* 4 (2013).

[24] In previous treatments of collective blameworthiness I have not discussed the matters indicated in this paragraph.

even in a dyad—a two-person group. The same goes for acting together itself. This can involve two people—or a vast number.

The fourth chapter is "Rationality in Collective Action." It connects two distinct topics: collective action in the sense of acting together, of which it gives an account, and collective action in the sense of rational choice theory.

Rational choice theory focuses on *collective action problems*, which include but are not limited to the famous "Prisoner's Dilemma." I argue that when collective action problems are couched in terms of the *inclinations* of the parties, an appropriate joint commitment—such as that I take to be involved in acting together—provides a stable solution to the problem, without changing the initial "matrix" of inclinations. In general, joint commitments are well-fitted to organize the lives of those who, left to follow their personal inclinations, would find themselves in trouble. This chapter includes a relatively full discussion of commitments of the will and a number of elaborations on the theme of joint commitment, including the normativity of joint commitment.

In both this chapter and the preceding, I take collective action in the sense of acting together to involve collective *intentions*---understood in terms of joint commitment. When I first approached the subject, and in "Acting Together" and more recently also, I invoked, rather, collective *goals*----also interpreted in terms of joint commitment, which is the crucial element in these analyses.[25]

I suspect that my appeals to collective intentions rather than collective goals have been influenced by the intense focus on such intentions generated by the work of other theorists of collective action including, in particular, Michael Bratman. It may well be that there is a good reason for such a move, but I am not certain that there is. For present purposes I leave the matter there.

There are doubtless other such variations between the chapters. That is, the same issue is discussed in somewhat different terms. This may be all to the good: an earlier approach or way of putting things may be found helpful by some readers, whatever my own current preferences.

The fifth chapter, the last in Part I, is "Two Approaches to Shared Intention." Its topic is the nature of shared intention in the sense of our intending to do something in the future. Building on earlier work of mine, it compares and contrasts a joint commitment approach to shared intention with that of a species of theorists who take what I refer to as the *personal intentions perspective*, making particular reference to the work of Michael Bratman, the most prominent personal intentions theorist.

First, three criteria of adequacy for an account of shared intention—the disjunction, concurrence, and obligation criteria—are argued for. It is then argued

---

[25] I initially invoked collective goals, as opposed to collective intentions, in my early treatments of acting together in *On Social Facts* and "Walking Together," and quite recently in the extended treatment in Gilbert, *Political Obligation*, ch. 6 and 7.

that the joint commitment account succeeds in satisfying these criteria where Bratman's, for instance, fails.

This chapter is prefaced by a brief history of contemporary work in the philosophy of social phenomena. This indicates the increasing interest that theorists in other disciplines from developmental psychology to economics have shown in this area of philosophy.

Part II: Collective Attitudes

While the topic of shared agency has attracted a great deal of attention from some contemporary theorists, a growing number have been focusing on collective attitudes, broadly construed. They have focused in particular on the topic of collective belief. Everyday ascriptions of beliefs to two or more people are rife. What is it for us, as opposed to me, on the one hand, and you, on the other, to believe something?

My work in this area, as in that of shared agency, has had both a negative and a positive side. Negatively, I have offered reasons for rejecting a number of accounts of the phenomenon in question that might, at first blush, be considered plausible. Positively, I have developed an account of what it is for us to believe something—according to our everyday understanding. At the core of this account lies a joint commitment.

On Social Facts offers an extended discussion of collective belief.[26] Since writing that and a shorter companion piece, I have further articulated my account of collective belief and discussed its applications in a number of places.[27] With respect to applications, I have, among other things, argued for the importance of the topic for understanding the development of science.[28]

Two of the chapters in Part II concern collective belief. Chapter six engages with a number of commentators on my account of collective belief, which I explain as a preliminary to discussing their position. I label them "rejectionists": what

---

[26] Gilbert, *Social Facts*, ch. 5. The companion piece mentioned in the text is "Modeling Collective Belief," *Synthese* 73 (1987), pp. 185–204

[27] See Gilbert, *Living Together*, Introduction, for discussion of the developing articulation of the account.

[28] Margaret Gilbert, "Collective Belief and Scientific Change," in *Sociality and Responsibility: New Essays in Plural Subject Theory* (Lanham, MD: Rowman and Littlefield, 2000). This has helped to generate a stream of science-related literature. See, for instance, the essays in *Episteme* volume 7, issue 3, 2010, edited by K. Bradley Wray, on the theme "Collective Knowledge and Science." I develop further the proposal in *On Social Facts* that everyday *conversations* are important contexts for collective belief formation in Margaret Gilbert and Maura Priest, "Conversation and Collective Belief," in *Perspectives on Pragmatics and Philosophy*, ed. Capone, A., Lo Piparo, E., Carapezza, M. (Dordrecht: Springer, 2013).

they reject is that collective belief, on my account, is belief. Rather, they aver, it is a form of acceptance. My discussion notes the way in which belief has hitherto been understood in epistemology—the study of knowledge, belief, and related cognitive states—and considers the phenomenon picked out by my account of collective belief in that light. My discussion suggests that this phenomenon is closer to that of belief—according to standard tenets of epistemology—and further from acceptance than rejectionists suppose. I also offer some critical remarks on the way in which epistemology has, traditionally, arrived at its accounts of such cognitive states as belief.[29]

Chapter seven, "Collective Epistemology", argues for the importance of the developing field delimited by its title, and offers an overview and some amplification of my previous work in that field, including some of the negative points I have made against a family of accounts of collective belief that I refer to as *summative* accounts. At the core of any summative account of a collective belief that p are beliefs of all or most members of the relevant group—beliefs, in particular, that p.

As the discussion in these chapters makes clear, if collective beliefs on my account are central features of groups, they are important and consequential phenomena, whatever we choose to call them.,

Chapter eight is "Shared Values, Social Unity, and Liberty." It approaches another significant features of groups—their values. Just as people often refer to what we believe, they often refer to what we value, to our values, and so on. Here I argue for a joint commitment account of what it is for us to value something. In so doing I provide a way to interpret a phrase that has often been used by political theorists invoking something they take to be of importance to the smooth functioning of a society: "shared values."

I point out some divergent implications for societies of shared values in the sense in question. On the one hand, they enhance social unity. On the other, there is a diminution of liberty.[30] Given its several connections with political life this chapter might have been included in Part IV.

Chapter nine, the last in Part II, offers a refined version of the account of social conventions sketched in *On Social Facts,* comparing and contrasting it with Lewis's account of convention in light of a range of proposed criteria of adequacy for an account of social convention.[31] The joint commitment account elaborated here does better than Lewis's in terms of these criteria. That said, there may well be conventions in Lewis's sense. Conventions in either his or the joint commitment sense will be consequential phenomena when they occur.

---

[29] A paper in preparation, co-authored with Daniel Pilchman, continues this discussion thread.

[30] For related discussion see Margaret Gilbert, "Can a Wise Society Be a Free One?" *Southern Journal of Philosophy,* 44, 2006, 1–17 and 'Corporate Misbehavior and Collective Values', *Brooklyn Law Review,* 70, 2005, 1369–1380.

[31] Gilbert, *Social Facts,* ch. 6.

As for social conventions in the joint commitment sense, though they can be of great value in the solution of coordination problems, they need not relate to such problems, and may enjoin actions that respond to no one's prior preferences. They may also enjoin actions that are wrong from a moral point of view, a point that has not received much attention.[32] Either way they are apt distinctively to shape the lives of those whose conventions they are.

Just as there are frequent references in everyday speech to what we believe and what we value, there are frequent references to what we feel, as in "We feel terrible about the way we treated you.' Such references are considered in "Collective Guilt and Collective Guilt Feelings" the tenth chapter and the last in Part II. It argues for a joint commitment account of the referent of a particular collective emotion ascription: the ascription to *us* of feelings of guilt.

The joint commitment in question may often be appropriate. It would clearly be appropriate in the aftermath of collective wrongdoing of the worst kind, involving atrocities a large scale. Insofar as its occurrence in practice is likely to lead to reparative action, it should be welcomed. Evidently, this chapter might have been placed in Part IV.

Part III: Mutual Recognition, Promises, and Love

The chapters in Part III focus on "small-scale" social phenomena that are of great importance to the way in which our lives go Though small-scale and ubiquitous, theorists have not found any of them easy to understand.

Chapter eleven, the first in this Part, was prompted by a striking claim that is often made about love, in particular marital love: in a love relationship, the parties somehow "merge" or "fuse" together "Fusion: Sketch of a 'Contractual' Model," suggests that, in effect, one plausible way of making sense of this idea is by appeal to joint commitment.[33]

The formation of any plural subject can be thought of as involving a kind of melding of the parties. A long-term marital relationship, however, is likely to give rise to a complex web of joint commitments, both long and short term, as myriad collective beliefs, values, and so on are formed. This is liable to make the fusion

---

[32] I discuss it in Margaret Gilbert "Responses to some questions on social conventions and related matters" *Convenzioni, Post* n.4, Milano-Udine: Mimesis.

[33] I say "in effect" since the phrase "joint commitment" does not appear in this chapter. The phrase "plural subject" does. The essay that constitutes this chapter was originally drafted in 1988 and published in 1990. I include it in this volume of more recent essays both because of a recently renewed interest in philosophical interest in love and further to emphasize the scope of explanations in terms of joint commitment.

involved particularly salient. Fusion of the kind in question is not always in the service of the good, but in the right context it can greatly improve a relationship.

The next two chapters concern two central and ubiquitous components of our daily lives: promises and agreements. These range from the trivial to the profoundly consequential. But what are these things? And how do they produce the obligations and rights that we take them to give us? Though philosophers have considered them extensively, I argue against the central contemporary approaches, offering a significantly different alternative in terms of joint commitment.

Chapter twelve, "Scanlon on Promissory Obligation: The Problem of Promisees' Rights", questions the well-known and influential account of promissory obligation offered by moral theorist Thomas Scanlon. According to Scanlon a given promisor's obligation is a matter of his subjection to a moral requirement deriving from a general moral principle that applies to him in his circumstances. While questioning Scanlon's account in particular, the chapter aims to throw doubt on all accounts of the same general type. Its main thrust is that such accounts are hard pressed to account for a promisee's rights.

Chapter thirteen is "Three Dogmas About Promising". Having characterized three standard opinions about promissory obligation—the three dogmas of the title—it questions them in light of two intuitive points. Then, starting with agreements, it argues for joint commitment accounts of promises and agreements. The account of promises allows for the two intuitive points. It does not support the prevalent opinions, one of which is that promissory obligation is a matter of moral requirement. On my account the obligations most closely associated with promising are obligations of joint commitment, not moral requirements.

Chapter fourteen, which concludes Part III, is "Mutual Recognition and Some Related Phenomena". It focuses on a joint commitment account of what it refers to as "mutual recognition," a highly significant though often fleeting occurrence between two people. This will often be part of what is going on when a given joint commitment of another type is formed.

This chapter also offers a joint commitment account of a phenomenon worthy of the label "shared attention," a phrase that psychologists introduced some while ago to mark what humans are capable of at an important developmental stage.

Part IV: Political Life

This part of the book focuses on topics germane to the public and political life of human beings, though several are also relevant to our more private lives.

The title of chapter fifteen, "A Real Unity of Them All", is a quotation from Hobbes's description of a political society. The chapter starts from questions inspired by the contemporary development of the European Union. What kind of unity can such a vast agglomeration of nation-states pretend to—if any? This leads to discussion of the general idea of social and political union. A plural subject or joint commitment account of social groups, large and small, is brought to bear on the perennial inclination to appeal to a contract of sorts in accounting for the unity of a given society. Some attention is paid to other conceptions of such unity, including a number of subjective conceptions.

Chapter sixteen "*Pro Patria*", tackles a topic that has provoked a fair amount of debate among philosophers: patriotism. Often it is held up as a great virtue; yet many find it morally suspect—something that promotes a disregard for our common humanity. The best way to approach this evaluative issue is to have a clear sense of what patriotism is. It is often defined as "love of country." It is argued that this definition is unsatisfactory. A patriotic act crucially involves a particular motive—it is action on behalf of one's country as such.

A further articulation of the basic patriotic motive is offered, given an interpretation of what it is for a country to be one's own in terms of joint commitment. A number of further questions are then addressed. These include the relation of patriotism to humanitarian concerns, and its common association with pride.

As with all of the chapters in this volume, including "*Pro Patria*," those in the section are not, or not intentionally, in any way partisan. My overarching concern, as said, is to understand the terms in which people conduct their everyday lives—the terms, more particularly, in which they live among one another and conduct their lives together. This concern, important as it is, is fairly far from the usual terrain of contemporary political philosophy, which is largely geared to justifying particular evaluative, moral judgments on the conduct of life within and between political societies. This is, of course, a vital project. Its virtually exclusive pursuit, however, can lead to an obfuscatory moralization of the whole domain of political life, something that blinds us to deeply important dimensions of political life, thought, and action. That is an implication of the last two chapters in Part IV, among others.

These chapters are lightly revised versions of lectures that have been widely presented. Chapter seventeen, "De-Moralizing Political Obligation," takes up a central theme of my book *A Theory of Political Obligation*. It makes the point that though familiar discussions of political obligation focus on the moral requirements, if any, on citizens as such, there is an equally important and closely related type of question that does not appeal to morality–or not obviously. This concerns what a citizen owes, and to whom, by virtue of his citizenship. "De-Moralizing Political Obligation" focuses on the type of owing that correlates with claim-rights and the standing to demand what one is owed. Interpreting citizenship as membership in a political society and the latter in terms of joint commitment, it is argued that citizens owe it to each other to support the political institutions of their society. Further, given these interpretations, these political obligations are *content-independent* in a strong sense.

Chapter eighteen, "Commands and their Practical Import" offers a non-moralized account of something that is central to all our lives in one form or another: command authority. Not only military commanders, but parents and teachers, for instance, frequently issue commands or, as we would more naturally put it, *instruct* or *tell us* what to do.

This chapter goes beyond the standard approach to the subject, arguing that if one issues an authoritative command the addressee of one's command owes one his conformity to that command. In other terms his commander has a right to his obedience.

On what basis does one accrue command authority? It is argued here that joint commitment is at least one source of such authority. This helps to explain a judgment that is otherwise hard to credit: there can be "dark duties" which enjoin the performance of unconscionable acts. We can owe such actions to our commanders. Though this does not tell us that we are to perform them, all things considered, it is still of considerable importance in practice, as I explain.

Concluding remarks

This collection as a whole demonstrates the wide array of topics that are fruitfully approached in terms of joint commitment. It explains why I have elsewhere referred to joint commitment as the "structure of the social atom."[34]

That said, there are relevant themes and topics that have received little or no attention in this book. Many of those that have been addressed are worthy of more extended treatment.

Among the themes that receive little or no attention here is the history of work in the philosophy of social phenomena including the work of the founders of sociology. I have paid some attention to this in previous work. *On Social Facts* contained extensive discussions of Max Weber's essentially singularist approach, probes Emile Durkheim's suggestive discussion of "social facts," and considers of Georg Simmel's intriguing claims in his classic article "How Is Society Possible?" In "Walking Together" I indicated the affinities I saw between my account of groups generally and some of the pronouncements of classic social contract theorists such as Hobbes and Rousseau, a theme that is lightly taken up here in "A Real Unity of Them All" and, with a focus on Rousseau, in more recent

---

[34] Margaret Gilbert, "The Structure of the Social Atom: Joint Commitment as the Foundation of Human Social Behavior," in *Socializing Metaphysics: The Nature of Social Reality*, Frederick F. Schmitt, ed. (Lanham, MD: Rowman and Littlefield, 2003).

work.[35] All of these thinkers, and more, are important resources for contemporary theorists.

A topic hardly discussed here at all is one on which I have not focused since writing *On Social Facts*, though it is certainly important. The reader is referred to the discussion of group languages in that work.

Among the topics that deserve a more extended treatment, though it is discussed in many of the chapters, is the nature and sources of claim-rights roughly as conceived of in those discussions. We value the possession of such rights, and it is important to understand how we may accrue them. I argue more or less briefly in several of these chapters that joint commitment is one source of claim-rights—as of the correlative directed obligations and associated standings. As some of these chapters also suggest, the question whether there are other sources is a pressing one. I am currently completing a book that focuses on the contemporary literature on claim-rights and addresses these questions in greater detail.

Many of the topics considered in these chapters are worthy of a book to themselves or at least a longer treatment. It is often helpful, however, to have shorter, more focused discussions offering a particular perspective on such topics. They can act as a stimulus to further reflections, and provide a more easily assimilable starting point.

[35] Margaret Gilbert, "Two Central Aspects of Association," presented to the Geneva University workshop celebrating the 300th year since Rousseau's birth, September 2012.

PART ONE

SHARED AGENCY

"Sir," said the nephew, "we have done wrong, and are reaping the fruits of the wrong."

"*We* have done wrong?" repeated the Marquis, with an enquiring smile, and delicately pointing, first to his nephew, then to himself.

"Our family; our honourable family, whose honour is of so much account to both of us, in such different ways. Even in my father's time, we did a world of wrong, injuring every human creature who came between us and our pleasure, whatever it was."

Charles Dickens, *A Tale of Two Cities* (New York: Barnes and Noble, 2003) 75. First published 1859.

1

Acting Together[1]

1. Introduction

Examples of what I shall refer to in this chapter as "acting together" include dancing together, building a house together, and marching together against the enemy, where these are construed as something other than a matter of doing the same thing concurrently and in the same place. I take it that people frequently see themselves as engaging in such acting together and that it is both an important and ubiquitous phenomenon in the life of human beings. It can be argued, indeed, that an understanding of this phenomenon uncovers the structure of human sociality. It illuminates not just acting together but also, among other things, intending, believing and requiring together. In sum, acting together is an important topic both in its own right and for its relevance to human sociality in general.[2]

The discussion of acting together in this chapter starts with some informal observations. It appears that, in everyday life, acting together is understood to involve a package of *rights*. There is a temptation to assume, for this and other reasons, that people can only act together after making an agreement, agreements being well-known sources of rights. I argue against this assumption. I then elaborate key elements of an account that accords with these points. The account I sketch here was first mooted in my 1989 book *On Social Facts*.[3]

---

[1] The original version of this chapter was presented as an invited lecture at the University of Leipzig in July 2000. It has been lightly revised for publication. I thank Professor Georg Meggle and his "Kommunikatives Verstehen" research group for their welcome invitation to Leipzig. Thanks also to my colleagues at the University of Connecticut for comments after a related talk, and to J. C. Beall and Paul Bloomfield for further related discussion.

[2] On sociality in general see Gilbert 1989, and, for a more compact discussion, Gilbert 1994.

[3] Those of my previous writings closest to the present topic include Gilbert 1989, chapter 4; Gilbert 1990, and Gilbert 1997. At various places I cite further sources on specific points. I make no attempt in this chapter to compare my own account with others. For such a discussion, see, for instance, Gilbert 1998a, and Gilbert 1998b.

2. Observations on a case: a package of rights

It is worth emphasizing at the outset that the word "together" in the phrase "acting together" should not be interpreted in terms of physical proximity. Thus
Ulrich and Anna may be investigating the murder together, and for this purpose
she may stay in Leipzig while he goes to Dresden.[4]

In what follows I shall sometimes refer to cases of acting together as cases of
"joint action" and "joint activity." The quoted phrases have the advantage of not
inviting an interpretation in terms of physical proximity.

In this section of the chapter I shall focus on the example of two people who
are going for a walk together, or, more briefly, walking together.[5] Clearly, two is
the smallest number of people who can engage in joint activity. Though a two
person case undoubtedly has special aspects, I don't believe that these will affect
the points being made in this essay.

Evidently, to say that two people are walking together in the sense at issue
implies that there is something, going for a walk, that they are doing together—
in a non-spatial sense.[6] That said, I shall assume that the people in my example
take walking along side by side to be the way for two people to walk together as
a joint activity. This is, if you like, the conventional behavioral form of walking
together as far as they are concerned.

I shall now describe what I take to be everyday understandings involved in
walking together. My warrant for the description is informal observation including self-observation.

Suppose that Heinrich and Andrea are going for a walk together. This is what
they rightly take themselves to be doing. They are walking up Fifth Avenue
toward Central Park. Suppose now that Heinrich suddenly claps his hand to his
brow, says "Oh No!" and, without further ado, starts walking rapidly away from
Andrea.

---

[4] Cf. Gilbert 1989, pp. 159–161.

[5] I don't regard this example as sacrosanct in any way. Gilbert 1989, focuses on traveling together.
Michael Bratman's favorite example is painting the house together (Bratman 1993). Searle refers to
the execution of a pass play (Searle 1990).

[6] It is worth noting that in common parlance one can properly refer to people as "walking
together," construed as a kind of acting together, who are not exactly going for a walk together. For
instance, Anna is walking somewhere and runs into Karl. It turns out that he is going somewhere
further away in the same direction. They link up for a while, but it is understood that Anna will leave
Karl when she arrives at her destination. Though for a certain period they can be said to be walking
together, this being a kind of acting together, they would not be said to be going for a walk together,
or out on a walk together. The difference seems to be that in the last two cases but not the former their
walking together is their primary project. The differences between these cases—between, in effect,
generic walking together and a special form—is evidently not material to their value as examples of
acting together. In any case I focus here on a case in which two people are going for a walk together.

Andrea may not be disappointed that he has gone. Barring special background understandings, however, she will understand that—to put it somewhat abstractly—the manner of his going involved *a mistake*. It is a mistake by virtue of the fact that they were walking together.

Heinrich's walking away will not have this effect if he first says to Andrea "I've just remembered I am supposed to be at the doctor's office in ten minutes!" and receives the reply "Go quickly, then!" In that case Heinrich would, in effect, have obtained Andrea's permission to leave.

Heinrich must obtain her permission if her sense of mistake is to be precluded. Thus, for example, it is not enough for Heinrich simply to *inform* Andrea that he is going to leave their walk, without any suggestion that her endorsement of his decision is needed.

Given that this is so, Andrea evidently understands that by virtue of their walking together she has a *right* of some kind to Heinrich's continuing to walk alongside her.[7] The right in question can be waived in certain contexts by Andrea's permitting him not to walk alongside her.

Further observations also suggest that Andrea understands herself to have a right to Heinrich's continued walking alongside her. In the original scenario where no permission has been given, Andrea might well call out to Heinrich in a rebuking tone: "Heinrich, what's going on?" She might also issue a related demand such as "Heinrich, wait!" She may not do either of these things, but she will understand that she has the standing to do each of them.[8] These understandings are natural accompaniments of an understanding that she has a right to his continued walking alongside her.

If they are walking together, both Andrea herself and Heinrich will have the understandings so far described: by virtue of their walking together Andrea has a right to Heinrich's continued walking alongside her, together with the standing to issue related rebukes and demands. This right can be waived in certain contexts if Andrea gives her permission to Heinrich to cease walking alongside her.

[7] Cf. Hart 1955, a classic philosophical discussion of rights, especially p. 180: "it is Y who has a moral claim upon X [to have his, Y's, mother looked after] is *entitled* to have his mother looked after, and who can *waive the claim and release* Y from the obligation. Y is, in other words, morally in a position to determine by his choice how X shall act and in this way to limit X's freedom of choice; and it is this fact, not the fact that he stands to benefit, that makes it appropriate to say that he has *a right*." [Emphases in the original.] In saying, in the text above, that Andrea understands herself to have a right "of some kind" I mean to leave it open whether or not the right in question is best referred to as a "moral" right. If "moral" is understood simply as a synonym for "non-legal" then it would clearly be appropriate to use it here. For some discussion of Hart's article with a focus on his discussion of obligations as opposed to rights see Gilbert 1999.

[8] To have the standing to rebuke someone is, I take it, to be entitled to do so or, in other terms, to have a right to do so. I forebear from talking of a right here so as to distinguish this right of rebuke from the right whose violation grounds it.

They will understand, also, that, on the same basis, Heinrich has the same right and standing in relation to Andrea.

Assuming that these understandings are well-founded, what is it about walking together that gives rise to them? In particular, what is it about walking together that gives the participants rights to each other's continued participation?[9]

3. How joint actions arise

In order to discern the basis of the noted rights one might inquire into the contexts in which people find themselves doing things together. How does joint activity get started? How are the rights in question established?

a. Agreements

Conse. How might Andrea and Heinrich have come to be walking together? Perhaps Andrea proposed that they go for a walk (as in "Shall we go for a walk?") and Heinrich accepted her proposal (as in "Yes, let's"). Having thus agreed to walk together, they set off on their walk.

Such an agreement is, indeed, a standard way of initiating joint action. As a result, one might propose the *agreement hypothesis,* that is, the hypothesis that we can best understand the rights involved in acting together as stemming from a prior agreement to engage in the relevant joint action. Agreements are, after all, an acknowledged source of rights. If you and I agree that I will cook dinner and you will wash the dishes, I acquire a right to your washing the dishes, and you acquire a right to my cooking dinner.

Though it has some plausibility, the agreement hypothesis must be rejected. For, as I now argue, a prior agreement is not a necessary condition for joint action. Suppose that on a beautiful spring day Heinrich runs into Andrea and tells her he is going for a walk to Central Park. She says "Oh, what a nice idea! Please wait a moment while I make a phone call!" Evidently pleased, Heinrich says "Sure!" Her phone call finished, Andrea turns to him and says "I'm ready!" This interchange could be enough to provide the foundation for a case of walking together, but it seems wrong to say that Andrea and Heinrich *agreed* to walk together.

In this case there is, indeed, an interchange between the parties that occurs prior to their walking together, an interchange that is apt to provide a foundation

---

[9] In previous writings I have tended to emphasize that the parties to an established joint action recognized *obligations* to continue their participation, in relation to which the other parties had corresponding rights. Though the present approach emphasizes rights it in no way denies the existence of correlative obligations. See the text below, section 8.

for it. To that extent it resembles an agreement and serves the purpose that an agreement would have served, had the parties made one.[10]

Perhaps for this reason, there may be a temptation to say that the parties "implicitly agreed" to go for a walk in this case. If one succumbs to it, however, one must admit that the parties made no agreement strictly speaking. In other words, examples such as this still present a problem for the agreement hypothesis.

In addition, there are cases of acting together that involve no such preliminary interchange. Thus people may begin to quarrel, for instance, without preamble. This is probably the most common way for quarrels to occur. They tend to erupt spontaneously, on the basis of feelings of anger. For example, Helga angrily bursts out "You never should have invited your sister to dinner!" Klaus offers a sarcastic retort, and more angry back and forth ensues. The premeditative quality of an agreement sets it at odds with this aspect of most quarrels.[11] It is not only joint actions precipitated by forceful emotions that occur without a prior agreement or other anticipatory preamble, but these are particularly suited for such an unheralded beginning.

A friend of the agreement hypothesis might point out that there is an agreement-like structure in the situation described. One could say that, in effect, by bursting out as she does Helga proposes a quarrel, and by "taking the bait" and returning hostilities Klaus accepts her proposal. This may be so, but it does not save the agreement hypothesis. In common parlance, as the story goes, Helga and Klaus did not *agree to quarrel.* They simply *started quarreling.*

It might be questioned whether the example of quarreling is sufficiently like walking together to qualify as an example of the type of acting together at issue here. One might wonder, in particular, if quarrels involve a package of rights analogous to those that appear to be present when people walk together. If they do not, that would make quarreling significantly different from walking together.

A package of rights analogous to those involved in walking together does seem to be involved when people quarrel. Once people understand themselves to be quarreling, there is liable to be a strong sense of mistake if one party suddenly tunes out, for instance. A sense of mistake is less likely to occur if one who wants to stop quarreling says something like "Let's stop this!," inviting a permission-granting response such as "Okay." One party may, of course, concede defeat, and have this concession accepted as in the following interchange. Helga: "I guess you are right. It was time to invite her." Klaus: "I'm glad you understand where I was coming from."

---

[10] This is not to say that everything achieved by an agreement is necessarily achieved in this case.
[11] On the premeditative quality of agreements see Gilbert 2000, pp. 112–113.

As long as an analogous package of rights is present, and without further reason to doubt its status, it seems reasonable to put quarreling alongside walking together as examples of the kind of acting together at issue here. Someone might perhaps wonder if the antagonistic aspect of quarrels disqualified them as joint actions. It is not clear why this should be so.[12]

As far as the agreement hypothesis goes, it is easy enough to provide non-antagonistic examples of joint actions beginning without a prior agreement or other anticipatory preamble. Thus people may quite spontaneously begin a conversation, or kiss. Either of these joint actions might more easily begin with an agreement than a quarrel would ("Shall we talk?" "Let's kiss and make up!") but neither need do so, nor need there be any related anticipatory preamble.

Unless for some reason we feel forced to accept the agreement hypothesis, there is no need to insist that there are agreements where common parlance would deny this. One might think that the agreement hypothesis is the best we can come up with because one believes that, in contrast to the rights associated with joint action, philosophers generally understand well the rights associated with agreements. There is reason, however, to reject this belief.

Agreements, as opposed to promises, have not been thoroughly considered by philosophers. The prevailing view has been that they are promise-exchanges. If promises are understood in the usual way, however, it is not clear that this view can stand.[13] As to the rights associated with promises, there is a large literature of conflicting views as to their foundation.[14] Though one of these views may of course be correct, there cannot be said to be general agreement among philosophers on this matter. I think it fair to say, then, that the rights associated with agreements are not so well-understood by philosophers that they would well understand the rights associated with a joint action if what they knew was that they stemmed from a prior agreement.

b. A more general condition

In order to give a general account of the genesis of acting together, it makes sense to consider what is common to three kinds of case: cases where the joint activity

---

[12] It may be pointed out that we tend to speak of people quarreling "with" each other rather than as quarreling "together." It is not clear what, if anything, is marked by this fact about usage. "With" does not of itself connote antagonistic feelings, since people can converse with one another, for instance, in perfect amity. Clearly there may be several useful distinctions to be made within the broad realm of acting together that includes quarreling, amicably conversing, and walking together. I shall not attempt to pursue this matter here.

[13] See Gilbert 1993b. The main response to this article on behalf of the promise-exchange view is Bach, 1995. Bach explicitly appeals to a richer but unanalyzed notion of exchange than that I consider. One problem with so doing is that the notion of exchanging itself stands in need of an account.

[14] For note of a variety of such accounts see, for instance, Vitek 1993.

is prefaced by an agreement, cases where there is some other preliminary inter-change, and cases where neither of these things is the case.

If we focus on the examples already considered, it appears that in all of these cases at least the following occurs. Each party to the ensuing joint action says or does something expressive of personal readiness to participate in that action with the other party. And this is "common knowledge" between the parties. To put the "common knowledge" requirement informally here, it is necessary that the relevant expressions be "out in the open" as far as the parties are concerned. Should Heinrich have his deaf ear turned to Andrea, for instance, she may express her readiness in speech, without his having access to her expression.[15]

With respect to Heinrich and Andrea's walking together, their agreement to do so, involving her explicit proposal of a joint walk and his acceptance of her proposal, clearly fits this description. Each thereby expresses a personal readiness to go for a walk with the other. So does the preliminary interchange between them that does not amount to an agreement. As to Helga and Klaus's quarrel, Helga's angry outburst expresses her personal readiness for a quarrel and Klaus's sarcastic retort indicates that he is ready also.

Agreements are, evidently, a particularly effective way of initiating joint actions insofar as they involve an explicit specification of what will be done together. They also serve well to organize the progress of ongoing joint actions.

I believe that a good way of characterizing an agreement is as a joint decision.[16] The decision may concern a future joint action or a personal action or actions of the participants.

In saying "Shall we go for a walk?," then, Andrea expresses her personal readiness to decide together with Heinrich to go for a walk together, and in responding "Yes," Heinrich expresses his readiness to do so. That is enough for them to have made the joint decision in question. They have agreed. At one and the same time each has, of course, expressed readiness to go for a walk with the other.

---

[15] There are numerous discussions of "common knowledge" and attempted technical accounts of it. The original philosophical discussions are Lewis 1969, and Schiffer 1972 (Schiffer's "mutual knowledge*"). Other discussions include the relevant sections of Gilbert, 1989. See also Gilbert, 2002.

[16] Making a joint decision may count as a case of "acting together" in a sense. However, deciding together to go for a walk, say, seems to be importantly different from walking together, just as one person's making a personal decision to go for a walk is importantly different from that person's going for a walk. Walking together, and so on, may be deemed cases of acting together in a narrow, central sense. As will emerge in the text below, I believe that whatever their differences, acting together (as in walking together) and deciding together (as in making an agreement) share crucial common features.

4. Two questions

These observations on the genesis of joint action give rise to at least the following questions. (1) Evidently when one person's expression of personal readiness for joint action is "met" by the corresponding expression of the other party or parties the foundation for joint action is laid. What happens, then, when one such expression is met by the corresponding expressions? What, in other words, is the outcome of these expressions? (2) How does the outcome of these expressions create the rights associated with joint action? In what follows I propose answers to these questions.

5. Collective goals

Consider someone who is acting alone, as opposed to acting together with another person. Heinrich, for instance, is going to his doctor's office. Taking this apart, at least the following elements seem to be present. Heinrich has the goal of reaching his doctor's office, he is acting in a way appropriate to the achievement of this goal, and he is doing so by virtue of the fact that it is his goal.

If acting together has something like this structure, we will need to know what it is for two or more people collectively to espouse a goal. In terms I shall explain, my proposal as to what it is for two or more people collectively to espouse a goal is this. They must be *jointly committed* to espousing that goal as a body.[17]

As I shall argue shortly, if one accepts this suggestion one can give a plausible account of the rights associated with acting together. I first briefly introduce the notion of joint commitment as I understand it.[18]

I should say at the outset that though I use the phrase "joint commitment" as a technical phrase of my own, I take the concept of a joint commitment as I understand it to be a fundamental everyday concept. More fully, I take it to be a fundamental part of the conceptual equipment of human beings functioning in social contexts. This is in part because I think it is a crucial element in the best accounts of such central social concepts as acting together, collective belief, and social convention.[19]

It will be helpful to start with some remarks on commitments in general and on what I refer to as *personal* commitments.

---

[17] In earlier work I have argued against some alternative accounts in part on the basis of their failure to give a satisfactory account of the rights associated with acting together. See, for instance, Gilbert 1989, chapter 4, 1990. See also Gilbert, 2002 (response to Bittner).

[18] For a longer treatment, see Gilbert, 2002, section 1.

[19] On collective belief and social convention, see Gilbert 1989, chapters 5 and 6.

a. Commitments in general

I shall not attempt a general account of commitment. Rather, I shall start with what I take to be a clear case of commitment in the sense at issue here, and note some of its features both negative and positive.

A clear case of commitment is provided by a personal decision. One who has decided to do something is thereby committed to do that thing. One need not have communicated that decision to anyone else. Nor need there be any weighty reasons for making it. Thus commitments in general need not have an obvious social dimension, nor need they arise on the basis of some pre-existing moral requirement.

I take it that commitments in the sense in question here rationally motivate in the following sense. If one is subject to a commitment, reason requires one to act in accordance with that commitment, all else being equal.

Thus suppose Andrea has decided to have lunch at the Nutmeg Restaurant today. Suppose she then sets off, absentmindedly, in the direction of Chang's Garden, which is where she usually eats. If she remembers her decision, it should seem to her that things are going off course: she should not be on her way to Chang's Garden, for she decided to go to the Nutmeg Restaurant. Quite likely she will decide not to bother to retrace her steps. She will then and there *change her mind* about where to eat. But until she does this, she has reason to go to the Nutmeg Restaurant by virtue of a standing decision.

More can be said about commitments in relation to reason and reasoning. The foregoing may suffice for present purposes.

b. Personal commitments

Having said this much about commitments in general, let me introduce the notion of a personal commitment. A personal commitment is a commitment that is brought into existence by one person alone. That person can, further, terminate or rescind it simply by changing his or her mind. A personal decision, for instance, generates a personal commitment.

c. Joint commitments

A joint commitment is the commitment of two or more people. Thus Heinrich and Andrea may be jointly committed to espouse a certain goal as a body. In this section I focus on the nature of joint commitment—what makes a commitment a joint one? I turn later to the interpretation of "endorsing a goal as a body." Heinrich and Andrea's joint commitment is not composed of a personal commitment of Heinrich's and a personal commitment of Andrea's. Rather, it is their commitment, the commitment of the two of them.

How might Andrea and Heinrich become jointly committed in this way? In a central type of case, Heinrich expresses to Andrea his readiness to be jointly committed to espouse the relevant goal as a body, in conditions of common knowledge, and Andrea does likewise. The joint commitment is then in place.

Note that in order to enter a joint commitment with another person one must know what a joint commitment is. One could not otherwise express one's readiness to enter such a commitment. This does not mean, of course, that the *phrase* "joint commitment" is part of one's vocabulary.

It is not the case that Heinrich's expression of readiness brings into being *part* of the joint commitment in question. A joint commitment is not a complex of personal commitments, nor does a joint commitment have parts in the way such a complex does, each part being a particular personal commitment. Rather than Heinrich and Andrea each creating part of their joint commitment by his or her expression of readiness to be jointly committed, their two expressions create the whole when and only when both expressions are in place.

Just as the readiness of each is required to bring the joint commitment into being so the concurrence of each is required in order to rescind the commitment. No one party can rescind it unilaterally. Nor can any one party rescind any part of it unilaterally, since it does not have parts.

Each of the parties to a joint commitment is indeed committed in the sense that each one is subject to a commitment. It is tempting then to refer to the parties' "individual commitments" when there is a joint commitment. If one does this, one must bear in mind that these individual commitments have important special features: they depend for their existence on the joint commitment; and the person who has a given individual commitment of this sort is not in a position unilaterally to rescind it. These individual commitments are clearly not *personal* commitments in the sense introduced earlier. It is true that one party can deliberately violate or break a joint commitment, but as long as the joint commitment survives, what is done amounts precisely to a violation, as each party will understand.[20]

d. The content of joint commitments

In stating my account of a collective goal I said that the participants must be jointly committed to espousing a goal as a body. As I understand them, all joint commitments are joint commitments to do something as a body, where "doing something" is construed broadly so as to include such psychological states as

---

[20] Exactly what a violation achieves in terms of the persistence or otherwise of a given joint commitment needs careful consideration. On this see Gilbert 1996.

belief, the acceptance of a rule or principle of action, and so on. The phrase "as a body" is not sacrosanct. One might use other phrases such as "as a unit" or "as one."

The complex idea of a joint commitment to espouse a goal as a body is to be interpreted roughly as follows. The relevant joint commitment is an instruction to the parties to see to it that they act in such a way as to emulate as best they can a single body with the goal in question. The idea of a single goal-endorsing body is not itself understood in collective terms. The concept of a body that endorses a goal is neutral with respect to the nature of the goal endorser and with respect to its composition.

6. The genesis of acting together reconsidered

I suggested earlier that acting together will have as an important component the collective espousal of a goal. I then proposed that in order collectively to espouse a goal the parties must be *jointly committed* to espousing that goal as a body. I have now explained what this proposal amounts to, in particular with respect to the concept of joint commitment as I understand it.

Prior to this, in discussing how people come to be acting together I raised the question of what seems to be common to the following range of cases: those where the joint activity is prefaced by an agreement, those where it is tempting to speak of a prior implicit agreement, and those where neither of these things is the case.

I proposed as a preliminary answer that each party must express something to the others, something that is expressive of readiness to participate in the joint action. At this point I propose the following more precise answer: each party must express his or her personal readiness to enter a joint commitment to endorse a certain goal as a body.[21]

7. Acting together: a sketch

Considering the case of one person acting alone I suggested that this involved at least the following elements: the espousal of a certain goal, and action

[21] I have sometimes written of expressions of "willingness" rather than "readiness." I use neither term in a special technical sense. A problem with the term "willingness" is that it may suggest that it involves, by definition, a state incompatible with strong pressure or coercion on the person who is willing. I did not intend this implication, which is not a part of a standard interpretation of "willingness." (Think of such a statement as "I know you don't want to go, but are you willing to do so?") In any case, "readiness" may have less of a tendency to suggest the lack of coercion.

appropriate to the achievement of that goal, this action being performed in light of the fact that it is his goal. It seems that the parallel account of acting together will run as follows: two or more people are acting together if they collectively espouse a certain goal, and each one is acting in a way appropriate to the achievement of that goal, where each one is doing this in light of the fact that the goal is their collective goal.

Assuming now the understanding of a collective goal that I have proposed, the above account of acting together can be unpacked as follows: two or more people are acting together if they are jointly committed to espousing as a body a certain goal, and each one is acting in a way appropriate to the achievement of that goal, where each one is doing this in light of the fact that he or she is subject to a joint commitment to espouse the goal in question as a body.

It would clearly support the proposed account of acting together, or something close to it, if the rights associated with acting together can be shown to be associated with it according to that account.

8. The rights inherent in acting together

It can be argued that there is an important sense in which a joint commitment, in and of itself, involves rights and obligations. I cannot explore this matter fully here, so a few words must suffice.

When two people enter a joint commitment each surely gains a special standing in relation to the other. If one violates the commitment, the other is in a special position to object. It was, this other may emphasize, *our* commitment that you violated, not a personal one.

From this consideration alone one can say that a joint commitment grounds mutual claims for conformity. In other words, it grounds rights of the parties against each other, rights to conformity to the commitment.

Clearly the language of obligation can also be used here, insofar as those against whom one has a right to some action are obligated to perform that action.[22] The obligations in question here are what are known in deontic logic as directed obligations. Such obligations involve three elements: an agent, who is obligated, a person or persons to whom that agent is obligated (the right holder or holders), and an action or actions that the agent is obligated to perform. Such

---

[22] For a longer discussion of the relationship of joint commitment to obligation see Gilbert 1999.

obligations must therefore be sharply distinguished from other so-called obligations that do not have this character.[23]

If I am right about agreements, and an agreement is constituted by an appropriate joint commitment, then the nature and source of the rights and obligations of agreement are no longer obscure. They are rights and obligations of joint commitment.[24]

I should emphasize that the rights and obligations in question appear to exist by virtue simply of the existence of a particular commitment that is joint. It may for this reason be misleading to describe them as *moral* obligations insofar as they need only the will of the parties to bring them into being. This may be capricious or arbitrary, and its content may bear little or no positive relationship to the true, the beautiful, or the good.

References

Bach, Kent (1995): "Terms of Agreement," *Ethics* 105, pp. 604–612.

Bratman, Michael (1993): "Shared Intention," *Ethics* 104, pp. 97–113.

Gilbert, Margaret (1989): *On Social Facts*, Princeton, NJ: Princeton University Press.

—— (1990): "Walking Together: A Paradigmatic Social Phenomenon," *Midwest Studies in Philosophy* 15, reprinted in Gilbert 1996.

—— (1993a): "Agreement, Coercion and Obligation," *Ethics* 103, pp. 679–706, reprinted in Gilbert 1996.

—— (1993b): "Is an Agreement an Exchange of Promises?" *Journal of Philosophy* 90, pp. 627–649, reprinted in Gilbert 1996.

—— (1994): "Concerning Sociality: The Plural Subject as Paradigm," in: J. Greenwood (ed.), *The Mark of the Social*, Lanham, MD: Rowman and Littlefield.

—— (1996): *Living Together: Rationality, Sociality, and Obligation*, Lanham, MD: Rowman and Littlefield.

—— (1997)"What Is It for Us to Intend?," in: G. Holmstrom-Hintikka and R. Tuomela (eds.), *Contemporary Action Theory*, vol. 2, pp. 65–85, reprinted in Gilbert 2000.

—— (1998a): "Review of Tuomela," 1995, *Ethics*.

—— (1998b): "In Search of Sociality," *Philosophical Explorations* 1, pp. 233–241, reprinted in Gilbert 2000.

—— (1999): "Obligation and Joint Commitment," *Utilitas* 11, pp. 143–163, reprinted in Gilbert 2000.

—— (2000): *Sociality and Responsibility: New Essays in Plural Subject Theory*, Lanham, MD: Rowman and Littlefield.

—— (2002): "Considerations on Joint Commitment: Responses to Various Comments," in: G. Meggle (ed.) *Social Facts and Collective Intentionality*, Frankfurt: Hansel-Hohenhausen, pp. 73–101. [Chapter 2, this volume]

---

[23] On one distinction among obligations see Gilbert 1993a.

[24] See Gilbert 1993a, 1999.

Hart, H. L. A. (1955): "Are there any Natural Rights?," *Philosophical Review*, pp. 175–191.

Lewis, David (1969): *Convention: A Philosophical Study*, Cambridge, MA: Harvard University Press.

Schiffer, Steven (1972): *Meaning*, Oxford: Oxford University Press.

Searle, John (1990): "Collective Intentions and Actions," in: P. Cohen, J. Morgan, and M. Pollack (eds.), *Intentions in Communication*, Cambridge, MA: MIT Press, pp. 401–415.

Vitek, William (1993): *Promising*, Philadelphia, PA: Temple University Press.

2

Considerations on Joint Commitment: Responses to Various Comments[1]

Introduction

My book *On Social Facts* (1989) proposes accounts of a number of important social phenomena. These include, in particular, group languages, acting together, social groups, collective beliefs, and social conventions. I argued that at the core of all these phenomena was what I referred to as a *joint commitment*. I refer to those who are jointly committed with one another in some way as constituting a *plural subject*, and have accordingly dubbed my general theory of social phenomena *plural subject theory*.[2]

Since the appearance of *On Social Facts* the interest taken in its central concerns and specific proposals has been gratifying and encouraging. In this chapter I respond to various points in recent essays that address these concerns and proposals. These points all relate in one way or another to joint commitment as I understand it.

The technical phrase "joint commitment" is open to different definitions, so where it may be helpful to clarify my intent I refer to joint commitment in my sense as "Gilbertian" joint commitment. In relation to what follows it will be useful first to emphasize and elaborate on certain key aspects of such joint commitment.

---

[1] I thank Georg Meggle for inviting me to respond to comments on my work in this volume. I have incorporated here material from an informal response written in December 2000 to the draft of an article by Abe Roth (Roth 2000ms). I am grateful to Professor Roth and to all the commentators on my work in this volume for thoughtful and stimulating discussions.

[2] See Gilbert 1989, and elsewhere. Gilbert 1996, pp. 7–15, gives an overview of relevant material to 1996. My own statements are, I hope, becoming clearer as time goes on. See sections 2.v.a and 2.v.b of this chapter.

1. *Preliminaries*

i. Characterizing "personal commitments"

An important preliminary matter is as follows. When I refer to a "personal commitment" I mean a commitment of a person X, such that X is in a position unilaterally to bring the commitment into being and unilaterally to rescind it. An example of a personal commitment is the commitment involved in a personal decision. For instance, if Joan decides to go shopping, she thereby creates a personal commitment to go shopping. She was the sole originator of this commitment and she is in a position unilaterally to rescind it by changing her mind.

I take it, evidently, that a personal decision such as Joan's does involve a commitment. Thus commitments as such do not essentially involve more than one person—at least on their face.[3] Nor are they essentially matters of morality. Nonetheless reason requires one to act in accordance with them, all else being equal.[4]

a. Personal commitments and answerability

An important aspect of personal commitments relates to what I shall call *answerability*. Suppose Joan decides to go shopping today and does not change her mind. Somehow, however, she fritters the day away on other activities and eventually it is too late to go shopping. Thus Joan fails to conform to her commitment. Absent special background circumstances, Joan is answerable for this failure to no one but herself. It seems appropriate to say that she is indeed answerable to herself. Such an understanding would be manifest were Joan to chide herself on realizing her failure to get out to the shops in time, as she might well do.[5]

The point about answerability, then, is this. If one fails to conform to an unrescinded personal commitment one is answerable to oneself and to no one else. One has a basis for chiding oneself by reason simply of one's failure to conform to the commitment in question.

---

[3] I say "at least on their face" to make it clear that my point is made at a level at which Wittgensteinian concerns about the extent of sociality are irrelevant. Gilbert 1989, chapter 3, discusses skeptically some Wittgensteinian arguments for the sociality of language and thought as such.

[4] See e.g., Gilbert (2002), section 5.a.

[5] I have argued elsewhere that one can see failure to abide by an unrescinded personal commitment as a kind of *self-betrayal*. I take it that if Ann feels *betrayed* when Ben does X, she supposes that Ben is *answerable* to her for doing X. Use of the term "betrayal" may tend to suggest that the matter at issue is a weighty one, and could lead one to question the point. Reference to "answerability" is likely to be less contentious, and is all that is needed for present purposes.

b. On the unilateral creation of a personal commitment

It will be useful to elaborate on what it is to be in a position *unilaterally to create a commitment.* Consider first the possibility that Joan decides to go shopping today if and only if the sun comes out. If she is to carry out her decision she must wait to see whether or not the sun comes out. Still, at the time of her decision she is already committed. She is, as we might put it, committed to *go-shopping-if-and-only-if-the-sun-comes-out.* Again, suppose that Joan decides to go shopping today if and only if her daughter Marcie goes out with some friends. If she is to carry out her decision she must wait to see what Marcie does. Her commitment exists in advance, however, irrespective of Marcie's decisions or actions.

What, though, if what Joan decides is this: if and only if Marcie goes out with her friends, I'll decide to go shopping today? Note that the decision in question is not that, if and only if Marcie goes out with her friends, Joan will decide *whether or not* to go shopping. Rather, the content of her possibly upcoming decision is already fixed: she will decide *to go shopping.*

One can imagine circumstances in which Joan's decision to decide a certain way would make perfect sense.[6] Perhaps Joan hates to shop and the decision to go shopping is always difficult. In order to make it she has to engage in various preliminary rituals. She needs to shop soon but Marcie's staying home would provide a good excuse not to shop today. She thus decides to make the decision to shop if and only if Marcie goes out with her friends. She will then to do whatever she needs to do in order to make that decision.

There are two decisions at issue in this case. The first is a decision to decide a certain way, if and only if certain conditions hold. The second is the decision decided upon. The conditions for making the latter decision involve the action of another person. Does that mean that the second decision is not a personal one?

It seems not, for Joan is surely in a position unilaterally to *make* the decision, even though she has made a prior decision to make it if and only if someone else, namely Marcie, first does a particular thing. Once having made it, she is in a position unilaterally to change her mind.

ii. Some central features of Gilbertian joint commitment

In this section I list some central features of Gilbertian joint commitment.[7] I might have labeled such commitments "holistic" which would, I feel, be appropriate, but there is some likelihood that label is overly ambiguous. I mostly leave aside such questions as how the features relate to each other, whether there are

---

[6] Here I am indebted to Pink 1996, p. 192.

[7] See also Gilbert, 2002.

any redundancies in the list, and how I would justify each feature's presence in it. Generally speaking, I take myself to be engaged in the articulation of a central everyday concept.

I start with what is presumably the core feature, feature (1). Others are numbered (1a), (1b) and so on, to indicate that (1) is indeed the core feature. For mnemonic convenience I give each feature a short label.

(1) [Holism] A joint commitment is a commitment of two or more people.

(1a) [Answerability] Each party is answerable to all parties for any violation of the joint commitment. This is a function of its jointness.[8]

(1b) [Creation] Creation of a joint commitment requires the participation of all the parties. A joint commitment cannot, then, be created by a single party acting unilaterally. In some cases there may be special background understandings or explicit preliminaries involving all the parties that allow, in effect, for creation of a joint commitment by some proper subset of the parties. This involves the authorization of a person or body to create joint commitments for the parties.[9] The situation described here is the "default" situation in which no such understandings or preliminaries are present.

Note that this point does not address *the means* by which a joint commitment is created, but rather *who must be involved* in its creation. With respect to the means see section iii.

(1c) [Rescission] A joint commitment is not rescindable by any one party unilaterally, but only by the parties together. Again, in some cases there may be special background understandings or explicit preliminaries that allow, in effect, for unilateral rescindability.[10] The situation described here is the "default" situation.

The *two-person case* has some special features. For instance, if one person violates the commitment the non-violator may have the option of "unilaterally" rescinding it. This would be because the violator has in effect indicated concurrence with such rescinding.[11]

---

[8] Cf. Gilbert 1999a, section 4. There I argue that properly so-called obligations and rights inhere in any joint commitment. Much of the argument can be applied to answerability. See section 3ii., this chapter, on the obligations and rights of joint commitment.

[9] Cf. Gilbert 1989, p. 206. The text there refers to the parties' "joint acceptance that X is to count as Y" which I parse as *"joint commitment to accept as a body* that X is to count as Y."

[10] See Gilbert 2000, p. 35 note 36 for an example.

[11] Gilbert 1996 discusses the consequences of violation of joint commitments of various kinds, and expresses my current inclination to understand violation in certain two person cases as rendering the commitment *voidable* rather than *void* (pp. 14–16; 381–383). This would not materially affect the argument in Gilbert 1993a, in which I supposed the alternative.

(1d) [Dependent "individual" commitments] When there is a joint commitment each of the parties is committed. One may therefore speak of the associated "individual commitments" of the parties. These commitments exist through the joint commitment: they are dependent on its existence for their own. As to the content of these individual commitments, each is presumably committed to promoting the object of the joint commitment to the best of his or her ability, in conjunction with the others. (On the object or content of a joint commitment see (1g) below.)

(1d') [Dependent commitments not personal] Given their existence through the joint commitment, these "individual commitments" are not *personal commitments*: they are not the unilateral creation of the respective persons, they cannot be unilaterally rescinded, and one is answerable to all for their violation, which is, in effect, a violation of the commitment of all—the joint commitment.

(1d'') [Interdependence of dependent commitments] The dependent individual commitments are interdependent in the sense that there cannot be a single such commitment, pertaining to a given individual, existing in the absence of any other such commitment. Thus given a two-person joint commitment, and *ceteris paribus*, one person's dependent individual commitment cannot exist unless the other's does. These commitments must arise and fall together. Again, this is because of the dependence on each of these individual commitments on the joint commitment (see 1d).

(1d''') [Simultaneity of dependent commitments] The dependent individual commitments of the parties come into being simultaneously at the time of the creation of the joint commitment. Some qualifications may be necessary here but this is at least true with respect to the dependent individual commitments of those creating an original joint commitment *de novo*. (In a two-person case, simultaneity follows from interdependence, though not conversely.)

[1e] [Content] Joint commitments are always commitments to "act as a body" in a specified way, where "acting" is taken in a broad sense. Thus people may jointly commit to deciding as a body, to accepting a certain goal as a body, to intending as a body, to believing as a body a certain proposition, and so on.

This list of features may of itself help to clarify various matters concerning Gilbertian joint commitment. I now address in light of it some issues raised by various authors.[12]

---

[12] I refer particularly to relevant discussions in Meggle, ed., 2002. See the text below..

2. *Creating joint commitments*

i. Robins's discussion

Michael Robins wonders how "two or more people could ever *become* jointly committed if they weren't already 'joined at the hip'!"[13] Robins explores this question in relation to several discussions including my own. I am not sure that I fully understand his positive proposal, and will not address that here. Rather, I focus on an assumption that may be central to his and many other discussions, and clarify my own view of it with respect to Gilbertian joint commitments.[14]

ii. The conditional personal commitments assumption (CPC)

Why might the possibility of creating a Gilbertian joint commitment *de novo* seem problematic? One possibility involves an assumption I call the "conditional personal commitments assumption," or "CPC."

According to the CPC, a joint commitment is created if and only if the parties make appropriate matching conditional personal commitments. Some clarification of the CPC as I shall be construing it here is in order.

Robins refers at one point to "an exchange of conditional intentions or promises...."[15] Intentions and promises are, of course, very different things. The CPC as I am construing it involves conditional personal *intentions* and the like.[16]

I take it that a conditional personal intention involves a conditional personal commitment in the sense of personal commitment characterized in the text above.[17] Focusing on conditional personal intentions accords with at least some of the proposals Robins discusses including the carefully considered proposal of Velleman.[18]

There is a good theoretical reason not to appeal to *promises* as part of the process by which joint commitments are created: it is quite plausible to see a promise as itself incorporating a joint commitment.[19] That cannot be said of personal intentions, decisions, and so on. There is a related problem about requiring an

---

[13] Robins 2002, p. 306 .

[14] Though Robins refers to and quotes my own discussions of joint commitment, it is not completely clear that he means to focus precisely on Gilbertian joint commitment. Thus at one point he refers, perhaps more broadly, to "a stronger sense of commitment, which can ... be found in the work of Gilbert and Tuomela." Robins 2002, p. 302.

[15] Robins 2002, p. 302.

[16] I mean here to include decisions, plans, and so on, all of which appear necessarily to involve intentions thought they are not necessarily present when an intention is.

[17] See section 1.i.b in this chapter.

[18] Velleman 1997.

[19] See Gilbert 1993a (Gilbert 1996, chapter 13, at pp. 333–334).

exchange, in any substantial sense, in the creation of a joint commitment: there is reason to think of such an exchange as itself involving one or more joint commitments.[20] The same goes, indeed, for standard everyday forms of communication, such as telling, informing, and so on.[21]

I shall take it that what is at issue is simply a pair of matching conditional personal intentions, where the existence of each member of the pair is common knowledge between the parties. One of the pair may, indeed, have been formed in reaction to the other.

Common knowledge in general may be understood roughly as follows: there is *common knowledge that p* among certain parties if and only if the parties *notice* that the fact that p is *open** with respect to all of themselves.[22] As I define it, openness* involves, roughly, many levels of potential knowledge of one another's knowledge.[23]

What is a conditional personal intention? One might initially characterize such an intention as one expressible by a statement of the form "I intend to do A, if (*or* only if) a certain condition holds." That granted, it will be helpful to distinguish among conditional personal intentions as follows. For simplicity I shall focus on sufficient conditions.

An *internally conditional* personal intention is expressible by a statement of the form: "I intend this: to do such-and-such if a certain condition holds." An *externally conditional* personal intention is expressible, rather, by a statement of the form: "If a certain condition holds, I intend to do such-and-such."[24] In other words, the condition of an externally conditional intention is a condition of the existence of the intention as such.[25]

An externally conditional intention can at the same time be internally conditional. The condition of an externally conditional intention is, in other words, the condition of an *actual* intention as opposed to one that is *categorical in form.* The condition of an internally conditional intention is a condition for an intention categorical in form.

---

[20] This connects with a worry I have about the positive proposal regarding *agreements* made in Bach 1995, a thoughtful and fine-grained essay that came to my attention only recently.

[21] See Gilbert 1989, p. 434.

[22] For a fuller exposition see Gilbert 1989, pp. 188–197. The report on my account of common knowledge in Baltzer, 2002, leaves out the "noticing" element which is important. Cf. Gilbert 1989, p. 195 and pp. 212–213. On openness* see the text immediately below.

[23] For a precise account of openness*, which uses some set theory, see Gilbert 1989, pp. 189–191.

[24] See Gilbert 1993a, for discussion of a parallel distinction between internally and externally conditional *promises* (Gilbert 1996, pp. 317–319). For present purposes the question whether there is something suspect in the idea of an externally conditional personal intention may be waived.

[25] Velleman 1997 appears to have externally conditional personal intentions in mind. See, for instance, p. 45, 3rd full paragraph. There are various questions about the status of externally conditional intentions that I shall waive here.

Suppose now that in Claire's presence Phyllis remarks loudly: "I intend to do what I can to promote my going for a walk with Claire, if and only if Claire so intends [that is, if and only if Claire intends to do what she can to promote our going for a walk]." Claire then remarks, in similar fashion: "I intend likewise [that is, I intend to do what *I* can to promote my going for a walk with Phyllis, if and only if *she* so intends]."

If the intentions expressed here are *externally* conditional, it is hard to see how the parties can end up with *actual* personal intentions or commitments. If the intentions are *internally* conditional, it is hard to see how the parties can end up with *categorical* commitments of each to do what she can to promote their walking together. At one point Robins suggests, indeed, that—given the CPC—the "real puzzle" about the creation of joint commitments is how to arrive at categorical commitments from conditional ones.[26]

In light of the above discussion we can discriminate two possible puzzles here. Putting them together one might say that—given the CPC—there is a puzzle as to how people can move from conditional personal intentions to actual, categorical personal intentions, and hence to actual, categorical commitments. Insofar as this is a puzzle, however, it is not the crucial puzzle that the CPC generates with respect to Gilbertian joint commitment.[27]

iii. The crucial problem for the CPC

Suppose for the sake of argument that the "actual, categorical commitments" puzzle has found a solution.[28] Suppose, in particular, that in the foregoing example the condition of each conditional personal intention has been satisfied and that each of the parties now intends to do what she can to contribute to their going for a walk.[29] The intention each now has is a personal intention. The fact that the condition of each party's original conditional personal intention was another person's conditional intention does not make either one's ensuing intention any less personal. Most important for present purposes: should the puzzle be solved we would be left with *a conjunction of personal commitments*.

Now a joint commitment—a Gilbertian joint commitment—is not, nor does it entail, a conjunction of *personal* commitments to promote the object of the

---

[26] Robins 2002, p. 304.
[27] Robins understands that there are other problems. See e.g. Robins 2002, p. 314, footnote 16, and p. 315, where he refers to an "interdependence operator."
[28] I shall not pursue the issue of its solution here.
[29] See the discussion in section 1.i.b. in this chapter.

joint commitment.[30] It does not, of course, rule out such a conjunction. There is no logical entailment either way.[31]

The CPC, then, is suspect in relation to Gilbertian joint commitments. It is plausible to suppose, indeed, that it can be ruled out *a priori*. It is at least hard to see how a combination of conditional *personal* commitments can, through satisfaction of their conditions, create a set of commitments such that the committed people are answerable to one another for violating them. Insofar as the "actual, categorical commitments" puzzle presupposes the CPC, then, it seems best to set that puzzle aside.

iv. The personal commitments assumption

One might be inclined to make the CPC if one understands a joint commitment to be something constituted by a set of personal commitments. This might be called the PC, or personal commitments assumption.

One may, indeed, think that an acceptable account of any so-called joint commitment must accord with the PC. This thought is consonant with a prevalent philosophical stance toward social phenomena that I have elsewhere called "singularism."[32] That is the view that social phenomena are all ultimately composed of the thoughts, attitudes, actions, and so on (including commitments) of single individual persons. Evidently, one who espouses singularism will not countenance any kind of commitment that is not, at base, either a personal commitment or a logical function of the personal commitments of the relevant parties.

As we have seen, the CPC is implausible in relation to Gilbertian joint commitments, which are not constituted by a set of personal commitments. Meanwhile, some of my own early statements have undoubtedly helped to suggest it.[33] In the next section I discuss my own understanding of the creation of joint commitments. I include some reference to those statements that may have helped to suggest the CPC.

[30] If we are jointly committed to doing A as a body then the *object* of the joint commitment is our doing A as a body.

[31] Recall that I distinguish between personal commitments and the *individual* commitments—which are *not* personal commitments—dependent on a joint commitment. See my characterization of joint commitment, section 1.ii above, especially point (1d').

[32] Gilbert 1989.

[33] See Velleman 1997, p. 31. This thoughtful article takes off from remarks of my own. Velleman sees that there is a problem as to how "distinct intentions of different people can add up to a single token of intention, jointly held" (ibid.). He aims to solve this problem, that is, to show how distinct intentions of different people can indeed add up to a single token of intention jointly held. I cannot address his proposal directly here. It may come up against what seems to be a general problem with attempts to construct a Gilbertian joint commitment out of conditional personal intentions.

v. Another story

In characterizing Gilbertian joint commitments earlier I noted just one thing about their creation: subject to some qualifications noted, it requires the participation of all the parties to the commitment. In fuller discussions I have claimed that the parties must *openly** express something, where these expressions must be *common knowledge* between the parties. Expressions *made openly** are expressions intended to be open* to all.[34]

The something that must be expressed is one and the same thing for each expressor, *mutatis mutandis*. We have already seen that something seems not to be a conditional personal intention. What is it, then?

a. An early formulation

When first exploring this question, I contemplated a number of different formulations of what needs to be expressed.[35] I was looking for the best description of a given process, rather than suggesting different processes that might be at issue. One such formulation refers to: "a *conditional commitment of one's will*, made with the understanding that if and only if it is common knowledge that the relevant others have expressed similar commitments, the wills in question are unconditionally and jointly committed" (Gilbert 1989, p. 198; italics in original).

I take this formulation to include crucial elements that any adequate account of the creation of a Gilbertian joint commitment should include. Insofar as certain background circumstances may change the picture, these may be considered elements of the basic case.

What is key is the incorporation of a holistic notion of joint commitment approximating that characterized earlier in this chapter.[36] The formulation correctly implies that the parties to any joint commitment must possess this notion. Also

This would apply also to the proposal from David Gauthier discussed in Robins 2002. In that article Robins makes some reference to Gilbert 1993a. I there argue against the idea that an everyday bilateral executory *agreement* is an exchange of conditional or unconditional *promises*. I should perhaps emphasize that I do *not* argue that a promise cannot give rise to a joint commitment insofar as I think a *single* promise may well be *constituted by* a joint commitment.

[34] Gilbert 1989, p. 197. See also pp. 182–184 which distinguishes and posits both an "expression" condition and an "expressed" condition.

[35] Gilbert 1989, pp. 197–198, 408–410, and elsewhere.

[36] That a holistic conception of joint commitment is at issue is indicated in the preceding discussion of plural subjecthood in Gilbert 1989, pp. 163–164. See also the summary discussion in the final chapter, especially pp. 409–411, and elsewhere. In Gilbert 1987, I wrote: "...if *all* openly express such a commitment they are then *committed as a body* in a certain way" (Gilbert 1996, p. 204; italics in original). I have subsequently clarified and consolidated points made somewhat roughly and scattered about in the initial though long-meditated discussion in Gilbert 1989. See Gilbert 1996, Introduction, section V.

rightly present is the idea that, as the parties understand, the existence of the relevant joint commitment and hence each one's being committed through it depends on each one's expressing the same thing, *mutatis mutandis*.

The reference to the expression of a "conditional commitment" by the parties could be misleading. It may tend to suggest the expression of a *conditional personal intention* whose condition is satisfied if and only if each of the relevant parties expresses a similar intention, the end result being a set of unconditional personal intentions. Though I have been so interpreted, I do not believe that it was ever my intention to suggest this.[37]

It is now some while since I have formulated matters in terms of "conditional commitments." From the outset, I have contemplated and tended to prefer other formulations.[38] As we shall see, this is not to say that there is no kind of *conditionality* in the picture.

b. Another formulation

Rather than referring to the expression of a conditional commitment, I often refer to expressions of willingness, or readiness, to be jointly committed.[39] I now tend to prefer the term "readiness" which is less suggestive of a strong form of voluntariness.[40]

Considering matters in these terms, I take it that, in the basic case, matching expressions of *readiness to enter a particular joint commitment* are necessary to create that joint commitment. These expressions must be made openly* and it must be common knowledge between the parties that they have occurred.

Suppose that Bob is personally ready to be jointly committed in a particular way with Lily and does his part in the creation of the commitment. That is, he openly* expresses his readiness. He understands that the relevant joint commitment will come into being only if Lily similarly does her part, and there is common knowledge between them that this has occurred. In other words, he understands that *only if a certain condition is satisfied* will he or Lily be committed through the relevant joint commitment.

---

[37] In several places I cautiously wrote of "a special kind of conditional commitment." See for instance Gilbert 1989, p. 198.

[38] See, for instance, Gilbert 1989, p. 18. See also the text of the present chapter below.

[39] The following note may be helpful for readers of Gilbert 1989: in chapter 4 of that work I invoke the notion of joint readiness to act together in some way. I also write of an individual's "quasi-readiness." An expression of one's *quasi-readiness* in that sense amounts to an expression of *personal* readiness to be jointly committed with the other person to being *ready as a body, or jointly ready.*

[40] On the relation of joint commitment and voluntariness see Gilbert 1989, p 140, Gilbert 1993b (joint commitment as embodied in a joint decision), and elsewhere

It is not clear that there is any very helpful way of breaking down the notion of expressing one's readiness to be jointly committed. It could be said that one makes it clear that *all is in order as far as one's own will is concerned* for the creation of the relevant joint commitment. Importantly, one understands that *a necessary condition of the creation of the joint commitment is corresponding contributions from the other parties.*

It seems plausible to maintain that this is pretty much the whole story regarding the creation of a basic case of Gilbertian joint commitment. What more could be necessary? What less could be adequate?

It is easy to construe familiar types of everyday interaction in terms of this account. Suppose that, in conditions of common knowledge between Bob and Lily, the following occurs. Bob says to Lily "Shall we dance?." Lily responds "Yes! Let's." Given a certain understanding of dancing together, the account suggests the following interpretation of the core of what transpires. In saying "Shall we dance?" Bob openly* expresses his own readiness to enter a Gilbertian joint commitment with Lily in favor of their dancing together.[41] Lily's "Yes! Let's." openly* expresses her own readiness to do so, and, as they both understand, this expression does all that remains to be done in order to create the relevant joint commitment. At this point, then, they are jointly committed. As a result, each one is answerable to the other for violation of the commitment, and all of the other features of a Gilbertian joint commitment are present.

c. Concomitant joint commitments

It may be observed that Lily is the *addressee* of Bob's question "Shall we dance?." And it can be argued that successfully *questioning* someone involves entering a joint commitment with that person.[42]

Bob's "Shall we dance?" may indeed play multiple roles, as can Lily's "Yes! Let's!." Each, in effect, openly* expresses readiness for a number of distinct joint commitments. As a result of this pairing, it seems that at a minimum a question is asked, an agreement made, a goal jointly accepted. All of these can be argued to be joint commitment phenomena, and all can apparently be created at one and the same time by one and the same pair of expressions. Also achievable within the same encounter is the important phenomenon that I have elsewhere called mutual recognition.[43]

---

[41] In the more elaborate terms I sometimes use, the joint commitment is to accept as a body the goal of their dancing together. In this case Bob and Lily make an explicit agreement, so there is a concurrent and intuitively primary joint commitment to accept as a body the joint decision to dance together, i.e. to accept as a body the goal of their dancing together. On agreements as joint decisions see section 3 of this chapter.

[42] See Gilbert 1989, p. 203. See also chapter 14, this volume.

[43] See Gilbert 1989, p. 218.

vi. Summary and conclusion on the creation of Gilbertian joint commitments

Robins raised the question of how people can enter a joint commitment if they are not already "joined at the hip." With respect to Gilbertian joint commitments, this will certainly seem to be a problem if one makes the assumption I have called here the CPC. It is not clear, however, that one should accept the CPC or what may drive it, the assumption I have called the PC. A proposal that involves neither assumption has been sketched.

3. *The relationship between joint commitments and agreements, obligations and rights*

Remarks by various authors suggest that it is worth clarifying certain points on the relationship between Gilbertian joint commitments and agreements, on the one hand, and obligations and rights on the other.[44]

i. Agreements

I have argued in several places that one can enter a joint commitment without making an agreement, where the phrase "making an agreement" is understood as in pretheoretical talk.[45] Nonetheless there is a close connection, as I understand it, between joint commitments and agreements.

Crucially, everyday agreements can be understood as *constituted by* Gilbertian joint commitments. Specifically, an everyday agreement can be understood as a joint decision, and a joint decision, in its turn, can be construed as constituted by a joint commitment to uphold a certain decision as a body.[46] On this account of agreements, then, if Sylvia and Paul agree to lunch together today, say, they jointly commit to upholding as a body the decision to lunch together today.[47]

ii. Obligations and rights

In the list of central features of Gilbertian joint commitment above I did not directly refer to an aspect of such commitments to which I have devoted considerable time elsewhere. This is the fact that—as I have argued—obligations

---

[44] I have in mind in particular remarks in Miller [Kaarlo] 2002, and Tuomela 2002.

[45] See e.g. Gilbert 2002.

[46] On agreements as involving joint commitments, see Gilbert 1993a; also 1993b.

[47] The remarks in this paragraph were prompted by note ii in Miller [Kaarlo] 2002.

and correlative rights inhere in any joint commitment.[48] In my view this is an extremely important aspect of Gilbertian joint commitments.[49]

It is of course closely related to a feature that I have emphasized here, namely, the fact that the parties to a joint commitment are *answerable* to one another for violations of the commitment. Those who are obligated to one another to satisfy the commitment are answerable to one another if they fail to do so. Thus answerability is entailed by obligations of the relevant sort. Similarly, if you have a right against me to the performance of some action, I will be answerable to you if I fail to perform that action.

Given my understanding of agreements, the obligations and rights everybody takes to be tightly connected with agreements can be explained as inhering in the joint commitment that constitutes the agreement. That is, indeed, my theory of the rights and obligations of agreement.[50]

Some writers who use such terms as "joint commitment" and "collective commitment" do not claim the same intimate connection with obligation—or with answerability—for the phenomena they subsume under these labels. This suggests that they are not talking about Gilbertian joint commitment.[51]

The term "obligation" is, of course, open to several interpretations. Thus, as I understand them *obligations of joint commitment* are, so to speak, inherent in any joint commitment. They are a function of its jointness. Their entrenchment in this particular basis differentiates them from other types of so-called obligation. Again, obligations of joint commitment are, in the parlance of deontic logic, "directed obligations." A logical correlate of my obligation *to you* to do such-and-such is your right *against me* that I do such-and-such. Not all so-called obligations are of this type.[52]

Clearly, in relation to such questions as whether joint commitments obligate and how the obligations of joint commitment relate to the undisputed obligations associated with agreements, it is important to be as precise about what is meant as possible.

[48] See Gilbert 1999a; see also Gilbert 2002.

[49] Among other things it provides the basis for a new approach to the classic problem of political obligation. See Gilbert 1999b.

[50] See Gilbert 1999a and elsewhere.

[51] Tuomela 2002, links obligation only with agreement-based "joint commitments" which, as he emphasizes, he does not see as exhausting the range of such commitments. On the face of it, then, Tuomela's general sense of "joint commitment" is not the Gilbertian.

[52] See Gilbert 1993b, for discussion of two different types of so-called obligation. See also Gilbert 1999a.

4. *Joint commitment in large populations*

In the cases so far considered, the creation of a joint commitment involved individuals who *knew of* each other, indeed *knew each* other, and could thus refer to each other as particular individuals, as when Bob openly* expressed his readiness to dance *with Lily*. In many populations, particularly large ones, members do not all know of one another as individuals—thus the inhabitants of a certain island may know that there are many people living on the island but may not know or know of all of them as individuals. Let us call such populations *distanced* populations, for the sake of a label.[53] The question arises whether the members of distanced populations can participate in a joint commitment together and if so how such a commitment can be formed.

Relevant to this is a distinction between two kinds of common knowledge. Recall that I am construing common knowledge roughly as follows: there is common knowledge that p among certain parties if and only if the parties *notice* that the fact that p is *open** with respect to all of themselves, where openness* involves, roughly, many levels of potential knowledge of one another's knowledge.

The above general account of common knowledge is intended to cover both of two possibilities. First, someone may *notice* that some fact is open* *among A, B, and C*, where A, B, and C are particular individuals referred to as such. Second, someone may notice that some fact is open* *among the Xs*, where one is an X if one possesses some general feature such as the feature of *living on this island*. Evidently we can distinguish between two corresponding forms of common knowledge. I shall refer to these as *individual common knowledge* and *population common knowledge*, respectively.[54]

Clearly the members of a distanced population cannot participate in *individual* common knowledge relating to each member of the population. Can they participate in population common knowledge relating to the whole population? In particular, can they create a joint commitment of the whole population by openly* expressing their readiness to do so and participating in population common knowledge of these expressions?

Ulrich Baltzer has questioned whether they can. Here I attempt briefly to defuse two concerns on this point suggested by his discussion.[55]

---

[53] It is hard to think of a good label for such populations. An existing one is imagined, which tends to suggest "imaginary." See Anderson 1991.

[54] Cf. Gilbert 1989, which introduces population common knowledge after initially introducing common knowledge in terms of individual common knowledge. See also Schiffer 1972, who proceeds similarly with respect to what he calls "mutual knowledge." The discussion of Lewis 1969, chapter 2, introduces common knowledge in his sense in terms of particular people who know of each other but also uses terms that apparently allow for population common knowledge.

[55] Baltzer 2002. There is no space to address other issues Baltzer raises relating to plural subjects.

One of these concerns relates to the possibility that though *most* members of a given distanced population may openly* have expressed themselves in the relevant way, *some* may not have done so. This possibility may, indeed, often be actualized. It does not, however, imply that the members of distanced populations *cannot* enter joint commitments in the way noted. It is, after all, possible that *all* members of a given distanced population have openly* expressed their readiness to participate in a certain joint commitment with the other members of the population, whoever they may be. There could surely be a population in which (a) this is true and (b) each of these openly* made expressions is open* to all, and everybody in the population notices this. In other words, it could be population common knowledge in the population that every member of the population has openly* made the relevant expression.[56]

It is perhaps worth emphasizing, in this connection, that one can have good evidence that p, even *know* that p, without it being the case that one's evidence positively *guarantees* that p. To think otherwise would be to set the standards for knowledge too high.[57]

Another of Baltzer's concerns is this. Correctly understanding me to require that in order to create a joint commitment people must *intentionally* express their readiness to participate such a commitment, he suggests that it is impossible to know the intentional state of a person without knowing of her.[58] Baltzer does not explain why he thinks this is so. In any case, the following example seems to refute it.

Suppose you know that the information I give you is generally reliable and that I obviously have every reason to tell you the truth on this occasion. I then tell you, truthfully, that there are several people next door all of whom intend to come into this room shortly. Failing special background circumstances, it seems you now know that all of those next door have a certain intention. Now suppose that Sue is one of those people. It is perfectly compatible with the story so far that you do not have a clue that Sue, that particular person, exists. You may never have seen her, heard her spoken of, and so on. In that sense you do not know *of* her. You may not know anything of any one of the relevant persons. You may only know that *whoever they may be,* they all have a certain intention.

The topic of joint commitments in large groups is an important one for plural subject theory. It is certainly worth extensive exploration.[59]

---

[56] This was how I intended my example of the tower-building islanders, to which Baltzer refers, to be taken.

[57] Relevant material on the development of population common knowledge can be found in Lewis 1969, and Schiffer 1972.

[58] Recall that my technical term "openly*" is defined in terms of intention.

[59] Baltzer cites a number of my own discussions.

5. *Joint commitments in acting together*

i. Bittner's skepticism

A central social phenomenon is acting together, where this is not a matter of the parties personally doing the same thing at the same time or in one another's vicinity.[60] Thus people may travel together, investigate a crime together, and so on. I have argued in several places that in order so to *act together*, people must constitute the plural subject of the appropriate goal.[61] Negatively, acting together is not to be understood in terms of the personal goals of the parties.[62]

Rüdiger Bittner has questioned this negative claim.[63] He does so by questioning a central contention of mine that, he allows, would support it. That is, he questions whether obligations and rights of some kind—not necessarily moral obligations and rights—are inherent in acting together. This is an important issue for the theory of acting together. My contention both argues in favor of a plural subject account and casts doubt on a variety of other proposals including some which do not appeal to personal goals.[64]

Bittner considers the type of behavior I argue to be in violation of some kind of obligation, such as striding ahead unconcerned for the whereabouts of one's companion when walking together. He says that such behavior seems to him to be no more than "unexpected, unusual, or indeed bizarre, in the ordinary sense of the term."[65]

ii. A response

Standard reactions of the parties in the contexts in question suggest that Bittner's sense of the matter is not common. These reactions express more than a sense of the unexpected, unusual, or bizarre in the sense of "strange."

Rebukes, for instance, are standardly uttered by and accepted from the other participants in such cases. Excuses are made and apologies given. It is hard to see such things as appropriate if the behavior in question is perceived merely

---

[60] The ambiguity of the English word "together" prompts this elucidation.

[61] See, for instance, Gilbert 2002.

[62] This would presumably rule out an account of acting together in terms of "collective ends" as Seumas Miller defines these. See, for instance, Miller [Seumas] 2002. The same goes for "shared intentions" on Michael Bratman's account (Bratman 1993).

[63] Bittner 2002.

[64] For instance that of Searle 1990. See Gilbert 1998. In response to my contention Michael Bratman, in particular, has made a sustained attempt to accommodate associated obligations within his own account of "shared intention." See in particular Bratman 1999, chapter 7.

[65] Bittner 2002, p.39. In the following paragraph Bittner alludes to rudeness. See the text of this chapter below.

as unusual and so on.[66] People can, of course, avoid such rebukes by obtaining advance permission for the behavior in question. But this strongly suggests the existence of a right in the person whose permission is requested.[67]

iii. Concerning rudeness and procedural conventions

At one point Bittner speaks of the behavior in question as "merely... rude." Now one might think that one who acts rudely in relation to someone else violates some sort of right in the person to whom he is rude.

Suppose for the sake of argument that Bittner himself thinks this. If his reference to rudeness is to support his skeptical position he will not claim that the rudeness he writes of violates a right *inherent in acting together* in the relevant way. He might claim, however, that this rudeness violates rights associated with a procedural social convention—a matter, if you like, of *etiquette*—that can be violated without the violation of any rights internal to acting together in the way at issue.[68] He might go on to propose that while this kind of rights violation may be associated with acting together, it is a mistake to think that there are any rights inherent in acting together. In short, the behavior to which I have alluded may be flawed, it may even—where it is clearly rude—violate rights, but it does not violate rights inherent in acting together.

This is an interesting argument, which Bittner may or may not have envisaged. Nonetheless I find its conclusion implausible.

Suppose that Roz and Dan are playing tennis together, and Roz leaves the court for a few minutes to get a drink of water. Failing special background circumstances, Dan's refusal to allow Roz back on the court, rude or not, would surely violate a right Roz has by virtue of her playing tennis with Dan, that is, her right to continue to play tennis with him until, in effect, they jointly so decide.

iv. On the importance of subtle differences

As is clear from Bittner's delicate discussion of a passage in Gilbert, 1989, it is important to get the details of one's examples right, since a subtle difference between cases can be all-important. A written text can be more problematic than a spoken one, where one can make use of a range of meaningful tones of voice. Thus, as Bittner suggests, there are ways in which one who merely has the

---

[66] Cf. the case of social rules, on which, in this connection, see Gilbert, 2000, chapter 5 ("Social Rules: Some Problems with Hart's Account and an Alternative Proposal" [1999]).

[67] This point is emphasized in Gilbert 2002. See also Gilbert 1997.

[68] I myself take it that violation of a social rule or convention does involve violation of a right: I take social rules and conventions to be plural subject phenomena. On this see Gilbert 1989, chapter 6, and Gilbert 2000, chapter 5.

same personal goal as another person might properly *urge the other on* as a way of meeting his own goal, irrespective of anyone's rights or obligations. But what of the person whose urging involves saying to the other "Come on!" or "Hurry up!" in a tone at once demanding and rebuking? This person needs the standing to rebuke and to demand, a standing which his personal goal or even the parties having the same personal goal surely does not provide.[69] Evidently my writing in the relevant passage of Jack's "urging" Jill to come quickly does not of itself differentiate between importantly different possibilities.[70]

v. On the fear of unfreedom

Bittner engagingly reveals a personal desire that may help drive a resistance to acknowledging that there are rights inherent in acting together: "In Gilbert's picture, once I have embraced an action for two, I am also bound, bound by the terms of the shared action itself, to do my share: and *I wish rather not to be so bound*" (Bittner 2002, p. ; emphasis mine).

I am sure that this wish is a common one

As I understand things, of course, Bittner cannot have his wish and, in the sense at issue, act together with one or more other persons. He must choose between his freedom and acting together.

Bittner suggests that there is only cost in such acting together, the cost of being bound. But there is benefit as well. If he and I were traveling together, as I understand things, not only would he be bound but I would also. Should I fail to do my share, he would have the standing to rebuke me, as I would understand. His freedom would to some extent be lost to him but to that same extent he would gain my freedom. In many circumstances, such a result is desirable. It, or what it hinges on, may even be pleasant.[71]

6. *Joint commitment and collective moral responsibility*

I conclude with a brief note on the important topic of collective moral responsibility, or, in its grimmer aspect, collective guilt. Boris Hennig writes: "Moral responsibility can only be undertaken by individuals, that is beings that cannot

---

[69] See Gilbert 1989 and 1990.

[70] Gilbert 1989, p. 162, quoted in Bittner 2002.

[71] It is desirable in coordination problems, for instance. See, for instance, Gilbert 1996, chapter 2 ("Rationality, Coordination, and Convention" [1990]). Bittner 2002, p. 40 says "I resist plural subjects...because I doubt that they...make life pleasant." That participation in a joint commitment binding the parties may be pleasant is argued in Gilbert 1989, pp. 223–225. See also Gilbert, 1990, chapter 11 this volume.

be split up into further parts any more. A collective as such cannot be liable to moral accusations."[72]

Can plural subjects be "split up into further parts"? On the one hand, one may think that they can. They are in some sense made up of individual human beings, who are in any case already "split up" insofar as they are separate physical units. On the other hand a joint commitment and hence a plural subject is in a sense unitary and indivisible. In particular, it is not an aggregation of personal commitments, one for each of the members of the plural subject.

In sum, if one accepts the point made in the first sentence quoted, one need not necessarily accept the point made in the second. Insofar as plural subjects are a type of "collective," the idea of an irreducibly collective form of moral responsibility may yet make sense.[73]

References

Anderson, Benedict (1991): *Imagined Communities*, revised edition, London: Verso.

Bach, Kent (1995): "Terms of Agreement," *Ethics* 105, pp. 604–612.

Baltzer, Ulrich: "Joint Action of Large Groups," (2002) in: Meggle (ed.), pp. 1–18.

Bratman, Michael (1993): "Shared Intention," *Ethics* 104, pp. 97–113.

—— (1999): *Faces of Intention*, Cambridge: Cambridge University Press.

Bittner, Rüdiger: "An Action for Two," (2002) in: Meggle (ed.), pp. 35–42.

Gilbert, Margaret (1987): "Modeling Collective Belief," Synthese 73, pp.185–204, reprinted in Gilbert (1996).

—— (1989): *On Social Facts*, Princeton: Princeton University Press.

—— (1990): "Fusion: Sketch of a "Contractual" Model," in: R.C.L. Moffat, J. Grcic, and M. Bayles (eds), *Perspectives on the Family*, Lewiston: Edwin Mellen Press, pp. 65–78, reprinted in Gilbert 1996. [Chapter 11 this volume.]

—— (1993a): "Is an Agreement an Exchange of Promises?" *Journal of Philosophy* 90, pp. 627–649, reprinted in Gilbert 1996.

—— (1993b): "Agreements, Coercion, and Obligation," *Ethics* 103, pp. 679–706, reprinted in Gilbert 1996.

—— (1996): *Living Together: Rationality, Sociality, and Obligation*, Lanham, MD: Rowman and Littlefield.

—— (1997): "Group Wrongs and Guilt Feelings," *Journal of Ethics* 1, pp. 65–84.

—— (1998): "In Search of Sociality," *Philosophical Explorations* 1, pp. 233–241, reprinted in Gilbert 2000.

—— (1999a): "Joint Commitment and Obligation," *Utilitas* 11, pp. 143–163, reprinted in Gilbert 2000.

—— (1999b): "Reconsidering the 'Actual Contract' Theory of Political Obligation," *Ethics* 109, pp. 236–260, reprinted in Gilbert 2000.

—— (2000): *Sociality and Responsibility: New Essays in Plural Subject Theory*, Lanham, MD: Rowman and Littlefield.

—— (2002): "Acting Together" in: Meggle (ed.), pp. 53-72. [Chapter 1 this volume]

---

[72] Hennig 2002, p. 122.

[73] For more along these lines see Gilbert 1997, Gilbert 2000, chapter 8 ("The Idea of Collective Guilt"), and elsewhere.

Hennig, Boris (2002): "Holistic Arguments for Individualism" in: Meggle (ed.), pp. 103–124.

Lewis, David (1969): *Convention: A Philosophical Study*, Cambridge, MA: Harvard University Press.

Meggle, Georg, ed. (2002): *Social Facts and Collective Intentionality*, Frankfurt: Hansel-Hohenhausen.

Miller, Kaarlo (2002): "Individual and Joint Commitment," in: Meggle (ed.), pp. 255–272.

Miller, Seumas (2002): "Against Collective Agency," in: Meggle (ed.), pp. 273–298.

Pink, Thomas (1996): *The Psychology of Freedom*, Cambridge: Cambridge University Press.

Robins, Michael (2002): "Joint Commitment and Circularity," in: Meggle (ed.), pp. 299–321.

Roth, Abe (2000ms): "Sharing Intentions."

Schiffer, Steven (1972): *Meaning*, Oxford: Oxford University Press.

Searle, John (1990): "Collective Intentions and Actions," in: P. Cohen, J. Morgan, M. Pollack (eds.), *Intentions in Communication*, Cambridge, MA: MIT Press, pp. 90–105.

Tuomela, Raimo: "Joint Intention and Commitment," (2002) in: Meggle (ed.), pp. 385–419.

Velleman, David (1997): "How to Share an Intention," *Philosophy and Phenomenological Research* 57, pp. 29–50.

3

Who's to Blame? Collective Moral Responsibility and Its Implications for Group Members

If *we* are morally responsible for something, what does that say about *me* and *you*—distinct individuals whose personal stories may widely differ?[1] In particular, what does it say about my personal moral responsibility, and yours?

The phrase "morally responsible" is importantly ambiguous, so I should at once say something to clarify my focus. There are both backward-looking and forward-looking claims of moral responsibility (or so I shall label them). An example of a backward-looking claim is: "We are morally responsible for the war," where the war in question may be taking place now or may have taken place in the past. An example of a forward-looking claim is: "We are morally responsible for cleaning this place up," where the cleaning up, it is understood, has yet to be done. These two types of claim may be closely related, but they are clearly distinct. Thus it is intelligible to say: "Though we are *not* morally responsible for what happened, we *are* morally responsible for ameliorating its effects." Think, in this connection, of the consequences of a natural disaster.

Roughly, the backward-looking kind of moral responsibility has to do with causation. One can cause something (the breaking of a vase, say) without being morally responsible for it in the backward-looking way (one was pushed so hard by another, that one fell on the vase). One cannot, however, be morally responsible for it in that way if one had nothing whatsoever to do with its coming to be. The forward-looking kind of moral responsibility has to do with obligation. It has to do with one's moral obligations or *responsibilities* with respect to some matter.

---

[1] Cf. Karl Jaspers, *The Question of German Guilt*, trans. H. B. Ashton (New York: Capricorn, 1947), 17: "we differ extraordinarily in what we have experienced, felt, wished, cherished, and done."

My focus in this chapter is on the backward-looking kind of moral responsibility. My opening question was intended to refer to that, as are the statements that follow here. Even so qualified, the question is a large one, and I shall concentrate on one particular aspect of it. In order to make clear what that aspect is, I first restate the question.

If moral responsibility for some state of affairs, S, is appropriately ascribed to some population of persons, P, what is the relationship of population P's moral responsibility to that of each member of P?[2] Does P's responsibility imply, for instance, that each individual member is personally responsible for S, or at least to some extent responsible for it? Does it imply, rather, that most individual members of P are to some extent responsible for S? Or that some are? Does it imply that no individual member is to any extent personally responsible for S? Or does it have no implications either way?

This restatement of the question is neutral with respect to an important aspect of population P. I do not say that population P is a *collective*. Here are a few examples of populations that—as far as I know—are *not* collectives: the worldwide population of people with blue eyes, the population of people named "Susan," the population of people currently capable of reaching high C, the population of people who were walking along Fifth Avenue in New York on November 22, 2005 at 3 p.m. I shall refer to such populations as *aggregates* which here will be used contrastively: An aggregate is any population that is not a collective.

What, then, is a collective? What might one learn about the worldwide population of people with blue eyes, for instance, that would make one decide that, after all, it was a collective? Rather than offering an account of a collective, at this juncture, I offer a list of examples. These are drawn from a list made by the economist Michael Bacharach: couples, families, workgroups, platoons, sports teams, street gangs, terrorist cells, and "three passers-by giving a motorist a push start."[3] I might have used the more common phrase "social group" instead of the more technical "collective," though the former phrase may be more open to different interpretations.[4] "Social group" should be understood as equivalent to "collective" when it occurs in what follows.

---

[2] I use the term "persons" here in a nontechnical sense without meaning to allude to any particular philosophical account of persons.

[3] Michael Bacharach, "Foreword: Teamwork," in *Teamwork: Multi-Disciplinary Perspectives*, ed. Natalie Gold (New York: Palgrave Macmillan, 2005), xx. Bacharach was giving a list of "teams" in what I take to be a broad sense such that it is equivalent to "collective" in the sense I have in mind here. See my "A Theoretical Framework for the Understanding of Teams," sec. 1.1, in the same volume, pp. 22–23.

[4] In Margaret Gilbert, *On Social Facts* (Princeton, NJ: Princeton University Press, 1989), chap. 4, I offered an account of social groups for which the same list of examples would have served. I noted there the importance of a list of examples to orient discussion. See, e.g., pp. 225 ff.

I take it that collectives are a species of population. In my restatement of it, I put the question of this chapter in terms of populations. The answer, I surmise, will differ depending on what type of population one has in mind. Thus suppose someone says "Rich people have a lot to answer for," or, in another familiar type of locution, "The rich have a lot to answer for." These may amount to ascriptions of moral responsibility to an aggregate. Assuming this construal, their truth may depend on whether or not at least some rich people have something to answer for in whatever domain was in question. Be that as it may, in this chapter I limit myself to consideration of *the moral responsibility of collectives*. Accordingly, as I shall use it in what follows, the phrase "collective moral responsibility" refers to such moral responsibility.

My focal question, then, is this: What is the relationship of the moral respon-sibility of a collective to that of its members?[5] It evidently presupposes that there is such a thing as collective moral responsibility. Is there? If so, what does it amount to? If these questions can be answered, an answer to my focal question should be forthcoming.

I shall first present a carefully articulated account or, for short, a *model* of col-lective moral responsibility. Assuming this model, I then consider the logical implications of collective moral responsibility for the members of the collective in question. I focus on the implications, if any, for their personal moral responsi-bility, but consider other matters as well.

Evidently, this is primarily a conceptual investigation. It explores the logical consequences of a particular idea—that instantiated by a particular model of collective moral responsibility. The *language* of collective moral responsibility has doubtless sometimes been associated with other ideas. This language has, moreover, often been accompanied by actions widely and plausibly regarded as unacceptable. All the more reason, then, carefully to explore particular ideas of collective moral responsibility, the better to understand the occurrence and the justifiability or otherwise of particular actions performed in light of them.

Modeling Collective Moral Responsibility

i. Blameworthiness

In everyday discourse, individual human beings and collectives are held mor-ally responsible for both good things and bad things. They are praised for the good, blamed for the bad. In philosophical discussions of collective moral

---

[5] I have previously published several discussions on this and related issues, beginning with *Social Facts*, esp. 425–27. Some of these discussions are cited in later notes.

responsibility, however, the focus tends to be on moral responsibility for the bad. I shall adopt this common focus here. The fact that there is a more heartwarming version of the issue, however, should not be overlooked. In other terms, common understandings suggest that collectives, like human beings, do much good, just as they do much harm.

Many of the philosophical discussions mentioned are concerned with moral *guilt*, a key issue being the viability or otherwise of the idea of collective moral guilt. This is true of two of the best-known discussions, both written shortly after the conclusion of the Second World War, both of which are skeptical of the idea.[6]

Because there is some question as to precisely what *guilt* amounts to, I shall focus on what is perhaps the thinner notion of moral blameworthiness or culpability. I say that it *may* be thinner for the following reason. Joel Feinberg, for instance, says that "the idea of guilt has always been *essentially connected* with the idea of 'owing payment.'"[7] It looks as if he is claiming a conceptual connection here. Perhaps there is such a connection given a standard understanding of guilt. It does not seem plausible, meanwhile, to posit a conceptual connection between moral blameworthiness and owing payment.

Let me say something, then, about what I take moral blameworthiness in general to be. *Blaming,* as I understand it, is a matter of *judgment* rather than a matter of doing or saying something. One can, then, blame someone for something without communicating with them. One might think to oneself, for instance, "I am not to blame for our rupture: she is." And one need say nothing about this to any other person. When is someone *worthy of* blame? In the discussion that follows I shall focus on an agent's blameworthiness *with respect to a particular action he has intentionally performed*—a particular intentional *action*.[8] Paradigmatic examples of intentional action at the level of an individual human being are: raising one's arm, running for cover, voting. Such blameworthiness would seem to be the central kind, at least if "action" is construed broadly to include omissions.

I take it that the less *free* an action is, the less blameworthy it is. Here I understand freedom as, roughly, freedom from external pressure, or *voluntariness*. An

[6] I have in mind Jaspers, *Question,* and H. D. Lewis, "Collective Responsibility," *Philosophy* 24 (1948): 3–18. Jaspers's skepticism comes out when he exclaims that a certain idea of co-responsibility goes "beyond conception" (pp. 80–81). Lewis's article is reprinted in: *Collective Responsibility: Five Decades of Debate in Theoretical and Applied Ethics,* eds. Larry May and Stacey Hoffman (Lanham, MD: Rowman and Littlefield), which includes contributions from Peter French, Virginia Held, May, and others.

[7] Joel Feinberg (1991), "Collective Responsibility," in *Collective Responsibility,* 60 (emphasis mine); originally published in Joel Feinberg, *Doing and Deserving* (Princeton, NJ: Princeton University Press, 1970).

[8] In this sentence the pronoun "he" is meant to be neutral with respect to the type of agent in question. Where human beings are in question, in this chapter, this pronoun is intended to be neutral with respect to gender.

intentional action need not be free or voluntary in the sense in question. Thus, with a gun to her head, Jane may intentionally lead the burglar to the house safe. She leads the burglar to the safe intentionally, but not freely. I take it that there are degrees of freedom, given that external pressures may vary in strength.

Suppose, now, that Clare intentionally torments her friend Leslie by pretending she has told others a particular secret of Leslie's. No one is forcing Clare to do this. Nor, as Clare knows, has Leslie done anything to deserve this torment. She does it because she desires to see Leslie squirm. She would admit, if asked, that her tormenting of Leslie in this context is morally wrong. In short, Clare freely torments Leslie, knowing that it is morally wrong of her to do so. I take it that Clare is fit to be blamed for tormenting Leslie as she does. The following account of blameworthiness suggests itself. One acts in a blameworthy fashion to the extent that one freely and knowingly violates a moral requirement in doing what one does.[9] This is the account with which I shall work in what follows.[10]

Questions may be raised about the knowledge requirement. It may be questioned whether it is necessary.[11] It may also be questioned whether it even makes sense, given that one acts as one does.[12] I shall set these questions aside, for the following reason. The account of blameworthiness has two central conditions. First, it requires an action, freely performed, that is in violation of a moral requirement or, for short, is morally wrong. Second, it requires the said agent to know the action in question is morally wrong. I take it that the first condition can be fulfilled even when the second is not.[13] These conditions are *separable*, then, to that extent.

---

[9] Cf. David H. Jones, *Moral Responsibility in the Holocaust: A Study in the Ethics of Character* (Lanham, MD: Rowman and Littlefield, 1999), chap. 1.

[10] In my exposition, this account issues from consideration of the individual human case. For present purposes, would it not be both possible and preferable to look directly at cases in which blame is attributed to a collective, and to consider what conditions for blameworthiness seem to be at issue there? It would indeed be possible to do this, and it may in some contexts be preferable. One reason for proceeding with an account of blameworthiness drawn from the individual human case, however, is that for many that case is the least problematic. In a discussion of collective blameworthiness that hopes to engage someone who feels this, it seems best to derive a general working account of blameworthiness from the individual case, and then to present a model of collective blameworthiness that fits it.

[11] This query may be developed thus: Do we not sometimes blame people for freely doing what is morally wrong *according to us*, whether or not *they* know that it is? This suggests that, though the account may give a sufficient condition, its conditions are not all necessary for blameworthiness.

[12] The thought is: Doesn't his freely acting in a certain way show that someone does *not* know that it is morally wrong so to act? Were the answer "Yes," no one would ever be morally blameworthy, on the account just proposed. This account would not be consistent, a problem that would be repaired if the knowledge condition were removed.

[13] This may not be true for all understandings of moral wrongness, but it surely is for at least one standard construal. I proceed on this assumption.

I shall offer accounts of the free action of a collective, and of a collective's knowledge that it violates or would violate a moral requirement if it acted in a certain way. Putting these together, one has a model of collective blameworthiness according to my working account. Suppose that for some reason, and contrary to appearances, it is impossible for *any* agent freely to do what it knows to be wrong.[14] Suppose, further, that freely doing what is in fact wrong is both necessary and sufficient for blameworthiness. There will clearly be no trouble amending the proposed model of collective moral responsibility accordingly. More generally, if a collective can be blameworthy on the proposed account of blameworthiness, that will most likely be true for whatever variants or supplements are plausible.

ii. Plural Subjects and Joint Commitment

At the core of any plausible model of a blameworthy collective will be an account of a collective's action. Prior to offering such an account, I introduce two technical notions that I shall invoke later. The first is the concept of a plural subject. I use the phrase "plural subject" as a technical one; it must therefore be understood, in what I write, in terms of the definition I give it.

By definition, any population of persons who are jointly committed in a certain way constitute a *plural subject*.[15] I must now explain what I mean by "joint commitment." In this connection, some pertinent matters will either not be touched on here or barely touched on. Longer, fuller treatments are available, and still longer, fuller treatments are in order.[16]

The relevant general concept of *commitment* is exemplified in the following judgment. If Pierre decides to join the resistance, he has *committed himself* to doing so. He is, then, committed to do so. In the case of a decision such as Pierre's, the commitment is *personal*: The one whose commitment it is creates it on his own and is in a position unilaterally to rescind it. I take it that one could say the same thing of an intention of Pierre's, such as his intention to tell his mother of his decision. Though an intention need not arise out of an intentional

---

[14] "Contrary to appearances"—the case of Clare in the text above seemed possible.

[15] The general term "plural subject" is useful in part because of the variety of contents that joint commitments may have, and the fact that one and the same population of persons may have multiple joint commitments. Thus plural subjects can have a variety of characters.

[16] See, in particular, Margaret Gilbert, "The Structure of the Social Atom: Joint Commitment as the Foundation of Human Social Behavior," in *Socializing Metaphysics*, ed. Frederick Schmitt (Lanham, MD: Rowman and Littlefield, 2003), 39–64; also Margaret Gilbert, *A Theory of Political Obligation: Membership, Commitment, and the Bonds of Society* (Oxford: Oxford University Press 2006), chap. 7.

act of commitment, if one intends to do something one is committed to do so, and the commitment is personal in the sense just noted.

For the sake of a label, I call commitments of the kind personal decisions and intentions produce *commitments of the will.* Such commitments, I take it, come in two varieties: personal and joint. In what follows when I speak of a "commitment" I should be taken to be speaking of a commitment of the will.

Speaking generally, I take it that one who is subject to a commitment has sufficient reason to act in accordance with it. As I am using the phrase, if by virtue of some fact I *have sufficient reason* to perform act A, then, in the absence of countervailing factors, this is what reason requires me to do. Thus one might be said to be "bound," in a sense, to do what one has decided to do. All else being equal reason requires one to do it.[17] I am of course not saying that, once I have decided to perform it, an action has something to be said in its favor, in and of itself. Deciding to do something does not make the action decided upon "a good thing to do" in and of itself. Nor am I saying that one is *morally bound* to do what one decided to do.

A decision's normative force remains until one rescinds the decision or fulfills it. That is, it continues to give one sufficient reason to act until such a time. The normative force of an intention has less persistence. Just as intention can just fade away, so can its normative force.[18]

I now come to the kind of commitment that is central to this chapter. A *joint* commitment, in the sense in which I understand the phrase, is a commitment of two or more people. It is not a conjunction of a personal commitment of one and separate personal commitments of the others. Rather, it is the commitment of them all. I say something about the way a joint commitment is created shortly.

Joint commitments can have a variety of contents. In general terms, it is always the case that the parties are jointly committed to X *as a body.* Acceptable substitutions for "X" are many: intend, believe, accept, value, despise, hate and so on. To focus on a particular example, what is it to *intend as a body* to do something? This can be spelled out roughly as follows: It is to *together to constitute, as far as is possible, a single body that intends to do that thing.* The guiding idea of *a single body,* here, includes nothing about the intrinsic nature of the body in question. In particular, it does not imply that it has a plurality of members. One who is party to a given joint commitment is thereby committed to act as best he can, in conjunction with the others, to fulfill the commitment. His commitment in this case is not a personal commitment in the sense introduced above.

---

[17] I mean to assume no particular *theory* of reason, having reason, and so on here. For further discussion and references, see Gilbert, *Political Obligation,* chap. 2.

[18] For further discussion see Gilbert, *Political Obligation,* chap. 7.

I have argued at length elsewhere that when people say that "we" intend to do something, "we" believe that such-and-such "we" despise so-and-so, and the like, where the word "we" is not elliptical for "we all" or "we both," the intended referent is understood to constitute a plural subject whose members include the speaker. I return to this point in due course. For now, I shall assume its truth. Except when it is obvious that I am not doing so, I should be taken to be construing "our" and "their" goal, and so on, in plural subject terms.

How are joint commitments formed? To put it very generally, in a situation where there are no special background understandings, each person must express to the others that he is in a certain broadly speaking mental state, such that common knowledge among them that all have made the appropriate expressions suffices to create a joint commitment of them all. I refer to this state as "readiness" for joint commitment.[19] As to common knowledge, suffice it to say that the expressions in question must be "out in the open" as far as the parties-to-be are concerned.[20]

There are many variations on this theme and it is impossible to encompass them all here. I briefly note a number of pertinent points. Entering an everyday agreement is one way to establish a joint commitment.[21] It is not the only way, however. The establishment of a given joint commitment may be considerably extended in time, as expressions are made by different people and, as necessary, disambiguated by reference to context or explicit avowals. Nor need the parties be able to point to a moment in time when it was finally established. That does not mean that they cannot be perfectly clear that it is in place.

A note on the demise of joint commitments may usefully be inserted here. A joint commitment that results from entry into an agreement may retain its normative force until it is rescinded, like a personal decision. Failing special background understandings, in this case the parties must rescind it together. I say more about the normative force of a joint commitment shortly. A joint commitment less formally entered does not need to be rescinded in order to lose this force. In other terms, it does not require a specific act of repudiation. Like an intention, it can just fade away. Absent special background understandings, again, in this case such "fading" requires the concurrence of all. Such concurrence may be established gradually through more or less subtle actions of the parties.[22] These

---

[19] See Gilbert, "Social Atom" for more on how this idea of "readiness" is (and is not) to be construed.

[20] For a more complex proposal, and some references to the literature, see Gilbert, *Social Facts*.

[21] On everyday agreements as joint commitment phenomena see, e.g., Margaret Gilbert, "Is an Agreement an Exchange of Promises?" *Journal of Philosophy* 90 (1993): 627–49, reprinted in Margaret Gilbert (1996), *Living Together: Rationality, Sociality, and Obligation*, chap. 13. See also Gilbert, *Political Obligation*, chap. 10.

[22] For further discussion see Gilbert, *Political Obligation*, chap. 7.

points about the demise of a joint commitment are of course consistent with the possibility that one party *violates* the commitment, for good reasons or bad, without the concurrence of the other parties.

People need not be physically in face of one another in order to create or to rescind a joint commitment. It is possible, indeed, that the members of a large population can be jointly committed in some way without each one *knowing of* each as an individual. If it is common knowledge in a population, P, that *everyone in P has expressed his readiness to be jointly committed in a certain way*, this suffices to create the relevant joint commitment. For instance, it may be common knowledge among the adult inhabitants of the coastal plain that all of them, that is, all of the adult inhabitants of the coastal plain, are ready jointly to commit with the others in some way.[23] This suffices for their joint commitment. The various inhabitants of the coastal plain need not know of one another as individuals. *A fortiori*, they need not know one another personally in the sense of being personally acquainted.

One's *readiness* to enter a particular joint commitment, along with one's expression of such readiness, may come about as a matter of considerable external pressure. Friends, family, teachers, and politicians, among others, may exert such pressure. The same is true for a personal decision. At the point of a gun, one may, and most likely will, decide to hand over one's money to the gunman. This decision may then be expressed though one's handing the money over.

It is possible for people to come to participate in, or *join*, a joint commitment after it has been formed.[24] Here is an example of such joining. At a certain point in time the adult inhabitants of a certain coastal plain are jointly committed, as such, to uphold as a body the goal of keeping out of the plain all who approach it from the sea. Some time after this, Tarzan, a stranger, comes to the plain from the interior and sets up home there. The current inhabitants learn of his coming, converge on his house and tell him of the established joint commitment. He makes it clear to them that, as long as he remains on the plain, he is ready to be jointly committed with the other inhabitants along the lines indicated. It seems

---

[23] For more on joint commitments in large populations see Gilbert, *Political Obligation*, chap. 8; this in part responds to Ulrich Balzer, "Joint Action in Large Groups," in *Social Facts and Collective Intentionality*, ed. G. Meggle (Frankfurt: Dr. Hansel-Hohenhausen AG, 2002), 1–18. See also *Social Facts*, 212–13.

[24] This is true for joint commitments in general and agreements—understood to be joint commitment phenomena—in particular. The point is important from the point of view of the evaluation of actual contract theories of political obligation. After a while at least, an "original" society-founding contract will lie in the past. It is sometimes assumed that, for this reason, such contracts cannot obligate people in the present. This supposes—falsely, I would argue—that people cannot "add their names" to preexisting agreements. Gilbert, *Political Obligation*, includes an extended treatment and *partial* defense of actual contract theory (chaps. 4, 5, and 10).

reasonable to say, in the circumstances, that Tarzan has joined an existing joint commitment.[25]

I do not say that all instances of a person's joining an existing joint commitment have to occur in exactly parallel circumstances. The example is supposed only to show how one can come to participate in an existing joint commitment.

iii. Collectives, Hierarchy, and Duration

I have argued in detail elsewhere that the concept of a joint commitment is a fundamental part of the conceptual scheme of everyday human life, embedded in many of the standard concepts relating to human social life and behavior.[26] These concepts include those of a collective, and a collective's action. Space limitations forbid me from attempting to reproduce these arguments here, so I focus on my conclusions.

As to collectives, I have argued that a collective, as exemplified in the list of examples given earlier, is a plural subject. Thus, any population of people who are party to a given joint commitment—thereby constituting a plural subject—constitutes a collective. Those who are jointly committed in one way can be jointly committed in many other ways as well. Collectives, then, can be richly textured, their texture changing as particular joint commitments are completely fulfilled, modified, or rescinded.

The idea that collectives are constituted by joint commitments resonates with a variety of statements made by theorists in different disciplines and, indeed, in different ages. Among other things, a joint commitment links people together or *unifies* them in such a way that it makes sense to say that they have *created something new*, something that is more, at least, than a mere aggregate of persons.[27]

With respect to this account of a collective, it is important to note that plural subjects can be hierarchical or non-hierarchical. In addition, they can endure for long periods of time, and, indeed, and through a wholesale change in their members, as is often thought to be true of collectives.

As to hierarchy, there are several ways in which the rule of some person or body can be established within a given collective.[28] I focus on two central types

---

[25] See also Gilbert, *Social Facts*, 219–21.

[26] See Gilbert, *Social Facts*, passim; also *Living Together, Sociality.*

[27] To cite but two classic texts, Thomas Hobbes (1982/1651) writes of the creation of a commonwealth as a matter of people "reducing all their Wills...unto one Will" making "a real Unitie of them all" in *Leviathan*, Harmondsworth: Penguin Books, part 2, chap. 17, p. 227. Sociologist Emile Durkheim emphasized that a social group was something "new" in relation to its individual members in Emile Durkheim, *The Rules of Sociological Method*, trans. W. D. Halls (New York: Free Press, 1982/1895).

[28] On this topic see also Gilbert, *Political Obligation*, chap. 9.

of case here. First, the members of a population can jointly commit to stipulate, as a body, that a certain person or body of persons has the standing or authority to do various things in the name of the jointly committed persons: to issue commands to members of the population, to make decisions for them, and so on. Restrictions of various kinds may, of course, be put on the standing in question. Thus Rex may be granted the standing to make decisions about internal affairs only, Regina may be granted the standing to make decisions about external affairs only.

In another important type of case, the stipulation in question ascribes the relevant type of standing to whoever fits a certain general description. For instance, the standing to determine the foreign policy of the population as a whole is stipulated for whoever shall receive a majority of the votes in a bi-annual election until the next election is completed. Once this type of commitment is in place, and the appropriate selection process has been carried out in light of it, a given individual or body will have received the authorization in question.

In the type of case last mentioned I shall say that the authorization of a given individual or body derives *ultimately* from the joint commitment in question, indicating that a number of intermediate steps may have been needed for this authorization to take place. In the type of case discussed first I shall say that it derives *immediately* from the joint commitment in question.

It is by means of such authorizing joint commitments that people can become jointly committed in ways that are presently unknown to them. This can occur on both a large and small scale. It is illustrated by this question from Peter to his wife Rita: "Where are we going on holiday this year?" Their holiday plans may already have been made by Rita, according to a joint commitment of the two to the effect that she may make these plans. They are now therefore jointly committed to going to wherever she has decided they will go to.

Joint commitments engendered by the acts of stipulated authorities will be referred to here as *non-basic* joint commitments. In contrast, the authorizing kind of joint commitment, along with other joint commitments that do not involve the acts of such authorities, will be referred to as the *basic* kind.

I turn now to the matter of duration. It is already clear that someone can join an existing joint commitment, becoming part of an existing plural subject. Given that this is so one can explain how it may be reasonable to judge that a plural subject has survived a wholesale change in its members. Once again, I use an example simply to show how something is possible. This allows that there may be examples that differ from this one in important ways.

Suppose that at a certain point in time the people of the plain, now including Tarzan, constitute a richly textured plural subject. They have the goal previously described, and have by now also jointly committed themselves to uphold as a body a set of rules intended to enhance their effectiveness against seafarers and, in addition, to preserve the orderly progress of their lives on the plain. These joint commitments are understood to hold between the people in question insofar as each inhabits the coastal plain.

Over time the membership of this plural subject changes in various ways. Some people join it after coming to the area, some members die, some leave the area and therefore cease to be members.

After a while none of the original members is part of the plural subject. The character of the plural subject has not radically changed during this time. In particular, its primary goal and its fundamental rules are the same. Under some such conditions, at least, it seems reasonable to say that the original plural subject has endured from one generation to the next. One can at least see what would justify such a statement. In principle, this process could go on indefinitely. The plural subject in question could endure through the ages.

iv. Collective Intention and Action

It is now time to sketch an account of collective intentional action. Formulations that differ somewhat from the one I provide give similar results in terms of the focal question of this chapter. So for present purposes it is not necessary to be concerned about matters of detail.

I shall assume, as is common, that a plausible account of *intentional action* in general goes somewhat as follows: An agent, X, *performs an action*, A, if and only if X intends to perform A, and successfully implements this intention.[29] I shall therefore first offer an account of collectively intending, and then an account of collective action that incorporates this account of collective intention.[30]

According to these accounts, the members of an established collective can collectively intend and act. So can those who did not previously constitute a collective. However, given the plural subject account of collectives, *those with a collective intention, whether or not they previously constituted a collective, do so now.* That is, they do so by virtue of their possession of a collective intention.

The account of collective intention runs roughly as follows:

Persons X, Y, and so on (or, alternatively, those persons with feature F) *collectively intend* to perform action A (e.g., get X's piano into a truck)

---

[29] To give an account of *doing A* in terms of the intention to *do A* may seem to involve a troublesome circularity. I here assume the propriety, at least in a rough description, of characterizing the intention as above. In everyday discourse we certainly speak both of someone *raising his arm* and of his intending to *raise his arm*.

[30] I have sometimes explicated collective action in terms of goals. See *Social Facts*, chap. 4, and *Living Together*, chap. 6. For present purposes, at least, the differences would seem to be immaterial.

if and only if X, Y, et al. are jointly committed to intend as a body to perform A.

In discussion of the general form of a joint commitment, I explained earlier what intending as a body amounts to.

Given the distinction between basic and nonbasic joint commitments, it is clear that a number of people can be jointly committed to intend as a body to do A even though some of them do not yet know this, and perhaps never will know of it.

Intentions can be of two kinds. They may relate to some future time, as when Jemima intends to become President of the United States some years from now. And they may be what Elizabeth Anscombe referred to as intentions *in acting,* as when Jemima raises her arm, intending to do so. Here the intention is part and parcel of the action. In other words, it is "in" the action. My account of a collective intention is neutral as between these two possibilities.

One can build an account of collective action on the foregoing account of collective intention somewhat as follows:

> Persons X, Y, and so on, *collectively perform action A* if and only if X, Y, et al. are jointly committed to intend as a body to perform A and, in light of this joint commitment, relevant persons from among X, Y, et al. act accordingly.

A situation that fulfilled the conditions of this account would be the following. Jane and Hilda agree to hike to the top of the mountain. They thus jointly commit to intend as a body to hike (as a body) to the top of the mountain. In light of this joint commitment each sets off, making sure not to leave her companion lagging behind. Perhaps Hilda stops to allow Jane to catch up, or encourages her to move more quickly: "It's not slippery, don't worry!" Or perhaps Jane calls out, in a tone of mild rebuke: "Don't go so fast, I can't keep up!" By dint of their various efforts, they arrive at the top of the mountain. They have fulfilled the conditions set out in the account, which will therefore judge them collectively to have hiked to the top of the mountain. In other terms, they hiked up the mountain together.[31]

It can be argued that an account like this, with a joint commitment at its core, answers well to everyday understandings of what is going on when people are *doing something together,* and when they say of themselves *"We intend..."* or *"We are doing...,"* without using "We" as elliptical for "We all" or "We both."[32]

[31] In this case the parties may have spent most of their hike walking abreast though hiking together, in this context, does not *mean* hiking side by side.

[32] See, e.g., Gilbert, *Social Facts,* chap. 4, *Living Together,* chap. 4, *Sociality,* chap. 2.

One aspect of the matter, which I cannot go into here, is that the participants in a joint commitment can be argued to owe one another actions that promote its fulfillment.[33] This allows a joint commitment account of collective action to explain a variety of phenomena one finds when people understand themselves to be doing something together, such as Jane's rebuke to Hilda, or Hilda's encouragement of Jane. Such behavior might well be considered inappropriate, in particular *interfering*, if the parties were not understood to owe one another certain actions. It is, indeed, hard to find a justification for it outside a joint commitment framework.[34]

The accounts of collective intention and action sketched in this section are, indeed, intended to capture everyday understandings of what it is for *us* to intend and to act. They are not intended as simple stipulations. The conjecture is that our intending and acting, according to a central everyday construal, is a matter of our being jointly committed to intend as a body, and so on.

On the assumption that people regularly fulfill the conditions of these accounts, it is obviously important to understand as best one can the nature and implications of collective intention and action as these have been characterized in this section. Precisely when and where those conditions are fulfilled in practice is, of course, an empirical matter.

v. Collective Belief and Knowledge

In order to complete this outline of the plural subject model of collective blameworthiness, I need to offer an account of collective knowledge, and to say something about freedom of collective action. As to the matter of collective knowledge, I take it that the core of such an account will be an account of collective belief, and shall largely restrict myself to offering such an account here.

I have argued at length elsewhere that something like the following account of collective belief accords well with everyday understandings as to what we (collectively) believe:

> X, Y, and so on, *collectively believe that p,* if and only if X, Y, et al. are jointly committed to believe as a body that p.

[33] See, e.g., Gilbert, *Sociality,* chap. 4, *Political Obligation,* chap. 7

[34] In *Sociality,* chap. 9, e.g., I argue against the capacity of a number of other proposals—including well-known accounts from Michael Bratman and John Searle—to account for the observations in question. Relevant also is my argument against a "moral principle" account of owing in Margaret Gilbert (2004), "Scanlon on Promissory Obligation: The Problem of Premisees' Rights," *Journal of Philosophy,* to be amplified in a work in progress, on rights, to be published by Oxford University Press. In "Shared Values, Social Unity, and Liberty" (2005), *Public Affairs Quarterly* 19, I argue, relatedly, that a special standing is needed to rebuke someone for the violation of a moral requirement as such.

From what has gone before in this chapter it should be more or less clear what it is for people to be jointly committed to *believe something as a body*, so I shall not pause to say more about that now.[35]

It may be questioned whether people can collectively believe something on the basis of evidence—as may be required for knowledge. It seems that they can. Certainly, people can collectively believe that a proposition that is already collectively believed entails a further proposition, and so on.

The following imaginary discussion exemplifies a process by which this may happen: A: "People will think badly of us if we do that." B: "*Why?*" C: "*Because there is so much negative talk about it in the wind just now.*" A: "True. We'd better do something else *then.*" B and C: "Agreed." That there is *collective reasoning* here is indicated by the italicized words. As their discussion proceeds, the parties jointly commit to believe as a body the relationships between the various propositions indicated by these words. In sum, the plural subject approach allows not only for collective belief but for collective reasoning.

Collective belief can relate to both theoretical and practical matters. In particular, a collective may have various moral beliefs. Allowing that there is such a thing as moral knowledge, it would seem that there can be collective moral knowledge also.

Now someone may argue that everyday references both to moral *beliefs* and to moral *knowledge* are misleading.[36] It may be proposed that one who says "Capital punishment is morally wrong," for instance, is doing little more than expressing his personal disapproval of capital punishment. So, it may be continued, to speak of moral beliefs is really to speak of a special class of attitudes or emotions. There is no such thing as moral knowledge, if by this is meant knowledge of something external to a given individual's attitudes.

In the present context this may be seen as an objection to the idea that a collective can have moral beliefs, let alone moral knowledge. It would then be an objection to the idea that a collective can be worthy of blame, given the general account of blameworthiness in terms of which I am working, even if this is modified to invoke moral beliefs as opposed to moral knowledge.

It can be argued, however, that even if one's blameworthiness depends on one's acting in a way that conflicts with a particular attitude or emotion of one's

[35] For more on collective belief see, for instance, Gilbert, *Social Facts*, chap. 5, and Margaret Gilbert (2002), "Belief and acceptance as features of groups," *Protosociology* (http://www.protosociology.de). There is now a burgeoning literature on the subject with contributions from (in alphabetical order) Alban Bouvier, Austen Clark, Christopher MacMahon, Anthonie Meijers, Frederick Schmitt, Deborah Tollefsen, Raimo Tuomela, K. Brad Wray and others. Gilbert, "Belief and acceptance" responds to proposals of Wray, Meijers, and Tuomela.

[36] This has of course been done, and different proposals about moral statements have accompanied such claims. For present purposes the details are not of concern.

own—so that, for instance, one disapproves of what one is doing, or would disapprove if one were not focused on the matter in hand—collectives can yet be morally responsible. This requires, of course, that they can have attitudes and emotions.

Now this is something that is certainly contemplated in everyday thought and talk. Attitudes and emotions are routinely ascribed to collectives. I have argued elsewhere that such talk, or at least a large swathe of it, can be explicated in plural subject terms. That is, when people talk about what a certain collective values and feels, just as when they talk about what a certain collective intends and believes, they refer to a situation of joint commitment.[37] They do not imply— and nor do I mean to imply—that there are "collective emotions" that exist outside the sphere of human action, emotion, and will.

It is possible, then, to give accounts of collective attitudes and emotions that do not force us into metaphysically extreme waters, any more than the corresponding accounts of collective belief and knowledge do. That said, I continue to focus on a model of collective blameworthiness that appeals to collective moral knowledge rather than collective disapproval and the like.

vi. A Collective's Freedom of Action

There is need now to say something about a collective's freedom of action. Evidently, it is one thing for an individual human being, as such, to be subject to external pressure, and another thing for a collective, as such, to be subject to such pressure. The question, then, is whether it makes sense to say that a given collective has been subject to external pressure and, conversely, whether it makes sense to say that a given collective was free to act as it did.

Without reference to any particular theory of collective action, it seems that both of these things make sense. It may be useful to present some pertinent examples.

Suppose that an emissary from a certain collective, known as Ax, comes to the small city in which the members of another collective, known as Pax, reside. He makes the following announcement in the public square: "Ax will destroy all of the buildings in this city in twenty-four hours, unless Pax hands over to me, the emissary of Ax, such-and-such an amount of gold before sundown." In light

---

[37] For accounts of collective emotions, the first I know of within contemporary analytic philosophy, see Gilbert, *Sociality*, chap. 7 (on collective remorse) and Margaret Gilbert, "Collective Guilt and Collective Guilt Feelings," *Journal of Ethics* 6 (2002): 115–43. Considering two main alternatives, I argue that everyday ascriptions of such emotions as remorse and guilt (feelings) to collectives can best be understood in plural subject terms. In Gilbert, "Shared Values," I contemplate an account of *valuing* in terms of believing that something has value. However, a plural subject account could allow for a less cognitive or cognitive-sounding account of valuing.

of this threat, the leaders of Pax assemble at their usual meeting place to discuss the matter and agree that Pax should give the emissary the gold, so as to save the city. This decision is then carried by those members of Pax to whom this task has been assigned. Here it seems right to say both that Pax gave Ax the gold, and that it did so under duress.

Now suppose that no emissary from Ax had come to the city. Rather, faced with more gold than was needed to keep Pax happily afloat, its leaders met and decided that they would give such-and-such an amount of gold to Ax, in a gesture of friendship. If this decision was implemented as before, it would seem that Pax has freely given the gold to Ax.

It might be questioned whether the last example is fully enough described to show that Pax acted freely. What if, prior to the crucial meeting, one member of Pax's government had privately put strong pressure on the other members to vote the way they did? Or, what if one member had put such pressure on the other members at the meeting itself?[38] I propose that the type of pressure in these cases does not yet amount to pressure *on the collective* as such. It is, precisely, pressure on those individuals whose actions are about to produce the decision of the collective. I am not, of course, endorsing such tactics. I am only considering what their implications are for the freedom of the group's action, as such, and, hence, the blameworthiness of the group itself.

Nothing like the kinds of intimidation just envisaged *need* be present when a particular collective's decision is established. Therefore the possibility of such cases does not take away from the possibility of freedom of collective action.

Membership in a Blameworthy Collective: What Follows?

I have argued that this concept of blameworthiness can be instantiated at the collective level: One freely engages in an action that, as one knows, violates a moral requirement. The nature of a collective, its intentions, actions, beliefs, and knowledge have been explicated in plural subject terms. The discussion that follows will assume this explication.

I return now to the initial question of this chapter, with a continued focus on blameworthiness. If *our* acting in a certain way was blameworthy, what does that say about *me*? In particular, what does it say about my personal blameworthiness? My discussion of this question is divided into two parts. First, I consider the situation of one who was a member of a blameworthy collective at the time

---

[38] Burleigh Wilkins contemplates such possibilities in "Joint Commitments," *Journal of Ethics* 6 (2002): 149, a thoughtful comment on Margaret Gilbert (2002), "Collective Guilt and Collective Guilt Feelings," in the same volume.

the relevant act was performed. Second, I consider the situation of a member who was not a member of the collective—perhaps he was not yet even alive—when the collective he is a member of performed the relevant act. As it turns out, these situations have much in common in relation to the matter at hand.

i. On Those Who Were Members at the Time of the Blameworthy Collective Act

What of those, then, who were members of a given collective at the time of its blameworthy act? What does the blameworthiness of the collective's act imply about the personal blameworthiness of any one member of that collective? From a logical point of view, the short answer is: *nothing.* Everything depends on the details of a given member's particular situation.

Such details can vary enormously from person to person. As a result, I may or may not be blameworthy in relation to my collective's blameworthy act. That said, there are certain obvious distinctions that may obtain among members of a collective.

A collective action occurs, roughly, when relevant members of a collective act in light of a joint commitment to intend as a body to perform some action, so that the action is performed. One or more members may have determined the relevant collective intention having been given the authority to do so by the others, who left such matters in their hands. Or the joint commitment may have been established through the general acclamation of the members.

Those who formed the intention in question will clearly be prime suspects in terms of those individuals who are personally to blame in connection with the collective's act. That is not to say that they must be to blame, as I discuss shortly.

In order for the collective action to occur, at least some of the members of the collective must act in light of the pertinent joint commitment. Their personal moral responsibility for doing so will, clearly, need to be examined. That they are subject to a joint commitment that requires them to do so cannot be the end of their story—whether or not they try to make out that it is. Though the joint commitment, as such, gives them sufficient reason to act as they do, and though they owe such action to the other parties, neither of these things either separately or in conjunction constitutes a conclusive argument for so acting unless "all else is equal." One may have been morally required to refrain from so acting, given one's overall situation, and one may have realized this. Then one's conforming to the joint commitment will have been morally culpable. Otherwise, it may not be.

Some members of the collective may play no role either in determining the nature of or in promoting the performance of this particular collective action. Among these, some may not even know that the collective action is taking place.

If their ignorance is in no way culpable, any personal blameworthiness of theirs must be for something relatively tangential to that act.

That is not to say that those who fall into these categories may not bear some blame in connection with their collective's blameworthy act. For instance, they may freely have voted for an elected official who was known for his advocacy of morally dubious policies, leaving the way clear for him to engage in such policies with or without their further help. In *The Question of German Guilt*, written shortly after the Second World War as lectures delivered to a German audience, Karl Jaspers describes a number of more or less "tangential" actions for which a given individual may be worthy of blame, though he is not directly involved in the collective commission of atrocities.[39]

That does not mean that every member of a blameworthy collective is blameworthy in some way in connection with a collective's blameworthy action. Some of those who did not know of the action, for instance, may have acted throughout their lives as well as anyone could expect of them. Of those who knew of the action, or sensed that it or something like it was on the cards, some may have done all they could reasonably be expected to do to prevent its happening. Some may have suffered significant deprivations in the process.

Is it possible that no member of a given collective is personally to blame in relation to the collective's blameworthy action or actions? This is perhaps unlikely, but appears to be possible. The following considerations suggest that *all* of the individual members may at least be *relatively* blameless.

The one who gave the order to perform the blameworthy collective action— if there is such a person—may have been under personal pressures that would at least to some extent excuse his action. Each member of a governing body may, too, have been faced with such pressures, when that body decided on a particular policy. Those who complied with the order of a governing body may reasonably have assumed that it was aware of facts unknown to them that justified this particular action. Those who failed to speak out against the collective action, knowing that it was under way and realizing that it was wrong, may have been under considerable pressure not to speak out. And so on.

Whether or not a particular individual is in any way blameworthy in the matter of a given collective's action—or anything else—may be debated even when the facts of the case are clear-cut. The main point for present purposes is that what is to be said about the blameworthiness of an individual member of a collective depends on what is true of him in particular. Little, if anything, can be assumed a priori, even given that the collective of which these people are members can be blamed for what it has done.

---

[39] See, e.g., Jaspers, *Questions*, 63–70.

I have said something about the possible blamelessness even of those who instigated a pertinent joint commitment, those who complied with it, and those who failed to speak out against it or its implementation, knowing full well what was happening. I turn now to two cases that raise a different kind of question. In both of these one might reasonably think that the person in question was blameless in the matter of a particular collective activity, and I shall not question this judgment. The question I shall ask is one that relates to the connection of these people with the activity in question.

Consider, first, one who does not know that the joint commitment in question exists or, *a fortiori*, that it is being implemented. Such people could be quite numerous. (Perhaps the leader of a given collective has made a decision on its behalf that is known only to a few people who carry it out in secret.) Let us assume that none of these people is personally blameworthy in the matter. Not only did they not know of the action, they would have protested at some risk to themselves, had they known of it. The question here is: Do they have any significant relationship to the collective action at all? In particular, do they have any basis for saying "We did it" when they were personally so distant from the action?

Consider, second, one who knew of the action in progress and did what he could do to stop it. Perhaps he could do little more than protest, and he did protest, at significant risk to himself. Perhaps he was subjected to a cruel process of interrogation by the police and then let go. Clearly he is totally against the collective action.[40] Is there any sense in which he can appropriately speak of it as "What we are doing," or "What we did?"

People do frequently speak in this way such cases. For instance, one who was ignorant of the action while it was going on, and then hears of it might well say, with great disapproval "We did that!" And a protestor might well continue emphatically to insist "What we are doing is evil!" So it would be good from an interpretative point of view to have a model of collective action that showed how someone in the position in question could appropriately say "We did that!" and the like. How might such locutions, in such contexts, make sense?[41]

Evidently, the plural subject model of collectives and collective action allows for sense to be made of them. On this account any member is party to one or

---

[40] For more on the relation of protests to joint commitments see Gilbert "Group Wrongs," 77–78 (a personal protest need not violate a joint commitment to, e.g., intend as a body to go to war).

[41] I do not say that all locutions that ever occur must make sense! I would not argue that "2 plus 2 equals 7" or "he discovered a round square" make sense, on standard construals of the terms in question. I take it that if someone says one of these things he has to be wrong. If, for instance, someone's saying "We did it" when he was ignorant of the collectives act at the time it occurred can be shown to be patent nonsense, so be it. Even then the possibility remains that the demonstration is in terms of concepts other than those the speaker was expressing. (This note responds to comments on a related discussion of mine from Jon Elster at the Mellon seminar, Columbia University, Spring 2005.)

more joint commitments that are constitutive of the collective in question. Particularly pertinent here is a basic joint commitment that ultimately or immediately authorizes a given person or body of persons to make decisions, to issue commands, stipulate rules and so on, for the jointly committed persons.

One's participation in such an authority-constituting joint commitment is a basis for his saying "We did wrong!" and the like, though he did not know of the action in question when it was happening, or did all he could to prevent it when it was being carried out. His participation in this commitment puts him squarely *inside the collective* as opposed to outside it. It also provides an objective basis for certain feelings he may experience in relation to the actions of the collective, including a feeling of guilt over what the collective, *as opposed to he himself,* has done.[42]

The words just emphasized are extremely important: saying that one's participation in an authority-constituting joint commitment puts him squarely inside the collective is not to say that makes him *in any way* morally responsible, personally, for the collective's action or, indeed, that he is morally responsible for his membership in the collective. In this connection the following points deserve emphasis.

People often point out that one may have had little choice as to one's membership in a given collective. As I indicated earlier, this is true of collectives understood as plural subjects. Consider the small-scale case of a family, for instance. No one is morally responsible for being born into a given family. If, coming to understand what is going on, young Betty joins various existing familal joint commitments, it is unlikely that she has much choice in the matter. Her parents may have threatened to withhold food or shelter, if she does not join these commitments. She can nonetheless become a party to them. All that is necessary for this is familial common knowledge of Betty's expression of readiness to do so. As noted earlier, one can be ready in this way in the presence of external pressure, and this may be clear to all involved. Thus there are circumstances in which one is not morally responsible for one's entry into a given collective-constituting joint commitment.[43]

Clearly this applies to both small and large units. Betty may at some quite early point have been pressured in various ways by those around her into joining a large plural subject, one whose members reside in a vast continent.

---

[42] I have discussed the phenomenon of feeling guilty for what one's group has done in a number of places, in particular, e.g., Margaret Gilbert, "Group Wrongs and Guilt Feelings," *Journal of Ethics* 1 (1997): 65–84, and *Living,* chap. 16.

[43] This point often comes up in discussions of consent or actual contract theories of political obligation. If I agree to support certain institutions under duress or something close to it, have I really bound myself? I discuss this question in Gilbert, *Political Obligation,* see esp. chap. 10, arguing that it is crucial to specify what type of "binding" is in question. See also Margaret Gilbert (1998), "Agreements, Coercion, and Obligation," *Ethics,* reprinted in *Living Together,* chap. 12.

As she matures, as the member of a particular family and as a member of the far larger collective, Betty will no longer be so vulnerable to individual people who might oppose her wishes. Perhaps all she needs to do to exit the large collective in question is to leave a particular geographical area. Nonetheless, she may have little money, and several young children to care for. Her parents and other relatives all live here too. It may be unreasonable to expect her to leave the area. She may fairly be said to have little choice but to stay. Her continuing membership in the collective when she is a mature woman may not be blameworthy either.[44]

In sum, Betty may not be blameworthy for becoming or continuing as a member of the collective. Nor need she have performed, or be blameworthy for, any action that contributed in one way or another to a given act of the collective. Nonetheless, her participation in its constitutive joint commitments put her in a position to say "We are to blame"—a way of speaking that automatically includes her as one of the "we," without implying her personal blameworthiness.[45]

ii. Present Members and Past Misdeeds

Suppose that I am a member of a collective that is morally to blame for something that happened *before I was born*. What bearing, if any, does this have on my personal blameworthiness? On the face of it one cannot be morally responsible in any way for malfeasance that occurred before one was born—not unless the present can causally affect the past. At the same time it seems that as a member of the collective in question I must be willing to allow that *we* did it, and, of course, that *I am one of us*.[46] People quite frequently speak in this way. The thought that membership in a collective can somehow saddle one with history of malfeasance that occurred before one was born, then, may seem both incredible and unassailable at once. The same issue arises, less dramatically perhaps, for one who, though alive at the time, only became a member of a collective after it had engaged in a particular misdeed.

Is there an appropriate basis, in either case, for my saying "*We* are worthy of blame for what *we* did then"? Intuitively, the basis for such claims is clear enough. It is, quite simply, the speaker's membership in the collective in question. But

---

[44] This point, also, is often made in discussions of political obligation.

[45] Echoing a phrase I used elsewhere one might say that one has accrued "membership blameworthiness" (Gilbert, "Group Wrongs"). This phrase would be unfortunate if it were taken to imply anything about one's personal blameworthiness. It is intended rather to reflect the fact that someone might appropriately say to an individual person "You (plural) are to blame," meaning to refer to a particular collective, and implying only that the person addressed is a member.

[46] In saying "We did it," I presuppose that I am one of us. In contrast, "They did it" presupposes, rather, that I am *not* one of them. *You*, my hearer, may or may not be included when I say "We did it": the linguists' distinction between the *inclusive* and the *exclusive* "we" relates to this.

how does that link *him* to these actions the collective performed in the past—perhaps the far distant past?

I have already indicated how the plural subject model of collective blameworthiness would respond to these questions, in my discussion of the cross-time identity of collectives. There is no space to explore this important issue in detail. Suffice it to say, then, that in the case of those who were not members—and perhaps were not even born—when a given collective misdeed took place, there will be a clear basis for talking of *what we did* if one now participates in the joint commitment, or set of joint commitments, that underpinned the collective intention in question. I have in mind here, in particular, a joint commitment of the type that endows with a stipulated authority those who fulfill certain generally specified criteria.

One clear difference between this case and that of those who were members at the time that the blameworthy act took place—call them *concurrent* members—is that, in this case, it is quite clear at the outset that one is not personally morally responsible for any kind of contribution to the blameworthy act—*our* act though it is. In the case of concurrent membership as well, however, the fact that it is *our* act does not entail anything about the personal moral responsibility of members of the blameworthy collective. This is so even though, as would seem to be true, concurrent members are more intimately connected to a collective's blameworthy action than those who become members after the action has been performed.

Concluding Remarks

I have made no claims in this chapter about anyone's moral *obligations,* or responsibilities in that sense, in relation to the morally blameworthy acts of a collective of which he is a member. The question of who has such obligations and what they might be goes beyond the scope of the present discussion.

The same goes for a number of other moral concerns, including the question of how if at all non-members are morally permitted or required to respond to a given collective's blameworthiness. Suffice it to say that given the model of such blameworthiness presented here, any steps directed against a blameworthy collective must be taken with extreme caution, on pain of harming numerous individuals who have little or nothing to answer for in connection with that collective's action. That is not to say that no such steps can ever be taken. The moral propriety of any such steps, however, must always be carefully examined.[47]

[47] I thank Peter French for inviting me to contribute to the volume of *Midwest Studies* in which this chapter was first published. I thank all of those who have commented formally or informally on my previous publications on collective moral responsibility and related matters. I hope to respond to comments not spoken to here, in a longer treatment.

Rationality in Collective Action

1. Introduction: Two Senses of "Collective Action"

The title of this chapter involves an ambiguous phrase: "collective action." In many discussions, it means little more than "combination of actions of different individuals." Thus consider a case made famous by David Lewis. Their telephone call interrupted, each of the two participants has to choose whether to call the other back or to wait for the other to call. Whatever each chooses, if each one acts on his choice, there will be a "collective action" in the sense in question.[1] Their concurrent actions, considered together, will be enough for this. This, or something like it, is the construal of "collective action" that predominates in what is known as "rational choice theory." It is not the only prevailing construal.

Another, more natural one associates the phrase with what would be referred to in vernacular terms as doing something together or acting together. In order for two or more people to do something together, it is not enough for them to perform concurrent actions, though what is needed is a moot point. As it happens, Lewis's telephone case provides an example of acting together. Before they were interrupted, his two agents were engaged in a telephone conversation. They were conversing together, or with one another. Conversing, in other terms, is what they were collectively doing—in the sense in question. This is the sense of the phrase "collective action" on which I shall concentrate, so my further unqualified uses of the phrase should be so understood.

Here is a short list of collective actions from the philosopher Alfred Shutz: marching together, dancing together, making love together, making music together. More recently analytic philosophers have used as their focal examples walking together (the present author), painting the house together (Michael Bratman), and executing a pass play (John Searle).

---

[1] For brevity's sake, I follow the convention of using "his" as short for "his or her."

It is hard to see how there can be anything problematic about collective action. After all, people take themselves to be engaged in it all the time. The very idea of collective action may, however, raise both metaphysical and moral concerns.

Consider how one speaks when doing something with another person. One says, for instance, "We are walking to the station." One may insist that one does not mean, "We are both walking." No: "We are walking." Implicit here seems to be the idea of a collective agent, and collective as opposed to individual human agency. In an article that focuses on other matters, Martin Hollis and Robert Sugden refer in this connection to "supra-individual units of agency."[2] However innocently intended, this phrase may suggest that something has gone horribly wrong.

Some associated worries are as follows. If we act—what happens to you, and me, and him? Is each of us somehow "swamped," somehow "taken over" by the collective agent that we constitute? Does each of us now cease to be an agent in his own right? Is each now the analogue of an individual human agent's arm or leg, his movements not dictated by himself but by the collective agent in question—just as my arm does not move itself, I move it?

If the answer to these questions is "Yes," the idea of collective agency may seem to be untenable, and happily so. Who wants to be taken over by anything or anyone? Yet, if the answer is "No," what justifies everyday talk of collective agency?

On reflection, then, it may seem that the idea of collective agency is metaphysically or morally dubious or vacuous—a poseur. There is, after all, no such thing as collective as opposed to individual agency.

In the article just mentioned, Hollis and Sudgen propose that if the idea of supra-individual agency makes sense, it implies deep revisions to rational choice theory. Whether or not this is so is best considered after one has better understood collective agency. In the next section I explain what I take the collective agency referred to in everyday discourse to be.[3] With an account of this in hand, I explore its relation to the reasoning and agency of its human participants.

2. Collective Agency

2.1. Collective Intention

I take a collective action to involve a collective intention. I start, therefore, with a proposal about what it is for us to have a particular intention or collectively to

---

[2] Martin Hollis and Robert Sugden, "Rationality in Action," *Mind* 102, no. 1993: 1–35. The title of this chapter is an intentional echo of Hollis and Sugden's.

[3] This discussion draws on much previous work, some of which is cited in later notes. My first published discussion on this matter was Margaret Gilbert, *On Social Facts* (Princeton, N.J.: Princeton University Press, 1989).

intend something as this is ordinarily understood. I say something in defense of this proposal later. I have made similar proposals about everyday references to what we believe, accept, and so on.[4] Any technical terms will be explained shortly. The proposal about collective intention runs as follows:

> Persons X and Y collectively intend to perform action A (for short, to do A) if and only if they are jointly committed to intend as a body to do A.

The technical terms in this account are, evidently, "joint commitment" and "intend as a body." Before focusing on the key notion of joint commitment, I say something about the relevant general notion of commitment.

2.2. Commitments of the Will

The term "commitment" appears in many contexts nowadays, both theoretical and practical, and it is clearly used in different senses. Therefore, in any given discussion, it stands in need of some degree of explanation.

To amplify the point, I first refer to some statements by economist Robert Frank. Thus Frank: "A person who has not eaten for several days is 'committed' to eat"[5] and "[C]ommitments of this sort... are merely incentives to behave in a particular way."[6]

Perhaps all so-called commitments are incentives, depending, of course, on how one construes "incentive." Be that as it may, I am concerned with commitments of a particular kind. For the sake of a label, I refer to them as "commitments of the will." One who has not eaten for several days need not have a commitment of this kind to eat. He may be hungry and thus have an incentive to eat. He may, however, have a commitment of the will never to eat again.

I shall in what follows refer to commitments of the kind on which I shall focus as "commitments," period. I shall not attempt a general account of this kind of commitment but will discuss a number of cases that I take to involve it and note some of their distinctive marks.

I take the personal decision of an individual human being to entrain a commitment. For instance, Helen decides to wear her yellow skirt today. She is thereby committed to wearing it today. To say this much is to make it clear that

[4] On collective belief, see Margaret Gilbert, "Modeling Collective Belief," in Margaret Gilbert, *Living Together: Rationality, Sociality, and Obligation* (Lanham, Md.: Rowman & Littlefield, 1996); and Gilbert, On Social Facts, ch. 5; on collective belief versus collective acceptance, see Margaret Gilbert, "Belief and Acceptance as Features of Groups," *Protosociology*, 2002, http://www.proto-sociology.de.

[5] Robert Frank, *Passions within Reason: The Strategic Role of the Emotions* (New York: W.W. Norton, 1988), 6.

[6] Ibid.

a commitment, in the sense in question, does not necessarily involve more than one person. It also makes it clear that an action to which one is committed need not be one that, in and of itself, one is morally required to perform. Indeed, one may rightly regard one's decision as essentially arbitrary.

I take it that in the case of Helen's decision to wear her yellow skirt, the associated commitment is solely a function of her having so decided. I take it, also, that if anything is an exercise of a person's will, his making a decision is. Hence the commitment a decision produces is apt for the label "commitment of the will."

In fact this label suggests two things, both of which are important features of the situation in which one has made a personal decision. First, the commitment is a "creature of the will"—an exercise of will produces it. Second—as I explain—it may be said to "bind" the will. In short, the commitment is of the will, by the will.

There are various ways in which one's will maybe "bound." The binding nature of personal decisions has two salient aspects, both of which merit discussion.

First, in an intuitive sense, by virtue of having made it, the one who makes the decision has sufficient reason to act in accordance with it. As I am using the phrase, if one has sufficient reason to perform Act A, this is what reason (in a broad, intuitive sense) requires one to do—all else being equal. I am not operating here with a theory of "reason," but propose that, intuitively, something along the lines suggested is right. One may be said to be bound to do what one has decided to do, then, in the following sense: All else being equal, reason requires one to do it.

I do not mean to imply that by deciding to wear her yellow skirt today, Helen thereby makes her wearing that skirt more desirable in and of itself, or in its consequences. Rather, there is something about the simple fact that she has so decided that makes it the case that, all else being equal, reason requires her to wear a yellow skirt.

This point may be supported by consideration of how Helen might react if she failed to wear a yellow skirt without having changed her mind about doing so. Having absentmindedly put on her standard attire—blue jeans— she may well speak to herself critically somewhat as follows: "Oh, I meant to wear my yellow skirt!" This suggests that her decision made it the case that, all else being equal, she ought to have worn her yellow skirt. I use the word "ought," here, as shorthand for "was rationally required to" in the sense at issue.

The second salient aspect of the way a decision binds is this. It binds one, in the above sense, with a specifiable degree of persistence. Given one's decision, one will continue to be bound in the first sense unless and until one has carried out the decision—unless or until one rescinds it. I take rescission to be a matter of intentional repudiation, as when one "changes one's mind"—deciding not to do what one had previously decided upon.[7] A decision that has been rescinded ceases to bind.

While a decision may be thought of as an act of will, an intention appears rather to be a state of will. I have argued elsewhere that personal intentions bind those whose intentions they are as decisions do but not with the same degree of persistence.[8] Intentions do not require rescission or deliberate repudiation in order to cease to bind prior to their fulfillment. One can decide not to do what one finds oneself with an intention to do and hence deliberately repudiate it. It will then cease to bind. It may cease to bind, however, without any such repudiation. It can simply go out of existence or be replaced by a contrary intention. I return to this distinction later.

One might wonder whether to think of an intention as in any sense committing its possessor to a given course of action. Insofar as an intention binds in the same sense a decision does, there is some plausibility in allowing—as I shall do here—that one with an intention is subject to a commitment of the same general type. Perhaps one might think of it as involving a "lower grade" of commitment.

The personal decision or intention of an individual human being is such that he can rescind it on his own and he is the only one who can rescind it. I shall say that it therefore creates a personal commitment: it is created by a single human being who alone has the capacity personally to rescind it.

2.3. Joint Commitment

I now turn to joint commitment. I take the concept of a joint commitment to be a fundamental everyday concept, in that it is a central element in many other such concepts. In addition, and relatedly, I believe that we need to appeal to joint commitment in order fully to understand the nature of obligations and rights.[9] For present purposes a full treatment will not be necessary. Some central points, however, must be sketched.

A joint commitment, as I understand it, is the collective analogue of a personal commitment of the will. Thus the joint commitment of Anne and Ben, say, is the commitment of Anne and Ben. It is not the conjunction of a personal commitment of Anne's and a personal commitment of Ben's. It is in an important sense simple or singular.

---

[7] The phrase "deliberate repudiation" may be pleonastic. I want, in any case, to emphasize the deliberateness of the repudiation here.

[8] See Margaret Gilbert, "Towards a Theory of Commitments of the Will: On the Nature and Normativity of Intentions and Decisions," in *Patterns of Value II*, edited by Toni Rønnow-Rasmussen and Wlodek Rabinowicz (Lund, Sweden: Lund University Press, 2005).

[9] See, for instance, Margaret Gilbert, "Obligation and Joint Commitment," in Margaret Gilbert, *Sociality and Responsibility: New Essays in Plural Subject Theory* (Lanham, Md.: Rowman & Littlefield,

As to the general form of a joint commitment, people are always jointly committed to do something as a body—in a broad sense of "do something." In the case of collective intention, on my account of it, the parties are jointly committed to intend as a body to perform some action. I understand this roughly as follows: the commitment is to emulate as far as is possible a single body (perhaps better, person) that intends to perform that action. Each party, then, has reason to do what he can to emulate, in conjunction with the others, a single body of the relevant kind. Evidently, discussion among the parties may be called for in order that individual efforts are effective.

In discussing the creation and demise of joint commitments, I focus on the basic case, where there are no special background understandings in play. In order to create a given joint commitment of the basic kind, each party must make clear to the others that he is ready to be jointly committed in the relevant way. Thus each must express a certain condition of his will.[10] Once these matching states of the will are mutually expressed, and this is common knowledge between the parties, the joint commitment has been created.[11]

To make this more concrete, here are some situations of the kind I have in mind. First example: Jessica says, "Shall we meet at six?" and Joe says, "Sure." I have argued elsewhere that this interchange is best parsed somewhat as follows. Each party expresses to the other his or her readiness to be jointly committed to endorse as a body the decision that they meet at six. These expressions are common knowledge between the parties. This interchange constitutes what would ordinarily be termed "an agreement" in English—an informal agreement, not a legal contract. I say more about agreements in due course.[12]

Second example: coming out of the factory one day, two factory workers, Polly and Pam, start a conversation about their day. Each lights a cigarette and they talk till a while after the end of their smoke. This happens again and again. The sequence is broken when one day Pam waits for Polly but she doesn't turn up. The day after this, Polly comes up to her and apologizes for her absence: "I was off sick."

2000); and Margaret Gilbert, *A Theory of Political Obligation: Membership, Commitment, and the Bonds of Society* (Oxford: Oxford University Press, forthcoming), ch. 7.

[10] For more fine-grained detail, see Margaret Gilbert, "The Structure of the Social Atom: Joint Commitment as the Foundation of Human Social Behavior," in *Socializing Metaphysics*, edited by Frederick Schmitt (Lanham, Md.: Rowman & Littlefield, 2003). See also ch. 2.

[11] "Common knowledge" is a term of art introduced into the literature in David Lewis, *Convention: A Philosophical Study* (Cambridge, Mass.: Harvard University Press, 1969). It has been defined in different ways by different authors, and I use it here in order simply to gesture in the relevant direction. As far as the creation of a joint commitment is concerned, one might say informally that the expressions in question must be entirely out in the open as far as the participants are concerned. For some further discussion, see Gilbert, *Social Facts*, 186ff.

[12] I argue for a joint commitment account of agreements in various places, including Margaret Gilbert, "Is an Agreement an Exchange of Promises?" *Journal of Philosophy* 90 (1993): 627–49.

"I wondered what happened," says Pam, accepting her apology. "Glad you're back." By this time, it would seem, it is common knowledge between the parties that each has expressed to the other her readiness jointly to commit with the other to uphold as a body the practice of their meeting daily outside the factory. At no point did the parties agree to start or engage in this practice. Yet their interchange suggests enough has passed between them jointly to commit them to uphold it.

A joint commitment is a commitment of two or more wills. It is true that mutual expressions in conditions of common knowledge are among the necessary conditions for the creation of a joint commitment. What is expressed, though, and what thereby becomes common knowledge, is the state of the will of each party (including each one's will to express his or her readiness to be jointly committed with the other party or parties) where each one's readiness to be jointly committed is key. I take it that a joint commitment can only be rescinded with the concurrence of all the parties, just as it requires their concurrence for its formation.

In what way or ways do joint commitments bind? First, a standing joint commitment binds the wills of the individual parties in the following way: Each has sufficient reason to act in accordance with the commitment. Thus the commitment has at least the binding force of a personal intention or decision for each of the parties.

What of the persistence of this binding? Is it the case that it persists until the joint commitment in question has been either satisfied or rescinded, as in the case of a decision? This is true of some joint commitments. Those created by an agreement are in this category. Agreements are, indeed, the closest cousins to decisions in the realm of joint commitment. Other joint commitments are open to deliberate repudiation but do not appear to require it in order that they cease to give anyone reason to conform to them, for they may go out of existence in much the way that they came in, by means that do not rise to the status of an agreement.

The joint commitment of the factory workers Pam and Polly is of this kind. Just as it came into existence by a subtle, gradual process, it may cease to exist in such a way. Perhaps Polly fails to appear several times, each time offering an excuse. The next day, as the factory closes, Pam says, "Well, I'm off for home now," waiting to see how Polly reacts. Polly says, "Me too." At this stage, if not sooner, their joint commitment is at an end.[13]

Such joint commitments are closer to the personal commitments involved in personal intentions than those involved in personal decisions. At the same time, I take it that no one party can unilaterally stipulate the demise of the commitment in these more intention-like cases either. Thus, should Pam say to Polly, "I

[13] See Gilbert, *Living Together*, 367–68, for an example of a similar practice that grows and then wanes.

shan't be joining you any more after work. I've got to get home earlier now," Polly is likely to give a concurring response, as opposed to a mere acknowledgment. Should Pam appear not to care to obtain her concurrence, Polly is likely to feel that something is amiss.

To summarize the discussion so far, a joint commitment binds each of the parties in at least the following way: It gives the parties sufficient reason to act in conformity to it unless and until the joint commitment has been satisfied, has been jointly rescinded, or has otherwise jointly been put to rest.

Though not all joint commitments have the persisting bindingness of personal decisions, they all have a kind of bindingness that personal decisions lack: once jointly committed, each party has sufficient reason to conform to the commitment subject to the appropriate exercise of both his own will and that of the other parties.

And there is more. Not only does a joint commitment give each party reason to act in a certain way, reason no one party can unilaterally remove; in addition, it constitutes an important form of relationship between the parties. To say something about this in summary form with the briefest of explanations here: Each party is answerable to every other party should he default on the commitment. Relatedly, each has the standing to demand an explanation of another's default, a standing that is grounded on the jointness of the commitment. Indeed, each party can be said to owe every other party conformity to the commitment and to have a right to each other's conformity. In other terms, each is obligated to the other to conform to the commitment and has a right against the other to his conformity.

These things will be understood by the parties, if not in so many words. Joint commitments bind, then, in the following three ways: they give the parties sufficient reason to conform to them, this reason persists subject to the concurrence of the rest, and they obligate the parties to one another.[14]

3.4. Collective Agency

Recall now my account of collective intention:

> Persons X and Y collectively intend to perform action A (for short, to do A) if and only if they are jointly committed to intend as a body to do A.

Why should one accept it? One reason is this. When people regard themselves as collectively intending to do something, they appear to understand that, by virtue of the collective intention, and that alone, each party has the standing to demand explanations of nonconformity and, indeed, to demand the

---

[14] Sometimes the concurrence of the rest has, in effect, been given in advance. See Gilbert, "Structure"; and Gilbert, Theory of Political Obligation.

conformity of the other parties. A joint commitment account of collective intention respects this fact. Though it would take too long to argue this here, accounts that do not appeal to joint commitment—such as those of Michael Bratman and John Searle—are hard-pressed to do so.[15]

A joint commitment account of everyday agreements accords with the fact that a standard way of creating a collective intention and, indeed, of initiating collective agency is by making an agreement. Those who jointly commit to uphold as a body the decision to paint the house, say, are thereby jointly committed to intend as a body to paint the house. Such an account is attractive independently of considerations on collective action and intention. One can argue, though I shall not do so here, that it is preferable to the standard approach in moral philosophy.[16]

Turning now to collective agency, one can say something along the following lines.

> Persons A and B are collectively doing A if and only if they collectively intend to do A (according to the previous definition), and each is effectively acting, in light of the associated joint commitment, so as to bring about fulfillment of this intention.

In other words, if the conditions posited in the analysans are fulfilled, A and B are in a position to say, "We are doing A," where this is not elliptical for "We are both doing A." Rather, "We (collectively) are doing A." In my technical phrase, we constitute the plural subject of doing A.[17]

Is there a collective agent here? There is reason to find an affirmative answer attractive. Consider the following. On this account, what does "We" refer to, in "We are doing A"? It refers to the jointly committed individuals as such. Thus it implies the real unity—in Hobbes's phrase—that a joint commitment creates. To echo Hollis and Sugden, we constitute a supra-individual unit. Further, in Rousseau's terms now, the joint commitment that unites us creates a single moving power. In a more modern phrase, it provides a single locus of control for the movements of each. These last points bring me to the third section of the chapter.

3. Rationality in Collective Action

Collective agents, as I understand them, act through their members. More precisely, in order for a collective to act, its members must correctly understand

---

[15] See Gilbert, Sociality, ch. 9, also ch. 2, for critical discussion of a number of alternative accounts whose authors include Michael Bratman, John Searle, Raimo Tuomela, and David Velleman.

[16] On the standard approaches in moral philosophy, see Margaret Gilbert, "Scanlon on Promissory Obligation: The Problem of Promisees' Rights," *Journal of Philosophy* 101 (2004) 83–109.

[17] Those who are jointly committed in some way constitute a plural subject in my sense.

their situation in a certain way and their behavior must be explicable in terms of this understanding. What is key is the understanding that the parties are jointly committed in the way in question.

The members of collective agents constituted by human beings are generally possessed of the following important capacities. First, they can make their own decisions, form their own plans, settle on their own goals, and act in light of these. In short, they have the capacity to act as "singular agents." Second, they are capable of considering the reasons that apply to them for acting in one way or another, and acting in accordance with what, if anything, reason dictates. Insofar as they act within the bounds of reason, they will be acting rationally.

As empirical evidence suggests, the capacity to reason and deliberate may sometimes be put "on hold" as people act on salient factors without consideration of the big picture. Clearly, a salient joint commitment might in this way lead to unthinking conformity to it. Given that the joint commitment was the only applicable factor, and there was no question in this case of rescinding it, conformity would, indeed, be the rational outcome.

What I want to touch on now is the relationship between commitments of the will generally and two other types of consideration: personal inclinations and moral considerations. What would it be rational to do when these factors are opposed to a given commitment of this kind? This is a large topic and open to disagreement. In particular, it may be unclear whether the claims made are ultimately matters of opinion or judgment, on one hand, or of logic, broadly speaking, on the other.

I turn first to inclinations—the label is intended to cover urges, promptings, leanings toward, and so on. It is plausible to suggest that commitments of the will, as such, "trump" inclinations with respect to what reason dictates. Why else, one might ask, would people make New Year resolutions?

A resolution, New Year's or otherwise, may be somewhat special. Rather than pursuing that question, we can consider humdrum personal decisions.

I think it was Christine Korsgaard who used the nice metaphor of inclination "proposing" that a certain act—such as buying an ice cream—be performed. One way of reacting to such a proposal is to decide to go along with it. "Okay," one says, "I'll buy the ice cream." Another way to react is to decide not to go along with it. "No, I won't buy that ice cream; I'm on a diet." Either of these things is supposed to close the case. In other words, the decision is assumed to be the last word on the subject, not the inclination.

Of course, in the case of a personal decision, one can change one's mind, and a nagging urge may well lead one to do so. This could be the story of many New Year's resolutions: They are rescinded rather than broken. The case of joint commitment is different. Absent special background understandings, no one party is in a position to rescind it or otherwise bring it to a close unilaterally.

In addition to the commitment side of things, there is the "owing" side of things. Suppose Mel owes Frank her sobriety. She's entered a joint commitment with him to the effect that she will abstain from alcohol in the future. How, then, could she reasonably judge that her personal inclination to drink is decisive from the point of view of what rationality requires?

Perhaps her urge to drink is so strong that she will say, "I've simply got to have a drink." She may mean simply that nothing is going to stop her, whatever the rational thing to do might be. Alternatively, her suggestion may be that a consideration outweighing the fact that she owes Frank her sobriety is in play: a consideration that goes beyond mere inclination in its rational effects.

I turn now to the matter of morality. Precisely what morality amounts to is a hard question. It is not clear, meanwhile, that my argument so far brings in any moral considerations. The trumping of inclinations by decisions, for instance, is not clearly a moral matter. It is a matter of the nature of decisions, on the one hand, and inclinations, on the other—and it is not clear that morality need intrude into the case. Again, the fact that those who are jointly committed with one another owe one another certain actions is a matter of the structure—or, perhaps better, lack of structure—of a joint commitment. It is not a matter of what one is morally required to do given considerations about important interests of another person, for instance.

Be that as it may, moral considerations can surely "override" joint commitments in terms of what rationality requires one to do. Suppose we are intent on doing something evil. It seems reasonable to say that, all things considered, we should not do this evil thing. Rather, each of us should make sure that it is not done. That is, rationality requires of each one that he do what he can to avert it.

Recall now the worries about collective agency mentioned earlier. How do things stand on my account? Does the collective agent "swamp" its individual members, and so on?

First, participation in collective agency—in particular, subjection to the underlying joint commitment—does not leave me free to do as I please from a rational point of view. Among other things, it gives me sufficient reason to act in a certain way, reason I cannot remove at will.

Second, it does not—how could it?—deprive me of my capacity to reason and to act according to my own best judgment. I may break away from a collective action in progress at any time—sometimes this may be rationally required, sometimes at least rationally permitted, sometimes not.[18]

Third, if I do break away, there will always be something amiss—something not quite right about the situation—that is more than a violated commitment of the will. I will not have given the other participants what I owed them qua parties to the underlying joint commitment.

---

[18] On how a personal decision, as such, "stacks up" against a joint commitment, see the next section of the chapter.

Precisely how this fact should affect my decision in a given case is, I take it, a significant matter of judgment. As is already clear from the case of the evil plan, some considerations may override it. Interestingly enough, Plato made this clear at the opening of the Republic. He suggests, in particular, that you should not return a weapon to someone who has gone mad since he left it with you. Precisely which considerations are in this category is another matter.

4. Collective Agency and Collective Action Problems

In this brief concluding section, I return to collective action in the "other" sense, and say something about the perspective on the "collective action problems" of rational choice theory suggested by the foregoing discussion. Rational choice theory has discussed a number of distinct problems—the best known perhaps being the prisoner's dilemma—each characterized by a particular "structure of preferences." Now, these structures can exist among inclinations if we allow—as seems reasonable—that inclinations can have different strengths. We can, then, consider the "inclination" versions of the various problems. This will have a degree of realism insofar as personal inclinations often are patterned in the way of these problems.

I start by considering a pure coordination problem. Everything that is posited is, we assume, common knowledge between the parties. A telephone call between Jill and Kate has been interrupted. Both would like to continue the conversation, and there is nothing to choose between the two relevant ways of doing so—as far as their personal inclinations are concerned. That is, neither cares which one calls back and which waits for a call. Thus far, neither Jill nor Kate has a rational basis for deciding to call back or to wait. Suppose the case is altered only in this way: Jill and Kate are jointly committed to espouse as a body the rule that if one of their calls is interrupted, the original caller is to call back. The original caller should then call back, and the person who was called should wait for his call. An appropriate joint commitment would, of course, have to be established by the usual means.

A joint commitment would do better in this situation than two concordant personal decisions (or intentions), even given that it is common knowledge that these have been made, for a personal decision is rescindable at will by the one who made it. As I wonder whether or not to push off from the shores of reflection, it may occur to me that you just might change your mind before you act, knowing that, after all, I might change mine.

Note that though a decision, as such, gives one sufficient reason to act, it does not bring it about that one owes that action to anyone else. Thus conformity to a joint commitment has more to be said in its favor than conformity to a personal decision: in the former case alone one is committed to conform and, in addition, owes conformity to the other party. It can be argued, therefore, that a joint commitment as such preempts a contrary decision as such.

What of other types of collective action problems? I am not sure what reason has to say about attempting to do as well as possible according to one's inclinations over the possible outcomes. Perhaps it has nothing to say about this. In other words, whatever you choose to do is okay. It's up to you. Suppose, though, that reason says one is to maximize inclination satisfaction, all else being equal. Given what has been said already, it seems that an appropriate joint commitment will, nonetheless, settle the issue in favor of conformity to it: each party is both committed to conform and owes it to the other to conform, and his personal inclinations do not rise to the level of these considerations. If this is indeed so, then we can see how agreements or other joint commitment phenomena—such as specific collective intentions or goals or rules with appropriate content—can lead to relatively good outcomes for all in collective action problems of all kinds, even when one otherwise consults only one's own inclinations. That is, one need not allude to morality.

Included here is the prisoner's dilemma. If (for instance) we intend to do as well as possible for each individually—and each is therefore committed through the underlying joint commitment to do what he can in conjunction with the others to achieve this aim—we have to work out what doing as well as possible for each individually in this situation amounts to. Quite likely this will mean that each must "cooperate" with the other, doing his part in a combination of actions that do not give him what he is most inclined to get.

A joint commitment may trump one's inclinations in the balance of reasons, but it does not obliterate them. An inclinations-plus-joint-commitment model of action in situations with the structure of collective action problems can therefore explain how, though rationality requires one to act in a particular way, there may remain a pull in the direction of acting contrary to reason's dictates.[19]

[19] The original version of this chapter, entitled "Collective Intentions, Commitment, and Collective Action Problems," appears in Rationality and Commitment, ed. Fabienne Peter and Hans-Bernard Schmid (Oxford; Oxford University Press, 2007). Related material has been presented in several places, including a decision theory seminar convened by Michael Bacharach and Gerry Mackie at Oxford University (1997), an expert seminar on rationality and intentions at the University of Amsterdam (1999), workshops on values at the Swedish Collegium for Advanced Study in the Social Sciences (2004) and rationality and commitment (with special reference to Amartya Sen's work) at the University of St. Gallen (2004), a conference in memory of Martin Hollis at the New School for Social Research (2004), the Roundtable on the Philosophy of the Social Sciences at Columbia University (2004), and colloquia at the Universities of Zurich, Frankfurt, and Oxford (2005). I thank all who contributed their comments. The bulk of the chapter was written when I was a fellow at the Swedish Collegium for Advanced Study in the Social Sciences (SCASSS). Warm thanks to that institution for its hospitality, and to the late Michael Robins and David Gauthier for their "official" comments on the paper discussed in Amsterdam. Responsibility for any claims made here is my own. I continue to reflect upon the issues, and comments are welcome.

5

Two Approaches to Shared Intention: An Essay in the Philosophy of Social Phenomena

Prologue: Analytic Philosophers on Social Phenomena

In the late 1980s and early 1990s analytic philosophy took an important new turn: it began to take a sustained and focused look at the nature of the social world and the distinctive phenomena that it includes.[1] There have, of course, been extremely important studies of particular social phenomena within analytic philosophy that predate this period, not to speak of studies outside that philosophical orientation. Influential examples of such earlier work in analytical philosophy are H. L. A. Hart's discussion of social rules in *The Concept of Law*, and David K. Lewis's game-theoretical account of social convention.[2]

These two works were in a broad sense individualistic in their approach. Just as, in the study of demonstratives, the analytic tradition had focused on "I" and not at all on "we," so the theories of these authors could be fully represented in terms of "I" rather than "we." Thus, according to Hart, there is a social rule in some population if and only if I, on the one hand, and you, on the other, have certain attitudes (often for a multitude of different "I"s).

There were also works that went beyond the "I" perspective. These are exemplified in the writings of Charles Taylor, who was influenced by the continental tradition. Using helpful concrete examples, Taylor advanced the important argument that in addition to the possibility that some fact is "common knowledge"

---

[1] Two points of clarification: (1) I do not take the distinction between "analytic" and other kinds of philosophy to be clear-cut. (2) The social world on which philosophers have so far focused is that of human beings rather than non-human creatures. I maintain that focus in this chapter.

[2] Hart 1961; Lewis 1969. In my own work I focus on Hart's discussion in Gilbert 2000, chapter 5; and on Lewis in many places including Gilbert 1989, chapter 5 and, most recently, Gilbert 2008, chapter 9 this volume.

between you and me—roughly, I know it, you know it, I know that you know it, and so on—there is the further possibility that it is "entre nous," "between us," "in public space."[3] Though the quoted phrases are not self-explanatory, Taylor's general message is clear. There is a way in which people can relate to one another with respect to their knowledge of some fact that goes beyond the "I" perspective of common knowledge and somehow pertains to "us."[4] Wilfrid Sellars had earlier appealed to thoughts couched in terms of "us' rather than "me" (Sellars 1963).

In saying that a new turn was taken after this, I mean that the philosophy of social phenomena, under various labels, began to attract large numbers of new researchers, from doctoral students and junior faculty to senior members of the profession. It is possible that this was in part because in the few years around 1990 a certain critical mass was reached in terms of distinct perspectives within the field.

I published "Modeling Collective Belief" in 1987 and my book *On Social Facts* in 1989.[5] This work offered novel accounts of a wide range of social phenomena including group languages, acting together, social groups, collective belief, and social convention. In 1990 John Searle published an article on "collective intentions and actions." Among other things he criticizes an article by Raimo Tuomela and Kaarlo Miller entitled "We-Intentions," published in 1988.[6] Michael Bratman published his articles "Shared Co-operative Activity" in 1992, and "Shared Intention" in 1993, citing the work of Searle, Tuomela and Miller, and myself.[7]

Following this period many new articles and books were written in the area. There was significant interest in the topic of collective belief, but topics in the area of acting together have so far predominated. That topic was addressed in

---

[3] See Taylor 1985. On "common knowledge" see Lewis 1969; for a proposal of my own see Gilbert 1989, chapter 4. A good general survey of the often quite technical literature is to be found in Vanderschraaf/Sillari 2007.

[4] This part of Taylor's work was an important influence on my own thinking. See Gilbert 1989, preface. Though there I see common knowledge as playing a significant role in human sociality, I saw a more central role for it in the doctoral dissertation of 1978 of the same title. The latter is, to my knowledge, the first attempt within analytic philosophy to attempt a general theory of social phenomena in the human world. Central references in the book were the sociologists Emile Durkheim, Georg Simmel, and Max Weber and the philosophers Peter Winch and David Lewis. The work of all three sociologists, in particular that of Simmel, can reasonably be thought of as comprising an important part of the philosophy of social phenomena.

[5] As it happens, the article was written after the book went to press.

[6] Tuomela/Miller 1988 maintains the basic thesis of Tuomela 1984, a substantial treatise which cites Sellars' work as a major influence, along with material in Rosenberg 1980, also inspired by Sellars. See Tuomela/Miller 1988, 388n2. More attention has been paid in the literature to the article, whose basic thesis is also represented in Tuomela/Miller 1985.

[7] Bratman 1999, 9n14, notes the particular influence of Searle 1990.

all of the above mentioned works, and was, indeed, the main focus of all but my own.

Two important aspects of the development of this general area of analytic philosophy are as follows. First, it is clearly pertinent to several other fields within philosophy, including political philosophy, the philosophy of law, and ethics. For example, theories of acting together can be expected to throw light on the topic of collective moral responsibility.[8]

A second important aspect of the development of this general area of analytic philosophy has been the interest taken in it by social scientists and others in a variety of fields. These fields include experimental social psychology, economics, management science, communication theory, political science developmental psychology, and anthropology, along with primatology and artificial intelligence.

This interest is not surprising, if only for reasons that Max Weber articulated at the turn of the 19th century. Centrally, the social sciences are concerned with processes involving human action. There is then a need to understand, with as much articulation as possible, the concepts that inform the actions in question. At least some of those engaged in the philosophy of social phenomena, myself included, aim precisely to articulate pertinent everyday concepts such as the concept of acting together. Their accounts may be viewed in some such light: they propose that acting together, say, as conceived by non-theorists who see themselves as so acting, amounts to such-and-such. Those who do not see their aim in precisely this way may yet, in their accounts of acting together and so on, go some way to articulate such vernacular concepts. And all may direct the community of scientists and scholars to important phenomena that might otherwise fail to attract its attention.[9]

Sometimes the account of a phenomenon such as acting together that has been produced by a philosopher has been directly applied to an issue within another discipline.[10] This process may itself constitute a contribution to the philosophical conversation. And theorists in other fields have sometimes entered that conversation more directly.[11]

This chapter will focus on a particular social phenomenon, which I refer to here as "shared intention."[12] I contrast my own approach to it with another, very

---

[8] For a recent volume devoted to this relationship see French/Wettstein 2006. Other pertinent topics include the problem of political obligation. See, e.g., Gilbert 2006.

[9] Cf. Gilbert 2008 on the distinct accounts of social convention offered by David Lewis and myself.

[10] See, for instance Bagozzi/Dholakia 2006.

[11] See, e.g., economists Sugden 1993; also Sugden/Gold 2007; Davis 2003; Bacharach 2006; Bardsley 2007.

[12] Other equally if not more appropriate phrases that have been used in the literature are "collective intention" and "joint intention."

common perspective which, I argue, is not apt to produce a satisfactory account of this phenomenon. As will emerge, the topic is rich and complex. Though the discussion that follows is intended to be relatively self-contained, it is inevitably sketchy in places. Where pertinent I sometimes cite more extended discussions of important points.

I first discussed the topic of shared intention, specifically, in "What Is It for *Us* to Intend?," having prepared the ground for it in *On Social Facts*, where my focus was on acting together and shared readiness to act.[13] Further material has amplified important aspects of the discussion.[14] The present discussion will pull together central elements of this earlier work while extending and clarifying it in various ways.[15]

1. Shared Intention

The technical phrase "shared intention," now in common use by philosophers, comes from Michael Bratman (Bratman 1993). It is best to specify how I shall understand it here. I do so by reference to an imaginary dialogue. For the sake of simplicity, here as elsewhere in this chapter, I use an example of shared intention involving two people.[16]

Suppose Alice asks Ben "What are you doing this afternoon?" and Ben, gesturing toward Celia, replies "We're going shopping." If Alice were—improbably—to respond "I see: you intend to go shopping and Celia intends to go shopping," Ben might irritably reply "No, no: *we* intend to go shopping!"

In this chapter I construe the phrase "shared intention" roughly as follows: a *shared intention* is what people refer to when—as in Ben's case—they utter everyday sentences of the form "We intend to do A," "We're going to do A," and the like, and are not using them elliptically for "We both intend to do A" or "We all intend to do A," and so on.[17] I shall refer to such sentences, when used to refer to a shared intention, as *shared intention sentences*.

[13] See Gilbert 1997; 1989. Also e.g. Gilbert 1990.

[14] E.g. Gilbert 2003 and 2006, chapters 6 and 7.

[15] Special features of this discussion in relation to Gilbert 1997 include: an explicit focus on future-directed shared intentions; emphasis on the problems three plausible criteria of adequacy pose for an account of shared intention in terms of corresponding personal intentions; expansion of my previous argument for the disjunction criterion, a further articulation of obligation criterion, and further discussion of the ability of a plural subject or joint commitment account to satisfy it (see the text below for explanation of technical terms used in this note).

[16] Cf. Bratman 1993. The perspective on shared intention that I advocate has no problem with larger scale cases. See, e.g., Gilbert 2006, chapter 8.3, which discusses a broader range of phenomena but whose general approach can be applied to the case of shared intention.

[17] The answer could in principle be disjunctive.

Shared intention sentences can take a variety of forms. For example, instead of taking the form "We intend to do A," and so on, they may take the form "Our intention is to do A," and so on. They may also take the form "We intend that p" e.g. "We (Diane and Ed) intend that Fern attend the best school in town." I shall focus here on the "intend to" form of shared intention sentence.

Shared intention sentences may explicitly or implicitly refer to particular individuals as parties to the shared intention. Or they may explicitly or implicitly refer to individuals insofar as they possess certain general features including relational features. Again for the sake of simplicity, my focus in this chapter will be on the kind of shared intention sentence that refers to particular individuals, and the corresponding shared intentions.[18]

Philosophers of action who are not concerned with shared intention specifically distinguish between intentions that regard the future and intentions in acting—such as my intention in raising my arm precisely to raise it. In this chapter I am concerned with shared intentions that regard the future, rather than shared intentions in acting. In what follows I shall take this as read.

In at least some cases of future-directed intentions, whether shared or not, it is natural also to speak of *plans*. I take it that, indeed, if one plans to do something in the future, then one intends to do it in the sense of "intention" pertinent here.[19]

Intuitively an agreement between the parties is sufficient to bring a shared intention into being. Thus one morning Gina may say to Harry, "Shall we go to the library this afternoon?" and Harry may reply, "Sure." Gina might now properly say to a third party, of Harry and herself, "We intend to go to the library this afternoon," in the shared intention sense of "We intend [. ..]." In at least this kind of case one might also speak in terms of planning. Thus, in the example, Gina might equally well say to the third party "We plan to go to the library this afternoon."

A future-directed shared intention need not stem from what is strictly speaking an agreement between the parties. In saying this I mean not to rule out the possibility that something akin to an agreement, strictly speaking, may be involved in the genesis of all shared intentions. In what follows when I write of "an agreement" I should be understood to be talking about an agreement, strictly speaking.

---

[18] My perspective on shared intention can accommodate cases involving populations individuated by one or more common features, something that is necessary when dealing with what Scott Shapiro has referred to as "massively shared intentions," that is, the shared intentions of very large populations. On this see Gilbert 2006, chapter 8.3.

[19] Bratman 1987, 29, offers a "planning theory" of intention and describes plans (as he conceives of them) as "intentions writ large." This implies, I take it, that plans and intentions do not differ in substance.

Here is an example of the formation of a shared intention without an agreement between the parties. In late spring Isobel is organizing a summer trip for her students in which they will work in teams helping the townspeople in local towns recently devastated by floods. She puts on a table a list of assignments, each for two people to accomplish together, and asks each student to sign up for one of these assignments. Jake signs up to go to Quiet Harbor, and so does another student, Kristen, who has not spoken to him before. Standing by the table, they start to talk about how they will help the people of Quiet Harbor. I take it that at some point in this process Jake and Kristen come to share an intention to help the people of Quiet Harbor that summer, though they have not made an agreement with one another to help them.

Clearly, though understanding agreements should help us to understand shared intention, understanding shared intention is not simply a matter of understanding agreements.

Shared intentions and the actions that proceed from them can be significant forces for both good and evil: we can intend to save the world, and we can intend to destroy it. Whatever we intend, we may succeed in doing. For practical purposes, it would be well to understand what such intentions amount to, as it is good to understand all such forces.

2. The Personal Intentions Perspective

In addition to the undoubted practical importance of shared intention, there is a more theoretical reason for caring about it. Shared intention sentences—though completely commonplace—may seem to raise a squarely philosophical puzzle.

On the face of it, one who says, for instance "Larry and Meg intend to paint the living room tomorrow" ascribes an intention to Larry and Meg, as opposed to Larry, on the one hand, and Meg, on the other. One may think that this cannot be right—things cannot be as they seem.

One may well think this if one assumes that the only intentions in the human domain are intentions of single human beings as opposed to intentions of two or more human beings, such as the putative intention of Larry and Meg. Perhaps one makes this assumption because one thinks that only a being with some feature possessed by individual human beings and not possessed by two or more human beings—a mind, perhaps, or consciousness, or a brain—can have intentions. In other terms, an intention must inhere in a mind, consciousness, or a brain (see, e.g., Searle 1990).

Suppose we refer to the intention of a single human being as a *singularist intention*. One may believe, with Wilfrid Sellars, for instance, that singularist intentions are not always *personal intentions*, that is, intentions expressible by sentences of the form "I intend [...]."[20] One may yet think that in the human domain intentions of whatever kind are correctly ascribable only to a given individual human being. I shall call this *the singularist assumption about intentions*, or, for short, *the singularist assumption*.[21] If it is true, either shared intention sentences are false, or they are not what they seem.

This assumption can be questioned in light of the prevalence of shared intention sentences. To be sure, a singularist intention and an intention ascribable to two or more human beings—to "us" or, correlatively, "them"—will have different substrata. One can accept this without being forced to deny that the latter kind of intention is possible. Perhaps, after all, an intention need not inhere in a feature of individual human beings that "we" or "they" inevitably lack.[22]

In theorizing about shared intention it is best, I suggest, to set aside the singularist assumption. That leaves us with the question: how best are we to understand what shared intention amounts to?

Recall that I am focusing in this chapter on cases in which a shared intention is ascribed to two or more particular individuals as such. In addition, I focus on cases in which there are no pertinent authority-relations between the parties. In particular, neither is in a position to stipulate a shared intention for the two. These may or may not be the most basic cases from a genealogical point of view, but, at the least, they are commonplace cases that it is important to understand.

It is natural to proceed by asking what shared intention amounts to *at the individual level*. What must each of us think or have thought, do or have done, and so on, in order that we intend to do such-and-such? Can a set of individually necessary and jointly sufficient conditions for a shared intention be given along these lines? In other words, can one give what I shall refer to as *an account of shared intention* in these terms? It is possible, of course, that the best we can come up with is a set or sets of conditions sufficient for a case of shared intention, as opposed to a set of conditions that are individually necessary and jointly sufficient. The latter would be most satisfying, however, so it is worth proposing as an initial target.

---

[20] Sellars 1963, 203; also Searle 1990. Both invoke intentions of individuals expressible by sentences of the form "We intend [...]." I have critically discussed Searle's approach to shared intention (insofar as he does approach it) in Gilbert 2007. See also (on Searle and others including Bratman and Tuomela/Miller) Gilbert 1998.

[21] I coined the term "singularism" in Gilbert 1989, for related purposes.

[22] For concordant discussion relating to the ascription of beliefs to two or more persons, as opposed to individual people, see Gilbert 2002a. I take Bratman's statements on his theory of shared intention 1993, 107, to be in the spirit of these remarks. He says, e.g. "shared intention, as I understand it, is not an attitude in any mind." (I take it he believes that shared intention is nonetheless intention; it is, in particular, our intention.)

It is not clear how many theorists who work in the philosophy of social phenomena have been concerned with shared intention in precisely my sense.[23] Even when their focus is the same, they may not aim to give more than sufficient conditions for a case of shared intention, or, whatever their initial aim, they may not claim to have given more than sufficient conditions.[24] Whatever precisely a given theorist's aim, one can usefully consider whether a given account of what is referred to by its author as "shared intention," "collective intention," or something with a similar flavor, does *in fact* constitute an account of shared intention as I have just characterized such an account. That will be my procedure here.

It is standard to proceed in terms of a set of singularist-intentions—a set of intentions ascribed, *seriatim*, to different human individuals. Within this framework, a popular option is what I shall call the *personal intentions perspective*, according to which the singularist-intentions in question are personal intentions. This is probably the most prevalent perspective among theorists.[25] That is hardly surprising. An appeal to personal intentions, in contrast to an appeal to any other form of singularist-intention, is an appeal to something relatively well studied and familiar from outside the philosophy of social phenomena.[26]

Among theories that adopt a personal intentions perspective, the most prominent and influential is that of Michael Bratman. In its initial presentation in 1993 it ran roughly as follows:

> "With respect to a group consisting of you and me, and concerning joint activity, J, *we intend to J* if and only if: (1) (a) I intend that we J and (b) you intend that we J; (2) I intend that we J in accordance

---

[23] Bratman 1993 opens with a reference to what I am calling shared intention sentences with the implication that these fix the topic (98). To this extent we are on the same page. He then moves to the question "What do shared intentions do, what jobs do they have in our lives?" (99) and couches his aim ("what we want to know") (99) as that of finding an appropriate complex of the attitudes of each participant whose proper functioning would do those jobs—coordinating our personal plans and actions and providing a framework for bargaining—since "we would have reason to identify shared intention with this complex" (100).

[24] Cf. Velleman 1997. Though clearly preferring to have developed a set of individually necessary and jointly sufficient conditions, Bratman 1993 allows that the conditions he has proposed may be sufficient but not necessary for a case of shared intention.

[25] Among those who do not adopt it in addition to Sellars 1963 and Searle 1990 is Bardsley 2007 who offers a version of Searle's approach. His particular interest is in how people might solve such coordination problems as the "Hi-Lo" game without prior interaction. On the latter, and Searle, Bratman, and Tuomela/Miller's work in relation to it, see also Gold/Sugden 2007. My own sense of "Hi-Lo" is that one does not need to bring "we" thoughts in to explain why people tend to go for Hi, though classical game-theory may not mandate it. That is a topic for another occasion, though see Gilbert 1981.

[26] Michael Bratman is a leading contemporary figure in this area. See Bratman 1987. His interest in shared intention was an offshoot of this earlier work. The same goes for John Searle. Raimo Tuomela also previously worked on action theory.

with and because of (1) (a), (1) (b), and meshing sub-plans of (1) (a), (1) (b); and you intend likewise. (3): (1) and (2) are common knowledge between us."[27]

Bratman proposes, then, that what our intention amounts to is a complex of, as he puts it, "interlocking" singularist-intentions. Since initially formulating his account Bratman has been developing a more complex set of conditions (see Bratman forthcoming). The fundamental condition remains condition (1), which posits personal intentions of you, on the one hand, and I, on the other, in favor of our J-ing. By now many other theorists working from a personal intentions perspective have offered accounts that differ in one way or another from Bratman's in its various versions.[28]

Starting with observations on the way people think and talk about shared intention in everyday life, my own inquiries have led in a different direction. As I explain, they have suggested to me three central criteria of adequacy for an account of shared intention. In what follows I spend most time on the criterion I introduce first. This very clearly rules out accounts of shared intention in terms of personal intentions. The other criteria also throw doubt on such accounts. I then sketch the account I have developed and explain how it meets the criteria. Finally I note some important aspects of its relationship to personal intentions accounts with special reference to that of Michael Bratman.

3. The Disjunction Criterion

The criterion I first introduce concerns the relationship of a given shared intention to a certain kind of personal intention. Recall that a *personal intention* is understood here as an intention of an individual human being that is expressible by him in a sentence of the form "I intend [. ..]." Before proceeding to the criterion I say something more about personal intentions generally.

I take it that one who makes a personal *decision* to do such-and-such in the future, and has not subsequently changed his mind, thereby has a personal intention to do such-and-such. He may be said, also, to plan to do it.

One is, indeed, in a position to change one's mind or, in more technical parlance, to rescind one's personal decision. Such rescission may not be appropriate in a given circumstance, but one is in a position to bring it about unilaterally,

---

[27] This derives from the recapitulation in Bratman 1999, 131.

[28] Other appeals to personal intentions in related contexts include MacMahon 2005; Miller 2005; Kutz 2000a; 2000b; Roth 2004 and Tuomela/Miller 1988. I discuss Kutz's approach in Gilbert 2002b.

at will. Moreover, no one else is in this position. I can persuade you to rescind your decision, but I cannot rescind it for you. I take this to be so, intuitively, and to be an important aspect of decisions and those personal intentions associated with them.

Some future-directed intentions may not be associated with decisions. Perhaps one just finds oneself with the intention. In that case, too, one is in a position to rescind it, and no one else can do it for one.

I need next to introduce one more technical phrase. Suppose that two people share an intention to go shopping tomorrow. Some theorists may think that, as a conceptual matter, each must then personally intend to contribute as best he can to their going shopping tomorrow. None are likely to deny that each *may so* personally intend. Setting that issue aside, if one party does so personally intend, I shall say that he has a (*personal*) *contributory intention* with respect to this personal intention.

I shall argue that, as a conceptual matter, when two or more people share an intention, none of them need to have a contributory intention. The point is not that generally speaking when there is a shared intention there are no such intentions. The point is, rather, that it is in principle possible correctly to ascribe a shared intention to the parties when one or more of them lack contributory intentions.

This point does need arguing, and a pertinent mode of argumentation is appeal to one or more examples.[29] So consider the following imagined retrospective report by one of the parties to a past shared intention. It should be considered, of course, without assuming the correctness of any particular account of what a shared intention is.

The parties are Ned and Olive, and Olive is speaking: "Our plan was to hike to the top of the hill. We arrived at the hill and started up. As he told me later, Ned realized early on that it would be too much for him to go all the way to the top, and decided that he would only go halfway. Though he no longer had any intention of hiking to the top of the hill, he had as yet said nothing about this to me, thinking it best to wait until we were at least halfway up before doing so. Before then we encountered Pam, who asked me how far we intended to go. I said that our intention was to hike to the top of the hill, as indeed it was."

I do not find that Olive's report is inconsistent. If it is not, one can conclude that people may share an intention though at least one of them lacks personal contributory intentions. I say "at least" one of them. In fact it seems that none of the parties need have such personal intentions. Thus I would not take Olive now to involve herself in an inconsistency if she went on: "As it happens, when we met Pam, I was in the same position as Ned: I'd also decided that I would

---

[29] See also Gilbert 1997. The discussion that follows here is more extensive.

not go all the way to the top of the hill, though I hadn't yet broached the subject with him."

There is a general argument to the conclusion that I have drawn from Olive's story in its longer version. This argument refers to the relationship between shared intention and agreements.

Michael Bratman has objected to the claim that an agreement brings a shared intention into being (Bratman 1993, 111 n31). He says that it "[…] seems to me wrong, since binding agreements do not guarantee intentions on the part of the individual agents to act accordingly." I take him to be referring here to personal intentions. I am not quite sure what he has in mind by a "binding" agreement as opposed to an agreement, period, but I shall assume for the sake of argument that he means an agreement on what is to be done by the parties, as opposed to an agreement on terms, and shall refer in what follows simply to agreements.[30] To be sure, agreements do not guarantee personal intentions of the kind in question.

Consider the following version of Olive's story: "Ned and I agreed to hike to the top of the hill that afternoon. Given our plan, we set off after lunch for the hill, and began to hike up it. As he told me later [...]" The story goes on as before.

One can imagine, indeed, that even while agreeing to hike to the top of the hill, thus intentionally cementing their shared intention, Ned was planning not to go to the top of the hill. Perhaps Olive was in the same position. That does not mean that he and Olive failed to enter a binding agreement to hike to the top of the hill.

In such a case one might want to say that neither party entered the agreement sincerely, meaning by this that neither intended to conform to it even while it was being made. By hypothesis, however, and compatibly with this, each did intend to make an agreement with the other. And we may assume that neither would ever think of denying that an agreement was made.

One can and, I think, should turn on its head Bratman's argument from the point that agreements do not guarantee contributory personal intentions. According to a firm pre-theoretical judgment, an agreement to do something immediately gives rise to a shared intention. Given Bratman's point, it follows that the parties to a shared intention need not have contributory personal intentions—either at the time the shared intention was formed or at any time prior to its satisfaction.

To endorse this argument is of course not morally or otherwise to endorse the creation with others of shared intentions for which one lacks the contributory personal intentions, or even guesses that one will lack them. Nor is it to

---

[30] An example of an agreement on terms: we agree that if you work for me, the pay will be $20 per hour.

approve one's deciding not to conform to a standing shared intention. All else being equal, these things should doubtless be discouraged. My point is only that these things are possible. That is what matters when the issue is the nature of shared intention.

As can easily be seen, my arguments here apply not only to personal contributory intentions, but also to the specific form of personal intention that figures in Bratman's account of shared intention, a personal intention *that we J*. It applies more generally to any personal intentions explicitly geared to the satisfaction of a given shared intention. I shall refer to such intentions as *correlative personal intentions*.

In light of the foregoing I propose the following criterion of adequacy:

> an adequate account of shared intention is such that it is not necessarily the case that for every shared intention on that account, there be correlative personal intentions of the individual parties.

I shall call this *the disjunction criterion*. In what follows I shall assume its correctness. Recall that I am here construing an adequate account of shared intention as one that provides individually necessary and jointly sufficient conditions on shared intention. The account I have developed, to be described shortly, does not entail that there are correlative personal intentions whenever there is a shared intention. Nor, quite properly, does it rule them out.

Accounts in terms of correlative personal intentions of one or another kind clearly fail to satisfy the disjunction criterion. They fail, therefore, to provide a set of conditions that are individually necessary and jointly sufficient for shared intention.

A set of conditions or structure whose core was a set of correlative personal intentions could yet be *sufficient* for shared intention. In speaking of *a structure whose core is a set of such personal intentions* I mean to rule out a structure with correlative personal intentions within it, such that it is indeed sufficient for shared intention but only by virtue of those parts of the structure not involving the correlative personal intentions.

The interesting question is whether a structure of correlative personal intentions, more or less, is ever sufficient for shared intention. The qualifier "more or less" here is intended to cover such further features as the parties' knowledge of each other's personal intentions, the mutual reinforcing influence of this knowledge, and so on. I shall henceforth construe the personal intentions perspective in these terms.

If some structure of correlative personal intentions is indeed sufficient for shared intention, then given the disjunction criterion, the hope of giving a set of individually necessary and jointly sufficient conditions on shared intention will have to be abandoned. This may not seem to be too large a cost. Remember, however, that I am focusing here on a particular class of shared intentions, those for which one might think that a personal intentions account would be most plausible: the class of shared intentions of particular individuals without pertinent authority relations. This is the class on which Michael Bratman, for instance, focuses. It is not implausible to expect that what is in my sense an adequate account of these, at least, can be found

I grant that in spite of this it is of interest to consider whether we can find a structure of correlative personal intentions that is sufficient for shared intention in these or other cases. That one cannot is suggested by two further criteria of adequacy for an account of shared intention.

4. The Concurrence Criterion

I shall call the two further criteria of adequacy to which I now turn "the concurrence criterion" and "the obligation criterion" (see also Gilbert 1997). The naturalness of the following story can be used in support of both.

Queenie and Rom intend to do some shopping in a nearby town. In order to get there in time they must walk some miles along a dusty road at a certain pace. They are now half way along the road. Queenie's pace begins to slow. In a tone of mild rebuke Rom says, "Can you hurry up a bit? We won't be able to get any shopping done at this rate!" Queenie says, "Sorry!" and moves more quickly for a while. Later she stops and for some reason announces: "That's it! I'm not going any further!"[31] Rom is likely to be taken aback. Whatever he says, his thoughts may well run along these lines: "You can't just decide to stop here, not just like that!" *Sotto voce* or not, he might add by way of explanation: "We're on our way to the shops!" Had Queenie said something like "Do you mind if I stop here?"— seeking his concurrence in her stopping—his reaction would have been different. Then she would not have been "simply deciding" to stop.

The likelihood of such thoughts and reactions in the presence of a shared intention suggests, for one, something like the following criterion of adequacy for an account of shared intention.

According to *the concurrence criterion,* to be further explained shortly:

> an adequate account of shared intention will entail that, absent special background understandings, the concurrence of all parties is required

---

[31] Perhaps, as a follower of ethnomethodologist Harold Garfinkel, she is bent on teasing out reactions to behavior she believes is "out of line."

in order that a given shared intention be changed or rescinded, or that a given party be released from participating in it.

I take it as read that the account should be such that the parties to the shared intention will understand that their concurrence is required as stated, and that, in addition, they will understand that this is a matter of what shared intention is. That the shared intention itself is understood to ground the need for concurrence is indicated by the naturalness of Rom's explanation of his "You can't just decide!" with "We're on our way to the shops!" This presents itself, indeed, as a complete explanation of the need for concurrence.

The qualifier "absent special background understandings" is important, and should also be taken as read in what follows. It allows that prior agreements such as the following are possible. Queenie is not sure she wants to walk all the way into town that afternoon, so before she and Rom set out on their shopping expedition she gets him to agree in advance that if at any time she feels like stopping, she is free to do so. Against this background, Rom would not react as in the original story. For now, given their agreement, Queenie *can* just decide, "just like that." The qualification is crucial: Rom can be considered to have concurred in advance with any proposal from Queenie that she not go all the way into town.[32]

The concurrence criterion in effect spells out the most plausible interpretation of Rom's "You can't just decide!" He means that Queenie is *not in a position* unilaterally to decide to stop where she does—not without coming up against their shared intention. What is required to render her action faultless in the relevant respect is Rom's concurrence with her stopping.

One can of course make a personal decision *not to act in accordance with a shared intention*; this is what Queenie does in the initial story. It is also what Ned does in the story of his shared intention with Olive to hike to the top of the hill. What neither Queenie nor Ned is in a position unilaterally to do by virtue of his or her own decision, in and of itself, is change, rescind, or release themselves from participation in the pertinent shared intention in such a way as to make faultless their acting contrary to it.

I shall now assume that the concurrence criterion must indeed be satisfied by an adequate account of shared intention.[33] Given that criterion, there is another significant problem for the personal intentions perspective.

As discussed earlier, one is a position unilaterally to rescind one's personal intentions. One is also in a position unilaterally to alter them with respect to

---

[32] A reader may be reminded of the duet-singers in Bratman 1993, to whom I recur later. Bratman's example is pertinent to both criteria though not, I think, adversely. For an extended discussion of background understandings of the kind in question here, see Gilbert 2006, chapter 6.

[33] There is a much longer pertinent discussion of a similar concurrence condition with respect to joint activity (as opposed to shared intention) in Gilbert 2006, chapter 7; see also Gilbert 1997.

some detail. One can "just decide" to do so, and it is done. Thus, though one might beg someone else not to change his mind, point out some undesired consequence of his doing so, malign him for doing so, and the like, it is not true as a matter of what a personal intention is that he is not in a position to do it without one's concurrence.

This criterion has, it seems, a sharper edge than the disjunction criterion. According to that criterion, there need be no correlative personal intentions given a shared intention. Though this means that there cannot be a correlative personal intentions account of shared intention that is adequate in the sense at issue here, the criterion leaves open the possibility that a structure of personal intentions may be sufficient for shared intention.

Given the concurrence criterion it is hard to see that such a structure can indeed be sufficient for shared intention. If a shared intention is such that one cannot unilaterally release oneself from participation in it by a simple change of mind, there must be something other than a structure of personal intentions at the core of any shared intention. For given any personal intention, the person with that intention is in a position to rescind it, and hence in effect demolish the shared intention itself, simply by changing his mind.

5. The Obligation Criterion

As I explain, a further criterion of adequacy for an account of shared intention is suggested by the following part of the story of Rom and Queenie's shopping expedition: when Queenie starts slowing down, Rom says, in a tone of mild rebuke, "Can you hurry up a bit? We won't be able to get any shopping done at this rate!" In other words, she is acting in such a way as to make it hard for them to fulfill their shared intention.

In speaking as he does Rom both mildly rebukes Queenie for slowing down, and implicitly demands that she hurry. Her "Sorry!" presupposes his standing to make this demand and to rebuke her as he does.

This suggests something like the following *obligation criterion*:

> an adequate account of shared intention will entail that each party to a shared intention is obligated to each to act as appropriate to the shared intention in conjunction with the rest.

In parallel with my assumption regarding the concurrence criterion, I take it as read here that the account should be such that the parties to the shared intention will understand that they have the stated obligations, and that they understand that this is so as a matter of what a shared intention is. Thus in explaining the rebuke and demand that are the focus here—as in explaining his "You can't just decide to stop!"—Rom might simply have said "We're on our way to the shops!"

I take the obligation criterion to imply that each has an obligation to form, as and when necessary, personal intentions that mesh appropriately with those of the other party or parties.[34] One can, of course, fail to satisfy these obligations: their existence is not disproved by such failure.

It is important to emphasize that the obligation criterion, as just set out, concerns obligations of a particular type. Thus in my formulation of the criterion each party is said to be obligated *to* the other parties to do something. I shall refer to obligations of this type as *directed* obligations, using an established phrase that is appropriate here. Before I say why the criterion is couched in these terms, it will be helpful to say more about directed obligations as I shall construe them here.

Rights theorists commonly use the language of directed obligation: one person's right against a second person to an action of the second person is said to be equivalent to the second person's obligation to the right-holder to perform the action. The word "duty" is often substituted for "obligation" in the formulation given here.[35] Rights of the kind in question are generally known as *claim-rights* or *claims*.[36]

The obligation criterion, indeed, could just as well have been labeled *the rights criterion*, as long as that is understood to refer to rights that are the equivalent of directed duties, as opposed to some other kind of right, such as a liberty-right. It might be thought that in order to understand better the nature of directed duties one can simply reach into the theory of claim-rights for an answer. There is great controversy among rights theorists, however, as to what a claim-right amounts to. The same goes, not surprisingly, for the nature of directed obligations.

As to the latter, as far as the theory of shared intention goes, I would argue that the interpretation we need is in terms of *owing*, an interpretation given by two distinguished rights theorists, H. L. A. Hart and Joel Feinberg. In this construal, the parties owe each other action appropriate to the shared intention (Hart 1955; Feinberg 1970). To say that, however, is not to conclude discussion.

---

[34] This point recalls the "meshing sub-plans" Bratman 1993 invokes, and emphasizes, in his account of shared intention. This is clearly pertinent to the relations between our accounts to which I turn later in the text.

[35] Hart 1955 explicitly prefers "obligation."

[36] The classic reference here is Hohfeld 1919/1964. That species of rights Hohfeld calls *claims* (rights against persons to actions of those persons) are said to have, as their "correlative and equivalent," duties toward the right-holder. I shall not here speculate on why Hohfeld chose the label he did, something he did not make explicit.

People use the term "owe" in different ways, not always in a way that is appropriate here. For instance, one may say "I owe him a favor" without meaning that he has a right to a favor from you. To say that for one person to owe another an action, in the present context, is for that other to have a right against him to the action in question is, of course, true. It is only helpful in the present context if it is clear what such a right amounts to.

I find an important clue in this. Feinberg suggests at one point that a right-holder's demanding what he has a right to can be thought of as a matter of demanding *his own* (Feinberg 1970, 251). This could be construed in various ways. We might take it to imply that if I owe someone a certain action, in the sense of "owe" in question here, he already in some intuitive sense *owns* that action. On hearing this one may wonder if it can be correct. In what sense can one own the future action of another person? I believe that something can be made of it. For now I explain how some pertinent and important intuitive ideas in addition to those of owing and claim-rights fit together with the idea of one's owning, in some intuitive sense, another's action.

I take Feinberg to offer us a way to amplify the nature of a demand, or, if you like, a demand that is something more than a seriously intended imperative. Anyone is in a position to address such an imperative to anyone else. Indeed, if one issues such an imperative while threatening some undesired consequence if its addressee does not conform to it—for example, if one is brandishing a gun while saying 'Hand over your money!"—one is likely to be successful in obtaining such conformity. For a demand in the sense in question here one needs a special standing. The same goes for the issuing of a rebuke, which might be thought of as a retrospective demand.[37]

The idea about demanding that I take from what Feinberg says is this: to be in a position to demand something from someone is already to be in some intuitive sense to own it. That is because demanding in the relevant sense *is* demanding what one owns. This suggests that there is an important and closely linked family of concepts here: the concept of *a right to some future action of the right's addressee,* one's current *ownership,* in some intuitive sense, of that action, one's being *owed* that action by the right's addressee prior to his performing it, one's being in a position to *demand* it of him prior to its performance, and one's being in a position to *rebuke* him if he has failed to perform it at the appropriate time. The linkage can be displayed as follows: one who has a right to someone's future action already owns that action in some intuitive sense of "own." Until the action is performed he is owed that action by the person concerned, thus being in a position to demand it of him prior to its being performed and to rebuke him if it is not performed. If it is performed, one might say that it has finally come into the possession of the right-holder, in the only way that it can.

---

[37] On concepts that can only be applied to one with a special standing see also Gilbert 2006, chapter 1.

This all suggests a way of interpreting the obligation criterion that fits the observable facts about shared intention and offers a plausible interpretation of them. Consider again the case of Rom and Queenie. Rom both rebukes Queenie (albeit mildly) for going too slowly for the satisfaction of their shared intention and demands that she speed up if she can. Queenie implicitly accepts his standing to issue such rebukes and demands when she says "Sorry!" In so doing she acknowledges, in effect, that at the time he spoke Rom had a right against her to actions appropriate to the shared intention; and that she owed him such actions, which he already in some sense owned. In other terms, she has the corresponding directed obligation to perform such actions. Intuitively the same goes, with appropriate changes, for the parties to any shared intention.

One who accepts the obligation criterion so interpreted—as I shall in what follows—could also posit as a criterion of adequacy a "standing to demand" criterion and a correlative "standing to rebuke" criterion. This is redundant, strictly speaking, once one has clarified the nature of the obligation at issue in the way just indicated. If you owe me your action in the sense that implies that I already in some sense own it, I am in a position to demand that action as mine and to rebuke you when you fail to perform it.

Standing, incidentally, must be sharply distinguished from justification. One may have the standing to demand something of someone, yet not be justified in doing so, in the circumstances. Thus were Queenie so sensitive to criticism that she would suffer a grave physical crisis if rebuked, in most circumstances it would be wrong to rebuke her even if one had the standing to do so.

So much, then, in explanation and justification of the obligation criterion. There are various ways in which it might be satisfied. An account of shared intention could list one or more other conditions from which the pertinent obligations of the parties did *not* follow and then explicitly posit, in addition, the existence of such obligations. That would be unsatisfactory because it would not explain the ground of the obligations.

More desirable would be an account such that the conditions it explicitly posits—which do not explicitly stipulate the necessary obligations of the parties—are such that *it follows* from them that the parties have these obligations. This way, the source of the obligation would be completely clear. It would also fit well with the observation made earlier that one who calls another on his inappropriate action may well justify his intervention *by reference simply to the shared intention.* This suggests that the existence of the necessary obligations—providing the standing to demand and rebuke—is understood to be grounded in other conditions the shared intention satisfies, the core conditions for shared intention. Thus no reference to further, "external" factors such as expectations or reliance generated by the shared intention, or to side or background promises or agreements, is needed.

The obligation criterion, like the concurrence criterion, argues against the sufficiency of an account of shared intention in terms of correlative personal intentions. For, though my personal intention constrains my behavior, it does not in and of itself entail that I owe you the intended action.

Michael Bratman has allowed that when there is a shared intention in his sense, there are not necessarily any mutual obligations of the parties. At the same time he has in various ways argued, in effect, against the obligation criterion. I briefly review and respond to three of those arguments here.[38]

One argument involves the example of two duet-singers who "each value their duet-singing but nevertheless have a clear understanding between them that neither is making any binding promise to or agreement with the other concerning their singing. Each publicly states that she reserves the right to change her mind" (Bratman 1993, 111). There are various ways of construing this example.

If we give the most natural reading to "their duet-singing" we should allow that these singers do have an established shared intention. At the same time we can construe their "clear understanding" as, in effect, a side agreement to the effect that each may proceed as if they have no obligations to one another with respect to their duet-singing. The possibility of such a side- agreement does not force us to reject the obligation criterion. A similar point was made earlier in relation to the concurrence criterion (see also Gilbert 2000, 35 n36).

Another argument alludes to a case involving coercion. Here is the version of it that best fits the present juncture in my own discussion. I tell you that unless you share with me an intention to sing a duet, I will blow up your house. This threat leads you sincerely to act in such a way as to establish that now we have the shared intention in question. Of this scenario Bratman says "it seems to me that in this case I have no entitlement to your playing your part" (Bratman 1999, 132–133).

I agree with Bratman that a shared intention can be established in these circumstances. I suggest, however, that once the shared intention has been established in the way described, you may well refrain from acting in a way inconsistent with it because you understand that, fortunately or not, you now owe me actions consistent with that shared intention. Perhaps there are considerations on the other side. And you may judge that all things considered it is rationally permissible not to fulfill your obligation to me. You are likely still to have it in view, and to recognize my standing to rebuke you for failing to fulfill it.

It is quite possible—likely, in fact—that Bratman is thinking of entitlements of a specific kind, and that the parties to a shared intention have rights against each other of another kind. Then his judgment on this case could be correct in its own terms, but it would not tell the whole story about shared intention and obligation.[39]

---

[38] In doing so I focus on material that was published prior to the completion of this chapter.

[39] I discuss the related case of coerced agreements at length in Gilbert 1996, chapter 12. See also Gilbert 2006, chapter 10.

Another argument alludes to shared intentions to do something bad. Bratman assumes that these cannot involve obligations to act in favor of the shared intention.[40] Yet those who share intentions to do bad things may well think otherwise; and, as in the previous case, it is possible that Bratman's negative conclusion is valid only for a kind of obligation other than that involved in shared intention—which is what I believe is the case. I return to this issue later in the chapter.

Though inclined to reject the obligation criterion, Bratman believes that the parties to a shared intention according to his account often have obligations to one another to act in favor of the shared intention. This could be due to prior agreements or promises. Or it may be due to factors downstream from the shared intention—perhaps not very far downstream—which trigger a moral principle such as the one argued by Thomas Scanlon to explain the moral wrong involved in promise-breaking, but not that alone, a principle he dubs "Principle F."[41]

All this may well be true. Allowing for the sake of argument that it is, it cannot be the whole story of the obligations associated with shared intention.

As Bratman would agree, shared intentions can arise without a background agreement or promise. Yet, as argued earlier, a shared intention is sufficient in and of itself for the obligations in question. What of downstream factors such as expectations and reliance, coupled with Scanlon's Principle F, or something like it? Since these are indeed downstream factors they cannot accommodate the intuition that obligations inhere in the shared intention. There is, in any case another problem with this move.

As I have argued elsewhere, the application of a principle such as Scanlon's Principle F to a given party does not show that the other party has a claim-right against him, along with the standing to demand as his what he has a right to. Rather, it shows that the first party is morally required to act in favor of the shared intention, subject perhaps to certain conditions.[42]

In sum, though Bratman and other personal intentions theorists may be able to argue for the existence of various obligations that are in the offing when there is a shared intention, they may not be able to account for the directed obligations that, intuitively, inhere in the shared intention itself.

---

[40] See Bratman 1999, 132 n6 Others have had this reaction in related contexts. For discussion of the related case of immoral agreements (along with case of coerced agreements) see Gilbert 2006, chapter 10.

[41] "F" stands for "fidelity." Since the details of this complex principle are not of central importance here I do not quote it. See e.g. Scanlon 1998.

[42] I argue at length that Principle F, in particular, does not suffice to explain the rights of promisees, in particular, in Gilbert 2004 (chapter 12 this volume). I also raise doubts there about the sufficiency for this purpose of moral principles more generally. In the case of an application of Principle F specifically, the condition that needs to hold is that the second party does not say it is fine with him that the first party not act in favor of the shared intention. See Gilbert 2004 on unhelpfulness of this clause in explaining the rights of a promisee.

6. The Plural Subject Account of Shared Intention

As I shall explain, the account I have been developing respects the disjunction, concurrence and obligation criteria. I first present the account without explanation. The ensuing discussion will explain the technical terms involved and clarify some further aspects of the account.

In its most general form the account runs as follows:

> Members of some population P *share an intention* to do A if and only if they are jointly committed to intend as a body to do A.

For two-person cases of the type on which I have been focusing in this chapter it would run, more specifically, thus:

> Persons X and Y *share an intention* to do A if and only if X and Y are jointly committed to intend as a body to do A.

Both formulations include some technical terms that require explanation. In particular I must explain what it is for people to be *jointly committed* in some way and what it is to intend *as a body* to do A. I start with joint commitment.

The relevant concept of *commitment* can usefully be introduced, albeit roughly and briefly, by reference to personal intentions and decisions, since people are committed by them in the appropriate sense of commitment. The cases of intention and decision are somewhat different. As to decisions, if I have decided at t to do A at time *t* + 1, *and have not subsequently rescinded my decision*, then I have sufficient reason to do A at *t* + 1. As to intentions, if at time t I intend to do A at *t* + 1, *and my intention has persisted to t* + 1, then I have sufficient reason to do A at *t* + 1.[43]

The central point for present purposes is that given either an un-rescinded decision or a standing intention, the person in question has sufficient reason to act in a particular way even without this having been the case prior to the formation of the intention or decision. In saying that one has *sufficient reason* to act in some way I mean that, if all else is equal, one ought so to act. The "ought" here is a matter of what might be referred to as *rational* requirement, such that one is not being appropriately responsive to the considerations that bear on the case if one fails to act as one ought.[44]

---

[43] I have elsewhere summarized this point by saying that decisions but not intentions have *trans-temporal reach*. Clearly the notion of trans-temporal reach is distinct from the notion of *relating to the future*. See Gilbert 2006, chapter 7, where there is a longer discussion of decisions versus intentions in the context of a discussion of joint commitment. On "having sufficient reason" see the text following.

[44] For concordant discussion see Verbeek 2007. For present purposes I shall not attempt to argue the point.

Sometimes, I take it, all else is not equal. That is, all things considered, I ought not to do A, in spite of my decision or intention to do it. Perhaps doing A is imprudent or immoral.[45] Then, all things considered, I ought not to do A.

I do not mean to imply that either decisions or intentions are "reasons" in a particular sense of "reason" on which many contemporary philosophers have focused. Such reasons are, we might say, considerations for and against a particular action that would appropriately be weighed *prior to making a decision whether or not to perform it.*

Personal decisions and intentions create commitments of a kind I shall call *personal commitments.* For present purposes the key salient feature of such commitments is that the one who personally formed or made the corresponding personal decision or intention is in a position unilaterally to expunge it as a matter of personal choice.[46]

A joint commitment is not a concatenation of personal commitments. Thus it is not formed by virtue of the formation of a personal commitment by each of the parties. In particular, as I have emphasized elsewhere, its formation is not achieved by the expression of a *conditional* personal commitment which is met by a clinching expression from the other party or parties.[47]

How, then, is a joint commitment created? In the basic case, on which I focus here, each of two or more people must openly express his personal readiness jointly with the others to commit them all in a certain way.[48] I mean to imply here that each is indeed personally ready for this, and that he expresses this readiness.[49] Once the concordant expressions of all have occurred and are common knowledge between the parties, the joint commitment is in place.

I make some further points regarding the creation of a joint commitment shortly. Before that I say something to clarify the idea that those who share an intention are jointly committed to intend *as a body* to do something.

[45] In the case of decision, even if all else is not equal, so that one ought not to act in accord with one's decision all things considered, I take it that something is amiss if one fails to change one's mind yet acts contrary to the decision. This could happen if one simply forgets one's decision and goes ahead and acts contrary to it—without explicitly changing one's mind. I shall not pursue this aspect of the matter here, though I take it to be significant.

[46] Perhaps this is true also of an individual's we-intention as Searle 1990 understands it—a different type of singularist-intention. To my knowledge Searle has not addressed this issue; I shall not attempt to pursue it here.

[47] Some tentative formulations in Gilbert 1989 may have led to misunderstanding in this respect; though see e.g. 282, which attempts to forestall such misunderstandings. The position involving conditional personal commitments criticized in Roth 2004, then, is not mine. See Gilbert 2003 for more discussion on this point.

[48] Non-basic cases involve authorities whose status derives from a basic joint commitment. See Gilbert 2006, chapter 7.

[49] In Gilbert 1989, chapter 4 I argue for an "expressed" condition as well as an "expression" condition.

I should say at the outset that there can be joint commitments not only to *intend* as a body to do something but also to believe as a body that such-and-such, to accept, as a body, a certain rule, and so on. The content of every joint commitment can be represented in a similar way. That is, whatever its content, a joint commitment can be represented as a joint commitment to "do" something as a body, where "doing" is understood in a broad sense so as to include intending, believing, accepting, and so on.

For the sake of a label, I say that those who are jointly committed in some way constitute a "plural subject."[50] Those who are jointly committed in one way may also be so committed in one or more other ways. In that case one can say that they constitute the plural subject of an intention, a belief, and so on, depending on the case. Given the meaning of my technical phrase "plural subject" I dub the account of shared intention I am discussing *the plural subject account* of shared intention.

There is doubtless more than one way further to articulate the idea of a joint commitment to intend as a body to do something. The way that I have tended to adopt keeps the word "body" in play. Thus one might put things roughly as follows: the parties are jointly committed *as far as possible to emulate, by virtue of the actions of each, with respect to its intending, a single body* that intends to do the thing in question.

In this formulation speech and deliberate inaction are understood to be included under "actions." Taking as read the qualifiers "as far as possible," "by virtue of their several actions" and "with respect to its intending" we have something a little more pithy: the parties are jointly committed to emulate a single body with a certain intention. I shall generally use this shorter formulation in what follows.

What is a "single body" as I construe the phrase? I take it that whereas a single human being constitutes a single body, in the sense I have in mind, a plurality of human individuals does not in and of itself constitute such a body. At least to some extent, however, such a plurality can *emulate* such a body—one with a plurality not only of limbs, eyes, and ears, but also of noses and mouths.[51]

As I have said in a number of places, I am not wedded to the use of the term "body" in my account of the content of a joint commitment or in the specific case of shared intention. One might substitute in the previous formulation the term "person," for instance, or "agent." Another possibility that retains any talk of emulation is to say something along the following lines: a joint commitment

---

[50] I first used "plural subject" as a technical term in Gilbert 1989.

[51] In previous writings I have tended to write of the parties being committed to "constitute as far as possible a single body that does such-and-such." I think an appeal to emulation is more helpful here, because what is at issue for the jointly committed parties is largely a type of behavior or performance.

to intend as a body to do something is a joint commitment *as far as possible to emulate, by virtue of the actions of each, a single instance of intending to do that thing.*

As to what precisely is intended, we need a felicitous way to deal with the fact that some of the things we may share an intention to do are designed for two or more participants—things such as playing a duet or a game of basketball or tennis—and some are not so designed. For instance, we may intend to prepare a meal, solve a problem and go for a walk.

Consider a case of the latter kind. Suppose that Sally and Tim share an intention to go for a walk. Understanding what it is to intend as a body along one of the lines suggested, we might articulate their situation as a whole roughly as follows: Sally and Tim are jointly committed to intend as a body to produce, by virtue of the actions of each, *a single instance of going for a walk with the two of them as the participants in that walk.*

One can expect this spare and basic idea to be filled out in concrete situations by background social conventions or explicit agreements between the parties as to how a walk for two is to proceed. Thus the social conventions to which I am a party dictate that when we go for a walk, we walk alongside each other, unless the terrain requires us to do otherwise. Other such conventions might require the parties to walk in single file, or for parties of one social class or gender to walk ahead of those from another social class or gender, and so on.

I turn now to a case of the other kind: Sally and Tim now intend to play a game of tennis. This can be understood in a parallel way, roughly as follows: Sally and Tim are jointly committed to intend as a body to produce, by virtue of the actions of each, *a single instance of a tennis game with the two of them as participants in that game.*

I return now to the question of how a joint commitment is created. As said, it is necessary and sufficient for the creation of a joint commitment that each party express his personal readiness jointly to commit them all in a certain way, in conditions of common knowledge. The necessary expressions of readiness can take various forms.

Some may involve a verbal agreement as in: "Shall we go to London together?" "Okay!" I have argued elsewhere for an understanding of everyday agreements generally in terms of joint commitment.[52] I propose more specifically that such an agreement is a *joint decision,* where such a decision is made by an explicit process such as that in the example, creating a joint commitment of the parties to endorse as a body a particular plan of action.

A less explicit process is also possible.[53] This may or may not be considerably extended in time. Then, what emerges will not involve a joint commitment to

---

[52] My argument is summarized in Gilbert 2006, chapter 10. For more detail, see Gilbert 1996, chapter 13.

[53] As in case described earlier of students Jake and Kristen. For further examples in the context of a discussion of joint commitment generally see, e.g., Gilbert 2006, chapter 7.

endorse as a body a certain explicitly formulated decision, but will simply be a jointly commitment to intend as a body to do something.

A practically important aspect of any joint commitment is this. Like a personal commitment it can only be rescinded by the "one" who created it: in this case, absent special background understandings, that "one" comprises those who jointly committed themselves by their concordant expressions. Together they constitute the creator of the commitment; the "one" who imposed the relevant normative constraint on each of the parties.

With respect to the ending of a joint commitment arrived at without an agreement it may be more apt to speak of something other than "rescission," which conjures another focused, dated process, with respect to its demise (see Gilbert 2006, 141–143). In order not to complicate matters I shall continue to write of "rescission" in what follows.

I have argued elsewhere that the concept of joint commitment just sketched lies at the foundation of many central everyday concepts including those of a social rule, an interpersonal agreement, a group's language and a group's belief.[54]

Its invocation as part of an account of shared intention, then, is by no means *ad hoc*. On the contrary, one reason for my initially proposing a plural subject account of shared intention was my prior recognition of the plausibility of such an account for other central social phenomena. Most of these accounts were argued for independently of the others.

7. Some Questions about the Account

Before turning to the relationship of the plural subject account of shared intention to the criteria of adequacy specified earlier, I address some questions that might be raised in response to what I have said so far.

Reflecting on the formulation in which one is jointly committed to intend as a body to do a certain thing, one might ask: do those who are jointly committed in some way *thereby* constitute a body in some intuitive sense of the word? In my technical terminology, is a plural subject itself a body of some kind? If so, is that a problem for my account of shared intention?[55]

Suppose, as I think is plausible, that that any plural subject, in my sense, is indeed a kind of body. We might call the kind of body in question a *collective* body, or *collective*, understanding this to be a body that somehow comprises a number of single bodies in the sense invoked in the previous section, or a

---

[54] In Gilbert 1989 with amplifications and further points made elsewhere. See Gilbert 1997 for a summary of the framework of analysis that has evolved therefrom.

[55] Thomas Smith raised these questions in conversation (personal communication, Helsinki, 2006).

number of persons.[56] My proposal—in one formulation—is that a shared intention is a joint commitment to intend as a body to do something, where a "body" here is understood to be a *non*-collective body.

Suppose then that certain persons constitute, by virtue of their joint commitment, a collective body that intends to do something. That clearly does not mean that their joint commitment requires no further action from them—that it is, in effect, pointless. On the contrary, each one must continue to act so that as far as possible they emulate, by virtue of their several actions, with respect to its intending, a single non-collective body with the intention in question.

I now briefly consider whether there is anything philosophically disreputable about the plural subject account of shared intention. Are there any sound ontological canons, for instance, that it transgresses? I think not.

Some people have, I think, read too much into my technical phrase "plural subject." For me, if and only if individuals X, Y and any others are jointly committed in some way then—by my definition of "plural subject"—they constitute a plural subject. If one finds joint commitment to be a philosophically acceptable notion, then there is nothing to quarrel with in my references to plural subjects, unless perhaps it is the label "plural subject" as such.

If anything, that label is intended to suggest something for which I have argued. Namely, when they are not susceptible of a simple distributive reading, when they refer to a set of statements about what one might call "singular subjects," each of which appropriately refers to himself as "I," everyday references to what "we" intend, and so on, are references to "plural subjects" in my sense.

What, then, of joint commitment? Is it a philosophically acceptable notion? Whether or not one is *committed* in the sense appropriate to joint commitment is a matter of one's normative situation and its source. One is *jointly* committed with another person or persons if and only if one is committed, along with him or them, as a matter of the readiness of each together to commit them all in a particular way, which readiness has been mutually expressed in conditions of common knowledge.

I see in this description nothing philosophically disreputable. In particular, it fails to posit any metaphysically suspect group mind—the scary monster that is often invoked in order to enhance the attraction of an account in terms of singularist-intentions, personal or otherwise.[57] At the same time, the plural subject account implies that a shared intention is not constructed out of singularist-intentions. It is possible, then, to give an account of shared intention

---

[56] I have long argued that a central everyday concept of "social group" is more or less equivalent to the concept of a plural subject as I define that. See Gilbert 1989, chapter 4; also Gilbert 1990, 2006, chapter 8. It is natural enough to think of a social group as a *body* of persons.

[57] Bratman 1993; Searle 1990, respectively.

that is not constructed out of singularist-intentions, but which fails to posit any metaphysically suspect entities.

8. Implications of the Account

I now justify my claim that the plural subject account of shared intention meets the criteria of adequacy mentioned. As to the disjunction criterion, since a shared intention (according to the account) is a matter of joint commitment, it is logically possible for it to exist in the absence of correlative personal intentions of the participants. Thus the disjunction criterion is satisfied.

What of the concurrence criterion? What parties to a shared intention cannot do is alter or rescind the foundational joint commitment without the concurrence of the other parties, absent special background understandings. That latter point shows that the concurrence condition is satisfied.

I turn now to the obligation criterion, and argue briefly that this also is satisfied by the plural subject account.[58] Recall what one needs to show according to this criterion: on the proposed account of shared intention the participants must owe one another future conforming actions, where that means that they already in some intuitive sense own these actions in advance of their performance. Accordingly, each is in a position to demand conforming actions of the others, and to rebuke the others for non-conforming actions. As indicated earlier one might be doubtful as to whether there is an intuitive sense in which one can own someone's future action. I propose that there is at least one such a sense, and that consideration of what happens when a joint commitment is made tells us what it is.

What I have in mind is roughly this. Crucially, in co-creating their joint commitment *the parties together impose on each other a constraint such that, all else being equal, a given party will not act as he ought should he fail to respect it.* It is to this extent and in this sense that the parties can be said to own the future conforming actions of each one.

Accordingly, any one party is in a position to demand conformity or rebuke for non-conformity as co-owner of the action in question. Making things explicit, he might say "Give me that, it's mine—qua one of us!"

I take it that when actions are owned in the sense now in question they are owed to their owners prior to performance. Thus the parties to a joint commitment owe one another conformity to it, qua parties to the commitment.

The foregoing line of argument for the obligating nature of a joint commitment is a matter of the authorship of the commitment and its constraining nature.

---

[58] One can argue for the obligating nature of joint commitment in other ways also. See, e.g., Gilbert 2000, chapter 4.

The obligations of the parties are, one might say, purely internal to the joint commitment. These obligations exist irrespective of the content of the commitment in question: they exist whenever a joint commitment is made, whatever else is true. I now briefly explore some of the implications of this particular point.

On the face of it, it is possible for people jointly to commit one another to intend as a body to do something that considered in itself, apart from the commitment is morally impermissible—something that is, for short, an evil act.[59] In saying this I do not mean that the action in question is seen by the parties as evil but that it is in fact evil. I shall assume for present purposes that such a joint commitment is indeed possible.[60]

Suppose, then, that Ulrich and Vance share an intention according to the plural subject account to do some evil thing. Each will then owe the other conformity to their intention, by virtue of the constitutive joint commitment. As each will understand, if the other wishes to call him on his non-conformity then he will have the standing to do so, since he is not being given what is owed him. In other terms, Vance and Ulrich are obligated to each other to conform to the constitutive joint commitment, though neither (I shall assume) ought to conform to it all things considered.

One may now be moved to say that there is a problem here for the plural subject account precisely because it implies that the parties to a shared intention to do evil are *obligated* in this way. That, one may say, cannot be the case.[61] In saying this, one may well have in mind a type of obligation that is not here to the point.[62] In particular, one may have in mind the obligations, duties, or requirements that accrue to those who fall under a moral principle such as Scanlon's principle F. Though I shall not attempt to argue this here, I would agree that it is impossible to have an obligation of *this* type to do evil. Call an obligation of this type a *moral requirement*. If one has a shared intention to do A, where A is an evil action in the sense at issue, then in my view it is *not* the case that one is morally required or obligated in *that* sense to conform to the constitutive joint commitment.

The directed obligations of joint commitment are another matter. As said above, if people can jointly commit to intend as a body to do some evil thing, it follows that they are obligated to one another to conform to that evil intention,

---

[59] I do not mean here to plump for some kind of deontological as opposed to consequentialist ethics. If you like read "morally impermissible" as "morally impermissible in normal circumstances," and read the rest of the discussion as assuming normal circumstances.

[60] Any argument to the effect that it is not would most likely imply that a personal commitment to do what is in fact evil is impossible also. Both positions are on the face of it implausible.

[61] Cf. Michael Bratman's reaction to the obligation criterion, discussed above.

[62] For some discussion of so-called obligations as a genus and at least two significantly different species of so-called obligation see Gilbert 2006, chapters 2, 7, and elsewhere.

whatever the circumstances.[63] As I have put it elsewhere, the obligations that ensue from a joint commitment are not context-sensitive; moral requirements, on the other hand, are (Gilbert 1996, ch.apter 7, 2006, chapter 7).

9. The Plural Subject Account and Personal Intentions

What is the relationship of shared intention on the plural subject account to personal intentions of the parties to the shared intention? In briefly considering the question here I start by reviewing the core of Michael Bratman's personal intentions account of shared intention, whose initial formulation was detailed earlier.

According to Bratman, if we two share an intention to paint the house together, for instance, then each of us personally intends that we paint the house together, personally intends that we paint the house together by virtue of his own and the other's personal intention that we paint the house together, and personally intends that we do this on the basis of meshing personal sub-plans of each.[64] Each is personally committed to act in accordance with his personal intention, in the sense of "personal commitment" introduced earlier. A central aspect of a personal commitment in this sense is that one with such a commitment is in a position unilaterally to divest himself of it as a matter solely of his personal choice.

A first point to make in comparing this personal intentions approach with the plural subject account involves an important contrast. On the plural subject account the individual parties to a shared intention are necessarily *committed* in related ways. The commitments in question, however, are not *personal* commitments but rather what one might refer to as "individual" commitments.[65]

Thus suppose that Will and Xenia have a shared intention according to the plural subject account. If he proposes a shared sub-plan to her, and it is reasonable, there is already some onus on her to accept it, as a party to the fundamental

---

[63] I have applied these points to the question of commands to do evil in chapter 17 this volume. For further discussion of joint commitments with immoral content see Gilbert 2006, chapter 10, which also discusses the related topic of joint commitments whose genesis involves coercion of one or more parties.

[64] That Bratman has in mind personal sub-plans rather than shared sub-plans is indicated by such references as "the other's relevant sub-plans" (Bratman 1993, 105). Meshing sub-plans were a key ingredient in the account of shared intention in Bratman 1993; the larger set of conditions he has been developing include, e.g., the parties' personal willingness to help one another if needed to carry out the shared intention. Given Bratman's personal intentions perspective I take the addition just mentioned to be plausible insofar as the parties to a shared intention, like those who act together, tend both to expect and to manifest such helping behavior. See e.g. Gilbert 1989, chapter 4.

[65] See Gilbert 1996, 11–13 for a detailed treatment of these "individual" commitments. See also Gilbert 2003 and the text below.

joint commitment.[66] In terms of commitment, she is already committed not capriciously to reject Will's proposal, an individual commitment deriving from the fundamental joint commitment of the two. The same goes for Will, of course, with relevant changes. I assume that something similar is true of those with the personal intentions at the core of Bratman's account, the derived commitments there being personal. There are important differences between the cases, however. I focus on one here.

In the case described, Xenia, for instance, cannot unilaterally revise or rescind the joint commitment from which her individual commitment derives, nor can she release herself from it. Thus her being subject to the derived individual commitment, also, is dependent on more than her own will and pleasure. This is not true of the personal commitments deriving from a personal intention, since the person with the intention is in a position unilaterally to revise or rescind that intention. This difference lends the derived commitments involved in shared intention on the plural subject account a greater stability in terms of revisability, rescindability, and release, than those involved in Bratman's or any other personal intentions account. Such stability is also possessed of course by a shared intention on the plural subject account.

There is, also, more reason to conform to a joint commitment as such than to a personal intention as such. Actions that conform to a joint commitment are owed by each party to every other. This is an additional consideration in favor of conforming to the joint commitment. Not only is conformity owed to the others but, because of this, they have the standing to make demands and issue rebukes in relation to threatened or actual non-conformity by a given party.

A second point to make in comparing the personal intentions account with the plural subject account of shared intention is this. When people have a shared intention on the plural subject account, they are likely to develop a variety of concordant *personal* intentions. These will arise under the guidance, so to speak, of the foundational joint commitment and the joint commitments involved in any shared sub-plans. For instance, if Will and Xenia now share the sub-plan he proposed (according to the plural subject account), and it involves his getting paint at the store, he may form the personal intention to go to the garage and start the car, as a means of fulfilling his commitment to go to the store.

If the parties have not arrived at such a shared sub-plan—perhaps they are no longer in touch—it is even more likely to be incumbent on each to form personal intentions that mesh well with the personal intentions of the other, so as appropriately to fill in any gaps in the shared master plan. As Michael Bratman

[66] Bratman emphasizes the role of meshing *personal* sub-plans of the parties in achieving coordination in the service of the shared intention. In fact, as Bratman may well allow, such coordination may best be achieved, where possible, by means of the co-creation of a *shared* sub-plan containing meshing roles for each.

has emphasized in his work on intention, most of our plans, both personal and shared, are partial, in that they do not specify everything that needs to be done in order that the plan be successfully carried out.

Though the plural subject account does not itself posit any particular personal intentions, then, one can predict that shared intentions on that account will be accompanied by a variety of meshing personal intentions of the parties when those parties act appropriately in light of their shared intention and any shared sub-plans they have consequently developed.

I should emphasize that in saying this I am not saying that when there is a shared intention according to the plural subject account there will be personal intentions *of the type at the core of Bratman's account,* that is, personal intentions "*that we J.*" Nor am I saying that the development of correlative personal intentions in the sense defined earlier is predictable. On the contrary, any need for *commitment* in that respect is already taken care of by the joint commitment at the core of the shared intention. The personal intentions that are needed, and hence predictable, are intentions to act in ways *not* implicitly specified by the shared intention.

Given the plural subject account, then, shared intentions are apt to play important roles emphasized by Michael Bratman as roles we understand shared intention to play, in advance of our development of an account of it (Bratman 1993, 99). In particular, they help to organize and coordinate our *personal* intentions and plans in ways that favor the fulfillment of the shared intention. They do this in part by providing a stable framework within which bargaining and negotiation about how things are to proceed may take place.

Bratman has argued, reasonably, that the structure of personal intentions described in his account plays these roles. It is important to note, however, that shared intentions on the plural subject account are even better suited for these roles. Shared intentions on the plural subject account are a more felicitous, because more stable framework for bargaining and negotiation and, relatedly, a more felicitous means of coordinating personal intentions and, more generally, the commitments of individuals, and keeping them on the track of the shared intention. This is because they are more stable in relation to rescission, revision, and release.

Suppose, then, that for the sake of argument one were to agree with Bratman when he says:

Can we describe an appropriate complex from whose proper functioning would emerge the coordinated action and planning, and the relevant framework for bargaining, characteristic of shared intention? If so, we would have reason to identify shared intention with this complex.[67]

[67] This and the following quotation come from Bratman 1993, 100.

Set aside his assumption that there is a "complex" in question that is a matter of the "attitudes of each of the individual agents—attitudes that have appropriate contents and are interrelated in appropriate ways," which may or may not rule out the conditions stipulated by the plural subject account. Think of the term "complex" as referring simply to a number of factors, possibly just one. One could then argue that since when functioning properly the plural subject complex is more efficacious in the pertinent way than a personal intentions complex—however complicated—it has a better title to be identified with shared intention.

Of course, I do not think that the criteria of adequacy for an account of shared intention are exhausted by the tendency of shared intentions to fulfill the roles mentioned by Bratman. I agree with him that they have this tendency, and allow that it might reasonably be invoked in a full set of criteria of adequacy for shared intention. Such a full set, meanwhile, will include others that the personal intentions perspective is harder put to it to satisfy.

Before concluding this section I consider another way in which the plural subject account and a personal intentions account may be compared. Though it is not I think necessary for an adequate account of shared intention that shared intentions on that account possess features that have been highlighted by theorists as features of personal intentions, it is certainly of interest to consider whether shared intention on a given account possesses such features.

To the extent that it does not, one might seek for features that have not previously been highlighted for personal intentions but which might be common to both personal and shared intentions and significantly so. Or one might simply rest with the interesting fact that shared intentions and personal intentions have quite radically different characters.[68]

Bratman considers this question in relation to his own account of shared intention and gives a positive answer. One should also give a positive answer with respect to the plural subject account. Consider the following important features of intentions at the personal level emphasized by Bratman, here described somewhat cursorily and to some extent in my terms for present purposes. Personal intentions are relatively stable states of their possessors and are subject to norms of coherence and consistency both synchronic and diachronic (cf. Bratman 1993, 101). Bratman contrasts them in this respect with personal goals.

One would think that shared intentions according to the plural subject account are at least as stable as the personal intentions of individuals. And insofar as personal intentions are subject to demands for coherence and consistency, and so on, these shared intentions would appear to be subject to similar demands. If Zena and her friends share such an intention to bring peace to the world, they

---

[68] Cf. Gilbert 2002a in relation to belief, where points supposedly criterial for belief in the individual case are explored in relation to the collective case.

have reason, by virtue of that intention, to develop concordant sub-plans, both synchronic and diachronic, at both the shared and the individual level.

10. Concluding Remarks

I have proposed three main criteria of adequacy for an account of shared intention specifically: the disjunctive, obligation, and concurrence criteria, along with several subsidiary criteria. The plural subject account satisfies these criteria. Something that I shall not pursue here is a conjecture that I am inclined to accept: if *and only if* we invoke joint commitment in one way or another are we in a position to develop an account of shared intention that meets these criteria. Certainly, an account of shared intention whose core is a set of correlative personal intentions does not seem capable of satisfying any of the criteria.

Whether or not it stands as the most adequate account of shared intention it is worth having in view a joint commitment account along the lines I have proposed. For whatever we call a situation in which the conditions it stipulates obtain, that situation is likely to be of great consequence for all concerned.

This is true, indeed, of any situation in which there is a joint commitment, in which sociality and an important form of obligation come together. Whatever we jointly commit ourselves to "do" as a body—decide, intend, believe, accept as a rule, and so on—we create for each one of us a relatively intractable, and hence relatively stable framework for his or her life, both in the short and in the longer term.[69]

Bibliography

Aristotle (circa 345 B.C./1998): *Politics*, trans. by C. D. C. Reeve, Indianapolis.
Bacharach, M. (2006): *Beyond Individual Choice: Teams and Frames*, Princeton: Princeton University Press.
Bagozzi, R./U. M. Dholakia (2006), Open Source Software User Communities: A Study of Participation in Linux User Groups, in: *Management Science* 52, 1009–1115.
Bardsley, N. (2007), On Collective Intentions: Collective Action in Economics and Philosophy, in: *Synthese* 157, 141–159.

[69] I have benefited from and am grateful to Anton Leist, Abe Roth, Frank Stewart, and two anonymous referees for *Analyse & Kritik* for detailed comments on various drafts of this chapter. Thanks also to Thomas Smith, and to the discussants at the invited symposium on shared intention that was part of the Pacific Division American Philosophical Association meetings in Pasadena 2008, where I presented a shorter version of this chapter under the title "Shared Intention and Personal Intentions," of which Gilbert 2009 is a revised version. Michael Bratman was my co-symposiast at the APA session. I have appreciated the attention he has given to my work over the years, while developing his personal intentions account of shared intention.

Bratman, M. (1987), *Intentions, Plans, and Practical Reason*, Cambridge: Harvard University Press.

—— (1992), Shared Cooperative Activity, in: *Philosophical Review* 101 327–340.

—— (1993), Shared Intention, in: *Ethics* 104, 97–113.

—— (1999), Shared Intention and Mutual Obligation, in: M. Bratman, *Faces of Intention*, Cambridge: Cambridge University Press, 130–141.

—— (1999), *Faces of Intention*, Cambridge: Cambridge University Press.

—— (2009), Modest Sociality and the Distinctiveness of Intention, in: *Philosophical Studies*, 144, 149–165.

Davis, J. (2003), Collective Intentionality, Complex Economic Behavior, and Valuation, in: *Protosociology* 18, 163–183.

Feinberg, J. (1970), The Nature and Value of Rights, in: *Journal of Value Inquiry* 4, 243–257.

French, P./H. Wettstein (2006) (eds.), Shared Intentions and Collective Responsibility, in: *Midwest Studies in Philosophy* 30, Malden, MA: Blackwell .

Gilbert, M. (1978), *On Social Facts*, D. Phil. thesis, Manuscript, Oxford.

—— (1981), Game Theory and Convention, in: *Synthese* 44, 41–93 (Reprinted in Gilbert 1996).

—— (1987), Modeling Collective Belief, in: *Synthese* 73 185–204 (Reprinted in Gilbert 1996).

—— (1989), *On Social Facts*, Princeton, NJ: Princeton University Press.

—— (1990), Walking Together: A Paradigmatic Social Phenomenon, in: *Midwest Studies in Philosophy* 25, 1–14 (Reprinted in Gilbert 1996).

—— (1996), *Living Together: Rationality, Sociality, and Obligation*, Lanham, MD: Rowman and Littlefield.

—— (1997), What Is It for Us to Intend?, in: G. Holmstrom-Hintikka/R. Tuomela (eds.), *Contemporary Action Theory* 2, Dordrecht: Springer, 65–85 (Reprinted in Gilbert 2000).

—— (1998), In Search of Sociality: Recent Developments in the Philosophy of Social Phenomena, in: *Philosophical Explorations* 1, 233–241 (Reprinted in Gilbert 2000).

—— (2000), *Sociality and Responsibility: New Essays in Plural Subject Theory*, Lanham, MD: Rowman and Littlefield.

—— (2002a), Belief and Acceptance as Features of Groups, in: *Protosociology* 16, 35–69 [Chapter 6 this volume].

—— (2002b), Collective Wrongdoing: Moral and Legal Responses, in: *Social Theory and Practice* 28, 167–187.

—— (2003), The Structure of the Social Atom: Joint Commitment as the Foundation of Human Social Behavior, in: F. Schmitt (ed.), *Socializing Metaphysics*, Lanham, MD: Rowman and Littlefield, 39–64.

—— (2004), Scanlon on Promissory Obligation: The Problem of Promisees' Rights, in: *Journal of Philosophy* 101, 83–109 [Chapter 12 this volume].

—— (2006), *A Theory of Political Obligation: Membership, Commitment, and the Bonds of Society*, Oxford: Oxford University Press.

—— (2007), *The Morality of Obedience*, Manuscript, Philosophy Department, University of California, Irvine [Chapter 18, this volume, is a version of this ms.].

—— (2007), Searle and Collective Intentions, in: S. Tsohatzidis (ed.), *Intentional Acts and Institutional Facts*, Dordrecht: Springer.

—— (2008), Social Convention Revisited, in: *Topoi* 27, 5–16 [Chapter 9 this volume].

—— (2009), Shared Intention and Personal Intentions, in: *Philosophical Studies* 144, 167–187.

Gold, N./R. Sugden (2007), Collective Intentions and Team Agency, in: *Journal of Philosophy* 104, 109–137.

Grosz B./L. Hunsberger (2006), The Dynamics of Intention in Collaborative Activity, in: *Cognitive Systems Research* 7, 259–272.

Hart, H. L. A. (1955), Are There Any Natural Rights?, in: *The Philosophical Review* 64, 175–191.

—— (1961), *The Concept of Law*, Oxford: Oxford University Press.

Hohfeld, W. N. (1913/1964), *Fundamental Legal Conceptions*, New Haven: Yale University Press.

Kutz, C. (2000a), Acting Together, in: *Philosophy and Phenomenological Research* 51, 1–31.

—— (2000b), *Complicity: Ethics and Law for a Collective Age*, Cambridge: Cambridge University Press.

Lewis, D. K. (1969), *Convention: A Philosophical Study*, Cambridge: Cambridge University Press.

MacMahon, C. (2005), Shared Agency and Rational Cooperation, in: *Nous* 39, 284–308.

Miller, S. (2005), Intentions, Ends, and Joint Action, in: *Philosophical Papers* 24, 51–66.

Rosenberg, J. (1980), *One World and Our Knowledge of It*, Dordrecht: Springer.

Roth, A. S. (2004), Shared Agency and Contralateral Commitments, in: *Philosophical Review* 113, 359–410.

Scanlon, T. (1998), *What We Owe to Each Other*, Cambridge, MA: Harvard University Press.

Searle, J. (1990), Collective Intentions and Actions, in: P. R. Cohen/J. Morgan/M. E. Pollack (eds.), *Intentions in Communication*, Cambridge, MA: Harvard University Press, 401–415.

Sellars, W. (1963), Imperatives, Intentions, and the Logic of "Ought," in: G. Nakhnikian/H. N. Castaneda (eds.), *Morality and the Language of Conduct*, Detroit: Wayne State University Press, 159–214.

Sugden, R. (1993), Thinking as a Team: Toward an Explanation of Non-Selfish Behavior, in: *Social Philosophy and Policy* 10, 69–89.

——/N. Gold (2007), Theories of Team Reasoning, in: F. Peter/H.-B. Schmid (eds.), *Rationality and Commitment*, Oxford: Oxford University Press, 280–312.

Taylor, C. (1985), *Philosophical Papers 2. Philosophy and the Human Sciences*, Cambridge: Cambridge University Press.

Tuomela, R. (1984), *A Theory of Social Action*, Dordrecht: Springer.

——/K. Miller (1985), We-Intentions and Social Action, in: *Analyse & Kritik* 7, 26–43.

——/(1988), We-Intentions, in: *Philosophical Studies* 53, 367–389.

Vanderschraaf, P./G. Sillari (2007), Common Knowledge, in: *The Stanford Encyclopedia of Philosophy*: http://plato.stanford.edu/entries/common-knowledge.

Velleman, D. (1997), How to Share an Intention, in: *Philosophy and Phenomenological Research* 57, 29–50.

Verbeek, B. (2007), Rational Self-Commitment, in: F. Peter/H.-B. Schmid (eds.), *Rationality and Commitment*, Oxford: Oxford University Press.

PART TWO

COLLECTIVE ATTITUDES

"Listen, Alexey Fyodorovitch. Isn't there in all our analysis—I mean your analysis... no, better call it ours—aren't we showing contempt for him, for that poor man—in analyzing his soul like this, as it were from above, eh? In deciding so certainly that he will take the money"

Fyodor Doestoevsky, *The Brothers Karamazov*, tr. Constance Garrett (New York: Random House, 1943), 257. First published 1880.

6

Belief and Acceptance as Features of Groups

1. Introduction

1.1. Collective belief statements

Statements such as the following are commonplace:

> "The United States believes that those responsible for these dreadful acts must be punished."
> "The teachers' union believes it can negotiate a significant pay raise for its members."
> "Our family believes that the best way to spend Christmas is at the beach."

In these and many other cases, a belief is ascribed to something—the United States, the union, our family—which is in some sense made up of individual human beings. For present purposes I shall refer to things of this kind as *collectives or groups*. I shall refer to such statements as *collective belief statements.*

1.2. What is collective belief?

To what phenomenon are collective belief statements intended to refer? I shall call this phenomenon, whatever it is, *collective belief.*[1]

In a classic social scientific discussion, Emile Durkheim includes the beliefs of groups among the phenomena he denominates paradigmatic "*faits sociaux*" or social phenomena. Among other things, he says that such beliefs are "independent of their individual manifestations" and possess a certain "coercive power"

---

[1] My writing of the "phenomenon" as opposed to the "phenomena" is not intended to rule out the possibility that there are importantly different types of collective belief.

and "authority."[2] Many have found Durkheim's discussion obscure. It does, indeed, cry out for further elaboration.[3]

Analytic philosophers, established purveyors of clarity and rigor, have traditionally paid no attention to collective belief. This includes those who focus on epistemology, for which a central issue is the nature of belief. More recently, even those who characterize what they are doing as social epistemology have neglected *collective* belief in favor of consideration of aspects of the beliefs of individuals.

1.3. The plural subject account of collective belief

In a number of places I have been developing and defending an account of collective belief. For reasons that will emerge, I refer to it as the plural subject account.[4] In this chapter I focus on some claims that have been made concerning collective belief when it is understood according to this account or in a roughly similar way.

1.4. "Rejectionism"

An antecedently discussed philosophical distinction has been brought to bear on the plural subject account of collective belief. This is a distinction between "belief," on the one hand, and "acceptance," on the other.

A number of philosophers working in epistemology have made a distinction in these terms. These include Michael Bratman, Jonathan Cohen, Keith Lehrer, Robert Stalnaker, and Bas Van Fraassen. Though they use the same terminology, they do not always have the same distinction in mind. In the case of Lehrer, for instance, "belief" is the broader term, acceptance a special form of belief.[5] For others, including Stalnaker, "accept" is the broader term, belief being a special

---

[2] Emile Durkheim, *Rules of Sociological Method*, ed. S. Lukes (New York: Free Press, 1982). First published in French 1895.

[3] For a proposed articulation of the core elements of Durkheim's account of social phenomena in general and collective belief in particular, see Margaret Gilbert, *On Social Facts* (Princeton: Princeton University Press, 1989), chapter 5; also Margaret Gilbert, "Durkheim and Social Facts" in *Debating Durkheim*, eds. Herminio Martins and William Pickering (London: Routledge, 1994a), 86–109.

[4] See Margaret Gilbert, "Modeling Collective Belief," *Synthese* 73 (1987): 185–204; *Social Facts*; "Durkheim"; "Remarks on Collective Belief" in *Socializing Epistemology*, ed. Frederick Schmitt (Lanham, MD: Rowman and Littlefield, 1994b), 235–256; "Collective Belief and Scientific Change" (2000a) in Margaret Gilbert, *Sociality and Responsibility: New Essays in Plural Subject Theory* (Lanham, MD: Rowman and Littlefield, 2000c), 37–49. "Modeling" and "Remarks" are reprinted in Margaret Gilbert, *Living Together: Rationality, Sociality, and Obligation* (Lanham, MD: Rowman and Littlefield, 1996), whose introduction is also pertinent.

[5] See, for instance, Keith Lehrer, *Self-Trust: A Study of Reason, Knowledge and Autonomy* (Oxford: Clarendon Press, 1997).

form of acceptance.[6] In yet others, there are no mutual entailments between belief and acceptance, though believing a proposition is compatible with accepting it on occasion.[7]

Referring to a distinction such that acceptance is *not* a form of belief, a number of philosophers have suggested that collective belief, according to my account of it, is not belief but rather acceptance.[8] For the sake of a label, I shall call their position "rejectionism."

The philosophers I have in mind are not opposed to my account of collective belief. That is, they do not reject the plural subject account of *the referent of collective belief statements.*[9] Rather, they reject the idea that *the phenomenon the account describes* is a form of belief, as opposed to acceptance. Thus according to K. Brad Wray, "... the phenomenon that concerns Gilbert is a species of acceptance [rather than belief]."[10]

For present purposes, then, I shall assume that my account of the referent of collective belief statements is essentially correct. I detail the account shortly. I shall henceforth refer to the phenomenon it delineates as *collective belief**. The asterisk is intended to indicate that the status of this phenomenon as a form of belief is in dispute.

I shall continue to refer to statements in which so-called beliefs are ascribed to collectives as collective belief statements. If rejectionists are right, these statements are at best misleading, at worse false. For, if they are right, in spite of the way it is referred to in everyday speech, the phenomenon in question is not belief but rather acceptance.

[6] Robert Stalnaker, *Inquiry* (Cambridge, MA: MIT Press, 1984).

[7] See Jonathan Cohen, *An Essay on Belief and Acceptance* (New York: Oxford University Press, 1992); Bas Van Fraassen, *The Scientific Image* (Oxford: Clarendon Press, 1980)

[8] See Anthonie Meijers, "Believing and Accepting as a Group," in *Belief, Cognition and the Will,* ed. A. Meijers (Tilburg: Tilburg University Press, 1999), 59–71; K. Brad Wray, "Collective Belief and Acceptance," *Synthese* 129 (2001): 319–333. See also Raimo Tuomela, "Group Beliefs," *Synthese* 91 (1992): 285–318; *The Importance of Us* (Stanford: Stanford University Press, 1995; "Belief versus Acceptance," in Meijers, ed. *Belief, Cognition,* 319–333, and elsewhere). This suggestion has also come up informally, once in the early 1990s in Dan Sperber's Princeton graduate class where the students were discussing my account of collective belief. I understand that Professor Meijers has a new discussion of the topic that will be published along with the present essay in *Protosociology.* He has not, however, given up rejectionism. I limit myself here to discussion of his 1999 article.

[9] Meijers and Wray do not question the broad outlines of my account. Wray explicitly accepts it and draws on it. Tuomela, *Importance,* grants it a measure of plausibility (310) and offers an account of his own that resembles it in various ways (450, note 9) He sees it as a consequence of his own account that so-called group beliefs are not beliefs proper (311). See also his "Group Beliefs."

[10] Wray, "Collective Belief," 319. See also Meijers, "Believing," 67–68.

1.5. Acceptance

I shall focus on what rejectionists say about belief, and the question of whether they have shown that collective belief* is not belief. A word might usefully be said at the outset, however, as to the nature of acceptance as they understand it. A canonical example of acceptance, for all concerned, I think, is a case of assuming something "for the sake of the argument," or "for present purposes." Thus, in the text above, I explained that for present purposes I shall assume collective belief* is the referent of collective belief statements. As it happens, this is what I believe, irrespective of present purposes. Importantly, one can assume something for the sake of argument *without* believing it.[11]

1.6. The argument of this chapter

In this chapter I question rejectionism. My argument proceeds along four different paths. The first concerns a fundamental methodological question for epistemology, in particular: how is one to arrive at an account of belief in general? Evidently this question is important for other fields of philosophy, including the philosophy of mind, as well as for other disciplines also. The second and third arguments concern two features that have been claimed to be key features of belief in general: a truth-seeking nature, and a particular relation to the will. Collective beliefs* have been said to lack these features. The fourth argument appeals to the difference between collective belief* and a related phenomenon that naturally attracts the label "collective acceptance."

I hope my discussion as a whole will encourage epistemologists and others to take collective belief statements seriously. I hope, also, that it will clarify in a number of ways the nature of collective belief*. In my view collective belief* is a widespread and consequential phenomenon under any name. That this is so is not disputed by rejectionists.

1.7. Cognitive states and collective mentality

Belief and acceptance are what I shall here refer to as *cognitive states*.[12] One rough and ready way of giving a general account of cognitive states is to say that they are states whose specification requires reference to a proposition, such as the

---

[11] Cf. Wray (referring to common ground between Stalnaker and Van Fraassen): "For example, one might accept something that one does not believe for the sake of an argument," 324; Meijers: "To accept that p is to make the decision to use a certain proposition as a valid premise in one's deliberations," 64.

[12] This phrase may sometimes be used more narrowly than I use it here. That does not matter for present purposes.

proposition that two plus two equals four, or the proposition that it is raining in Dubuque right now. This is not the place to attempt to characterize propositions, so that idea must remain at an intuitive level here.

Cognitive states, on this account of them, may vary widely in their specific character. Where the letter "p" stands for some proposition, cognitive states will include believing that p, wondering whether p, doubting whether p, and accepting that p.

It is natural to think of cognitive states as mental states, though not as the only species of such states and perhaps not the paradigmatic ones. Now it is quite common for people to argue against the possibility of collective mental states in general or, to use a phrase usually intended to raise hairs, *group minds*. What is one to make of the rejection of group minds? What bearing does it have, if any, on the present inquiry?

Those who argue, or simply state, that there are no group minds often forbear from explaining their position. They tend to take it to be obvious. At first blush, however, it appears to fly in the face of everyday attributions of belief and so on to groups.

One construal of the no-group-minds thesis that fits at least some versions is a form of reduction. The position is roughly this: insofar as collective beliefs and so on exist they are a function of facts about individuals. Individuals are, if you like, the *bedrock* of collective beliefs.

If so construed, the no-group-minds thesis is not obviously antagonistic to everyday attributions of belief or other cognitive and mental states to groups. Nor does it clearly stand in opposition to my own views. There is at least a sense in which I would not be averse to describing the bedrock of collective beliefs* as individuals.[13] However, to say that is to say very little about them. For present purposes, much more must be said.

2. Collective belief*

2.1. The range of collective belief statements

When we consider the collective belief statements of everyday life, the supposed believers are quite diverse, at least on the surface. Two strangers, for instance, having conversed for a while, might say to a third party "We think a defensive war is justified." This might also be said of a family, a political party, a committee, a governing body.

---

[13] On the issue of "individualism" versus "holism," see Gilbert, *Social Facts*, chapter 7.

Presumably, all families, political parties, governing bodies—all relatively long-lasting, more or less organized or hierarchically structured groups—have come about ultimately through small-scale, short-term, informal processes involving a few individuals in face-to-face contact. There is reason, then, to consider collective belief statements made on the basis of such processes as the basic cases and to start with them. It can be argued that the account I sketch shortly is adequate both for these basic cases and at least some others.[14]

2.2. Collective belief statements and the distributive condition

Consider the case of the strangers who explain to a third party what "we" think. Suppose Roz and Mark are the two people involved. Some may claim that this is not really what I am calling a collective belief statement. That is, contrary to appearances, it is not *the ascription of a belief to a collective* comprising Roz and Mark. It is, rather, an ascription of the belief in question to Roz, on the one hand, and to Mark, on the other, expressed elliptically. The non-elliptical way of expressing this ascription in English would be "We both believe that p." The only alleged believers in the situation, therefore, are two individuals. One of these individuals is Roz, the other is Mark. There is no further believer, comprised of Roz and Mark.[15]

Sentences of the form "We believe that p" may sometimes be uttered as elliptical expressions. Suppose Jeb has just said to Roz and Mark "I don't know what Roz thinks about this, and I don't know what Mark thinks about it either…?" In responding "We think a defensive war is justified" Roz may mean, and reasonably assume she will be understood to mean, that both think a defensive war is justified.

Insofar as, in these cases, sentences of the form "We think that p" are elliptical for "We both think that p," or "We all think that p" then one is not dealing with what I am referring to as collective belief statements. So we may set them aside for present purposes.

A collective belief statement is canonically expressed in English by a non-elliptical sentence of the subject-predicate form where the subject term refers to a collective and the predicate ascribes a belief to that collective. In English, in the case of "We believe that p" the verb is plural, given, perhaps, the overt constitution of the subject by a plurality of persons. In the case of "The union believes that p" and so on, the verb is singular.

It can be argued that it is neither necessary nor sufficient for all (or most) of the members of the collective to believe that p. In other words, for these cases

---

[14] See, for instance, Gilbert, *Social Facts,* chapter 5.
[15] See Anthony Quinton, "Social Objects," *Proceedings of the Aristotelian Society,* 76 (1975): 1–27.

fulfillment of what I shall call *the distributive condition* is neither necessary nor sufficient. I have argued this at length elsewhere, and the interested reader is urged to consult the more extended discussions.[16] A brief account of some main points follows.

With respect to the insufficiency of the distributive condition, a central argument is this. When Roz and Mark understand that "We believe that p" the following is true. If she goes on to say to him, without preamble, that p is not the case, he will judge her as having *offended against* him in some way. She will understand the appropriateness of this reaction. It is hard to argue that satisfaction of the distributive condition can ground these understandings. The same goes for certain more complex conditions I have discussed elsewhere.[17] The necessity of the distributive condition is also open to doubt. The following scenario seems possible. Roz personally believes that it is never justified for one country to take up arms against another. When Mark asserts the justifiability of a defensive war, he speaks very forcefully. Rather than argue, Roz decides to agree with him. So she says, "Yes, indeed." It seems that now either of them could properly make the collective belief statement "We believe that a defensive war is justifiable." And this is true even if Mark was for some reason asserting the opposite of *his* personal view when he spoke. In other words, it may be true, for Roz and Mark, that "We believe that p" though neither of them personally believes that p. Evidently, the distributive condition is not a necessary condition of the truth of the collective belief statement "We believe that p."

I have developed an account of the referent of collective belief statements that does not require satisfaction of the distributive condition. To this I now turn.

2.3. The plural subject account of collective belief

According to my account, and in terms to be further explained:

The members of a population, P, collectively believe that p if and only if they are jointly committed to believe that p as a body.[18]

As presaged earlier I shall, for present purposes refer in what follows to the phenomenon that this account describes—a joint commitment to believe that p as a body—as collective belief*. In other words, by stipulative definition, the

---

[16] See, in particular, Gilbert, *Social Facts*, chapter 5; also "Modeling," "Remarks."

[17] See Gilbert, *Social Facts*, chapter 5.

[18] My earlier formulations of the account were somewhat different. See Gilbert, *Living*, Introduction, and also the text here, below.

members of a population P *collectively believe** that p if and only if they are jointly committed to believe as a body that p.

2.3.1. Joint commitment

A key element in this account is *joint commitment.* I have explained what this is at length elsewhere.[19] For present purposes a brief account should suffice.

It is useful first to introduce the conception of a personal commitment. If Maureen decides to do something, she is now personally committed to do that thing. That is, her commitment is such that she has unilaterally brought it into being and she can unilaterally get rid of it by changing her mind. In short, she is the sole author, and has sole authority over, the commitment.

A joint commitment can be characterized negatively as follows: it is not a sum or aggregate of personal commitments, one for each of the parties. Rather, it is a commitment of the parties, of Jim and Lisa, say. Each of the parties is committed, but these commitments are not personal commitments in the sense characterized above. Absent special background understandings, the joint commitment can only be brought into being or rescinded by the parties acting together. Nor does any one bring a part of it into existence. Only when all have acted does it, or any "part" of it exist. All "parts" then come into being simultaneously.

2.3.2. The general form of joint commitment

We can think of the general form of a joint commitment as follows:

Persons xi, xii, . . . xn are jointly committed to @ as a body.

Substitution instances for "@" will be terms for psychological states, such as "believe that p," "feel grief over X," "accept goal G."[20] The general idea of a joint commitment to @ "as a body" is this. The parties take it upon themselves to emulate, as far as is possible, a single body that @s, by virtue of the actions of each. The term "body" is not sacrosanct. It could be replaced by "person" or "entity." I say more about what it is jointly to commit to *believe* as a body shortly.

---

[19] See, for instance, Gilbert, *Living,* Introduction; Gilbert, "Aspects." I first invoked the relevant idea in "Modeling."

[20] On collective emotions see, for instance, Margaret Gilbert, "Collective Remorse," (2000b) in *Sociality,* 123–140. On goals and intentions see "Walking Together: A Paradigmatic Social Phenomenon," in Peter French, Theodore Uehling, and Howard Wettstein, eds., *Midwest Studies in Philosophy,* 15 (Notre Dame, Indiana: University of Notre Dame Press, 1990): 1–14, reprinted in *Living Together,* and Margaret Gilbert, "What Is It for *Us* to Intend?" in *Sociality, 14–36.*

I have given the following technical meaning to the phrase "plural subject":

> By stipulative definition, persons xi, xii,...xn form a *plural subject* of @-ing if and only if they are jointly committed to @ as a body.

Hence I refer to my account of the referent of collective belief statements as the plural subject account.

2.3.3. Forming joint commitments

How are joint commitments formed? Roughly, each of the parties must express—in conditions of common knowledge—his or her readiness to be jointly committed with the others in the relevant way.[21] There are different cases that need to be distinguished, but for present purposes that brief description may suffice.

An important aspect of all cases has to do with the way a given joint commitment is understood. The point may be illustrated by reference to the following two cases.[22] Case 1: Ellen and Sylvie are fellow-students who have been conversing. Each has expressed her personal readiness to be jointly committed with the other to believe as a body that there needs to be a café on campus. Case 2: Phil, Cass, Ben, and Ted are the members of the campus improvement committee. In a session of the committee they discuss what new amenities might be needed on campus. Each then expresses his readiness to be committed with the other members of the committee to believe as a body that there needs to be a café on campus.

These cases appear to differ in at least the following way. In Case 1, the resulting joint commitment holds *between certain individuals without qualification*. That is, it holds between Sylvie and Ellen, period. In Case 2, the commitment holds *between the members of the improvement committee as such*.

This has consequences for the *correct description of the subject of a given collective belief statement*. One may baldly say of Ellen and Sylvie that they collectively believe that a new café is needed. This would not be appropriate for the parties in Case 2. There one might baldly say that *the improvement committee* believes a new café is needed.

In Case 2 there may be a temptation to say something like this: Phil, Cass, Ben, and Ted believe that a new café is needed, in their capacity as members

---

[21] On "common knowledge" see David K. Lewis, *Convention: A Philosophical Study*, (Cambridge, MA: Harvard University Press, 1969); Stephen Schiffer, *Meaning* (Oxford: Oxford University Press, 1972); Gilbert, *Social Facts*.

[22] The second case does not involve a basic case of joint commitment. Informal analogues of Case 2 can be found. See "Remarks."

of the committee. This mode of description may tend to suggest that there is a special mode of believing, "believing in a certain capacity." That there is such a thing, however, is unclear.[23] If one adopts this mode of description in the present context I suggest that it should always be seen as a cumbersome way of ascribing the belief to the collective in question.

One can highlight the contrast between the cases thus. Suppose Phil and Cass—two members of the improvement committee—are friends, and are meeting for lunch near the campus. Implying a negative response to the question, Phil might ask Cass: "Do we really need a café on campus?" He poses this question to Cass as an individual, rather than as a member of the improvement committee. The committee is not in session and they are meeting as friends. One might say that a new subject of a new collective belief is being proposed here. The question is: will Cass jointly commit with Phil to believe as a body that a café is not needed, contrary to the belief of the committee of which they are both members?

Were the same thing to transpire between the parties to Case 1, after they have settled on collectively believing that a café is needed, it would have a special character. Ellen and Sylvie collectively believe that p, and Sylvie, say, is proposing that the question be *re-opened between them*.[24]

2.3.4. The joint commitment in collective belief*

How are people to act so as to emulate, as far as possible, a body that believes that p? As I understand it, they are not required personally to believe that p, nor to *try* personally to believe that p. Nor are they required to act *as if* they personally believed that p, whether or not they do. Rather, they are to act as would any one of several *mouthpieces* of the body in question, thus uttering *its* beliefs, as opposed to the beliefs of any of its members, including the utterer.

This understanding accords with the following observation regarding everyday collective belief statements. While acknowledging that she and her friends collectively believe a certain thing, Rose might add, without a sense of fault, that she, *personally*, does not believe it. Here she certainly does not act as if she has the belief herself. On the contrary, she avows, in the most emphatic way, that she does not have it.[25]

---

[23] On this see Gerald A. Cohen, "Beliefs and Roles," *Proceedings of the Aristotelian Society* (1966–70): 53–66. Cohen argues that "whatever produces his belief, it is *his* belief, rather than his only *qua* stockbroker..." 63.

[24] For related discussion see Gilbert, *Living*, 353–354; 359 note 15.

[25] See Gilbert, *Social Facts*, and elsewhere.

2.3.5. A historical note

In the above account of collective belief* the parties are jointly committed to believe that p as a body. In my earliest formulations of the account, I wrote rather of the parties *jointly accepting* that p, implicitly parsing this as *jointly committing to accept as a body that p.*[26] In the present context someone might ask why I originally made use of the term "acceptance." Was there a conscious choice of this term as more appropriate than "belief"? To the best of my knowledge the answer is negative. There is, I think, a non-technical sense of "accepts that" such that it is more or less synonymous for "believes that." Without evidence to the contrary, I assume that I was using "accept" in that sense, when talking of joint "acceptance" and so on.

There is one reason to prefer the phrase "joint acceptance" to "joint belief" that might have been influential. It has nothing to do with meaning. The former is more euphonious, the latter involving a babble of consonants between the terms.

2.3.6. No circularity

According to the plural subject account, a collective belief that p requires a joint commitment to believe that p as a body. The concern may be raised: is there a circularity here? The issue would seem to be this. Is speaking of "believing that p as a body," or "emulating, as far as is possible, a single body that believes that p" not simply another way of speaking of "believing collectively"?

I would say not. Consider the case of an individual human being. If Lois, say, believes that p, she constitutes a single body that believes that p. Which is to say this: a belief that p is correctly ascribable to *her.* One can understand what it is, then, for a single body to believe that p, without understanding what it is for a collective to believe anything.

Suppose now that Tom and Alice Jones are jointly committed to emulating as far as is possible a single body that believes that p. In order to carry out this commitment, they need only to understand the idea of a single body that believes that p. Being jointly committed to emulate as far as is possible a single body that believes that p, they are committed to behave in ways appropriate to such a body. According to the plural subject account, they require just such a commitment in order to constitute a *collective* body that believes that p.

3. The question of method

Most theorists of belief focus on the beliefs of individual human beings, or, to put it briefly, on the individual case. While their views of the nature of belief may

---

[26] See Gilbert, *Social Facts*, "Modeling," *Living,* Introduction, and elsewhere.

to some extent be based on intuitive judgments about belief as such, these intuitions are standardly tested out on thought experiments regarding hypothesized cases. For instance, one might ask, "Would I judge that someone believed something if I knew he had no evidence for it whatsoever?" Theorists have focused on the individual case in this respect. In other words, the "someone" in question is standardly an individual rather than a group.

It is not surprising, then, that rejectionists draw on an understanding of belief that derives from consideration of the individual case.[27] Rejectionism's reliance on such an understanding, however, is open to the objection that it begs an important methodological question.

Why do most theorists of belief focus on the individual case alone? There are several possibilities. One is that a given theorist's interest is in how human beings, as opposed to human groups, function. The theorist is interested precisely in the beliefs of individuals. Another possibility is that the theorist has not considered that there are—or are commonly said to be—collective cases. Ignoring the collective case is not then a principled matter. Yet another possibility is that the theorist is aware of how common collective belief *statements* are, but for some reason assumes at the outset that such statements *cannot be taken at face value.* "Of course there are no genuinely collective beliefs" the implicit argument may run. "So—assuming that they are not deluded—those who make these statements cannot be understood as claiming that there are." Collective belief statements may then be accounted for in some way—as *"facons de parler,"* perhaps—but they are not taken seriously in constructing an account of belief.

It might be argued that a well-founded account of belief in general will take collective belief statements seriously. The argument I have in mind runs somewhat as follows.

An important criterion of adequacy for a philosophical account that is not merely stipulative is a degree of responsiveness to the use of the relevant terms. In this case, the central terms are "belief" and its cognates (believes, believer, and so on). An adequate account of belief must, in particular, accommodate all phenomena that are referred to without question as cases of "belief," unless some good reason can be given for excluding some of these phenomena. Thus, the argument concludes, unless some good reason can be given for excluding collective belief statements, it would be better to consider their referents in formulating an account of belief, and not to pronounce as to the nature of belief as a result of considering only individual belief statements and their referents. A similar

---

[27] Thus Meijers, "Believing" makes use of a list of properties that beliefs have "in the individual case," using this list as a touchstone for deciding whether or not collective beliefs* are beliefs. See Meijers, 63. Meijers cites Pascal Engel, "Believing, Accepting, and Holding True," *Philosophical Explorations* I (1998): 140–151, 143–144 and 146–147. Engel, in turn, draws on the work of Michael Bratman in "Belief and Acceptance in a Context," *Mind* (1993).

argument can be made for the whole range of attributes that are ascribed both to individual human beings and to collectives.[28]

One could, of course, decide to focus on the individual case, asking what it is for an individual human being to believe something. Suppose one called the resulting account an account of *individual belief*. It is not clear that it would then be legitimate to argue that if the so-called beliefs of collectives lack features of individual belief, then such so-called beliefs are not in fact beliefs. The proper conclusion would surely be that a collective's believing something differs in important ways from an individual's believing that thing.

A famous example of the more inclusive procedure is that of Plato in the *Republic*. Plato's guiding question was the nature of an individual human being's justice, and whether or not it was of benefit to its possessor. Shortly after raising this question, however, he turns to the question of a just society. His most salient argument for doing so is probably the least persuasive. He says that since a society is larger than an individual, it should be easier to make out the lineaments of justice in a society than in an individual. A related, deeper point he makes is this. We ascribe justice to both individuals and societies. It seems, then, that there is a general idea of justice that applies to both. We can investigate justice in a society independently of any considerations of justice in the individual. Suppose we do so, and come up with a certain account of it. We then investigate justice in an individual human being, and find the results tally nicely. In other words, the account of justice in the society corresponds in a salient fashion to the account of justice in the individual. These accounts mutually reinforce each other. Were justice in the individual not importantly analogous to justice in society, according to our accounts of them, we would have reason to doubt at least one of these accounts.

Plato's accounts of justice in the individual and in society are indeed analogous. At the same time, they respect obvious differences between societies and individuals. The psyche of a human individual, in Plato's scheme, has its own elements and ideal structure. A society too, has its own elements and ideal structure. In both cases there are just three such elements, and the ideal structures have the same shape. Obvious differences are not ignored. The elements of a society are themselves individuals, albeit individuals in which one or another of the central psychic elements tends to hold sway. With respect to a society there is room for discussion of such matters as censorship of the arts, or the ideal marriage institution. There is no room for such discussion in the individual case.

---

[28] I do not mean to imply that ascriptions to individual humans and to collectives exhaust the field. For present purposes, however, these are the ascriptions at issue. Another case is ascriptions of belief to non-human animals. On the whole there is more receptivity among epistemological theorists to discussing the animal case than to discussing the collective case. See, for instance, Bernard Williams, "Deciding to believe" in his *Problems of the Self* (Cambridge: Cambridge University Press, 1970): 136–151.

There is a case, then, for taking collective belief statements seriously as part of an enquiry into the nature of belief itself. One consequence of doing so would be the following. Instead of arguing, where appropriate, that "since individual belief has feature F, and so-called collective belief does not, so-called collective belief cannot be genuine belief," we may argue "since so-called collective belief does not have feature F, though individual belief does, feature F cannot be a necessary feature of belief as such."

Perhaps there are good reasons for privileging so-called individual belief in the search for an adequate account of belief. I shall not pursue that question here. What I propose is the following. First, this question requires more attention than it has to date been accorded. Second, unless and until a satisfactory answer is available, an account of belief that fails to take collective belief statements seriously cannot be used in support of rejectionism.

The broader method envisaged in this section itself suggests the following question, among others. What do the phenomena picked out by collective belief statements, on the one hand, and ascriptions of beliefs to individual humans, on the other, have in common? Much of what follows is germane to this issue.[29]

4. Taking collective belief statements seriously

Suppose we take collective belief statements seriously, that is, we take them to be ascriptions precisely of *belief*. What happens to the various assumptions epistemologists and others make about belief, based on their understanding of the individual case? Do these assumptions have to be changed? Assuming the plural subject account of the referent of collective belief statements, do collective beliefs* have the relevant properties, or not?

Rejectionists argue, in effect, for particular *disanalogies* between belief in the individual case and collective belief*. They go on to conclude that collective belief* is not belief. The inference may or may not be defensible on methodological grounds. Setting that question aside, are the rejectionist claims about particular disanalogies correct?

In the next two sections I scrutinize two central rejectionist claims. Both are of the form: beliefs as such have feature F, and collective beliefs* lack F. The supposed features of all beliefs that I consider, though often taken to be central, do not exhaust the features that have been ascribed to beliefs as such by those focusing on

---

[29] Gilbert, *Social Facts*, chapter 5, 313, briefly notes some commonalities between the individual and collective cases. Austen Clark argues for parallelisms between the individual and the collective cases of beliefs and desires, with particular reference to Dennett's analyses ("Beliefs and Desires Incorporated," *Journal of Philosophy* (1994), 404–425).

the individual case. The points made in discussion indicate how other features may be approached.

It has to be said that there is continuing controversy among those epistemologists who, focusing on the individual case, have come up with characterizations of the nature of belief. Indeed, the status of the very features to which rejectionists appeal has been questioned.

My strategy here will hopefully sidestep such issues. I start by setting out the relevant rejectionist claim to the effect that beliefs as such have a particular feature F. I attempt to arrive at an interpretation of the nature of F such that the rejectionist claim appears to be relatively plausible on the face of it. I then explore whether or not collective beliefs* lack F, as the rejectionist claims. If, contrary to the rejectionist, collective beliefs* have F, then rejectionism will not follow from the premise that beliefs as such have F. Rejectionism may also be forestalled as follows. It may be possible to show that insofar as it is unclear whether collective beliefs* have F, it is *equally unclear* whether individual beliefs do, and for similar reasons. In other words, it may still be possible to show that the claimed *disanalogy* does not exist. My discussion involves counters to rejectionism of both these kinds.

5. Is truth the "aim" of collective belief*?

Belief, it is often said, "aims at truth." This phrase may have been introduced by Bernard Williams in his well-known essay "Deciding to Believe."[30] To say that belief "aims at" something may suggest that believing is a form of goal-directed activity.[31] Williams, however, does not obviously suppose this.

In spelling out what he means, Williams emphasizes three things. First, "truth and falsehood are a dimension of the assessment of beliefs." Second, to believe that p is to believe that p is true. Third, to say, "I believe that p" "conveys the message that p is the case."[32]

Do collective beliefs* aim at truth in something like Williams' sense? Anthonie Meijers, for one, argues that they do not.[33] He himself summarizes the idea that belief in general aims at truth as follows: "beliefs represent the world

[30] Williams, "Deciding."

[31] Cf. Peter Railton, "Scientific Objectivity and the Aims of Belief," in Pascal Engel, ed., *Believing and Accepting* (Dordrecht: Kluwer Academic Publishers, 2000), 179–208.

[32] Williams, "Deciding," 137. Williams says "This trio of points constitutes the [feature of belief] which I vaguely summed up by saying 'beliefs aim at truth.'"

[33] Meijers, "Believing," 64–66. Meijers is operating with an account of so-called collective beliefs that he calls "contractualism." This is very close to my plural subject account, and I consider his arguments in relation to that. On the "contractualism" inherent in the appeal to plural subjects see, Gilbert, *Social Facts*; also Margaret Gilbert, "Reconsidering the 'Actual Contract' Theory of Political Obligation," *Ethics* 109, (1999b): 236–260, reprinted in *Sociality*.

as it is; they have a mind-to-world direction of fit."[34] He goes on to make several points in support of his claim that collective beliefs* do not aim at truth. I now consider these one by one.

5.1. Are collective beliefs* necessarily "context-bound"?

First, Meijers claims that collective beliefs*, unlike individual beliefs, are "context-bound." He writes: "we as a group believe[*] that p...always given a particular situation, role, or point of view. Genuine beliefs, on the other hand, are not context-bound. A person believes that p regardless of the context she is in" (Meijers 1999, p. 64).

One might, I think, restate the point in terms of a contrast with acceptance. Suppose one accepts that p *for the purposes of some argument.* This is what one sees oneself as doing. One then *explicitly or implicitly ties one's acceptance that p to a context,* in this case, the pursuit of a particular argument. This kind of intentional binding to a specified context, it is claimed, shows that one is dealing with acceptance rather than belief. Belief, it is alleged, is never so context-bound. Collective belief*, on the other hand, is said always to involve such binding to a context, so it is never to be identified as belief. Setting aside the claim about belief, we can consider whether collective beliefs* are necessarily context-bound in the way at issue.

Surely they are not. We can quite unproblematically suppose, for instance, that the campus improvement committee believes* that there should be a café on campus—or, for short, believes* that c—period. That is, we can quite unproblematically suppose that the committee neither explicitly nor implicitly ties its belief* that c to a particular context.

It should be emphasized that what the committee believes*, along with any associated qualifications on the context of the belief*, is determined by the content of constitutive joint commitment. In the case in question, the joint

---

[34] Meijers, "Believing," 64. The claim that beliefs have a "mind-to-world direction of fit" is common in epistemology, along with the idea that desires, in contrast, have a world-to-mind direction of fit. Others have made what look like closely related points, e.g. Stalnaker, *Inquiry,* 80, "Correct beliefs are beliefs the contents of which are true. A correct desire or hope, however, is not one that will in fact be satisfied." Note that what Stalnaker says of beliefs here may not be said of acceptance in the sense at issue here. At least, acceptances are not appropriately evaluated by reference to their truth—though they are, of course, truth-evaluable—but rather by reference to the accepter's purposes. Williams explanation of his first point tends to obscure the distinction between being *appropriately evaluated* in terms of something and being *evaluable* in terms of that thing. (Compare the irrelevance of a mathematician's weight to the evaluation of excellence as a mathematician.) After stating that "truth and falsehood are a dimension of the assessment of beliefs" he goes on "when someone believes something, then he believes something which can be assessed as true or false." I take it that he means to claim not only that beliefs *can* be so assessed but also are *appropriately* so assessed.

commitment is, simply, to believe that c as a body. There is no explicit or implicit qualification as to context.

Whether or not any such qualification would *make sense* appears to depend entirely on whether or not such a qualification ever makes sense for *beliefs*. The joint commitment is, after all, a commitment precisely to *believe* that c as a body. I shall not attempt to address that issue here.

The committee's situation in the case of its belief* that c appears to be exactly parallel to that of an individual person who *believes* that c. Suppose that Pam presently believes that c, period. This does not mean that in all—or indeed, in any—future contexts she will continue to believe that c. She may come to doubt that c or simply cease to believe it, for a variety of reasons. It does mean that she cannot later *consistently* come to believe that it is not the case that c without giving up her belief that c. All this may surely be said, *mutatis mutandis*, of the improvement committee's belief* that c. The committee may, at some time in the future, come to believe* that it is not the case that c. If it has not first given up its belief* that c, it will hold inconsistent beliefs*.

I conclude that, contrary to Meijers's suggestion, collective beliefs* are not always context-bound in the sense at issue. It is unclear, indeed, if they are ever context-bound in that sense. If they sometimes are, that would strongly suggest that belief in general may be sometimes be context-bound also. I cannot enter into that issue here. However it turns out, collective beliefs* certainly cannot be argued to be acceptances, rather than beliefs, on the grounds that they are *always* context-bound.

Before leaving this particular topic, it is worth noting the following. To claim that collective beliefs* are not always, and may perhaps never be, context-bound in the sense at issue, is not to say anything against the point, explained earlier, that the *subject* of a given collective belief* will depend on the situation or context in which it is formed.[35]

5.2. Collective beliefs* and evidence

Meijers writes "Beliefs...require that all the relevant evidence be taken into account..."[36] I am inclined to gloss this as a normative statement, somewhat as follows: the belief that p is open to criticism if it does not reflect all the relevant evidence. Thus, to take an extreme case, if all the relevant evidence points strongly in the direction of not-p, the belief that p is open to criticism for that reason.

---

[35] See section 2.3.3 above.
[36] Meijers, "Believing," 64.

Meijers goes on (and this is what he sees as his second point in favor of rejectionism): "We may give up our...collective beliefs[*] for reasons not related to the epistemic evidence we have but, for example, because of prudential concerns."[37] I take it that he means that people are not open to criticism for giving up—or, for that matter, adopting—a collective belief* for reasons that do not relate to the evidence for or against the belief in question, in short, for non-epistemic reasons. Such a belief*, indeed, may fly in the face of the relevant evidence without being open to criticism.[38]

In the example with which Meijers illustrates his point, the members of an alliance of states fear the political repercussions at home of a particular bombing campaign, "and consequently the alliance may give up its belief[*]" that the bombing will achieve a certain desirable result.[39] What is the import of "consequently" in the statement that "consequently the alliance may give up its belief*"? It could mean "as a causal consequence" or "for this reason." Meijers is evidently focusing on reasons, the reasons for which the alliance may give up its belief* about the bombing.

His claim, then, would seem to be something like this: the alliance may properly—that is, without violating any appropriate standards of assessment—give up its belief* for the reason that doing so would be politically advantageous to the member states. In that case, he argues, its belief*, whatever it may be called, is not a *belief*. For one cannot properly give up a belief for purely prudential reasons. The following should be noted, however.

Suppose that each member of an alliance of states thinks it will gain an important political advantage if the alliance gives up its belief* that p.[40] Each member is, indeed, fearful of the outcome if the collective belief* is not given up. Subsequently, the alliance gives up its belief* that p. That the giving up of the alliance's belief* *follows in the footsteps of* these thoughts and fears on the part of its members does not entail that *the alliance's reasons for giving it up* had to do with the political advantage of doing so for its members, or with their fears. It does, of course, strongly suggest that the noted beliefs and fears of the members played *some* role in the process that led to the alliance's giving up its belief* that p. But that is not enough for them to count as the alliance's reasons for giving it up.

[37] Meijers, "Believing," 65.

[38] Cf. Wray, "Collective Belief" who claims very clearly that "plural subjects are and should be responsive to different reasons than the reasons individuals are responsive to when they are deciding what to believe" (327). He specifies that—generally—the reasons plural subjects should be responsive to are not "epistemic" but rather "practical" (327).

[39] Meijers, "Believing," 65.

[40] In order to keep close to Meijers's example, I am writing as if the members of an alliance of states—particular states—think certain things. If that seems bothersome in the present context, the reader is invited to substitute an example in which the members of the relevant group are individual human beings.

How are we to tell why a collective gives up a certain belief*, or why a collective comes to a given belief*? How do we know what epistemic reasons it takes into account, or what practical reasons, if such reasons are at issue? These are important questions, and it is beyond the scope of this chapter to explore them fully.

Evidently, one cannot stop with an examination of the reasons, epistemic or practical, that individual members of the group have for trying to create or change the group's belief*. These reasons may certainly be sought and knowledge of them may help to fill important gaps. But they do not speak directly to the issue.[41]

Consider the following imaginary scenario. There are three states in a particular alliance. Each is represented by a particular official around the conference table, the officials being Peter, Antoine, and Karl. Previously the alliance had come to believe* that the way to achieve its goal G was to bomb country C, or, for short, it had come to believe* that g. Now each member prefers, for its own reasons, that the alliance's bombing of C be discontinued. It therefore wants to bring it about that the alliance cease to believe* that g.

Karl speaks first, in the name of his own country. He is quite likely to say: "Is bombing C really going to achieve G?" In other words, he is likely to *question the truth of g.* How might Peter or Antoine react, if Karl asks this question? Like Karl, they both want the bombing stopped, and therefore they both want the alliance to change its mind on whether the bombing will achieve G. Meanwhile, *the form of Karl's question constrains the appropriate responses.* Peter might appropriately say "It's not clear that it is!." Antoine might add "Hardly!" Peter might push on: "I'd say that bombing *isn't* likely to achieve G. Given the people we are up against, it is just as likely to have the opposite effect!" Karl and Antoine might eagerly approve this, thus establishing for the alliance a new collective belief*, the belief* that the bombing is unlikely to achieve G. Any one of them can then reasonably continue: "Then we should stop the bombing...!"

It would clearly have been *off the point* for Peter or Antoine to have said, "Well, my country would prefer that we didn't believe* that g." Either of them *could* have said this, but, in the context, it would have had to be taken *as an aside.* The business of the conversation has already been established. It is to consider the truth or falsity of the alliance's current belief* that g. The preferences of any member of the alliance are simply irrelevant to that.

Given this scenario, *on what basis did the alliance give up its belief that g? It did so for this reason: given the character of the people the alliance is up against, the bombing of C is not—after all—likely to achieve goal G. The alliance discarded its belief that g, then, on the basis of epistemic as opposed to practical reasons.*

---

[41] Cf. Margaret Gilbert, review of Jon Elster, *Ulysses Unbound, Mind* (2002b).

These epistemic reasons, one might add, were believed* *by the alliance* to be epistemic reasons for discarding its belief* that g. For, in the course of their discussion, the members of the alliance mutually expressed their readiness jointly to commit to believing as a body that the character of the people, etc., was evidence in favor of the claim that the bombing would not achieve G. This was, we may assume, common knowledge.

That a group gives up—or takes on—a belief* for epistemic reasons is, I propose, a very common situation. One could, indeed, predict that this would be so if *collective beliefs* are open to criticism if they do not reflect all the relevant evidence.* And that they are is, surely, a plausible claim given what collective beliefs* are. A collective belief* is constituted, after all, by a joint commitment to *believe* something as a body. It is plausible to suppose that it is required of the parties or would-be parties to such a commitment to make some effort to support the giving up or taking on of the relevant collective's beliefs* with what are collectively believed* to be epistemic reasons.[42]

Meijers might attempt to counter this by emphasizing that even if the type of situation in my story about the alliance is a common one, it is not the only possible one. Karl might, in principle, have said "Is it in our—the alliance's—interest to believe* that bombing will achieve G?" He would then have posed a prudential rather than an epistemic question. And perhaps this line of questioning could have resulted in the formation of a collective belief* that accorded with what the alliance believed* was in its interests, without recourse to epistemic reasons.

It is should be noted, in response, that individual human beings, also, may question and assess their beliefs from a purely prudential point of view. Thus Joe may wonder if it is in his interests to believe that his wife is unfaithful. He may decide that it is not, since the belief is making him miserable. And perhaps it could come about, in consequence, that he believes the opposite, without recourse to epistemic reasons.[43]

What conclusion can we draw from Joe's case? Does it show that the belief of individuals is not always open to criticism on the basis of its relation to the relevant evidence? On the face of it, it does not show this. And this is what seems to be at issue in the passage from Meijers under discussion.[44]

It is not necessary for present purposes to pursue the question whether Joe's case shows that belief in the individual case is not always open to criticism on the basis of its relation to the relevant evidence. For suppose, as I am inclined to

---

[42] For a detailed exploration of the justification of group beliefs and a "joint account" of group justification see Frederick R. Schmitt, "The Justification of Group Beliefs," in Frederick R. Schmitt, ed., *Socializing Epistemology* (Lanham, MD: Rowman and Littlefield, 1994).

[43] On this see also section 6 below.

[44] As it is in the passage from Wray quoted above, note 38.

think, that it does *not* show this. Then the existence of parallel collective belief*
cases does not show that collective beliefs* are not open to criticism on such
grounds. Suppose, however, that it *does* show this. Then the existence of the *parallel* collective belief* case shows nothing that takes away from the idea that collective beliefs* are *any the less* beliefs than are the so-called beliefs of individual
human beings.

I take the claim that belief as such is open to criticism if it does not reflect all
the relevant evidence to be quite plausible. It is, I think, relatively weak, not ruling out the possibility of such cases as Joe's. I cannot, however, attempt to assess
it here. Suffice it to say that there appears to be no radical *disanalogy* between
collective belief* and individual belief in relation to this particular matter.

5.3. Would people form collective beliefs* if truth were all that mattered?

The joint commitment underlying a collective belief* is, indeed, a commitment. In addition, it allows for claims from any one party against any another for
baldly gainsaying what is collectively believed* in the relevant context.[45] Meijers
argues that, if the truth of a collective belief* were the only thing that mattered,
"it would be incomprehensible why there are inter-individual commitments
involved in these beliefs...."[46]

His concern here seems to be with the motivations of the individuals who
participate in the underlying joint commitment. It is unclear, however, what
the details of these motivations have to do with the nature of collective beliefs*,
once formed.

It is worth noting, in this context, that people who are all *personally certain*
that p can collectively believe* that p. Thus a group of mathematicians can collectively believe* that the square on a triangle's hypotenuse is equal to the squares
on the other two sides, while individually being certain that this is so. In such a
case, even if they wish not to be constrained from speaking the truth, the people
in question may have no reason for not participating in the collective belief* that
p. There may, meanwhile, be good reasons to do so.[47]

As I have argued elsewhere, people who, *not* being certain that p, participate
in a collective belief* that p, may indeed find this frustrating, should they later
discover that p is not true. This aspect of collective beliefs* can play an inhibitory

[45] For extended discussion of this point see Margaret Gilbert "Obligation and Joint Commitment,"
Utilitas 11 (1999a): 143–163, reprinted in *Sociality*.

[46] Meijers, "Believing," 65, see also 68.

[47] On reasons for participating in collective beliefs* in general, see Gilbert, "Remarks," 253, *Social
Facts*, 225, cited and discussed in Wray, "Collective Belief," 322.

role in the development of the sciences, among other things.[48] Nonetheless, the balance of reasons may justify participating in a potentially false collective belief*. In the case of scientists, one of these reasons may be that participation in a *collective* truth-seeking enterprise is arguably the best way overall to reach the truth, whatever its hazards and, in particular, the potential of the collective beliefs* that arise for repressing new ideas that may prove to be correct.

Indeed, truth may not be the only thing that matters *to the individuals* who participate in a particular collective belief*. This is a matter of the aims of those individuals. These aims are not strictly relevant to the claim that collective beliefs* aim at truth. This is, after all, a claim about *collective beliefs*,* not the individuals who make them up. It is, moreover, not really a claim about "aims" but rather about *appropriate standards of assessment*.

5.4. Collective beliefs* and the beliefs of the participants

Meijers argues, finally, that collective beliefs* do not aim at truth because "we as a group may believe[*] a proposition that no-one takes to be *true* individually" (65). This surely does not rebut the claim that collective beliefs* aim at truth.

Suppose the campus improvement committee believes* that a café would improve the campus, or, for short, believes* that c. Suppose, further, that this collective belief* emerged in spite of the fact that no member of the committee personally believed that c, and the members have not personally changed their minds on the matter. What happened was that everyone knew that the Chancellor was wedded to the idea of a campus café, and, in the committee's discussion, no one dared propose anything contrary to the Chancellor's view.

If one looks at the members of the committee, they do not, indeed, take c to be true. This, however, is not relevant to the stance of the collective they constitute, namely, the committee itself. It is a mistake to look at to the personal situation of the members of the committee when what is at issue is the stance of the committee as a whole.

How are we to assess the situation of the committee as a whole, when it believes* that c? We would do well to consider what the members express, or are likely to express, when acting in light of the joint commitment to believe that c as a body. They are then acting, in effect, as the mouthpieces of the whole their commitment tells them to emulate, as far as is possible.

If one looks at these expressions as a clue to the committee's stance, does it seem to take the proposition that c to be true? Well, one might well find

---

[48] For discussion of the potentially unfortunate role of collective beliefs* in the progress of science see Margaret Gilbert, "Collective Belief and Scientific Change," in *Sociality*, 37–49. Wray, "Collective Belief" discusses the role of collective belief*—which he prefers to label "collective acceptance"—in the scientific laboratory, 327–330.

expressions of the claim that *c*. One might well find expressions of the claim that *it is true that c*. And one might well find expressions of the form "We believe that c," which, according to Williams, would convey the message that *p is the case*, at least as far as *we* are concerned.

Presumably the same can be said, *mutatis mutandis*, of an individual who believes that c. If so, with respect to "taking p to be true," it is not clear that there is any distinction to be made between the case of a collective that believes* that p, and an individual human being who believes that p.

5.5. Collective beliefs* and truth

I have considered the situation of collective belief* in relation to Williams's criteria for "aiming at truth," and in relation to several related points from Meijers. The conclusion that suggests itself is that collective belief* holds much the same relation to truth as the beliefs of an individual do.

6. Belief and the will

6.1. "Involuntarism"

It is often claimed that belief cannot be willed. That is, I cannot bring a belief of mine into being by an act of will, or not directly.[49] I shall call this claim "involuntarism." I shall not here examine the reasons people have adduced in favor of involuntarism.[50] Nor shall I attempt to assess it in any detail.

Involuntarism has provoked the following rejectionist argument: collective belief* is necessarily willed, hence it is not belief.[51] I shall question the claim about collective belief on which this argument is premised.

6.2. Collective beliefs* need not be willed by the collective

It is crucial to understand that collective beliefs* need not be willed into being *by the relevant collective*. They are, indeed, *constituted by* what could be referred to as

---

[49] See, for instance, Williams, "Deciding," 147f. Meijers, "Believing and Accepting," 64; Engel, 1998, 143; Tuomela, "Belief versus Acceptance," 86; Wray, 2002. Sometimes the claim is put in slightly different terms. The details will not matter for present purposes.

[50] On this see, for instance, Williams, "Deciding," 147f. Williams suggests that "...I cannot bring it about, just like that, that I believe something. Why is this? One reason is connected with the characteristic of beliefs that they aim at truth..." (148).

[51] See, for instance, Meijers, "Believing," 64, section (1), discussed in the text below. See also Wray: "the goals of a plural subject determine" what its members collectively believe*, "Collective Belief," 7.

a collective will, but that is a different matter. I have in mind, of course, the joint commitment that constitutes the collective belief*. To say that there is a sense in which a collective belief* involves a collective will, however, is not to say that a collective belief is necessarily willed into existence by the relevant collective.

Compare the case of an individual's belief. One may suppose that this, also, to some extent is constituted by that individual's will. There may be something passive about an individual's beliefs, insofar they are responsive to something outside the control of the believer, in particular, to evidence for the beliefs. Arguably, however, there is always something active about them also. There may be a need for judgment, for instance, where judging is an active rather than a passive matter. If performing an action, such as raising one's arm, is completely active, and having a sensation, such as feeling pain, is completely passive, then believing would seem to lie somewhere in the middle.

To say that an individual's belief is in part constituted by an exercise of that individual's will is not to say that the belief—constitutive judgment and all—is necessarily willed into existence by that individual. Indeed, it could be true that, in some sense, a given individual *cannot* believe *at will*, though believing necessarily *involves* that individual's will. The same goes for the collective case.

Meijers says that the main reason for thinking that involuntarism supports rejectionism is that collective beliefs*: "...require some sort of voluntary assent, agreement, or decision by the members of the group for the belief."[52] Again: "members of a group...express their commitment to certain beliefs in their practices..."[53] The focus here is, evidently, on the individual members of the group and the involvement of their wills in the production of a collective belief*.

Consider the case of Sam, who helps to create a collective belief* in his department that costs must be cut. On the one hand, his input to the creation of this belief may not be *fully voluntary*. Conscious that his boss would disapprove of the group's thinking otherwise, he feels under great pressure to propose that costs must be cut.[54] On the other hand, in setting out to help create the collective belief*, he expresses a certain state of his will. He expresses his readiness to be jointly committed with the others to believe as a body that costs must be cut. In order for the department to believe* that costs must be cut, the other members must express themselves likewise, in conditions of common knowledge.

In the sense exemplified in this case, then, the wills of the individual group members are involved in the production of a collective belief*. This does not show however, that collective beliefs* must be willed *by the collective in question*

---

[52] Meijers, "Believing," 64.

[53] Meijers, "Believing," 64.

[54] On the possibility of entering joint commitments in coercive circumstances, see Margaret Gilbert, "Agreements, Coercion, and Obligation," *Ethics* 103 (1993): 679–706.

and or even that they can be so willed, contrary to involuntarism. As far as the story goes, the collective belief* in question was not created by the will of the collective whose belief it is. So, contrary to Meijers suggestion, there is no confrontation with involuntarism here.[55] I have argued, what seems firm, that a collective belief*, is not *necessarily* willed by the relevant collective. According to Meijers, acceptance, as opposed to belief, is "voluntary. To accept that p is to make the decision" to use p as a premise in one's deliberation.[56] Contrary to Meijers proposal, then, collective belief* is not a case of acceptance so characterized.

6.3. Can collective belief* be willed by the collective?

Someone might raise the question whether a collective belief* *can* be willed into existence by a given collective. More precisely, can a collective belief* arise *directly* as a result of the collective's willing it into existence?

It may be proposed, along lines that Bernard Williams has traced out for the individual case, that insofar as belief aims at truth, there is something rebarbative about the idea of adopting *as a collective goal* what is, in effect, a joint commitment to *believe* as a body that p.[57] The idea in question, more specifically, is that these people would have as their goal their emulating as far as possible, a body that *believed* that p, *without that body's having any inkling of the truth of p.* There may, then, be a hedge of sorts around collective beliefs* just as there may be such a hedge around individual beliefs, tending to prevent people from wantonly creating or indeed trying to create such beliefs just because they want to have them, or because it would be in their interests to have them.

Let us suppose that, in spite of these considerations, and perhaps *per impossibile,* Fran and her friend Trudy explicitly adopt as their collective goal their collectively believing* that their future is bright, without concern for whether or not their future actually is bright. It would be good for them, they think, to believe* this. Thus they become the plural subject of the goal our believing* that our future is bright.

This situation is interestingly different from that of familiar collective goals where, once the goal is set, all that needs to be done is that the individuals in question personally act in light of the relevant joint commitment so that the goal be achieved. An example might be the goal of walking along the beach side by side for a while; once the parties have jointly committed to adopting this goal as a body, all they have to do is perform relevant actions in light of the joint commitment in question. Thus each must simply walk along the beach monitoring

---

[55] See also Wray, "Collective Belief," 7, cited earlier.

[56] Meijers, "Believing," 94.

[57] See Williams, "Deciding," 147f.

her spatial relationship to the others, if necessary urging the other to walk faster, and so on, and their goal is achieved.[58]

In the present case, by hypothesis, a *new joint commitment must be made*. It is true that the parties are creating this commitment in light of another such commitment. Nonetheless, the group's wanting to believe* that p does not lead to its believing* that p *with the same immediacy* with which it may lead to the beach walk. One might put the point this way: a group cannot directly bring its beliefs* into being by an act of its own will. In other words, one can argue that this case does not present a counterexample to involuntarism.

6.4. Collective belief* and involuntarism at the collective level

In the last two sections, I have argued that the will of the collective—as would be found in a collective goal—is not necessarily involved in the production of a collective belief*. So it is wrong to consider collective belief* a form of *acceptance*, if that involves something that is *necessarily* willed by the subject of the acceptance. To see this one needs clearly to distinguish between the individual wills of the members of a collective and the will of the collective itself. That is an important distinction that needs to be made, irrespective of the issue of rejectionism.

I have also suggested that there may be something rebarbative about a group's setting its possession of a certain collective belief as a goal, just like that, just as there may be something rebarbative in the individual case. The two cases would seem to be on a par in relation to this matter, which is the main point for present purposes.

Finally, I argued that a collective belief* cannot be *directly* willed into being by the collective, even if the collective does, perhaps *per impossibile*, form the goal of possessing that belief*. There is no reason in particular for me to want this to be true. However, if it is true, it goes against the view that collective beliefs* are not beliefs because—as it is often supposed—genuine beliefs cannot be directly willed into existence by the believer.

6.5. Collective belief* and involuntarism at the individual level

I said earlier that the joint commitment involved in collective belief* does not, as I understand it, require the participating individuals personally to believe

---

[58] For detailed discussion of the case of walking together see Margaret Gilbert, "Walking Together"; also "Acting Together," in *Social Facts and Collective Intrentionality*, ed. Georg Meggle (Frankfurt: Hansel-Hohenhausen, 2002a) [chapter 1 this volume].

something, nor even to *try* personally to believe it. Hence it does not involve the denial of involuntarism at the individual level. It may be worth elaborating upon this point here.

I have characterized the joint commitment in question as a commitment to emulate, as far as possible, a single body that believes that p. It may be observed, first, that insofar as a given collective belief* that p exists once the relevant joint commitment does, *the existence* of a collective belief* cannot depend on the participants personally believing that p. Even if that were what the commitment *required of them*, the commitment in and of itself suffices for the collective belief*, whether or not it is conformed to.[59]

However that may be, the commitment, as I understand it, does not require that anyone do anything impossible. Suppose Judy is jointly committed with certain others to constitute, as far as is possible, a single body that believes that p. Suppose, further, that involuntarism about belief is true. Then it is not possible for Judy to believe that p *at will*. It follows that she is *not required* to believe that p at will.

It is often suggested that there are things one can do in order to get oneself to believe something, even if the means of creating the belief are indirect. One can avoid places where contrary evidence is likely to be found, and so on. I said earlier that a joint commitment to believe that p as a body does not require that one do what one can personally to believe that p. I shall assume, for present purposes, that this is not because such an attempt is impossible.

Why would a joint commitment to believe that p as a body *not* require the individual participants personally to believe that p or at least to attempt personally to believe that p? Presumably this is why: the focus of the commitment is on the emulation of a body that believes, not on the components of the body in question, or their personal states of mind.

Though this is so, it is presumably easier to conform to a joint commitment to believe that p as a body if one does oneself believe that p. It will be easier, and less internally stressful, to give voice to the view that p when it is one's personal view. In this sense collective beliefs* are likely to influence what people think: they have what Durkheim called "coercive power." They are, in short, extremely consequential.[60]

---

[59] The question of how lack of conformity impacts on the existence of a joint commitment cannot be entered here. See Gilbert, *Living*, chapter 16, for some discussion.

[60] See Durkheim, *Rules*, chapter 1; Gilbert, *Social Facts*, chapter 5, and elsewhere.

7. Collective belief* and acceptance

7.1. Collective belief* and individual acceptance

If the participants in collective belief* are not required to believe that p, are they required to *accept* that p in some sense in which acceptance does not entail belief? In other words, when the collective belief* that p is "in full flower," with the relevant individuals all complying with the joint commitment, are we confronted with a population of individuals all of whom accept that p, in relevant contexts, as opposed to believing that p?

Note that whatever the answer to this question, it does not appear to have an impact on the question whether collective belief* is belief or, rather, acceptance. Suppose, for the sake of argument, that in order to participate in a fully flowering collective belief*, the members of a population must in some appropriate sense accept that p, in relevant contexts, though they need not believe it. This would not seem to show that collective belief* was acceptance, in the relevant sense, and not belief. To say that it did would seem to be confusing what is going on at the level of the individual with what is going on at the collective level.

Does collective belief*, in full flower, involve a set of acceptances on the part of the participants? That depends, of course, on precisely what acceptance is, and authors vary in their detailed descriptions of acceptance. For Meijers, following Engel and others, acceptance is a propositional attitude which, unlike belief, has at least the following properties. It is the result of decision, aims at utility rather than truth, need not, even ideally, be shaped by evidence, and is context-dependent. The paradigm case of "accepting for the sake of the argument" would appear to have all of these properties.

Now it is not clear that a collective belief* that p involves the participants, personally, in having *any* particular propositional attitude to p. More precisely, emulating as far as is possible a body that believes that p does not appear to require *any* such attitudes on behalf of the participants. Their acts and expressions are, in a sense, *representational*; they act and utter expressions as representatives of the body in question. It does not seem that this requires them to have any particular attitude toward the proposition that p themselves.

7.2. Collective belief* as belief as opposed to acceptance

The above considerations strongly suggest that there is no particular reason to say that collective belief* is acceptance as opposed to belief. For one thing, it seems that there need not be acceptance of the relevant proposition p at the individual level. That is, there need not be personal acceptance of that proposition, any more than there need be personal belief that p at that level. For another, there is no obvious reason to say that there is acceptance rather than belief at the *collective* level.

Why, though, say that collective belief* is *belief*? For one thing, it is, I am assuming, the referent of everyday collective *belief* statements. For another, it involves a joint commitment to *believe* something as a body, not to accept something as a body. And a joint commitment to *accept* as a body a proposition, in contrast, is perfectly possible. I discuss this shortly. If one has to choose between saying that collective belief* is belief and saying that it is acceptance, I propose that one should say it is belief.

7.3. Collective acceptance

Accepting a proposition, where this does not involve believing it, is sometimes a useful thing to do. Often one wants to consider the consequences of some state of affairs without investigating whether or not it obtains. This is certainly true in science, it is true in various branches of scholarship, and it is true in everyday life as well. Thus people regularly say things like this: "Suppose she has left already. What would I do then?"

Collectives can, surely, accept propositions, in this sense. People make *collective acceptance statements* just as they make collective belief statements. And I would propose an analogous account of them.

Cases are easy to imagine. The campus improvement committee is discussing whether the campus needs a café. Cass says, "Look, let's suppose, for the sake of argument, that Café Sunshine—the only café in town—is going to close in the next year." Phil says, "Okay," and the others nod in agreement. The committee members have now expressed their readiness to be jointly committed to accept as a body, for the purposes of their discussion, that Café Sunshine is going to close in the next year. And this is—we can assume—common knowledge between them. They have, in other words, now constituted themselves, in their capacity as members of the committee, a plural subject of acceptance, in the sense at issue.

It is worth emphasizing that collective beliefs* are unlikely to be brought into existence in an analogous way, that is, with the suggestion "Let's believe that..." Rather, a proposition is put forward as a candidate for collective belief*: "Nice day!" "Yes, indeed." It is a proposal for acceptance, I would think, that needs to be specially marked as such. Normally to put a proposition forward in conversation without qualification is an invitation to one's fellow conversationalists collectively to believe* it.

Insofar as there are several viable ideas of acceptance in the individual case, they should *all* be susceptible of exemplification in the collective case. The whole range of cognitive states possible for individuals would appear to be attributable to groups in relevant circumstances. Groups can surely doubt that p, wonder whether p, be certain that p, consider whether p, and so on. And a distinct plural subject account seems to be available for each one of these, the underlying joint commitment having a different content in each case.[61]

8. Concluding remarks

What is most important about collective belief*? I would say not that it is—or is not—a kind of belief, but rather the following. It is a phenomenon of which one might say, in Durkheimian terms, that it has "coercive power" over individuals. Once again in Durkheimian terms, in the context of collective beliefs* the individual is liable to be pressured by other group members, acting as such, into speaking, acting, and, ultimately, thinking in certain ways. Indeed, the individual is liable eventually personally to believe what the collective believes*—*whether the collective is properly said to believe* it or not. I have argued for all these things elsewhere.[62]

The issue discussed in this chapter, then, does not impinge on the importance of collective beliefs* under whatever label, nor does it throw their existence into doubt. The present discussion suggests that ordinary language, in referring to them as *beliefs* has not been shown to be in error. It is not clear that it could be shown to be in error, if, as I have suggested, collective belief statements are part of the data for an account of belief in general. If, for some reason, one refuses to allow this, it appears that, nonetheless, collective beliefs* behave much like beliefs in the individual case, and certainly more like such beliefs than rejectionists have supposed. It is hard to see why the learned should not speak with the vulgar, and go ahead and call them beliefs.[63]

---

[61] Cf. Gilbert, "Remarks."

[62] See, for instance, Gilbert, *Social Facts,* chapter 5; "Durkheim."

[63] Selected sections of this chapter were presented to the Department of Philosophy at the University of Connecticut, Storrs, November 2001. I am particularly grateful to Jerome Shaffer for his contribution to the lively discussion. I have in response made more of the distinction between *reasons for* and *causes of* belief. Ruth Millikan helpfully emphasized the intrinsic interest of analogies and disanalogies between the individual and the collective cases. I am most grateful also to Donald Baxter, Paul Bloomfield, Simon Evnine, Anne Hiskes, Saul Kripke, Scott Lehmann, Giovanna Pompele, K. Brad Wray, and Nick Zangwill, for related discussion. Finally, I thank those authors I have discussed, Anthonie Meijers, Raimo Tuomela, and K. Brad Wray, for provoking me to consider the topic. Though I resist their conclusions, I have found much of merit in their discussions.

References

Michael Bratman, "Belief and Acceptance in a Context," *Mind* 101 (1993): 1–16.

Gerald A. Cohen, "Beliefs and Roles," *Proceedings of the Aristotelian Society* 67 (1966–70): 53–66.

Jonathan Cohen, *An Essay on Belief and Acceptance* (New York: Oxford University Press, 1992).

Austen Clark, "Beliefs and Desires Incorporated," *Journal of Philosophy* 91 (1994): 404–425.

Emile Durkheim, *Rules of Sociological Method*, ed. S. Lukes (New York: Free Press, 1982).

Pascal Engel, "Believing, Accepting, and Holding True," *Philosophical Explorations* I (1998): 140–151.

———, ed., *Believing and Accepting* (Dordrecht: Kluwer Academic Publishers, 2000).

Margaret Gilbert, "Modeling Collective Belief," *Synthese* 73 (1987): 185–204

———, *On Social Facts*, (Princeton: Princeton University Press, 1989)

———, "Walking Together: A Paradigmatic Social Phenomenon," in Peter French, Theodore Uehling, and Howard Wettstein, eds., *Midwest Studies in Philosophy*, 15 (Notre Dame, Indiana: University of Notre Dame Press, 1990): 1–14, reprinted in Gilbert, *Living Together*.

———, "Agreements, Coercion, and Obligation," *Ethics* 103 (1993): 679–706.

———, "Durkheim and Social Facts," in *Debating Durkheim*, ed. Herminio Martins and William Pickering (London: Routledge, 1994a), 86–109.

———, "Remarks on Collective Belief," in *Socializing Epistemology*, ed. Frederick Schmitt (Lanham, MD: Rowman and Littlefield, 1994b), 235–256.

———, *Living Together: Rationality, Sociality, and Obligation* Lanham, MD: Rowman and Littlefield, 1996.

———, "What Is It for Us to Intend?," in Raimo Tuomela and Ghita Holmstrom-Hintikka, *Contemporary Action Theory*, vol. 2, Social Action (Dordrecht: Kluwer Academic Publishers, 1997): pp-pp, reprinted in Gilbert, *Sociality*, 14–36.

———, "Obligation and Joint Commitment," *Utilitas* 11 (1999a): 143–163, reprinted in *Sociality*, 50–70.

———, "Reconsidering the 'Actual Contract' Theory of Political Obligation," *Ethics* 109, (1999b):236–260, reprinted in Gilbert, *Sociality*, 97–122.

———, "Collective Belief and Scientific Change," (2000a) in Gilbert, *Sociality*, 37–49.

———, "Collective Remorse," (2000b) in Gilbert, *Sociality*, 123–140.

———, *Sociality and Responsibility: New Essays in Plural Subject Theory* (Lanham, MD: Rowman and Littlefield, 2000c).

———, "Acting Together," in *Social Facts and Collective Intentionality*, ed. Georg Meggle, (Frankfurt: Hansel-Hohenhausen, 2002a), 53–72 [Chapter 1, this volume].

———, review of Jon Elster, *Ulysses Unbound*, *Mind*, 111 (2002b) 339–403.

Keith Lehrer, *Self-Trust: A Study of Reason, Knowledge and Autonomy* (Oxford: Clarendon Press, 1997).

Anthonie Meijers, "Believing and Accepting as a Group," in Meijers, ed., 1999): 59–71.

———, ed. *Belief, Cognition and the Will* (Tilburg: Tilburg University Press, 1999).

Anthony Quinton, "Social Objects," *Proceedings of the Aristotelian Society*, 76 (1975): 1–27.

David K. Lewis, *Convention: A Philosophical Study* (Cambridge, MA: Harvard University Press, 1969).

Peter Railton, "Scientific Objectivity and the Aims of Belief," in Engel, 2000:179–208.

Stephen Schiffer, *Meaning* (Oxford: Oxford University Press, 1972).

Frederick R. Schmitt, "The Justification of Group Beliefs," in Frederick R. Schmitt, ed., *Socializing Epistemology* (Lanham, MD: Rowman and Littlefield, 1994): 257–288.

Robert Stalnaker, *Inquiry* (Cambridge, MA: MIT Press, 1984).

Raimo Tuomela, "Group Beliefs," *Synthese* 91 (1992):285–318.

———, *The Importance of Us* (Stanford: Stanford University Press, 1995).

———, "Belief versus Acceptance," in Meijers, ed., *Belief, Cognition*, 319–333.

Bas Van Fraassen, *The Scientific Image* (Oxford: Clarendon Press, 1980).

Bernard Williams, "Deciding to believe," in his *Problems of the Self* (Cambridge: Cambridge University Press, 1970): 136–151.

K. Brad Wray, "Collective Belief and Acceptance," *Synthese* 129 (2001): 319–333.

7

Collective Epistemology

The traditional focus of philosophical epistemology

Philosophical epistemology is concerned with knowledge and related phenomena such as belief. In order to have a general label for such phenomena I shall refer to them as *cognitive states*. Differing accounts of a variety of cognitive states have been produced. For instance, according to one venerable—if debated—account of knowledge, it is justified true belief. Belief has been contrasted with acceptance, though the belief-acceptance contrast has been drawn in a variety of different ways.

In nothing I have said so far has the following question come up. Who (or what) is capable of knowledge, belief, or, to use a general label for all of the relevant cognitive states, *cognition*? The question concerns not particulars but kinds. What kinds of entity are capable of cognition?

Most epistemologists would confidently include human beings in this class. One basis for this confidence is simple enough: everyday thought routinely ascribes such states to individual human beings. The detective asks his colleague: "What does she know?" An informant says, "I believe he went that way." As a result the denial that individual human beings are subjects of knowledge and belief is counterintuitive. Such denial has occurred in the history of epistemology, but it needs to be argued.

Epistemologists largely focus on the individual human case, and few spend much time on the question "Who (or what) knows?" and so on. There is no problem with this focus in itself. It has a consequence, however, that may be less innocuous.

Following an examination of the individual human case epistemologists standardly go on to offer general accounts of knowledge, belief, and so on that are based on that case. Then the question whether, for instance, animals have beliefs is answered in terms of an account of belief that has been derived from reflection on the individual human case. What justifies this procedure?

If everyday thought routinely ascribes particular cognitive states to entities other than human beings, one might take that to be crucial evidence for a general account of these states. To allow this would not be to deny that the cognitive states of human beings have a distinctive character. On the contrary, one would expect them to have such a character, given the distinctive nature of human beings. It would be to allow that the various cognitive states, as these are conceived of in everyday thought, may not be restricted to human beings.

It is possible that all or some ascriptions of cognitive states to other kinds of entity are metaphorical, or that they are understood to involve some kind of pretence. That they are of this kind, however, cannot simply be assumed. It needs to be argued or shown by reference to examples that make it clear. Sometimes it may be clear enough that those who make them do *not* see them as either metaphorical or as involving some kind of pretense.

Again, it is possible that in all or some cases some kind of mistake is involved. This too will need to be argued. It will not do simply to insist that human beings alone are capable of cognitive states—so that some such mistake must be involved.

Everyday ascriptions of collective cognitive states

Everyday life is full of statements such as the following: "The union believes that management is being unreasonable," "In the opinion of the court, this law is unconstitutional," "Our discussion group thought it was a great novel," "Our family believes in ghosts," "Bill and Jane have concluded that it would be wrong," "We knew we had to stop."

These appear to be ascriptions of *collective* cognitive states. That is, what is claimed to have a given cognitive state is understood to comprise *two or more* human beings. It is understood, further, that these people could properly ascribe the cognitive state in question to "us."

Thus construed, the examples given fall into two broad classes. There are ascriptions of cognitive states to two or more people who are understood to constitute an established group of a specific kind such as a union, court, discussion group, family, and so on. There are also ascriptions of cognitive states to two or more people without any presumption that they constitute an already established group.[1]

Though they differ in important ways, both expressions such as "The union," on the one hand, and expressions such as "Bill and Jane" on the other, can be

---

[1] I take it that if what is referred to on a given occasion as a "family," for instance, is understood to have but a single member, the ascription of a cognitive state to it would not count as the ascription of a *collective* cognitive state. Nor would a single-membered "family" count as a paradigmatic *group*.

thought of as referring to a *population*. Clearly, a population, in the sense in question, need not be an already constituted group, or social group, in the narrow sense in which courts and unions and discussion groups are paradigmatic examples.[2]

Populations may be specified not only by means of expressions such as "the union" and reference to particular individuals, but also by reference to some feature possessed by all of their members. For example, the phrase "haemophiliacs" picks out a particular population, comprising all haemophiliacs.

Particular collective cognitive states can be referred to in either of the following ways. With respect to belief, one might say either, "Population P believes that p," or, equivalently, "The members of population P (collectively) believe that p."

I take it that those who make everyday ascriptions of collective cognitive states do not generally regard these ascriptions as metaphorical or as "pretend" ascriptions. I shall assume that they are innocent of mistake unless and until they are proved guilty.

Collective epistemology

To what phenomena are ascriptions of collective cognitive states intended to refer? In other terms, what are *collective* knowledge, *collective* belief, and so on?

Until very recently this question has been largely been neglected by philosophers. Those who have neglected it include many of those who have focused to some extent on what they refer to as *social epistemology*.[3] In order both to emphasize its distinctiveness and to indicate its character I shall refer to the study of collective cognitive states as *collective epistemology*.[4]

Around 1980 Charles Taylor made some suggestive points relevant to collective epistemology in several publications. In particular he persuasively argued that to say it was common knowledge that such-and-such in a certain context

---

[2] On the relatively narrow sense of "group," or "social group," in question see *On Social Facts*, chapter 4. I also explore there the conditions for the appropriate use of the first-person plural pronoun "we," which had been neglected by theorists of other such expressions.

[3] See for instance the essays in Frederick Schmitt, ed., 1994, *Socializing Epistemology*, Rowman and Littlefield: Lanham, MD; see also, in Italian, *Esperienza e Cognoscenza*, 1995, ed. Gianguido Piazza, Milan: Citta Studi, which translates a number of texts that are generally taken to be contributions to social epistemology. Each of these collections includes at least one essay on a collective cognitive state, but the majority of the essays are concerned with other matters.

[4] Deborah Tollefsen uses this phrase in a roughly similar way in a paper presented at Leipzig University, June 2004, "Collective Epistemic Agency and the Need for Collective Epistemology" (2004 ms).

was not to say that anything was yet, in his terms, *entre nous* or, again in his terms, *in public space.*[5]

In my 1987 article "Modeling Collective Belief" I argued for a relatively full-blown account of collective belief, a closely related version of which is my book *On Social Facts*, 1989.[6] Since then there has been a steady increase in studies in collective epistemology.[7] Nonetheless it has not yet achieved the recognition from epistemologists and other philosophers that it deserves.[8]

One reason that it deserves such recognition has already been indicated. If epistemologists are to offer a plausible of account of cognitive states in general, as opposed to the cognitive states of individual human beings, they need to consider in a more than cursory way the nature of collective cognitive states.

Irrespective of this consideration, and whatever precisely they are, collective cognitive states would seem to be a significant aspect of the social world. Their importance was emphasized by one of the founders of sociology, Emile Durkheim, in his classic work *The Rules of Sociological Method.* Though there may be earlier pertinent discussions, Durkheim has some title to be considered the founder of collective

---

[5] See, for instance, Charles Taylor, 1980, Critical notice, Jonathan Bennett's *Linguistic Behavior,* Dialogue, vol. 19; Charles Taylor, 1985, *Human Agency and Language,* Cambridge University Press: Cambridge, chapter 10, "Theories of Meaning," section III. 1. "Common knowledge," undoubtedly an important topic for epistemology, has been variously defined. For present purposes what is important about these definitions is that they generally refer to individual human beings, what each knows, what each knows about each one's knowledge, and so on. Two classic sources are David Lewis, 1969, *Convention: A Philosophical Study,* Harvard University Press: Harvard; and Stephen Schiffer, 1972, *Meaning,* Oxford University Press: Oxford. See also Margaret Gilbert, 1989, *On Social Facts,* Princeton University Press: Princeton.

[6] Margaret Gilbert, "Modeling Collective Belief," 1987, *Synthese,* reprinted in Margaret Gilbert, *Living Together: Rationality, Sociality and Obligation,* 1996, Rowman and Littlefield: Lanham, MD, and Gilbert, *Social Facts.* Due to the vagaries of publishing, the 1987 article was written after the 1989 book was sent to the press. I have developed my position in a number of subsequent publications including, most recently, "Belief and Acceptance as Features of Groups," 2002, *Protosociology,* vol. 16, 35–69. [Chapter 6 this volume.]

[7] Raimo Tuomela, 1992, "Group beliefs," *Synthese* vol. 91, 285–318, responds to my proposals in "Modeling" and *Social Facts* and presents an alternative but in many ways similar account. See also his book *The Importance of Us,* 1995, Stanford University Press: Stanford. Other philosophers who have addressed one or more aspects of the topic in the 1990s or later include, in alphabetical order, Alban Bouvier, Austen Clark, Angelo Corlett, Christopher MacMahon, Anthonie Meijers, Philip Pettit, Gianguido Piazza, Gerhard Preyer, Abraham Sesshu Roth, Frederick Schmitt, Deborah Tollefsen and K. Bradley Wray. Preyer edits the online journal *Protosociology* in which relevant publications by a number of these authors have recently appeared in special issues: web address: www.protosociology.de.

[8] Relatively few of the authors mentioned in the last footnote specialize in mainstream epistemology.

epistemology. His suggestive words on the topic, however, badly stand in need of further development.[9]

In the rest of this chapter I sketch my own approach to collective epistemology, with some reference to related discussions. I hope to encourage those who have not yet engaged with collective epistemology to do so. There are many avenues to pursue. These include the refinement of existing proposals, the development of alternatives, and examination of the consequences of these proposals for general epistemology.

Philosophers tend to be modest about the relevance or effect of their work in relation to science—the tendency nowadays is to think of philosophy as informed by the sciences rather than the other way round. Many social scientists, meanwhile, are keen to avail themselves of the results of philosophical investigations. Philosophical investigations in collective epistemology, then, are likely to constitute an important contribution to the social sciences.

Method

My own approach to collective cognitive states has been as follows. Examine the contexts in which everyday ascriptions of such states are generally considered true or false with the aim of arriving at a perspicuous description of the phenomena people mean to refer to when ascribing collective cognitive states.[10] I have largely drawn on my own understanding of when it would or would not be in order to ascribe a particular cognitive state to a given population. My own focus to date has been on collective belief and I shall focus on that here.[11]

---

[9] See Emile Durkheim, 1982, *The Rules of Sociological Method*, translated from the French by W. D. Halls, Free Press: New York (first published 1895). I suggest an interpretation of key passages in this work in *On Social Facts*, chapter 5, and subsequently in "Durkheim and Social Facts," 1994, in *Debating Durkheim*, Herminio Martins and William Pickering, eds., Routledge: London, reprinted in French translation in Margaret Gilbert, *Marcher Ensemble: Essais sur les Fondements de la Vie Collective*, 2003, Presses Universitaires de France: Paris. As I interpret him Durkheim presents us with an intriguing, nuanced proposal that requires further elaboration. My own proposals on the topic indicate one way in which such elaboration out might proceed.

[10] In *On Social Facts* I referred to my approach as "conceptual analysis," a phrase open to various construals. The preceding description of my approach may be less tendentious. The main point is that everyday judgments about when, say, a group believes something, and when it fails to believe something are carefully considered to arrive at a description of what (according to everyday understandings) collective belief is. No substantive "theory of concepts" is presupposed.

[11] Angelo Corlett pays attention to the question of collective knowledge in his book *Analyzing Social Knowledge*, 1996, Rowman and Littlefield: Lanham, MD.

The simple summative account

The first hypothesis about the nature of collective belief that occurs to many people is what I have called the *simple summative account*. This maintains that—according to everyday understandings—the members of a population, P, *collectively believe that p* when and only when all or most of its members believe that p. For instance, to say that the union believes management is being unreasonable is to say that all or most members of the union believe this.[12]

It can be argued, however, that most of a population's members believing that such-and-such is neither necessary nor sufficient for their collectively believing it. I now briefly argue this.[13]

Consider first the question of necessity. That is, consider whether most members of P must believe that such-and-such in order that they collectively believe it.

If one looks at examples like those of a union or a court, the answer appears to be negative. One relevant consideration is this.

Often what is taken to determine the collective belief in such cases is a formal voting procedure where the opinion that receives the most votes is deemed, for that reason, to be the opinion of the court, the union, or whatever. What counts as far as any individual member is concerned, then, is his or her *vote*—not what he or she personally believes.

Evidently, one's voting in favor of the proposition that Jones was the best candidate does not entail that one personally believes that Jones was the best candidate, whether or not others might be inclined to think one does believe this, given one's vote. In other words, it cannot be argued that because one did not believe that Jones was the best candidate one did not really vote for him. Nor can one generally argue that the absence of correlative personal beliefs invalidates the result of the voting procedure.

Less formal processes can determine a collective's belief. These can be argued to be analogous to the case of voting at least insofar as public expressions as opposed to private thoughts are what counts. It is worth considering one such case in some detail.

Suppose that the members of a poetry discussion group have been focusing on Sylvia Plath's famous poem, "Daddy." After a lengthy discussion of its content and structure has taken place someone asserts that it is a very powerful poem.

---

[12] See, for instance, Anthony Quinton, 1975, "Social Objects," *Proceedings of the Aristotelian Society,* vol. 75. Quinton assumes the simple summative account *en passant*. Related assumptions have been made for specific forms of belief or judgment, such as moral judgment. On this see Margaret Gilbert, 2005, "Shared Values, Social Unity, and Liberty" *Public Affairs Quarterly*, vol. 19, 25–49.

[13] More extensive discussions are to be found in Gilbert, "Modeling," and Gilbert, *Social Facts*.

The other members respond in a positive way. One says "Yes, indeed," another "That's so true," and so on. On some such basis a group member might reasonably say, "Our discussion group thinks this is a powerful poem."[14]

Why would this collective belief ascription be in order? One thing to consider here is what the positive responses in question amount to.

Suppose you are in this group and don't particularly admire the poem in question. However, you don't want to get into an argument, so you refrain from expressing your own view. Indeed, at the crucial juncture you nod your head in an approving way. There is perhaps some likelihood that people will take you to think the poem powerful if you do this. In that case you are doing something that is likely to mislead them. You may in no way intend to mislead anyone, however.

Your primary intention may best be described along the following lines. You intend to express your readiness to see the belief that the poem is a powerful one established as the belief of the group. Your having an intention of this kind will be entirely reasonable insofar as the aim of the discussion as a whole is primarily a matter of developing a collective perspective on the poem.[15]

I return now to the question: why would the collective belief ascription at issue here be in order? My conjecture is roughly as follows. It is in order insofar as the members of the poetry discussion group have all indicated their readiness to let the belief in question be established as the group's belief. I say more later by way of explanation of precisely what is expressed by the participants. For now the main point is this. In this informal type of case, also, there may be a collective belief that p without all or most—or indeed any—members of the population in question believing that p. This stark conclusion follows from my understanding of the process of collective belief formation, and seems true to the facts. Precisely which members of a population believe that p when the members collectively believe that p will need to be determined empirically.[16]

To go back briefly to the case of voting, though this has special features, it too can be argued to involve concordant expressions of readiness with respect to a group's belief. Participating in the voting process, whichever way one votes, is a

---

[14] I develop an example involving a poetry discussion group in more detail in Gilbert, "Modeling." The example derives from an actual, unexpectedly long-standing group founded by the author together with Mairi McInnes and Priscilla Barnum.

[15] I take interpersonal discussions generally to be a form of acting together or collective action. I offer accounts of such action in *On Social Facts*, chapter 4, and elsewhere. See, for instance, "What Is It for *Us* to Intend?" 1997, in *Contemporary Action Theory, vol. 2, The Philosophy and Logic of Social Action*, G. Holmstrom-Hintikka and R. Tuomela, eds., reprinted in Margaret Gilbert, 2000, *Sociality and Responsibility: New Essays in Plural Subject Theory*, Rowman and Littlefield: Lanham, MD. These accounts are formally similar to the account of collective belief sketched here.

[16] For an example of how there might be a complete lack of corresponding personal beliefs see Gilbert, *Social Facts*, p. 290.

way of indicating one's readiness to accept as the belief of the group that belief picked out by the voting process.

I turn now to the question of sufficiency: is the fact that all or most members of a population believe that such-and-such sufficient for the members collectively to believe it? It is easy enough to argue for a negative answer.

Consider a court. A certain matter may not yet have come before it. It would then seem right to say that, as yet, the court has no opinion on the matter. The individual justices may, at the same time, have definite personal opinions about it. What they now think, however, is not relevant to the question of what the court now thinks.

Similarly, every single member of a poetry discussion group may personally think a certain poem is a powerful one, but the group may not have discussed it yet. It would seem, therefore, that there is as yet nothing that the group believes about this poem.[17]

To further the point, note that if discussion does take place, the resulting "opinion of the court" or "judgment of the poetry group"—based on the relevant expressions—could be opposed to that of the majority of its members both before and after the formation of the collective belief. Were the contrary personal views of the members to come out into the open after the formation of the collective belief it might cause some degree of shock or at least surprise. It is unlikely, though, to be seen as a rebuttal of the claim about what the group believes or to show that the group is "of two minds."

The intuitive disjunction between personal and collective beliefs may be further brought out by considering an example in which two (or more) distinct groups have the same members. Suppose the members of a certain court also constitute a poetry discussion group. (The justices decided it would be a good thing for them to get to know each other better outside the courtroom and since all liked poetry they decided to form such a group.) One day the court has to decide the merits of a certain poem, in connection with a certain legal action. While in session it brings various expert witnesses before it, and so on. At a certain point it may be reasonable to judge that the court believes that the poem has great merit. The justices' poetry discussion group, meanwhile, has not yet discussed the poem. Failing special circumstances, then, it may *not* be reasonable to judge that the poetry discussion group believes the poem has great merit. (If it ever does come to discuss the poem, it might come to a different conclusion. That would not necessarily affect the opinion of the court.) In short, one group believes that such-and-such, another doesn't, and the members of both groups are the same. That these members personally believe that such-and-such, if they

---

[17] This might not be so in special circumstances. For instance, the group has previously opined that a given poet is so talented he is incapable of writing a poem that is less than brilliant.

do, cannot be what determines the beliefs of either group, logically speaking. This example is instructive in various ways but for now I use it only to emphasize the intuitive disjunction at issue.

My discussion so far argues for the rejection of the simple summative account of collective belief statements, according to which these are in place when all or most members of the relevant group have a given belief.

This conclusion accords with central statements of Durkheim in the *Rules*. He says there that the generality of a given belief—that the group members generally have the belief—is not what makes it collective. He also makes the following point: a belief's being collective may *account for* its generality. One may be helped to see how this second point could hold by considering the observation discussed in the next section.

An observation concerning the standing to rebuke

In attempting to formulate an alternative to the simple summative account the following should be borne in mind. Once a group belief is established, the parties understand that any members who bluntly express the opposite belief lay themselves open to rebuke by other members. Opposed to a "blunt" expression is one that makes it clear that the speaker is, as he might well say he is, "speaking personally."[18]

A rebuke is a form—albeit a mild form—of punishment.[19] One needs a special standing to rebuke someone just as one needs a special standing to punish him or her in other, less verbal ways. In other terms, if asked "what puts you in a position to punish me?" one cannot answer "nothing" and still reasonably claim that one is indeed *punishing* the person in question. One can, of course, act in a "punishing" manner without any special standing. That is, one can inflict some kind of unpleasantness upon the people in question in response to some action of theirs. But a special standing is required for punishment proper.

That one has the standing to punish someone for certain behavior does not mean that in a given situation punishing him will be *justified* all things considered. It means only that one's punishing that person is *possible*.

Why is this matter of standing important? I take it that many people would hesitate to respond in a "punishing" way to someone's behavior without an understanding that they had the standing to punish that person. In other words, *given* such an understanding, they are more likely to respond in a punitive fashion. If one is averse to unpleasant treatment, then, the knowledge that certain

---

[18] See Gilbert, "Modeling"; also "Remarks."

[19] Cf. H. L. A. Hart, 1961, *The Concept of Law*, Clarendon Press: Oxford. Hart sees "informal reproofs" and legal punishment as in the same category.

others have the standing to punish one for certain behavior is apt to dissuade one from engaging in it.

Here is a hypothetical example of these processes in action. Bob and Judy collectively believe that the conservation of species is an important goal. When this collective belief was formed Judy herself personally believed the opposite. Now that the collective belief is in place, Judy recognizes that Bob has the standing to rebuke her for expressing a view in conflict with it. This leads her to suppress any inclinations bluntly to assert that the conservation of species is unnecessary. Such inclinations initially come to her at times, but their incidence diminishes as a result of such regular suppression. Indeed, the belief that prompts them subsides. This will leave the field open for what she and Bob collectively believe to become her personal belief. If she regularly mouths the collective belief, or hears Bob mouthing it, this may well happen.

Thus the collectivity of a belief may lead to its being generally held at the personal level in the population in question. The process envisaged accords with Durkheim's characterization of collective beliefs (and related phenomena) as having *coercive power* and certainly helps to substantiate his claim that the collective nature of a belief may lead to its generality.

That the other parties have the standing to rebuke the member in question appears to be a function of the collective belief itself. An adequate account of collective beliefs as these are ordinarily conceived of, then, should explain how a collective belief gives the members this standing. In addition to the other problems with it, it is hard to defend the simple summative account in light of this consideration.[20]

More complex summative accounts may be proposed. These take the simple summative account and add further conditions such as common knowledge of the widespread nature of the belief in question. I shall not pursue any such account here. As I shall explain, I believe that a quite different type of account is more promising.[21]

The plural subject account of collective belief

Three criteria of adequacy for an account of collective belief are suggested by the foregoing discussion. It should explain how the existence of a collective belief that p could give the parties the standing to rebuke each other for bluntly expressing a view contrary to p. It should not suppose that all or most of the

[20] For related discussion see Gilbert, "Modeling"; Gilbert, *Social Facts*, chapter 5.

[21] For detailed discussion and critique of two such complex summative accounts see Gilbert, *Social Facts*, chapter 5.

parties must personally believe that p. Nor should it suppose that if all or most of them believe something then they collectively believe it.

Among other things, the account of collective belief that I have developed meets all of these criteria. It also respects an important suggestion derived from examples like those considered here. Roughly, it is both necessary and sufficient for members of a population, P, collectively to believe something that the members of P have openly expressed their readiness to let the belief in question be established as the belief of P. In its present formulation, this suggestion begs for some unpacking. Its gist is evidently this: the members must express *something* such that—as all understand—once all have openly expressed it, the truth conditions for the ascription of the relevant belief to population P are satisfied.

So, what is this something that must be expressed? This question is best approached by first elaborating the *outcome* of the giving of these expressions. To be sure, one way of describing this outcome is "The members of population P collectively believe that p." There is another way of describing it, however, that is more helpful. In terms I shall shortly explain: "The members of Population P are jointly committed to believe as a body that p." In other words, my account of collective belief is roughly as follows.[22]

> *A population, P, believes that p* if and only if the members of P are jointly committed to believe as a body that p.

The phrase "joint commitment" is a technical one.[23] I take the *concept* it expresses to be implicit in everyday discourse.[24] Indeed, I have argued that it is fundamental to our everyday conceptual scheme concerning social relations.[25] It is not, then, a technical concept.

First I should say something about the relevant general concept of *commitment*. This is the concept involved in the intuitive judgment that if Pam, say, decides to go shopping today, she is committed to doing so. In the case of a personal decision, the commitment is *personal*. By this I mean that the one whose commitment it is creates it unilaterally and can unilaterally rescind it. I take it

---

[22] I have formulated this account differently on different occasions. Essentially the same idea is expressible in different ways. The Introduction to my book *Living Together: Rationality, Sociality, and Obligation*, 1996, Rowman and Littlefield: Lanham, MD, pp. 7–10, explains the way the main formulations I have used relate to one another. See also Gilbert, *Social Facts*, chapter 7, on different formulations of the general schema of which this is an exemplification.

[23] Other theorists have used the same phrase; sometimes they have not indicated what they mean by it; at other times the sense explicitly given has been different to the one I give. In any case I am concerned with joint commitment in my own technical sense here.

[24] For a more extended discussion see the Introduction to *Living*, pp. 7–15.

[25] See Margaret Gilbert, *Social Facts, Living,* and *Sociality and Responsibility: New Essays in Plural Subject Theory*, 2000, Rowman and Littlefield: Lanham, MD.

that, once committed, Pam *has sufficient reason* to go shopping today, unless and until she changes her mind. Her commitment does not make her shopping today more valuable in itself; unless and until it is rescinded, however, she is rationally required to go shopping, all else being equal. For the sake of a label such commitments may be termed *commitments of the will.*[26]

I do not claim to have plumbed the depths of the general concept of commitment at issue here. Doing so is an important task. Meanwhile I find promising the idea that commitments of the will may usefully be represented as involving a type of self-directed order or command.[27]

The concept of a *joint* commitment is the concept of a commitment of two or more people. A joint commitment so conceived is not something composite, a conjunction of the personal commitment of one party with the personal commitment(s) of the other(s). Rather, it is simple. A joint commitment is the creation of all the parties to it, rescindable only with the concurrence of all. Insofar as it involves a type of self-directed order, it involves an order issued jointly by all the parties to all the parties.[28]

Generally a given party will be physically capable of acting against an unrescinded joint commitment, if he or she so desires. But then the commitment will have been violated, as all of the parties will understand.[29]

A joint commitment is created only when each of the parties has, in effect, openly expressed his or her personal readiness to be party to it. That these expressions have been made openly must be common knowledge in the relevant population.

By virtue of their participation in a *joint* commitment, the parties gain a special standing in relation to one another's actions. Here I summarize without argument important aspects of that standing.

---

[26] For more on such commitments see Margaret Gilbert, forthcoming, "Towards a Theory of Commitments of the Will: On the Nature and Normativity of Intentions and Decisions," Wlodek Rabinowicz, ed., *Patterns of Value 2*, Lund University: Lund. For a distinction between "reasons" and "rational requirements" see John Broome, "Are Intentions Reasons? And How Should we Cope with Incommensurable Values?," 2001, in *Practical Rationality and Preference: Essays for David Gauthier*, eds. Christopher Morris and Arthur Ripstein, Cambridge University Press: Cambridge, pp. 98–120.

[27] On this see Margaret Gilbert, 1999, "Obligation and Joint Commitment," *Utilitas*, reprinted in Gilbert, *Sociality*; this cites Anthony Kenny, 1963, *Action, Emotion, and Will*, Routledge and Kegan Paul: London.

[28] For a more extended discussion of joint commitment see Margaret Gilbert, 2003, "The Structure of the Social Atom: Joint Commitment as the Foundation of Human Social Behavior," in Frederick Schmitt, ed., *Social Metaphysics*, Rowman and Littlefield: Lanham, MD; see also the Introduction, *Living*, pp. 7–15, and "Obligation."

[29] For discussion of the consequences of such violation see the Introduction, *Living*, pp. 14–15. I there incline to the view that generally speaking violation by one or more parties renders a joint commitment rescindable by the remaining parties, as opposed to nullifying it.

The parties to a joint commitment are *answerable* to one another with respect to their non-conformity. Further, one who violates a joint commitment has *offended against* all of the parties to the joint commitment, as such. The offense in question can plausibly be characterized in terms of a *violation of right*. In other words, when I am subject to a joint commitment requiring me to do certain things, all of the parties to the commitment have a right to the relevant actions from me.[30] Correlatively, I am *under an obligation* to all of them to perform these actions.[31] These are obligations and rights of a distinctive kind, deriving immediately from the joint commitment. Once it exists, they exist also, irrespective of the surrounding circumstances.[32]

In consequence of the existence of these rights and obligations, failing special background circumstances, those who are party to a joint commitment have the standing to demand that others conform to it, if non-conformity is threatened, and to rebuke one another for defaults that have taken place. As to that, the following can be argued.Conformity to the commitment is or was owed to him as a party to the commitment. It is therefore in an important sense his. This gives him the standing to demand that it be "given" to him or to rebuke one who has withheld it from him.[33]

A given joint commitment can always be described in a sentence of the following form: the parties are jointly committed *to X as a body*. Acceptable substitutions for "X" are psychological verbs such as "believe," "intend," and so on.

What is it to be jointly committed to *X as a body*? As I understand it, this joint commitment has two related aspects. First, the parties are jointly committed to bring it about, as far as is possible, that the parties emulate a single body that Xs. Second, it is understood that their doing so is to be a function of the joint commitment in question.

Putting these points together: the joint commitment to X as a body is a joint commitment to bring it about that, as far as is possible, the parties emulate a single body that Xs, and to do so in light of the joint commitment in question. Evidently, the end in question—bringing it about that, as far as is possible, the parties emulate a single body that Xs—is to be brought about by virtue of the combined activity of the individual parties, each acting in light of the joint commitment.

The guiding idea of *a single body that Xs* includes nothing about the intrinsic nature of the single body in question. In particular, it does not imply that it is in some way made up of two or more distinct bodies that are capable of X-ing on their own.

---

[30] I focus on the relationship of joint commitment and rights in a book on rights in preparation, to be published by Oxford University Press.

[31] See Gilbert, "Obligation," and elsewhere.

[32] For discussion of the distinctiveness of these obligations see my article "Agreements, Coercion, and Obligation," *Ethics*, 1993, vol. 103, reprinted with some revisions in *Living*.

[33] I assume here that a rebuke is the after-the-fact correlate of a demand.

I use the phrase "plural subject" as a technical term to refer to those who are jointly committed to X as a body, for some X.[34] Those who are jointly committed to X as a body constitute, by definition, the *plural subject* of X-ing. Accordingly, I shall dub my account of collective belief the plural subject account.

As should be clear from the previous paragraph, I am *not* supposing that those who are jointly committed to X as a body are jointly committed to emulate, as far as is possible, a *plural subject* of X-ing in my technical sense, or, indeed, in any *other* appropriate sense. By definition, they already constitute a plural subject of X-ing, in my technical sense, once they are jointly committed to X as a body.[35]

Those who are jointly committed to X as a body, then, have as their guiding idea that of a single body that Xs. They are to bring it about that, as far as is possible, they emulate such a body. It is up to them to figure out exactly how this may be done.[36]

What the joint commitment requires of each party is that *he should do what he can* to bring it about, *in conjunction with the other parties,* that they emulate, as far as is possible, a single body that Xs. This is likely to involve some degree of monitoring of others' behavior on his part.

My account of collective belief involves a joint commitment to *believe* something as a body. I shall now focus on this particular form of joint commitment.

A joint commitment to believe that p as a body does *not* require each participant personally to believe that p. It would seem to follow from the fact that the requirement at issue is precisely to emulate, as far as is possible, a single body that believes that p. It does not concern any *other* bodies that may bear some relation, however close, to the body in question.[37]

More positively, the joint commitment will be fulfilled, to some extent at least, if those concerned say that p in appropriate contexts, with an appropriate degree of confidence, and do not call p or obvious corollaries into question. Their behavior generally should be *expressive of the belief that p,* in the appropriate contexts. That does not mean, as said, that they must personally have that belief. In other words, this expressive behavior need not be *the expression of a personal belief that p.*

As just indicated, certain contextual conditions are likely to be understood. Thus, for example, members of a seminar on human rights may in the course of a meeting form a joint commitment to believe as a body that the notion of a group right is a viable one. This would involve a requirement to express that belief at least within the confines of the seminar when it is in session. More broadly, it would require that each party express that belief *when acting as a member* of the

---

[34] See Gilbert, *Social Facts, Living,* and other writings.
[35] I emphasize the point in response to various comments.
[36] For more on this see the text below.
[37] See Gilbert, "Shared Values."

seminar. Presumably the parties are not always so acting. If a friend who is not a member of the seminar engages one of them on the topic while they are out on a hike, it would presumably be appropriate for each to speak *in propria persona,* without preamble.[38]

Suppose one is in a context where it is appropriate to act in accordance with a given joint commitment to believe something as a body. It is then open to one to use such qualifiers as "Personally speaking" to preface the expression of a belief contrary to the collective one. This makes it clear that one is indeed now speaking for oneself and not as a member of the relevant collective.

Thus the plural subject account of collective belief accords with the logic of "We (collectively) believe that p" as this is understood in everyday life. In particular, it allows for the possibility that a party to the collective belief aver without fault that he *personally* does not believe that p.

Though such avowals are not ruled out, there is likely to be some cost attached to them. One thereby makes it clear that one's personal view differs from that of the collective in question. Other members may subsequently regard one with suspicion, thinking one more liable to default on the joint commitment, either inadvertently or deliberately. They may begin preemptively to think of one as an "outsider," as no longer "one of 'us.'" If one does default, of course, they have the standing to rebuke one for doing so. All of this accords with Durkheim's perception of "social facts" generally as having coercive power.

It is clear that collective beliefs according to the plural subject account are likely to suppress the development of contrary ideas at both the individual and the collective level. This has many practical implications. For instance, it suggests that groups of researchers in various fields of science are likely to benefit from the less constrained insights of outsiders and neophytes—assuming that these fields involve a collective characterized by a network of collective beliefs. There are, certainly, well-known cases in which the insights of such people have transformed a field.[39]

Further questions

I have offered an account of the phenomenon I take to correspond to everyday ascriptions of collective belief. I have argued that this phenomenon, where it exists, is extremely consequential with respect to human thought and behavior.

[38] On the question of context see also Margaret Gilbert, "Remarks on Collective Belief," 1994, in Frederick Schmitt, ed., *Socializing Epistemology*, Rowman and Littlefield: Lanham, MD (revised as "More on Collective Belief" in *Living*).

[39] For further discussion of the role of collective beliefs in science see Gilbert, 2000, *Sociality*, chapter 3, "Collective Beliefs and Scientific Change," first published in Italian in 1998.

It is, in other words, a highly significant phenomenon. In what follows I shall refer to this phenomenon as *collective belief*, assuming the accuracy of the account.

Is there any reason that the epistemologist should refuse to take collective beliefs seriously? In concluding, I briefly consider three concerns that might be raised on this score.

The first concern goes back to everyday collective belief ascriptions. It was on the basis of a variety of data relating to such ascriptions that an account of collective belief was proposed. The concern runs as follows. Why should the epistemologist take everyday collective belief ascriptions seriously? After all, there are many ascriptions of belief that should not be so treated.[40] Consider the following possibilities. In a story for children a train is said to believe something. A computer user finds himself saying in response to an error message that his computer thinks he is stupid. Someone says of his cat: "She thinks she is the President of the United States."

I agree that many belief ascriptions can be excluded from consideration by epistemologists as not *intended* to be taken seriously or literally. Collective belief ascriptions, in contrast, are commonly made with serious, literal intent. That does not necessarily let them off the hook. As I said at the beginning, they could involve some kind of mistake. That they do involve some kind of mistake, however, needs to be shown.

I suggest that showing it is going to be a harder task than is often assumed. Consider this. A tempting way of arguing that collective belief ascriptions involve a mistake would be to bring up some feature alleged to be essential to belief and to argue that, since so-called collective beliefs lack that feature they are not beliefs—nor, perhaps, can they be counted as any other kind of cognitive state. One who wishes to maintain that collective belief is indeed belief can argue that, on the contrary, if collective beliefs lack the allegedly essential feature of belief, that throws doubt on the claim that this feature is indeed essential to belief.

Another concern that several philosophers have raised both informally and in print is whether collective belief—on the plural subject account—is better thought of as *acceptance* rather than *belief*.[41] I have dubbed this position "rejectionism" and replied to some initial statements of it elsewhere.[42] Discussion on

---

[40] I make this point in response to a query from the developmental psychologist Letitia Nagles in discussion at a University of Connecticut cognitive science colloquium. A related point was brought up by the anthropologist Maurice Bloch in discussion at a roundtable on collective belief held at the Sorbonne, Paris.

[41] See, for instance, K. Bradley Wray, 2002, "Collective Belief and Acceptance," *Synthese*, 129: 319–333; Anthonie Meijers, 1999, "Believing and Accepting as a Group," in *Belief, Cognition and the Will*, ed. A. Meijers. Tilburg University Press: Tilburg. 59–71; also A. Meijers, 2002, "Collective Agents and Cognitive Attitudes," *Protosociology*, 16: 70–86.

[42] See Gilbert, "Belief and Acceptance."

the topic has continued.[43] I shall not attempt to summarize this material here. Indeed, I have not yet had a chance myself to review all of it. Suffice it to say that my own tendency is to go with everyday discourse, as I understand it. If such-and-such a phenomenon is referred to, seriously and literally, as belief, it is hard to argue that it is not, after all, belief as *this is ordinarily understood*. Four related points follow.

First, given that individual human beings differ in important ways from populations comprised of such beings, it is likely enough that collective beliefs differ in important ways from the beliefs of individual human beings. If there are significant contrasts to be made between beliefs of these two kinds, that is certainly worth pointing out.

Second, it is possible that the claim that collective "belief" is acceptance rather than belief could be argued for, given one or more pairs of stipulative definitions for the relevant terms. I have taken the issue to concern the everyday concept of belief whatever precisely that amounts to. It should be noted, in connection with this point, that different philosophers have proposed a wide variety of contrasts between "belief" and "acceptance."

Third, it is interesting to note that many of the features traditionally claimed to characterize belief in general can be argued to characterize collective beliefs. In order to see this it is important carefully to distinguish what is true of the members collectively and what is true of them as individuals.[44]

Fourth, I do not deny that there is such a thing as *collective acceptance* according to the various accounts of acceptance that have been proposed. Though I have focused on collective belief in this chapter, I assume that, generally speaking, there is a collective cognitive state that corresponds to a given cognitive state of individual human beings: we believe, we know, we accept, we doubt, we conjecture, and so on.

The final concern I address here returns us to the question of the relevance of collective epistemology to general epistemology. I proposed that epistemologists should consider what it is for the members of a population collectively to believe something, before settling on a general account of belief. Now it turns out that if I am right about collective belief those who collectively believe something must have the general concept of belief. Is there a problem here?

On the contrary, the plural subject account of collective belief suggests a certain test for an acceptable account of belief in general. Suppose that according to a proposed account of belief in general S believes that p (for any S) if and only if

---

[43] See K. Bradley Wray, 2003, "What Really Divides Gilbert and the Rejectionists," *Protosociology* 17, and related papers, in the same volume, by Christopher MacMahon, Anthonie Meijers, and Deborah Tollefsen. See also Abraham Sesshu Roth, 2003 ms, "Remarks on Collective Belief and Acceptance."

[44] See Gilbert, "Belief and Acceptance."

S Fs (for some particular F). This will be acceptable only if a population whose members are jointly committed to F as a body thereby Fs.

Here is an example of the application of this test. Suppose one holds that S believes that p if and only if S is generally disposed to act as if p is true. Is it the case that a population whose members are jointly committed to be disposed-as-a-body-to-act-as-if-p-is-true is thereby disposed to act as if p is true? If so, the account passes the test in question. That does not mean, of course, that it is the correct account of belief, only that it is consistent with the plural subject account of collective belief. That an adequate account of belief in general is so consistent is quite possible in principle.

Summary and conclusion

I have argued for the importance of collective epistemology both in its own right and in relation to general epistemology. As to the latter, if we are to develop adequate general theories of knowledge, belief, and so on, we need to take the collective versions of these phenomena into account.

Apart from the matter of such general theories, if we are to make sense of the human world, we need to understand the nature and functioning of collective cognitive states as well as the nature and functioning of the cognitive states of human individuals. We also need to understand the relationship between these two types of cognitive states, for example, the ways in which they may influence one another.

In this chapter I focused on the topic of collective belief. I argued against an account that is likely to spring to mind when one first considers the question, and in favor of the account I labeled the plural subject account. This alone satisfies the criteria of adequacy for such an account that I specified.

The subject of collective epistemology is still in its infancy. It is to be hoped that more and more theorists will pay it the attention it deserves, so it grows to maturity.*

* A version of this chapter, "Collective Belief as a Subject for Cognitive Science," was given to the cognitive science group at the University of Connecticut, Storrs, CT, February 14 2003, and to the Roundtable on Collective Belief at the Sorbonne, Paris, April 4 2003. I thank those present for discussion, and Ludger Jansen for some pertinent conversation on a related topic, August 2004.

8

Shared Values, Social Unity, and Liberty

I. Introduction: Shared Values and Social Unity

Shared values are often invoked in contemporary political philosophy.[1] They are invoked in other, less philosophical, contexts as well.[2] What *are* shared values? This is not usually explained with any precision. There are several distinct accounts that might, on reflection, be proposed. Since their implications are quite different, the assessment of any argument about shared values requires a decision as to which account is in question.

One context in which shared values are invoked is in discussion of the question: what creates the kind of *unity* that characterizes a society as opposed to a mere aggregate of individuals?[3] Many people, in different parts of the world, are concerned with what is essentially the same issue. Thus, in 2003, a European journal opined "The real issue for European society is not how to keep new foreigners out but how to integrate the minorities they already have."[4]

Following various authors, this chapter will refer to the kind of unity at issue as *social unity*. The qualifier "social" rather than "societal" will seem particularly apt if one assumes that social groups generally involve a similar kind of unity. This conceives of social groups in a relatively narrow sense, such that typical examples include discussion groups, political parties and labor unions, along

---

[1] A variety of related phrases involving "sharing" are also used more or less interchangeably. Thus in the index of Will Kymlicka's *Liberalism, Community and Culture* (Oxford: Clarendon Press, 1989), p. 280, one finds "shared values *see* conceptions of the good (sharing of)." Phrases with what may be a somewhat broader extension include "shared meanings," "shared sensibilities," and "shared intuitions," all found in Michael Walzer, *Spheres of Justice: A Defense of Pluralism and Equality* (Oxford: Blackwell, 1983).

[2] This would include disciplines such as management science and family studies, and more practical contexts such as that of politics.

[3] This echoes Rousseau's statement of the question at the outset of the *Social Contract*.

[4] "Forget Asylum Seekers, It's The People Inside Who Count," *The Economist* (May 10 2003), pp. 22–24, esp. p. 22.

with those larger, more complex groups for which the label "society" tends to be reserved.[5]

Philosophers have taken up a variety of positions on the relationship of shared values to social unity. Will Kymlicka cites Rawls's claim that "public agreement on questions of political and social justice secures the bonds of association." He then himself asserts that, on the contrary, "shared values are not sufficient for social unity."[6] It is possible, even likely, that the authors who oppose each other on this question are operating with different conceptions of shared values, so that their disagreement is more apparent than real.

Is there a way of *sharing values* such that such sharing is sufficient for social unity? Call this the *social unity* question. This chapter focuses on three accounts of shared values in relation to it.

Two of these accounts are individualistic or what this author has elsewhere referred to as *singularist* accounts.[7] They appeal to nothing other than the beliefs, desires, intentions and so on of single or, in that sense, individual human beings. The third account goes beyond the conceptual scheme of singularism. It incorporates a notion of joint—as opposed to personal—commitment that the present author has invoked in other contexts. This chapter argues that it alone supports a positive answer to the social unity question.

The present discussion will make use of several points made by Lord Patrick Devlin in a well-known lecture delivered in 1959.[8] This lecture has been strongly criticized in certain respects. In relation to the present enquiry it makes several pertinent points of a less contentious nature.

One of Devlin's central theses is the importance of, in his words, a *common morality* to social unity.[9] In a statement akin to that just quoted from Rawls,

[5] Cf. Margaret Gilbert, *On Social Facts* (Princeton, N.J.: Princeton University Press, 1989), pp. 8–10.

[6] See Will Kymlicka, *Multicultural Citizenship: A Liberal Theory of Minority Rights* (Oxford: Clarendon Press, 1995), pp. 187–192. The quotation from Kymlicka is from p. 183. He quotes from John Rawls, *A Theory of Justice* (Cambridge, Mass.: Harvard University Press, 1980), p. 540.

[7] The label "singularism" was introduced in *On Social Facts*.

[8] Devlin's lecture was read at the British Academy on 18 March 1959 as the Maccabaean Lecture in Jurisprudence, and printed in the *Proceedings of the British Academy*, vol. 45, under the title "The Enforcement of Morals." It was reprinted by Oxford University Press in 1965 in a volume of Devlin's essays with the same title, the original lecture being retitled "Morals and the Criminal Law." Page references here are to the 1965 volume.

[9] Devlin himself does not use the term "sharing"; he refers to "collective moral judgments" and to a "common morality." In expressing agreement with Devlin on this particular point, his best known contemporary critic H. L. A. Hart does use the term "sharing": "some shared morality is essential to the existence of any society" (Hart, 1963, *Law, Liberty and Morality*, Stanford, Calif.: Stanford University Press). All of these locutions carry some risk of ambiguity, though some evidently feel that "collective" and "common" are less ambiguous. Cf. Charles Taylor, "Interpretation and the Sciences of Man," in *Interpreting Social Science*, ed. Paul Rabinow and William Sullivan (Berkeley: University

Devlin claimed that, in effect, a common morality *binds people together*. In his sonorous words:

> Society is not something that is kept together physically; it is held [*sic*] by the invisible bonds of common thought. If the bonds were too far relaxed the members would drift apart. A common morality is part of the bondage. (p. 10)

Clearly Devlin does not regard a common morality as the *only* source of the type of binding that he has in mind. He writes, in the above quotation, of the bonds of "common thought."[10] Elsewhere in the lecture he emphasizes ideas political as well as moral. His primary concern was, indeed, with political societies, and, in particular, the England of his time. It would be natural to regard these as involving a multiplicity of common ideas, and hence a multiplicity of factors serving to bind the people together.

Is there any significance in the fact that both Devlin and Rawls refer to "bonds" in this context? One might think that anything that was properly said to unify a number of different people could also be said to bind them together. At the same time, reference to bonds, binding, or, as in Devlin, "bondage," could be intended to have implications beyond that of unification. To put it generally, it could be intended to imply that the way in which people are unified into a society is for some reason particularly apt to be described in terms of bonds.

This chapter considers the social unity question from both of these angles, articulating it now as follows. Is there a way of sharing values such that this can plausibly be said specifically to bind the parties together or otherwise unify them, in a way sufficient for social unity?

II. Shared Values: the Summative Account

i. Preliminaries: Values

Before turning to the accounts of *shared* values that will be interrogated here, something must be briefly said about *values*. For the sake of the argument here it will be assumed that, if someone asks about one's values, they are interested in what one *takes to have value*. In order that one have values, then, one must

of California Press, 1979), p. 51. Taylor writes of "common meanings," which he sees as the "basis of community." Insofar as a common meaning is "shared," he says, "its being shared is a collective act." In other words, common meanings are "shared" in a particular way. In effect, the discussion in the present essay elaborates on the idea that *sharing a value may be a collective act*.

[10] See also Devlin, "The Enforcement of Morals," p. 9: "What makes a society of any sort is community of ideas."

have *beliefs* or *opinions*. More specifically, one must have beliefs or opinions to the effect that some item or items have a certain value. The question about the nature of shared values will then be understood as a question about *shared beliefs or opinions to the effect that some item or items have a certain value.*

Some might prefer to understand a person's values in terms of that person's attitudes rather than their beliefs.[11] There is no reason to think that doing so here would significantly affect the thrust of this chapter.[12] The same goes for other accounts of one's values that might be proposed. The structure of the various accounts of shared values considered in what follows can be carried over, with appropriate substitutions, into accounts adopting other versions of what it is to value something in general.

ii. The Summative Account

The first account that is likely to come to mind when one is asked what it is for people to share a value is as follows:

> The members of a population P *share value V (in the sense of believing that some item I has a certain value)* if and only if all or most members of P believe that item I has that value.

For the sake of a label let us call this the *summative* account. According to the account, to say that the members of a population share a certain value is, in effect, to present a summary of their individual views, namely, all or most of them believe that some item I has a certain value.[13]

The summative account may be found appealing in part because of its simplicity. In addition, it may be hard to think of any other account.

Probably many of those who write about shared values and the like would, if questioned, offer something like this account of them. Some are relatively explicit. Thus, for instance, in the discussion of shared values mentioned earlier, Kymlicka refers to the "convergence" of values and to a shared conception of

---

[11] Cf. Gary Watson, "Free Action and Free Will," *Mind*, no. 196 (1987), pp. 145–172, p. 150.

[12] Pertinent to some extent here is the discussion of collective emotion in, for instance, Margaret Gilbert, "Collective Guilt and Collective Guilt Feelings," *The Journal of Ethics*, vol. 6 (2002).

[13] The label "summative" is taken from Anthony Quinton, "Social Objects," *Proceedings of the Aristotelian Society*, vol. 75 (1975). In previous work, including Gilbert, *Social Facts*, the present author discusses a parallel account of collective belief with a focus on its intuitive plausibility as an account of *collective* belief. The other accounts of shared values considered here also parallel accounts of a group's belief considered in *Social Facts*, chapter 5, and elsewhere, with the same focus. This chapter is more concerned with the consequences for social unity of the phenomenon delineated in a given account.

justice "throughout" a particular community.[14] And in one place Richard Brandt asserts "It seems relatively uncontroversial that for there to be a social moral code of a certain kind is for something to be true of the personal moral codes of the society's members—all of them, or most of them, or on the average."[15]

iii. Devlin on the Summative Account

Before assessing the summative account, it will be useful to turn again to Devlin and spend some time on points he makes that are pertinent to this assessment.

Devlin makes it clear that, for his part, he does not accept a summative account of what he refers to as *common values* or *collective value judgments*. He does not mean to argue, then, that common values in the sense of that account are sufficient to bind people together. He explicitly distinguishes a *collective* judgment from "a large number of individual opinions" with the same content.[16]

In this connection he makes two observations about the situation in which *a number of individuals are of the same opinion*. First: "nine men out of ten may disapprove of what the tenth man is doing and still say it is not their business."[17] Second: "sensible people may even refrain from pronouncing [these opinions] at all"[18]

In other words, many people in a society may personally disapprove of a particular form of conduct, religious, say, or sexual. At the same time, they may not find it appropriate to *express* their views to anyone. Even if they are willing to *reveal* their opinions, they may regard what that person does as *none of their business*.

Devlin appears to have in mind the rejection of something that goes beyond mere censorious judgment, and he adds, in his own voice: "Without a collective judgment there can be no case for intervention." How are we to construe "intervention" in the present context?

Devlin would surely include as interventions *rebuking* others for certain actions and, in advance, *demanding* that they act in a particular way. If one thinks something is "none of my business" one will not act in such ways. In what follows such rebukes and demands are taken as paradigmatic *interventions*.[19]

---

[14] Kymlicka, *Multicultural Citizenship*, p. 188. Taylor, "Interpretation," writes "we can speak of a shared belief...when there is convergence between the subjective beliefs...of many individuals." However, as what he goes on to say indicates, it is possible to construe "shared belief" differently, or, in other words, there are different ways of sharing belief.

[15] R. B. Brandt, "The Concept of a Moral Right and its Function," *The Journal of Philosophy*, vol. 80 (1983), pp. 29–45, p. 32.

[16] Devlin, "The Enforcement of Morals," p. 8. Though Devlin himself does not write "with the same content," his intention is clear from the context.

[17] Ibid.

[18] Ibid.

[19] This chapter makes no attempt to say more about what something's being one's "business" might amount to. So far it appears to be at least a necessary condition for appropriate intervention. It

Devlin says that without a collective judgment "there can be no case" for intervention. To say that there can be no case for performing action A suggests that there can be no reason to do so. In the present context, however, Devlin should be taken to be talking about *standing*: without a collective judgment, others lack the standing to intervene. If one lacks the standing to do A one is not yet in a position to do A. In that sense, therefore, "there can be no case" for one's intervening.

On this understanding, Devlin is suggesting, then, that when values are not common one lacks the standing to intervene in the behavior of others. When they are common, one has such standing. How might common or in some sense shared values give those who share them the standing to intervene in one another's lives?

One possibility, evidently, is this. Shared values involve a type of binding such that each of those who are bound together *thereby* have the standing to intervene when any one of their number acts contrary to the shared value. That the values are shared thus makes any one participant's actions "the business" of the others.

III. Interlude on Intervening

Does one have the standing to intervene in another person's life merely by virtue of the fact that, in one's own estimation, someone is acting in a morally bad way?[20] The question can initially be elaborated in terms of two imaginary dialogues. Assume that Anne has just witnessed Ben, who is a stranger to her, doing X. Anne believes that doing X is morally wrong, and is addressing Ben in a tone of rebuke.

In Dialogue 1, Anne implicitly justifies her rebuke by alluding to the fact that *she believes that doing X is morally wrong*. It is perhaps unlikely that anyone would do this, but let us see how this case plays out.

---

may or may not be a sufficient condition as well. The best interpretation will depend upon the answer to that question.

[20] This calls to mind some of J. S. Mill's discussion in *On Liberty*. I say more about this later in the text. Related points are made in some more recent discussions. In "Is There a Right to Do Wrong?" *Ethics*, vol. 92 (1981), pp. 21–39, Jeremy Waldron distinguishes between "moral guidance" and "coercive interference" in the face of another's moral wrongdoing. Waldron proposes that another's "right to do wrong"—a general right for which he argues—would preclude the latter, though not the former. See, especially, pp. 38–39, also p. 30. Roger Wertheimer, "Constraining Condemning," *Ethics*, vol. 108 (1998), pp. 489–501, argues that "the propriety...of wrath toward the wrongdoer may be tenuous if our relation to the situation is" (p. 499). See also A. J. Simmons's "Justification and Legitimacy," *Ethics*, vol. 109 (1999), pp. 739–771, which, in opposition to a standard practice of political philosophers, plausibly distinguishes between the moral attractiveness or *justification* of a given state and its right to, among other things, "coerce noncompliers" with its laws, that is, its *legitimacy* in a Lockean sense.

Dialogue 1:

Anne (in a tone of rebuke): "I think that doing X is wrong!"

Ben (skeptically): "You are entitled to your own opinion. However, how does your being of that opinion entitle you to tell me off?"

In the absence of further information bearing on the situation, one might find Ben's response quite reasonable. At the same time, it may be observed that Anne is more likely to put things more objectively: not in terms of *her opinion*, but in terms of *what is the case morally speaking*. This brings us to Dialogue 2.

Dialogue 2:

Anne (again in a tone of rebuke): "Doing X is wrong!"

Ben (skeptically): "Supposing for the sake of argument that you are right, how does that entitle you to tell me off?"

Does Anne have a convincing reply to Ben's skeptical response here? Or is it the case that, without further information, we must allow that even though X is indeed wrong, Anne *does not have the standing to* rebuke Ben for doing X or to demand of him, in advance, that he not do X? Call the claim that it is *the no-standing claim*.

It is worth noting precisely what this claim amounts to. Given that, in Anne's eyes, Ben's doing X would be morally wrong, she may wish to consider *how she might act so as to bring it about that Ben refrains from doing X*. She will presumably need to consider, with respect to those things it is in her power to do, which are morally acceptable for her to do. According to the no-standing claim, assuming there is no further information that bears on the case, there is at least one thing it is not in her power to do, for *she is not in a position to do it*. In particular, in the situation as described the fact that Ben's doing X is or was wrong does not suffice to put her in that position. She is not in a position to *demand* of Ben that he not do X or *rebuke him* for doing X, for *she does not have the appropriate standing in relation to Ben*.

She can, of course, pretend or purport to have that standing. She may say, demandingly, "Don't do X," or she may speak reprovingly to Ben: "How could you have done X!" This brings us back to the foregoing dialogues. According to the no-standing claim, Ben would not be mistaken in arguing that she lacks the standing to reprove him, or to demand of him that he not do X.

Can he grant her that standing? It is consistent with the present point to allow that he can. That will, however, be up to him. The no-standing claim raises an important question. One might formulate the issue in general terms as follows. If one has the standing to make demands on a person or to rebuke them, it must come from somewhere. So, where?

The following may usefully be noted in the context of the present discussion. Anne and Ben were described as strangers. Two people could be strangers in an everyday sense yet known to one another to be members of the same club, for instance. They could be strangers in the sense that they have never met face-to-face before or otherwise interacted with one another. Meanwhile club membership might in some cases be intuitively sufficient to ground the standing to rebuke for immorality in general. Thus consider a club that describes itself as follows: "Our goal is to prevent immoral action."[21] Or particular kinds of immorality, at least, might be taken care of in this way, as with the club whose stated goal is the prevention of cruelty to animals. If, therefore, one phrases an inquiry into the no-standing claim in terms of "strangers" in some such everyday sense, one will need to bring in qualifications as to the lack of further factors bearing on the case. This has been my procedure here, and will be in related contexts in the text below.

For present purposes there is no need to pursue the no-standing claim beyond this point. Its main interest in the context of this chapter is as follows. Devlin suggests that there is a way of sharing values such that this provides people with standing to rebuke one another for behavior contrary to those values. This would be particularly *important* from a practical point of view *if* the no-standing claim were correct. Shared values would then provide people with a basis for intervention in the life of another person that was not available on the basis of that person's wrongdoing alone, and they may well wish to have such a basis.

IV. The Summative Account Assessed

Returning to the summative account of sharing values, let us start with a new question. Does the fact that people share values in the sense of the account *bind them together in such a way that they gain the standing to intervene when one of them acts contrary to the shared values*? Devlin thinks not, and that seems right.

It may be observed that to share values with someone in this sense is not necessarily to know that one does. Suppose, though, that Anne comes to know that she and Ben, a stranger, share a certain value in this sense.

Consider Dialogue 3:

Anne (in a rebuking tone):You think that doing X is wrong, and so do I.
Ben:You're right about me. It's interesting that you are of the same opinion.
I fail to see, though, how either of these things, or their conjunction, entitle
    you to tell me off for doing X!

---

[21] Someone may propose that *all or most human beings* are the members of just such a club, or, in other terms, constitute a *moral community*. This chapter will not attempt to evaluate this proposal, which clearly needs some unpacking. It is clearly germane to the evaluation of the no-standing claim. But see the next paragraph in the text.

Failing further information on the case, it is hard to see what Anne can say to convince him. In short, it is hard to see how sharing values or the summative account brings people together in such a way that it gives each the standing to intervene when any of them acts contrary to the value in question.

Does sharing values in the sense of the summative account *bind people together* in any other way? It seems not. More specifically, no constraints on a given party with respect to the other parties seem automatically to be involved in such sharing. One pertinent consideration is this. Suppose that Sylvia and Maureen share some value in this sense. Perhaps each believes that it is good to impose the death penalty for certain crimes. As far as this supposition goes, either can *change her mind* on the relevant matter as and when it pleases her to do so. Neither is *bound to the other* in the sense that she needs her permission to change her own mind. One may wonder, indeed, whether such binding would make sense. After all, one's beliefs are liable simply to change in the light of considerations that strike one as relevant.

What kind of *unity*, if any, do people have through sharing values in the sense at issue? If two or more people each have a certain view they have, evidently, a degree of qualitative identity. In general however, such identity provides human individuals with only a superficial kind of unity, if it provides them with anything that is properly viewed as a kind of unity at all. To use a phrase from Hume, one might say that if the only way certain people share a value is in the summative sense, their views are still "entirely loose and separate" from each other. And so, as far as that goes, are they.

Of course, people may be drawn together when they realize that they value the same thing or things. Sharing values in this way may be a basis, and a good basis, for people to come together or stay together in some more substantial way: to become friends, for instance, or to marry. It may, indeed, be a necessary condition of the most stable, solid kind of unity.[22] But that is not to say that sharing values in the sense under discussion has *already* brought them together in any such way.

Suppose that those living on a particular island all have a distinctive moral opinion, an opinion, perhaps, that nobody anywhere else holds. Perhaps each believes that it is evil to eat leafy green plants. It might be quite natural for an observer to lump these people together in thought and refer to them by a common name, "leafers," say. At the same time, the simple fact that each of these people holds this moral view is not something that—without more—shows that they are bound together or unified in more than the superficial sense of having the same opinion.

---

[22] See Margaret Gilbert, *Living Together: Rationality, Sociality, and Obligation*, chapter 8, "Fusion: Sketch of a 'Contractual' Model" (Lanham, Md.: Rowman and Littlefield, 2000).

It may be reasonable to suppose that these people all make the same moral judgments on these cases by virtue of the fact that have interacted in certain ways, and so on. Indeed, it may be reasonable to suppose that they are bound together or unified in some substantial way. But there is nothing in the logic of the case that requires this.

Quite possibly these people don't interact, or not much. There may be families among them and interaction between the members of these families but otherwise little or no interaction within the population at large. And the moral judgment they share, in the sense we are looking at, could be shared for reasons having nothing to do with interactions between members of the wider population. Perhaps all of the leafy green plants on the island are delicious but tend to produce highly unpleasant temporary effects once they have been eaten. Each island dweller has, consequently, learned from personal experience, or that of his or her family, to leave these plants alone. Over time, the original reason for avoiding the plants has been forgotten, and each island dweller has come to believe simply that eating leafy green plants is evil. Clearly, this could happen without the leafers interacting with one another beyond the boundaries of individual families. Even if the convergence in the leafers' moral views occurred through a variety of inter-familial interactions, this would not necessarily be enough to bind all of the islanders together or otherwise unify them in a substantial way.

It follows from the above considerations that those like Kymlicka who deny that shared values are sufficient for social unity are right, *if shared values are construed according to the summative account*. Shared values in this sense unify only in a superficial way—in the sense of qualitative identity. This kind of unity may tend to promote a more substantial kind of unity. It cannot, however, plausibly be claimed of itself to bind the participants together, or otherwise to be enough to constitute a social group as opposed to a mere aggregate of persons.

V. Adding Common Knowledge

Is there some relatively small amendment that might transform the summative account so that it characterizes a way of sharing values that binds those involved together, thereby creating a substantial kind of unity? Can a small amendment provide grounds, perhaps, for the claim that those who share values thereby gain the standing to intervene when one of their number acts contrary to the values in question?

A relatively small but significant addition to the summative account would be a condition of "common knowledge" of the type introduced into the philosophical literature by David Lewis. To put this informally, we could stipulate that *it is entirely out in the open among the members of the relevant population* that everyone has certain values in common. Let us call the resulting account the *complex summative* account.

The addition of common knowledge to a situation in which the conditions of the summative account obtain would be quite consequential. Where it is absent, those who share values in the sense of the simple account might be loath even to express their views publicly, let alone interfere with another for acting against the value in question. For instance, they may fear that they are alone in having the value in question, and that they will be thought ridiculous or simply to be in error and viewed with suspicion for that reason.

Once the fact that all have the *same* value is out in the open, this fear will most likely vanish, and each will be able comfortably to express the value without fearing that they will provoke disapprobation or even discomfort in the others.

Suppose, now, that our friends Anne and Ben—still strangers to each other—share a value in the sense of the complex account. Both think that doing X is wrong and this is common knowledge between them. Does the existence of this complex state of affairs, without more, give Anne the standing to intervene if she finds that Ben has done X?

It is hard to see that it does. Though the common knowledge itself may seem to connect the parties together in a more substantial way than does their simply having the same values, it does not appear to give the parties *a new basis for intervening*. Further, people who share values in this sense are more connected than those lacking the relevant common knowledge, all else being equal, but they are not *bound together* in any obvious way, any more than in the summative case. Finally, such sharing is not intuitively sufficient for *social unity*.

VI. The Plural Subject Account of Shared Values

This section presents an account of shared values that differs from the foregoing summative accounts in significant ways. For one thing, it does not have at its core a set of individual valuings, as do the summative accounts. For another, the summative accounts appeal to nothing but the beliefs, desires, and so on, of individual human beings. They are in this sense individualistic or, in my terms, *singularist* accounts. This account is not.

As we shall see, this account of shared values is such that they *unify* and, indeed, *bind together* the participants *in such a way as to justify interventions*. Moreover, in order to understand this, the parties need do no more than understand that the conditions of the account are fulfilled. This chapter will not attempt to argue this, but it is plausible that no form of summative or singularist account will have these features.[23]

Here, in terms to be shortly explained, is the account:

> The members of a population P *share value V (in the sense that they share the belief that item I has a certain value)* if and only if the members of P are jointly committed to believe as a body that item I has that value.

The key idea here for present purposes is that of joint commitment.[24]

i. Joint Commitment

The phrase "joint commitment" is used in a sense the author has developed elsewhere. In order to clarify that sense it will be useful first to say something about another kind of commitment.

If Anne makes a decision, she has made a commitment. She may change her mind, of course. Her commitment is then at an end. She has, in effect, rescinded her commitment. Let us say that one is subject to a *personal* commitment if and only if one is subject to a commitment that one has created for oneself and is in a position to rescind unilaterally.

The broad notion of *commitment* as it is understood here, then, is not automatically *social* in that a given person's being committed must implicate other people. Nor is it automatically *moral* in that one is only committed if there are some weighty reasons for acting in the way at issue. One may make a particular decision lightly, for no particular reason. (For instance, one's eye lights on a particular shirt and one decides to wear that shirt today.) One is then committed

---

[23] This would seem to be true of Michael Bratman's recent account of shared valuing ("Shared valuing" [2002 MS] presented at the Collective Intentionality Conference III, Rotterdam, December 2002). This account is not summative but is singularist. It involves, roughly, a generalized personal commitment to give weight to a given value in deliberations within the group in question. The relationship between his account and the one to be elaborated in the text below is quite interesting. When the conditions posited in the latter account hold, central conditions in his do also. James Lenman (personal communication, May 15, 2003) suggested a complex summative account such that—he proposed—parties to a shared value would have the standing to intervene when one of their number acted contrary to that value. Roughly, this adds to the original summative account the shared (in a summative sense) acceptance of a norm, N, that any member of the population in question may rebuke any other member for acting contrary to value V, and so on. Setting aside the question whether the parties here do indeed have the standing to intervene—which can be doubted—sharing values in this sense does not intuitively produce a substantial kind unity, or bind the parties together.

[24] For further explanation see Gilbert, *Living Together,* Introduction, and, most recently, Margaret Gilbert, "The Structure of the Social Atom: Joint Commitment as the Foundation of Human Social Behavior," in *Social Metaphysics,* ed. Frederick Schmitt (Lanham, Md.: Rowman and Littlefield, 2003).

to acting in light of the decision unless and until one changes one's mind. A personal decision gives a special type of commitment. One might refer to it, for the sake of a label, as a *commitment of the will*.[25] Joint commitments, also, are of this type.

What, then, of *joint* commitments? To start with a negative point, a joint commitment is not a sum or aggregate of personal commitments. The joint commitment of Anne and Ben does not have as components Anne's personal commitment and Ben's personal commitment. Rather—to continue with a positive point—this commitment is the commitment *of Anne and Ben. It is theirs.*

One aspect of this jointness is as follows. Absent special background understandings, neither party is in a position unilaterally to rescind the commitment. It can only be rescinded by the two of them together. Of course each one is capable of *violating* the commitment without the concurrence of the other. What one cannot do alone is rescind the commitment so that violation is no longer a possibility.

To say that a joint commitment is not a sum of personal commitments is not to deny that those individuals who are party to a particular joint commitment are committed by it. Once a joint commitment is in place—how this comes about will shortly be described—each of the parties is subject to it, and in that sense committed through it. Each is committed to do what he or she can so that the joint commitment is fulfilled. This does not amount to each one's having what is here called a personal commitment since, among other things, a personal commitment is unilaterally rescindable by the person whose commitment it is. Since Anne cannot rescind the joint commitment she has with Ben, she cannot rescind the commitment she herself has through it.

All joint commitments are of the same form. X and Y (and Z and so on) are jointly committed *to do something as a body.* Here "doing something" is construed broadly enough so as to include believing that such-and-such and feeling thus-and-so. What is it to do something "as a body"?

The joint commitment in the case we are considering is a commitment to believe as a body that some item I has a certain value, v. This would be achieved by each of the committed parties doing such things as: confidently stating that item I has value v; refraining from calling this or its obvious corollaries into question; suggesting by actions and emotional expressions that item I has value v; not, therefore, acting contrary to the shared value, nor reporting such contrary actions with bravado. Thus, were each of the parties the mouthpiece or representative of a single person, one would judge that single person to believe that

---

[25] For further discussion see the present author's "Towards an Account of Commitments of the Will: The Nature and Normativity of Intentions and Decisions" (2004 MS) to appear in *Patterns of Value II*, ed. Wlodek Rabinowicz and Toni Ronnow-Rasmussen.

item I had value v. To put things more abstractly, those who participate in a joint commitment to believe as a body that some item I is of value v are committed together to emulate, as far as possible, a single person—a single body—who believes that item I has value v. Alternatively, their commitment is together to emulate, as best they can, a single person who believes item I is of value v.

The context in which a joint commitment arises is relevant to its precise implications. Consider the members of a committee, call it committee A. Suppose that in a meeting of this committee the members jointly commit to believing as a body that some item I has value v. Failing rescission of the commitment, each committee member will now be committed to confidently stating, without preamble, that item I has value v, and so on, not in all contexts but rather in a limited set of contexts. One might roughly specify these contexts as those in which these individuals are acting as members of committee A. Obviously relevant contexts are the rest of the current meeting of committee A and its subsequent meetings.[26]

One has an option of clarifying the context in which he is speaking by using certain preambles. Thus suppose Peg, a member of committee A, is also a member of committee B in which the members are jointly committed to believe as a body that item I lacks value v. In a session of committee A she might preface a derogatory remark about item I with "Speaking as a member of committee B,..." She would thus make it clear that she was not speaking as a member of committee A. It would then be inappropriate to judge her post-preamble "...item I lacks value v" as if she were speaking as a participant in the joint commitment linking the members of committee A.

A point that may need emphasis is this: those who are jointly committed to emulating, as far as is possible, a single person who believes that p are not individually committed to believe that *p* themselves. That may be just as well, insofar as it is at best not easy to bring it about that one believes something. Some have been inclined to deny that one can believe something "at will," though one might be able to manipulate one's circumstances in such a way that one comes to believe it.

There are various reasons for accepting this point about the joint commitment in question apart from the fact that it is at best not easy to believe something at will. Primary, perhaps, is the fact that the idea of a given person who believes that p does not seem to have anything to say about the beliefs of anyone or anything other than *that person*. To echo Gertrude Stein: Jill's belief is Jill's belief is Jill's belief; it is not the belief of any other person or body. To amplify the point, suppose someone claims that Jill believes that it is raining. The fact that Jill's toe does not believe it is raining or—to be fanciful—that Jill's

<hr/>

[26] For an example involving a more informal situation than a committee meeting see Gilbert, *Living Together.* pp. 353–354.

toe believes it is not raining would not, surely, militate against the truth of this. Jill is one thing, her toe is another. Similarly, the single person or body we are committed together to emulate, as far as possible, is one thing. Each of us is another.

Another consideration is this. When in everyday life, people talk and think about what *we* believe, as they often do, the idea that these people are parties to a joint commitment together to emulate a single person with the belief in question seems to explain a number of related phenomena. These include the kinds of offended responses that follow if one of us baldly gainsays what we believe.[27] In these contexts, meanwhile, people seem willing to accept that, for any one of us, *our* believing that p is compatible with *my* not believing it, or *my* believing that p is not the case. This is indicated by their acceptance without similar offense of such statements as "I realize that the department, of which I am a member, is against this, but, speaking personally, I am still convinced it a good thing."[28] In order to capture what people have in mind in these everyday situations, one's account of the joint commitment in question must allow that one may conform with the commitment while personally not believing that p. As it is understood here, a joint commitment together to emulate, as far as possible, a single person that believes that p satisfies this constraint.

Given the present specification of the joint commitment at issue when people share values, it is clear that, from a logical point of view, a number of people can share a value on the account now in question without personally espousing that value. Indeed, even were one to suppose that, in general, a joint commitment to believe that p as a body *committed* the participating individuals to believing that p, people could be jointly committed to believe as a body that item I is of value v without believing that item I is of value v. For one can be committed without having yet managed to fulfill one's commitment.

As an empirical matter, conforming participation in the joint commitment here in question will presumably have some tendency to produce corresponding personal values. Again, corresponding personal values will help to give rise to the relevant joint commitment.[29]

---

[27] See the text, below, on how appeal to a joint commitment can justify offended responses.

[28] On the use of the qualifier "personally," see also Margaret Gilbert, "Modeling Collective Belief," *Synthese* (1987), reprinted in Gilbert, *Living Together*. On the contingent dangers of expressing a personal view contrary to that one is jointly committed with certain others to believe as a body, see Gilbert, "Collective Belief and Scientific Change," in *Sociality and Responsibility: New Essays in Plural Subject Theory* (Lanham, Md.: Rowman and Littlefield, 2000).

[29] Amplification of the points in this paragraph is to be found in several places including Gilbert, *On Social Facts,* and *Living Together,* chapter 7.

ii. Joint Commitment Formation

How are joint commitments formed? In order that Anne and Ben become jointly committed it is clearly not enough for each of them to make a personal decision, form a personal plan, espouse a particular value, and so on. Only a sum of personal commitments would emerge from that. What, then, would suffice to create a joint commitment?

It is sufficient for the creation of a joint commitment between Anne and Ben if the following conditions hold. Ben has expressed to Anne his readiness *to be jointly committed* in the relevant way. This, in effect, is to make it clear to Anne that all that is required for them to be thus jointly committed is for her to do likewise. Anne does likewise. And these things are common knowledge.

The creation of a joint commitment is therefore quite strongly analogous to the creation of a personal commitment through a decision. One might bring out the analogy as follows. In the latter case, the party in question may be thought of as, in effect, issuing to him- or herself an edict of the form: I am to do X. In the case of joint commitment, the parties in question may be thought of, likewise, as jointly issuing to themselves, considered "as one," an edict of the form: We are to do X. A single person can issue such an edict by means of his own thought alone, without saying or communicating anything to anyone else. In the case of something that can plausibly be thought of as the joint edict of two or more parties, however, more than a concurrence of private thoughts is required.[30]

In the case of large populations people will not so much make it clear to particular individuals that they are ready jointly to commit with them, as make it clear to particular individuals that they are ready to commit with them—and the relevant others—insofar as they fit some general description, such as "person living in such-and-such a geographical area." In this way it can become common knowledge that all in a certain geographical area have expressed their readiness to be jointly committed in a certain way with the others. This is sufficient, as they understand, for the formation of the relevant joint commitment.

In the case of joint commitments to believe that some item I has value v, how might these be formed in a concrete case? In a face-to-face interaction it is enough for this type of interchange to take place: Anne says "Ugh!" gesturing toward the behavior of a certain person. Ben nods, as we say, in agreement. This type of interchange is standardly interpretable as the proposal and acceptance of a joint commitment to believe something, whether or not it can at the same time be construed in other ways as well. Such proposals need not be verbal. Anne might turn up her nose, raise her eyebrows, or behave in other ways endorsed by her interlocutor. The parties may be known to each other personally or rather responding to one another as members of a particular group or large population.

---

[30] Cf. Gilbert, "Obligation and Joint Commitment," *Utilitas* (1999), reprinted in Gilbert, *Sociality*.

iii. Plural Subjects

People can be jointly committed in a variety of ways. That is, they can be jointly committed not only to believing as a body that such-and-such, but also to accepting or pursuing a goal as a body, to accepting as a body that A is to be done in circumstances C, and more. In my technical terminology those who are jointly committed to X-ing as a body constitute the *plural subject* of X-ing.[31] Hence the account of shared values that just presented may be labeled the *plural subject account* of shared values.

The present author has argued in *On Social Facts* that a variety of central everyday concepts of social phenomena are plural subject concepts. More specifically, everyday references to *our* beliefs, goals, intentions, language, conventions and rules are standardly interpretable as references to the beliefs and so on of a particular plural subject, namely, *us*. There is no space to repeat these arguments here. If their conclusions are right, however, it would not be surprising that references to "our values" and the like often had this connotation. That this is in fact so is suggested by Devlin's pronouncements on the subject, among others. For, as will be argued below, Devlin's pronouncements can all be justified in terms of a plural subject account of our values.

iv. The Plural Subject Account and Devlin on Collective Moral Judgments

Devlin proposed that that if there is a collective moral judgment, as opposed to a sum of personal moral judgments, other members of the relevant population have the standing to intervene—with rebukes, for instance—if one acts in a way that is incongruous with that judgment. He does not attempt to explain what collective moral judgments amount to except in a negative way. A plural subject account would justify his proposal, and would also render plausible the idea that shared values are constitutive of societies, unifying and, indeed, binding the members together. Arguments for these points follow.

Those who are jointly committed are clearly unified in a way that goes substantially beyond any unity bestowed by having the same values. Each is subject to a commitment that each understands to be joint. This joint commitment appears by its very nature to unify them and in that sense bind them together. It—one and the same commitment—holds sway over each of them.

In addition, without the concurrence of the others no one can unilaterally dissolve the commitment in question. Each is, therefore, not only unified and in

---

[31] The author first used the phrase in this sense in Gilbert, *On Social Facts*.

that sense bound together with the others, but also bound to that union subject to the approval of the rest.[32]

This last point is of considerable practical importance. Though commitments need not ensue from weighty reasons, they are standardly understood to "trump" mere inclinations in at least the following way: *violation* of a standing commitment is not excused or justified by saying "I didn't feel like it."[33] So each is "pinned down" by all in a practically significant way.

Further, even if certain reasons may excuse one's violating a joint commitment, the commitment gives the other parties the standing to intervene, if they wish, should one violate it or threaten to do so.

Consider that a joint commitment in which I participate is precisely not *my* commitment or *his* or *her* commitment but one of which each of the parties can say it is *ours*. If I violate our commitment, rather than my own, each of the other parties has a special standing in the matter. Each has, one might say, a lien on my will with respect to a certain range of actions.

Through the joint commitment I am committed to doing what I can to satisfy the requirements of the joint commitment as best I can. If fail to do this, I am answerable to each of the others for this failing. Any one of them is in a position to demand an explanation. More, in face of threatened failure, each of them is in a position to demand that I act in conformity with the commitment.

After the fact, each is in a position to rebuke me for non-conformity. Each can say: actions of a certain kind were due to me, as a party to the joint commitment. Absent this joint commitment, and any others with overlapping requirements, you were free to do as you pleased in these respects, at least in the sense that no other person had a relevant lien on your will. Given our commitment, you were no longer free in this sense. In violating it, you have offended against each of us in his capacity as a party to the joint commitment.[34]

So far the following points have been made about the relationship of the plural subject account of shared values to assertions made, but not explained, by Devlin. By virtue of the underlying joint commitment, those who share values on the plural subject account are (a) unified in a relatively substantial way, (b) in an important sense bound to this union, and (c) possessed of the standing to intervene in one another's lives in related respects. For instance, they have the standing to rebuke one another for action that contravenes the joint commitment.

---

[32] Depending on the content of the commitment, someone may undergo a change such that he or she no longer falls under the description specified for the parties of a given joint commitment. For instance, the joint commitment of the inhabitants of a certain island, as such, will not apply to one who leaves the island. This type of situation is not supposed to be ruled out by the remark in the text.

[33] Of course, not feeling like it might lead you to change your mind, in the case of a personal decision, and to seek the concurrence of the other parties, in the case of a joint commitment.

[34] For further discussion idea see Gilbert, "Obligation."

It may be helpful to note that not all of the actions for which the parties to a joint commitment have the necessary standing in relation to one another have the unpleasant punitive or coercive flavor of rebukes and demands for compliance. For instance, the parties also have the standing to commend one another for conformity to the commitment in difficult circumstances.[35]

A joint commitment not only gives the parties the standing to intervene in the behavior of others with rebukes, demands, commendations and so on. Any commitment is in an important sense reason-providing.[36] Thus, insofar as such interventions will help to bring about the satisfaction of the commitment, a joint commitment gives the participants a reason for intervening.

Such interventions will, in other words, be required by the commitment in these circumstances. Failures to express useful rebukes, demands and so on would then amount to contraventions of the commitment. As with all such contraventions, these might be excusable in the circumstances but would be open to the usual type of reaction. Thus one person's failure to engage in relevant interventions could justify such "meta-interventions" as: "Aren't you going to say anything?" "How could you not say anything when she...?"

v. Shared Values and Social Unity

What, finally, of Devlin's suggestion that the unification and, indeed, binding together of persons that sharing values effects is the unity and binding constitutive of a society or other social group? This suggestion accords with the argument in *On Social Facts* that there is a central sense of the everyday phrase "social group" such that social groups are plural subjects.[37] For present purposes the following point may be made.

The common ideas that a society or other social group as opposed to a mere aggregate involves the unification, indeed, the binding together, of a number of individual persons is acceptable given a conception of social groups as plural subjects whose unity is the unity of joint commitment. There may be other ways of giving substance to this idea—that there are not is something of which one can hardly be certain—but an understanding of social groups as plural subjects is certainly one such way.

---

[35] This remark responds to a comment from Jennifer Nadelsky, Toronto, October 4, 2003. It is perhaps more compelling to focus on less pleasant aspects of the situation because people are more likely to object to purported rebukes without standing than to purported commendations. In Devlin's case, his ultimate interest was of course with the scope of the criminal law, in other words, in the standing to punish.

[36] On commitments as reason-providing see Margaret Gilbert, "Agreements, Coercion, and Obligation," *Ethics* (1993), reprinted in Gilbert, *Living Together.*

[37] See Gilbert, *Social Facts*, chapter 4.

The plural subject idea of a social group is, to be sure, a relatively narrow one. The term "social group" may be used of those who are not unified in any substantial sense. It may be used, for instance, of populations individuated by reference to their members' possession of some salient common feature: hemophiliacs, for instance, or the elderly.[38] Clearly, however, thinkers who affirm the unity of a society, the group-constituting nature of "social bonds," the difference between a society and a mere aggregate of persons, and so on, have a narrower notion in mind.

Assuming, then, a plural subject account of social groups, we have an answer to the question: is sharing values sufficient for social unity? The answer is yes—*if sharing values construed according to the plural subject account.*

It seems that the sharing of but a single value in the plural subject sense would be enough to unify the individuals in question socially. They would then, after all, be subject to a joint commitment with all that implies. It is perhaps unlikely in practice that a single value will be all that is shared in the plural subject sense, but there are real cases where a group is characterized in terms that suggest that the sharing of one predominant value is its core.[39] Consider, for example, the pro-choice lobby, the National Rifle Association, or the peace movement.

To say this is clearly not yet to consider precisely what serves to keep a given social unit together, to consider, that is, the question of stability. Given a single collectively shared value, the creation of further such values or other joint commitment phenomena will presumably enhance the stability of a given social unit. This chapter says more about this below.

As noted, there is reason to think that a plural subject understanding of what it is to share values corresponds to a standard everyday construal of references to "our values" and the like. It certainly accords with Devlin's sense of this matter, and this is presumably not entirely idiosyncratic.

For the sake of a label, let us now refer to values shared in the sense of the plural subject account as *collectively shared* or more briefly *collective* values. The rest of this chapter notes and briefly addresses some important aspects of the collective sharing of values.

---

[38] Of course, such so-called social groups or populations, including those mentioned in the text, may have further important features in common by virtue of their possession of the feature by means of which the population is singled out. The life course of those in such a population may be affected in gross and similar ways by virtue of their possession of the relevant feature. They may, for instance, be discriminated against by some or all of those who lack the relevant feature. They may have particularly pressing special needs. That this is so does not of itself necessarily *unify* the individuals in question rather than making their individual lives have further important commonalities.

[39] "Shared in the plural subject sense": as yet uninterpreted talk of *sharing* values, beliefs, goals, intentions, emotions, and so on is all open to a plural subject interpretation just as it is open to a summative interpretation and others.

VII. Collective Values and the Freedom of the Person

Collective values unify the participants in a substantial way, and insofar as such unity has positive aspects, they may be regarded as valuable properties of human populations. They may be regarded as valuable properties of human populations for other reasons also. One such reason is as follows. In Durkheim's terms, each and every collective value will serve to reduce the amount of *anomie* in a given society.[40] It will provide members of the society with a framework for their own life choices, choices they can expect to mesh with those of other members. Each member will not only expect this but understand that he is in a position to demand it of the others, should he so wish.

This section reviews some important aspects of the analytical relationship of collective values to something else that has been considered an important societal value, liberty, or *personal freedom*. For present purposes assume that one's personal freedom is diminished to the extent that one is pressured or liable to be pressured by one or more others to act in certain ways, irrespective of one's own stance with respect to those ways of acting. The personal freedom at issue here is that of those with a particular collective value: they will be referred to in what follows as the *parties* to that value.

i. The Prior Freedom of the Parties

As to what might be called the "prior freedom of the parties," one cannot assume of any given party that he or she *freely embraced* the values in question as collective values. One may come to participate in a joint commitment to believe as a body that something is of value without having much real choice in the matter.

Suppose, for example, that one's parents, powerful figures in one's eyes, speak with great despite of a particular type of person. Perhaps they utter with relish certain racist remarks. One might, of course, go ahead and question these remarks. But clearly one is under some psychological pressure not to do so. In a given case one may know that questioning one's parents leads to all kinds of punitive reactions, some quite severe. The same goes for the pronouncements of teachers, political leaders, and so on. If all of these are in accord, expressing their readiness to jointly commit with you to believe that members of a certain race are inferior, and holding ready relatively severe punishments if you refuse their offers, you will have to be quite a forceful character to go ahead and refuse to participate, assuming that you understand that you have reason so to refuse.

---

[40] In his classic work, *Suicide*, sociologist Emile Durkheim suggested that "anomie" or the relative paucity of established guides for action in a society was positively correlated with the amount of suicide in that society.

If one sincerely expresses one's readiness jointly to commit with these others, one becomes jointly committed. To say that one's expression is sincere is not to say that one must believe that the collective is correct in valuing whatever it is. It is simply to say that one is genuinely ready to enter the relevant joint commitment. And one may be, in circumstances of strong pressure, among others.[41]

The sense in which collective values must involve the prior freedom of the parties is, therefore, minimal. One may come to participate in collectively valuing something with others, in circumstances of strong pressure. In expressing one's readiness to participate, one does intentionally express what may be referred to as a *state of one's will*—one is, after all, ready to participate. This is the minimal sense in which one must be free to participate in collective values.

ii. The Posterior Freedom of the Parties

What of the "posterior freedom of the parties" once a given collective value is formed? This chapter has emphasized that each now has the standing to pressure the others to act appropriately to the collective espousal of the value in question. The parties are therefore continuously liable to experience interventions from others that they cannot rebuff as coming from those without the appropriate standing. In other words, if for its existence a society requires collective values—or other phenomena founded in joint commitment—membership in a society automatically involves a loss of personal freedom.

One can bring this point to bear on ideas expressed in Mill's classic essay *On Liberty*. Mill there proposed a "very simple principle"—the harm principle—that he felt would be upheld in all societies properly referred to as *free*. According to Mill's principle, and roughly, the only thing that could justify the criminalization of behavior or informal punitive pressure (such as informal rebukes) was that behavior's harmfulness to people other than the agent.[42]

In light of his principle, Mill strenuously objected to the punitive actions of those he sardonically referred to as the "moral police."[43] He had primarily in

---

[41] For amplification on this point see Gilbert, "Agreements."

[42] Though this point is not pressed in the present essay, it is very plausible that rebukes are informal analogues of legal punishments. It is clearly endorsed by H. L. A. Hart, *The Concept of Law* (Oxford: Clarendon Press, 1961). Both informal rebukes and legal punishments raise the question of *standing*. This does not tend to be discussed in the philosophical literature on punishment, perhaps because the focus is on *justification*, which is a distinct question. The question of standing is more likely to be addressed under the rubric of political authority or political obligation. (Cf. Simmons, "Justification.")

[43] J. S. Mill, *On Liberty*, Hackett, p. 82.

mind self-appointed individual enforcers of morality *as the majority of individu-als personally saw it.*[44]

Could he object in the same manner to punitive actions on behalf of *col-lectively shared* moral values? He does not approach this question. That is, he does not ask what would be the case if moral values were shared in the plural subject sense.

In developing his *harm principle*—as it has come to be called—in chapter 4 of *On Liberty*, Mill elaborates on what counts as harm. It is the violation of a "dis-tinct and assignable obligation."[45] If a person violates an obligation to you, that takes that action out of the self-regarding class. The kind of obligation he has in mind includes that created by business contracts and informal agreements, both of which create obligations that are "assignable" to particular persons. It seems also to be the kind of obligation created by collectively shared values.

This chapter argued earlier that the parties to a joint commitment can prop-erly be said to *owe each other* actions that conform to the commitment. In the case of a collective value, they owe each other, among other things, actions that respect that value. In this sense, at least, action inappropriate to a collective value violates a distinct and assignable obligation.[46]

If this is right, then Mill would have to admit that action inappropriate to a collective value constitutes harm to the other parties to the relevant joint com-mitment, so that—all else being equal—it could justify punitive pressure. In other words, in Millian terms, a society that enforced its collective moral values could still be deemed a *free* society, in not yet contravening the harm principle.

iii. The Morality of Enforcement

It is appropriate immediately to say something about the morality of the enforce-ment of collective values. The point emphasized here is analytical rather than moral: questions concerning the morality of the enforcement of collective val-ues go beyond the analytical aims of this chapter.[47] Evidently, the fact that one has the *standing* to pressure others for acting in disregard of some value does not entail that one should exert such pressure all things considered. Nor does the fact that one has *reason*, by virtue of a commitment, to do it. One may have

---

[44] Cf. his reference to those who "make *their own personal feelings* of good and evil, if they are *toler-ably unanimous* in them, obligatory on all the world" (p. 82, my emphases).

[45] Mill, *On Liberty*, p. 79.

[46] See Gilbert, "Obligation."

[47] A classic debate relating to the morality of criminalizing behavior contrary to collective values is that involving Hart and Devlin. See Hart, *Law, Liberty, and Morality*; Devlin, "The Enforcement of Morals."

reason, but other reasons may make it clear that one should not act accordingly, all things considered.

One question here is how to treat those who live "in" a society but are not "of" it, in terms of being parties to the joint commitment in question. This is an important question in practice, but it can be set aside here. Even if there are no such people in a given case, the question of when punitive pressure is justified all things considered, and what kind of pressure is appropriate, remains.

Mill would presumably say the same for those actions that came within the scope of his harm principle. If more harm than good to society and its component individuals would be achieved by seeking punishment for those who had trespassed beyond the acceptable bounds of liberty, it could be argued in utilitarian terms that they should not be punished.

Deciding to put the weight of the criminal law behind a collective value judgment is clearly a major step in terms of external pressure on an individual—a major blow to personal freedom. As Mill emphasized, other institutional and more informal pressure can also be consequential. Hence there is need even in informal contexts to examine the merits of making authoritative demands or engaging in punitive action when action contrary to a collective value is in question. Should we collectively value, initially and perhaps for the duration, the gentlest means of bringing each other on course with respect to our collective values as such—including this one? Should we completely eschew even informal demands and rebukes in the matter of action contrary to these values? Whether or not those with the standing to intervene should exercise it, all things considered, and how they should do so, are important normative questions.[48]

VIII. Collective Values in the Life of a Society

This chapter has argued that a collective value is in principle enough to unify people into a social group as opposed to a mere aggregate. It would seem that such values are not necessary, however, for social unity. A plural subject, founded in a joint commitment, need not be the subject of values as opposed to other beliefs, rules of the fiat form, and so on.

Thus a group of roommates may adopt a set of "house rules" but little in the way of collective values or goals beyond what might be implied by those rules themselves, if anything. Some may personally see the justification of a given rule one way, some another. A larger population may adopt a set of rules, laws, or a constitution, in the same way.

[48] For an important scholarly discussion of rules regarding how to "command right" and "forbid wrong" in one religious tradition, see Michael Cook, *Commanding Right and Forbidding Wrong in Islamic Thought* (Cambridge: Cambridge University Press, 2000).

Devlin recognized that collective moral judgments were not the only factors binding people together into a society. He spoke of "common thought" in general as what was needed, collective moral judgments being only "part of the bondage." Nonetheless, as he recognized, collective moral values, and collective values more generally, are liable to be an especially powerful component of collective life.

Suppose, for instance, that the roommates are jointly committed to upholding as a body a non-smoking rule. Should they add to that a joint commitment to the belief that smoking is an *evil* practice, they can now do more than rebuke one another because, as they may say, "You have broken our rule!" to one they find smoking. They can rebuke the rule-breaker in terms appropriate to the collective value in question. In this case they can say, of what the rule-breaker is doing "That's evil!" The same goes for sexual practices, religious views, fashions in dress, and so on.

Collective moral judgments as to the evil nature of certain practices may well enhance the life of a community and its members insofar as *the judgments are correct.* If some practice is indeed evil, it is more likely to be rooted out, and the community and its inhabitants the better for it. Insofar as *the judgments are incorrect,* however, they may themselves be the agents of evil, causing untold pain and suffering. And, of course, they help to constitute not a wise society, but an ignorant, perhaps a culpably ignorant one. As is clear from the above, though people are in one sense bound to uphold their collective values, being jointly committed to do so, there may be weighty moral reasons not to uphold them, or reasons to attempt to change them.

Whether or not one mourns the passing of a particular collective value or set of values will depend on various things. One may have a tendency to nostalgia, or be inherently conservative. One central reason for mourning the passing of some value or set of values, however, will surely be one's sense that these were the correct, genuine, or true values.

That these values are *our* values, now, is clearly no guarantee that they are correct or genuine, insofar as there is such a thing as a correct or genuine value. Collective values do change, and in retrospect progress is often deemed to have been made. Does this mean we should rein in our collective valuings? Certainly the personal freedom of each one of us would to that extent then be enhanced—but the costs to this must be reckoned also.[49] This chapter has shown that these questions press on the parties to one or more collective values—whatever these values are.

---

[49] Related thoughts are developed in Margaret Gilbert, "Can a Wise Society be a Free One?" *Southern Journal of Philosophy* vol. 44 (2006), pp. 1–17.

IX. Summary and Conclusion

Shared values are frequently invoked in political philosophy, but the nature of shared values is generally taken for granted and not explained. This chapter has presented and explored three accounts of shared values in relation to the social unity thesis. One, the plural subject account, supports a number of related points suggested by Lord Patrick Devlin: sharing values unifies people, it binds them together, and it provides them with the standing to intervene in one another's lives. Shared values in the sense of the plural subject account were labeled *collective* values, to differentiate them from shared values in other senses. The kind of unity in question comes at a cost to the personal freedom of the individuals so unified, since it gives each of them the *standing* to intervene in the lives of the others.[50]

[50] Versions of this chapter have been presented at the University of Connecticut, Storrs; the Seminar on the Political Economy of War and Peace at Columbia University; and the University of East Anglia in 1999; at the Technical University of Dresden in 2000; at Yale University; the University of California, Berkeley; M.I.T.; and the University of Toronto in 2003; and at SCASSS, Uppsala; Stockholm University; Lund University; and the University of Copenhagen in 2004. I am grateful for the probing comments I have received from many members of these different audiences. Thanks to James Lenman for extensive discussion and to Paul Bloomfield for helpful comments. The paper was completed while I was a Fellow at the Swedish Collegium for Advanced Study in the Social Sciences (SCASSS) in the spring semester, 2004. I am most grateful to the Collegium for its generous hospitality, and to the University of Connecticut for granting me a leave of absence that semester.

9

Social Convention Revisited

1. Introduction

What is a social convention? This question arises in many fields, among them law, economics, and other social sciences. It received a detailed treatment in David Lewis's book *Convention: A Philosophical Study*. Since its publication in 1969, Lewis's account of social convention has been influential. Many theorists have endorsed accounts that retain one or more of its central elements.[1] Most have also retained one particular aspect of Lewis's account: its individualism. An account that is individualistic in the sense I have in mind makes reference only to the personal inclinations, expectations, commitments, and so on of individual human beings.[2] A non-individualistic or holistic account is not limited in this way.

The account I have developed is holistic in that it crucially appeals to a concept of joint commitment that is not reducible to facts about what the individuals in question are personally committed to. The present discussion compares and contrasts my account of social convention with Lewis's.[3]

It may be observed that Lewis describes himself as seeking an account of "our common, established concept of convention."[4] Neither here nor elsewhere, as far as I know, does he write of "social" convention. Moreover, he aimed to contribute to our understanding of the conventionality of language—of the fact, in

---

[1] See, e.g., Schiffer (1972), Burge (1975), Schotter (1981), Miller (1992), Marmor (1996), Millikan (1998). Lewis tells us that the game-theoretical side of his own account was inspired by Schelling (1960). Indeed, Schelling came close to a Lewisian account of social convention, associating "institutions and traditions" with "coordination games" (1960, p. 91).

[2] In Gilbert (1989a) I used the technical label "singularist" instead of "individualistic" as I am construing that here.

[3] I have previously published several discussions of Lewis's work, including criticisms of several of his game-theoretical points. See, e.g., Gilbert (1974, 1981, 1983a, b, 1984, 1989a: Ch. 6, 1989b, 1990). This chapter draws on some of this material but makes no attempt to encompass it all. My own account of convention was first presented in Gilbert (1989a, Ch. 6). It is more finely articulated here.

[4] Lewis (1969, p. 3).

one description, that "[w]ords might be used to mean anything."[5] On the face of it, this is not a specifically social matter.[6] Be all that as it may, the sample conventions Lewis presents, and much else besides, suggests that his quarry is indeed a common, established concept of social convention.[7] I shall myself often write here of "convention" rather than "social convention," for brevity's sake.

Lewis sees himself as having described "an important phenomenon" whether or not any established concept applies to it.[8] He doubtless thinks that conventions in his sense are ubiquitous phenomena that play an important role in human life. He would also presumably say that they are apt to play such a role, however ubiquitous they actually are. The latter type of importance is evidently the easiest to gauge prior to empirical investigation.

Not unreasonably, Lewis sees exploration of "our common, established concept" as one way to arrive at the description of an important phenomenon. Perhaps, though, "not all of us do share any one clear general concept of convention."[9] What then? Even if a theorist does not capture a universally shared pretheoretical concept, he (or she) may articulate a central one.[10] This too may well pick out something of importance.[11]

In what follows I first offer some starting points about social conventions in what I take to be a—if not the—central everyday sense.[12] They derive from the way people think and talk about convention in the course of their everyday lives. An adequate account of convention in the sense in question will explain these points. I argue that my account of convention does better than Lewis's in relation to this particular explanatory project. I conclude by discussing the relationship of the phenomenon described by my account to that described by Lewis's.

[5] Lewis (1969, p. 1).

[6] Such conventionality can be seen as a matter of the sound-sense links or conventions incorporated in a given language considered as an abstract system of rules. On the face of it, a single individual can adopt such a convention for his private use, as in a diary, including his use on a single occasion. See Gilbert (1983a). Also Gilbert (1989a, pp. 385–390).

[7] The sample conventions are at Lewis (1969, pp. 42–51)

[8] Lewis (1969, p. 3).

[9] Both of the preceding quotations are from Lewis (1969, p. 3).

[10] Instead of "pretheoretical" I sometimes use the adjectives "intuitive" and "everyday" in roughly the same sense. For something to be "intuitively" the case, as I use the term, is for it to be true given the intuitive concepts in question. No unusual faculty of "intuition" is implied, nor is it implied that "commonsense" views on empirical matters are authoritative.

[11] As Lewis indicates, even one person's idiosyncratic concept may do this. (1969, p. 3). He has larger hopes. Thus Lewis (1975) argues that some putative counterexamples to his account fail because we may say the phenomenon in question is a "convention" by virtue of the more or less close relationship in which it stands to conventions in his sense—it is apt to become such a convention, for instance.

[12] Cf. Gilbert (1989a, Chap. 5). Here I emphasize an important point not mentioned there.

2. Starting Points on Social Convention

2.1. Social Conventions Are "Our" Conventions

In everyday speech people say such things as: "The convention in this department is that we dress formally for department meetings"; "Our convention is more complex"; "Jane and I often eat out together. We need a convention as to how we split the tab." Conventions in the sense at issue, then—for short, now, "conventions"—may be said to be "in" groups such as academic departments, which may be said to "have" them, and whose several members may refer to them as "ours."

Conventions may also be ascribed to two or more particular individuals considered together—to "Jane and I," and so on. Such individuals, also, may refer to their conventions as "ours." I refer to the group members or the individuals in these cases as the "parties" to the convention.

2.2. They May Be Instigated by Agreement—or Not

Two or more people may adopt a convention by means of an agreement. Thus Julia may say "I suggest we adopt the convention that…" and her friends respond "Agreed." At this point, Julia may truly say: "Our convention is that…" One of Lewis's main aims in developing his account of convention was to show how people could come to have a convention without having adopted it in this way—as they surely can.

2.3. They May or May Not Offer Specific Protections

Consider Lewis's drivers who: "…are driving on the same winding two-lane roads…. if some drive in the left lane and some in the right, everyone is in danger of collision."[13] One can imagine one of these drivers truthfully saying, of himself and the others, "Our convention is that we drive on the right." (This is most likely, I think, in the absence of a law to the same effect.)[14] The convention he speaks of presumably serves to prevent many crashes, injuries and deaths.

Other conventions do not offer the parties such obvious, specific protections or benefits.[15] Consider a department's convention that people dress formally for

---

[13] Lewis (1969, p. 6).

[14] Precisely what a law amounts to is a matter of great debate within jurisprudence. For some brief remarks on the topic that relate it to my account of convention see Gilbert (1989a, 405–407). See also Gilbert (2006a, Chap. 9).

[15] By "specific" protections, etc., I mean those that are provided by a particular convention rather those that would be provided by any convention whatsoever. I say this mindful of the proposal in Durkheim (1951) to the effect that a certain critical mass of social conventions and the like is necessary to the human individual's well-being.

department meetings. It may be hard to argue that there needs to be any particular dress code for these meetings, or that anyone thinks this is so. Perhaps one member suggested the convention as a matter of caprice, and others, feeling concessive, agreed to adopt it. Perhaps, prior to that, no one cared how anyone dressed. They simply had no interest in the matter. As I now explain, the violation of even such a convention can have significant consequences for the violator.

2.4. One Party's Non-conformity Offends Against the Others: The Offense Criterion

Suppose Molly is a member of the department just imagined. I take it that if Joe, another department member, turns up for a meeting in a tee-shirt and shabby jeans, Molly may well react negatively to his behavior. I have a particular negative reaction in mind, whose specifics will play an important role in the argument of this chapter. Molly may well judge that Joe has offended against her in her capacity as a party to the convention. As a result, she may give Joe a look of rebuke or speak to him in a rebuking tone.

I take it that whether or not Molly does this, or is justified in doing so, all things considered, she is in a position to do so, since, as she judges, Joe has indeed offended against her.[16] If she does rebuke him, she may appropriately cite the fact that the department has this convention as a complete justification for the rebuke—which is not to say that it justifies it all things considered.

Generalizing: if one party fails to conform to a given convention, this offends against the other parties, as such. They are then in a position to rebuke him for this failure, and may appropriately cite the fact that their group has the convention as a complete justification for their rebukes. Conventions, then, are clearly forces to be reckoned with at least because they lay each party open to the rebukes of the other parties if he fails to conform.

If all this is granted, we have a fairly demanding criterion of adequacy for an account of convention: the account must explain how, for any convention, the non-conforming action of one party offends against the other parties, as such, who are for this reason in a position to rebuke him, their having the convention being a complete justification for the rebuke. I shall call this the offense criterion.[17]

---

[16] Clearly I do not think that everyone is in a position to rebuke any given person as and when they have reason to respond negatively to what that person has done. People may sometimes speak of "rebukes" when what is at issue is only purportedly a rebuke in the sense I have in mind. The terms "order," "command" and "punish" are similar in this respect. Cf. Gilbert (2006a, pp. 4–5).

[17] I say more about what I take offending against to be when discussing how Lewis's account fares in light of this criterion.

3. Lewis on Social Convention

What is the relationship between conventions-according-to-Lewis—for short, "Lewisian conventions"—and conventions according to the everyday concept of convention I have just characterized—those I am referring to simply as "conventions"? In particular, are the conditions necessary and sufficient for Lewisian conventions also necessary and sufficient for conventions? If they are not necessary, are they at least sufficient?

There are reasons for giving a negative answer on both counts. Before discussing this, I briefly review the nature of Lewisian conventions, drawing on Lewis's "first, rough definition" of convention and on later discussion that adds a "common knowledge" condition.[18] For present purposes it suffices to say, roughly and informally, that there is common knowledge in population P that p when and only when it is entirely out in the open among the members of P that p.[19]

According to Lewis, roughly:

> a regularity R in the behavior of members of a population P when they are agents in a recurrent situation S is a convention if and only if in any instance of S among members of P it is both true and common knowledge in P that

(1) everyone conforms to R,

(2) everyone expects everyone to conform to R,

(3) (a) everyone prefers that any one more conform to R, on condition that all the others do, and (b) there is another regularity, R*, such that everyone prefers that any one more conform to R* provided everyone else conforms to that. In Lewis's phrase, S is a "coordination problem."[20]

Several questions of interpretation arise. I briefly discuss four here.

First, what is a regularity? I once asked Lewis this question. He replied "a regularity is a pair of properties."[21] Accordingly, I shall take it that a given regularity R can be abstractly represented as "phi-ing in situation S" (or more abstractly

---

[18] Lewis (1969, p. 42) (the first rough definition); pp. 52–57 (common knowledge—in itself a major contribution to philosophy).

[19] Vanderschraaf and Sillari (2007) carefully review several accounts of common knowledge, including that in Gilbert (1989a).

[20] On difficulties with the precise interpretation of Lewis's "coordination problem," see Gilbert (1981). Lewis ultimately relaxes the universal quantifications within conditions (1) through (3) (1969, pp. 76–80). In this article, for simplicity's sake I present both his and my account of convention in what might be referred to as their "ideal" versions.

[21] Probably circa 1980.

as "phi in S") where phi-ing is a type of action (for instance, driving on the left) and S is a type of situation.

Second, situation S is said to be "recurrent": this could simply be emphasizing that situation S is a type of situation—which may have several tokens or instances. Or it could be intended to imply that situations of type S "recur" in P, perhaps frequently.[22] However the question is resolved, the account of convention presented above requires that there is a type of situation S and a type of action phi-ing, such that whenever an instance of S occurs among members of P every member of P phi-s.

Third: what is a "population"? I take it that a given population may be fully characterized by reference to the possession of a particular feature or features by its members—as in "those who live north of the Equator"—or by reference to the particular members as individuals—as in "Peter, Paul and Mary."

Fourth: what is it for one to "prefer" one outcome to another? In the context of Lewis's discussion I take one's preferred outcome to be "the resultant of all the more or less enduring forces that go into determining his choices."[23] In other terms, the outcome that he ranks most highly—all things considered. In my own discussion here I shall adopt this construal of "preference."

4. Critique of Lewis

What, then, is the relationship between Lewisian conventions and conventions according to the everyday concept of convention now in question?

4.1. None of Lewis's Conditions Are Necessary

Must any of Lewis's conditions (1) through (3) be fulfilled with respect to a regularity R in the behavior of a population P in order for R to be P's convention? For present purposes, the following example may suffice to cast doubt on the necessity of any one of them.[24]

I imagined earlier that at a meeting of Molly's department someone suggested the department adopt the convention that members dress formally for

---

[22] In Gilbert (1983b) I reported the impression from Lewis's discussion as a whole that in clear cases at least the situation in question occurs fairly frequently among members of P, and offered a counterexample to this position. See also Gilbert (1989a, pp. 326, 344–346).

[23] Lewis (1969, p. 93).

[24] These points hold, mutatis mutandis, for the version of Lewis's account in which the universal quantifications within conditions (1) through (3) are relaxed. For further discussion see Gilbert (1989a, Chap. 6) and elsewhere. Other critics of one or more of Lewis's conditions include Schiffer (1972), Jamieson (1975), Robins (1984), Miller (1992), Marmor (1996), Millikan (1998).

department meetings, and everyone explicitly concurred with the suggestion. As noted earlier, Molly could at once appropriately say: "our convention is that we dress formally for department meetings." This would seem to be so irrespective of whether anyone has yet conformed to it, and irrespective of whether it is in some sense true that whenever there is a department meeting the department's members conform to it.

Further, it may not be true that whenever a department meeting is upcoming, everyone expects that everyone conform to the convention. Knowing her colleagues well, Molly predicts that few will dress formally at the next meeting. Jack will want to upset people by dressing very informally, contrary to the convention. That's the way he is. Joe has nothing but shabby jeans in his wardrobe and will probably not get round to buying something special for some time, if he ever does. He will apologize, perhaps, but still not conform to the convention. Kate will probably forget to conform to the convention, though she will be disappointed to have done so when she realizes what has happened. Dave may forget—or he may intentionally conform to the convention; it is a toss-up what he will do. He tends to have his mind on other matters. Most others either have no particular expectations about who will conform to the convention and who won't, or their expectations are in line with Molly's, who will herself conform because she wishes to respect the fact that the department has, indeed, adopted this convention.

As to condition (3), this has two parts or sub-conditions, both of which must be satisfied for condition (3) to be satisfied. I focus on condition (3) (b). In my first description of the situation in which Molly's department had a convention—a description that did not seem to be self-contradictory—this condition was not satisfied. It seems, then, that it is not a necessary condition on convention.

It is true that the sample convention on which I am focusing has a special origin which is not necessary to conventions in general: its existence depends on its adoption by means of an agreement.[25] Nonetheless, there can certainly be such conventions, and it is possible that none of Lewis's conditions are satisfied with respect to them. It cannot be said that Lewis himself had no interest in this type of case. He was expressly concerned to give an account of convention "in its full generality."[26]

Possibly the convention envisaged here will not last long in the imagined circumstances. Nonetheless it is hard to doubt that it exists, and that it can exist without any of Lewis's conditions (1), (2), and (3), being satisfied.

---

[25] That is, an agreement proper as opposed to something akin to one.

[26] Lewis (1969, p. 3). Lewis's discussion of the relation of conventions to agreements comes after and presupposes his account of convention. See the text, below.

4.2. Lewis's Conditions Are Not Sufficient

Given that none of Lewis's conditions are necessary, are they jointly sufficient? In discussion elsewhere I focused on two reasons for thinking they are not.[27] These reasons constitute, in effect, two further criteria of adequacy for an account of convention. I review them briefly before turning to the offense criterion, on which I focus here.

4.2.1. The Appropriate-"Ought" Criterion

Intuitively, if something is our convention, then for that reason, all equal, I ought to conform to it, and this will be apparent to me and the other parties.[28] I take it that to say that I "ought" to conform, all equal, is to say that I have reason sufficient to mandate action in the absence of overriding considerations to the contrary. In short, I have sufficient reason to conform.[29] What mandates action here is rationality in a broad intuitive sense such that it is a matter of responding appropriately to relevant considerations. For short, it is a matter of reason-responsiveness.[30]

Now, one can infer that something ought to be done on a variety of bases. When the considerations in question are moral ones, the "ought" is sometimes said to be the "moral ought," and so on. An adequate account of convention will positively and convincingly characterize what we may pretheoretically dub the "ought" of convention. In other terms, it will explain the normativity of convention. Call this the appropriate-"ought" criterion.

Lewis says that "according to our common opinions" one who is party to a convention in his sense ought to conform to it, all equal: for it answers both to his own preferences and to those of the others involved.[31] Let us allow that this is so. This may, then, be an "ought" associated with some conventions and appreciated by at least some parties to some such conventions.

It is hard to see, however, how it can be the "ought" of convention, given that a convention can exist in the absence of an underlying coordination problem structure of inclinations or Lewisian preferences. This leaves open, of course, the precise nature of the "ought" of convention, something of which I say more in due course.

---

[27] Gilbert (1989a).

[28] See Gilbert (1989a, pp. 349–351).

[29] Care is needed to distinguish one's having sufficient reason for acting a certain way from one's having reasons for such action. See Gilbert (2006a, Chap. 2).

[30] I deliberately avoid saying "reasons-responsiveness." See the previous note.

[31] Lewis (1969, p. 97).

4.2.2. *The Collectivity Criterion*

Intuitively, if the members of a population, P have a convention, they thereby constitute a collectivity or social group in a central, relatively narrow, intuitive sense—the sense represented in many of the lists of social groups offered by social scientists and others, where a typical list might include families, discussion groups, and sports teams. They might of course have constituted a collectivity on other grounds, before developing the convention. If this were not the case, they constitute one now. One feature of the collectivity so constituted—perhaps its most salient feature—is that it has the convention.

One might think this point was already implicit in the starting point listed earlier to the effect that social conventions are "our" conventions.[32] In any case I take the point about collectivity to be fleshing that starting point out in acceptable way.

I take it, then, that an adequate account of convention should be such that its proposed conditions on convention are sufficient for collectivity-hood in the relevant sense. Call this the collectivity criterion. I have argued elsewhere that it is not satisfied by Lewis's conditions on convention.[33]

The point that conventions are essentially collectivity-constituting has been questioned by Andrei Marmor.[34] He argues that many conventions "cut across societies and cultures." There surely is a sense in which many conventions do cut across societies and cultures. It is less clear that this militates against the idea in question. Suppose that many societies have the convention that men wear trousers and women wear skirts, where "trousers" and "skirts" are defined by some rough and ready physical parameters. In that sense, then, this convention "cuts across" all the pertinent societies. This supposition allows that there is more than one society, however, and that each society has the convention. There is nothing here, as yet, that refutes the proposed collectivity criterion.[35]

With respect to his own example of a "cross-cutting" convention, Marmor asks: "Does it make sense to suggest that by complying with this convention, all of us become a collectivity?" This question is not clearly to the point. One

---

[32] See Gilbert (1989a, Chap. 4).

[33] Gilbert (1989a, pp. 355–361).

[34] Marmor (1996, p. 360). Unless otherwise noted my quotations from Marmor come from this page. He raises other questions about my 1989a discussion of convention. I cannot attempt a full response here: some of the points made may nonetheless be pertinent. The same goes for some other critical discussions e.g. Latsis (2005).

[35] Marmor's own example of a "cross-cutting" convention is this: "in most cultures the sign of an arrow is a conventional means of pointing to a certain direction in space." It is not clear that whatever is properly referred to as a "conventional means" of doing something is associated with a convention of the type I am focusing on. The same goes for linguistic, notational, and signaling conventions. Though there may be a version of Marmor's example that would clearly address the point at issue, I focus on a different example in the text.

may understand compliance with a given convention as a matter of generally conforming to a particular regularity in Lewis's "pair of properties" sense.[36] In proposing the collectivity criterion I did not mean that those who generally comply with a given convention in this sense thereby constitute a collectivity. Rather, members of a population that has a convention thereby constitute a collectivity. That is not, of course, to say what it is for a population to have a convention.

4.2.3. The Offense Criterion

There are still other problems with Lewis's account with respect to the sufficiency of its conditions, some of which will be mentioned later.[37] I focus here on the offense criterion.

Suppose that in June's department Lewis's conditions on convention are fulfilled with respect to the regularity of dressing formally for department meetings. Now suppose that June fails to dress formally for today's meeting. Will Bob, another department member, appropriately feel offended against, and does he consequently have the standing to rebuke her? I suggest that he will not, given only the situation as described so far.

He may reasonably be surprised, even disappointed. After all, June acted contrary to his personal preferences. He may have reason to judge her to have acted badly. After all, she acted contrary to most people's preferences. Nonetheless, she has not offended against him in such a way that he now has the standing to rebuke her for doing so.

When, one might ask, has one person offended against another, in this way? I propose that X has in the relevant sense offended against Y by failing to phi on some occasion only if X owed Y his phi-ing on that occasion, where one who is owed an action is in a position to demand it as in some sense his.[38] One who was owed an action that has not been performed on the pertinent occasion is therefore in a position to rebuke the one who failed to perform it, a rebuke being the after-the-fact counterpart to a demand.

There is reason to think that the standing to demand an action is quite generally the standing to demand it as (in the pertinent sense) one's own. In that case

[36] Marmor may not mean this; but it is a natural way to construe what he says.

[37] These problems include the intuitive relation of convention to agreements, rules, and arbitrariness.

[38] Another way of saying that X owes Y his phi-ing is to say that Y has a right against X to X's phi-ing. For further discussion see Gilbert (2004), which critiques the account of promissory obligation in Scanlon (1998) as not explaining why the promisee has a right against the promisor to performance. Since a right can be waived, I do not say that X has offended against Y if X owed Y his phi-ing, etc.

one way of specifying the kind of owing at issue is simply to say that one who is owed an action is in a position to demand it.[39]

One might wonder under what circumstances, precisely, such owing occurs. For now the question to be addressed is whether it occurs, in the right way, when Lewis's conditions on convention are satisfied. I should explain why I have just said "in the right way."

Some philosophers argue or simply judge that if one person is about to violate a moral norm or principle, all others have the standing to demand that he does not violate it; they also have the standing to rebuke him if he violates it.[40] I am doubtful of the truth of this.[41] Even if it were true, however, that would not help Lewis's account of convention.

Suppose for a moment that the point about moral norms is right. Suppose, further, that failing to conform to a Lewisian convention is failing to conform to a moral norm (however that might be argued). Then non-conformity offends against everyone, not just the parties to the convention. Suppose that it does. That does not speak to the intuitive point that drives the offense criterion: non-conformity offends against the parties to the convention as such. If you like, they have been offended against in a special way. In other terms, there is a particular, special right here, a right of each party to the convention, as such, against every other party as such. I propose that Lewis's conditions on convention do not have the resources to explain this: in the example Bob is not in a position to demand June's dressing formally

5. A Radically Different Account of Social Convention

I turn now to the radically different account of convention first presented in *On Social Facts* and more fully elaborated here. It does well according to the various criteria of adequacy mentioned so far, and more also. It is worth listing several of its significant features at the outset.

First, it is a holist or non-individualist account in the sense introduced earlier. In particular, it crucially appeals to a concept of joint commitment that is not reducible to facts about what the individuals in question are personally committed to. Perhaps I should add, in order to defuse immediate concerns about the philosophical acceptability of this crucial concept, that it does concern what the individuals in question do in relation to one another, and how that affects

---

[39] I write of "the kind of owing that is at issue here" to make it clear that people including philosophers use the words "owe," etc., in a variety of senses. For what appears to be a different use to that at issue here see the title of (and elsewhere in) Scanlon (1998).

[40] Cf. Darwall (2006) who cites others with similar views.

[41] See Gilbert (2005) for some discussion.

them. In short, there is nothing "supraindividual" in a metaphysically questionable sense about this idea. Second, the account eschews the austere conceptual palette of game theory.[42] Third, it includes none of Lewis's three central conditions, positing neither conformity, nor expectations, nor a coordination problem structure at the level of personal inclinations or Lewisian preferences. Fourth, it concerns commitments of the kind I have elsewhere labeled "commitments of the will."[43] A familiar example is the commitment made when one makes a personal decision.

I turn now to the details of my account. I originally proposed that a social convention was a jointly accepted fiat.[44] I am ready still to phrase the account in terms of joint acceptance, as long as that is understood in terms of joint commitment as follows:

> Members of a population, P, jointly accept a given fiat if and only if (by definition) they are jointly committed to accept as a body that fiat.[45]

Some immediate explanation of the technical terms in the definiens are in order.

What is joint commitment? I have written extensively on this topic elsewhere, and cannot attempt a full exposition here.[46] I hope that the following points will be helpful. They concern in particular the founding of a basic case of joint commitment.[47]

A joint commitment is to be contrasted with both a single, personal commitment and a conjunction of personal commitments. A personal commitment, such as that created by a personal decision, is created by one person who is in a position unilaterally to rescind or cancel it. In contrast, a joint commitment is created by two or more people, neither of whom is in a position unilaterally to rescind or cancel it. One's participation in a given joint commitment commits

---

[42] As indicated earlier, there is reason to understand Lewis's account in such reductive terms.

[43] See e.g. Gilbert (2006a).

[44] Gilbert (1989a, p. 377f).

[45] I now prefer to couch my accounts of various social phenomena in terms of an underlying joint commitment, whose content varies with the phenomenon in question. See Gilbert (1996, pp. 7–9). This both usefully "regiments" the accounts and facilitates explanation of the normativity of the phenomenon at issue. In my original proposal about convention joint commitment was not mentioned though it had been introduced within a long prior discussion at Gilbert (1989a, p. 198).

[46] Some relatively detailed sources are Gilbert (2003) and Gilbert (2006, Chap. 7). This is not to say that I have covered all aspects of the matter or that those I have covered cannot be further clarified.

[47] The non-basic case depends on a basic joint commitment authorizing a given person or body to create new joint commitments for the parties. See Gilbert (2006a, Chap. 7).

him to promote its fulfillment in conjunction with the others, but this commitment of his is not personal in the sense just noted.

Two or more people are needed in order to create a conjunction of personal commitments: each must commit himself. In the case of a joint commitment, all commit all. In order that this happen, each must express to the others, in conditions of common knowledge, his readiness to participate with the others in committing them all—perhaps under some general description such as "person driving on this island." All need to participate, likewise, in rescinding or otherwise concluding the commitment.

The expressions of readiness may be verbal or not, clear as the day or quite subtle. They may take place in a one-shot face-to-face interaction or, rather, over a longish period of time.[48] The latter process is most likely in a large population.[49] As I understand it, an everyday verbal agreement is one way to create a joint commitment. I say more about this later.

Moving on to the content of the joint commitment in question here: what is it to accept some fiat as a body?[50] Briefly, the parties must emulate, as far as possible, a single body or person who accepts the fiat in question—call it "F." Conformity to F, except in special exculpating circumstances, is understood to be a major part of what it is incumbent upon each to do in order to conform to this joint commitment.

Having explained how the joint commitment construal of joint acceptance is to be understood, I now offer an account formulated somewhat to echo Lewis's:

> A population P has a convention of conformity to some regularity in behavior R in situations of type S if and only if the members of P jointly accept, with respect to themselves, the fiat: R is to be conformed to.

I add the clause "with respect to themselves" to indicate that the fiat is understood to apply to members of P as such. It is not held to be universally applicable. The expanded version (in terms of joint commitment) runs:

> A population P has a convention of conformity to some regularity in behavior R in situations of type S if and only if the members of P are jointly committed to accept as a body, with respect to themselves, the fiat: R is to be conformed to.

---

[48] For an example of the generation of a jointly accepted fiat that involves a number of stages see Gilbert (1989a, p. 398). On the role of initiatory expressions of "we" in the process of generating joint commitments generally see Gilbert (1989a, Chap. 4).

[49] On joint commitments in large populations, see Gilbert (2006a, Chap. 8). Both Lewis's and my account can cope with this kind of situation, and in similar ways.

[50] The content of every joint commitment can be represented as follows: to phi as a body, where "phi" stands for a verb such as "accept," "believe," "seek" and so on. I focus on the case in point here.

This representation of the fiat in question is supposed to show that it is simple in the following sense: no particular rationale for it is presupposed.[51]

According to my understanding of social rules, conventions on this account are a type of social rule: all such rules involve the joint acceptance of a fiat of some kind.[52] If the account is right, what distinguishes conventions from other types of rule is the simplicity—in the above sense—of the involved fiat.

Here is a fiat whose form is not simple in the relevant sense: R is to be conformed to because morality requires this. One would naturally refer to this as a moral principle, as opposed to a (mere) convention.[53] Here is another example: R is to be conformed to on account of our generally conforming to it. Those who jointly accept a fiat of this form may be said to have a "custom," as opposed to a convention. And another case: R is to be conformed to because it has been conformed to in the past. It has been handed down. Those who jointly accepted this fiat may be said to have a "tradition" as opposed to a convention.

In the case of a convention, on the account proposed, it is of course possible that R is generally conformed to in P, and it may have been conformed to for a long time. Members of P may be morally required to conform to R, irrespective of the convention, and so on. Whether or not any of these things is true, the parties to a convention, by definition, conceive of it as a simple fiat.

In so conceiving it, there is a sense in which they conceive it as arbitrary. Thus this account offers an explanation for the intuitive idea that conventions, as such, are in some sense arbitrary—an explanation different from that suggested by Lewis and, I suggest, a more plausible one.[54] If that is correct then the present account may be considered better to have satisfied a further criterion of

---

[51] Cf. Gilbert (1989a, pp. 373–374).

[52] For a discussion of social rules starting from Hart (1961) and leading to a new proposal see Gilbert (1999a). See also Gilbert (1989a, p. 405). I might have proposed as a further criterion of adequacy for an account of social convention in the sense I have in mind that it imply that conventions are rules. For some concordant discussion see Marmor (1996, p. 352f), and various dictionary entries. See also the quotation from Lewis about words, in the text below. I take it that my account does better than Lewis's on this "conventions are rules" criterion.

[53] Morality itself need not be referred to in order for us to consider this a moral principle. An appeal to justice, or charity, would have the same effect.

[54] Lewis claims to have made precise the pretheoretical judgment that "it is redundant to speak of an arbitrary convention" (1969, p. 70). Here, "Lewis-arbitrariness" seems to be a matter of a convention's role in a coordination problem according to his technical definition. In describing concrete examples of coordination problems, however, Lewis generally uses the language of indifference (Lewis 1969, pp. 5–8). Over and over he says that "It matters little" to the parties which of two or more alternative combinations of their actions (the "proper coordination equilibria") is the outcome. For only three of eleven examples does he not say this, and in one of those he says "it matters comparatively little." Thus it is not surprising that some have taken the mark of Lewis-arbitrariness to be "a certain indifference" (see Gilbert 1989a, pp. 340–342; the phrase is from W. V. 0. Quine's

adequacy for an account of convention: that it offers a plausible explanation of the intuitive idea noted.[55]

Though simple in the sense just defined, the fiat in convention may not be simple in another way: it may involve some kind of qualification. For example, it might run: R is to be conformed to, unless one lacks the financial means to conform. Or: R is to be conformed to—if one wishes to mark the fact that it is Christmas by one's color scheme.[56]

I now turn to the assessment of my joint acceptance account of convention. Regarding the first three starting points mentioned earlier, I have suggested that the point about conventions being "ours" can be elided with the collectivity criterion. I turn to that shortly. Clearly the point that conventions may or may not be particularly beneficial to the parties is covered by the present account. It neither requires that the convention is beneficial nor precludes this. What of the points about conventions and agreements?

There is reason to see the making an agreement as a matter of jointly committing to uphold as a body a certain decision.[57] Supposing this is so, we can see how a convention on the present account can be initiated by agreement. If you and I jointly commit to upholding as a body the decision to accept (as a body) a certain fiat, we are thereby jointly committed to accepting as a body that fiat. In other words, we have the convention in question at once. This is the intuitive result.

Lewis's account does not do well in this respect. He notes that those who agree to conform to a given regularity may initially so conform out of respect for the agreement, without concern for the actions of the others or their impact on themselves. In this situation, as Lewis allows, there would not yet be a convention on his account.[58]

On neither of our accounts are agreements necessary to convention. As already indicated, in relation to my account, the necessary expressions of readiness for joint commitment need not be such that one would properly describe the parties as making an agreement. Both accounts, then, accord with pretheoretical judgement here.

I turn now to the collectivity criterion. My account does well according to this: it can be argued that when the members of a particular population, P, have

"Foreword," Lewis 1969, p. xii.) As Marmor (1996, p. 355) brings out, there is tension between these two interpretations, given Lewis's technical definition of "coordination problem." In either case the Lewis-arbitrariness of a convention is a matter of its allegedly necessary relationship to a coordination problem of some kind. If conventions are not necessarily related to coordination problems, an alternative explanation of their intuitive arbitrariness is called for.

[55] Luca Tummolini emphasized this point, personal communication (2008).
[56] This is one way of bringing an example in Millikan (1998) within the purview of my account.
[57] See e.g. Gilbert (1989a, pp. 380–382) and, most recently, Gilbert (2006a, Chap. 10).
[58] See Lewis (1969, pp. 45, 83–88).

a convention according to the joint acceptance account, they constitute a collectivity or social group in the relatively narrow, intuitive sense in question. Indeed, a central argument of On Social Facts is that any joint commitment founds a group in this sense.[59]

This may be a good place to note that my account accords well with something Lewis says prior to the development of his own. He writes: "somehow, gradually and informally, we have come to an understanding that this is what we shall use them [i.e. particular words] to mean."[60] It is then plausible to see him as proposing to offer an account of how, quite generally, people come to an understanding that, as they would put it "this is what we are to do."[61] In effect, the joint acceptance account of convention offers an account of what it is for us to come to an understanding about what we are to do, where no particular rationale for doing what we are to do is presupposed.

It is not clear, meanwhile, that any of the individual parties to a Lewisian convention are in a position to have an understanding about what we are to do. Even if each one individually comes to some understanding, and this is common knowledge, that is not enough, intuitively, for any one of them to say "we have come to an understanding that..." as opposed to "each one understands that...."[62]

Next I address the offense criterion. It can be argued that on the proposed account those with a convention will indeed offend against one another in their capacity as parties to the convention, should they fail to conform to it. The argument I have in mind, outlined below, focuses on the underlying joint commitment.

A background assumption concerns all commitments of the will. I take it that these are such that one is rationally required, all equal, to conform to them. I take this to be a matter of what a commitment of the will is.[63] I take this to be neither a moral nor a prudential matter. Evidently the notion of morality invoked here—as elsewhere in this chapter—is such that moral considerations do not comprise all of those that generate requirements of rationality. Such a notion is quite standard, though broader notions, including residual notions, are also current.[64]

---

[59] Gilbert (1989a, esp. Chap. 4); see also Gilbert (2006a, Chap. 8). My technical term for a population of people who are jointly committed in some way with one another is "plural subject."

[60] Lewis (1969, p. 1).

[61] Lewis writes of "what we shall use them to mean." I take this to be imperatival in force: it is not a mere prediction. My point, in any case, relates to that interpretation of Lewis.

[62] For an argument along these lines relating to Hart's conditions on social rules, see Gilbert (1999a).

[63] I take the point to be intuitive: precisely why it is rationally required to conform to one's commitments, as such, all equal, is a good question I set aside here. For some discussion see Gilbert (1999b).

[64] When is "all equal"? I assume that commitments of the will, generally, can be "trumped" by moral considerations in terms of what rationality—in the sense of reason-responsiveness—requires, though they will not necessarily be trumped by all moral considerations. There is reason to think

Those who create a joint commitment, then, together impose a constraint on each of the parties with respect to what it is open to him to do, rationally speaking, in the future. For each is now committed, through the joint commitment, to conform to it. In the specific case of convention each party is now committed at least to conform to the pertinent jointly accepted fiat.

It is therefore appropriate to say, in the vernacular, that the parties have together and as one put their dibs on those actions of each that will result in fulfillment of the joint commitment. Though to speak this way is to speak metaphorically, the metaphor fits well. This is another way of saying that there is an intuitive sense in which the co-creators of a joint commitment, as such, can appropriately see as *theirs* the conforming actions of them all.[65]

One can then say that before conforming actions occur they are owed to the other parties in the sense of "owe" here in question. Should one party threaten not to conform, any other can demand conformity of him saying, in effect, "I demand that you give me what is *mine—in my capacity as one of us!*" Again, the others can rebuke him if he fails to conform.

One who fails to conform to a joint commitment, then, offends against the other parties in the requisite sense: he did not give them what was theirs jointly and severally as co-creators of the joint commitment—what, consequently, he owed them. They have the standing to demand his conformity if non-conformity is threatened, and to rebuke him for non-conformity.

Note that this argument appeals essentially only to the normativity of any commitment—including personal decisions—and the jointness of the commitment in question. It does not constitute a moral argument except in some very broad or residual sense. Nor is it a prudential argument that appeals to the self-interest of the parties. I shall now assume that the conclusion of the argument has been made out, and that the offense criterion is satisfied by the joint acceptance account of convention.[66]

What of the appropriate-"ought" criterion? On the joint acceptance account: is there an "ought" of convention and what is the argument for it? In short, how—if at all—does the account explain the normativity of conventions?

---

that commitments of the will generally trump a person's personal inclinations and welfare in terms of what rationality requires of them. The general case is not important here, as I argue in the text below.

[65] Clearly if this involves a kind of ownership, it is a special kind of ownership, as it is ownership of a special kind of thing, a kind of ownership I take to be fundamental to the social existence of human beings. I make no attempt here to relate it to the many kinds of "ownership" and "property" that have been identified, including those that relate to the ownership of land and material things.

[66] For further discussion see, e.g. Gilbert (1999b; repr. 2000) and Gilbert (2006a, Chap. 7).

There is indeed an "ought" of convention on the joint acceptance account. According to this account, the normativity of convention, at its core, is the normativity of joint commitment. At this point a few words on that may suffice.

First, each party to a joint commitment is subject to a commitment of the will, and therefore has sufficient reason to conform to it. All equal, then, he ought to conform. Perhaps, too, his subjection to a commitment of the will "trumps" his contrary personal inclinations and welfare as such, in terms of what he has reason to do. Be that as it may, since the commitment here is joint, we need to consider the normative implications of that fact.

Here, centrally, each party owes every other his conformity to the commitment. Intuitively your owing me an action constitutes sufficient reason for you to perform the action. That does not mean that you must perform it whatever else is true. All else being equal, however, you ought to perform it. Thus there is an "ought" of owing, as there is an "ought" of commitments of the will generally. The former goes beyond the latter in its grounds. It too, however, is not the "ought" of morality or of prudence, for neither moral nor prudential considerations are involved either in arguing that you owe me the action or in the derivation of the "ought."[67]

Intuitively, again, your owing me an action "trumps" your contrary inclinations, as such, in terms of what rationality requires you to do. If you owe me this action, how can you plausibly argue that your personal inclinations or, indeed, your personal benefit, as such, permit you not to perform it? As noted above personal commitments may also trump the agent's contrary inclinations and welfare as such. This will then be for a different reason though these reasons will have some connection with each other. And it will be of less moment since the personal commitment can be rescinded unilaterally. Be all this as it may, there is a consideration over and above one's being committed that can be brought into play in the case of joint commitment—one owes the action in question to another. And this is something that cannot be changed by a change of one's own mind.

Of course your owing me an action does more than give you sufficient reason to perform that action, where your inclinations and welfare as such take second place in terms of what rationality requires. It also gives me the standing to demand the action and to rebuke you if it is not performed. And this is something both of us have sufficient reason to acknowledge.

Not only do I have the standing to demand the action, however, I surely have some justification for doing so. After all, you owe me that action. This, too,

---

[67] It is implausible to suggest that my owing someone an action is, in and of itself, a matter of moral requirement. This latter is worth pointing out in light of a great tendency in the literature on rights to interpret "owing" in terms of moral requirements of a certain sort. Cf. Gilbert (2004).

you have sufficient reason to acknowledge. I may of course forebear from making the demand, and be justified in doing so all things considered.

It may be that if you owe me an action, then you ought morally to perform that action, all equal. In other words, you may be not only rationally but also morally required, all equal, to perform those actions that you owe. Be that as it may, there is on the joint commitment account a non-moral, non-prudential "ought" of convention. That there is such an "ought" is all to the good for convention, since the moral perspicacity of its followers may fluctuate, as may their personal inclinations and rankings of the outcomes.[68] This way, convention has a separate, and relatively stable normative leg to stand on.[59]

Given what has been said about the normativity of convention according to the present account, one can see how such conventions are apt to prompt the parties to conform to them. Assuming that they are reason-responsive, they will so conform in the absence of countervailing considerations that override those the convention provides. Given common knowledge among the parties of their reason-responsiveness, they will expect each other to conform to the convention absent countervailing considerations that override it.

I take it that sometimes moral considerations will override the convention from the point of view of what rationality requires. And if one decides a particular convention is itself immoral—a convention that excludes certain classes of persons from important opportunities, for instance—one may well judge that one ought not to conform to it, all equal. Widespread willful non-conformity in such circumstances—and a general abstention from responsive rebukes—may serve to terminate the convention as the parties gradually manifest their readiness to do so.

I conclude that the joint acceptance account of convention does well with respect to all of the intuitive tests I have proposed in relation to social convention according to a particular central everyday concept. Clearly it fares far better than Lewis's account in that regard. In the next section I discuss further the relationship between these accounts.

6. The Two Accounts Related

Lewis's is an individualistic account. The joint acceptance account is holistic as a result of its appeal to joint commitment. Though this may seem to be a cost to some, it may be necessary if the pertinent everyday concept is to be properly

---

[68] Robins (1984) emphasizes the latter point.

[59] Clearly, then, the parties to conventions in the sense of the joint acceptance account need not be "moralisers" in any but a very broad sense. Nor need their participation in the convention be a matter of deliberation or "voluntaristic" in any strong sense. On the latter point see e.g. Gilbert (2006a, pp. 223–234). The quoted terms are from Latsis (2005, p. 720).

articulated. It may also be necessary to capture what is a consequential and ubiquitous social phenomenon, whatever its name.

Some may wonder about the possibility of joint commitment. I see no reason to deny that people can jointly commit one another by virtue of their readiness to do so, expressed in conditions of common knowledge. In order to do this they need the concept of joint commitment. That does not mean that they need to have a word for it. Nor need it be easy to extract it from the way in which they explicitly think, talk, and act. Nor need it be easy to explain. It may still inform their thoughts, talk, actions, and interactions. Indeed, as I have argued elsewhere, it is plausible to see it as a fundamental everyday concept, embedded in many of the central concepts with which human beings approach one another.[70]

I propose, then, that with respect to the possibility of their instantiation in the world the concepts described by Lewis's and by my proposed accounts are on a par. In other terms, both are realistic and equally so.

According to the version of Lewis's account I presented earlier, all of the parties to a convention conform to it, and everyone expects almost everyone to conform. Call these the conformity and expectation conditions. The joint acceptance account incorporates neither of these conditions. Nonetheless, its relationship to them is close. As I have just argued, on my account, reason-responsive parties to a convention will conform to it, all equal. If the reason-responsiveness of the parties is common knowledge, they will also expect each other to conform, all equal.

Further, reason-responsive parties are likely to find conventions on the present account extremely useful if and when their inclinations constitute, in effect, a coordination problem. For suppose that one way or another they jointly commit to accept as a body a fiat that dictates actions for each such that each is inclined to act accordingly provided the others do. This will resolve the coordination problem, because a standing joint commitment "trumps" inclinations with respect to what one is rationally required to do. It will therefore set the course of the parties to the convention.[71]

7. Summary and Conclusion

I have focused here on two accounts of social convention, David Lewis's, as set out in 1969 in his influential book Convention, and my joint acceptance account, further elaborated since its first presentation. Mine is neither a minor nor a major variant of his. One radical difference between our accounts is the individualism of his account versus the holism of mine. In the main body of this

---

[70] See Gilbert (1989a, Chap. 7) and elsewhere.

[71] For further discussion along these lines, with allusion to other "problems of collective action" including the prisoner's dilemma, see Gilbert (2006b).

chapter I have argued that my account answers better to what is at least a central everyday concept of social convention, emphasizing a particular criterion of adequacy—the offense criterion.

Social scientists do well to arrive at an articulated understanding of central everyday concepts such as that, or those, corresponding to everyday talk of "convention." One reason is the relevance of such concepts to Verstehen in something like the sociologist Max Weber's sense: social scientists do well to understand the terms in which people understand their own lives—the terms in which they act. If my account does capture a central everyday concept, therefore, it is worth the social scientist's attention. The same goes, of course, for Lewis's account. These accounts clearly latch on to different concepts. Though I have my doubts about Lewis's in this respect, both could in principle be central everyday ones.

An account of convention need not be judged in terms of its representation of a particular everyday concept, however central. It may usefully latch on to an important phenomenon, actual or possible, whether or not some everyday concept does so as well. Looked at in that way, also, the two very different accounts discussed here could both be successful. In that case neither should be ignored by those wishing accurately to describe the human condition.

Acknowledgments

For extensive responses to a late draft of this chapter I thank Giacomo Sillari, Matthew Noah Smith, Luca Tummolini, and two anonymous referees. Thanks also to Cara Gillis and Chad Kidd for suggestions on a later draft. I have responded to their comments as best I could in the allotted space and time.

References

Burge, T. (1975) On knowledge and convention. *Philos Rev* 84: 249–255.
Darwall, S. (2006) *The second person standpoint*. Harvard University Press, Cambridge, MA.
Durkheim, E. (1951) *Suicide: a study in sociology* (trans: Spaulding JA, Simpson G), Free Press, New York.
Gilbert, M. (1974) About conventions. *Second-Order* 3:71–89.
Gilbert, M. (1981) Game theory and convention. *Synthese* 44:41–93. Reprinted in Gilbert (1996).
Gilbert, M. (1983a) Agreements, conventions, and language. *Synthese* 54:375–407. Reprinted with some revisions in Gilbert (1996).
Gilbert, M. (1983b) Notes on the concept of a social convention. *New Lit Hist* 14:225–251. Reprinted in Gilbert (1996).
Gilbert, M. (1984) Coordination problems and the evolution of behavior. *Behav Brain Sci* 7:106–107.
Gilbert, M. (1989a) *On social facts*. Routledge and Kegan Paul, London (Reprinted 1992, Princeton University Press, Princeton).
Gilbert, M. (1989b) Rationality and salience. *Philos Stud* 55:223–239. Reprinted in Gilbert (1996).

Gilbert, M. (1990) Rationality, coordination, and convention. *Synthese* 84:1–21. Reprinted in Gilbert (1996).

Gilbert, M. (1996) *Living together: rationality, sociality, and obligation.* Rowman and Littlefield, Lanham, MD.

Gilbert, M. (1999a) Social rules: some problems with Hart's account, and an alternative proposal. *Law Philos* 18:141–171. Reprinted in Gilbert (2000).

Gilbert, M. (1999b) Obligation and joint commitment. *Utilitas* 11: 143–64. Reprinted in Gilbert (1996).

Gilbert, M. (2000) *Sociality and responsibility: new essays in plural subject theory.* Roman and Littlefield, Lanham, MD.

Gilbert, M. (2003) The structure of the social atom: joint commitment as the foundation of human social behavior. In Schmitt F (ed) *Social metaphysics.* Roman and Littlefield, Lanham, MD.

Gilbert, M. (2004) Scanlon on promissory obligation: the problem of promisees rights'. *J Philos* 101:83–109 [Chapter 12 this volume].

Gilbert, M. (2005) Shared values, social unity, and liberty. *Public Aff Q* 19:25–49 [Chapter 8 this volume].

Gilbert, M. (2006a) *A theory of political obligation: membership, commitment, and the bonds of society.* Clarendon Press, Oxford.

Gilbert, M. (2006b) Rationality in collective action. *Philos Soc Sci* 36:3–17 [Chapter 4 this volume].

Hart, H. L. A. (1961) *The concept of law.* Clarendon Press, Oxford.

Jamieson, D. (1975) David Lewis on convention. *Can J Philos* 5:73–81.

Latsis, J. S. (2005) Is there redemption for conventions? *Cambridge J Econ* 29:709–727.

Lewis, D. (1969) *Convention: a philosophical study.* Harvard University Press, Cambridge, MA (Reissued 2002, Blackwell Publishers Ltd, Oxford).

Lewis, D. (1975) Languages and language. In Gunderson K (ed) *Language, mind and knowledge.* Minnesota Studies in the Philosophy of Science 7:3–35, University of Minnesota Press, Minneapolis.

Marmor, A. (1996) On convention. *Synthese* 107:349–371.

Miller, S. (1992) On conventions. *Australasian J Philos* 70:435–445.

Millikan, R. (1998) Language conventions made simple. *J Philos* 95:161–180.

Robins, M. (1984) *Promising, intending, and moral autonomy.* Cambridge University Press, Cambridge.

Scanlon, T. (1998) *What we owe to each other.* Harvard University Press, Cambridge, MA.

Schelling, T. (1960) *The strategy of conflict.* Harvard University Press, Cambridge, MA.

Schiffer, S. (1972) *Meaning.* Oxford University Press, Oxford.

Schotter, A. (1981) *An economic theory of social institutions.* Cambridge University Press, Cambridge.

Vanderschraaf, P., Sillari, G. (2007) Common knowledge. The Stanford Encyclopedia of Philosophy (Fall 2007 edn): http://plato.stanford.edu/entries/common-knowledge/.

Collective Guilt and Collective Guilt Feelings

1. Introduction

i. *The Commonplace Nature of Holistic Talk about Groups*

Nations, firms, families, and other such groups are often accused of wrongdoing, both informally, and in the more formal context of legal action. Charges are brought, demands for compensation are made, apologies are sought, not from particular individuals, but from the groups themselves. As Christopher Kutz observes in a recent monograph:

> Political and legal life would be...unrecognizable without...holistic talk of groups, and without holistic systems of accountability.[1]

In spite of the evident truth of this observation, there has been considerable philosophical dispute as to whether or not such "holistic talk" is legitimate when taken at face value.[2]

Thus, though in the previous quotation Kutz acknowledges the ubiquity of ascriptions of accountability to groups, in the following he appears to express opposition to "treating [the group itself] as the culpable party":

> The law of complicity and conspiracy in effect applies an organicist conception of collective action, treating the acting group as conceptually

---

[1] C. Kutz, *Complicity* (Cambridge: Cambridge University Press, 2001), p. 192.

[2] Philosophers who have focused attention on the topic of collective moral guilt in various contexts include Peter French, Virginia Held, Larry May, and the other authors whose work is collected in L. May and S. Hoffman (eds.), *Collective Responsibility: Five Decades of Debate in Theoretical and Applied Ethics* (Lanham: Rowman and Littlefield, 1991). This chapter makes no attempt to review the literature but rather delineates the author's own approach to the topic.

prior to its individual members. This is, in effect, to naturalize the group itself, treating it as the culpable party... This reifies the joint intention that underlies all concerted action, treating it as a thing in itself rather than an overlap among individual participatory intentions...[3]

For Kutz, as for others before him, a collective or joint intention exists when there is a certain kind of overlap in the content of a number of individual intentions, that is, in the intentions of individual members of the relevant group.[4]

Kutz allows that ascriptions of culpability to groups may *have a point* in some circumstances—presumably in his view such ascriptions would be literally false. In this connection, he argues that:

> There is an important difference between expressing recrimination at an organization and expressing it at an individual...a collective cannot respond affectively to these expressions, only its constituent members can. The lack of an affective counter-response is troubling, because the efficacy of responses of accountability partially depends upon affect. The responses of shame, guilt, and regret help to register the significance of the harm.[5]

Kutz is surely not the only philosopher who would endorse the claim that "a collective cannot respond affectively, only its members can." In this chapter I attempt to counter that claim. In particular, I argue that there is an important sense in which a collective can feel guilt.

ii. *The Practical Importance of Guilt Feelings*

There is clearly a case to be made for a relatively sustained examination of the possibility of collective guilt feelings. In effect, Kutz himself makes a case for exploring this question.

[handwritten marginalia: Kutz is perhaps most pragmatic & applicable than Gilbert, who may be more absolutely correct.]

---

[3] Kutz, *Complicity*, p. 236.

[4] Views of collective intention with some similarity to Kutz's include those of Michael Bratman and Seumas Miller. See, for instance, relevant essays collected in M. Bratman, *Faces of Intention* (Cambridge: Cambridge University Press, 1999), S. Miller, "Intentions, Ends and Joint Action," *Philosophical Papers* 24 (1995), pp. 51–66. John Searle rejects the idea that collective intentions involve a set of "I intends" with similar content. He opts rather for a set of "We intends"—each member of the set in the mind of one of the individuals involved. See J. Searle, "Collective Intentions and Actions," in P. R. Cohen, J. Morgan, M. E. Pollack (eds.), *Intentions in Communication* (Cambridge: MIT Press, 1990), pp. 401–415. Searle's view is similar to that of W. Sellars, see, e.g., W. Sellars, "Imperatives, Intentions, and the Language of 'Ought,'" in G. Nakhnikian and H.-N. Castaneda (eds.), *Morality and the Language of Conduct* (Detroit: Wayne State University Press, 1963), pp. 401–415.

[5] Kutz, *Complicity*, p. 196.

Appropriate affective responses he says "help to register the significance of the harm." I am not entirely sure precisely what he has in mind here, but the following may be an illustration of his point, and it seems to be true. Were an agent to respond with a feeling of guilt to the blame it encounters for what it has done, this response would act as an acknowledgement of its guilt by the agent itself.

An agent does not need to respond to others in order to acknowledge its guilt. A spontaneous feeling of guilt would surely suffice.

A feeling of guilt for harms done is apt to have important practical effects. It is particularly galling for victims to meet with self-righteousness and self-justification from those who have wronged them. Such a stance is likely to harden the victims' feelings toward these wrongdoers. In contrast, a feeling of guilt—and even better, its close cousin remorse—is liable to promote the restoration of good relations.[6]

Those not directly affected, also, are likely to be more kindly disposed toward a wrongfully acting agent after the fact if it feels guilt over its wrongful action. In addition, an agent's guilt feelings are apt to provoke the agent to engage in constructive self-examination and change, to offer help to the victims, and so on.

Were collective emotions such as guilt feelings possible, then, they would be of great practical importance. They would help to ameliorate relations between wrongfully acting collectives, their victims, and others. They would also be apt to improve the relevant collectives themselves. This does not mean, of course, that there are such emotions. It just means that whether there are or not is a matter of consequence.

iii. *In Favor of the Possibility of Collective Guilt Feelings*

Is there a case for thinking that a group can feel guilt, for example? One might start from the fact that, just as groups are routinely accused of wrongdoing in everyday life, emotions are routinely ascribed to them. Perhaps one should put it more cautiously, though without intending a presumption either way: people talk *as if* they are ascribing emotions to groups. These emotions include guilt feelings along with other emotions responsive to what a group has done.

Thus the member of a political party might say, "The party feels great guilt. It had no idea this would happen." A family member might say, "This family has treated you very badly. We feel terribly guilty." Similarly, a responsive emotion may be called for, or its lack decried. Thus critics of a nation *N*, might say, "*N* should feel guilt for what it has done." Or "*N* has never felt any guilt for its wrongful actions."

---

[6] On guilt versus remorse, see H. Morris, "Guilt and Suffering," *Philosophy East and West* 21 (1971), pp. 107–108.

What can one learn from such statements? That people are prepared to speak in this way, and frequently do, at least suggests that they think that there is something, something real, to which they refer: the feelings of a group. Rather than casually writing off this assumption as due to ignorance, or writing off these ways of speaking as fanciful, we can approach both more carefully. We can attempt to explore the circumstances in which ascriptions of guilt feelings to groups are judged to be in place.

iv. *Skepticism about the Possibility of Collective Emotions in General and Collective Guilt Feelings in Particular*

Why might one write off the assumption that there are collective guilt feelings as Kutz, for instance, seems to do? Kutz puts it this way: only the constituent members of a collective can respond affectively, feeling guilt, shame, regret, and so on. Presumably he means that only individual human beings can so respond.

Why might one think this? One possible reason is this. Emotions generally may be thought of as essentially involving something with a distinctive "feel" to it. Thus people talk of "surges" of anger, of joy "welling up," of the "sting" of jealousy, of "pangs" and, for less vivid cases, "twinges" of guilt.

Pangs and twinges, in particular, seem to be something like a sensation, such as the sensation of pain. It may be thought that to feel guilt is to experience a "pang of guilt" conceived of as a particular kind of "feeling-sensation"—nothing more and nothing less than that. In that case, if feeling-sensations are something only individual humans can have, the case against collective guilt feelings seems to be closed. If groups cannot have pangs of guilt, they cannot have guilt feelings. It may seem obvious that while individual human beings can have feeling-sensations, groups cannot.

v. *Some Counters to Skepticism about Collective Emotions in General and Collective Guilt Feelings in Particular*

a. *Particular emotions may not require a specific phenomenology*

There are a number of ways to defuse the certainty that the case against collective guilt feelings is closed. With respect to the issue of feeling-sensations, one may ask whether a feeling of guilt is only, or indeed necessarily, a matter of sensation-like feelings.

In order to feel guilt an individual human being must, surely, have certain thoughts about his or her situation and perhaps be disposed to act in certain ways. Thus one who feels guilt over what she has done must take what she has done to be wrong to some degree. Perhaps, then, such cognitions lie at the heart of the emotion. Perhaps specific "feeling-sensations" are not essential, but only frequent concomitants.

In accord with this line of thought, Martha Nussbaum has recently argued that "... emotions are forms of evaluative judgment that ascribe to certain things and persons... great importance."[7] In the course of so arguing she disputes the idea that particular emotion types necessarily have specific phenomenological concomitants.

One of the points she makes is this: "... if we are prepared to recognize non-conscious emotional states, such as nonconscious fear of death... then we cannot possibly hold to any necessary phenomenological condition for that emotion type."[8] She also cites her own experience, observing that "[m]y anger... is at times entirely asymptomatic... [it does not have] the phenomenology of 'boiling' so many people report."[9]

Others, too, have contemplated the possibility of an account of emotions that does not assume phenomenological conditions for specific emotion types.[10] This is not to say that there is no room for discussion of the issue.[11] Nonetheless, there are reasons to question the idea that, in general, specific emotion types have phenomenological conditions. These reasons allow us to regard it as at least open whether guilt feelings necessarily involve a qualitatively special "pang of guilt," a generic type of "pang," or any phenomenological condition at all.

How do things seem to stand with guilt feelings at the level of the individual? Without attempting a fine-grained discussion, I can imagine saying that I felt guilty about something without meaning to imply that any particular phenomenological condition was satisfied. The central if not the sole thing at issue would be my judgment that I was wrong to do whatever it is I say I feel guilty about. The very nature of any associated pangs or twinges as pangs or twinges of guilt could only be assumed if this judgment were present.

---

[7] M. Nussbaum, *Upheavals of Thought* (Cambridge: Cambridge University Press, 2001), p. 22.

[8] Nussbaum, *Upheavals of Thought*, p. 61. The quotation is from a section headed "Are There Necessary Noncognitive Elements?," pp. 56–64.

[9] Nussbaum, *Upheavals of Thought*, p. 61.

[10] See J. Shaffer, "An Assessment of Emotion," *American Philosophical Quarterly* 20 (1983), pp. 161–172. Shaffer moots the possibility of an analysis of emotion purely in terms of beliefs and desires at p. 171. He argues for an analysis in which beliefs and desires are essential to emotion, but not exclusively so.

[11] Nussbaum cites M. Stocker, *Valuing Emotions* (Cambridge: Cambridge University Press, 1996), as one who would oppose her view. She also offers criticism of Stocker (see Nussbaum, *Upheavals of Thought*, p. 61).

must guilt be based emotion?
a bored emotion?

b. A matter of method

Another consideration, this time a methodological one, is this. How is one to decide what it is to feel guilt? Should one first arrive at an account of guilt feelings by considering the so-called guilt feelings of individuals solely, and then ask whether groups can feel guilt according to that account? Why, though, should things be done this way? Why not consider the so-called guilt feelings in both individuals and groups, and extrapolate from both of these? I shall refer to the latter method as the *broad* method of investigating the nature of guilt feelings.

If the broad method is used, it is unlikely to result in the judgment that there is no such thing as a collective feeling of guilt. Possibly the conclusion will be along these lines: for an individual human being to feel guilt, this and this must be the case; for a group, that and that must be the case, where there are both significant similarities and significant differences between "this and this" and "that and that." One might then want to say that groups did not feel guilt in quite the same way that individuals did. It would not be necessary to say that they did not feel guilt at all.

I shall not here try to argue carefully for or against the broad method. It should be said, however, that insofar as people refer without a sense of fantasy or metaphor to the guilt feelings of groups, there is good reason not to rule these out as impossible from the start of enquiry. Again, since a narrower method of understanding such phenomena as guilt feelings is the prevailing one and has been for a very long time, there is much to be said for using the broad method as a possible route to fresh insights and understandings.

c. The scope of psychology

The methodological remarks just made are relevant to another objection that might be made to the very idea of collective emotions in general, and collective guilt feelings in particular. The idea that many if not all emotions involve a kind of belief or judgment evidently has some plausibility.[12] As noted earlier, one who feels guilt over what she has done, for instance, must surely believe at some level that she has done something wrong.

Thus it might be argued that whether or not guilt feelings necessarily involve feeling-sensations of one kind or another, they involve a kind of belief. It may then be contended that collectives cannot have their own beliefs, and, therefore, cannot feel guilt.

Here again one can raise a pertinent methodological question. How is one to decide what it is to believe something? Are cases of so-called belief in human beings to be taken as the only paradigmatic ones, or are cases of so-called belief in

---

[12] See, for instance, Shaffer, "An Assessment of Emotion"; Nussbaum, *Upheavals of Thought*.

collectives to be taken into account? Beliefs are certainly ascribed to collectives in everyday life. People speak—without any sense of fantasy or metaphor—of the judgments of courts, of the beliefs of unions, families, nations, and so on. On what grounds, then, is one entitled to rule out the possibility of collective belief *a priori*?[13]

Once again, there is reason to adopt a broad method in this case. And if collective belief ascriptions are taken as part of the data for an account of belief, it is hard to see how the conclusion will be that there is no such thing as collective belief.

d. Summary

In sum, if experiencing a feeling-sensation is essential to feeling guilt, one may have to grant that groups do not feel guilt. But it is not clear that even a human individual must experience a feeling-sensation in order to, as we say, feel guilt over some matter. Nor is it clear that we should decide *what it is to feel guilt* on the basis of considering what it is for an individual human being to feel guilt. Should we not look at what are taken to be cases of group guilt feelings, and consider what they seem to amount to, as well? The same goes for other psychological properties, including belief.

vi. *Collective Guilt Feelings Assume Collective Guilt*

Collective guilt feelings over the relevant group's wrongdoing would evidently be misplaced were there no collective guilt to serve as its appropriate object. I shall take it that we are talking about collective *moral* guilt here, as opposed to legal guilt or any other kind.

Collective moral guilt appears to require collective moral responsibility. Can a collective be morally responsible? Many have found this idea troubling, though there is little doubt that people frequently ascribe such responsibility to collectives, whether rightly or wrongly in a given case. Thus Franklin Roosevelt, in the wake of the Second World War:

> Too many people here and in England hold to the view that the German people as a whole are not responsible for what has taken place—that only a few Nazi leaders are responsible. That unfortunately is not based

[13] For more on collective belief ascriptions see M. Gilbert, "Modeling Collective Belief," *Synthese* 73 (1987) pp. 185–204, reprinted in M. Gilbert, *Living Together: Rationality, Sociality, and Obligation* (Lanham: Rowman and Littlefield, 1996), pp. 195–213; M. Gilbert, *On Social Facts* (Princeton: Princeton University Press), 1989, Chapter 5, and elsewhere. See also the text below.

on fact. The German people as a whole must have it driven home to them that the whole nation has been engaged in a lawless conspiracy against the decencies of modern civilization.[14]

The root worry over the idea of collective moral responsibility may be a worry over the possibility of genuinely collective action and intention. A central question relating to collective moral guilt, then, is the question whether collective intentions are possible or, less skeptically—as I prefer—what collective intentions amount to.

Unlike Kutz, Bratman, and others, I do not see a collective intention as a certain kind of overlap among the intentions of individuals. If doing anything other than this is to "treat it as a thing in itself," as Kutz puts it, then I do that.

Moreover, I do not want to assume that it is a falsification of the facts concerning a group sometimes to "treat it as the culpable party" and hence, to use Kutz's term, to "naturalize" it. Though this may involve a kind of "organicism" about groups, it is not clear that such organicism is erroneous. Nor is it clear that it involves "treating the acting group as conceptually prior to its individual members." Since I am not sure precisely what such treatment is supposed to involve, I shall neither avow nor disavow it here.

I shall preface my discussion of group guilt feelings with a sketch of an account of collective moral guilt. In addition to giving some substance to the notion, this account will include some of the groundwork for the account of collective guilt feelings that I prefer.

vii. *A Distinction among Groups*

The above discussion sometimes refers to "groups," sometimes to "collectives." "Collective" is the more technical of the two terms.

I refer to populations as "collectives" when I conceive of them as genuinely collective subjects of intention, action, and so on. I take it that a population is a *genuinely collective* subject of intention if and only if, roughly, it can plausibly be regarded as having an intention *of its own*, an intention, if you like, of the population *as a whole*.

[14] Quoted in G. J. Bass, *Stay the Hand of Vengeance: The Politics of War Crimes Tribunals* (Princeton: Princeton University Press, 2001), p. 154. M. Gilbert, "Collective Wrongdoing: Moral and Legal Responses," *Social Theory and Practice*, forthcoming, reviews Bass's book along with Kutz, *Complicity*. B. Wilkins, *Terrorism and Collective Responsibility* (London: Routledge, 1992), notes that after the Second World War, Konrad Adenauer, the German Chancellor, "acknowledged an obligation on behalf of the German people to make moral and material amends for crimes perpetrated in the name of the German people..." (p. 20). Wilkins later remarks, of the German case, "...the example does fit, however awkwardly, the classic picture of guilt, confession, and repentance in the form of attempts to make reparations" (p. 21).

As long as so-called collective action is conceived of as having as its intentional base some sort of amalgam of the intentions of the individuals involved, it does not seem plausibly to be thought of involving a collective subject. This will be so even if the intentions involved have what is in some sense a collective object or end—such as an end requiring the actions of many persons, as in the so-called collective ends invoked by Kutz, Seumas Miller, and others.[15]

The populations I argue to be potential subjects of moral guilt constitute collectives in the sense indicated above. Often, when people discuss the topic of so-called collective moral responsibility or guilt, they are thinking of individuals who constitute no more than an aggregate, as opposed to a collective. In particular, they are thinking of sets of individuals with certain features in common, such as people with skin of a certain color, of the same sex, economic class, social status, beliefs, propensities, and so on. Often such populations are referred to as groups. Given that one does so refer to them, one might do well to call them something like *feature-defined* groups to explain how they are individuated.

I should emphasize that *a feature-defined group is not necessarily a collective subject.* In order that the members of a given feature-defined group come to constitute such a subject, they must have taken an important step. What I take this step to be will be made apparent shortly. Whether or not it has been taken may not be altogether easy to discern, but that this step has been taken must be assumed before culpability can properly be ascribed to the group as a collective subject.

The term "group," as applied to human populations, may tend to conjure more than what I am calling a feature-defined group. It may tend to suggest a collective subject. The same goes for "social group."[16] "Population" is probably a better term for feature-defined groups that are not collective subjects, or for any aggregates of individuals that lack collective subject-hood. There is little point in trying to legislate against popular usage. I shall myself, however, tend to use the terms "collective" and "group" to refer to collective subjects, using "population" for sets of people who do not necessarily, as referred to, form such subjects.

2. Collective Moral Guilt

For present purposes I shall take it that moral guilt in general paradigmatically involves an agent that freely acts wrongly believing its act to be wrong. I shall take it, therefore, that in order for a collective to bear moral guilt it must be able to *act, act freely,* and *believe* its act to be wrong.

---

[15] For relevant discussion in this regard of Kutz (in particular Kutz, *Complicity*), see Gilbert, "Collective Wrongdoing: Moral and Legal Responses"

[16] For a discussion arguing that, in a central sense, "social group" refers to collective subjects as such, see Gilbert, *On Social Facts*, Chapter 4.

In what follows I briefly argue that collectives can fulfill these conditions.[17] The considerations adduced are likely to support the possibility of collective moral guilt given some variation from the above description of its elements.

i. *What Are Collective Intentions and Actions?*

I take it that a genuinely collective action, as opposed to the concordant action of several people, requires a goal or intention with what I referred to before as a genuinely collective subject. The account of collective action that I have been developing for some time meets this condition.[18] I refer to it, and to the associated accounts of collective goals and intentions as *plural subject* accounts. They seem to capture the idea of a subject that is in an important sense singular though its constitution requires a plurality of individual participants.

The account of collective intention I delineate below allows for a radical disjunction between the specific intentions of groups and those of their members. I have argued in favor of this account at length elsewhere.[19] I say something about these arguments shortly. My main aim here is simply to sketch the account and explain the key technical terms involved.

My account of a collective intention runs as follows:

> A population *P* has a collective intention to do *A* if and only if the members of *P* are *jointly committed* to intending *as a body* to do *A*.

I say that a population *P* constitutes a *plural subject,* by definition, if and only if its members are jointly committed to do something as a body, where "doing something" is construed very broadly so as to include intending and being in various cognitive states. Populations fulfilling the above conditions constitute the plural subject of an intention to do *A*.

The key term here is "joint commitment." What is a joint commitment?[20]

---

[17] Cf. M. Gilbert, *Sociality and Responsibility: New Essays in Plural Subject Theory* (Lanham: Rowman and Littlefield, 2000), Chapter 8.

[18] See Gilbert, *On Social Facts,* and elsewhere, most recently, in M. Gilbert, 'Acting Together' (2002) in G. Meggle (ed) *Social Facts and Collective Intentionality* (Frankfurt: Hansel-Hohenhausen, 2002). [Chapter 1 this volume.]

[19] See, in particular, M. Gilbert, "What Is It for Us to Intend?," in R. Tuomela and G. Holmstrom-Hintikka (eds.), *Contemporary Action Theory* (Dordrecht: Kluwer Academic Publishers, 1997).

[20] Some treatments of joint commitment other than that given here may be found helpful supplements to what follows. See, for instance, Gilbert, *Living Together,* Introduction. Particularly detailed in certain respects is M. Gilbert, "Considerations on Joint Commitment," in *Social Facts and Collective Intentionality,* ed. G. Meggle (Frankfurt: Hansel Hohenhausen, 2002).

ii. *Joint Commitment*

It is helpful to begin an explanation by considering something other than a joint commitment, namely, the personal decision of a human individual. Suppose that Alison has decided to flee the country. Her decision can be seen as involving a *personal* commitment. Failing a change of mind, she is now committed to fleeing the country. She is, of course, in a position to change her mind. But as long as she does not do so her commitment stands. That is important because, as a commitment, it has some force from a normative point of view. Should she stray from the course she is personally committed to, without a prior change of mind, she has in some sense done what she was not supposed to do.

A joint commitment is not created by a set of personal decisions. It is not a set of personal commitments, but a truly joint commitment, a commitment of two or more persons. Those initiating such a commitment do not each create a part of it by making a personal decision. Rather, they participate in creating the whole of it along with the other parties. A joint commitment does not have parts, though it certainly has implications for the individual parties. That is, each is committed through the joint commitment.

Importantly, without special side understandings no individual party to a joint commitment can rescind it unilaterally. All must participate in its rescission. Since it does not have parts, no one is in a position to rescind just part of it.

Two or more people enter a joint commitment in much the same way as an individual creates a personal commitment through a personal decision. To put it generally, and somewhat roughly, each must openly express his or her readiness to be jointly committed with the relevant others, in conditions of common knowledge. The common knowledge condition requires, roughly again, that the expressions must be out in the open for all concerned.[21]

Thus Joshua may say to Martin, "Shall we meet at six?" In standard circumstances, should Martin reply "Sure!" they will have created a joint commitment. Here one can describe the joint commitment as a commitment to uphold together the decision that the parties will meet at six. It also counts as an explicit agreement. That is not true of all cases of joint commitment. Some may be arrived at in a less explicit manner, and over a period of time.

In a large group where people do not know one another personally, or even know of one another as individuals, they must openly express their readiness to be jointly committed with others of the relevant type. They must do this in such a way that knowledge of these expressions can be expected to filter through to those others generally. Indeed, the occurrence of these expressions should in all cases become common knowledge in the sense noted earlier.

---

[21] For a much more detailed discussion see Gilbert, *On Social Facts*, Chapter 4. See also other references given there.

For two or more people to intend *as a body* to do A is for them as far as is possible to emulate a single "body" which intends to do A. Putting things in some such way makes it clear that what is at issue is not a plurality of intentions of individual members of group G.

iii. *Collective Action*

Turning now to collective action, one can say that, roughly,

> A population P *collectively performed action A* if and only if the members of P were jointly committed to intending as a body to do A, and, acting in the light of this joint commitment, relevant members of P acted so as to satisfy this intention.

Note that the members of P may be jointly committed to intending as a body to do A, without everyone in P knowing or even conceiving of the content of their commitment. This can happen if there is a joint commitment to authorize as a body some person or body to make decisions, form plans, and so on, on behalf of the jointly committed persons. For the sake of a label, one might call this an *authority-producing* joint commitment. Thus a leader and his henchmen may formulate and carry out a plan in the group's name, and, given the appropriate background, the group's members can say of the group as a whole "We did it."

iv. *In Favor of the Plural Subject Account of Collective Action*

In everyday life when people understand that "We collectively intend such-and-such," or that "We are doing such-and-such together," they understand themselves to have a special standing in relation to one another. In particular, they understand that they have rights against and obligations toward each other. They also understand that they are not in a position unilaterally to change the collective's mind, though they may do so by mutual consent. I have argued elsewhere that the perception of an underlying joint commitment would explain all these understandings. Since this matter is not directly relevant to matters at the center of this chapter, I shall not say more about it here.[22]

v. *Collective Belief*

I have argued at length elsewhere that, according to our everyday conception of collective belief, roughly:

---

[22] Gilbert, *Sociality and Responsibility*, Chapter 4, contains a lengthy discussion of the obligating and rights-grounding nature of joint commitments as I conceive of them.

Members of a population *P collectively believe that p* if and only if they are jointly committed to believe as a body that *p*.

There is no room in this chapter to go through the arguments in behalf of this plural subject account of collective belief.[23] A key point, however, is that here, as in the case of collective action, those who take themselves collectively to believe something also take themselves to have a special standing in relation to one another. The details of this standing can be further spelled out in much the same way as that involved in collective action. A plural subject account of collective belief provides an explanation for the parties' belief that they have a special standing in relation to one another.

Collective beliefs can include moral beliefs. Hence it seems to make sense to say that a group did something it, as opposed to any individual members of the group, believed to be wrong.

vi. *Freedom of Collective Action*

Is there a basis for distinguishing between the free and the coerced actions of groups? Surely there is. In particular, a group may be subject to strong external pressure from another group. In the opinion of many thinkers, this could provide the first group with a justification for carrying out actions that would otherwise be reprehensible. In other words, the external pressure could ground a rebuttal of the charge of moral guilt.

This line of thought is presumably a large part of what lies behind traditional just war theory. If a nation is attacked or under immediate threat of attack, it may—according to the theory—justly defend itself, where necessary engaging in actions that in other circumstances could be described as heinous.[24]

Where there is no external pressure on a group, there can surely be circumstances in which it would be appropriate to say that it acted freely. This would presumably be when, at a minimum, a collective intention was arrived at without any external interference, and implemented by members of the group acting in light of it.[25]

One question arising is whether in order for a group to act freely the members of the group must act freely with respect to all relevant matters.[26] I shall not

[23] See Gilbert, *On Social Facts*.

[24] For a well-known account of just war theory that links it to ideas about the nature of collectives concordant with my own, see M. Walzer, *Just and Unjust Wars: A Moral Argument with Historical Illustrations* (New York: Basic Books, 1977), p. 54 and elsewhere.

[25] For more on the topic of freedom of group action, with a relatively fine-grained elaboration of cases of coerced and free group action, see Gilbert, *Sociality and Responsibility*, Chapter 8, Section 8, pp. 149–150.

[26] Fabio Maldonado-Veloza brought this good question to my attention during my graduate seminar, 1998.

attempt carefully to investigate this here. On the face of it, however, there are cases of "internal coercion" which would seem not to impact on the freedom of action of the group itself. Thus suppose some individuals were subject to strong pressure to participate with certain others in a joint committment to intend as a body in a certain way. Nonetheless, as long as they were indeed ready so to be committed, and expressed their readiness to do so, the joint commitment could have been established, providing the basis for a collective action.[27] Again, some may have been under strong pressure from others to participate in the collective action, the collective intention having been established. Though reluctant to do so, they may yet participate. As long as they act in light of the relevant joint commitment, or, if you like, as members of the group, it seems that one can with justification say that the group acts through them, and, given that *it* is not under strong pressure, acts freely.

vii. *The Impact of Collective Guilt on Individual Members*

For a number of reasons the guilt of a group must be sharply distinguished from the guilt of any of its individual members. Consider a version of the possibility just mentioned. Joe is put under strong pressure by his parents to join the army and participate in the collective waging of a war that their country is engaged in. They threaten to disown him if he does not join the army. Now suppose that the waging of this war by this country is morally wicked, and both the country, and Joe, believe this. Suppose, finally, that the country in question freely entered the war. The collective itself appears unequivocally to meet the suggested standards for collective guilt. Joe's situation, however, is more nuanced. He does believe his country is in the wrong, but he stands to lose his inheritance if he fails to participate. If the loss of an inheritance does not seem sufficient to excuse him, one can imagine stronger pressure. Perhaps a government official has credibly threatened to kill Joe's wife and child if he refuses to join the army. Then perhaps we will not fault him for participating in the war. He may be morally blameless, or, if not that, he is not properly the object of harsh blame, as is his country.

There are other cases, where direct participation in the performance of the collective act is not at issue, where the blameworthiness of a particular group member is different in degree, or wholly absent, in the context of clear-cut collective moral guilt. Some of these will be mentioned later.

---

[27] On the possibility of entering a joint commitment in coercive circumstances see M. Gilbert, "Agreements, Coercion, and Obligation," *Ethics* 103 (1993), pp. 679–706, reprinted in Gilbert, *Living Together*, pp. 281–311.

3. Collective Guilt Feelings

What is it for us, collectively, to feel guilt about what we have collectively done?[28] In this section I articulate three possible answers to this question. These differ in interesting ways from one another. All describe possible phenomena, and important phenomena at that. In discussion of each one I focus on the question of how well it seems to represent "a collective feeling of guilt."

The most important thing about these answers, however, is that they all detail possible phenomena that are apt to be consequential. None should be overlooked in a discussion of the possible concomitants of collective guilt. The first phenomenon, or range of phenomena, is likely to be the most familiar. The other two are more recondite, but of at least equal significance.

i. *The First Aggregative Account. Feelings of Personal Guilt*

One who is considering for the first time what the phenomenon of so-called collective guilt amounts to is likely to suggest an account in terms of the feelings of individual human beings, feelings of a particular kind that I shall refer to as feelings of *personal guilt*.

What is a "feeling of personal guilt?" By definition:

> For A to feel *personal guilt* is for A to feel guilt over an action that A personally has performed.

In other words, the *object* of the guilt feeling, what it is about, is an action of the one who feels the guilt. The one who feels the guilt is the *subject* of the guilt feeling, the one whose feeling of guilt it is.

It may seem obvious that collective guilt feelings will be a matter of the feelings of personal guilt of individual members of the relevant collective. Two common assumptions suggest this. First, one may assume that the only possible subjects of guilt feelings are individuals as opposed to collectives. This is Kutz's assumption. Second, one may assume that a feeling of guilt is—as a matter of logic—guilt over one's own actions. Thus Gabriele Taylor writes: "Feelings of guilt...cannot arise from the deeds or omissions of others."[29] Others make

---

[28] I shall focus on collective guilt feelings over what the collective itself has done without reference to the actions of particular members. We might also feel guilt over what one of our members has done, acting as one of us. We might also feel guilt over what a group of which we, as a group, are a member, has done. I discuss this latter type of guilt feeling—which I refer to as "membership guilt"—in the text below, focusing on its occurrence in individuals with respect to the groups of which they are members.

[29] G. Taylor, *Pride, Shame, and Guilt: Emotions of Self-Assessment* (Oxford: Clarendon Press, 1985), p. 91.

concordant remarks. R. Jay Wallace, for instance, asserts: "Guilt is appropriate to one's own violations."[30]

Later discussion in this chapter will question both assumptions. For now I mean only to suggest that together they seem to recommend an account of collective guilt feelings in terms of the feelings of members of the collective, in particular, their feelings of personal guilt.

The first account I shall consider construes collective guilt feelings in terms of an aggregate of individual members' feelings of personal guilt. It runs thus:

> For us *collectively to feel guilt over our collective action A* is for each of us to feel guilt over something he or she did that directly contributed to our doing *A*.

There are two main problems with this account. First, the object of guilt in the *analysandum* is our collective act, something we have done together. It is hard to see how an account in terms of personal guilt can accommodate this consideration.

Suppose that Linda and Phil together kidnapped Sally. Perhaps Linda masterminded the affair, and feels guilt over doing so. This is not the same as feeling guilt over the collective act of kidnapping Sally. What if the plan to kidnap Sally was both jointly executed and jointly authored? With regard to what can either Linda or Phil appropriately feel personal guilt? Each one could appropriately feel guilt over having personally participated in the planning and execution of the kidnapping. That, of course, is not the same as feeling guilt over Sally's kidnapping.

Suppose that both Linda and Phil feel guilt for participating in the planning and execution of Sally's kidnapping. Is that enough to warrant the claim that they collectively feel guilt over their collective act? It does not seem so, since even now no one is feeling guilt over what they did together.

Apart from the fact that this first aggregative account does not seem to capture the object of the guilt in the *analysandum,* there is another problem with it. The account requires that all members of the relevant population feel guilt in relation to some contributory action of their own. There surely are cases of collective action where we cannot expect all of the members to feel this way, or in which they simply do not feel this way, cases in which—at the same time—it is not obvious that a collective feeling of guilt is ruled out.

---

[30] J. Wallace, *Responsibility and the Moral Sentiments* (Cambridge: Harvard University Press, 1994), p. 66, note 22. See also J. Feinberg, "Collective Responsibility," in May and Hoffman (eds.), *Collective Responsibility,* p. 60 [*"There can be no such thing as vicarious guilt"* (emphasis in original)].

Suppose the commander of a small battalion of soldiers orders the battalion to destroy a certain village along with its inhabitants. One of the men decides that it would be morally wrong for them to destroy the village. He pretends to have a bad knee and takes no part in the action. Another stumbles, breaks his ankle, and is genuinely unable to participate. A third, also having had a change of heart, pretends to be taking part in the carnage but in fact tries to help the villagers escape with some of their belongings. And so on. Perhaps in the event less than half the men contribute directly to the destruction of the village.[31]

Suppose now that all who did contribute substantially to the destruction of the village feel guilt over personally contributing to its destruction. The majority, however, do not feel any personal guilt in connection with the destruction of the village. We need not assume that this would be reasonable of them, though it is plausible enough to think that it would.

According to the present account of collective guilt feelings, the situation just described is one in which, as things presently stand, the collective in question cannot feel guilt, as a matter of logic. This does not seem to be the case, however, in relation to an intuitive notion of collective guilt feelings. Suppose one of the soldiers, referring to the whole battalion, observed "We feel guilt over our destruction of the village." He would surely not *have to be wrong* in the circumstances so far described. In other words, even though the conditions posited by the account are not met, it seems that the battalion could feel guilt over its act. What the basis of the soldier's claim would be is still obscure; yet it seems that such a basis could be present even given the distribution of feelings of personal guilt currently envisaged.

It will be tempting here to amend the present account in the following direction. Do not require that all members feel personal guilt in relation to the collective action. Require, instead, that those who contributed directly to it feel personal guilt for having done so. This may seem like the obvious way to proceed, but there is still a problem. The unamended account logically ruled out group guilt feelings on what seemed like insufficient grounds. The amended account seems logically to rule them *in* on insufficient grounds.

Is it enough for a *group* to feel guilt over its action if less than half of the group members directly contributed to the action and these members feel guilt over having done so? I would say not.

---

[31] The notion of "direct contribution" is both intuitive and somewhat vague. I am taking it that the soldiers who took no part in the action, by virtue of such things as falls and deliberate holdings off, count as not having contributed directly. This is not to say that they were necessarily in no way "involved in" the action. Insofar as they can properly refer to it as "our" action it seems that they were in some way involved. It does mean to suggest that whatever involvement they had might well not make a feeling of personal guilt appropriate.

I have considered two versions of an account of collective guilt feelings in terms of the personal guilt feelings of the directly contributing members of the relevant collective. Neither seems wholly plausible. Given that this is so, it looks very much as if one cannot give a satisfactory account of a collective's feeling guilt over its act in terms of the personal guilt feelings of the directly contributing members.

A query may arise here. Is it correct to say, in the case of the battalion of soldiers, that the battalion destroyed the village? Would it not be more accurate to say that those particular soldiers who directly contributed to the destruction of the village destroyed it? I suggest that though one could, of course, say this, one can also with perfect propriety say that the battalion destroyed the village. This would surely be plausible, if each member is party to a joint commitment that created the relevant collective intention and subsequent action. In this case, that might be the joint commitment to accept as a body that the commander is to decide what the group's intentions are to be. Given that he has commanded the destruction, and enough group members have acted in such a way that the command is fulfilled, there is a basis for saying that the group destroyed the village. For enough of its members, acting in light of its intent, fulfilled its intention.

However the first account is modified, the core idea that is likely to drive all versions of the account is that collective guilt feelings must ultimately be a matter of feelings of personal guilt on behalf of some or all members of the relevant collective. If this is all there ever is to a collective feeling of guilt, it would appear that no one ever actually feels guilt over a wrongful collective action. This may seem regrettable. Is it not possible for some person or body to feel guilt in regard to it?

ii. *The Second Aggregative Account: Feelings of Membership Guilt*

a. Feeling guilt over what one's group has done: Feeling membership guilt

Is there an alternative account of collective feelings of guilt that does not appeal to feelings of personal guilt, but, rather, to something which has the action of the collective as its object? That might seem impossible, at least if we are dealing with feelings of guilt whose subject is an individual human being. Recall the doubts philosophers have expressed about the possibility of guilt feelings that are not directed toward the personal guilt of the subject of these feelings.

A problem with rejection of such feelings is that people seem to have them. In particular, they sometimes seem to feel guilt and other supposedly "self-directed" emotions in relation to the actions of a group to which they belong. And this may be so even when they would not warrantably feel guilt over anything they themselves had done in relation to the group's action. Perhaps as soon as they realized it was afoot they tried to prevent it from happening. Perhaps they simply never made any direct contribution to it. Perhaps they did not even know that it was going on. Thus Herbert Morris, in relation to pride and shame:

> A man may take pride in the accomplishments of his countrymen when all he appears to share with them is his nationality...And do we not feel shame and think it appropriate, at least sometimes, over *actions of our country with which we may not have been involved*. (The emphasis is mine.)[32]

And thus Karl Jaspers, philosopher and psychiatrist, writing soon after the end of the Second World War in his nuanced and sensitive essay *The Question of German Guilt*:

> We feel ourselves not only as individuals, but as Germans. Everyone, in his real being, is the German people. Who does not remember moments in his life when he said to himself, in opposition and in despair of his nation, "I am Germany" or in jubilant harmony with it, "I, too, am Germany!"

and

> ...I feel co-responsible for what Germans do and have done. I feel closer to those Germans who feel likewise...and further from the ones whose soul seems to deny this link.[33]

I shall take it that people sometimes feel guilt over what a group of which they are members has done. I shall call this feeling a feeling of *membership guilt*.[34]

b. Membership guilt versus personal guilt

What is it *like* to feel membership guilt? How does it compare with feeling personal guilt?

I assume that a feeling of membership guilt may not be distinguishable from a feeling of personal guilt in terms of whatever pangs and twinges may be involved.

---

[32] H. Morris, *On Guilt and Innocence* (Berkeley: University of California Press, 1979), p. 117. Morris writes here of shame rather than guilt. Did he think that feeling guilt over one's country's action was ruled out on logical or conceptual grounds? It is not clear to me that it is. People claim to feel such guilt, though it puzzles them. See the discussion of Karl Jaspers below.

[33] K. Jaspers, *The Question of German Guilt*, trans. E. B. Ashton (New York: Capricorn Books, 1947), p. 80.

[34] This may not be the best label, but I am not sure what would be better. "Participatory guilt" may suggest too close a connection with the collective action, that is, the status of a direct participant. Since I have used this label before, e.g., in M. Gilbert, "Group Wrongs and Guilt Feelings," *Journal of Ethics* 1 (1997), pp. 65–84, I continue to use it here.

More generally, these feelings will not have distinguishable phenomenological conditions. They will, however, be distinguishable, by reference to the requisite judgment or thought. A feeling of membership guilt will at some level involve the judgment that a collective of which the subject of the guilt is a member has done something wrong, whereas a feeling of personal guilt involves the judgment that the person whose feeling it is has done something wrong.

c. Karl Jaspers' dilemma

Are feelings of membership guilt intelligible? Jaspers thought not. I omitted the words that express his judgment from the second passage quoted above. The penultimate sentence reads, more fully, as follows:

> ...in a way which is rationally not conceivable, which is even rationally refutable, I feel co-responsible for what Germans do and have done.

In effect, Jaspers is confronted with a dilemma. There is a way that he "cannot help feeling" which is "rationally refutable." Being a philosopher, he finds this extremely problematic:

> As a philosopher I now seem to have strayed completely into the realm of feeling and to have abandoned conception...[35]

As a philosopher he would prefer not to have emotions that are "rationally refutable." He would prefer not to "abandon conception," presumably leaving concerns with logical coherence and consistency, and stray completely into the realm of feeling.

The several careful distinctions among kinds of guilt that he has made in the course of his essay do not appear to help him with this problem.[36]

d. The intelligibility of membership guilt

Jaspers can be rescued from his dilemma. Or, at least, a related dilemma can be resolved. That is, given that a group has acted in a blameworthy fashion, one

---

[35] Jaspers, *The Question of German Guilt*, p. 81.

[36] Jaspers distinguishes criminal guilt, political guilt, moral guilt, metaphysical guilt. I comment on Larry May's discussion of the last mentioned kind of guilt in Gilbert, "Group Wrongs and Guilt Feelings." See L. May, *Sharing Responsibility* (Chicago: University of Chicago Press, 1992), section reprinted in May and Hoffman (eds.), *Collective Responsibility*. Gilbert, "Group Wrongs and Guilt Feelings" focuses on the elucidation of feelings of membership guilt, as does Chapter 16 of Gilbert, *Sociality and Responsibility* ("On Feeling Guilt for What One's Group Has Done").

can argue that it is indeed intelligible for group members to feel guilt over the action in question. My argument for the intelligibility of these feelings utilizes the account of collective action introduced earlier in this essay. To repeat it here:

A population *P collectively performed action A* if and only if, roughly, the members of *P* were jointly committed to intending as a body to do *A*, and, acting in the light of this joint commitment, relevant members of *P* acted so as to satisfy this intention.

Given this analysis of collective action, there is an argument for the intelligibility of membership guilt for any member of the collective. Even group members who do not directly contribute to the group's action are linked to it through their participation in the foundational joint commitment. This joint commitment is crucial to the argument. It grounds each member's ability to say, "We did it" with some justification. He, as a party to the foundational joint commitment, is indeed one of *us*.

A member can say this, on this basis, whether or not he or she made a direct contribution to the performance of the action. A member can say this, indeed, whether or not he or she knew at the time that the action in question was being performed. For one can be part of a population whose members are jointly committed to intend as a body to do *A* whether or not one is aware of the content of the intention in question. One's being jointly committed in this way can be a function of an authority-creating joint commitment. Thus the relevant intention may have been brought into effect by virtue of the acts of a person or body authorized to make decisions for the group. It is not necessary that everyone in the group knows that the intention has been brought into effect or implemented. Nonetheless the authorization may be one in which everyone has participated.

Similarly, one can say "We did it" appropriately, even if one has done whatever one could to subvert the course of the collective action. One's participation in the relevant joint commitment still ties one inextricably to the group. If what "we" did was morally wicked, one can appropriately in these circumstances admit that too, and appropriately feel guilt over what we did. This is not, of course, to feel guilt over what one did oneself. One may have been entirely guiltless, personally, in the matter.

e. Joint commitment and identification

What of Jaspers' thought, "I am Germany?" Can the above account of collective action help to explain it? One might say that Jaspers here *identifies* with Germany. There is a clear sense in which a joint commitment provides a basis for *identification* with the group as agent. A party to the joint commitment is not literally identical with the agent, of course, but to some extent it is as if a party is the agent. If my group bears guilt, then my participation in the relevant joint commitment means that I cannot disassociate myself from that guilt: from my point of view it is *our* guilt, not *their* guilt. To be jointly committed is to be, in a substantial sense, an "associate" of the other parties.[37] In terms from J.-J. Rousseau's *Social Contract,* one is "an indivisible part of the whole."

f. Intelligibility versus accuracy

I have argued, contrary to Jaspers' doubts, that feelings of membership guilt are intelligible, and can find a clear rationale in the joint commitment that underlies a collective action. One might be comfortable with this conclusion, but raise the following question. Were "the German people," comprising millions of people, parties to a joint commitment to authorize the Nazis to do what they did? If not, then Jaspers' own feeling of membership guilt has not been rationalized at all.

The details of Jaspers' situation are an empirical, historical matter. As I have indicated earlier, there are mechanisms for the creation of large-scale joint commitments. Hence it is in principle possible, for any given large population, that there is a joint commitment in that case. Jaspers suggests that many—though not all—Germans feel as he does. They feel "coresponsible" for what Germans do and have done. Insofar as he and others have this feeling, my guess would be that what underlies it is a sense of joint commitment. This sense would be misplaced only insofar as there is no such commitment in fact. Given that many do share it, however, it there may be something approximating a relevant joint commitment.

I suspect Jaspers thought the problem was worse: that for a person to feel guilt over acts in which he was not directly involved, and so on, is simply unintelligible. It is against this concern that I have argued here.

g. Feelings of membership guilt and collective guilt feelings

Can one give an account of collective feelings of guilt in terms of an aggregate of feelings of membership guilt? Is it plausible to think of a group as feeling guilt over one of its actions if all of its members feel membership guilt over the action in question?

I suggest not. It is true that, here, a group's action is the object of a feeling of guilt. But the feeling does not have a collective subject. One might put it this way. Certainly individual members of the group feel guilt over the group's action. But

---

[37] Cf. May, *Sharing Responsibility,* on "metaphysical guilt." May thinks I can disassociate myself from my group's guilt relatively easily.

one can still ask: what of the group itself? The group itself does not seem to be the subject of a feeling of guilt.

To point up the problem, consider that no one may know that everyone feels guilt over the group's action. Perhaps each member believes that she or he alone feels membership guilt over the group's act. Perhaps he or she believes that everyone else would laugh or be scornful on hearing that anyone felt the group's act was culpable. It would surely be quite odd to say that the group felt guilt under such circumstances, even though the conditions posited by the account of collective guilt feelings under scrutiny are met.

We could amend the account in terms of a generalized feeling of membership guilt by adding a condition to the effect that the existence of the feelings in question should be common knowledge.

This would rule out the scenarios just mentioned, though it would still not introduce a collective subject of guilt.

In addition, a common knowledge condition could be fulfilled without anyone having publicly expressed a feeling of membership guilt. It does not rule out the following state of affairs. The group in question believes that it can do no wrong. That is, the members are jointly committed to believe as a body that they can do no wrong. Such self-righteousness may be as common with groups as it is with individuals. Unless this joint commitment is rescinded with the concurrence of all, it stands as a barrier to anyone's expressing guilt feelings over what the group has done. For such feelings involve a judgment of group wrongdoing.

In this situation group members, discussing the group's act with one another, are likely to refer to its fineness, justice, appropriateness, and so on. All will realize that they stand to be rebuked in the name of the joint commitment should they baldly assert a contrary judgment.

Few may be willing even to say something carefully qualified like "I personally think that we acted badly when...."[38] Though this does not amount to a violation of the joint commitment, it could be seen as subversive. Hence one risks being faulted for disloyalty even then. Such a situation, given common knowledge that people personally feel guilt over the group's action, may be inherently unstable. Nonetheless, as far as it goes, it seems some distance from a situation in which one would want to speak of the group feeling guilt.

One might be unwilling to give up an account in terms of feelings of membership guilt, if there were no plausible alternative. As I shall now argue, however, there is a plausible alternative.

---

[38] Regarding the use of such qualifiers in the context of collective belief, see Gilbert, *On Social Facts*, especially pp. 288–292; also Gilbert, *Living Together*, pp. 200–203.

iii. *A Plural Subject Account of Collective Guilt Feelings*

People constitute a plural subject in my sense when they are jointly committed to doing something as a body, where "doing something" is construed broadly enough to include intending, believing, and the like. An alternative to any of the aggregative accounts of collective guilt feelings that have been considered is, evidently, a plural subject account. I now consider such an account.

a. The account

A plural subject account of collective guilt feelings would run as follows:

> For us *collectively to feel guilt over our action A* is for us to be jointly committed to feeling guilt as a body over our action *A*.

Alternatively, with my definition of "plural subject" understood:

> For us *collectively to feel guilt over our action A* is for us to constitute the plural subject of a feeling of guilt over our action *A*.

What exactly are the parties committed to here? One might spell this out as follows. They are to act as would be appropriate were they to constitute a single subject of guilt feelings. Or, perhaps better, they are to act so as to emulate, as far as is possible, a single subject of guilt feelings. This does not mean that they are to act so as to emulate, as far as possible, a single *individual human* subject of guilt feelings. Thus this conception of collective guilt feelings does not entail that the guilt feelings of individual human beings are logically prior to those of collectives.

How will the individual members act if they act in the way required by their joint commitment? For one thing, when talking among themselves they will characterize the action in question as morally wrong. They will say and do only what accords with this judgment. For example, they will refrain from proposing that it is morally acceptable for the group to engage in an obviously similar action. Should one of their number propose such a thing, they will feel free to remonstrate with the person in question. In addition, they feel free to ascribe guilt feelings to the group, and to remonstrate with a group member who denies that the group feels guilty.

b. The importance of the phenomenon

Collective guilt feelings according to this account would be important phenomena under any name. Suppose that Ted and the other members of his gang understand that they are jointly committed to feel guilt as a body over their unprovoked attack on a rival gang. This is liable to make a significant difference to what happens next. Perhaps their credo is: "Attack other gangs when you get the chance." Accepting the wickedness of its last attack, Ted's gang will be under pressure from the point of view of self-consistency to question its credo. Perhaps it will modify its credo, or even decide to disband. Someone might propose that Ted's gang tender an apology to the other gang. A wrong done might be righted as far as is possible. A cycle of violence may be closed.

Evidently collective guilt feelings—on the plural subject account—provide an analogue of personal guilt, at the collective level. This is not surprising, since a joint commitment precisely to *feel guilt* as a body is at issue.

c. The genesis of collective guilt feelings

How might collective guilt feelings, according to the plural subject account, arise? It will be neither necessary nor sufficient for members of the group to feel membership guilt over an act of the collective. It will be neither necessary nor sufficient for members to feel personal guilt over their participation or other act relating to the collective act. In cases in which there is no relevantly authoritative person or body involved, what is needed, to put it abstractly, is expressions of readiness on everyone's part to be jointly committed to feel guilt as a body. Common knowledge of these expressions completes the picture.

Take a small-scale case. Lisa and Joe have been looking after Phyllis's daughter Mary for the weekend. Preoccupied with their own problems, they neglect Mary, leaving her to her own devices. She becomes depressed, as is obvious when Phyllis comes to collect her. Later, speaking on the phone to Phyllis, Lisa says, "We feel really guilty about letting Mary get so depressed.." Joe, who is listening, says to Lisa, *sotto voce,* "No we don't..." Lisa flashes back "Yes, we do..." and Joe concurs.

This may be enough to establish a joint commitment between Joe and Lisa, a joint commitment to feel guilt as a body over their treatment of Mary. In Lisa's presence, at least, Joe will now feel constrained to do and say things that echo or conform to Lisa's claim that she and Joe feel guilty about the way they treated Mary.

A different kind of case appears to be possible. This involves constitutionally elected governments. Addressing a third party through its emissaries, an official of such a government may say something like this: "The whole nation feels guilt over the way it treated you."[39]

---

[39] Such statements may tend to be rare. That it takes a rare person or body to feel guilt over an act performed does not, of course, mean that it is impossible.

It may be understood by all that the government, acting through its officials, is entitled thus to determine the emotional state of the citizen body, in effect, jointly committing the citizens to feel guilt as a body. A special feature of this case is that many particular citizens may be unaware of the official's pronouncement, and be found expressing contrary feelings without understanding that they violate a joint commitment they are subject to. Clearly this is a complicated type of case, dependent on an understanding of the simpler case without authorities. It seems there may be cases of analogous complexity involving a single human being.

d. The phenomenology of collective guilt feelings

On the plural subject account, are collective guilt feelings such that they have no associated phenomenology? The question here need not be interpreted in terms of a necessary phenomenological condition of feeling guilt. As I have argued, there is reason to doubt whether any such conditions are necessary in the case of an individual human being. If they are not, then they are not necessary for guilt feelings in general. There is then no issue for an account of collective guilt feelings that does not require that some phenomenological condition be met.

Meanwhile, it is worth considering the following fact about collective guilt feelings according to the plural subject account. To put it generally, it seems most likely that there are phenomenological accompaniments of collective guilt feelings. These will include feeling-sensations experienced by individual human beings and occurring, in that sense, in the minds of these individuals.[40] Nonetheless, they may best be thought of as pangs, and so on, of collective guilt.

Let me explain. Suppose Joe is conforming to the joint commitment he has with Lisa to feel guilt as a body over their treatment of Mary. His conformity involves such things as saying, in light of the joint commitment, "We acted wrongly," and "We feel guilty about what we did." In the course of saying such things and acting accordingly, Joe may experience a sudden pang.

How is one best to describe such feeling-sensations? Are they pangs of personal guilt, or pangs of membership guilt?

Clearly, from a phenomenological point of view there may be no way of deciding this issue: a pang is a pang is a pang. One needs to look at the context in which the pangs occur.

---

[40] I say that feeling-sensations will be *included*, bearing in mind that there may be qualitative states of mind that typically accompany guilt feelings in the case of individual humans that are not as salient as feeling-sensations.

As far as Joe's story goes, Joe's pang is responsive to his and Lisa's collective feeling of guilt, rather than to any feeling of membership or personal guilt of his own. Had he and Lisa not come to collectively feel guilt, he might never have had this pang. And his pang may not correspond to any judgments he has made in his heart as to the wrongfulness of what he and Lisa did or any associated act of his own. In the above story, insofar as he made any personal judgments on what they did these were not censorious.

It may be, then, that Joe's pang is best described as a "pang of collective guilt." To argue that there can be pangs of collective guilt, in this sense, is not to fly in the face of reason or science. Pangs of collective guilt, in this sense, exist in and through the conscious experiences of individual group members. Nonetheless, this way of labeling them makes sense.

iv. *How to Feel Guilt: Three Different Ways*

I have considered three accounts of what it is for people collectively to feel guilt in the context of collective wrongdoing, one in terms of feelings of personal guilt, one in terms of feelings of membership guilt, and the plural subject account.

The plural subject account alone posits an irreducibly collective subject of guilt feelings—a plural subject created by a joint commitment. With other accounts, the so-called collective guilt feelings come down to an aggregate of guilt feelings attributable to individual group members. I am therefore inclined to think that it captures the gist of everyday attributions of collective guilt feelings, attributions that appear to imply the existence of a collective subject.

Each account appeals to a different way of feeling guilt in the context of collective action. An individual member of a collective can feel personal guilt over what he or she has done in relation to the collective action. The individual member of a collective can feel membership guilt over what the collective has done. And people can constitute themselves the members of plural subject of guilt feelings, the object of these feelings being the collective act. This last seems most plausibly to be considered a collective way of feeling guilt. In what follows, when I refer to *collective guilt feelings* I understand this in terms of the plural subject account.

There are important connections between collective guilt feelings and feelings of personal and membership guilt. No one of these feelings seems to carry another with it as a matter of logic. The existence of guilt feelings of any of the three kinds, however, will tend to be associated with guilt feelings of the other kinds. People who feel membership guilt, for instance, are likely to express this feeling to one another in such a way that they constitute themselves a plural subject of guilt feelings. Hence, whether or not one continues to believe that the true subjects of guilt feelings are individuals, one can allow that collective guilt feelings *in the plural subject sense* are likely to occur and to play an important role in the life of groups, their victims, and their critics.[41]

[41] This chapter connects with several others works I have published in the area of collective guilt, collective emotions, and related matters. It greatly extends "How to Feel Guilt: Three Different Ways," an invited talk given at the "Guilt, Shame, and Punishment" conference in honor of Herbert Morris, Columbia Law School, 1998. I thank those present for lively discussion, and Kent Greenawalt for written comments. I am grateful also for comments on related talks at Providence College, the State University of New York at Purchase, the University of Illinois, Urbana-Champaign, the University of Connecticut, Storrs, and elsewhere. I thank Angelo Corlett for prompting me some time ago to extend my consideration of these matters beyond the discussion in Gilbert, *On Social Facts*, pp. 425–426.

PART THREE

MUTUAL RECOGNITION, PROMISES, AND LOVE

...thoughts that I had had before, about the fusion of our souls into one higher-level entity, about the fact that at the core of both our souls lay our identical hopes and dreams for our children, about the notion that those hopes were not separate or distinct hopes but were just one hope, one clear thing that defined us both, that welded us into a unit, the kind of unit I had but dimly recognized before being married and having children.

Douglas Hofstadter, *I Am a Strange Loop* (New York: Basic Books, 2007), 228.

Fusion: Sketch of a "Contractual" Model

"...love...is neither you nor him. It is a third thing you must create."
(D. H. Lawrence)[1]

"...[In] a good love relationship...to some extent the two people have become for psychological purposes a single unit, a single person, a single ego." (A. H. Maslow)[2]

"...fusion...central to all loving." (W. Gaylin)[3]

I. Introduction

The terms "fusion" and "merging," and related phrases, are often used to describe a common and desirable feature of long-term intimate relationships such as marriage. Such terms occur in theoretical contexts in sociology and psychology, as well as in poetry, fiction, and private thoughts. Sometimes it is said that two "selves" or "egos" merge or fuse.[4] And people may be said to become "a single unit," even "a single person" or "a single ego." (All three phrases are used by Maslow, quoted above.) Often merging is associated with phenomena such as responsibility, care, and concern. The sociologist Pitirim Sorokin writes: "The successes and failures of one party are shared by the others and elicit their concurrence, aid, and sympathy."[5]

Reference to the merging of two selves may be fine as a "picture" of a real process, but how much theoretical illumination does it give us? What is a "self" or "ego" and how can two distinct egos fuse?

In *The Symposium* Plato envisions the fire-god Hephaestus asking two lovers: "Do you desire to be joined in the closest possible union?...I am ready to

---

[1] Lawrence, *The Rainbow*, p. 176; quoted in Gaylin (1987).

[2] Maslow (1953), pp. 75–76.

[3] Gaylin (1987), p. 116.

[4] See Sorokin (1947), p. 100: "a complete merging of their selves," and (of a contrasting case) "the egos of the parties remain unmerged" (p. 103). I learned of Sorokin's discussion from Lindgren (1988).

[5] Sorokin (1947), p. 99; cf. Maslow (1953), p. 76.

fuse and weld you together in a single piece."[6] Lovers may indeed sometimes imagine a complete *bodily* merging of one with the other. But we know *this* does not actually happen. Is there something that *does* happen that might aptly be referred to as the fusion of two people?

In the literature of clinical psychology and family therapy, terms such as "fusion" are often used to refer to an actual phenomenon. However, when the parties involved are an adult couple, this phenomenon is commonly deemed pathological, or at least a sign of immaturity. Thus according to M. Karpel, the term "fusion," when applied to adult couples, refers to the "transactional and experiential phenomenon that is created when two minimally individuated persons form a close, emotional relationship." Karpel contrasts fusion with "dialogue": "a mature relationship between individuated partners."[7] And M. Bowen writes, "In mature families, individual family members are contained emotional units who do not become involved in emotional fusion with others."[8]

The term "fusion" may be an apt label for certain problematic forms of marital relationship. At the same time, many people have obviously thought that something aptly referred to as "fusion" has the capacity strongly to enhance a marriage. Witness my opening quotations from Gaylin, Maslow, and Lawrence. It is this thought that provokes the present essay.

Can one describe an actual phenomenon for which the label "fusion" is apt, and which has the capacity strongly to enhance a marriage? To echo Wittgenstein on meaning, "Is there a model for this?" In this chapter I propose one such model.[9]

Fusion in my sense is an actual state of affairs necessarily involving two persons in a symmetrical fashion. It is a state of affairs of which the parties may be expected to be aware: they may be expected to have a "sense of fusion." But fusion is not simply a matter of two persons having a certain sense of their relationship to one another.[10]

---

[6] Plato, *Symposium*, p. 192.

[7] Karpel (1976), pp.70–71. Karpel aims to summarize the trend in a body of literature on "fusion" in clinical psychology.

[8] Bowen (1965), p. 219.

[9] This is based on work that was not itself focused on this particular theme. See in particular *On Social Facts*. The topics of love and marriage are briefly touched upon at pp. 223–25 and 471.

[10] Cf. Gaylin (1987), p. 103: "The concept of fusion as I will use it literally means the loss of one's identity in that of another; a confusion of ego boundaries; the sense of unsureness as to where I end and you, the person I love, begin; the identification of your pain with my pain and your success with my success; the inconceivability of a self that does not include you; and the inevitability that your loss will create a painful fracture of my self-image that will necessitate a long and painful rebuilding of my ego during a period of grief and despair."

In this account a particular subjective state appears to be central to fusion. In fact it looks as if fusion can be wholly one-sided (unilateral). It also looks as if our being fused one with another is a matter of each of us having the relevant sense of how things are, while this sense is not answerable to the world in any way. (It could not be mistaken.)

The model I shall propose can be characterized as a "contractual" model in a broad sense. Some may find this surprising. Sorokin, for instance, labels relationships involving a high degree of fusion "familistic" while the contrast case is labeled "contractual." Can fusion itself be a function of something resembling a contract or agreement? People may, of course, espouse different ideas as to what is essential to a contract or agreement. Suffice it to say that the model of fusion presented here has some clear affinities with models of human association in classical contractarian political philosophy.[11]

I take the phenomenon I shall refer to as "fusion" in this essay to be central to human social relationships in general. It can be long or short-lived, and admits of degrees: two or more people can be more or less fused together at a given time. Meanwhile, a lasting marriage may well involve an intensive, continuing fusion. Though all fusion has inevitable cost in terms of individual freedom, an intensive continuing fusion has the capacity strongly to enhance a marriage.

In the second section I argue for and sketch a model for the general idea of the fusion of two or more persons. In the third section I discuss why one might think of fusion in my sense particularly in connection with marriage and family relations, and indicate how fusion can enhance matters in these contexts. I stress that fusion can co-exist with a variety of background states of the self, and that this is relevant to the evaluation of the total situation in which it occurs.

II. Fusion

How might we interpret the phrase "fused egos" in the present context? Let us start with an account of a "self" or an "ego." For present purposes I shall make use of the first person singular pronoun "I." An individual person can represent herself as "I," and her qualities, including her goals, values, and beliefs, as "mine." (What we call an "ego"-centric person, by the way, appears to be one who *focuses* to some high degree on what is *hers:* her thoughts, needs, wants, achievements, and so on.) I shall stipulate that a person who makes explicit references to herself in terms of "I" and "mine" *has an ego*, or, equivalently, *is an ego*. Now consider two egos (as defined), Jill and Jack. How might they "merge" or "fuse"?

One idea might be that Jack must make Jill's ideas his own, while retaining his own ideas, and vice versa. An obvious problem arises, though, if, say, Jack is a

---

A realistic definition of fusion does not have to make it a function of subjective states in this way. On the account I develop below, *the fusion of two persons is not purely a matter of each party's sense of things*. Fusion in my sense may lead to the type of sense of things Gaylin alludes to, as will emerge.

[11] That connection will not be pursued here. But see *On Social Facts*, especially pp. 197–98 and 415–16. See also Chapter 6, this volume.

Democrat and Jill is a Republican. Without difficulty Jack himself can hardly be both a Democrat and a Republican. If, to avoid generating a whole set of inconsistencies in belief, we insist that Jack take on Jill's ideas *while discarding his own*, and vice versa, there seems to be no more reason to call Jack and Jill "merged" than when they had their original ideas. They've just switched sides.

It may be suggested that "fused egos" are (by definition) those who care for each other's well-being: I care both for my own well-being, and for yours, equally, and vice versa. Here again there is the problem of seeing why we should talk of "fusion." It is perfectly consistent with the idea of an ego developed so far that egos care deeply about others. (This is also the case with the resembling notion of an agent in game theory with a personal utility function.) I may want you to be happy. I may intend to provide for your future, whatever else I do. If we want some appropriate general definition of "fused egos" or "merged egos," then, this seems the wrong way to go.

It is true that one fairly natural way of expressing the thought that I care for your welfare as I care for my own is to say that I "identify" with you, or, indeed, that I love you. In spite of this, "fusion" seems too strong a term in this connection. In addition, if we define fusion in terms of mutual concern and caring, we cannot explain instances of the latter in terms of fusion. Yet in many discussions fusion is seen as an explanatory concept, something that can help to explain at least some instances of concern and caring. Though its development was not influenced by this idea, the model of fusion that will be presented below will give it such an explanatory character.

I shall now stop focusing on the first person singular pronoun, and turn to the first person plural pronoun—"we." This is quite often invoked in connection with love and marriage, and Sorokin refers to "the egos of the interacting parties" as being "fused together *in one "we."*"[12] Use of "we" cannot of itself solve the problem of providing an articulated model of merging. However, as I shall argue, one can provide a perspicuous account of a phenomenon one might well name "fusion," if one focuses carefully on certain uses of "we" along with the pronominal adjective "our," and so on.[13]

Clearly, someone may represent herself as *part* of a "we" and may represent herself as *participating* in "our" opinions, goals, values, and so on. When is this justified?

Consider "our opinion." Is Jill's use of this phrase justified just in case she and Jack individually hold the same opinion? Perhaps sometimes "our opinion" is used in this way. But in many cases the appropriate interpretation for "our

---

[12] Sorokin (1947), p. 142, my emphasis; see also pp. 100 and 103.

[13] There is a detailed discussion of the semantics, broadly construed, of "we" and cognate terms, in *On Social Facts*. See in particular Chapter 4, pp. 167–203, and Chapter 7, pp. 417–27. What follows in the text draws upon that discussion.

opinion" is not of this "summative" kind. Nor, indeed, is it a necessary condition for the proper use of this phrase that at least some of the parties hold the opinion in question.

As I have argued elsewhere, a paradigmatic situation for "our opinion" is roughly as follows: each of a set of people has openly expressed personal willingness to accept a certain view *jointly* with the others. Once this has happened, joint acceptance of the view is established. It is then appropriate to speak of "our opinion." The process that generates a jointly accepted view is *agreement-like*, though it does not have to involve any explicit agreement. Like those who explicitly agree on something, the participants are, by their own acts, *simultaneously* and *interdependently* "bound" to behave in certain ways. In particular, *it is now incumbent upon the parties to act as the members of a (single) being with the view in question,* at least in certain relevant circumstances. Rebukes of one participant by another are in place for failures to comply with this requirement.[14]

Those who jointly accept a certain view have, in effect, jointly constituted themselves the single subject of a view. They will understand this (since they have the concept of joint acceptance) and now see themselves as constituting in effect, the members of a single being, or, as we might put it, a single "body" or "person."

For an example of this complex phenomenon on the ground, consider a typical statement made in the context of a family. Mr. Jones says, "We think you should be home by midnight, Johnnie." Mr. Jones may himself see no reason why Johnnie should not come home any time he pleases. Ms. Jones, meanwhile, thinks Johnnie should be home by ten, and, if it was up to her, would still make this ruling. But the Joneses have discussed the matter and compromised. They have arrived at what they may properly characterize as "our view"—not his, nor hers, but "ours," and in this case, ours only. Each understands that it is now incumbent upon each one to express "their" view (that is, the compromise view) in front of Johnnie. For instance, if Johnnie says to Ms. Jones, "Must I *really* be home by midnight?," she must answer affirmatively if she does not qualify her answer in some way (see below). Thus the Joneses may be expected to express the compromise view, and behave appropriately. For all Johnnie knows, both hold it personally.

It is important to see that the change in each of the Joneses in generating a view that is, as they say, "ours," is not a superficial one. This is so even when, as above, each personally holds a conflicting view. In particular, neither one is *pretending personally to believe something.* Rather, they now conceive themselves as the members of a single body (or person) that does believe that thing, a status

---

[14] For further elaboration of these ideas see Chapters 7 and 14, and the introduction, this volume. See also *On Social Facts,* especially Chapter 5.

requiring specific behavior on each individual's part. This behavior, not surprisingly, coincides to some extent with that of one who personally believes the thing in question. Consider, however, that Mr. Jones could tell Johnnie, with *logical* propriety, "I personally still think we do not have to be so restrictive." (Most likely it would be imprudent of Mr. Jones to make his own view known.)

"We" may not only have opinions, but also *values, principles of action,* and *aims.* Bob and Sue could have the *joint aim* of cycling from Storrs to Willimantic together. A salient aspect of this case is that Sue and Bob will need constantly to monitor each other's behavior, making sure that they are keeping up with one another. If Bob has a fall, it will be incumbent upon Sue to do something about it. A plausible course of action will be to stop herself, help him up from the ground, and ask if he needs to stop and rest for a while. Here, then, at least the simulacra of caring and concern are likely to come into play.[15]

Those with a joint aim are only obligated thereby to behave in a caring manner insofar as this is necessary to promote their joint aim. Thus the primary joint aim of a given couple, Belle and Ben, could be "keeping Ben happy," and Ben may derive pleasure from hurting Belle. Insofar as Belle has to exist and be capable of suffering pain in order that Ben have his pleasure, Belle's continued survival and her continuing sensitivity to pain, at least, will be a matter of concern for both. This will tend to produce a minimal degree of caring behavior on Ben's part. Clearly, though, that may be all the caring behavior that Belle receives from Ben (or from herself).[16]

I have elsewhere referred to those who participate in a joint belief, or a joint goal, principle, or the like, as the members of a *plural subject.* I have also argued that there is a correlative central sense of the pronoun "we" such that "we" refers to a plural subject.[17] I now suggest that one possible model for *fusion* is that of *plural subject formation,* or *"we"-formation* in the correlative sense. I propose that two egos may be said to have fused just in case the people in question form a plural subject of some kind.

Note that, on this account, an alternative to the phrase "fused egos" is *persons with egos, who fuse* (that is, come to constitute a plural subject). As the example of the Joneses makes clear, the fusion of two egos, on this construal, *does not require the obliteration of the egos in question.* Mr. and Ms. Jones can still be egos, on my definition, while being fused relative to the belief that Johnnie should be

---

[15] For further discussion of joint aims or goals see Chapter 6. See also *On Social Facts,* Chapter 4, especially pp. 157–202. On jointly accepted (or group) principles, see Chapter 2 here, and *On Social Facts,* Chapter 6, pp. 373 ff.

[16] These last remarks suggest that there is nothing in the concept of a joint aim or jointly accepted view that prevents these from amounting on occasion to a *folie à deux.*

[17] "We" may sometimes be used more broadly, but this narrower sense is often at issue. See *On Social Facts,* Chapter 4.

home by midnight; that is, while jointly believing this. Indeed, each can maintain a personal belief antithetical to their group belief. Their fusion does entail corresponding constraints on their behavior, of course. Some previously possible plans become inadmissible. For instance, Mr. Jones cannot now appropriately plan to tell Johnnie that he is welcome to stay out as long as he likes.

According to this account, it is part of the structure of all fusion that the parties accept an obligation to attend to one another and to act in such a way as to promote their joint "cause." This is most obvious in the case of joint pursuit of an aim, but it is true of jointly accepted beliefs, values, and principles also. Mr. Jones will need not only to watch his own words but to pay some attention to what Ms. Jones is doing. (It is, one might say, his business.) If he sees that she is about to say the wrong thing to Johnnie, he is both entitled and obliged to step in and do something, if he can, to prevent her from slipping up.

It appears that there is a sense in which the parties to any instance of fusion are obligated to come to one another's aid. By definition, each one is committed to promoting their "cause." When he intervenes with Ms. Jones, Mr. Jones is helping her to fulfill her commitments, along with his own. "Thanks," Ms. Jones might respond, "I nearly slipped up."

All fusion, then, will promote a particular species of aid to another, with a concomitant gratitude on behalf of the person helped. This is one inherent comfort of fusion in general. There can also be some comfort in being noticed. If another person is providing these comforts, one is likely to feel a degree of affection and kindness toward them.

There is, of course, another structural aspect of fusion that seems apt to generate positive emotion. Every instance of fusion provides a basis for a *sense of unity*, even a sense of *intimacy* or *closeness* within the single "we" that is involved. Human beings may tend to find this sense of things gratifying and those gratified in this way are likely to feel some affection and kindness toward those with whom they are fused.

In sum, on my account fusion in general is such that for structural reasons a degree of positive emotion stands to occur between the parties.

III. Fusion in Marriage

On the above construal, fusion is a matter of degree. That is, two (or more) people can be fused together to a greater or lesser extent.[18] Fusion can also be of

---

[18] The idea that there are *degrees* of fusion is assumed by Sorokin (1947). Though he writes (of such relationships as that of a landlord and tenant) that the egos of the parties "remain unmerged in any real 'we'" (p. 103), he does accept that in such relationships there is a degree of fusion or merging. Cf. Max Weber on "communal" versus "associative" relationships in *Economy and Society*.

long or short duration. Two strangers might start talking on a bus and converse until one has to leave. A conversation generally involves a joint aim (conversing with one another) and generates various views that are jointly accepted at least for the duration of the encounter.[19] These conversationalists will, then, be fused temporarily to a degree, in relation to a certain goal and a certain set of views.

If strangers can fuse, why think of fusion in relation to marriage in particular? The answer is clear. Marriage is liable to produce an intensive, long-term fusion.

There is no obvious reason to think that fusion of the kind common in marriage cannot exist without benefit of legal marriage. Marriage, though, is its usual locus in our culture as things stand. There are familiar aspects of marriage in our culture that will help both to encourage and to make salient the special kind of fusion it can involve. Marriage is often entered into in an emotionally charged public ceremony with a public exchange of vows, often under religious auspices, and has legal implications at least some of which are known to the parties.

Marriage, I suggested, is a fruitful field for fusion. Of course a given marriage may contain more or less fusion. But many will involve the following components. First, the parties have one or more major long-term joint projects, such as living together harmoniously for the rest of their lives ("'til death do us part"), creating and maintaining a comfortable home, raising a family, and so on. Such projects generate a plethora of smaller joint projects, both long- and short-term, such as maintaining a joint bank account, buying a car, visiting parents, and taking the kids to the zoo. Second, over time negotiations take place and agreements are reached on a multitude of issues, major and minor, such as whether we can afford to buy a house, who is the best babysitter, and how often we should eat fish. Such agreements arise in part in the course of carrying out joint projects. There are also many random conversations that result in joint acceptance of some proposition, value, or principle. A given issue may be debated many times, and the parties may agree to differ more or less often. (Joint acceptance of the view that you disagree on some issue is itself, of course, an agreement of sorts.) In any case, the parties come continuously jointly to accept numerous beliefs, values, and principles of action. In addition, there is a variety of beliefs and so on that are jointly accepted for a time.

In a situation like this, a host of major and minor projects, and a host of views, values and principles, characterize the same pair, the same "we" at a given time. The parties, then, are fused in many respects. I shall say that the fusion is *intensive*. They are also fused in this intensive way over time. This intensity and continuity of intensity can be expected sharply to stimulate the sense of unity and closeness fusion in general supports.

---

[19] In *On Social Facts* I argue for a model of conversation in general as the negotiation of jointly accepted views, pp. 294–98.

It is also significant that, in a situation like that described, there is a lot of stability in the way the parties are fused: they continuously sustain certain particular long-term projects, and certain particular views, values, and principles. What I shall call *stable* fusion has its own special import. Even when difficult compromises have been made over an opinion or a principle of action there is some likelihood that when a couple continuously cohabits and interacts, personal preferences will pale or get converted. The couple's practices may, as a psychological matter, so predominate that the individual has no countervailing tendencies any longer. Being committed to acting and speaking a certain view in Mr. Jones's presence, Ms. Jones may eventually lose hold of her own original view: it may cease to be her personal view. Indeed, there is some normative pressure upon her to let this happen. For each party will probably better sustain "our view" in being if they have no countervailing tendencies, and they are committed to sustaining that view as best they can. There is some likelihood, then, that stable fusion will also be *untrammelled*. There will be no countervailing tendencies within the individuals concerned.

Stable untrammelled fusion is likely to be reflected in a fully justified, strong sense of mutual trust. For over time each has trusted the other to do his or her part in promoting their jointly accepted "causes," and the trust has regularly been fulfilled. Moreover, by hypothesis, it has become easy for each one to fulfill that trust. That this is so will most likely be common knowledge between the parties.[20] This will increase their trust in the domains in question. Trusting the other will likely become second nature. This strong mutual trust will itself most likely be common knowledge.

Any situation involving a good deal of stable untrammelled fusion stands to provide both a sense of unity and common knowledge of mutual trust irrespective of what the fusion relates to. Essentially structural or formal features of the situation ensure that this is so. Insofar as a sense of unity and mutual trust themselves provide a degree of comfort or subjective satisfaction, then all such situations stand to engender some positive emotion in the participants, including a degree of positive feeling one for the other.

Meanwhile, it should be recognized that there are a number of importantly different possibilities in a situation where there is much stable untrammelled fusion.

It may be that in a given marriage practically everything is "ours" and the parties have no views, goals, interests, and so on, of their own, or little to speak of.

---

[20] Roughly, something is common knowledge between two persons if it is entirely out in the open between them. For references to the literature, see Chapter 1, note 4. For discussion of the role of common knowledge in plural subjecthood, see *On Social Facts*, Chapter 4, especially pp. 186–97 and 202–3.

This is a case where the people concerned barely have egos in the sense defined here. Plato sometimes seems to have something close to this as an *ideal* for the members of his "guardian class" in *The Republic*. The opposite pole will be the totally "unfused" ego, the "unjoined person," to use a phrase from Carson McCullers.[21] These types seem possible at least in the abstract. The case of "ego-less" fusion may deserve to be seen as pathological, or simply bad, something that is dangerous at least from the point of view of individual survival. That is something worth pondering. However, it should be stressed that it is not necessary in principle that a large amount of stable untrammelled fusion involve the virtual demise of the ego.

First, in principle each party may personally endorse all the joint values and so on. As already indicated, there exists some normative pressure to organize one's mental life so as to satisfy the commitments of joint acceptance with ease. But this need not involve leaving oneself with no personal views at all. One will satisfy this demand simply by bringing one's own views into line with the jointly accepted views. And, of course, in many cases one will do this easily or not need to change at all. Let us call the case where a joint value or whatever is personally endorsed by each of the parties *positively correlated fusion*. It might be labeled *deep* fusion. One would expect this particular form of fusion to be particularly comfortable for the parties.

Note that each person may or may not have views of their own outside the areas of fusion. This brings us to the other possibility. Even if there is much stable fusion that is completely uncorrelated with any personal views on the topic in question, there may be areas of thought and value that simply do not overlap the areas of fusion. Hence there may not be a total loss of ego. One's spouse may know little about one's work, for instance. One may love going to the ballet and one's spouse may hate it. One hundred years of living together may be incapable of changing these preferences. There is much space for the ego, then, even given the comforts of much stable untrammelled fusion.

Conclusion

Whether a relationship in which much fusion occurs is good overall depends on a number of facts extraneous to the presence of fusion itself. While this is undoubtedly so, fusion as such clearly has the capacity emotionally to enhance a marriage or similar relationship. Particularly when it is stable, it provides a ground for important positive experiences, and, through these, a basis for cherishing and caring for the other person or people. A marriage (or any relationship)

---

[21] McCullers (1985).

in which little fusion develops may have many charms. But, by hypothesis, it will mostly lack ideas, values, principles, and goals shared in the strong sense of joint acceptance. There may be a coincidental complementarity of ideas and values. But there will not be the interlocking commitments of plural subjecthood, with its capacity to generate a sense of partnership (as opposed to mere similarity) and mutual trust. The parties may well feel "loose and separate" from each other, lacking the sense of unity that fusion engenders.

It is clear that fusion does not guarantee that the parties will be subjectively comfortable overall (however others evaluate their union). There could be a marriage involving much fusion in my sense, but where there is also much conflict between the fused and unfused (ego) portions of the individuals concerned. In the extreme case, each of the parties personally strains against each of the jointly held opinions, values, and so on. Here we have much *negatively correlated fusion*. For obvious reasons, this is likely to be uncomfortable for the parties. Perhaps most importantly, each party is likely to be conscious at some level of inner conflict. They may feel "stifled" or "suppressed" all the time. Clearly there can be degrees of conflict here. Even in a situation of negatively correlated fusion, if there is real fusion there, particularly stable fusion, this may help to explain how the situation could still have some attractions in terms of a sense of partnering and "knowing where one is" with the other person.

Fusion as an ideal must, clearly, be viewed with caution. The main point of this chapter is to indicate how something aptly named "fusion" is possible, something that has the capacity strongly to enhance a marriage from a subjective point of view.

The word "love" was used in all of my opening quotations. George Eliot has aptly referred to it as that "jack of all words." One hesitates to say "what love is." Meanwhile, it seems quite plausible to suppose that at least the most comfortable cases of stable fusion will involve something worthy of the name "love."[22] Even in cases repugnant to outsiders the sense of unity and mutual trust may be valued, and the parties may see themselves as loving each other—not entirely bizarrely. Love is often associated with a sense of unity, with "being one." And wherever there is much genuine fusion, particularly that which endures, one can see why someone might feel moved to say: "We have created a third thing, and each of us is one of the parts."[23]

[22] Cf. Lurie (1985).

[23] The original version of this chapter was drafted as a comment on Lindgren, "Models of Marriage," 1988ms. A version was presented to my colleagues at the University of Connecticut, Storrs, December 1988. I thank everyone present for their comments. Particular thanks to Susan Anderson, Len Krimerman, and Carol Masheter for written comments. I alone am responsible for the views expressed here. In addition, I thank Bob Moffat for his recent reference to Lon Fuller (1969), Chapter 1, in connection with my discussion of the not-necessarily-explicit agreement-like process by which jointly accepted views and such, and their associated obligations, are formed. I have

References

Bowen, Murray (1965) "Family Psychotherapy with Schizophrenia in the Hospital and in Private Practice," in I. Boszormenyi-Nagy and J. Framo, eds., *Intensive Family Therapy: Theoretical and Practical Aspects*, New York: Hoeber Medical Division, Harper and Row, 213–244.

Fuller, Lon (1969) *The Morality of Law*, New Haven: Yale University Press.

Gaylin, Willard (1987) *Rediscovering Love*, New York: Penguin Books

Gilbert, Margaret (1989) *On Social Facts*, London: Routledge and Kegan Paul.

Gilbert, Margaret (1996) *Living Together: Rationality, Sociality and Obligation*, Lanham, MD: Rowman and Littlefield.

Karpel, M. (1976) "Individuation: from Fusion to Dialogue," *Family Process*, vol. 15, pp. 65–82.

Lawrence, D. H. (1949) *The Rainbow*, New York: Penguin Books.

Lurie, Alison (1985) *Foreign Affairs*, London: Michael Joseph.

Maslow, Abraham H. (1953) "Love and Healthy People," in A. Montagu, ed., *The Meaning of Love*, New York: Julian Press, 57–93.

McCullers, Carson (1985) *The Member of the Wedding*, London: Penguin Books.

Plato (B.C./1925) *The Symposium*, tr. W.R.M. B. Lamb, in Plato, vol. 3, Loeb Classical Library: Cambridge, MA: Harvard University Press.

Sorokin, Pitirim (1947) *Society, Culture, and Personality*, New York: Harper.

Weber, Max (1922/1978) *Economy and Society*, Berkeley: University of California Press.

not yet had a chance carefully to study Fuller's discussion at this point, but there does seem to be at least some congruence in our thoughts. See for instance Fuller's reference to "the patterns of a social fabric that unites strands of individual action." He goes on: "A sufficient rupture in this fabric must— if we are to judge the matter with any rationality at all—release men from those duties that had as their only reason for being, maintaining a pattern of social interaction that has now been destroyed" (p. 22; see also the following paragraph). Tempting though it is, there is neither space nor time, at present, to compare and contrast my views and Fuller's.

Scanlon on Promissory Obligation: The Problem of Promisees' Rights[1]

When promises give rise to clear obligations, these can be accounted for
on the basis of general moral principles....

—Thomas Scanlon[2]

Promises, along with their close cousins, agreements, are a ubiquitous feature of human life, and not surprisingly.[3] Promises and agreements are powerful tools. One aspect of their power is this. Failing special circumstances, at least, if you have promised to see me at five, and nothing more has transpired between us, I have a special standing in relation to your actions. Should you remark that you are thinking of not showing up at five, I have the standing to insist that you do. Should you fail to show up, I have the standing to rebuke you on that account. By virtue of your promise, your showing up at five becomes my *right*.[4]

---

[1] Material related to this chapter was presented to the University of Connecticut philosophy department in the spring semester 2002, and to the University of Connecticut Humanities Institute in the fall semester of that year. I thank those present for their comments. I am grateful to Richard Arneson, Paul Bloomfield, David Brink, Christopher Clark, Scott Lehmann, David Slutsky, Tim Scanlon, and John Troyer for discussions on other occasions. I dedicate this chapter to the memory of Michael Robins (1941–2002).

[2] *What We Owe to Each Other* (Cambridge: Harvard, 1998) p. 315; hereafter W.W.

[3] For some reason the philosophical literature has focused on promises rather than agreements. This may be because it has long been thought—wrongly in my view—that agreements are constructed out of promises. On this see Margaret Gilbert, "Is an Agreement an Exchange of Promises?" The *Journal of Philosophy*, XC, 12 (December 1993): 627–49, reprinted with some revisions in Gilbert, *Living Together: Rationality, Sociality, and Obligation* (Lanham, MD: Rowman and Littlefield, 1996), pp. 313–38. The precise nature of the relationship between promises and agreements is an interesting issue: my use of the phrase "close cousins" is not intended to beg any questions.

[4] This last point, which I take to be intuitive, is common ground between theorists of otherwise different persuasions with respect to the nature of rights. See, for instance, H.L.A. Hart, "Are There Any Natural Rights?" *Philosophical Review*, LXIV, 2 (April 1955): 175–91; Joseph Raz, "On the Nature of Rights," *Mind*, XCIII, 370 (April 1984): 194–214 (reprinted in Morton Winston, ed., The

As it happens, the philosophical literature has not focused on the way in which promising creates rights in promisees. Rather, the focus has been on how a promisor is obligated by a promise.[5] There is, evidently, nothing wrong with asking how promises obligate as, indeed, they seem to do. If you have promised to see me at five, and nothing more has transpired between us, you are surely in some sense obligated to do so. Something along these lines has been seen, indeed, as a self-evident or a priori truth.

Thus H.A. Prichard:

> Once call some act a promise, and all question whether there is an obligation to do it seems to have vanished.[6]

Intuitively, a promise obligates the promisor in a particularly direct way, and likewise directly gives rise to a right in the promisee. It is tempting to say that both the right and the obligation are part and parcel of promising.[7]

Since making a promise appears to involve little but the expression of the promisor's will, one might well think that promissory obligation is somehow directly willed into being. As David Hume observed, such an idea is "entirely conformable to our common way of thinking and expressing ourselves."[8]

How, then, do promises obligate? Thomas Scanlon's thoughtful treatment of this topic begins by discussing a popular type of account that he wishes to reject. Scanlon characterizes this type of account as a "two-stage" matter, the first stage being a "social practice" of promising (WW 295).

Here is a version of such a social practice account. First, there is a valuable social practice of promising. That is, there is a social norm or rule in a given

---

Philosophy of Human Rights (Belmont, CA: Wadsworth, 1989), pp. 44–60; page references here are to the original). Cf. Michael Robins, *Promising, Intending, and Moral Autonomy* (New York: Cambridge, 1984), p. 99. The qualification regarding special circumstances is intended to set aside, in particular, the cases of coerced promises or promises to perform immoral acts. I take it that these are best considered after one has an articulated understanding of less complicated cases. In what follows, the reader should assume that coerced promises or promises with immoral content are not at issue. I discuss coerced agreements in Gilbert, "Agreement, Coercion, and Obligation," *Ethics*, CIII, 4 (July 1993): 679–706, reprinted in *Living Together*, pp. 281–312.

[5] As can be seen from the titles of many articles—see, for instance, "The Obligation to Keep a Promise" (H.A. Prichard, circa 1940) and "Promises and Obligations" (Raz, 1982).

[6] "The Obligation to Keep a Promise," in Prichard, *Moral Obligation and Duty and Interest* (New York: Oxford, 1968), pp. 169–79, here p. 169.

[7] If this is correct, it would seem that the special circumstances discussed in note 3 above either invalidate the promise—in other words, there is no promise in spite of appearances—or the promisor and promisee have the usual obligation and right, the special circumstances notwithstanding. I would argue for the latter alternative, but will not do so here—see Gilbert, "Agreements, Coercion, and Obligation," on the case of coercion.

[8] *A Treatise of Human Nature* (New York: Oxford, 2000), 3.2.5.3.

society to the effect that one who does a certain thing under certain conditions (thereby "promising to do a certain thing") is to do something further (thereby "fulfilling the promise"). In addition, members of that society generally conform to this rule and expect one another to do so, and the existence of the social practice as a whole promotes an important good. Second, in the circumstances comprising the first stage, it is morally wrong for members of the society in question to violate the relevant social norm.

Suppose that these two stages have been reached in my society. All else being equal, it will then follow that if I say "I promise to feed your cat tomorrow," it would be morally wrong for me not to feed your cat tomorrow.

Scanlon does not directly attack "social practice" accounts, but argues in favor of an account of a different sort.[9] He proposes to argue that "the wrong of breaking a promise" is an instance of "a more general family of moral wrongs which are concerned ... with what we owe to other people when we have led them to form expectations about our future conduct" (WW 296). He adds "Social practices of agreement-making, when they exist, may provide the means for creating such expectations ...," but, he will argue, "these practices play no essential role in explaining why these actions are wrong" (WW 296).

I am inclined to agree with Scanlon that one should reject accounts of promissory obligation that appeal to social practices in the way described. One motive for developing such accounts has been the difficulty of understanding how—as our common way of thinking has it—the obligation of a promise can directly be *willed* into being. It is now standard to assume that another story about the genesis of promissory obligation must be found.[10] A problem with any other story, however, is that it is likely to be found counterintuitive.[11]

Its counterintuitiveness is not the only problem with an approach that appeals to social practices. Another problem is that such approaches are not clearly free,

---

[9] Scanlon has developed this position in (at least) three places: "Promises and Practices," *Philosophy and Public Affairs*, XIX, 3 (Summer 1990): 199–226 (hereafter PP); "Promises and Contracts," in Peter Benson, ed., *The Theory of Contract Law* (New York: Cambridge, 2001), pp. 86–117 (hereafter PC), and chapter seven of *What We Owe to Each Other*. See also Scanlon's reply to John Deigh in Scanlon, "Reasons, Responsibility, and Reliance: Replies to Wallace, Dworkin, and Deigh," *Ethics*, CXII, 3 (April 2002): 507–28, pp. 522–28.

[10] One contemporary philosopher who has argued against this assumption is Robins—see, for instance, "The Primacy of Promising," *Mind*, LXXXV, 339 (July 1976): 321–40.

[11] This would hardly worry Hume, whose own account of promissory obligation in the *Treatise* appeals to a social practice along the lines indicated in the text. He famously argued that the idea of willing an obligation into being was unintelligible (3.2.5.3–7). His skepticism about the pretheoretical conception of promissory obligation has found favor among many Anglo-American philosophers. We should surely see it as both troubling, and challenging, however, if outside our studies, we understand the obligations of our promises to be willed into being.

in their initial assumptions, of something akin to a "prior promise."[12] One needs to ask in what the existence of a social practice in a society consists: Might some kind of social acceptance be necessary, and might that involve something akin to a promise or agreement? If the assumption of anything akin to a promise is avoided, it may be harder to make the moral argument. If it is not avoided, then, at the least, more will need to be said about the thing-akin-to-a-promise that is involved in social practices.[13]

It may be observed that, as sketched in the previous quotation, Scanlon's own account of promissory obligation itself has too many "stages" to accord with the intuition that promissory obligation is somehow directly willed into being. First, there is a certain set of circumstances, in part created by the promisor, that include, importantly, certain expectations of the promisee. Second, in the circumstances comprising the first stage, it is morally wrong for the promisor not to do what was promised.

Thus, though it does not invoke social practices, on Scanlon's account promissory obligations are not directly willed into being. This is one concern one might have with his account, as with any account sharing the feature noted.

I will focus here on a different concern: that Scanlon's account of promissory obligation does not explain the existence of promisees' rights. As I shall explain, if this is the case, his account of promissory obligation is inadequate.[14]

I. Promisees' Rights: Intuitive Points

I.A. Hart on moral rights. In a classic article, "Are There Any Natural Rights?" H.L.A. Hart sets out an array of intuitive points on the nature of the rights of promisees. He refers to such rights as falling into a broad class of "moral rights." Precisely how he intended the qualifier "moral" need not detain us here. A central aspect of his intent is the differentiation of moral from *legal* rights. Certainly the rights of promisees are not in and of themselves legal rights, though coupled with special circumstances, such as the intent to create legal relations, they may give rise to legal rights.

---

[12] Cf. Prichard. The existence of this problem for a variety of theories of promissory obligation is a theme of Robins's "Primacy of Promising." For the relevance of the problem to Scanlon's theory, see the text, below.

[13] Observations in Hart, *The Concept of Law* (New York: Oxford, 1961), suggest that on a central everyday conception of a social rule something akin to a promise or agreement underlies social rules. I focus on these observations in developing a new account of social rules in chapter five of *Sociality and Responsibility: New Essays in Plural Subject Theory* (Lanham, MD: Rowman and Littlefield, 2000).

[14] Is a promisee necessary for there to be a promise? For present purposes, I waive this question. Like Scanlon, I focus specifically on the case of a promise with a (single) promisee, that is, someone to whom the promise is made, someone who can say "You promised *me* that you would...."

Hart lists the following features of moral rights in his sense: one *has* or *possesses* such a right, and corresponding to a right is another person's *obligation to* the right holder. This person *owes* the right holder what he (or she) has a right to: it is the right holder's *due*. If the obligated person fails to fulfil his obligation to the right holder he will have done *wrong* to the right holder. The right holder has a *claim* on the person who is obligated to him, and is *entitled* to have his right respected. He can *waive* the claim and *release* the person who is obligated to him from his obligation.

The emphasized terms—all emphasized in Hart's text—are central, closely related elements of what one might call the *language of rights*. Thus, Joe may *act wrongly* in relation to Jean. Or he may *do wrong to her, do her wrong,* or (even more briefly) *wrong* her. In the second set of cases, but not the first case, the words suggest that Joe has infringed a right of Jean's.

I.B. *The "correlativity" of rights and (directed) obligations.* The rights that Hart is talking about here are nonlegal analogues of what, in law, the eminent jurist Wesley Hohfeld called "claims." Hohfeld regarded claims as rights in the strict sense of the term.[15] In discussing Hohfeld, and consonantly with Hart, I shall refer to them simply as "rights."

Hohfeld insisted that there was a *duty* corresponding to every right. This duty was a duty *toward* the right holder, the person with the duty being the person the right was *against*.

There are, then, three elements that figure in the specification of each right and of the corresponding duty (in Hohfeld's terminology) or (in Hart's terminology) obligation. In the case of the right, there is a right holder, something the right is a right to, and someone the right is a right against. In the case of the duty, there is a duty holder, the thing it is a duty to do, and the person towards whom it is directed.

Duties or obligations of the type in question will be referred to as *directed* duties or obligations.[16] The duties or obligations corresponding to rights are, it may be said, intrinsically directed, as are rights themselves.

As is now common, I shall not here distinguish between duties and obligations.[17] The directed nature of certain duties (or obligations) will be indicated by the prepositions "toward" or more briefly "to." A general term that would seem to serve as well as the unqualified "duty" or "obligation" is "requirement," which I shall use on

---

[15] "Some Fundamental Legal Conceptions," *Yale Law Journal*, XXIII (1913–14): 16–59, see especially pp. 30–32.

[16] This follows the terminology of deontic logic. Other qualifiers used include "relational."

[17] Hart prefers to restrict the use of the term "obligation" for the directed duties that correspond to rights. He notes a broadening use of the term "obligation," however, such that "duty" and "obligation" are used interchangeably. See also Richard Brandt, "The Concepts of Obligation and Duty," *Mind*, LXXIII, 291 (July 1964): 374–95.

occasion. The "correspondence" between rights and directed duties is extremely tight. You cannot have a right without a corresponding directed duty, and vice versa. They are, if you like, two sides of the same coin.[18]

I.C. *Hart on special rights.* In "Are There Any Natural Rights?" Hart distinguishes between *general* and *special* rights, the rights of promisees being "the most obvious cases" of the latter kind (*op. cit.,* p. 183). Special rights "arise out of special transactions between individuals or out of some special relationship in which they stand to each other" in such a way that "both the persons who have the right and those who have the corresponding obligation are limited to the parties to the special transaction or relationship" (*op. cit.,* p. 183). As to promising:

> We voluntarily incur obligations and create or confer rights on those
> to whom we promise; we alter the existing moral independence of the
> parties' freedom of choice in relation to some action and create a new
> moral relationship between them, so that it becomes morally legitimate
> for the person to whom the promise is given to determine how the
> promisor shall act. The promisee has a temporary authority or sover-
> eignty in relation to some specific matter over the other's will which
> we express by saying that the promisor is under an obligation to the
> promisee to do what he has promised (*op. cit.,* pp. 183–84).

I.D. *Hart on the character of directed obligations.* The last sentence in the above quotation is of particular importance. As Hart sees it, being obligated toward another person is to be explicated in terms of that person's having a limited authority over one's will.

Hart sometimes writes of an obligation's being "owed" to the holder of the corresponding right.[19] Presumably what is owed is an action rather than an obligation. Thus Hart also speaks of a right holder as the person "to whom performance is owed or due."[20] He suggests, then, that an obligation of the type in question is a matter of the person with the obligation owing something to the right holder.

---

[18] For emphasis of this point and discussion of its implications for moral theory see Hugh Upton, "Right-Based Morality and Hohfeld's Relations," *Journal of Ethics,* iv, 3 (January 2000): 237–56. Roman law expresses the sense of such a tight relation by using one and the same word (*Obligatio*) for the duty of one party and the corresponding right of the other party to a contract. There was no special word for a right against a determinate person or persons. See George Long, *"Obligationes,"* in William Smith, *A Dictionary of Greek and Roman Antiquities* (London: John Murray, 1875), pp. 817–21.

[19] See "Are There Any Natural Rights?" p. 179, note 7, also p. 181. Others sometimes write of "owing a duty."

[20] See, for instance, Hart, "Are There Any Natural Rights?" p. 181.

Suppose that if I—somehow—owe you performance of a certain action, then there is a sense in which that action is already yours. Suppose, indeed, that in relation to that action you are in a position to act toward me in ways appropriate to one who owns it.

This conception of things is consonant with a variety of aspects of the situation of a promisee and, suitably developed, may help to throw light on it. For instance, suppose a promisor asks his (or her) promisee for release from the promise. The promisee is in a position to grant this request, and thus to release the promisor from his obligation. If the promisee owns the promised action—or is in a position to act in ways appropriate to one who does—then he is in a position to give it back, should he so choose.[21] Again, the promisee is in a position to keep the promisor's obligation in force. If the promisee owns the promised action, then he is in a position to keep it if he so chooses.

Pertinent here, also, is a statement of Hart's about rights in general prior to his discussion of promises. He says, "there is no incongruity, but a special congruity in the use of force or the threat of force to secure that what is someone's right to have done shall in fact be done; for it is in just these circumstances that coercion of another human being is legitimate" (*op. cit.*, p. 178).

Contemplating the exercise of "force" in connection with everyday promises and agreements may seem to go too far. It is reasonable, however, to include under the rubric of force the kinds of thing noted at the outset of this chapter: such things as informal rebukes and demands. Informal rebukes lie at the thin end of the wedge of force: nonetheless, they are a form of authoritative chastisement.[22] Likewise, informal demands are a form of authoritative pressure to act in a certain way.

As applied to promises, one can take Hart's central point here to be about *standing* rather than *justification*. Whatever the merits of a forceful response in a given situation, if you fail to give me what I have a right to through your promise, I have the standing, as your promisee, to rebuke you on that account. Similarly, should you threaten to break your promise, I have the standing, as your promisee, to demand or insist that you act as promised and thus pressure you to perform.[23]

---

[21] It may be that what the promisee has by way of ownership of the promised act is joint ownership with the promisor rather than sole personal ownership. He may then need the concurrence of the promisor in order to rescind the promise. Be that as it may, if the promisor has already sued the promisee for release, the latter is surely in a position "unilaterally" to release the promisor.

[22] In his classic work, *The Concept of Law*, Hart associates such rebukes with the punishments imposed through the formal processes of law as versions of one form of human activity—see p. 10 and elsewhere.

[23] Compare the description Scanlon gives of (claim-) rights in general as rights to "command" particular things, where others have a correlative duty to "comply" in "Rights, Goals, and Fairness," in Stuart Hampshire, ed., *Public and Private Morality*, (New York: Cambridge, 1978), pp. 93–111.

Consider a case of such insistence. Suppose that after lunch forgetful Fred casually remarks to his companion, Vera, "I'm off for a long hike!" and Vera authoritatively responds, "No, you're not!" explaining: "You promised me you'd help clean the house this afternoon!" If Fred's promise has brought it about that Vera owns his action of helping her clean the house, she would surely have the standing to insist that he does not withhold that action from her but rather performs it. She would also surely have the standing to rebuke Fred should he fail to give her what is hers.

In what follows I shall make the following assumptions about the directed obligations of promisors. In order to understand how a given promisor, A, comes to have an obligation *toward* his promisee, B, we need to understand how B comes to have a limited authority over A's will, where this involves the promised action's being owed to A, its being already in a sense *his*. B will have the associated standing to effect the release of A from the promise if requested to do so or to hold him to it, and to command and rebuke A in the ways mentioned above. The same goes, of course, for our understanding of how B comes to have a right *against* A to performance of the promise. In what remains, I consider whether Scanlon's account of promissory obligation helps us to understand these things and hence, in effect, to understand the rights of promisees.

II. Scanlon On Promissory Obligation

According to Scanlon, promissory obligations are a function of a moral principle that requires certain actions in specified circumstances. He labels this "Principle F" because he sees it as a principle of fidelity. He tells us that the conditions it specifies can be fulfilled in many ways other than by making a promise. "Promising is a special case, distinguished in part by the kind of reason that the promisee has for believing that the promisor will perform" (WW 306).

It appears, then, that in Scanlon's scheme a given promisor's obligation to do what he promised will exist, if it does exist, by virtue of the application of Principle F, as will the obligations of all who fulfill the relevant conditions. I shall not, therefore, spend time here on what, according to Scanlon, differentiates making a promise from acting in one of the other ways that fall under Principle F.

Let us assume that a given promisor will have an obligation—indeed, a moral obligation—that derives from Scanlon's Principle F. It is not at all obvious that this obligation corresponds to a right of the promisee against the promisor to performance of the promise.

In order for it to do so, it will have to be not just an obligation, but an obligation toward the promisee, an obligation that is the other side of the coin from the promisee's right against the promisor to performance. An obligation that exists by virtue of the application of a moral principle requiring certain actions in specified circumstances, though indeed an obligation, is not, or not necessarily, a directed obligation.[24]

One might sum up this line of thought by saying that there is an important challenge for any "moral principle" account of promissory obligation. Such accounts must show that what flows from the principle in question is not just an obligation, period, but a directed obligation.

At this point in the discussion someone may say "Whoa! What other kind of account can there be?" I believe that there is another kind of account, and a plausible one. In this chapter, however, I shall not go beyond the territory of moral principle accounts.

A variety of moral principle accounts is possible, and Scanlon's Principle F contains an interesting wrinkle such that it might be thought to be immune from criticism in terms of the rights of promisees. Scanlon may, indeed, have included this wrinkle in part so as to avoid criticism of this kind. There is some merit, therefore, in discussing the issue in relation to Scanlon's Principle F in particular.

I start with some observations on Scanlon's discussion preliminary to his presentation of his principle. In particular, I note some judgments on promises that help to motivate the principle.

II.A. Observations on promising. In the discussion preliminary to the introduction of Principle F, Scanlon introduces the "car and lawn" case:

> Suppose, for example, that I promise to drive you to work if you will mow my lawn, and that you accept this arrangement. Then, a day or so later (but before the time has come for either of us to begin fulfilling the bargain) I think better of the deal and want to back out. On most people's understanding of promising, I am not free to do this. I am obligated to drive you to work unless you "release" me, even if I warn you before you have undertaken any action based on our arrangement. If I am going to break my promise then it is better to warn you than not to do so, but even if I do, this is a case of breaking a promise, not fulfilling one (WW 301, see also PP 205; PC 92).

Scanlon's emphasis here is on the fact that one cannot fulfill the obligation of a promise to do a certain thing by a timely warning to the promisee that one will not, after all, do that thing. He makes a similar point about compensation.

---

[24] Concordant thoughts are found in Hart, "Natural Rights," pp. 180–81; also Joel Feinberg, "The Nature and Value of Rights," *The Journal of Value Inquiry,* IV (1970): 243–51, reprinted in Winston, ed., pp. 61–74, see p. 62.

If one fails to fulfill a promise, one should compensate the promisee if one can, but the obligation one undertakes when one makes a promise is an obligation to do the thing promised, not simply to do it or to compensate the promisee accordingly (WW 301).

In other words, having failed to do what one promised to do, one cannot bring it about that one has, nonetheless, fulfilled the obligation incurred by one's promise by compensating the promisee.

The quoted passages differ in relation to Scanlon's positive characterization of the obligation of the promisor. In the first passage, one is said to be obligated to do the thing promised unless "released" by the promisor. In the second, one's obligation is said to be an obligation to do the thing promised, period.

I take it that what is intuitively correct here is this. The content of the obligation of the promisor is, indeed, to do the thing promised, period. But that obligation stands as long as the promisee has not released the promisor from the promise. At this point, it seems reasonable to construe Scanlon's first positive characterization of the obligation of the promisor along these lines.[25]

II.B. *Principle F.* Scanlon concludes that in order to explain the obligations arising from promises: "we need a principle stating a duty specifically to fulfill the expectations one has created under certain conditions" (WW 302). The quoted words are somewhat ambiguous, but I take it that what Scanlon has in mind here is a principle stating a duty (or obligation) of the following form: if, under certain conditions, one has created expectations to the effect that one will do such-and-such, one must fulfill those expectations.

The principle Scanlon has in mind is understood to be a moral principle. When *is* a principle a *moral* one? The gist of Scanlon's own answer may be found in this statement of the core of his carefully argued and articulated form of "contractualist" moral theory: "an act is [morally] wrong if its performance under the circumstances would be disallowed by any set of *principles for the general regulation of behavior that no one could reasonably reject as a basis for informed, unforced general agreement*" (WW 153, my interpolation and emphasis).

I shall not attempt to discuss Scanlon's contractualism here. Nor shall I discuss his assumption that the moral principle that will explain promissory obligations has to do with *expectations* that have been induced in the promisee. Perhaps he

---

[25] Scanlon's statement that (in effect) a promisor is obligated "unless released" by his promisee may be thought to imply that action on the part of the promisee alone suffices to get rid of the obligation, whereas, according my (deliberate) characterization in this paragraph, action on the part of the promisee is necessary but may not be sufficient. For some congenial remarks on the insufficiency of action on the part of the promisee alone, see William Vitek, *Promising* (Philadelphia: Temple, 1993), pp. 101–02.

does not so much assume this as infer it from the fact that he can, as he believes, explain promissory obligation in terms of such expectations.

After some further discussion Scanlon proposes "a principle of fidelity that requires performance" (WW 304), namely, Principle F:

> If (1) A voluntarily and intentionally leads B to expect that A will do X (unless B consents to A's not doing so); (2) A knows that B wants to be assured of this; (3) A acts with the aim of providing this assurance, and has good reason to believe that he or she has done so; (4) B knows that A has the beliefs and intentions just described; (5) A intends for B to know this, and knows that B does know it; and (6) B knows that A has this knowledge and intent; then, in the absence of special justification, A must do X unless B consents to X's not being done (WW 304).

At this point I am not going to question the truth of Principle F. Rather, I want to argue that, if it is accepted, it is not sufficient for an understanding of promisees' rights.

II.C. *Scanlon's consent clause.* Principle F is more nuanced than Scanlon's description of it as "a principle of fidelity that requires performance" suggests. It requires performance *unless the promisor consents to lack of performance.* I shall refer to the emphasized clause as the "consent clause."

How does the consent clause get into Principle F? In terms of the progress of Scanlon's discussion, it gets there as a reflection of the nature of the expectations that he takes to be at issue.

Prior to the presentation of Principle F, Scanlon writes that, in the car and lawn case, "the expectation you reasonably want to be able to form is the expectation that I will drive you to work *unless you consent to my not doing so*" (WW 302). The expectation Scanlon then takes to be at issue when one promises is the expectation that the promisor will do a certain thing unless the promisee consents otherwise.

Principle F reflects this characterization of the expectation at issue. According to the principle, when this expectation is produced in the appropriate conditions, the promisor must do the thing in question unless the promisee consents otherwise. The promisor will in this way act precisely in accordance with the promisee's—internally conditional—expectation.[26]

One suspects that Scanlon's consent clause—and, indeed, his characterization of the expectation in question—is also intended to reflect the fact that, as he wrote earlier of a particular promise, "I am obligated...unless you 'release' me..." (WW 301). In other words, my "consenting" to your not doing the thing

---

[26] On the intended internal/external distinction as applied to intentions, see section VI below.

you led me to expect you to do, in the conditions specified by Principle F, is intended to be tantamount to my releasing you from your promise.

Scanlon puts the term "release" in quotation marks. I am not sure why, since the general idea of the promisee releasing the promisor from his promise is unexceptionable. I have just put the term "consenting" in quotation marks, though Scanlon does not do likewise. As I see it, the term "consent" may carry a load that is undesirable in this context. More specifically, it may seem to imply that I am in a position of authority in relation to you, something that would be true if you had, in effect, promised me something, or done something akin to that. This is presumably not something Scanlon either wants or needs to assume in the formulation of Principle F (where the term "consent" appears twice).

In what follows, therefore, I shall construe "consent" in such a way that my simply saying "I'm fine with your not doing it" or something to that effect is enough to count as my consenting to your not doing it. In other words, I can be in a position to consent—in this sense—to your not doing something even if I have no pre-existing authority over you with respect to your doing that thing.

III. Why Scanlon's Principle F is Not Sufficient for Promisees' Rights

Let us suppose the conditions of the protasis of Principle F are fulfilled in relation to Anne (who is in A's position) and Ben (who is in B's position), and that "doing X" in this case is phoning Ben on Monday. Now suppose that Anne does not phone Ben on Monday, Ben did not consent to this, and there was no special justification for it. Does Ben have a special standing to rebuke her for not phoning him—a standing that is not generally held, or, at least, not held for the same reason? Again, were Anne to suggest to Ben, before Monday, that she did not plan to phone him, would he have a special standing to insist that she did—a standing that was not generally held, or, at least, not held for the same reason? If Ben had, in effect, a promisee's right to Anne's phoning him on Monday, then he would have both of these special standings.

For simplicity's sake, I shall focus on the question of a special standing to issue a rebuke. I shall consider four possible grounds that Ben might be thought to have for rebuking Anne. For each of these I shall argue either that it does not, after all, give him the standing to rebuke Anne, or that it does not give him a special standing to do so. These grounds are: (a) Anne's violation of a moral principle; (b) Principle F's consent clause; (c) Ben's "right to rely" on Anne's performance; (d) Ben's being the intended beneficiary of Principle F.

III.A. Anne's violation of a moral principle. On what grounds might Ben rebuke Anne for not phoning him on Monday? The ground that Scanlon's principle most clearly suggests is this: *Anne has violated a moral principle she has not done that which, according to Principle F, she must do in the circumstances.* What she had to do was phone Ben on Monday, unless he consented to her not doing so.

For present purposes there is a problem with a ground of this nature. Either it is liable to give the standing to rebuke Anne to many other people, as well as to Ben, or it gives nobody that standing.

What I have in mind is this. There appear to be the following two options as to who has the standing to complain just because a moral principle is violated.

First, there may be a general "right to do wrong" such that *no one* has the standing to rebuke a person merely on the grounds that he or she has *violated a moral principle.*[27] In that case neither Ben nor anyone else—on those grounds alone—has the standing to rebuke Anne for violating Principle F. It obviously follows that Ben has no *special* standing to rebuke Anne on these grounds.

Second, there may be no general "right to do wrong" of the kind in question. In that case, it seems likely that *everyone* has the same standing to rebuke Anne merely on the grounds that she has violated a moral principle. Then, once again, Ben is in the same position as everyone else. He has no *special* standing in the matter.

Perhaps not absolutely everyone will have this equal standing in the second case. Perhaps some classes of people will be ruled out. It is implausible, however, to argue that *everyone but Ben* will be ruled out, if the basis for the rebuke that we are considering is simply the moral wrongness of what Anne has done.

It is an important question—both theoretically and practically—whether or not people generally have the standing to rebuke someone merely on the grounds that he has violated a moral principle.[28] There is no need to pursue that question here, however. For it seems to follow from the available positions that Ben has no *special* standing to rebuke Anne if we assume that his standing to rebuke her is grounded simply in the moral wrongness of what she has done, or, to put it differently, in her violation of a moral requirement.

This seems to be so however nuanced the requirement in question is. In particular, *the existence of Scanlon's consent clause appears to make no difference when matters are considered in this light.* That clause, embedded as it is within Principle

[27] Jeremy Waldron has argued in favor of a right to do wrong. See Waldron, "A Right to Do Wrong," *Ethics*, XCII, 1 (October 1981): 21–39; see also William Galston, "On An Alleged Right to Do Wrong: A Response to Waldron," *Ethics*, XCIII, 2 (January 1983): 320–24. Waldron responds in "Galston on Rights," *Ethics*, XCIII, 2 (January 1983): 325–27.

[28] I am myself inclined to the negative position. If one takes that position, and one believes, at the same time, that wrongdoers could do with rebukes from others, at times, one is likely to take a special interest in discovering how, in general, people gain the standing to rebuke one another that promises, among other things, seem to provide. This is a theme of Margaret Gilbert, "Shared Values, Social Unity, and Liberty," (2005) *Public Affairs Quarterly*, 19 (2005): 25–49. [Chapter 8 this volume]

F, only has the effect of qualifying what Anne must do, if she is to conform to the principle, or, in other words, if she is to act morally.

Does the consent clause really not give Ben a special standing to rebuke Anne? Perhaps its implications should be investigated more carefully.

III.B. Principle F's consent clause. Suppose Anne has failed to phone Ben on Monday, in the circumstances envisaged, and Ben later upbraids her for not calling him. Suppose, further, that it is common knowledge between Anne and Ben that each accepts Principle F, and each believes that no one has the standing to upbraid a person for simply contravening a moral requirement.[29] Anne asks Ben by what title he, in particular, sees fit to upbraid her in this case.

Suppose Ben observes, with emphasis, "Well, it wasn't just anyone's consent that was at issue, it was *mine.* You were supposed to call me unless *I* consented to your not doing so, and I did not consent." It seems that Anne can reasonably reply: "It is true that your consent was at issue in the way described. I don't see, however, how that gives you a special basis for upbraiding me for not calling you. Since you did not consent, I have, clearly, violated Principle F. In other words, what I did was morally wrong. We are agreed, however, that *that* does not give you the standing to upbraid me for what I did. I can't see how the fact that *your* consent was at issue does."

Anne might go on: "Consider the following case. Jane promises Diana that she will stay in the house with Timmy that night unless he consents to her not doing so. Later that night she leaves the house without Timmy's indicating that this is fine with him. She has broken her promise to Diana, and, intuitively speaking, Diana, the promisee, has a special standing to rebuke her for so doing. What about Timmy? Does he also have a special standing to rebuke Jane? I don't see that he does. Where would this standing to rebuke come from? Not, as far as my story goes, from her breaking a promise to him, or doing anything analogous. After the fact, he can certainly observe, as you, Ben, can observe: 'It was *my* consent that was at issue, and I did not consent.... But I do not see how that gives him a special standing to rebuke Jane, or to demand that she stay home when she prepares to go out."

Suppose Ben responds: "Consider this, then. Timmy had the power to bring it about that Jane lacked an obligation she otherwise had—the obligation to stay in the house with him on the night in question. All he had to do was consent to her not staying, and she would no longer have an obligation to stay. Similarly, by withholding his consent he was able to keep her obligation in force. In short, he had the power to release her from her obligation as a promisor—or hold her to it. Such power is a function of the right that gives a promisee the standing to

---

[29] I use the phrase "common knowledge" in roughly the sense of David Lewis, *Convention: A Philosophical Study* (Cambridge: Harvard, 1969). For an elaboration of my own, see Gilbert, *On Social Facts* (Princeton: University Press, 1989).

rebuke a promisor for failing to fulfill his promissory obligation. So Timmy has that standing—and so, by parity of reasoning, do I."

Anne could surely reply: "Jane's obligation through her promise is conditional. Timmy cannot release her from that conditional obligation, or hold her to it. Diana can. In other words, if Jane pleadingly asks Diana, '*Must* I stay with Timmy unless he consents?' Diana's saying, 'No, you need not,' brings Jane's conditional obligation to an end. Timmy does not have the power to do that. Timmy's power is only the power to fulfil or fail to fulfil a condition of Jane's conditional obligation. That he has this power does not imply he has the standing to rebuke Jane if she fails to fulfill her obligation."

III.C. Ben's "right to rely" on performance. Scanlon says that "the obligation to keep a promise is *owed to* a specific individual" (WW 316; emphasis mine). This may be thought to imply that the individual in question has a special right to performance of the promise, and, consequently a special standing to rebuke the promisor. Scanlon may or may not mean his reference to what is *owed* to imply this.[30] However, he does seem to allude to such a special right when he says the following:

> When the conditions of Principle F are fulfilled, it would be wrong, in the absence of special justification, for the party in A's position not to perform. In addition, the party in B's position has a "right to rely" on this performance: that is to say, the second party has grounds for insisting that the first party fulfill the expectation he or she has created (WW 305).

I am not sure why Scanlon puts quotation marks round the phrase "right to rely." In any case, he evidently—by his use of the words "that is to say"—wants us to interpret this phrase in terms of grounds for insisting that the first party fulfill the expectation he or she has created. In other words, he interprets a "right to rely" on a performance as, in effect, a right to that performance itself.

There is another way of interpreting the phrase "right to rely," a way such that having a right to rely is not equivalent to having a right to the thing relied on, and does not, or at least not obviously, entail having such a right. According to this interpretation, "having a right to rely on a performance" means the same as "being epistemically justified in thinking that a performance will occur (and hence to act as if it will occur)."

---

[30] For some observations that suggest that he does not, see the discussion of Scanlon's use of "owing" in Frances Kamm, "Owing, Justifying, Rejecting," *Mind*, CXI, 442 (April 2002): 323–54, at pp. 333–36.

I am not sure that fulfillment of the conditions of Principle F entails that—in the case of Anne and Ben—Ben *will* be epistemically justified in thinking that Anne will perform as expected unless he consents to her not so performing. For present purposes I shall assume that it does. While there is, in that case, no doubt that Ben has a right to rely on Anne's performance in the epistemic justification sense now in question, one must distinguish between this kind of right to rely and a right to rely that is equivalent to, or entails, a right to the performance itself, a right that gives one a ground for insisting on performance. I doubt that Scanlon was under any other impression, but it is worth pointing out the possibility of making an inadvertent slide from a claim that a right to rely in the first sense is present to a claim that a right to rely in the second sense is present.

Is it worth pursuing, in the present context, the idea that one might somehow argue from a right to rely in the epistemic justification sense to a right to rely in the right to performance sense? I think not, in part for this reason. In the present case, an observer of the situation may, presumably, have as good an epistemic justification as Ben for expecting Anne's performance. If an observer—Ben's trusty bodyguard, for instance—can for that reason have a right to Anne's performance, this will not be an argument to the effect that Ben has a special right to Anne's performance, a right he holds by virtue of being the person to whom something analogous to a promise was made.

III.D. Ben as beneficiary of Principle F. Suppose Ben says: "I am—surely—the intended beneficiary of the duty specified in Principle F, as that principle applies to you and me. Hence I had a right against you to your fulfillment of this duty. This right gave me the standing to rebuke you for not fulfilling the duty, a standing that, in this situation, is special to me."

Anne might surely reply: "I will agree, for the sake of argument, that there is a sense in which you are the intended beneficiary of the duty specified in Principle F. I would still draw the line at saying you had a right against me to my fulfillment of the duty. To my mind, it is possible—without contradiction—to accept that I have acted contrary to a moral requirement that was in some sense intended to benefit you, while not accepting that you have a right against me to my acting in accordance with the requirement in question."

Ben appealed, in effect, to a *beneficiary theory* of rights. According to his version, the intended beneficiary of someone's moral duty is the holder of a right against that person to the fulfillment of the duty. Related theories of rights are quite popular, so it would be well to go into this matter further here.[31] In the next section, I briefly consider one such theory in relation to the question of a promisee's rights.

---

[31] Often "beneficiary theories" are contrasted with "choice theories" and both seen as theories of the function of rights. However, in some cases (see the text below) the notion of a beneficiary is used to explain what a right is, and how to determine whom a given right is a right against.

IV. Beneficiary Theories and Promisees' Rights

A distinguished exponent of a type of beneficiary view of rights is Joseph Raz.[32] In a well-known discussion, Raz prefaces his account as follows:

> . . . a philosophical definition of "a right" like those of many other terms, is not an explanation of the ordinary meaning of a term. It follows rather the usage of writers on law, politics, and morality, who typically use the term to refer to a sub-class of all the cases to which it can be applied with linguistic propriety (*op. cit.*, p. 194).

Raz may mean to suggest, plausibly, that terms can get used so widely in everyday discourse that philosophers and others should be comfortable developing partial accounts of their referents, accounts that pick out an important sub-class of everyday uses. And one can, of course, introduce any term or phrase, including "a right," in any technical sense one pleases. This is something that philosophers, among others, often do. If, however, one is specifically interested in the rights of promisees, one would presumably want to give an account that was consonant with an intuitive characterization such as that given by Hart.

Raz presents the following fairly complex definition:

> "x has a right" if and only if x can have rights, and, other things being equal, an aspect of x's well being (his interest) is a sufficient reason for holding some other person(s) to be under a duty (*op. cit.*, p. 195).

This may capture a prevailing use of the phrase "a right" among writers in the areas Raz specified, as he intended. It has certainly had some influence over the way in which rights are understood in moral theory.[33] However, it is hard to see how it captures the nature of the rights of promisees.

A central thought about a promisee's right that seems to have no real place here is the thought that the person (s) who are under the duty referred to *owe* the

---

[32] See "On the Nature of Rights." I here include under the broad label "beneficiary theory" all those theories that make central to their account of rights the benefits, intended benefits, or interests of the putative right holder. Such theories may differ in important ways among themselves. Raz notes that his definition of a right "draws on several elements of analyses of rights which stem from Bentham's beneficiary theory" (p. 195, note 3). Among contemporary theorists, Raz cites Ronald Dworkin, *Taking Rights Seriously* (London: Duckworth, 1977), p. 100; D.N. MacCormick, "Rights in Legislation," in P.M.S. Hacker and Raz, eds., *Law, Morality, and Society* (New York: Oxford, 1977), pp. 189–209; and, especially, Keith Campbell, "The Concept of Rights" (D.Phil. thesis, Oxford University, Bodleian Library, 1979).

[33] See, for instance, Richard Arneson, "Against Rights," *Philosophical Issues*, XI (2001): 172–201, see third paragraph.

action that fulfills it to the so-called right holder. There seems to be a logical gap between its being the case that I have a (moral) duty whose ground is an aspect of the right holder's interest, and its being the case that I owe performance of that duty to the right holder. It seems that it would be perfectly intelligible for me to say: "Okay, this duty I have is grounded in an aspect of your interest … but I do not *owe* you its performance. It's just my duty, period."

If I were to allow that I owe you performance, then I would recognize that you have the standing to upbraid me for nonperformance, or to insist on performance. Before the fact you could pressure me, saying in effect: "Give me that! It's *mine!*"

It is true that a bystander could say, "Give her that! It's *hers!*" The case in which I command you to give me what is *mine* is special, however. The bystander's standing to command you to give it to me can be questioned. My standing surely cannot be questioned. In the bystander's case, the riposte "It's none of your business!" makes sense. In my case, it does not.

In a discussion of promises that follows his definition of "a right," Raz focuses briefly on the rights of promisees. He seeks an account of these according to which there is such a right corresponding to every promise. He therefore favors the view according to which, though anyone may lose interest in having a given promisor fulfill his promise, each person has a general interest that promises made to him shall be kept. This is the interest "to have voluntary special bonds with other people" (*op. cit.,* p. 203).

Of the promisee he says that "It is always up to him to waive his right under the promise and thus terminate the binding force of the promise" (*op. cit.,* p. 203), in other words, terminating the duty of the promisor. It seems that he might have suggested, though he does not, that the promisor's duty to perform is subject to a consent condition akin to Scanlon's.

There is nothing in Raz's discussion so far that seems to imply that a right is held *against a certain person* or that it corresponds to a *directed* duty. Nonetheless Raz says that "Rights are held against certain persons" (*op. cit.,* pp. 209–10). In his eyes, this seems to come down to the question of who can satisfy the interest that grounds the right. Thus, "since contractual rights are based on an interest in being able to create special relations, they give rise to rights against other parties to the agreement as they are the only ones who can satisfy that interest on that occasion" (*op. cit.,* p. 210).

If one wishes, one can stipulatively define "right R is held *against person P*" in some such way. Nonetheless, the points already made suggest that where rights are held against persons, in *this* sense, the right holder does not necessarily have the special standing associated with the rights of promisees as ordinarily understood. I conclude that the idea of explicating rights of the latter kind in terms similar to those of Raz is problematic, and shall not pursue it further.

V. Additional Principles

Suppose it is accepted that Scanlon's Principle F does not in and of itself account for the rights of promisees. It may be suggested that Scanlon can plausibly account for these rights by introducing some kind of subsidiary principle, in addition to Principle F. I think this is doubtful, as I shall argue with respect to two rather different kinds of proposals that might be made in this regard.[34] I consider these proposals in relation to the example of Anne and Ben.

V.A. A social rule in the context of Principle F. The first kind of proposal invokes a social rule. A version of it might run roughly as follows. Assume that situations in which Principle F applies are common within a particular society, S. It is predictable that S will adopt a rule for behavior in such situations—call it *Rule R*— which has the following implication in the case of Anne and Ben: if Ben chooses to speak in a rebuking tone to Anne for not phoning him on Monday, she is not to object to his doing so on the grounds that he lacks the standing to rebuke her. In other words, she is to behave as if he has such standing. Indeed, she is to behave for all the world as if he has a right to her phoning him. The existence of Rule R in S would tend to promote the interests of those members of S who find themselves in Ben's position, interests that Principle F itself promotes. The ubiquity in human societies of Rule R would help to explain the intuitive judgment that promisees have the standing to rebuke promisors, and, indeed, the intuitive judgment that this standing derives from a right against the promisor, who owes the promised performance to the promisee.

To this proposal the following objection may be raised. Whether or not it is apt in some sense to explain them, the ubiquity of Rule R would not seem to *justify* the intuitive judgments in question. Rule R requires Anne to act *as if* Ben has a certain right. Intuitively, however, he actually has such a right. If what we are looking for, then, is an account of our intuitive judgments that provides a justification of them rather than a debunking explanation, this proposal must be rejected.

One who accepts this aim may counter that the existence of a rule in one's society to the effect that in certain circumstances one is to be treated as if one has a certain right is a sufficient basis for allowing that, in that society, one actually has that right. Or a rule understood in somewhat different terms may be invoked: if, in a given society, it is allowed that a promisee is to *count as* having a right to performance against the promisor, then, in that society, the promisee has such a right.[35]

---

[34] In informal discussion of an earlier version of this chapter, the first was suggested by Arneson, the second by David Brink (La Jolla, November 2002).

[35] The formula "*X* counts as *Y*" plays a large role in the account of social institutions in John R. Searle, *The Construction of Social Reality* (New York: Free Press, 1995). See also Searle, *Speech Acts: An Essay in the Philosophy of Language* (New York: Cambridge 1969).

There is a familiar problem common to both of these responses: they are not clearly free of the assumption of a "prior promise." What, after all, does the existence of a social rule in a given society amount to? According to at least some accounts, something akin to a prior promise or agreement is among the existence conditions of a social rule.[36] Thus these responses are open to the objection that they are attempting to explain a puzzling feature of promising by reference to something with that very feature. Suppose we set this problem aside, and allow, at the same time, that the existence of an appropriate social rule would actually give Ben a right against Anne. This still leaves the proposal at issue with serious problems. In particular, it detaches promisees' rights from promises, and from promissory obligation, in an unintuitive way.

Intuitively, a promisee's rights are part and parcel of promises. They are on a par, in this way, with a promisor's obligations. According to this proposal, however, a promisor's obligation may exist when a promisee's right does not: that right depends on the existence in the promisee's society of an appropriate rule. To say this is to say something in the spirit of Scanlon's doubts about practice theories of promissory obligation: promises and the like appear to obligate independently of any background social practices, rules, or understandings as to what counts as what. In the same way, they give promisees rights.

Relatedly, from an intuitive point of view, a promisee's right is the obverse of a promisor's obligation (and vice versa), a promisor's obligation being, by its nature, a *directed* obligation. The proposal at hand, meanwhile, starts with a nondirected obligation—that which is a result of Principle F—and puts it together with a social rule that is supposed independently to generate a right. Clearly this right is not simply the obverse of the obligation in question.

The proposal under consideration, then, has several problems. These are the problem of whether and how a social rule could give a promisee a genuine right, the prior promise problem, and the structural problem. Even if the first two problems are set aside, the relationship between an obligation derived from Principle F and a right supposedly the product of a social rule is not structurally the same as the intuitive relationship between a promisee's right and a promisor's obligation.

V.B. Subsidiary moral principles. Rather than appealing to a contingent social practice, can Scanlon plausibly appeal to a subsidiary moral principle? A beneficiary theorist of rights may point out, as did the proponent of the previous proposal, that it is in the interests of someone in Ben's position to be able with impunity to act as if he had a right to Anne's performance. Might one not argue, indeed, that Ben's interest in being able so to act is sufficient to ground a moral duty in Anne, and that Anne has, therefore, a moral duty to allow him so to act?

---

[36] See Gilbert, *Sociality and Responsibility,* chapter 5.

What exactly is Anne's duty according to this argument? It seems to be a duty to allow Ben to act as if he had a right to her performance. Does this mean that Ben does in fact have a right to her performance? That is at best not clear.

Perhaps someone will say that if certain others morally ought to act as if I have a given right against them, then, whatever else is true, I have a *moral right* against them with the same content. Perhaps it will be said that that is *what it is* to have a moral right—or one type of moral right—against certain others.

Suppose that for the sake of argument one accepts these points. One must then observe that a moral right of the kind in question is, intuitively, of a different type to the rights of promisees. Promisees' rights are not, at base, only rights-people-morally-ought-to-act-as-if-the-promisee-had. They are—in addition—rights the promisee has. The same can be said of similar understandings of what a moral right is. It can be said, for instance, of the understanding that to have a moral right against someone is for it to be the case one morally ought to have a right against him. A promisee's right is a right the promisee has.

Another problem with this proposal has to do with the relationship between a promisee's right and a promisor's obligation. Once again, we have a proposal that starts with a nondirected obligation—unlike a promisor's obligation—and adds to the mix a type of right of the promisee—a right-people-morally-ought-to-act-as-if-the-promisee-had. Though it may not be correct to say that the right of the promisee is in this case only contingently present when the obligation of the promisor is, it is not simply the obverse of the promisor's obligation. It is something additional. For the promisor's obligation derives from Principle F, whereas the promisee's right relates to a different, here unnamed, principle, concerning an interest of Ben's that—according to the principle—morally ought to be protected.

VI. Principle F as the Source of a Secondary Obligation Presupposing Promisees' Rights

There could be more than one obligation, and perhaps more than one *type* of obligation, associated with promises. I take it that, first, there is a (primary) obligation that is part and parcel of promising, a directed obligation correlated with a right of the promisee against the promisor. Then there could be one or more other obligations, always or perhaps only sometimes present when promising occurs. These (secondary) obligations would perhaps reflect the existence of the obligations that are part and parcel of promising. The secondary obligations would not necessarily be directed obligations with correlative rights.

The gist of my argument so far has been that Scanlon's Principle F is not the source of the primary obligation, given the directed nature of that obligation or, in other words, its correspondence to a right in the promisee. Principle F could, however, be the source of a secondary, nondirected obligation that obtains in some or all cases of promising.

There is, indeed, reason to think that Principle F is least debatable, as a moral principle, if one of its assumptions is the making of what is, in effect, a promise, complete with the primary directed obligation of the promisor. This may be argued roughly as follows.

Scanlon's statement of the principle starts with the assumption that a person A voluntarily and intentionally leads another person B to expect that A will do X (unless B consents to A's not doing so). But there are many ways in which A might lead B to believe this. Thus A might express an appropriate personal intention. But A's personal intention is surely A's to change as A wishes. If all that A has done in bringing about the truth of the assumption is express a personal intention, then it is not at all clear that there will be any moral onus upon A to the effect that A must do X unless B consents to A's not doing so.

Scanlon's second assumption is that B wants to be "assured" that A will do X (unless B consents to A's not doing so), and his third is that A acts with the aim of providing this assurance, and has good reason to believe that this has been done. Now it may be that a simple expression of personal intention is not enough to *assure* anyone of one's future actions, because one may always choose to change one's mind. In that case, it seems that A must have done more than express such an intention.

In Scanlon's discussion, he at one point refers to a "settled intention," but it is not clear on the face of it what a "settled" intention is, other than a genuine one. However genuine my intention, I am surely at liberty to change my mind when I wish to, if my intention is the only relevant constraining factor. So the expression of a genuine intention is unlikely to be enough to assure someone that I will indeed do the thing intended. Rather, I will do it unless I change my mind.[37]

What is the appropriate intention here? Presumably it will incorporate a consent clause. Might the inclusion of this clause make a difference, constraining A from changing course?

Consider the statement "I intend to do X (unless you consent to my not doing so)." The stated condition, your consenting to my not doing so, may in principle

---

[37] A similar drift, not directed at Scanlon in particular, is to be found in various writings—see, for instance, Prichard, "The Obligation to Keep a Promise"; Robins, "The Primacy of Promising"; and, in relation to Scanlon, Michael Pratt, "Scanlon on Promising," *Canadian Journal of Law and Jurisprudence*, XIV, 1 (January 2001): 143–54, of which I learned after formulating similar points (Gilbert, "Moral Obligation and Agreement" (manuscript), presented at the University of Connecticut/Storrs, spring semester 2001). A focus of previous writing of mine has been the unilateral rescindability of personal intentions and other sources of personal commitments. See, for instance, my 1997 essay, "What Is It for Us to Intend?" reprinted in Gilbert, *Sociality and Responsibility*, pp. 14–36.

be construed as internal or external to the intention. What I have in mind is this: when it is construed as internal, the quoted sentence comes out as equivalent to "I intend this: to do X (unless you consent to my not doing so)." When construed as external, it comes out as "Unless you consent to my not doing X, my intention is to do X."

As to the first construal, there seems no bar from the consent clause to my changing my mind, and canceling or otherwise amending my intention. To cite two possibilities, the intention that results from my change of mind might be the intention not to do X whether or not you consent to my not doing so, or to do X whatever you say.

As to the second construal, it seems to imply that I have an intention to do X that will persist unless you consent to my not doing X. It is not clear, however, how a personal intention can become subject to another person's consent. Is my claim that my intention will persist absent your consent an empirical one? Then how can I be sure it is true? Is it or does it presuppose an undertaking of some kind? If so, then it seems that there is, in effect, a promise in the background, a promise complete with a directed obligation of the promisor and its correlative right in the promisee.

In short, it is not easy to see how the assumptions with which Scanlon introduces Principle F lead to a nondirected obligation of the person in A's position unless they implicitly include what is, in effect, a promise of A's to do X, complete with the directed obligation of the promisor. If we assume—contrary to Scanlon's drift—that this is so, then Principle F may hold. I shall not attempt to decide if it does here. If it holds when and only when these amplified conditions are met, then it will indeed describe an obligation that promisors often, if not always, have. It will not, however, describe the primary, directed obligation of a promisor.

VII. Summary, Conclusions, Prospect

Scanlon's account of promissory obligation is one of a certain general type, a type that appeals to a moral principle applied in a noninstitutional context. It is intended to apply on the basis of facts about personal intentions, expressions of such intentions, expectations, and preferences. I have briefly argued, concordantly with other authors, that in order to be valid such a principle needs a different basis. It may well need a promise or something like it as part of the basis on which it will apply. Be that as it may, my central argument in this chapter has been that Scanlon's principle is not equipped, in and of itself, to account for promisees' rights and the correlative directed obligations of promisors. My argument strongly suggests, if it does not show, that no account of this type will adequately account for the nature of a promisee's rights as these are intuitively understood.

If so, and if one agrees with Scanlon that social practice accounts are implausible, one might wonder: How are a promisees' rights possible? And if it is hard to see how rights of this nature are possible, their actuality may be doubted. One might then be tempted to stick with a noninstitutional, moral principle account of promissory obligation such as Scanlon's. And one may give up the search for a source of a promisees' rights.

I think this would be a mistake, since I believe that it is possible to give an account of promisees' rights that is neither a practice account nor a noninstitutional, moral principle account. I shall not describe nor discuss the account I have in mind here.[38] I shall, however, make some points relevant to it.

On the topic of promissory obligation, people may seesaw between noninstitutional moral principle views and practice views that, also, appeal to a moral principle because they take seriously Hume's worry that there is no sense in the idea of willing an obligation into being. Now this may seem to be absolutely clear if we are thinking of an obligation, duty, or requirement that derives from a moral principle, a principle, roughly, of the type that Scanlon's contractualism attempts to characterize. Call such obligations, and these alone, *moral* obligations. One may think, plausibly: How could anyone will a moral obligation into being, just like that, just because they wanted to? A moral obligation simply is *not* that kind of thing. One has or does not have such an obligation, in the circumstances. Given such-and-such circumstances, the obligation is or is not there. In a given context one may be able to create the relevant circumstances by an exercise of will, but that is not willing the *obligation*.

Supposing this is right, it need not end discussion of the possibility that the directed obligations of promisors are directly willed into existence. For it could be that the obligations associated with promises, while being genuine and indeed paradigmatic obligations, are not moral obligations (nor legal obligations either).

---

[38] I have sketched such an account in various publications. These focus on agreements rather than promises, but suggest an interpretation of promises as well. See, for instance, my articles, "Is an Agreement an Exchange of Promises?" "Agreements, Coercion," and "Obligation and Joint Commitment," *Utilitas*, xi, 2 (January 1999): 143–63, reprinted in Gilbert, *Sociality and Responsibility*, pp. 50–70. I return to it in my book, *Rights Reconsidered* (to be published by Oxford University Press). Robins, in *Promising, Intending, and Moral Autonomy*, emphasizes the need to account for a promisee's rights (at pp. 99–102) and pays careful attention to that need in developing a proposal as to the nature of promising (see pp. 102–03). My own proposal has some affinities with that of Robins—for whom the notion of *commitment* is key. There are important differences too, in particular, my invocation of a commitment that is *joint* in the sense I articulate.

Though one might be unclear as to how this could be, it can surely not be thought unintelligible. That there are nonmoral, nonlegal obligations and rights would only be unintelligible if by "moral" one meant "other than legal." Then the categories of "moral" and "legal" would be exhaustive, by definition. But a moral obligation is not being conceived of here in such a residual fashion, but rather in terms of an intuitive idea of the moral realm. Perhaps a sense of the problematic nature of moral principle views, along with practice views, will allow those otherwise skeptical of a *via media* to view such a possibility more favorably.

Evidently, the discussion here is relevant to more than the rights of promisees and the correlative obligations of promisors. It bears on the general question of the nature and source of rights in the sense of Hohfeldian claims or rights "in the strict sense of the term." When their directionality is construed as in this chapter, such rights—for short, *rights*, period—are clearly valuable possessions. If I have a right against you, I have the standing to put pressure upon you to do certain things. I have a certain, if limited, authority over your will. How, then, do people come by such rights?

Insofar as legal rights are *stipulated* rights, they raise immediate questions about the authority of law itself. The same goes for any other stipulated rights, including the rights, if any, that are created by nonlegal rules. Setting such rights aside, many moral philosophers have been inclined to suppose that some rights—which they would refer to as *moral* rights—are constructed out of purely moral materials such as moral requirements. These philosophers do not think of moral rights as rights that ought to be, or some such thing. They think of them as real, existing rights constructed out of purely moral materials. The discussion in this chapter suggests that there are no moral rights in this sense.[39]

If that is right, it leaves us with the question: Where do nonlegal, nonstipulated rights come from? One source of such rights is, evidently, the source of promisees' rights. Clearly, it would be good to know what that is.

---

[39] I explore this issue further in *Rights Reconsidered*.

13

Three Dogmas About Promising

The topic of promising connects with several broader issues. Among these is the question of how human beings can constrain or bind themselves with respect to their future actions. By promising, one binds oneself in a particularly intractable way: one who promises another that he (or she) will do something cannot unilaterally unbind himself but awaits release from the person to whom he has promised, his "promisee."[1]

There is a vast and expanding philosophical literature on promising. My main negative aim here is to highlight and question the three interrelated dogmas of the title, dogmas—more politely, assumptions—that prevail in that literature. I question them in light of two points that many (myself included) take to be intuitive.

My main positive aim is to demonstrate that there is a plausible theory of promising that respects the two intuitive points that render the three dogmas suspect and allows one to replace those dogmas with more intuitively plausible counterparts. According to the theory of promising I shall delineate, one who promises creates together with the person to whom the promise is made a *joint commitment* with a particular type of content.

Some Preliminary Points

I start with some preliminary points. First, in speaking of a *promise,* I do not mean to limit myself to situations in which someone utters the words "I promise," or an

---

[1] Here and elsewhere in this chapter I focus on the case of one person promising to another. Typically, this other is a single human individual. One can also promise something to a group of people, as when someone promises his parents, collectively, to take good care of himself. I shall focus on the case of a single individual promisee in this chapter. I take this to be the paradigm or clearest type of case. For some remarks on other types of case see the text below.

equivalent in a language other than English. A few words in support of this point may be useful, though it is not an uncommon one.[2]

Suppose that Jeremy says to Julia, "I'll phone you tonight," and Julia responds, "Okay." If Jeremy then fails to call, Julia may remonstrate with him: "You said you'd call." In other words, she may treat Jeremy's "I'll phone you" much as she would have treated his "I'll phone you—I promise," and she may be right to do so.

Supposing that she is, it would not be appropriate for Jeremy to respond that his "I'll phone you..." was a mere expression of intention or decision, or, as if it were, that "I changed my mind."[3] Nor could he appropriately respond "Well, I guess I was wrong, since I didn't call!" as if his "I'll call you" was a mere prediction. Nor would it be appropriate for him to say: "Well, I didn't *promise* to call!" and back this up with the observation: "I didn't say 'I promise'!" For the fact that he did not use the words "I promise" would not be enough to get him off the hook.

Perhaps Julia is less likely to say "But you promised!" in the case imagined. If so, that could be because Jeremy did not, indeed, say "I promise..." Otherwise, the two situations appear to be on a par.

This is not to deny that there are interesting things to say about the utterance "I promise." One of these is that it is a "performative" utterance in the sense of Austin (1962). Roughly, with a performative utterance one does what one says one is doing by saying that one is doing it. Thus one can also say "I hereby promise..."

No such thing can be said of Jeremy's "I'll phone you tonight." Yet, as said, what transpires between him and Julia when he says this and she says "Okay" may be much the same as it would have been had he said "I'll phone you tonight—I promise." In speaking of "promises," I mean to speak of what is common between these cases.

The second preliminary point is this: promises and *agreements* are "close cousins." I return to this point later in the chapter.

---

[2] Anscombe (1978) berates Hume for not realizing that you can promise without saying "I promise" or, indeed, using the word "promise." Among others who say that one can promise without using the word "promise" is Raz (1977).

[3] Had Julia initially understood Jeremy to be informing her of his intention, and herself as acknowledging receipt of this information, she might have responded to his saying he had changed his mind, in explanation of not calling, in some such way as this: *"You should have let me know* that you had changed your mind." Should she take him to have promised, she would be discountenanced in a particular way by the information that he had changed his mind. Indeed, were he to tell her that is what he'd done, she might well say "What do you mean 'I changed my mind'?" implying that *he was not in a position* to do such a thing.

The third preliminary point is that the focus of my discussion, like that of most philosophers who work on promises, is on everyday promises of the kind that Jeremy made to Julia in my opening example, as opposed to the smaller class of promises that fall into some category—in particular, contract—with which the law concerns itself. Those who make everyday promises may have no intention to create legal relations and may not create such relations in fact.

The law has its own reasons for allowing one or another transaction to establish a legal relation. Good as these reasons may be from the point of view of the law, the resulting judgments may or may not be helpful to those seeking to understand the nature and implications of what goes on outside the legal arena. Thus, though legal judgments may bear on whether or not a particular point is indeed an intuitive one, they cannot determine that question.

The fourth and final preliminary point has to do with the way in which a promise binds the one who makes it—the "promisor." It is generally assumed that there is at least one central intuitive sense in which a promisor is *obligated,* by virtue of having promised, to act as he has promised, at least if all else is equal. I shall not dispute this assumption.

Theorists often speak of a promisor's "promissory obligation," in the singular. This suggests that, when a promisor is obligated by virtue of having promised, obligation in just one sense of the term is at issue. Indeed, as I shall explain, different theorists of promising tend to focus on one and the same sense of "obligation."

In what follows I shall use the phrase "promissory obligation" on account of its familiarity. In using that phrase, however, I mean to allow that a promisor may be obligated, by virtue of his promise, in more than one sense.

I shall in due course distinguish two radically different senses of "obligation." I shall argue, in effect, that one must distinguish between the two senses in question if one is to understand the ways in which a promisor may be bound by his promise.[4]

One can put *the problem of promissory obligation* thus: in what sense or senses, if any, does one who promises thereby obligate himself to do the promised act—at least all else being equal?[5] The discussion in this chapter bears closely on this issue.

---

[4] I don't say that there are *only* two prevalent senses of "obligation." That is probably not the case. I have written of "senses of obligation," rather than "kinds of obligation," because I have found it hard to discern the genus of which these two senses might pick out two species, and speaking of "kinds of obligation" may suggest that I think there is such a genus. Cf. Gilbert (2006: ch. 2).

[5] There is a parallel with one version of the classic problem of political obligation, both in terms of the question, and in terms of the answer I am inclined to give. See Gilbert (2006).

I. Three Dogmas About Promising

The three dogmas I discuss are points that contemporary philosophers of promising tend to accept—either explicitly or implicitly.[6] To call them dogmas is not to say that philosophers have no reason to accept them. It is rather to say that they tend not to be examined with a critical eye. Their acceptance is consequential: they have helped to shape most contemporary theories of promising. All three dogmas concern promissory obligation. Taking each one in turn, I summarize it, then amplify the summary somewhat.

The Moral Requirement Dogma

The Moral Requirement dogma may be summarized thus: promissory obligation is a matter of moral requirement. More fully, it runs as follows: the obligation that a promisor incurs by virtue of his promise, when he does indeed so incur an obligation, is a moral requirement deriving from a general moral principle or several such principles. Thus, almost in so many words, Thomas Scanlon:

> When promises give rise to clear obligations, these can be accounted
> for on the basis of general moral principles. (1998: 315)[7]

It is understood that promisors may not be the only class of persons covered by the general moral principle or principles in question.[8]

Different theorists have different accounts of what a specifically moral requirement amounts to. They would generally agree that a moral requirement is to be distinguished from a legal requirement, and from a prudential requirement, among others. They would also generally agree that such requirements do not depend on contingent human agreements or other arrangements. More positively, it is common to argue for the existence of a moral principle or requirement by reference to significant values or interests that are, it is claimed, promoted by one's conformity to it.[9]

---

[6] Dissenting voices with respect to one or more of the dogmas include Raz (1977: 225) and Searle (2001: 194). In spite of such discussions, the dogmas are still generally entrenched.

[7] Though Scanlon mentions "principles" here, and discusses several pertinent principles in the course of his discussion, he focuses on his Principle F (see the text below) in his explanation of promissory obligation. His initial discussion of promising is Scanlon (1990).

[8] Cf. Scanlon (1998).

[9] In connection with promissory obligation, Scanlon (1998) appeals to the value that "assurance" has to human beings; and, among those who have most recently critiqued him, Owens (2006) appeals to an "authority interest" (as opposed to an "information interest"), and Shiffrin (2008) to the "values of trust."

Both the "social practice" theories that he opposes, and Scanlon's own theory, among others, appeal to moral principles in their explanations of promissory obligation.[10] Scanlon's complex "Principle F" takes certain carefully specified empirical conditions to be the crucial aspects of promising, and says that, when those conditions are satisfied then, morally speaking, and subject to a further condition, the promisor must act as promised in the absence of special justification for not doing so.

In one of its formulations Principle F runs as follows:

If (1) A voluntarily and intentionally leads B to expect that A will do X (unless B consents to A's not doing so);

(2) A knows that B wants to be assured of this;

(3) A acts with the aim of providing this assurance, and has good reason to believe that he or she has done so;

(4) B knows that A has the beliefs and intentions just described;

(5) A intends for B to know this, and knows that B does know it; and

(6) B knows that A has this knowledge and intent; then, in the absence of special justification, A must do X unless B consents to X's not being done. (Scanlon, 1998: 304)

I take it that Scanlon might equally well have written "is morally required to" instead of "must," as far as his intentions went.

The No Willing Dogma

I turn now to the second dogma. Its first proponent, to my knowledge, was David Hume. In a famous passage in the *Treatise* (2000: 322), Hume notes that, according to "our common ways of thinking and expressing ourselves…the obligation [of a promise] arises from our mere will and pleasure." He proceeds to argue, skeptically, that the obligation of a promise is not and cannot simply be willed into being. In his words, more generally: 'Tis impossible that we cou'd ever will a new obligation" (2000: 332, n. 2).

---

[10] The most prominent contemporary practice theorist is John Rawls (1955, 1971). More recent proponents of this approach include Kolodny and Wallace (2003); Scanlon cites Joseph Raz, Neil MacCormick, and Judith Thomson as taking nonpractice positions similar to his own.

Hume's skeptical conclusion about promises is the second dogma. I will refer to it as the *No Willing* dogma.[11] I think it fair to say that it has been a large part of the inspiration for contemporary theories of promissory obligation.[12]

Given that one accepts the Moral Requirement dogma, one is likely to accept the No Willing dogma for something like the following reason: the obligation of a promise is a moral requirement. As such, it is not the kind of thing that can be brought into being by a mere act of will—justified or not.[13]

The Immoral Promises Dogma

I now turn to the third dogma: in and of itself, one who makes an immoral promise is not thereby obligated to act as promised. I label this the *Immoral Promises* dogma.

An example of an immoral promise is Diana's promise to Sue that she will kill Clarence. The mere fact that Diana made this promise does not, surely, make it morally permissible for her to kill Clarence. On the contrary, if there are no other considerations bearing on the case, it is morally impermissible for her to do what she promised in this situation. Hence—in the sense of "immoral promise" at issue—her promise is an immoral one. According to the third dogma, Diana is not obligated to act as promised—all else being equal.[14]

The Immoral Promises dogma on my characterization of it is intended to be agnostic on the question of what kinds of obligation there are. Hence it is not intended to be implied by that characterization that obligation is therein

---

[11] Note that my specification of what the No Willing dogma rejects, and Hume's specification of our common way of thinking, does not obviously limit the workings of the human will specifically to *the promisor's willing an obligation for himself*, the main option Hume considers. I shall later argue that there is another option that allows us to reject the No Willing dogma as stated here, and to justify the "common ways of thinking" to which Hume alludes. This invokes a sense of "obligation" that differs from that with which Hume was operating—he had his own version of the Moral Requirement dogma. See the next paragraph in the text, and the next note.

[12] Theorists often suppose that what a promisor does, crucially, is express an *intention to obligate himself*. Precisely what further factors allow an obligation to accrue to the promisor is then seen as the issue, given that, as Hume argued, one's intention to obligate himself does not in and of itself do the trick. Other theorists attempt to show how promises can obligate without appealing to the promisor's intention to obligate himself—an intention Hume has after all discredited as the sole basis of promissory obligation. See Raz (1977) on the "intention conception" versus the "obligation conception," which Raz prefers.

[13] Hume presents a specifically Humean version of the Moral Requirement dogma.

[14] Altham (1985) offers a focused discussion of immoral promises. He invokes Anscombe (1978). Raz (1977: 212) suggests the prevalence of the immoral promises dogma.

understood to be a matter of moral requirement. Still, it is worth pointing out that one who holds the Moral Requirement dogma may be led by it to the Immoral Promises dogma.

According to the Moral Requirement dogma, the obligation of a promise, when it arises, is a moral requirement to keep the promise. Given its content, meanwhile, an immoral promise is such that one is not morally required to keep it, all else being equal. Rather, one is morally required not to keep it. Given the Moral Requirement dogma, then, an immoral promise, in and of itself, does not obligate the promisor.

This assumes something I take to be correct: if at this point in time, given current circumstances, I am morally required *not* to perform some action, A, then at this point in time, given the same circumstances, there is no moral requirement on me to *perform* A. Perhaps there would be such a moral requirement on me, if some of the current circumstances were not present; but that is a different matter.[15]

It is worth pointing out that given this assumption certain situations that have been described as involving conflicting *obligations* cannot be construed as involving conflicting *moral requirements*. Interestingly enough, such situations often involve conflicting promises. An example would be Jane's having promised Phyllis that she will attend Phyllis's wedding, and her also having promised Bob that she will drive his mother to an important appointment with the doctor— when it turns out, regrettably, that the doctor's appointment is at the very time of Phyllis's wedding. Evidently, the nature of these particular situations will be clearest when we have a satisfactory theory of promissory obligation.

II. Two Intuitive Points About Promising

I now introduce two intuitive points about promissory obligation that might be thought firm in advance of one's acquaintance with the three dogmas. The problem for the dogmas is that these points undercut them.

At this moment in time, of course, the three dogmas may seem as firm as any other points. They may also seem to be irreplaceable. With respect to the first dogma, for instance: if promissory obligation is not a matter of moral requirement, what is it? If one can give an account of promissory obligation that is otherwise plausible and respects the two intuitive points, while failing to support the three dogmas, those dogmas should seem less compelling.

---

[15] Cf. Gilbert (1993a): moral requirements, qua *requirements*, are "context-sensitive"; given the original basis for a given requirement, it may disappear when something is added to that basis. This is not the same as its "remaining" though "overridden." See also Gilbert (2006: ch. 7).

In saying that these points are "intuitive" I mean roughly this: given only one's understanding of them, it is hard to doubt their truth. Indeed, they may appear to be knowable a priori, or (more specifically) to be true by virtue of the meanings of the terms involved, or true by definition. Such judgments, being judgments, are open to pressure from arguments to the contrary. Such arguments are necessary, however, if they are to be discredited.

Prichard's Point

What, then, are these two points? The first is suggested by the Oxford philosopher H. A. Prichard when he writes: "Once call some act a promise, and all question of whether there is an obligation to do it seems to have vanished" (1968: 198).

I shall myself phrase the point I have in mind with more certitude, as I believe is appropriate, and in the material as opposed to the linguistic mode. I believe that it is intuitive *for at least one central sense of the term "obligation."* The point is this: if someone has promised to do something, then he is obligated to do it, by virtue of his promise. For the sake of a label, I shall call this: "Prichard's point."

Several philosophers have made statements that suggest it.[16] Some say that the statement that a promise obligates the promisor to perform the promised act is true by definition, or that it is analytic.[17] In either case Prichard's point as I have characterized it would be correct—and knowable a priori.[18]

Prichard's point seems to present a problem for the Immoral Promises dogma. According to that dogma, an immoral promise, in and of itself, *does not obligate the promisor.*[19] According to Prichard's point every promise obligates the promisor.

Perhaps the conflict between Prichard's point and the Immoral Promises dogma is only apparent. One pertinent issue here is this. On the face of it, an immoral promise is *possible.* Is that correct?

---

[15] Concurring authors include Searle (1964: 45) and Beran (1987: 6). Feinberg (1966: 138) speaks of the promisee's rights in such terms. (On promisees' rights see the second intuitive point, below.)

[17] Raz (1977: 221) allows that explanations of an action taken or intended "in terms such as 'But I promised I'll do it' do sound complete. To add 'therefore it was my duty to do it' is, we feel, to unpack what is already contained in the first statement, not to add to it."

[18] That it is indeed an intuitive point is suggested by this reference to it in Anscombe (1978: 319): regarding the idea that all promises obligate the promisor. "We might indeed argue that it was not so.... *Showing this might however leave someone puzzled;...*" (emphasis mine).

[19] Recall that the Immoral Promises dogma as represented in this chapter is couched simply in terms of "obligation," not in terms of moral requirement. Those who hold it may well believe that the only obligation that could be at issue is obligation in the sense of moral requirement, but that is a separate issue.

Though there is not a great deal of discussion of immoral promises in the literature, there is some, and it is generally agreed that immoral promises are indeed possible. One argument for this goes as follows: if what seems to be an immoral promise has not been kept, it can intelligibly be invoked by the promisee as a basis for complaint against the promisor. If it had not been made, it could not be invoked.[20] Having granted the possibility of an immoral promise, authors generally say that such promises do not obligate the promisor. In other words, they endorse the Immoral Promises dogma.

Let us grant, with the consensus, that immoral promises are possible. Whether or not there is indeed a conflict between the Immoral Promises dogma and Prichard's point depends, further, on precisely how that point is understood.[21]

Consider what I shall call the *weak reading* of Prichard's point, which runs roughly thus: it is a truth knowable a priori that, if one has promised to do something, then by virtue of his promise, as such, he is obligated to act as promised, *in the absence of sufficiently powerful countervailing considerations.* Given sufficiently powerful countervailing considerations, which are possible, he is not obligated to act as promised. On the weak reading, then, Prichard's point allows that a given promisor may *not* be obligated to fulfill his promise. In particular it allows that *the obligation of a promise may depend in part at least on the content of that promise.*

On the weak reading of Prichard's point it does not in itself constitute a challenge to the Immoral Promises dogma. It remains to ask whether Prichard's point should be given the weak reading. This I take not to be a question about Prichard's own intent, but about what is intuitive.

I propose that what is intuitive is this: promising is a source of obligation such that if one has made a promise one is in some sense obligated to do what one has promised, *all things considered.* In particular, a promise obligates *irrespective of its content.* I shall call this the *strong reading* of Prichard's point.

I make this proposal without attempting to specify the sense of "obligation" in question, while taking it to be a central, standard sense. I do take it that obligation in the sense of moral requirement is not at issue, if only because one who makes a promise is *not* morally required to act as promised irrespective of its content.

Recall now Prichard's own way of putting things: "Once call some act a promise, and all question of whether there is an obligation to do it seems to have vanished." On the face of it, he is not talking about an obligation "to do it, depending

---

[20] Anscombe (1978), cited approvingly by Altham (1985).

[21] I am indebted to Julie Tannenbaum for pressing this point, and for related discussion (personal correspondence, November 2008). The issue here was noted by Anscombe: in her terms, it is the possibility that the obligation of a promise is defeasible.

on what it is." Admittedly, given Prichard's use of the word "seems," his statement is somewhat tentative. This could be because he finds the point puzzling. He makes it clear that he does find it puzzling as he proceeds through the essay from which the quotation is taken. In short, I conjecture that Prichard's own tentativeness stems from his finding an apparently a priori truth hard to square with other things he believes. As I understand him, one of these is the Moral Requirement dogma. Another is the No Willing dogma.[22]

Be that as it may, in what follows I focus on the strong reading of Prichard's point: if one knows that someone has promised to do something, one knows that he is in some central, standard sense obligated to do it, *all things, including its content, considered.*

According to the Immoral Promises dogma, an immoral promise, in and of itself, does not obligate the promisor to act as promised. According to Prichard's point, one's promise obligates one to act as promised irrespective of its content. Thus an immoral promise obligates the promisor to act as promised irrespective of its immorality. It seems, then, that we must give up the Immoral Promises dogma if we accept Prichard's point.

Since the Immoral Promises dogma follows from the Moral Requirement dogma, we shall have to give both up, if we stick with Prichard's point. And then one clear basis for the No Willing dogma crumbles.

Promissory Obligations Are Directed

I now turn to a second intuitive point that creates a problem for the three dogmas. Though personally I find Prichard's point to be compelling, I take this second point to be the firmer of the two. It is in any case an important supplement to Prichard's point. In a brief statement to be amplified shortly: promissory obligation is relational or *directed* obligation.

If Olive has a *directed obligation,* there are one or more persons toward whom that obligation is directed. Her obligation is an obligation to Roger, say. It will be an obligation to Roger to do such-and-such.

It is generally understood that, correlative and equivalent to any directed obligation is a right. This is a right of a particular kind, sometimes referred to in the literature as a claim-right. Thus, if and only if Olive has a directed obligation *to Roger* to go to Chicago tomorrow, Roger has (in a common phrase) a *right against* Olive to her going to Chicago tomorrow.

If a promisor's obligation is directed to the promisee, then, a promisee will have a right against his promisor to the fulfillment of the promise. Intuitively,

[22] Prichard does not cite Hume, but his discussion resonates closely with Hume's skepticism about the willing of an obligation.

indeed, promisees have such rights.[23] Notably, these are "special" rights: the promise endows the promisee alone with a right to the promised action as such.[24]

Now philosophers frequently refer to "obligations to" and "rights against" without going further. And once one goes further, what one says may not correspond to what everyone who uses these phrases has in mind. There is, however, a well-known connection that has been made and that is pertinent to the case of promising. This is the connection between directed obligation and *owing*. Such a connection was assumed by H. L. A. Hart and Joel Feinberg among others. In terms of the previous example: If Olive has a directed obligation to Roger to go to Chicago tomorrow, then, equivalently, Olive owes Roger her going to Chicago tomorrow.

What, though, is owing? There is no doubt that this term is ambiguous. In the present context I shall amplify it at least to this extent: Olive owes Roger her going to Chicago tomorrow, if and only if, in an as yet unspecified intuitive sense, Roger can appropriately regard Olive's act of going to Chicago tomorrow *as his*.[25]

This may sound strange, if not impossible. In what sense can an action that is one person's to perform be another's? If there is more than one such sense, which sense is at issue here? I return to these questions later.

This construal of owing suggests a particular amplification of an important further point about promising. This is the intuitive judgment that by virtue of one's status as a promisee one is in a position to demand the promised act from the pertinent promisor if, say, he expresses an intention not to perform it in advance of the time for performance.

Evidently, given the sense of "demand" at issue here—and in what follows— it is not the case that everyone is in a position to demand any action he likes of any other. Anyone can of course *purport* to be in a position to demand a given action of another, in this sense of "demand," without actually being in a position to do so. And "demand" is doubtless sometimes used in a weaker sense, such that everyone *is* in a position to demand any action of any other.[26]

---

[23] Raz (1977) discusses two conceptions of promising, according to each of which the promisee has a right to performance of the promised action. The larger part of the literature focused on promising has not, in fact, emphasized the existence of rights in the promisee. The focus has almost exclusively been on the obligations of the promisor, whose intuitively "directed" nature is often ignored. Robins (1984) is another exception.

[24] See, for instance, Hart (1955: 183).

[25] Cf. Feinberg (1970: 251): "If Smith owes Jones five dollars, only Jones can claim the five dollars as his own." Here Feinberg is at least ostensibly talking about owing money rather than owing an action. That said, the suggestion is that there is a close connection between what is *owed* and what is *one's own*. In some recent discussions I have written of the right-holder as in some sense *owning* the action to which he has a right. This way of putting things has provoked some resistance, and may be unnecessarily strong, insofar as it goes beyond talk of the action being in some sense *one's own*. Here I stick to what may be the weaker of the two locutions, thus following Feinberg more closely

[26] Cf. the discussion of commanding and other authority-presupposing terms in Gilbert (2006: ch. 1).

Given my construal of owing, the suggested amplification of the intuitive point about promising just noted involves understanding *demanding* as follows: I am in a position to demand a certain action of someone if and only if that action is mine—in the sense at issue in the case of owing.

Independently of my construal of owing, one may find it intuitive that a promisee is in a position to demand the promised act as in some sense his. Given that construal, it is plausible to assume that the sense of "his" involved in each case is the same.

Intuitively, a promisee is in a position to *rebuke* the promisor for nonperformance of the promise after the time for performance has passed. Such rebukes can be seen as after-the-fact counterparts of demands in the sense at issue here.

These considerations throw doubt on the Moral Requirement dogma. Some pertinent concerns are as follows.[27]

Suppose that the obligation a promisor accrues is a matter of moral requirement deriving from a suitable moral principle. That is, he is now morally required to keep his promise. Now suppose that a promisor, Joe, appears to be about to break his promise to Mary. Does Mary have the standing to demand of Joe that he keep his promise on the grounds, simply, that a *moral principle is about to be violated*? Perhaps so. What needs to be shown, though, is that she has a *special* standing to demand of Joe that he keep his promise, given her position as Joe's promisee.

It is plausible to suppose that if anyone has the standing to demand conformity to a moral principle on the grounds, simply, that a moral principle is about to be violated, then everybody does—or at least everybody capable of making a demand in the first place. Suppose, then, that everybody has the standing to demand compliance whenever a moral principle is violated—several philosophers believe that something like this is the case. This does not help us understand how Mary comes to have a special standing to demand of Joe that he do what he promised to do. Suppose, alternatively, that the violation of a moral principle is not in and of itself enough to ground in anyone the standing to demand compliance—as I am myself inclined to think. Then again, obviously, we have not explained Mary's special standing to demand of Joe that he keep his promise. We can, then, set aside the matter of the standing that all—or none—have to demand compliance with any moral principle by virtue of its status as a moral principle.

What if the moral requirement in question is grounded in the interests of a particular person? Does that give the person in question a special standing to demand that the moral principle be conformed to?

---

[27] For a more detailed treatment see Gilbert (2004). My discussion there and in what follows resonates with some of the material in Thomson (2004).

Suppose that Jill, a healthy young student, is morally required to give up her seat on the subway to Jack, a frail professor, for the sake of saving him from unnecessary strain. It is by no means obvious—to me at least—that by virtue of this fact Jack, has the standing to *demand* of Jill that she give up her seat to him. It maybe reasonable for Jack to purport to be in this position—that may be a good way to get Jill to do the right thing, but that is another matter.

At this point the Moral Requirement dogma may seem to be in trouble: Intuitively, promissory obligation is a matter of owing, such that the promisee, as such, has the standing to demand the promised act from the promisor. How, then, can promissory obligation be a matter of moral requirement—or of moral requirement only?[28]

Here is one way, someone might think. Consider something like the consent clause in Scanlon's moral Principle F, and the moral requirements on particular people that derive from it. According to Principle F, if A fulfills its conditions with respect to B, he is morally required to do X "unless B consents to X's not being done." Is it the case that a person, A, owes a person, B, in particular, his doing X, if A is morally required to do X *unless B consents to X's not being done*?

Normally we would take it that for the promisee to "consent" to non-fulfillment of the promise is, in effect, for him to waive the right to fulfillment that he has as promisee. For present purposes, however, we cannot interpret the consent clause in terms of a notion of consent that presupposes B's right to fulfillment of the promise. The pertinent question is, in effect, whether invocation of a moral requirement conditional on a type of consent *that does not presuppose such a right in B* suffices to make it the case that B *has* the pertinent right. For present purposes, then, this question must take "unless B consents to X's not being done" to mean something like: "unless B says it is fine with him that X is not done."

In devising his consent clause Scanlon may both have interpreted it in terms of B's "saying it is fine with him that X is not done" and thought that given its presence B would have a right against A to A's doing X. Whether or not he thought this, it seems not to be true. More precisely, it seems not to be true given the construal of B's right such that it is correlated with A's owing B his (A's) doing X, in the sense of "owing" at issue here.[29]

Apparently, the two intuitive points about promissory obligation that I have noted pose problems for the Moral Requirement dogma. If that dogma is false, the other two dogmas require support from elsewhere, if they are to be

---

[28] In saying "moral requirement only" I mean to allow that more than one kind of obligation may accrue or tend to accrue to promisors.

[29] Cf. Gilbert (2004: 94). The sense of "owe," and so on, that are at issue in Scanlon (1998) may well be a different sense from that with which I am working here.

supported. Insofar as they draw all their force from the Moral Requirement dogma, they are problematic.

I should emphasize that the falsity of the Moral Requirement dogma would not imply that a promisor is never morally required—and in that sense obligated—to fulfill a given promise. Nor would it imply that one is not morally required to keep each of one's promises, all else being equal. The falsity of the Moral Requirement dogma would imply, rather, that *the full story of promissory obligation cannot be told in terms of one or more moral requirements*. In fact the arguments I have deployed so far tend to the stronger conclusion that the *primary* story of promissory obligation cannot be a moral requirement story. They suggest, that is, that whatever moral requirements most firmly accrue to a promisor are founded on an obligation that is not a moral requirement.

Suppose that the Moral Requirement dogma is indeed false. We are then left with a problematic gap. What could go in place of the moral requirement approach to promissory obligation? Is there an alternative approach that respects both Prichard's point, and the point that a promisor incurs an obligation directed to the promisee? Assuming that both of these points relate to a single obligation, is there a plausible account of promissory obligation that respects the point that every promisor incurs a directed obligation to his promisee?

Before arguing for a positive answer, I note that the directedness of promissory obligation rules out an approach that construes such obligation as engendered by no more than a personal decision to act in a certain way.

One might be led to this approach by virtue of an important aspect of personal decisions, something that will be relevant later in this chapter. One who decides to do something has, by virtue of his decision, sufficient reason to do that thing. By this I mean that rationality requires him to do it, all else being equal, where rationality is a matter of appropriately responding to relevant considerations. All else being equal, then, he ought to do it, in an appropriately broad sense of "ought."[30]

Given that this is so, there may be a sense of "obligated" in which he is obligated to do what he decides to do—though that use of "obligated" is not, I think, a central one. Be that as it may, it seems impossible to argue that someone's decision to act in a certain way, as such, makes it the case that he *owes anyone else* the action in question.

There are other arguments against a personal decision account of promissory obligation. One of these was alluded to at the outset of this chapter: one who binds himself by a promise cannot then unbind himself but must wait for release from his promisee. This is not the case for one who binds himself through

---

[30] I do not say that by deciding one gives oneself *a reason* for doing the thing decided on. For further discussion see Gilbert (2006: ch. 2). See also Robins (1984); Verbeek (2008).

a personal decision. He is in a position unilaterally to rescind the decision or, in the vernacular, to change his mind.

A promisor can, of course, decide not to keep his promise, and sometimes he may have good grounds for so deciding. What he cannot do unilaterally is rescind the promise, and hence destroy its obligation.

III. Joint Commitment

I now sketch what I take to be a plausible alternative approach to promising. As I shall explain, this respects the two intuitive points I have brought into this discussion: Prichard's point, and the directedness of promissory obligation. It also speaks against each of the three dogmas. At the same time, it gives what I take to be reasonable results with respect to immoral promises.

According to this alternative approach, promising is a matter of what I call a *joint commitment*. I have written about joint commitment extensively elsewhere, and continue to develop my understanding of it. My aim in this section is to introduce it in sufficient detail for present purposes.[31]

I start with some discussion of the type of commitment I have in mind. Consider again the decisions of an individual human being, or *personal* decisions, as I shall put it. I take it that just by deciding to do something, there is a sense in which one *commits* oneself to doing that thing. To say that one is committed in the sense in question is not to say that one is morally required to do something; nor is it to say that one owes another some action. Rather, to commit oneself is to make it the case that one has sufficient reason to do a certain thing, in the sense explained earlier.

Commitments of the kind one incurs by making a personal decision may be referred to as "commitments of the will," insofar as they come into being simply by virtue of an exercise of will in some intuitive sense. In the case of a personal decision, all the person has to do is decide, and he is committed.

A personal decision creates what I call a *personal commitment*. Such commitments are unilaterally rescindable by the human being who makes them. They can, of course, be made in private without the knowledge of any other party.

There is reason to suppose that commitments of the will come in two versions: personal and joint. A *joint* commitment is not a composite of two or more personal commitments. It is a commitment *of* two or more persons *by* two or more persons.

---

[31] For more detailed treatments see Gilbert (2003, 2006: ch. 7).

I focus here on the basic case of a joint commitment.[32] Further, I focus on cases that involve parties who know and are in direct communication with each other.[33]

In order to *create* a new joint commitment each of the would-be parties must openly express to the others his readiness together with the others to commit them all in the pertinent way. Once these expressions are common knowledge between the parties, the joint commitment is in place—as they understand.[34] Each is therefore now committed to do what he can to promote satisfaction of the joint commitment in conjunction with the actions of the rest. For the sake of brevity I shall say that each is now committed to "conform" to the commitment.

Absent special background understandings, a single party cannot *rescind* a joint commitment unilaterally; the concurrence of all of the parties is needed. Thus he cannot unilaterally remove his own dependent commitment.

Any joint commitment can be described in a statement of the following form:

A, B and so on (or those with property P) are jointly committed to do X as a body.

This formulation can be more fully articulated roughly as follows:

A, B, and so on (or those with property P) are jointly committed as far as is possible (by virtue of their several actions) to emulate a single doer of X.

"Does X" is understood here in a broad sense so as to include "believes that p," for instance.

These formulations are intended to make it clear that the individual parties are not committed, through the joint commitment, *personally* to do X. Thus a joint commitment to believe that p as a body, for instance, does not require that each personally believe that p. If you like, the aim of this joint commitment is *to create a certain situation at the collective as opposed to the individual level: a situation that as far as possible approximates a single case of belief.* The same goes, with appropriate changes, for joint commitments with other contents.[35]

[32] Roughly, a nonbasic joint commitment is created for the members of a population by some party or parties who have been authorized to do so by means of a basic joint commitment of those members. See Gilbert (2006: 140–1).

[33] For more general discussion see e.g. Gilbert (2006: ch. 7).

[34] On "common knowledge" see Gilbert (1989), also references therein.

[35] For more on collective belief see e.g. Gilbert (1989: ch. 5) and Gilbert (1996). When speaking without such a qualifier as "Personally" as in "Personally I don't think that p" a party to a collective belief that p must say things consistent with a belief that p, in order to conform to the constitutive joint commitment.

I take joint commitment to be a fundamental everyday concept that is an integral part of many central everyday concepts. These include those concepts expressible in nondistributive readings of such sentences as "We intend to go shopping," "We believe democracy is the best political form," and other ascriptions of psychological states whose grammatical subject is the first person plural. This has long been my position independently of any consideration of agreements or promises.[36]

The concept of joint commitment is a holistic or nonindividualistic one in the sense that it goes beyond the conceptual scheme of an individual human being's thoughts, beliefs, desires, and personal commitments.[37] It is not clearly holistic in any other sense.[38]

IV. Joint Commitment And Obligation

To every joint commitment corresponds a set of obligations. These are directed obligations with correlative rights. The parties are obligated to each other to conform to the commitment. In other terms, they owe each other their conformity. In this section I argue for the truth of this proposition.

Recall the sense of "owe" elaborated earlier. As initially put forward, the elaboration ran as follows: Olive owes Roger her going to Chicago tomorrow if and only if in an as yet unspecified sense Roger can appropriately regard Olive's act of going to Chicago as *his*. Subsequent discussion added, in effect, the following: Roger is in a position to demand of Olive that she go to Chicago if and only if he can appropriately regard Olive's act of going to Chicago as his—in the same sense.

It is easy enough to argue on this basis that those who are parties to a given joint commitment owe each other actions that conform to the commitment: Intuitively, the parties to a joint commitment are severally in a position to demand conforming actions from the other parties, by virtue precisely of the joint commitment itself. The actions in question, then, are owed to them by the other parties.

One can take this argument further. My initial elaboration of owing raised questions to which I said I would return. *In what sense* can another person's future action currently be mine? If there is more than one such sense, what sense is at issue in the case of owing?

---

[36] Gilbert (1989) can be seen as a long argument to the effect that joint commitments are a fundamental feature of everyday life. See Gilbert (1996).

[37] In Gilbert (1989) I referred to this conceptual scheme as "singularist."

[38] See Gilbert (1989: ch. 7) for discussion.

We now have a basis for an answer to the last question, and hence at least a partial answer to the first. Apparently, there is a sense in which the parties to a joint commitment are severally justified in regarding actions that conform to the commitment as *theirs*.[39] What, then, is that sense?

If such a sense can indeed be found it will help to firm up the intuitive judgment that the parties to a joint commitment are in a position to demand conformity from one another, and so on. In order to find it, we need to examine what the joint commitment achieves and how it does this.

By jointly committing the two of us, and by that alone, you and I make it the case that each of us has sufficient reason to perform actions that conform to the commitment. Thus, all else being equal, each is rationally required to conform to the commitment. In at least this way, then, *we have together bound each one of us* to perform the actions in question. This binding was, indeed, the immediate consequence of the expression of the will of each in conditions of common knowledge.

I propose that, given these facts, there is an intuitive sense in which any one party to the joint commitment can appropriately say of the other's conforming actions: "They are mine—in my capacity as co-creator of the commitment." I shall not try to say what that sense is in other terms. Rather, I propose that the sense in question is clearly—indeed paradigmatically—exemplified in the circumstances just described.

If this is right, we have tracked down the intuitive sense in which one who is owed an action by another, where that correlates with his standing to demand that action, can appropriately regard the action as his.[40]

One final point about the obligations of joint commitment is in order here. I take it that the directed obligations and the correlative rights of joint commitment are content- and context-independent in the following way: as long as there is a joint commitment, there are corresponding directed obligations. That is not to say that in all cases one ought to fulfill these obligations all things considered. It is to say that when a joint commitment comes to be these obligations come with it and remain irrespective of their content and changes in the circumstances of the parties—unless and until the joint commitment is rescinded or fulfilled.[41]

---

[39] I say this on the basis of the intuitive standing of each one to demand such conformity of each one, plus the assumption I am making that one has such standing if and only if there is an intuitive sense in which the conformity is one's own, the sense also involved in the statement that one is owed conformity.

[40] Though I have been assuming the contrary, as is plausible, I suppose that in principle there could be more than one such intuitive sense. Should this be the case, the argument to this point has shown, at a minimum, that *one* of the pertinent senses has been tracked down.

[41] For further discussion see Gilbert (2006: ch. 11).

V. Promises as Joint Commitment Phenomena

On the Kinship of Promises and Agreements

Recall now the second preliminary point with which this chapter began: promises and agreements are close cousins. In this section, I begin by saying something about the kinship of agreements and promises. I go on to propose a particular understanding of agreements, and a related account of promises.

It will be useful to have a sample agreement in view. I shall focus on the following case. After some discussion with Belle, Anne says "How about my doing the laundry after dinner, and your going to the store for groceries?" Belle responds "Okay." They have now made an agreement in which one future action is specified for each of the parties.

Each of them is now obligated to perform the action specified for her in the agreement. Anne is obligated to do the laundry; Belle is obligated to go to the grocery store. I shall call these obligations the parties' *performance obligations.*[42] A promisor may also be said to have a performance obligation or obligations the details of which are specified in the promise. In other terms, what I have been referring to, following custom, as his "promissory" obligations are performance obligations in the sense now in question.

I take it that an analogue of Prichard's point about promises holds for agreements—a point that appears to be knowable a priori: if one has agreed with another person that one will do something, then one is obligated to do it. Here, too, the obligation is content-independent: it derives from the fact that one is party to an agreement, and holds irrespective of the content of that agreement. Again, just as the performance obligations of a promisor are directed obligations, so are the performance obligations of the parties to an agreement. Thus in my example Anne is obligated to Belle to do the laundry. In other words, Anne owes Belle her, Anne's, doing the laundry. Belle, in turn, owes Anne her, Belle's, going to the grocery store.

Here, then, are some striking aspects of the cousinhood of promises and agreements. Both give rise to directed performance obligations that are content-independent, and this is knowable a priori.

Agreements

Theorists have tended to see promises as logically prior to agreements. I say this in light of the common proposal that a two-party agreement by virtue of

---

[42] These are the most salient obligations associated with an agreement and can reasonably be regarded as the primary obligations of the parties. That said, I mean to allow that other obligations may ensue from the agreement—I have in mind in particular obligations not to prevent the other's fulfillment of his performance obligations.

which each party accrues a performance obligation is constituted by a pair of promises, one from each party to the other.[43] It is often said that these promises are "mutual," or that they have been "exchanged," without further elaboration of what such mutuality or exchange is taken to involve.[44]

One might reasonably object to this proposal by saying that the example agreement, for one, does not *look* like a pair of promises, mutual, exchanged, or whatever.[45] This objection may not be conclusive, but it does show that the pair of promises view has a case to answer.

It is not clear why philosophers have almost universally adopted the assumption that a pair of promises is involved in agreements in which both parties take on one or more performance obligations. They tend not to present any argument for it.

Possibly the thought is that if—and only if—we can build agreements out of promises, we may be able to give an account of both in terms of the personal beliefs, intentions, and commitments of individuals, an account of a type that may seem to be the only feasible kind. I do not mean to imply that one can give such an account of *promises,* but it may be thought that one can, in view of the fact that "I" promise whereas "we" make an agreement. Be that as it may, one can argue against "pair of promises" views roughly as follows.[46]

Intuitively, my sample agreement, like many others, has the following three features. First, the parties' performance obligations are *unconditional* in form: Anne is obligated to do the laundry tonight; Belle is obligated to go to the grocery store. There can of course be agreements such that one or more of the parties accrue *conditional* obligations through them. An example is Polly's agreement with Sue that each will go to the tennis court at five if and only if it is not raining. The point is that in the sample agreement (and many others) the obligations are not conditional. Second, the performance obligations of the parties are *accrued simultaneously*—at the time the parties would be said to have agreed. Finally, these obligations are *interdependent* in a sense I now briefly explain.

Suppose that after Belle and Anne have had dinner, Belle tells Anne that she has decided not to fulfill her obligation under the agreement, in order to do something that accords better with her current inclinations. All else being equal, it seems that Anne is now in a position unilaterally to rescind the agreement.

---

[43] The idea of a pair of promises can presumably be extended to a triad of promises and so on, given more and more parties to the agreement, though there are some decisions to be made as to how this would go.

[44] See Gilbert (1993b) for a number of references

[45] Ashley Dressel emphasized it in my Promises and Agreements graduate seminar, University of California, Irvine, November 2008.

[46] For an extended treatment see Gilbert (1993b). See also Gilbert (2006: ch. 10). In a thoughtful response, Kent Bach (1995) has argued that an "exchange of promises" approach will work given a particular, rich notion of "exchange." I am not confident that this is so.

In particular, she does not need to petition Belle for her concurrence in such rescission. Thus she is in a position unilaterally to do away with her own obligation under the agreement. This is a matter of what an agreement is. It needs no grounding in "external" considerations such as fairness. Anne might reflect these points by responding, decisively "So much for our agreement!"

It is not clear that any promise pair has all of these three features. Discussion of the following pair of simple promises may serve here to illustrate the problem.[47] Suppose Cath has promised Dee that she will do the laundry that night. Dee has subsequently promised Cath that she will go to the store. True, Cath now has an unconditional obligation to do the laundry that night and Dee has an unconditional obligation to go to the store. However, these obligations are not accrued simultaneously. Cath accrues her obligation first. Further, the obligations in question are not interdependent in the pertinent sense, as I now argue.

Suppose that at this point Cath announces that she will not be acting as promised, since she wants to do something else. How, if at all, does this affect Dee's situation? Dee may of course decide not to *keep* her promise. After all, Cath will not be keeping hers. But she cannot unilaterally *rescind* her own promise and so bring it about that she has no obligation through it. That is—still—not up to her. She is not going to say "So much for my promise!" in parallel with Anne's imagined "So much for our agreement!" In sum, the performance obligations of these two promisors are not interdependent in the sense in which the performance obligations of the parties to the sample agreement are.

An account of agreements in terms of joint commitment allows one to account for the three features of the example agreement just noted and is otherwise plausible. To see this, consider again my sample agreement: Anne says "How about my doing the laundry after dinner, and your going to the store for groceries?" Belle responds "Okay."

It is easy to interpret what transpires through this dialogue roughly as follows: in conditions of common knowledge, Anne expresses to Belle her personal readiness to be jointly committed to endorse as a body the decision that she do the laundry that night and Belle go to the grocery store, and Belle does likewise. "Decision" in this formulation is used as roughly equivalent to "plan of action."

This is sufficient to jointly commit Anne and Belle in the way in question. Articulating that way along the lines detailed earlier: by virtue of their several actions they are to emulate as far as possible a single endorser of the decision in question. Anne thereby accrues an obligation to do the laundry, and Belle thereby accrues an obligation to go to the store; these unconditional obligations are accrued simultaneously, when the joint commitment is established.

[47] Gilbert (1993b) considers a wide range of possible promise-pairs in relation to the combination of features noted, and finds none of these pairs accounts for all three features. The promises in the example here are "simple" in the sense of "unconditional."

Now suppose that after this happens Belle makes it clear that she has decided not to go to the store in order that she might better fulfill her personal inclinations of the moment. Anne can reasonably take her thereby to have expressed her personal readiness to join with Anne in rescinding the joint commitment. Anne's position in relation to her own obligation, then, has changed: she is now in a position to do away with it, by unilaterally completing the rescission of the joint commitment that grounds it.

In legal parlance my sample agreement is a *bilateral executory* agreement: each party has at least one performance obligation. What if Julia asks "Will you phone me tonight?" and Jeremy responds "Sure"? This is not a *bilateral* executory agreement, since only one person has a performance obligation. Yet one could quite naturally say that, in this case, Julia and Jeremy *agreed* that he would phone her that night. And their transaction can plausibly be construed along the lines proposed for the example of Anne and Belle. In this new case the parties jointly commit themselves to endorse as a body the decision that Jeremy is to phone Julia that night.

I propose that, quite generally, and somewhat roughly: for two or more people to enter an agreement is for them jointly to commit themselves, by an appropriate, explicit process, to endorse as a body a certain decision with respect to what is to be done by one or more of the parties. I shall not attempt here to specify the nature of the explicit process in question. In practice it is easy enough to say, given an example, whether or not it is of the right kind clearly to constitute an agreement between the parties. The most important feature of the proposal, for present purposes, is the joint commitment that lies at its core.

For the sake of a label, I refer to the proposal just detailed as the *joint decision account* of agreements. In what follows I shall assume its correctness.[48]

Promises

The example just given of Jeremy and Julia's agreement concerning what he will do is very close to the example of a promise considered at the outset of this chapter. There Jeremy tells Julia "I'll phone you tonight," and Julia responds "Okay." In the example just given Julia asks "Will you phone me tonight?" and Jeremy responds "Sure."

This closeness suggests the following rough *joint decision account* of promises: for one person to make a promise to another is for them jointly to commit

[48] When there is a joint commitment to endorse as a body a certain decision (i.e. plan) that was not arrived at with the kind of explicit process requisite for an agreement the parties are aptly referred to as having formed a "joint intention" or, to use a more standard phrase (though this phrase has received other stipulative meanings), a "shared intention." For discussion of some of the literature on joint or shared intention see e.g. Gilbert (2009). See also chapter 5, this volume.

themselves, by an appropriate, explicit process, to the decision that one of them ("the promisor") is to perform one or more specified actions. As in the case of the joint decision account of an agreement, I shall not attempt here to specify the nature of the appropriate explicit process in question.

One point in favor of the joint decision account of promises is that, in the paradigm case, one person makes a promise to another, and *both are active in the process of constructing the promise.* More precisely, the promisee must do some-thing of an accepting rather than a rejecting nature. Thus, in the example, with-out Julia's "Okay" or some such response, possibly nonverbal, Jeremy would not have promised anything to Julia.

Acceptance, one might add, is to be distinguished from simple acknowledge-ment. If Jeremy were to make a prediction, such as "I think I'll be calling you tonight, it's going to be hard being home alone," Julia might respond with "I hear you." This would be a case of acknowledgement without acceptance in the sense at issue.

Another point in favor of the joint decision account of promises is that even the promisee appears to take on some obligations, though not performance obli-gations. That is, these obligations are not specified in the promise. They, like the performance obligations of the promisor, are directed obligations. In this case they are directed to the promisor. Thus, in the example, given Jeremy's promise to Julia, if she takes her phone off the hook that night he may well rebuke her as follows: "I said I'd call you tonight—what were you doing taking the phone off the hook?" This suggests that he understands that she was obligated to him not to make his calling her that night impossible.

Someone might now voice the following concern: surely the promisee has the power of unilateral rescission of the promise? And surely that would not be true if promissory obligation was founded on a joint commitment—as in the joint decision account?[49]

In response, one might question whether the promisee does have the power unilaterally to rescind the promise. In many cases this may appear to be so because of the circumstances of the promise. For instance, the promise is solic-ited by the promisee because of the promisee's desires or needs, the promisor having no personal desire to perform the promise. The promisee having stated that there is no need for the promisor to act as promised, thus implying his readiness to rescind the promise with the promisor's concurrence, the promisor promptly concurs and the promise is canceled.

In some cases, however, the promisor might resist. Thus suppose Joe prom-ises to return Jane's book on Tuesday. Jane calls him to say that it is not that

---

[49] This concern was voiced in discussion by Maggie Little when I presented related material some years ago at a meeting of the British Society for Ethical Theory.

important for her to have the book, so he may keep it. He might then say "No, I promised to return the book on Tuesday and that's what I'll do." It is at best not clear that Jane is a position to say "But the promise is over, I just said so."[50]

Sometimes people write of the promisee's "power of release." I think this is sometimes considered to be a power unilaterally to rescind the promise. In that case, its general existence can be doubted for the reasons given above.

There is, however, a clear sense in which the promisee does have the power of release with respect to the promisor—something that in no way runs counter to the joint decision account. Should the promisor wish the promise to be rescinded, he has only to ask the promisee.

In this case, the promisor's own concurrence in its rescission has been manifested, and all that is necessary is for the promisee to concur also. This state of affairs accords perfectly with a joint decision account. The same goes for the point, implied above, that the promisee's release is indeed *required* for the promise to be rescinded. The promisor is not empowered unilaterally to cancel the promise.

One who continues to insist that the promisee has the power of unilateral rescission or something very like it is not precluded from accepting a version of the joint decision account of promising. Thus he may feel able to accept something like the following account: a promise is a joint decision that one party, "the promisor," is to do something—a joint decision entered into by an appropriate explicit process—with which is associated the understanding that it stands at the pleasure of the other party—"the promisee."

As I now briefly explain, an account of promises as joint decisions does well when brought up against the two intuitive points that present problems for the three dogmas. This is another reason for taking the account seriously.

Consider first Prichard's point: if someone has promised to do something then he is obligated to do it by virtue of his promise. A joint decision account accords with this and, indeed, offers an explanation as to how it can be true—without exception—and knowable a priori. As long as the pertinent joint commitment has been created, and not rescinded, the promisor has an obligation of joint commitment to act as promised. There may be reasons not to fulfill this obligation in its particular circumstances or given its particular content. Its existence is not affected, however, even by the existence of factors such that all things considered one ought not to fulfill it.

Given the joint decision account of promising, what we may think of as the *primary* obligation associated with a promise is an obligation of joint commitment. This obligation is in a clear sense *intrinsic* to the existence of a promise as such. That said, it is possible that given an obligation of joint commitment, one is

[50] For concurring discussion see Vitek (1993).

morally required to fulfill it all else being equal. Then, on the proposed account of promising, the promisor will have an obligation of joint commitment to act as promised *and* be morally required to so act, all else being equal. If that is so, it may help to explain the pull both of Prichard's point and of the moral requirement dogma. I return to the latter in the next section.

What of the second intuitive point: promissory obligation is directed obligation? That was amplified in terms of a particular understanding of owing—an understanding such that, as I have argued, the parties to a joint commitment owe each other conformity to that commitment.

Given the joint decision account of promising, then, the promisor owes it to the promisee to act as promised. In other terms, he is obligated to keep his promise; his obligation is directed to the promisee, and the promisee has the correlative right. Thus the primary, intrinsic obligation of a promisor is directed.

In this chapter I have focused on what I take to be the paradigm case of promising: one person makes a promise to another, both being active in the process of constructing that promise. Promises may be spoken of in contexts that diverge from this paradigm in various ways. Thus someone may report that he "promised himself" to do something or that in his mind he made a certain "promise" or that he "promised" something to someone who turned a deaf ear to him, or who listened but offered neither an accepting nor a rejecting response.

An adequate account of the paradigm case of a promise may well be able to shed light on how such less than central cases come to be talked of as promises, as it may be able to shed light on why they are less than central. What is crucial, however, for any account of promising is that it illuminate the nature of paradigmatic promises and the obligation, or obligations, to which they give rise. I take the joint decision account of promising to have much merit in this connection. More generally, there is much merit in the idea of an account of promising in terms of joint commitment, however precisely the details are spelled out.

In my technical terminology all and only those who are jointly committed in some way constitute a "plural subject."[51] Some label is useful in the context of the wide variety of joint commitment phenomena. In this section, then, I have sketched a *plural subject account* of promising and explained some of the merits of some such account.

---

[51] See Gilbert (1989) and elsewhere. I do not intend to connote by the use of this phrase that some special kind of "subjectivity"—distinct from that possessed by individual human beings—arises in the context of a joint commitment. Rather, use by the parties of the first person plural pronoun as the subject term in certain sentences that refer to all of them is made appropriate in that context.

VI. Reconsidering the Dogmas

Acceptance of a plural subject account of promising allows us to jettison the three dogmas outlined earlier. Let me go through each, briefly, in turn.

The Moral Requirement Dogma

According to the first dogma, promissory obligation is a matter of moral requirement, where this, in turn, is a matter of the application of one or more general moral principles of conduct such as Scanlon's "Principle F," or a principle relating to conformity with a just and useful social practice. A plural subject account does not appeal to any such principle to explain the obligation of a promisor to perform the promise.

As said above, a plural subject account allows for the possibility that every promisor is morally required to do what he promised, all else being equal. This account allows therefore for the possibility that a given promisor has two distinct kinds of obligation as a result of his promise: he has an obligation of joint commitment to fulfill the promise, and he is morally required to fulfill it given its content and circumstances. Only the first of these kinds, of course, is such that every promisor has an obligation of that kind, irrespective of the content and circumstances of the promise.

Further, the possibilities just stated do not tend to justify the Moral Requirement dogma (though, as said earlier, they may help to explain it). That dogma would be false even given that they are more than possibilities. The dogma countenances only one kind of obligation as associated with promises—moral requirement. But, if the correct account of promising is a plural subject account, there are two kinds of obligation so associated—and the primary kind is not the kind on which the dogma fixes.

The No Willing Dogma

According to the second dogma, the obligation of a given promisor is not, and cannot, be directly willed into being. If the obligation in question is an obligation of joint commitment, however, it is in an important sense directly willed into being.

It is not willed into being by the will of the promisor alone, or by his promisee's will alone, but by the conjunction of their wills: each expresses that condition of his will that is preparedness to enter into the relevant joint commitment. Given only common knowledge of these expressions, the joint commitment and its inherent obligations are set.

The Immoral Promises Dogma

The third dogma is that immoral promises do not obligate. A plural subject account of promising will reject this.

By my definition of "immoral promise," one is not morally required to fulfill such a promise. A plural subject account can, of course, allow that this is so. Yet it entails that one who makes an immoral promise has an obligation to fulfill it. This is an obligation of joint commitment. The account thus neatly resolves the apparent conflict between Prichard's point in its most intuitive construal and the third dogma: all promises obligate, but one is not morally required—or obligated in *that* sense—to fulfill an immoral promise, all else being equal.

Briefly to summarize the argument of this chapter: The three dogmas of the title are hard to reconcile with two intuitive points I detailed. There is a type of account of promises that both accommodates these intuitive points and implies the falsity of each of the dogmas. That is an account in terms of joint commitment—a plural subject account.

The first version of this chapter was presented as an invited symposium talk at the Pacific meetings of the American Philosophical Association in March 27, 2005, where the commentator was Niko Kolodny. Subsequent versions have been presented at the University of California, Irvine, as the Zeno Lecture at the University of Utrecht, and at the University of Austin, Texas, in 2006, at the Graduate Center, CUNY, and the University of Southern California, in 2007, at the promises and agreements conference at Rice University, at California State University at Northridge, and to the students in my *Promises and Agreements* seminar at the University of California, Irvine, in 2008. I thank all of the discussants on those occasions, and Jonathan Adler, Hanoch Sheinman, Frank Stewart, Julie Tannenbaum, and Gary Watson for their comments on written material.

References

Altham, J. 1985. "Wicked Promises." In I. Hacking (ed.). *Exercises in Analysis*. Cambridge: Cambridge University Press, pp, 1–22.

Anscombe, G. E. M. 1978. "Rights, Rules, and Promises." *Midwest Studies in Philosophy* 3: 318–323.

Austin, J. L. 1962. *How to do things with words*, Cambridge, MA: Harvard University Press.

Bach, K. 1995. "Terms of Agreement." *Ethics* 105: 604–612.

Beran, H. 1987. *The Consent Theory of Political Obligation*. London: Croom Helm.

Feinberg, J. 1966. *Rights, Justice, and the Bounds of Liberty*. Princeton: Princeton University Press.

——— 1970. "The Nature and Value of Rights." *Journal of Value Inquiry* 4: 243–257

Gilbert, M. 1989. *On Social Facts*. London: Routledge.

———. 1993a. "Agreements, Coercion, and Obligation." *Ethics* 103: 679–706.

———. 1993b. "Is an Agreement an Exchange of Promises?" *Journal of Philosophy* 90: 627–649.

———. 1996. "Introduction: Two Standpoints—The Personal and the Collective." In *Living Together*. Lanham, MD: Rowman and Littlefield. 1–20.

———. 2003. "The Structure of the Social Atom." In F. Schmitt (ed.), *Socializing Metaphysics*. Lanham, MD: Rowman and Littlefield. 39–64.

———. 2004. "Scanlon on Promissory Obligation: the Problem of Promisees' Rights." *Journal of Philosophy* CI: 83–109. [Chapter 12, this volume.]

———. 2006. *A Theory of Political Obligation*. Oxford: Oxford University Press.

———. 2009. "Shared Intention and Personal Intentions." *Philosophical Studies* 144: 167–187.

Hart, H. L. A. 1955. "Are There Any Natural Rights?" *Philosophical Review* 64: 175–191.

Hume, D. 2000. *A Treatise on Human Nature*. Oxford: Oxford University Press.

Kolodny, N. and Wallace, J. 2003. "Promises and Practices Revisited." *Philosophy and Public Affairs* 31: 119–154.

Owens, D. 2006. "A Simple Theory of Promising," *Philosophical Review* 115: 51–77.

Prichard, H. A. 1968. *Moral Obligation and Duty and Interest*. Oxford: Oxford University Press.

Raz, J. 1977. "Promises and Obligations." In P. M. S. Hacker and J. Raz (eds.), *Law, Morality, and Society: Essays in Honour of H. L. A. Hart*. Oxford: Oxford University Press, 210–226.

Rawls, J. 1955. "Two Concepts of Rules." *Philosophical Review* 64: 3–32.

———. 1971. *A Theory of Justice*. Cambridge, MA: Harvard University Press.

Robins, M. 1984. *Promising, Intending, and Moral Autonomy*. New York: Cambridge University Press.

Scanlon, T. 1990. "Promises and Practices." *Philosophy and Public Affairs* 19: 199–226.

———. 1998. *What We Owe to Each Other*. Cambridge, MA: Harvard University Press.

Searle, J. 1964. "How to Derive 'Ought' from 'Is.'" *Philosophical Review* 73: 43–58.

———. 2001. *Rationality in Action*. Cambridge: MIT Press.

Shiffrin, S. 2008. "Promising, Conventionalism and Intimate Relationships." *Philosophical Review* 117: 481–524.

Thomson, M. 2004. "What Is It to Wrong Someone? A Puzzle about Justice." In J. Wallace et al. (eds.), *Reason and Value* Oxford: Oxford University Press, 333–384.

Verbeek, B. 2008. "Rational Self-Commitment." In H. B. Schmid and Fabienne Peter (eds.), *Rationality and Commitment*. New York: Oxford University Press, 150–174.

Vitek, W. 1993. *Promising*. Philadelphia: Temple University Press.

14

Mutual Recognition and Some Related Phenomena

Introduction

In this chapter I discuss three important, distinct phenomena. In my terminology, one is *common knowledge of co-presence*. Another is *mutual recognition*. I shall spend the most time on that. The third phenomenon is *joint attention*. As we shall see, common knowledge of co-presence is essential to mutual recognition; this, in turn, is essential to joint attention.[1]

There is reason to say that only with mutual recognition do we arrive at genuine *sociality*. Further, one can argue that such recognition constitutes the simplest form of existence of a *social group* in an important, central sense. Whether or not these points are correct, the occurrence of mutual recognition is of great practical, and theoretical, significance.

I start with three preliminary points. First, the phrases "common knowledge," "mutual recognition," and "joint attention" have all been defined differently by different authors. I am not concerned to argue that one or another definition is to be preferred. I believe that the phenomena I characterize through my own definitions are important and want, simply, to focus on them.

Second, the phrase "mutual recognition" is often associated with Hegel. So it is worth saying at the outset that my discussion will not attempt to engage with his work. I shall have something to say about some important passages in the work of one of Hegel's interpreters, Charles Taylor. These passages in Taylor's work had a significant impact on my own thinking.[2]

---

[1] This chapter is a revised version of a paper published online in a Festschrift in honor of Wlodek Rabinowicz: M. Gilbert, "Mutual Recognition, Common Knowledge, and Joint Attention," http://www.fil.lu.se/hommageawlodek/index.htm I thank Heikki Ikäheimo and Arto Laitinen for their comments.

[2] See M. Gilbert, *On Social Facts*, Princeton, Princeton University Press, 1989, p. ix.

Third, this discussion is not intended to be highly fine-grained. It is more of a sketch. My aim is roughly to specify the phenomena in question, to emphasize their distinctness and to discuss some of the relations between them.

1. Common Knowledge of Co-Presence

I start with common knowledge of co-presence. Consider this—very humdrum—situation.

> Two women find themselves briefly walking alongside one another on the pavement in a certain town. There has been no communication, by word or gesture, between them, nor is there any in what follows. One is walking faster and soon draws ahead of the other.

This is the kind of situation in which all of the following conditions are satisfied, the participants being here referred to as "A" and "B":

(1) A and B are currently physically close to one another. For the sake of a label I shall say that A and B are *co-present*.
(2) It is entirely out in the open between A and B that (1) is true.
(3) A and B both realize that (1) and (2) are true.

Some clarificatory notes on the above are now in order. In the example, the parties are walking side by side. I take it that they are at least peripherally visible to one another. Such visibility is not a necessary feature of cases of the type I have in mind. The parties might be audible to each other though not visible.

It is not clear that the parties must naturally be describable as "being in the same place." It may be better then to say, in cause (1), that A and B are "physically manifest" to one another, rather than that they are "physically close" to one another, insofar as the latter suggests more strongly than the former that they are "in the same place."[3]

What is it for something to be "entirely out in the open" between A and B? This is not the place to investigate all of the possible developments of this idea. So, for now, the following may suffice.[4]

---

[3] This paragraph responds to Heikki Ikäheimo and Arto Laitinen (personal communication, 2009).

[4] There is a longer, more detailed discussion in Gilbert, *Social Facts*, esp. p. 185f. The classic philosophical sources on this topic are D. K. Lewis, *Convention: A Philosophical Study*, Cambridge, Harvard University Press, 1969, and S. Schiffer, *Meaning*, Oxford, Oxford University Press, 1972. For a recent overview of the considerable and often highly technical literature see P. Vanderschraaf & Giacomo Sillari, "Common Knowledge," *The Stanford Encyclopedia of Philosophy*, http://plato.stanford.edu/ entries/common-knowledge.

First, A and B both have enough evidence from experience to be sure that A and B are co-present. Of course neither need know "who the other is," in terms of his (or her) name, station in life, and so on, but each has evidence that justifies his certainty that he and the other person, *whoever that person is,* are co-present.[5] In addition, each has enough evidence to be sure that each has the evidence just noted. And so on.

In saying this I do not mean to imply that either A or B is capable of contemplating an enormous number of propositions about what each has evidence for, let alone an infinite number of such propositions. Rather, each has evidence from which he could infer that any one of the pertinent propositions is true, given the principles of reasoning to which he adheres, and absent any restrictions on the processing of information such as memory or reasoning capacity that prevent him from doing so.

According to condition (3), each must *realize* that it is entirely out in the open between A and B that they are co-present. He need not have articulated the point. He must, one might say, have "a sense" of the openness.

Let us suppose that a situation accords with the three conditions just sketched. I shall say, here, that there is then *common knowledge* between A and B that A and B are co-present. So much, for now, on the phenomenon I shall call *common knowledge of co-presence.* Of course there can be common knowledge between persons of facts other than their co-presence. For present purposes, however, that is the case I focus on.

2. Charles Taylor: Beyond Common Knowledge

Some while ago now Charles Taylor argued in various places for the existence of a type of situation that goes beyond common knowledge in the sense explained in the last section.[6] He does not himself invoke common knowledge in precisely that sense, but his arguments apply to it, and I shall write as if he is speaking of it in what follows.

Taylor's focus is not common knowledge of co-presence, but more general. For instance, he considers common knowledge of the fact that the day is a hot one, or the fact that one of the parties is not enjoying the opera.

The central example in one of Taylor's discussions involves two strangers traveling on a train on a hot day. One turns to the other and says "Whew, it's hot!"

---

[5] I assume here only a non-technical concept of "person," such as the participants in such a humdrum situation might apply.

[6] I have in mind, in particular, C. Taylor, "Critical notice: Jonathan Bennett's *Linguistic Behavior,*" *Dialogue,* vol. 19, 1980, and C. Taylor, *Human Agency and Language,* Cambridge, Cambridge University Press, 1985, ch. 10, sec. 3.1.

This, Taylor points out, does not tell the other anything that was not previously common knowledge between them. Certainly it was already common knowledge between them that it was hot.

To invoke the French phrase Taylor prefers for what *is* achieved by the speaker's utterance, the fact that it is hot in the train compartment is now *entre nous*.[7] Alternatively, in terms of other locutions he uses, the fact that it is hot today is now "in public space," "for *us*," within the purview of a "common vantage point."

What is it, though, for something to be *'entre nous,'* "in public space," and so on? What precisely is achieved, in the example, by the one character's saying to the other "Whew! It's hot!"?

Taylor himself explicitly rejects an answer in terms of communication, where this is conceived of as the transmission or attempted transmission of states of knowledge or belief and where nothing but individual knowers and believers are involved. I don't think Taylor wishes to deny that such transmission is or may be part of the story when such scenarios occur. What he wants to emphasize is that something else goes on.[8]

As Taylor sees it, and as he emphasizes several times, an exchange like that in his example does not only place certain matters before us, in public space.[9] It *founds* or *constitutes* that space—or a particular part of that space. In his conception, then, public space is constructed, not discovered. To say this is still not to explain what public space is.

In the discussion on which I am drawing, Taylor focuses on the power of *language* to "found public space" or to "place certain matters before us." And, clearly,

---

[7] See for example Taylor, *Human Agency*, p. 265: "the crucial distinction between what is *entre nous* and what is not."

[8] The writer-reader relationship may be a version of the situation on which Taylor focuses. The writer purports, implicitly or explicitly, to "address" the reader with his words. The reader is supposed to "get" what he is saying: but more than this. This is not just the transmission of information or pretend information (cf. Saul Kripke on pretense in fiction, *John Locke Lectures* 1973 (unpublished ms)). It is more like a conversation—if you like, it is a *would-be* conversation—in which one by one certain things are made *"entre nous."* (It is of course a one-sided conversation; the reader may have no way to say anything to the writer, as each will understand. The writer may be long dead.) So there is a style in which one might write "Now that we are agreed that…" "Now we have seen that…" "Now it has been established [between us] that…," and a style in which one writes "You, dear reader…" and so on. And one can speak of a writer "drawing his reader's attention" to something. The flavor of such locutions is, I take it, to invoke something more like the creation of a common vantage point than the transmission of information from one mind to another.

[9] I say "exchange" though only one party seems to have spoken. It is best to construe Taylor's case as involving some form of acknowledgement on the part of the person spoken to. Something like a brief "Yes, indeed," or some concurring facial expression would suffice. If the other person was looking in the other direction and apparently deaf to the utterance, I take it that nothing would have been achieved—or, better, there would have been a failed attempt to achieve what the case with acknowledgement does achieve.

a linguistic act may perform the transformation—whatever precisely it is—that Taylor wishes to place before his readers. He allows, however, that this transformation may occur through any mode of "expression"—where expression need not be linguistic. Thus one party might turn to the other and, catching his eye, ostentatiously—as we say—wipe the perspiration off his face.[10] These points, though helpful, also leave open the question as to what it is for something to be *entre nous,* in public space.

Taylor's discussion is an important one. It is necessary to go beyond it, however, to get a better grasp of what is at issue. Taylor makes both a negative and a positive point. The negative point is clear enough. If we want to understand what "Whew, it's hot!" achieves we must go beyond the idea that its being hot, or the speaker's being hot, is common knowledge between the speakers. As he puts it in one place, here alluding to *our awareness* of some fact:

> We completely miss the point if we remain with the monological model of the subject, and think of all states of awareness, knowledge, belief, attending to, as ultimately explicable as states of individuals. So that our being aware of X is always analyzable without remainder into my being aware of X and your being aware of X. The first person plural is seen here as an abbreviated version of a truth-functional connective.
>
> What I am arguing here is that this analysis is terribly mistaken; that it misses the crucial distinction between what is *entre nous* and what is not.[11]

It is the positive point—the introduction of "what is *entre nous*"—that demands further clarification. Indeed, unless and until it is clarified and seen to be correct the negative point may, of course, seem more problematic. I return to Taylor's discussion shortly. I first introduce the phenomenon I shall refer to as *mutual recognition.*

---

[10] Taylor's example (p. 264) has one party both saying "Whew!" and also mopping his brow. It seems unnecessary, though, that any words be uttered in such a scenario. I doubt that Taylor would deny this.

[11] Taylor, *Human Agency,* p. 265.

3. Mutual Recognition

3.1. *An Example*

I start with a humdrum example.[12] I was sitting at a table in the Merton Street Library in Oxford, reading a book. I noticed that someone had come to my table and had sat down opposite me. I took it that it was now common knowledge between this person and myself that he and I were sitting at this very table. However, we had not yet communicated in any way. At a certain point, I looked up and gazed at him until he too looked up. I caught his eye (as we say); we looked at each other. I nodded toward him and briefly smiled; he did also. We then returned to our respective concerns and had no further interaction. What went on here?

3.2. *Mutual Recognition Defined*

In terms to be explained, I suggest that, crucially, this man and I made it the case that *we were jointly committed to recognize as a body that he and I were co-present*. This is at least a good provisional description of a situation in which mutual recognition as I understand it has occurred.[13]

Something must be said about *joint commitment*.[14] One who invokes *joint* commitment in the sense I have in mind allows that just as an individual can commit himself, by forming a decision, for instance, so two or more individuals can commit themselves *as one*. For this to happen, something must be expressed by each of the would-be parties, namely, his *personal readiness* jointly with the rest to commit them all in a particular way. Further, these expressions must be common knowledge between the parties.

My proposal about the Merton Street Library case, then, is that it fulfilled these conditions with respect to the joint commitment referred to. As I understand it, these two conditions are individually necessary and jointly sufficient for them to be jointly committed in the way in question.

---

[12] Cf. Gilbert, *Social Facts*, pp 217–218. The following discussion draws on *Social Facts*, pp. 217–219.

[13] In using the phrase "mutual recognition" here I follow my earlier usage, in *Social Facts*. As I explain later in the text, the phenomenon I have in mind could also aptly be referred to as *collective* recognition. This phenomenon is grounded in a communicative exchange whose immediate outcome it is. Introducing a more nuanced terminology one might refer to the exchange as such as "the process of mutual recognition," and to its immediate outcome as "the state of mutual recognition."

[14] I have written at length on this elsewhere. For a recent discussion see M. Gilbert, *A Theory of Political Obligation*, Oxford, Clarendon Press, 2006, ch 7.

As to the notion of *recognizing*, in this context, I take this to be a more or less enduring state like believing, as opposed to an event like noticing. What I am calling "mutual recognition," meanwhile, is an event, one that occurs precisely when the joint commitment in question is established.[15]

To say that mutual recognition is an event, is not to deny that it has normative consequences, consequences that extend through time. I say more about this shortly.

Quite generally, when I say that A and B are jointly committed to *recognize that p as a body*, for some proposition, p, I mean roughly this: they are jointly committed to emulate as far as possible, by virtue of their several actions with respect to one another, a single, embodied individual—a single body—that recognizes that p. To put the point another way, they are committed to act (and talk) in relation to one another as if they are, literally, "of one mind" with respect to the recognition that p.

I take it that *a joint commitment to recognize as a body* that, say, Kant was a great philosopher, does not require the parties personally to recognize that Kant has this stature. They may, or they may not personally recognize this; their joint commitment, meanwhile, relates to their public actions, including their communications, rather than to their personal judgments. That is just as well. There is little doubt that one can generally, at will, "act the part" of one who recognizes that Kant is a great philosopher, either in cooperation with another or on one's own. It is at least not so clear that one can personally recognize this at will.

When there is mutual recognition, then, what is required of the parties from the point of view of the constitutive joint commitment is certain public actions, including communicative actions, rather than private thoughts. It is in their public actions with respect to one another that they must attempt together to emulate as far as possible a single, embodied individual that recognizes that they are co-present or were co-present at the time in question. In the alternative formulation, they must act as if they are literally "of one mind" with respect to the recognition of this fact.[16]

So, in the Merton Street Library case, the joint commitment there established required among other things that if I were to see the man in question again on a later occasion, I do not say to him "You were in the library, then?" in a surprised tone. Of course I might end up saying this, if I do not realize at the later time that I am speaking to the man who was in the library then, or if I have forgotten the whole incident. I might also end up saying this had the following interchange transpired in the interim. After our moment of mutual recognition, the man in question comes up to me and says, with a meaningful wink "You did not see me

---

[15] Paragraph added in response to questions from Ikäheimo and Laitinen.
[16] Paragraph added in response to questions from Ikäheimo and Laitinen.

here this afternoon," to which I reply, "Oh, fine!" This new interchange may be understood as rescinding of the initial joint commitment, thus effacing all of the requirements that still flow from it.[17]

In what follows I am going to assume that mutual recognition as I have defined it is a regular occurrence—to put it mildly—and that the Merton Street Library case is an example of such mutual recognition. I now say more about mutual recognition in this sense.

3.3. *Taylor's* Entre Nous

I first briefly return to Charles Taylor's references to what is *entre nous*, "in public space," and so on. As I now explain, mutual recognition as I have defined it is a plausible context for talk—in French—of *nous*, and, therefore, of what is *entre* nous.

I have argued at length elsewhere that in a large class of cases in which people speak of what *we* are doing, thinking, or feeling this is best construed as referring to a joint commitment of an appropriate kind. I have in mind those cases in which it is not appropriate to construe what is being said in terms of what *we both,* or *we all,* are doing. Rather, we are doing it collectively. For those cases, a joint commitment interpretation recommends itself.

Those who are jointly committed to recognize as a body the co-presence of the parties, then, could properly describe their situation as follows: "We (collectively) recognize that you and I are co-present." This will not mean that you, on the one hand, recognize that you and I are co-present, and that I, on the other hand, recognize this. More generally, it cannot be broken down in terms of the way things are for me, on the one hand, and the way things are for you, on the other, because it is not about me, on the one hand, and you, on the other. It is about something else.

In saying "something else" I do not mean something whose existence is somehow independent of you and me. Of course it isn't. That "something else" is constituted by *you and me in a particular relationship*: that of joint commitment. This unifies us. It makes us *us*. For this particular kind of thing I have used the label "plural subject." According to my technical definition, those who are jointly committed to do X as a body constitute the *plural subject* of X-ing.[18]

---

[17] As I understand joint commitments in general, they require the concurrence of all parties on their rescission, absent special background understandings.

[18] My choice of the phrase "plural subject" has had some unfortunate consequences. It seems to suggest to some people something metaphysically suspect, whereas I do not believe there is anything suspect in the idea of a number of jointly committed persons, which is all that the idea of a plural subject (in my sense) amounts to. I take the phrase to be apt in part because, roughly, I take the first person plural pronoun "we" in its "collective" uses, to presuppose the joint commitment of the members of the "we."

Going back to Taylor's references to what is *entre nous*, consider a joint commitment to recognize as a body that such-and-such is the case. Generalizing, if you and I are thus jointly committed, then the fact that such-and-such can plausibly be referred to as *entre nous*, in public space, and so on.

3.4. *Mutual Recognition and Social Groups*

I argued in *On Social Facts* that social groups, in a central sense of the term, are a matter of joint commitment: those who are jointly committed with one another constitute a social group. If so, then those who mutually recognize one another constitute a social group—albeit one which may lack aims, values, or, in a word, character. Indeed, they constitute a fundamental kind of social group. Once people have mutually recognized one another, they have begun to pave the way for the creation of groups *with* character.[19]

In defining mutual recognition I have invoked a joint commitment to emulate as far as possible a single, embodied individual that recognizes the co-presence of the parties: in short, a joint commitment to recognize as a body this co-presence. I take it that a central use of the label "collective body" is to refer to social groups of the kind in question here.

It is worth pointing out that the content of the joint commitment required for mutual recognition does not involve the idea of a collective body. However, *once the parties are jointly committed* in the way required for mutual recognition the parties do constitute a collective body in what I take to be a standard sense of the phrase.

3.5. *Pure and Mixed Cases of Mutual Recognition*

The Merton Street Library case is what one might think of as a pure or simple case of mutual recognition. I take it, however, that mutual recognition is often achieved as part and parcel of a wider achievement.

Thus someone who is approaching another on a town street might call out "Nice day!" and the other return "Yes, indeed!" Here two things may be achieved at one and the same time. First, they jointly commit to recognizing as a body that the two of them are co-present. Second, at one and the same time, they jointly commit to believing as a body that it's a nice day.[20]

---

[19] On joint commitment as fundamental to social groups, see *Social Facts*, ch. 4 and *Political Obligation*, esp. ch. 8.

[20] On collective belief, see for example the Introduction and various essays in M. Gilbert, *Living Together: Rationality, Sociality, and Obligation*, Lanham, MD, Rowman and Littlefield, 1996.

There are, then, both pure and (shall we say) mixed cases of mutual recognition. In the mixed cases mutual recognition is brought about at the same time that some other joint commitment is created for the parties.

3.6. *Presuppositions of Mutual Recognition*

What is presupposed by mutual recognition? One pertinent issue concerns the relationship of mutual recognition to previously established social conventions, norms, practices and so on.[21] In the Merton Street Library case, each person nods and smiles. This is a socially established procedure for creating an instance of mutual recognition. A different procedure might have prevailed in their culture. In that case the parties might have behaved differently, each clearing his or her throat, perhaps, or clapping his or her hands.

How fundamental, then, can mutual recognition be? Can it take place between those who are not already parties to a social convention—total strangers who meet on a desert island, for instance?

This at least is clear: what one needs is some way of attracting the other person's attention, and then, or at the same time, engaging in whatever behavior will communicate one's readiness jointly to commit with the other to recognize as a body that you and he are co-present. It is not obvious that such behavior must follow socially established procedures or engage with previously established conventions.

It is plausible to argue, indeed, that social conventions themselves arise, in many cases at least, on a basis that involves mutual recognition. For instance, many conventions are set up by a face-to-face verbal agreement, which involves mutual recognition. Again, the establishment of the language in which the agreement was made may well have involved mutual recognition.

Though mutual recognition may not presuppose social convention, it presupposes something. It presupposes, for one, that the parties have the concept of joint commitment. The concept of joint commitment may well be a peculiarly human one, but some humans may lack it or have it in only in an inchoate or imperfect form. Some of those who have been labeled "autistic" may be in this category.

My assumption is that most adult human beings have this concept. That is because it allows one plausibly to explain much of what human beings think and do. If this is so, it may well be common knowledge among adult human beings that by and large beings of their kind have the concept of joint commitment. When two or more mature human beings approach one another, then, it will be

---

[21] On social conventions, which I take to be a species of social rule, see Gilbert, *Social Facts,* ch. 6. On social rules, with special reference to H. L. A. Hart's discussion in *The Concept of Law,* see

common knowledge that mutual recognition may well be possible. It may not happen, but it will make sense to attempt it.

Each of those who mutually recognize one another, in my sense, has expressed his readiness to be jointly committed in a certain way with the other. Such expression presupposes at least the following: the other exists; the other is a being with the concept of joint commitment; the other is capable of co-creating with him a joint commitment. Thus I shall assume that where there is mutual recognition in my sense, in being jointly committed to recognizing as a body their co-presence as persons, the parties will be jointly committed to recognize as a body their co-presence as, at a minimum, beings capable of joint commitment.

3.7. *Mutual Recognition and Care, Concern, and Respect*

To what extent, if at all, does mutual recognition promote care and concern for each other, or mutual respect, among the parties? Off the cuff, one might think "None." That may be a little too quick. Here are three observations that point in the other direction.

First, if we are jointly committed to recognize as a body our co-presence as beings capable of joint commitment, each of us is committed to see to it that *together* we emulate as far as possible a single body that recognizes this co-presence.[22] Thus one might argue that the situation involves certain safeguards for the parties. At the least, both parties are committed not to go ahead and render the other incapable of conformity to the joint commitment.[23] In a given case, this commitment may not be sufficient to determine the outcome, even for a fully rational agent. Though a joint commitment may "trump" certain other considerations in terms of what a proper responsiveness to relevant considerations requires, it does not trump all. In particular, certain moral considerations may trump it. Thus someone may enter a situation of mutual recognition with another, yet be prepared to kill him in self-defense, believing this to be morally justified in spite of the mutual recognition that has previously occurred.[24]

Second, one who has participated in an episode of mutual recognition, and then treats his opposite number in a way inappropriate to a being capable of mutual recognition in particular and joint commitment in general, has similarly failed to do what he is committed to doing. It would have to be argued, in

M. Gilbert, *Sociality and Responsibility: New Essays in Plural Subject Theory*, Lanham, MD, Rowman and Littlefield, 2000. I argue that social rules as conceived of in everyday life are joint commitment phenomena.

[22] This just spells out an entailment of the joint commitment in question.

[23] See my 1990 essay on marital relationships—"Fusion: Sketch of a 'Contractual' Model"—reprinted in *Living Together*. The pertinent passage is on p. 220.

[24] See *Political Obligation*, ch. 11. See also the third point in the text below.

amplification of this last point, that there are ways of treating such a being that are inappropriate to its nature, and that these are instances of uncaring, unconcerned, or disrespectful behavior. This can surely be done.

Third, as I have argued elsewhere, the parties to any joint commitment understand that they owe one another conformity to the commitment and have a corresponding right to conformity from the other. For these things can be inferred from the existence of the joint commitment itself.[25] Each is therefore not only constrained by the joint commitment in the way he would be given a standing personal decision to act in a certain way. He also understands that his not so acting would be a failure to respect the right of another. It is sometimes said that simply seeing another as having rights is a matter of respecting them.[26] In that case those who mutually recognize each other automatically respect one another.

There is, then, some basis for connecting this rather cognitive account of mutual recognition with behavior that is at least minimally caring, concerned and respectful of the parties concerned. That is harder to argue for the simpler situation in which there is only common knowledge of co-presence.

4. Joint Attention

I turn now to my third topic: *joint attention*. In contemporary developmental psychology, there is a great deal of literature on what is called "joint attention." One important source is the work of Michael Tomasello.[27] Nonetheless, there is some question as to precisely what is going on in paradigmatic situations of joint attention, and (relatedly) as to how "joint attention" should be defined.

Though developmentalists focus on parent-child interactions, it could be better to focus on adult-adult interactions to begin with, in working this out, since there are issues as to what precisely children are capable of at various young ages. That said, I start with a slightly abbreviated quotation from Tomasello as to the kind of situation he has in mind.

> Suppose that a child is on the floor playing with a toy, but is also perceiving many other things in the room. An adult enters... and proceeds to join the child in her play with the toy. The joint attentional scene becomes those objects and activities that the child knows are part of

---

[25] See Gilbert, *Sociality and Responsibility*; also Gilbert, *Political Obligation*, ch. 7.

[26] Joel Feinberg, "The Nature and Value of Rights," *Journal of Value Inquiry*. 4, 1970, pp. 243–260, suggests this in a famous discussion.

[27] For example M. Tomasello, *The Cultural Origins of Human Cognition*, Cambridge, MA, Harvard University Press, 2001. Another leading figure in these discussions is Simon Baron-Cohen.

the attentional focus of both herself and the adult, and they both know that this is their focus (. .. it is not joint attention if, by accident, they are both focused on the same thing but unaware of the partner).[28]

He concludes:

> Joint attentional scenes... gain their identity and coherence from the child's and the adult's understandings of "what we are doing."[29]

Before the last quoted sentence, Tomasello was anxious to distinguish a situation of joint attention to some object (say) from each one's personally focusing on that object without awareness that the other was also focusing on it. Yet the last quoted sentence suggests something that goes beyond each one's focusing with awareness that both are focusing. It also goes beyond common knowledge between the parties that each one is focusing on the object. It refers to "what we are doing" something I have argued elsewhere to be a phenomenon involving joint commitment.

There is much to be said for analyzing acting together or, to use another common phrase, "joint, action" along such lines as these: the parties are jointly committed to intend as a body to do a certain thing and they act in accordance with that joint commitment. For them to be jointly committed to intend as a body to do the thing in question is, in more familiar terms, for *them* to intend to do that thing. Or so I have argued.[30]

Now suppose that a child, Claire, and her mother, Maureen, are playing with Claire's doll Teddy. As Maureen or Claire might put it: "We are playing with Teddy." One might say, then, that their focus is Teddy. Maureen (or Claire) might put this as follows: "We are attending to Teddy." One way of construing this, in parallel with my proposal about joint action would be this (from Maureen):

---

[28] Tomasello, *Cultural Origins*, p. 98. Tomasello continues to write on this topic; I use these quotations as illustrations of one stance towards the phenomenon that has been adopted, and that might be attractive initially. I thank Michael Tomasello for discussion of joint attention on several occasions in Cracow and Leipzig.

[29] Ibid.

[30] See for example *Social Facts*, ch. 4; *Living Together*, ch. 6. In the form of analysis of joint action just presented I begin with an account of our *intending* to do something (in terms of our being jointly committed to intend as a body to do that thing) and add that each of us acts in accordance with this joint commitment, to make up our joint action. An alternative, perhaps better, is to say simply that we are jointly committed to do (as a body) a certain thing. Then presumably we will also be jointly committed to intend as a body to do that thing, and will act in accordance with the latter joint commitment in order to do the thing in question.

Claire and I are jointly committed to attend as a body to Teddy

What this means, as indicated earlier, is that they are jointly committed to emulate as far as possible a single body that attends to Teddy (and, in this case, plays with him).

I propose that joint attention, understood in terms of a joint commitment to attend as a body to some particular in the environment of the parties, is an important part of human life in society. Once we have gone beyond common knowledge of co-presence, and engaged in mutual recognition, we are ready jointly to attend to things, and to act upon those things together. Among other things, we are ready to create some kind of a group language, negotiating labels for particular things and kinds of things.[31] In short, we are ready to live recognizably human lives.[32]

---

[31] On group languages see Gilbert, *Social Facts*, ch. 3, sec. 6.

[32] A version of this chapter was presented at the conference on social ontology and constitutive attitudes held in Helsinki, August 29–30, 2006. At the subsequent collective intentionality conference in the same place (August 31–September 2), Clotilde Calabi of the University of Milan presented a paper "Joint Attention, Common Knowledge, and Ephemeral Groups" with significant points in common with this one. Calabi criticizes Christopher Peacocke's recent account of joint attention (C. Peacocke, "Joint Attention: Its Nature, Reflexivity, and Relation to Common Knowledge," in *Joint Attention: Communication and Other Minds*, eds N. Eilan, C. Hoerl, T. McCormack, J. Roessler, Oxford, Oxford University Press, 2005), and draws on my published work to argue, congenially, for an approach to the topic similar to that proposed here.

PART FOUR

POLITICAL LIFE

To understand political power right, and derive it from its original, we must consider, what state all men are naturally in, and that is a state of perfect freedom to order their actions, and dispose of their possessions and persons, as they think fit, within the bounds of the law of nature, without asking leave, or depending upon the will of any man.

John Locke, *Second Treatise of Government* (Indianapolis, IN: Hackett, 1980). Original 1690.

15

A Real Unity of Them All

1. Introduction

The gradual emergence of the European Union in the wake of the Second World War has raised important questions of a general nature. Thus in a recent article Dirk Jacobs and Robert Maier write:

> The problem of the constitution of a European identity can now be reformulated in the following way: are we in presence of the constitution of a new "we," a new people with the characteristics of Europeanness?[1]

These authors refer specifically to Europe, but there is a general question that is conjured by what they say: how is a "we" constituted?

Given an answer to this general question, several more specific ones will be easier to deal with. These include empirical questions such as those raised in the opening quotation regarding the situation in Europe and practical questions of a more or less general nature relating to the means by which a new "we" can intentionally be created or produced, to the extent that this is possible. In this chapter I pursue an answer to the general question mostly in general terms.

I shall assume that the question "how is a 'we' constituted?" is pretty much identical to an age-old question in political philosophy. Echoing Jean-Jacques Rousseau, we might ask: what differentiates a mere *aggregation* of individual human beings from an *association*?[2] Yet another way of putting the question invokes a phrase from Thomas Hobbes: if pre-theoretically, an association is a "real unity of them all,"[3] how does such *social unity* come about?

---

[1] Jacobs and Maier (1998, p. 20). See also the questioning title of Balibar (2004): We, the People of Europe?

[2] Rousseau (1983, p. 23).

[3] Hobbes (1982, p. 227).

In what follows, I first roughly describe and contrast two possible ways of answering the question, "how is a 'we' constituted?" as it has been construed above. I refer to these two ways of answering as the *subjectivist* and the *objectivist* stances. Having noted problems with the former and with one version of the latter, I develop a different, though related, version in some detail. Finally, I briefly consider what this particular development suggests for the following practical question: by what means can a new "we" be intentionally created or produced?

2. Two Approaches to the Question, "How Is a 'We' Constituted?"

I. The Subjectivist Stance

One general type of answer to the question of social unity in all of its various guises is in terms of the subjective states of the individuals involved. An answer of this type is in terms of *how these individuals see themselves and their relation to the other individuals in question.* Perhaps, it suggests that it is necessary and sufficient for the constitution of a "we" that every one of the individuals in question is disposed to think of the pertinent population of persons as "us" or "we." In short, these individuals are disposed to think *"we"-thoughts* of the population in question. For instance when referring to the constitution of the United States, he (or she) may speak of "our constitution" as opposed to "your constitution" or "the United States constitution."[4] Answers that speak of a sense of "belonging together" or to a subjective state of "identification" with the other members of a particular population also fall into this class. For the sake of a label I call this very broadly characterized approach the *subjectivist* stance.

In the realm of contemporary philosophical social theory, sometimes referred to as *social ontology*, or, again, *collective intentionality* theory, the work of John Searle exemplifies quite well the subjectivist stance. When he writes, for instance, about the "collective acceptance" in a population of a rule about how that population is to be organized, he seems to have in mind, roughly, that each member of the population individually thinks, with respect to this very population, "We accept that such-and-such," or, alternatively, that each member "we-accepts" that such-and-such, where we-accepting something is a purely subjective matter.[5]

If this state of affairs exists, that it exists is of course an objective fact about what people individually think. It is unclear from what Searle says whether *what* they think is answerable to anything else in terms of its justification. One gets the impression that, in his view, either it is answerable to nothing or it is

---

[4] He may of course use the last mentioned phrase but he will be disposed also to use the first.
[5] See Searle (1990; 1995). I offer a detailed critique of Searle's approach in Gilbert (2007).

answerable only to the existence of corresponding thoughts among the other members of the population in question. In the latter case, if I think, "We accept that such-and-such," this thought is impeccable as long as each of the people in question thinks the same way with respect to the members of the same population.[6] Alternatively, my "we-acceptance" co-exists with the "we-acceptance" of each of the relevant others.

Searle does not focus on the question of social unity as such. His account of collective acceptance and the like, however, suggests an account of such unity in terms of essentially subjective phenomena.

An example from contemporary political theory that suggests such an account is John Horton's theory of political obligation which is couched in terms of "identification."[7] According to Horton, one manifests one's identification with a certain population if one is ready to use the pronominal adjective "our" in relation to an action ascribable to the population as a whole, and liable to feel pride, or guilt, and so on, with respect to what "we" do. Further, one's taking up this stance, or at least one's taking it up when all or most other members of the "us" in question take it up, is enough to endow one with obligations to act in ways favorable to "our" aims and so on. The suggestion is that such widespread identification suffices for social unity.[8]

A subjectivist stance may also be common in more practical contexts such as a concern for what is often referred to as European "integration." That this is so is suggested by Jacobs and Maier when they write:

> For over almost three decades supporters of European integration have been seeing the promotion of a European consciousness... as a crucial policy goal.[9]

They have in mind specifically "a European consciousness among ordinary citizens." Consciousness can of course be consciousness of something objective; but it is possible to think of it as a subjective state of the person whose consciousness it is. Talk of a European consciousness may, then, suggest a subjectivist take on what is needed for the sake of European integration or unity.

One practical concern about the subjectivist approach to social unity is this. If the subjective states in question are not rooted in something outside the minds

---

[6] Cf. Sellars (1963) whose approach to "collective intentionality" is very close to Searle's.

[7] I refer here to Horton (1992, ch. 6).

[8] For more extended discussion of Horton, see Gilbert (2006, chs. 4 and 11). I argue there that he does not make good the identification-obligation connection, though there may be a way to do so, depending on the conception of obligation at issue.

[9] Jacobs and Maier (1998, p. 22).

of the people concerned, how stable are they likely to be? Setting this concern aside, there are also related theoretical concerns with the subjectivist approach.

Crucially, as I now argue, a proliferation of "we"-thoughts or the like does not seem to move the people involved from a mere aggregation to an association. Hence invocation of such a proliferation of thoughts does not suffice as an answer to the question of how to constitute a real unity of the people concerned.

Consider a population of people sharing some significant feature in common, such as the world-wide population of hemophiliacs. I assume that the fact that the members of this population are all hemophiliacs is not enough to make them members of an association. Assume that up until now they do not constitute an association on other grounds and that none of them think that they do.

Now suppose that privately each hemophiliac develops a special feeling of belonging together with other hemophiliacs. As I shall interpret that here, each often thinks in terms of "we hemophiliacs" where, in his use of "we," *he presupposes that the population of hemophiliacs somehow constitutes an association.* (In what follows, also, I shall construe "we"-thoughts generally in this way.) Can one say that on account of the prevailing sense of belonging together the population of hemophiliacs now constitutes an association as opposed to an aggregate of persons?

It is true that they have more in common than a population of hemophiliacs, otherwise the same, all of whom lack the pertinent sense of belonging together. This does not yet bring them to the point of social unity—or so I propose.

Of course people are unlikely simply to find themselves with "we"-thoughts and the like, either individually or *en masse.* Their thoughts are likely to be justified by something on the basis of which they occur. The point at issue here is that *a proliferation of "we-thoughts" and the like in a population, and that alone,* do not make that population an association.

As such, "we"-thoughts and feelings are little more than fantasy and illusion without some objective foundation. In the example, the individual hemophiliacs have no basis for their "we"-thoughts insofar as they neither constitute an association before these thoughts develop nor constitute an association by virtue of these thoughts. A crucial presupposition of their "we"-thoughts, then, is false.[10]

II. The Objectivist Stance

The second approach I have in mind does not in any way deny the importance of subjective states among the people in question. Rather, it proposes *an objective basis* for one's thinking in terms of "us" as opposed to "me," "you," and all the rest. I shall therefore refer to it, for the sake of a label, as the *objectivist* stance.

---

[10] Cf. Simmons (1996), criticizing views on political obligation such as Horton's.

One particular objective basis for such thoughts has been proposed by many authors of different philosophical and political persuasions over many centuries. This is the social pact, contract, or agreement. Thus, in Plato's dialogue *Crito*, Socrates imagines the laws of Athens invoking undertakings by which he agreed to live as a member of the Athenian polity [1] Later political philosophers of the Western tradition also invoked agreements, Rousseau answering his question about the transformation of an aggregate into an association in the appropriately named *Du Contrat Social.*

Without attempting any detailed account of the matter, one can see why reference to an agreement is an attractive one in this context. On the face of it one can plausibly claim that any agreement creates a "we." Its members can appropriately refer at least to the agreement itself as "ours." This is so even if the agreement is an agreement to differ or to go our separate ways. In the case of a political association, we would of course be looking, at a minimum, at something like an agreement to stand behind a certain constitution or system of laws—the type of agreement that Socrates imagines the laws of Athens to invoke.

Note that to say that an agreement of all to stand behind a particular constitution is sufficient for social unity is not to say that, without more, such unity will be particularly stable, long-lasting, or life-enhancing for the participants. It is only to say that it exists. Though this is a limited claim, it is still a claim of considerable interest.

Interpreted strictly in terms of agreement, the social contract approach faces the following problem. An agreement such as that envisaged may be sufficient, but it is not necessary for social unity that the people in question have made or signed on to any pertinent contract or agreement.

As evidence for this one may be inclined to cite the fact that while the naturalized citizens of a given nation may have done something akin to signing on to an agreement, most native-born citizens of most nations have done no such thing. I prefer to argue for it somewhat differently, in part because, whatever the implications of the terms "nation" and "citizen" themselves, one cannot assume that every so-called nation's so-called citizens together constitute an association.

Consider, then, the following small-scale example. Suppose that a small book discussion group has formed as the result of an agreement. Jack, a member of the group, invites his friend Sally to come to one of the meetings, as his guest. As the meeting ends, Jack says to Sally "See you next month?" and Sally replies "You bet!" There is a general murmur of pleasure at her response.

Sally has not agreed to join the group, but it may be clear at this point that she is ready to join it, and the existing members show that they are happy to have her. In some such way the group may expand from its five original members to fifteen. The unity of the final fifteen members is not, then, a matter of their all being parties to a given agreement.

One may be tempted to say that they are parties to an "implicit" agreement. If, however, one allows that an implicit agreement is not actually an agreement—as one must—then one has gone beyond social contract theory when this is understood to invoke a contract or agreement literally speaking. Be that as it may, the nature of an "implicit" agreement is not especially clear. It raises the following question: what is common to agreements on the one hand and "implicit agreements" such as that Sally enters into with the original members of the discussion group?

In addition to the invocation of an implicit agreement, it is worth noting another possible way of moving on from social contract theory without falling into subjectivism: invocation of not an actual but a *hypothetical* agreement—as in the claim that the people in question would enter a pertinent agreement if one were mooted. This may be an important fact about them, but it does not seem to suffice to make them into an association. The same goes for the claim that it would be unreasonable for them not to enter such an agreement if one were proposed. They need actually to enter such an agreement socially to unify themselves or they need to find some other route to social unity.

3. Joint Commitment as a Ground of Social Unity

What other route is there? Perhaps there are several. In the rest of this chapter, I focus on one such route. It is not that far distant from that of the social contract theorist. My proposal—which I shall shortly explain in more detail—is that "we"-thoughts, and so on, are well founded at least when they refer to a set of people who are *jointly committed* with one another in some way. These people, at least, constitute an association rather than an aggregate. Here there is a real unity of them all.

As a foundation for "we"-thoughts, this particular foundation is, I would argue, extremely widespread. I have argued elsewhere that everyday agreements are joint commitment phenomena.[12] If this is correct, then my joint commitment proposal accords quite well with the proposal of those classical theorists who claim that social unity is a matter of a pact or agreement. As I have already observed, that claim is fine as far as it goes, but it is too narrow. My proposal respects that observation, insofar as joint commitment is to be found in many contexts other than the context of an agreement. Further, it suggests a plausible

---

[12] See Gilbert (2006, ch. 10) and further references there.

interpretation of the idea of an "implicit" agreement that is not an agreement strictly speaking.

What is a joint commitment? This is a topic on which I have written extensively elsewhere. I have argued that the concept of a joint commitment is a fundamental everyday concept, incorporated in many central social concepts such as those of a social rule, a tradition, and an action performed together with another person.[13] Here I attempt roughly to indicate some of the important features of joint commitment as I understand it.[14]

A joint commitment is importantly analogous to the personal commitments that come from personal decisions and intentions. It is worth saying something about such personal commitments first; since intentions and decisions differ somewhat from one another I focus here on decisions.[15]

One who makes a personal decision commits himself to do what he decided to do. One way of explaining the applicable notion of commitment is this: all else being equal, as long as his decision stands, this person has acted in error should he fail to act in accordance with it. This might happen if, say, he is trying to carry out his decision but fails or he has temporarily forgotten his decision.[16] One who makes a personal decision unilaterally commits himself and he can unilaterally terminate his commitment prior to fulfilling it, by changing his mind.

A joint commitment is created by two or more people. In the *basic* case, on which I focus initially, all of these together commit them all. All are needed again for the termination of the commitment. Thus no one can unilaterally terminate the commitment. Evidently there is a sense in which the parties to a given joint commitment are united or *bound together*: together they commit or in that sense bind one another, and each continues to be so bound until all jointly decide otherwise. This gives the *joint commitment hypothesis* some plausibility. That is, it helps to support the idea that joint commitment is a, if not the, source of social unity.[17] Rather than arguing on behalf of this hypothesis further in this chapter, I shall focus further discussion here on its nature and implications.

As I have argued elsewhere, an important practical aspect of joint commitment is this: those who create a given joint commitment thereby obligate themselves one to the other to act as appropriate to the joint commitment, and have corresponding special rights against one another to such action. This gives each

---

[13] For my arguments see Gilbert (1989 and 1996), and elsewhere.

[14] See Gilbert (2003 and, 2006, ch. 7) for more extended discussions.

[15] For some differences between them see Gilbert (2006, ch. 7). What I say below represents my own position on the matter. There is some debate in the philosophical literature as to the "intrinsic" normativity of a given decision.

[16] I do not say and would not claim that the error in question is a moral one in any standard understanding of "moral."

[17] For further discussion see, e.g., Gilbert (1989 and 2006).

the standing to demand of the others conformity to the commitment and to rebuke the others for nonconformity.[18]

How do people manage to commit one another in this way? In essence, the matter is simple enough. In order to create a new joint commitment, two or more people must openly express their readiness together with the others to commit them all in a particular way, and each must know that this has been done. The parties may be specified as particular people, for instance, as Roy and Gilda, or in general terms such as "residents of this island," or "citizens of the member states of the European Union." In what follows I shall write as if this is all that is required, since further fine-tuning will not affect the argument.[19]

A joint commitment can be created with the kind of explicitness that makes what is happening an agreement, as in "Shall we go for a walk?"; "Yes, let's!" Or it can be done in a more subtle fashion. Thus consider the example previously given of Jack, Sally, and the book discussion group. Though there is no pertinent agreement, it may be clear from what transpires between the people present that Sally is ready to "sign on" to the existing joint commitments of the group's members respecting the group's goals and rules, and each of them is ready to have her so sign on.

It is possible to describe any joint commitment according to the following formula: X, Y and whatever others are jointly committed *to* x *as a body*. Substitutes for "x" are broadly speaking psychological terms such as "believe that such-and-such," "endorse such-and-such a goal," and so on. What is it to be jointly committed to x *as a body* as I intend this phrase? One way of further articulating the idea abstractly is as follows. To be jointly committed to x as a body is to be jointly committed to bring it about as far as is possible that the parties emulate a *single x-er*. It may help to use a concrete example in further clarification of this idea.

Suppose that John and Doris are jointly committed to believe as a body that Doris, who is ill, will get well. What must each of them now do, in order that the joint commitment is fulfilled? It is not the case that each must personally believe that Doris will get well, something it would be hard if not impossible for either one deliberately to bring about. Rather, in the appropriate circumstances—in particular, when they are together—each is to act in such a way that together they emulate a single believer of the proposition that Doris will get well. Among other things, whatever he or she personally thinks, neither will in the other's presence baldly declaim that Doris will not recover.[20]

---

[18] See Gilbert e.g. (2006, ch. 7).

[19] I generally posit also the parties' "common knowledge" of their expressions in roughly the sense of Lewis (1969). For discussion see Gilbert (1989, ch. 4).

[20] For more on this topic see, e.g., Gilbert (1987[] and 1989, ch. 5).

I refer to situations in which people are jointly committed to believe something as a body as cases of "collective belief." I have argued elsewhere that such situations are targeted by everyday assertions of the form "We believe...." when these are not understood as elliptical for "We all believe..." or "We both believe...."[21] Similarly, I have argued that everyday assertions of the form "We value...," "We feel...," "Our rule is...," "Our goal is...," and so on refer to situations of joint commitment.[22]

I sometimes use the technical phrase "plural subject" to refer exclusively to any set of jointly committed persons.[23] Use of this label allows me to refer to such persons more briefly and without risking the inevitable ambiguity of terms in common use. My use of it is not intended to have any more metaphysical implications than does the idea of a set of jointly committed persons—with which it is, by definition, equivalent.

In *On Social Facts* I proposed that the concept of a plural subject has been marked in everyday speech by a familiar noun phrase. More precisely, a central everyday concept associated with the English phrase "social group" is the concept of a plural subject, or, equivalently, a set of jointly committed persons.[24] This is the concept indicated by lists of groups such as the following: families, sports teams, discussion groups, labor unions, army units and so on. Such lists are often offered by sociologists and others.[25]

In order to allow myself some variety of language in what follows, I shall generally use the terms "social group," "association," and "social unit" as equivalent in meaning to "plural subject" as I have defined that phrase. In some contexts it will be clear that I am using one or another of the former terms without reference to this specific interpretation.

4. Social Groups as Plural Subjects

I take it that a given social group may be characterized by a single joint commitment—perhaps a joint commitment to believe that such-and-such as a body or a joint commitment to accept a certain system of rules—or by several joint commitments with distinct contents. Thus we may not only be jointly committed to

---

[21] See Gilbert (1987 and 1989).

[22] On our valuing see Gilbert (2005); on our feeling something (in this case remorse) see, e.g. Gilbert (2000); on our rule see Gilbert (2000); on our goal see e.g. Gilbert (2006).

[23] Introduced in this sense in Gilbert (1989, ch. 4).

[24] The English phrase "social group" is undoubtedly also used on occasion with respect to a broader range of populations than is my technical phrase "plural subject."

[25] Gilbert (1989, ch. 4). See also Gilbert (2006, ch. 8).

accept as a body a particular system of rules but also to believe as a body certain propositions, to endorse as a body certain values, and so on.

Presumably both the group's unity and the stability of its unity will be enhanced the more such commitments characterize it. The fading of a single judgment, value, aim, or rule may not, then, jeopardize the existence of the group it once characterized, as it might in other cases. Such an idea is suggested by the following quotation from Lord Patrick Devlin:

> Society is not something that is kept together physically; it is held [sic] by the invisible bonds of common thought. *If the bonds were too far relaxed* the members would drift apart. A common morality is part of the bondage.[26]

The idea of a joint commitment to believe as a body that such-and-such is a possible articulation of the idea that there can be "bonds of thought." Among the beliefs in question may be moral beliefs.

It has often been suggested in contemporary political philosophy that "shared values" are sufficient, and perhaps necessary, to transform a mere aggregation into an association. As I have argued elsewhere, whether or not this is so depends on what shared values are.[27]

Consider an understanding of "shared values" as a matter of each of the individuals in question personally espousing a particular value, such as freedom of speech. Given this construal the proposal about shared values is not plausible with respect to sufficiency. What we have when a number of people share a value according to this construal is an aggregation, not an association.

On an understanding of "shared values" in terms of joint commitment, and perhaps only then, the proposal is plausible. On such an understanding people share values (by definition) if and only if they are jointly committed to espouse as a body a certain value or values.

With respect to necessity, it is likely that in any association of human beings there will be some sharing of values in the aggregative sense. This, though, is not what constitutes the association, as already argued.

As to sharing values, in particular, in the joint commitment sense this is not, I think, necessary for the constitution of any association. Consider for example the members of the Flat Earth Society who are jointly committed to believe as a body that the earth is flat and, thereby, constitute a social group. It is at least not obvious that they must share any values in the joint commitment sense.

---

[26] Devlin (1965, p.10), my emphasis. My belief that Devlin makes an important observation here does not imply endorsement of any of his own personal value judgments or of his views on the British society of his time. For the most famous critique of Devlin, see Hart (1963).

[27] Gilbert (2005).

Perhaps most pertinent to a concern with the specific case of European Union is the possibility of an association that is wholly constituted by a joint commitment to uphold as a body one or more rules of governance. Such rules may explicitly or implicitly express certain values. Unless this is inevitable, however, there need be no shared values in such an association—a political association by virtue of the type of commitment that constitutes it.[28]

As the foregoing reference to political associations suggests, social groups founded on joint commitments can in principle be very small or very large. All that is needed is that the pertinent expressions of readiness be openly made and that members of the population in question know that this has occurred. In a very large population these expressions will presumably relate to the other members not as particular individuals but as possessors of a particular feature or features.

It may be implausible to assume that in a very large population every single member of the population has expressed his readiness for a particular joint commitment. Nonetheless, there may be good evidence that such readiness is sufficiently widespread for one to judge that there is a plural subject whose boundaries at least approximate that of the population in question.[29]

In what follows, for the sake of simplicity, I shall assume that every member of the designated population is party to the joint commitment in question. If you like, I shall operate in terms of a Weberian "ideal type," such that though reality may conform to it exactly, it is likely to conform to it only to some approximation.

Social units founded on joint commitments can exist within other such units. For example, a religious organization founded on the joint commitment of members to endorse as a body a certain creed may include many families each of which is held together as a social group by its own particular set of joint commitments.

Such *inclusiveness* does not entail a harmony of the associated joint commitments. On the contrary, these may be significantly at odds with one another. This can pose significant practical problems for the individuals involved. Thus, in the context of the example just given, Joyce may reveal to her parents that she has done something that is decried by their religious group. Are the parents to react negatively toward their child, as their membership in the religious group dictates, when a joint commitment within the family requires them to treat their children's choices with respect? If they prefer not to act as their religious

---

[28] On the idea of a political society or association see Gilbert (2006, ch. 8). The points made in this paragraph of the text link with the idea of "constitutional patriotism." See Habermas (1992), Ingram (1996); also Dworkin (1989). Ingram appears to Searle's perspective on society, discussed earlier in the text here. For a take on patriotism generally, inspired by a joint commitment model of political society, see Gilbert (2010).

[29] For discussion see Gilbert (2006, ch. 8).

group dictates, should they seek membership in a different group? Should they try to cover up the fact that they are failing to fulfill their obligations to their co-religionists? Such questions may crowd in upon them.

5. Basic and Derived Joint Commitments

It is important to note that a given joint commitment of the kind I have so far described—the kind I have referred to as the basic case—can lead to the generation of further joint commitments by the acts of designated authorities. These latter joint commitments may be termed *derived,* resting as they do on a basic joint commitment to accept the designated authorities as such.[30]

Once authorities have been designated in several associations, it is possible that the authorities from the different associations make an agreement or treaty on behalf of their associations. In so agreeing they may be said to create a further social group—one of a special kind. This is a group whose constituents are groups. According to my interpretation of agreements, the constitutive groups have together jointly committed themselves to endorse as a body the decision expressed in the agreement.

One can bring this last possibility to bear on the topic of the harmony or conflict of joint commitments mooted earlier. Suppose that the leaders of several different associations make an agreement to the effect that each is to institute certain rules in his own group. Each then does what he agreed to do. One of these rules may not sit well with a core value of one of the constituent groups.

Clearly this will lead to problems for its members. Previously and still jointly committed to value as a body certain things, they are now also jointly committed, derivatively, to conform as a body to rules that require them to act otherwise. All else being equal, the leader in this case would evidently have done well to avoid agreeing to institute this particular rule in his group, if he had been able to do so.

Notably, it is possible that those who are subject to particular derived joint commitments may not know that they are. Being participants in a joint commitment to accept that, say, a given body of persons may institute rules for the group, they know that in general they will be subject to rules appropriately instituted. Yet they may not know of a particular rule that they are now subject to. Perhaps for some reason, news of this has not reached them.

The last point makes it clear that as important as derived joint commitments are, the ultimate binding together of a population into an association by way of joint commitment depends on the existence of basic joint commitments. The

---

[30] See Gilbert (2006, ch. 8), and elsewhere.

ability of particular persons and bodies to introduce new joint commitments for the members of a given population is, indeed, derived from one or more basic joint commitments.

6. Ways of Creating Social Unity

I have argued that joint commitment is a—if not the—primary way of producing social unity, and thus offers a way of grounding "we"-thoughts in something that goes beyond the subjective states of the individuals in question. How might such commitments be induced or encouraged? The question can be put in terms of what has already been said about how joint commitments are created: how can one induce or encourage people openly to express their readiness to participate in a particular joint commitment? This is a large part of what is needed for a joint commitment to be established. The capstone is, roughly, knowledge throughout the population in question that the open expressions in question have been made.

One obvious answer is to offer them participation in a joint commitment or set of joint commitments that resonates with the joint commitments they are already party to, along with their personal aims, values, and so on. There are various ways in which such an offering might be made and accepted. In this section I focus on just one, noting the potential of certain special uses of *the language of joint commitment*—the language (in English) of the collective "we," "us," and "our."[31]

Suppose a member of the European Parliament begins a speech in his home country as follows: "We, the people of Europe, endorse this goal...." Perhaps there is as yet no such people, no such social unit, but rather a set of distinct social units approximating the various member nations that comprise what is referred to as the "European community." Insofar as this politician falsely presupposes that the citizens of the European nations together constitute a single, inclusive social unit or association, his use of "we" may be considered *tendentious*. Nonetheless, it may be accepted by those to whom he is speaking, and they may carry his thought throughout the nation in question, until it has been generally, and openly, accepted.

Of course, this may not happen. I mean only to argue that it may. What happens in practice may well depend at least on the concordance of the implicitly proposed joint commitment with existing joint commitments within the nation, along with existing personal aims, values, and the like of its citizens. The charisma of the speaker, meanwhile, may have its impact. Other factors also could

---

[31] Here I draw on Gilbert (1989, ch. 4).

move things along in spite of disparities between the proposed joint commitment and existing ones.

I now continue the story as it was left before the caveat just mentioned. Suppose that other European Parliamentarians are doing the same thing in their respective countries. Their words may also be accepted by their hearers, and so on. In some such way as this, through a process considerably extended in time, the citizens of the different member nations of the European Union could, in effect, openly express in their words and actions their personal readiness *jointly to commit with the citizens of other member nations to endorse as a body the goal in question.* This could gradually become known to all through various mechanisms. Some will travel widely within Europe and note the way people speak and act, bringing this information home. Others will write and read media reports, and so on.

Once it is known to the members of the different member nations that all have indeed openly expressed their readiness to enter the pertinent joint commitment, the people in question will be jointly committed in the pertinent way. Thus a large-scale social unit that was originally tendentiously presupposed in uses of the words "we," "us," and "our" could come into existence at least in part by means of that tendentious presupposition: the pertinent joint commitment would have been created from that starting point.

At this point the phrase "We, the people of Europe" could be used in a *full-blooded* way, with the knowledge that there is indeed a corresponding social unit. Now the "we"-thoughts, the sense of belonging together, the subjective identification, the feelings of pride over what we are doing, and so on—*all those things to which those who take the subjective stance on social unity refer—are likely to occur, and will have an appropriate objective ground.*

Such a process need not, of course, be started with the pronouncements of one or more politician. It need not depend on the existence of a particular "opinion-leader." It can start at the grass-roots level, with people tendentiously or in a more tentative, *initiatory* fashion using such locutions as "our constitution," "our belief that...," "our values...," and so on, with respect to the population in question. As such language and concordant behavior spreads, and its spread becomes known, the pertinent joint commitments would eventually be established. Subsequently such language and concordant behavior would help to maintain it.

In speaking of "concordant" behavior I include such things as pertinent demands and rebukes. Someone who takes "us" to espouse democratic ideas, for instance, will appropriately frown on one of us who baldly expresses antidemocratic sentiments. Likewise it will be appropriate for him to speak approvingly of one who makes an emphatically democratic speech.

It is worth repeating that even if it is not the case that every single citizen of each of the member nations has been involved in the kind of process described, it may be clear that there is a plural subject whose boundaries closely approximate that of the pertinent population. This would then be a good candidate referent for the phrase "We, the people of Europe."

7. Concluding Remarks

It is hard to say whether there is or can in practice be a real unity of the citizens of the member states of the European Union. Presumably this is truer now that there are so many more such states than there were originally. In this chapter, I have focused on the general question of what such a real unity would amount to, that is, what suffices for social unity, in general terms?

According to the subjectivist stance, enough concordant "we"-thoughts or other such subjective states among the members of a population suffice to constitute a real unity of them all. This stance is problematic for the simple reason that a concordance of "we"-thoughts is not plausibly argued to constitute a real unity out of the involved parties.

One might be tempted to take up this stance for the following reason. It suffices for social unity that, roughly, concordant "we"-thoughts, truly *or falsely* presupposing a given joint commitment, have been *expressed*, and *known to have been expressed*, among the people in question. For this suffices to establish the pertinent joint commitment of the parties.

That, however, does not show that the *subjective states* that the subjectivist invokes suffice for social unity. A joint commitment requires more than a proliferation of subjective states. Once it is established, however, it allows for full-blooded "we"-thoughts, as opposed to the "we"-thoughts of the tendentious or initiatory kinds. For then one can plausibly speak of a real unity of them all.[32]

References

Balibar, Etienne, 2004. *We, the People of Europe?* Princeton, NJ: Princeton University Press.
Devlin, Patrick, 1965. *The Enforcement of Morals*, Oxford: Oxford University Press.
Dworkin, Ronald, 1989. "Liberal Community," *California Law Review*, 77, pp. 479–504.
Gilbert, Margaret, 1987. "Modeling Collective Belief", *Synthese*, 73, pp. 185–204.
———, 1989. *On Social Facts*, Princeton, NJ: Princeton University Press
———, 1996. *Living Together: Rationality, Sociality, and Obligation*, Lanham, MD: Rowman and Littlefield.

[32] I thank Chad Kidd and Luca Morena for comments on a draft; and Aaron James for related conversation.

——, 2000. *Sociality and Responsibility: New Essays in Plural Subject Theory*, Lanham, MD: Rowman and Littlefield.

——, 2003. "The Structure of the Social Atom," in *Socializing Metaphysics*, Frederick Schmitt (ed.), Lanham, MD: Rowman and Littlefield, pp. 39–64.

——, 2005. "Shared Values, Social Unity, and Liberty," *Public Affairs Quarterly*, 19, pp. 25–49. [Chapter 8 this volume.]

——, 2006. *A Theory of Political Obligation: Membership, Commitment, and the Bonds of Society*, Oxford: Oxford University Press.

——, 2007. "Searle on Collective Intentions," in *Intentional Acts and Social Facts*, Savas Tsohatzidis ed., Dordrecht: Springer, pp. 31–48.

——, 2010. *"Pro Patria*: An Essay on Patriotism," *Journal of Ethics*, 13, pp. 319–340. [Chapter 16 this volume.]

Habermas, Jürgen, 1992. "Citizenship and National Identity: Some Reflections on the Future of Europe," *Praxis International*, 12, pp. 1–19.

Hart, H.L.A., 1963. *Law, Liberty, and Morality*, Stanford, CA: Stanford University Press.

Hobbes, Thomas, 1982. *Leviathan*, Harmondsworth: Penguin (orig. 1651).

Horton, John, 1992. *Political Obligation*, London: MacMillan.

Ingram, Attracta, 1996. "Constitutional Patriotism," *Philosophy and Social Criticism*, 22, pp. 1–18.

Jacobs, Dirk and Robert Maier, 1998. "European Identity: Construct, Fact and Fiction," in *A United Europe. The Quest for a Multifaceted Identity*, M. Gastelaars and A. de Ruijter (eds.), Maastricht: Shaker, pp. 13–34.

Lewis, David K, 1969: *Convention: A Philosophical Study*, Cambridge, MA: Harvard University Press.

Plato, 1978. *Crito*, in *The Collected Dialogues*, E. Hamilton and H. Cairns (eds.), Princeton, NJ: Princeton University Press (orig. circa 360 bc).

Rousseau, Jean-Jacques, 1983. *The Social Contract and Discourses*, D.A. Cress (trans.), Indianapolis, IN: Hackett (orig. 1792).

Searle, John, 1990. "Collective Intentions and Actions," in *Intentions and Communication*, eds. P.R. Cohen, J. Morgan, M.E. Pollack, Cambridge, MA: MIT Press, pp. 90–105.

——, 1995. *The Construction of Social Reality*, New York: Free Press.

Sellars, Wilfrid, 1963. "Imperatives, Intentions, and the Logic of 'Ought'," in *Morality and the Language of Conduct*, G. Nakhnikian and H-N Castañeda (eds.), Detroit, MI: Wayne State University Press, pp. 159–214.

Simmons, A.J., 1996. "Associational Obligations," *Ethics*, 106, pp. 247–273.

16

Pro Patria: An Essay on Patriotism

Introduction

"Dulce et decorum est pro patria mori" (Horace[1])

Patriotism: here is a topic around which swirl great poetry and oratory. A topic, then, about which it is all the more difficult to think clearly. This chapter aims to contribute to the discussion of *what patriotism is.*

Thinking about this can help one to engage with a controversy in contemporary political philosophy as to whether patriotism is a *good thing.* Indeed it is a desirable preliminary to such engagement.

I take patriotism to concern political societies—countries, in a broad sense of the term.[2] Such societies can vary enormously in size. In principle at least there could be a patriotism relating to a political society comprising all or most human beings.[3]

In this chapter I focus on what I call *"the basic patriotic motive."* By definition, one acts with this motive if one acts on behalf of one's country. Before saying more about it, I argue that from a pre-theoretical or intuitive point of view, it suffices in terms of motivation for a patriotic act. I then explain how this can be, in terms of a particular interpretation of what it amounts to. Finally, in light of the foregoing, I discuss the nature of patriotic acts and persons, and the relationship of patriotism and pride.

---

[1] Rough translation from the Latin: "It is a sweet and proper thing to die for one's country." This is line 13, of Ode 2, Book 3 of Horace's *Odes* (Horace 1901, p. 84). For a suggested interpretation of Horace's line, and reference to Wilfrid Owen's use of the line, see the text, below.

[2] Primoratz (2002b, p. 188) refers to a "political entity."

[3] Here I allude to the cluster of doctrines that fall under the rubric of "cosmopolitanism." One sometimes finds in the literature on that subject a preference for "the moral community" over other political societies. Though the quoted phrase appears to conjure a genuinely collective entity, it is not, I think, generally so construed in the cosmopolitan literature.

In the course of my discussion I make several claims about the intuitiveness of points about patriotic acts and so on. I should therefore say something at the outset about the basis and status of such claims.

The primary basis of the claims about intuitiveness I make here is my own sense of the matter in hand: Would I myself judge that such-and-such is a patriotic act, and so on? I have made some inquiries of others as to whether the judgments I make seem right to them. Such inquiries have so far at least firmed up these judgments. Still, there has been no random sampling of a representative population, and my claim is not statistical.

In effect, in proposing that this or that is so intuitively, I invite each reader to consider if this is true according to his (or her) own judgment. If it is, then there is some evidence that we share an idea of patriotic acts, for instance, and that further discussion will relate to an idea that we share. If some reader's intuitive judgment differs from mine, then he may take this text as developing a particular idea of patriotism—not his own, apparently—and its implications. In both cases the idea may have something to recommend it. It may, for instance, help to direct our attention to an important phenomenon, perhaps one more valuable than patriotism on other existing construals.

A final note on the matter of appeal to intuitive judgments may be helpful. I take it that the most useful pre-theoretical judgments for present purposes are not judgments about what patriotism is. Such judgments will either be stipulative or, already, to some degree theoretical, and may not correspond to the lower-level, less theoretical judgments that I take to be crucial here. These are judgments on cases, real or imaginary. Thus one might ask: "If someone did this, on this basis, would you say his action was patriotic?" I take one's answers to such questions to be better indicators of the idea of patriotism with which one is operating than a definition one might offer. At the least, there may be two quite different ideas of patriotism in question: the one expressed in the definition, which one may simply have taken over from others who have offered it, including the authors of dictionaries, and the one—if there is but one—expressed in one's intuitive judgments.

To begin, I argue for the intuitiveness of the following two negative points. First, in order to perform a patriotic act one need not ascribe any specific virtues or achievements to his (or her) country or see himself as in part aiming to promote these. Second, one need not be prompted by any particular emotions, or related positive attitudes toward his country.[4] More positively, the discussion

---

[4] In these initial sections I respond, to some extent, to Primoratz's discussion (Primoratz 2002a, pp. 10–11) which itself reflects common positions on patriotism. More recently, Keller citing Primoratz, accepts that the patriot will "conceive of the beloved country as having certain valuable characteristics" (Keller 2005, p. 574). The common assumption that a patriot is one who loves his country and/or believes it to have important virtues strongly suggests that a patriotic act will in part at least be prompted by love of and/or admiration for one's country.

in these sections suggests that the basic patriotic motive suffices to make an act patriotic at least as far as motivation is concerned.

Patriotism and the Ascription of Virtue

Consider a soldier who goes out to battle in his country's army. Assuming that any necessary non-motivational factors are present, what thoughts would suffice for us to deem his act a patriotic one?

I take it that quite a wide range of thoughts would suffice. He might simply invoke his country in some such way as this: "For France!" He might go further as in: "God for Harry, England, and St. George!" This invokes king, country, and that country's patron saint at once.[5] Going further, again, he might invoke one or more virtues of a political society—freedom, perhaps, or justice, or democracy—and ascribe this virtue, or these virtues, to his country as he invokes it. Or he might invoke past achievements of his country or what he sees as its glorious future.

The negative point I want to emphasize here is that, intuitively, our soldier's unadorned "For France!" taken as expressing an uncomplicated intention to act on behalf of his country, France, does not need to be supplemented by his ascription of some specific virtues, achievements, or the like, to France in order for us to deem his act a patriotic one. More positively, what we have is enough.

Let me briefly amplify the last point. Our soldier could be thinking of France as the country that will reward him financially for his efforts. He is then not thinking of it specifically as his country. Or it could be that he thinks that France is his country, though it is not. Then his unfortunate situation is such that we might call him a patriot-in-intention-only. Suppose, though, that France is his country and his thought "For France!" expresses his intention to act on behalf of it, seen as such.

Then, I propose, his act is intuitively a patriotic one from a motivational point of view.

Perhaps someone will attempt to save the view that one must at some level have in mind one's country's virtues or achievements with the claim that one cannot grant *that a country is one's own* without ascribing to it any particular virtues or achievements. This is surely implausible. I allow, of course, that one who finds his country's virtues and achievements to be few or non-existent might well try to rectify that state of affairs by public action. Or, if he can, he may well sever his ties with it, and find another country. Whatever he does, however, he is

---

[5] *The Life of King Henry the Fifth*, Act III, Scene 1, line 34 (Shakespeare 1900, p 33).

likely to find it less than honest to deny—in literal terms—that this country is, or was, his own.

I should emphasize that I am not here pressing the case for what Igor Primoratz has called "*egocentric* patriotism" in contrast to what he calls "*value-based* patriotism." He defines "egocentric patriotism" thus: "…an adherent of egocentric patriotism…loves her country as her country, rather than as a country that lives up to certain standards of value" (Primoratz 2002a, p. 11). In this quotation egocentric patriotism is linked to love of one's country. I have not in this section alluded to such love, and in the next I argue that it is not helpful to invoke it in one's account of a patriotic act.

Here I have argued against invoking the ascription of virtues and achievements to one's country in a description of the motivational component of a patriotic act as such. If we want to give an account of patriotic acts that has intuitive plausibility we should not insist that to be properly deemed patriotic an act must be undertaken on behalf of a country not only seen as one's own, but also seen as in at least some ways virtuous or successful.

Patriotism and Love of One's Country

People quite commonly invoke love when asked what patriotism amounts to: The patriot is one who loves his country.[6] This idea is reflected in informal conversations, in dictionaries and in theoretical discussions. The question I now discuss is whether a reference to love is an appropriate part of the characterization of a patriotic act. I propose that it is not, something that is true also for references to concern or devotion.[7] In discussion I focus on the question of love in particular.

One problem here is that the meaning of the term "love" is notoriously unclear, if indeed it means any one thing. In the present context, the pertinent question is precisely what, if anything, can be made of the invocation of love as associated with patriotic acts and, more strongly, as essential to them.

I propose that this question can be answered, and can only be answered, by means of a deeper understanding of the basic patriotic motive. One might put the point thus: from the point of view of an account of patriotic acts, one should not treat love as an independent variable; it is our better understanding of the basic patriotic motive that will properly drive our understanding of the love, if any, that is involved in any patriotic act. The same goes for the role in such acts of concern, devotion, and similar attitudes and emotions.

---

[6] Primoratz (2002a, p. 10) urges that the love of a patriot will be a love expressed in action.

[7] Primoratz (2002a, p. 10) prefers to speak of concern in connection with patriotism.

Prior to a clear understanding of the basic patriotic motive, appeal to love of country is likely to conjure up a particular array of emotions, inclinations and evaluative attitudes. Thus if asked what it would be to love one's country one might, off the cuff, suggest any or all of the following: it is to regard it with reverence; it is to reflect on its institutions, when one does, with pleasure; it is personally to desire the flourishing of its institutions and endeavors; it is to be downcast at its defeats and to glory in its victories; it is to miss it when one is traveling abroad, to rejoice in one's return to it, and to prefer living within its borders to living outside them; it is to attend with affectionate interest when it is mentioned, and to find one's thoughts of it suffused with sympathetic concern.

Emotions and inclinations such as those referred to in this list are often associated with love in one or another of its incarnations, and may sometimes be regarded as constitutive of it. It may well be common for people to experience such emotions and have such inclinations toward their country. It is surely implausible, however, to claim that any of these emotions or others like them must be expressed when one performs a patriotic act. Recall the example of the soldier who cries "For France!" when his intent is to act on behalf of his country, France. Must he be experiencing or expressing any of the emotions listed, or others like them? Surely not. If he does not experience them, does this make his action any the less patriotic? Again, surely not. If, for instance he experiences a combination of fear and determination, or excitement at the thought of battle, that would not seem to detract from the patriotism of his thought "For France!"

This proposal may seem to leave little room for any intrinsic association of love with patriotism. I do not wish to rush to that conclusion. Here is one reason why.

It is common to contrast acting out of a sense of duty with acting out of love.[8] I am not sure, though, that one can always properly distinguish the two. Think of someone who without thought or hesitation flies to spend his vacation sitting for weeks with a sick friend. He explains himself by saying simply that this is something he has to do. He invokes no emotions or evaluative attitudes and we can assume that he is right not to do so: The prompt for his action was the sense that this is what he must do. It may seem churlish—or simply inaccurate—to insist that his is not an act of love.[9]

If we can talk of love in such a case, perhaps we can talk of it in connection with the patriotic act, *understood initially in other terms*. Indeed, it may already seem that this is so. One who acts on behalf of his country, as such: does he not *thereby* manifest a love of country? If so—and this is not something I care to

---

[8] Cf. Nash (1938), in "Kind of an Ode to Duty": "Oh Duty/Why hast thou not the visage of a sweetie or a cutie?"

[9] Cf. "I am going to use the terms 'love' and 'loyalty' almost interchangeably" (Keller 2005, p. 567n14).

challenge—it is important to see that he need not, at the same time, manifest any of those warm, enlivening emotions, attitudes, and inclinations so commonly associated with love. Similarly, as argued earlier, he need not see as particularly virtuous the country on behalf of which he acts. It may, in his opinion, simply be "muddling through," or worse. In sum, an account of patriotism as a matter of love of country is either doubtful or unhelpful as it stands.

The Basic Patriotic Motive

I have argued that in characterizing a patriotic act from a motivational point of view we can restrict ourselves to the basic patriotic motive so far roughly characterized as follows: one acts from this motive if one acts on behalf of one's country. Can one say more about what it is to do this?

One might start by emphasizing that acting *on behalf of* one's country is to be distinguished from acting *in favor of* one's country. I take it that in both cases one will act as far as possible in consonance with one's country's institutions, goals, values, and so on. So to act on behalf of one's country is *to that extent* to act in its favor. To act in a way favorable to one's country, however, is not necessarily to act on its behalf. It is not, if you will, to act as its representative or agent.

One way of reflecting the dual aspect of acting on behalf of one's country noted in the text would be to say that one acts *in behalf of* one's country insofar as one acts *on its behalf.* Having clarified what I understand by it I shall stick with the phrase "on behalf of."[10]

Why would one act on behalf of one's country, assuming that one is in a position to do so? One can see why someone might be inclined to appeal, here, to one's admiration for one's country, however, qualified, or to similar factors. Can action on behalf of one's country make sense in the absence of such factors?

This depends to a large extent on *what a country is* and *what it is for a country to be my country.* One needs, therefore, a working account of these matters. I now sketch the account I shall work with here.[11] I believe that it is reasonably intuitive.[12] One aspect of its intuitiveness is precisely that it allows us to see acting on behalf of one's

[10] I thank Primoratz for pointing out the existence and meaning of "in behalf of" in English usage (personal communication, 2008).

[11] I draw on the more detailed discussion in Gilbert (2006), which further develops the account of social groups introduced in Gilbert (1989), attempting to bring out what is important for present purposes. As will emerge, my approach has something in common with that in Ingram (2002, 223–225). We differ in that she draws on Searle's account of "collective intentionality" (Searle 1990) whereas I draw on my own distinct approach to the pertinent phenomena, and follow out the consequences of that approach. For a critique of Searle, see Gilbert (2007).

[12] See Gilbert (2006), Chap. 8 and elsewhere.

country as intelligible without appeal to admiration for or love of one's country, or the like.

To begin, one may plausibly characterize a country as a political society or, for short, a *polity*. A country's *citizens*, in the sense I shall adopt here, are the members of the polity in question.[13]

What is a polity? The account I develop here describes an *ideal type* in the non-normative sense of the sociologist Max Weber: It describes a clear case to which real life situations will correspond more or less perfectly. For the sake of simplicity in what follows I do not generally consider possible deviations from the case that is represented. I shall offer similarly "ideal-typical" accounts of pertinent phenomena throughout this essay.

Briefly put:

> a number of persons together constitute a *polity* if and only if, at a minimum, they are jointly committed to support and uphold as a body a particular set of political institutions.

I have inserted the phrase "at a minimum" to indicate that though it is sufficient for people to constitute a polity that they be jointly committed in the specified way, their *polity-constituting joint commitments* may extend beyond the supporting and upholding as a body of a set of political institutions.[14] I say more about this shortly.[15]

I discuss the nature of joint commitment in the next section. Setting that aside for now, I develop a little further some other aspects of the above idea.

With respect to *political institutions* I take three central possibilities to be as follows. First, there may be no more than a number of "ground-level" social rules and edicts pertaining to the organization and defense of the population, or *governing rules,* for short. Or there may be ground-level rules that include one or more stipulations to the effect that some particular person or body of persons may make further rules and issue edicts of the governing type, rules and edicts that will count as issuing from the population as a whole. Such stipulations set up what may be called someone's or some body's *"personal rule."* Finally there may be ground-level rules that do not refer to particular persons or bodies of persons but explain in general terms who may make further rules and edicts of the governing type. These may be referred to as *"rules of governance."*

---

[13] I do not mean to imply that a country cannot fail to recognize a *legal status* of citizenship.

[14] In the ideal case, *all* members of some population are parties to *all* of a particular set of joint commitments some or all of which sustain a set of political institutions.

[15] One of its implications is that the kind of patriotism I discuss embraces but is not restricted to "constitutional patriotism" construed as a patriotism whose focus is a set of political institutions. On constitutional patriotism see e.g., Ingram (2002); she cites as a central reference Habermas (1992).

I take it that there may or may not be explicit or implicit reference within these kinds of rule-system to the function or purpose that a particular rule or the system as a whole is supposed to serve. The same goes for the invocation of specific values, moral principles, or religious doctrines within the political rule system. Indeed, some values, principles, or doctrines may be fundamental in the sense that, roughly, the authority of other rules of the system is understood to be contingent on their respect for these values, principles or doctrines.

I assume that one who is party to a joint commitment to *support and uphold as a body a particular set of political institutions* is not required by virtue of that commitment to do *everything* that would count as supporting and upholding the rules in question.[16] I say more about this later. For present purposes it will be useful to define some terms on the basis of this assumption. I shall say that whatever counts as supporting and upholding the rules is *in the spirit* of the commitment but may outrun what it *requires*. I shall say that an action *conforms* to a joint commitment to which one is a party if is in the spirit of the commitment, and an action *complies* with a joint commitment if it fulfills one of its requirements.

I stated earlier that the joint commitments constitutive of a polity may go beyond those that relate to a particular set of political institutions. This allows the proposed account of a polity to respect the following intuitive point: A given polity may have features that go beyond its political institutions. For instance, it may have goals, values, a moral outlook, religious convictions, and so on, that are not part and parcel of those institutions.

I have argued at length elsewhere for joint commitment accounts of a group's goals, values, and so on.[17] It follows that the intuitive point just noted can plausibly be represented as follows: Those who are jointly committed to support and uphold as a body a particular set of political institutions may at the same time be jointly committed to espouse as a body certain goals, to endorse as a body certain values, and so on, in such a way that both the political institutions and the goals and so on may be said to belong to the polity.

That noted, I take the core of any polity, as such, or the constitution of a *minimal polity*, to consist in one or more joint commitments of the members of a given population to support and uphold as a body specific political institutions.

There is nothing about what I have said here that implies that a polity cannot change its character in more or less radical ways. Change at the level of the institutions, goals, values and so on of the polity will occur, on the current understanding of them, as one or more joint commitment is to some extent altered, replaced by another, or simply given up.

---

[16] Compare a commitment to "look after" someone when they are ill. One is obviously required to make sure various basic needs of theirs are fulfilled. It is less obvious that one must cater to their every whim.

[17] See e.g., Gilbert (1989, 1996).

It is in principle possible that a given set of polity-constituting joint commitments may be such that inconsistent requirements may issue from it. For the sake of simplicity I shall assume that this is not so. Thus one who acts so as to conform to the requirements of one such joint commitment is not in danger of acting contrary to another. I shall continue with this simplifying assumption except in some special contexts where I shall make it clear that I have set it aside.

What then is it for a country to be *my* country? Given that a country is a polity, understood as just proposed, the following account suggests itself:

> A country is *one's own* if and only if one is party to those joint commitments that constitute it.

This ideal-typical account is the one I shall work with here.

I take it that on account of his participation in the pertinent joint commitments a citizen is in a position to refer to a given country and its institutions, values, and so on, as "ours" or (when he is considering only himself) as "mine." Thus to say that the country is *his*, on the proposed account, is to say in effect that he helps sustain it in existence by virtue of his participation in the joint commitments that constitute it.[18]

As to how one might now construe the basic patriotic motive, the related suggestion I shall work with is this:

> One acts *on behalf of one's country* if and only if, being party to the joint commitments that constitute it, one acts in light of these commitments in order to conform to them.

This could be somewhat fine-tuned, but for present purposes I leave it there, except to note that I shall take one to act in light of the pertinent joint commitments if one acts in light of one or more particular members of the total set of commitments.

Referring with the first person plural pronominal adjective to oneself and one's co-participants in the pertinent joint commitment, one might express oneself in terms such as these: "Our constitution requires this;" "The fulfillment of our goal requires this;" "This is in the spirit of one of our most important values." In what follows, unless I say otherwise, I construe such locutions accordingly.

There will be no need to appeal to one's personal admiration for or endorsement of the pertinent constitution, goals, and so on in explaining why one would act in terms of it, *if one's participation in a given joint commitment is itself complete from a motivational point of view*. This is what I argue in the next section. The matters to be dealt with there are, first, what joint commitment is, and, second,

---

[18] This observation has a number of implications some of which are discussed below in the section on patriotism and pride. On the English pronoun "we," see Gilbert (1989) Chap. 4.

what are the implications of one's participation in a given joint commitment for practical reasoning.

The Motivational Completeness of the Basic Patriotic Motive

It may be helpful to begin by considering something very familiar and relatively simple: a personal decision. Suppose I live in California and have decided to spend July in Italy. It would then be odd for me to buy a non-stop return ticket to Moscow for the first of July, returning at the end of the month. Indeed, it would surely be in some sense erroneous for me to do this, unless I have figured out that my Italian plan will not be hampered by my doing so. Of course, if I changed my mind about Italy before buying the tickets to Moscow, the problem in question would not arise. But suppose I have not changed my mind. I somehow forget my decision and find myself with the Moscow tickets. Remembering my decision I say, with some consternation, "Why have I done this, I am supposed to be going to Italy!" Such considerations suggest a point I take to be intuitive: My decision in some sense mandates my conforming action, provided I have not previously changed my mind.[19]

In what sense does my standing decision mandate my conforming action? One may say that it *commits* me, but must then say something about what that amounts to. I propose that it commits me in the sense that on account of it I now *have sufficient reason* to act that way, where this in turn means that all else being equal rationality—in a broad sense—requires me so to act. In other words, I will so act, all else being equal, if I am a person who acts (or attempts to act) appropriately all things considered.

I now stipulate a sense of "ought" that captures this situation, so that one can also say that when I have decided to act and not changed my mind, I *ought* so to act, *all else being equal.* This, then, is not the moral "ought" unless the qualifier "moral" is stretched quite wide.

I have elsewhere argued that human beings operate not only with the concept of a *personal* commitment such as that engendered by personal decisions, plans, and intentions regarding the future, but with the concept of a *joint* commitment engendered by certain kinds of open expressions made by each of two or more people.[20] These expressions, made in conditions of common knowledge, commit

---

[19] Theorists who seem to take a contrary position include Broome (1992). On the other side see Verbeek (2008). This is not the place to argue the point further.

[20] See e.g., Gilbert (1989, 1996).

the parties in much the way a personal decision, plan or intention would commit them, but with at least two important differences.[21]

One has to do with the way in which each party comes to be committed. In the basic case, on which I shall focus here, each one is committed as a result of the public process as a whole, involving all of the parties.[22] The people in question together commit one another. The basic joint commitments underlying personal rule and constitutional rules, mentioned earlier, allow for the generation of many non-basic joint commitments.[23]

The other difference between being committed through the joint commitment process and being committed through a personal decision or the like has to do with an individual's ability, or lack of ability, unilaterally to rid himself of his commitment. In the case of a personal decision one can rid oneself of it simply by changing one's mind. In contrast, no one party can remove the constraints of a joint commitment without the concurrence of the rest, at least in the absence of special background understandings. In other terms, with the same proviso, having imposed the commitment together the parties must remove it together if it is to be removed.

That stated, it is worth noting that in many cases one is committed *qua* person with some general feature, e.g., *qua* person living between the ocean and the mountains. Then, if one can deliberately give up the feature in question without the concurrence of anyone else, one can unilaterally rid oneself of the constraints of the joint commitment in question.[24]

I take the making of a regular everyday agreement to be an example of such a process of joint commitment, but it is not the only one.[25] People can become jointly committed through a process considerably extended in time, and with nothing as clear-cut as an explicit proposal such as "Shall we begin?" followed by an explicit acceptance: "Yes."[26]

What difference does one's being party to a given joint commitment make in terms of one's practical reasoning? All else being equal, once I understand that I am committed through it, and I am responsive to rationality's requirements, I will act accordingly. In other terms, I ought to do it. An important implication,

---

[21] On "common knowledge" see Gilbert (1989, Chap. 4); the best known philosophical source on the topic is Lewis (1969).

[22] For a more fine-grained discussion, see Gilbert (2003).

[23] See Gilbert (2006).

[24] A wrinkle here is that one may be jointly committed with others, *qua* persons with feature F, to accept as a body the rule "Do not deliberately give up feature F." But this need not be the case. For a longer discussion of ways of ceasing to be party to a given joint commitment see Gilbert (2006, Chap. 7).

[25] For discussion of agreements in this context see e.g., Gilbert (2006, Chap. 10).

[26] See e.g., Gilbert (2006, Chap. 7).

for present purposes, is that I do not need warm feelings or positive judgments of value to prompt me to action.

Sometimes, I take it, all is not equal *by virtue of the content of the commitment itself.* Both in principle and in practice the content of a given joint commitment may be such that the parties ought not to conform to it, absent special circumstances. In what follows I shall take this to be understood. The points I shall make concern the appropriate impact of a given joint commitment *as such* on one's practical reasoning.

One can argue that a joint commitment to which one is a party trumps one's personal inclinations, desires, and self-interest as such in terms of what one ought to do. Perhaps the best way to argue this is by invoking the central point that the parties to a joint commitment are in an important sense *obligated* to conform to the commitment. Notably, the obligation in question is *directed:* One is obligated *to* or *toward* the other parties. To put the point fully: one is obligated *to the other parties* to conform to the commitment.

Directed obligations are generally understood to correlate with rights, in particular with so-called *claim-rights.* There is much dispute in the literature on rights as to what either directed obligations or claim-rights amount to.[27] So it is best to consider what seems to be at issue in the case of joint commitment.

Here I take the following two-stage understanding of a directed obligation to be appropriate. First, *person P1 has an obligation to person P2 to perform action A if and only if P1 owes P2 that action.*[28] Second, P1 *owes* P2 an action if and only if P2 in some intuitive sense *owns* that action prior to its performance. Alternatively, it is in some intuitive sense *his.*[29] It is owed until it is performed.

It can be argued that if P1 and P2 are party to a joint commitment such that P1 must perform action A in order not to run afoul of the commitment, then P2 can appropriately regard P1's performance of A as in an intuitive sense *his.* Briefly to suggest the sense in question, it is apposite to say that in together maintaining the joint commitment—and accordingly *imposing a constraint on each other in terms of what it is open to them to do*—the parties have together "put their dibs" on certain actions of each.[30]

It can be argued, then, that the parties to a joint commitment *owe* each other actions required by that joint commitment, or, in other terms, *are obligated to*

---

[27] Among other things there is a long-standing and well-known debate between "interest theories" and "will theories" in the literature. See e.g., Sreenivasan (2005). I discuss this literature and problems I find in it in my book *Rights Reconsidered* to be published by Oxford University Press. For some pertinent discussion see Gilbert [Margaret] (2004).

[28] Hart (1955) is one who associates claim-rights and owing.

[29] Feinberg (1970) refers to the right-holder demanding *as his* what he has a right to.

[30] For some further discussion see Gilbert (2006, Chap. 7). I say more about it in *Rights Reconsidered.*

each other to comply with it, on the interpretation of these terms now at issue.[31] If this is so, as I shall now assume, it follows that if a number of persons are jointly committed together to support and uphold a particular set of political institutions, each one owes the other his supporting and upholding those institutions. Correspondingly, each is in a position to demand such support if another threatens to withhold it, and to rebuke another who has withheld it.[32]

This, then, is one way to argue that a joint commitment to which one is a party trumps one's personal inclinations, desires, and self-interest, as such, in terms of what one ought to do (in the sense of "ought" noted previously). Intuitively, if you owe me some action, you are not properly justified in refusing to perform it simply on account of your inclination or desire not to, or even by the fact that it is not in your interest to do so.

What if one is able to bring the weight of morality in? Consider the example Socrates gives at the opening of Plato's *Republic*, when evaluating the proposition that it is just to give someone what you owe him.[33] It goes roughly like this. Suppose someone has deposited his weapon with you, and then returns to get it, but now he has gone mad. Are you to return it then? The point of the example is to suggest a negative answer: the weapon's owner might well use it to maim or kill someone, and it cannot be right, all things considered, to give back his weapon in these circumstances, though one owes it to him.

It can be argued then, that it is sometimes wrong, all things considered, to give someone what you owe him, in the sense at issue here, and what, correspondingly, he has a right to be given. You will still owe him, he will still have the corresponding right, and he may choose to demand that you give him what is his or to rebuke you for not doing so: He will have the standing to do that. Yet all things considered you should not give him what you owe him in this particular instance.[34]

In sum, given that people ought to conform to a joint commitment, all else being equal, it looks as if one can further spell out when all else is equal, and when it is not, in terms of two kinds of consideration as follows. A joint

---

[31] For other ways of arguing that the parties to any joint commitment are obligated to one another to conform to it see e.g., Gilbert (2000).

[32] "Correspondingly:" if we think of demanding as demanding *as mine,* and rebuking as the "after the fact" version of a demand. I think this is the correct construal of the central narrow sense of "demand" and "rebuke." See Gilbert (2006), Chap. 7 on different senses of these terms.

[33] See Plato (1974). Though this example may be thought of as a matter of owing the man his weapon, it can easily be thought of in terms of owing an action: the action of returning the weapon. What was implicitly or explicitly agreed by the parties was that the person with whom the weapon was deposited would *give it back.*

[34] For some interpretations of "owe" the points in this paragraph are not correct. Cf. Oldenquist (2002), p. 35, on gratitude. Unless otherwise stated, I use the interpretation offered in the text above throughout this chapter.

commitment *trumps one's personal inclinations, desires, and self-interest, as such.* But it *may be trumped by at least some moral considerations.* I shall assume this to be so in what follows.

The point that a joint commitment trumps one's personal inclinations and so on, as such, does not preclude arguments to the effect that it is morally permissible or even required not to conform to a given joint commitment on account of the cost to oneself *qua* human being or human being of a particular general kind. The point is essentially this: one must move beyond a simple reference to one's conflicting inclinations and the like in order to argue that it is fine to ignore the requirements of a given joint commitment. And a given argument of this kind may or may not be plausible.

Before leaving the topic of joint commitment in general I should make one final point of clarification. I have characterized a polity as a number of persons jointly committed, at a minimum, to support and uphold *as a body* a set of political institutions. I understand that a joint commitment is always to do something—in a broad sense of "do"—as a body, though sometimes it is less cumbersome to omit the phrase "as a body" in discussion. This phrase is not sacrosanct: Other phrases might do just as well, for instance, "as one," "as a unit." One way of expanding the phrase as I understand it is this: the parties are jointly committed to emulate a single body or person that does whatever it is.

It is arguable that, in order to fulfill the requirements of a joint commitment to support and uphold as a body certain rules, it is not enough to follow the relevant rules oneself. One also needs on occasion appropriately to intervene in the lives of the other parties. Thus suppose that Alice is party to such a joint commitment herself and abides by the rules. She notices that Boris, another party to the commitment, has broken one of the rules. All else being equal, it may now be incumbent upon her to rectify that as best she can.

At a minimum she could offer a kindly reminder "I think we have a rule that says..." or, if she sees fit, she could straight-away rebuke Boris for his rule-breaking. Assuming that Boris recognizes that Alice is one of the parties to the joint commitment he will know that she has *the standing* to rebuke him for not following the rules—for "breaking rank" as may be said—and that she has reason to do so in light of the joint commitment.

One may of course not take advantage of this standing. And one may have good, perhaps humane, reasons for this. Or one's reasons may not be so good— Alice may be afraid to stand up to anyone.

One's failure to rebuke, and so on, may be required by another joint commitment to which one is a party. Thus Boris and Alice may be parties to a joint commitment with various others to accept as a body the rule "live and let live." Then Alice's participation in each of the two pertinent joint commitments puts her in a quandary. There is a particular kind of inconsistency in play here: It is not as if one joint commitment is to do X as a body, and another is to do not-X as a body. It is rather that the joint commitment to accept as a body the rule "live and let live" requires one not to act in ways required by any joint commitment—even itself.

Pertinent here are these remarks by Michael Walzer concerning what he refers to as "republican politics:" "....because it rests on a shared commitment it is often more bitter and divisive than politics in other regimes. *Civility and tolerance serve to reduce the tension, but they do so by undercutting the commitment... they make for quiet and passive citizens, unwilling to intrude on others...*"[35]

This is a good time to pull together the main threads of the argument so far. I have defined key terms and argued roughly as follows. One acts in terms of the *basic patriotic motive* if and only if one acts on behalf of one's country. This motive is sufficient, intuitively, to make an act patriotic from a motivational point of view. Needing a working account of what it is for a country to be one's own, I have adopted the following ideal-typical construal: *a country is one's own if and only if one is party to those joint commitments that constitute it.* I have therefore explicated the basic patriotic motive roughly thus: one acts *on behalf of one's country* if and only if, being party to the joint commitments that constitute that country, one acts in light of these commitments in order to conform to them. One *conforms* to a given joint commitment if and only if one either satisfies its requirements or goes beyond them, in the spirit of the commitment. One *complies* with it if and only if one satisfies one of its requirements.

I have argued, in effect, that a joint commitment as such is *motivationally complete* from a rational point of view, though it is not conclusive in all circumstances. Hence the basic patriotic motive, on the proposed construal, does not need supplementation with considerations relating to the virtues of one's country or from independently grounded positive emotions.

There need be nothing irrational or inexplicable about one's acting on behalf of one's country, just because it is one's country, given my construal of what it is for a country to be one's own. In particular, one's so acting need not be a matter of egocentricity, or unreasonable partiality, but may rather be a matter of responding appropriately to polity-constituting joint commitments to which one is a party.

That is the central argument of this chapter. In the following sections I consider its bearing on some closely related matters. These matters are delicate and my remarks are intended largely as pointers in the direction of a satisfactory final position. I begin with the nature of a patriotic act.

---

[35] Walzer (2002, p. 267), emphasis mine. I do not say that for Walzer a "shared commitment" is equivalent to my "joint commitment." It is possible that he has no explicit articulation of "shared commitment" in mind.

Patriotic Acts

Can we develop a reasonably intuitive account of a patriotic act by appealing to the basic patriotic motive construed as above? In what follows, this construal will be assumed unless otherwise indicated.

In considering this question something like the following *simple account* (P) is an obvious place to start:

(P) One's act is *patriotic* if and only if one acts in light of the joint commitments that constitute one's polity, in order to conform to them.

Recall that I take one to *act in light of the pertinent joint commitments* if one acts in light of one or more particular members of the total set of commitments.

I now consider some concerns one might have with this account. Three of them question the sufficiency of the conditions posited for a patriotic act.

The first concern is this. Assuming—as I have proposed—that the basic patriotic motive is sufficient to make an act patriotic *as far as motivation goes,* may we not need to look beyond an action's motive before we nominate an act a patriotic one?

As a preliminary to discussion of this concern, I note that a very wide range of actions may be performed from the basic patriotic motive. This is so even if we restrict ourselves to action in light of a joint commitment to support and uphold a particular set of political institutions—a joint commitment of the kind that is required in order that a society be a polity specifically, but which may not exhaust the joint commitments that constitute a particular political society. In what follows I limit my examples to citizens of a minimal polity unless I say otherwise.

Consider Ali, who is jointly committed with others to uphold and support a particular set of political institutions and thereby committed to joining the army when he is ordered to do so by the duly constituted authorities. He may join the army in light of these facts, and, subsequently, go out to battle in light of the fact that, again, a duly constituted authority has ordered him to do so. In doing so, he risks his life. Consider Brenda, who scrupulously pays the taxes that she owes according to the tax laws of her country, in light of her participation in the pertinent polity-constituting joint commitments; she does this in spite of the fact that, as she knows, she could have avoided paying so much in tax without any real chance of being found out, and spent the money thus saved on a pressing domestic project. Finally, consider Claire, who brings her car to a halt at a stop-sign in the desert by reason of the fact that this is dictated by a law she is jointly committed with others to support and uphold, as a matter of their joint commitment to uphold and support a particular system of laws. If the basic patriotic motive is enough to make an act patriotic, then Ali, Brenda, and Claire would all be performing patriotic acts when acting as described.

It is not clear to me that there is anything untoward about this result. Perhaps, though, someone might hesitate to call Claire's act patriotic, because the cost of the action, in terms of her self-interest, is likely to be minimal.

In that respect, he might point out, her act contrasts with those of the others. Assuming that she would not have stopped her car but for the sign, Claire has acted contrary to her inclinations, and in doing so she has expended the extra attention and effort needed to bring her vehicle to a stop at the sign, as opposed to simply breezing through it. Given what we have been told, then, she has incurred some costs, but they are minimal. In the other cases there is a significant cost or potential cost to the agent in acting in light of the pertinent joint commitment. Ali risks his life, not to speak of any other risks to his person or his peace of mind, and Brenda cannot undertake a pressing domestic project.

There is indeed this striking difference between the cases. And perhaps the patriotic act that is most likely to come to anybody's mind is *"pro patria mori."* That is not surprising given the very high personal cost of the act in this case.

The salience of this example does not itself answer the question: is the patriotic act intuitively *defined* in part in terms of the relatively high personal cost of the action? In other words, is a "relatively cost-free patriotic act" a contradiction in terms? Do we need to amplify the simple account by, at least, requiring that the act in question is not more or less cost-free? Should we rule that Claire's action is not a patriotic one?

Against such a ruling one might note the following. Claire has acted on behalf of her country: She stops at the sign because, as she might have put it, "Our laws require it," not because "The cops may be hidden somewhere, ready to give me a ticket" or "I like to abide by the laws of whatever country I happen to be in." Further, she has given every sign of understanding that from a rational point of view the pertinent joint commitment trumps the personal inclinations and self-interested considerations, as such, that are at issue in her case, and that she is ready to act appropriately in terms of the pertinent requirement of reason.[36]

If one is inclined to think of Claire's action as patriotic, her apparent readiness to respect the trumping quality of the pertinent joint commitments as they affect her case may make a contribution to one's sense of things. Consider in this connection the case of Claire's twin, Claes.

Approaching the stop sign, Claes realizes that the polity-constituting joint commitments to which he is a party require him to stop. He immediately thinks to himself "But... do I feel like stopping?" All else being equal, he will only stop if the answer is positive. Finding that he feels like stopping—perhaps he is thirsty

---

[36] My discussion of Claire's case has benefited from conversation with Aaron James.

and this will enable him more easily to drink some water—he stops. He would not have stopped, but for the joint commitments; yet in spite of them, he would not have stopped had he not felt like stopping.

I take it that Claes's case is at best not a clear case of patriotic action. Certainly Claire's case is more plausibly thought of as patriotic. In order to reflect this difference, the simple account—intended as ideal-typical—can be amended accordingly. Something like the following version of the account would do the trick. The extra material is italicized:

> (P1)One's act is patriotic if and only if one acts in light of the joint commitments that constitute one's polity, in order to conform to them, *and in so doing respects the fact that rationality requires those joint commitments to take precedence over any concurrent contrary self-interested considerations or inclinations as such.*

In referring to "the simple account" in what follows I should be understood to be referring to P1.

If someone thinks that Claire's act should not be deemed patriotic because it is relatively cost-free, though it fulfills the conditions stipulated in P1 the simple account can, of course, be amended in the proposed direction.

A second concern about the sufficiency of the conditions posited by the simple account relates to the results of one's action. Someone might wonder if one would say that an act was patriotic if, however, intended, it completely misfired. Consider Don, who intends to promote his country's goal of victory in battle over a certain enemy by doing such-and-such. As things turn out his doing such-and-such gives that enemy information that enables it to defeat his country.

I do not see why one should not say that Don performed a patriotic act but unfortunately for him and for his country things turned out badly for the latter. That said, it would clearly not be difficult to modify the simple account of a patriotic act in the direction just noted.

The third and final concern that I shall discuss with respect to the sufficiency of the conditions posited by the simple account is as follows. It appears that an act may be patriotic according to that account though there are moral considerations such that the act *should not have been performed, all things considered.*

Consider Ed, who goes out to fight for his country in a particular war, his act counting as patriotic according to the simple account. In his case, however, there are moral facts about his country's waging this war such that all things considered he should have refused to fight, taking the consequences.

Perhaps he has not looked beyond the polity-constituting joint commitments in question along with his own inclinations and self-interest, as such, as far as his purview of considerations relevant to what to do are concerned. If so, this may have been inadvertent. Or perhaps he believes, wrongly, that there is never any reason to look beyond these commitments, once it is clear that they require a certain action, or even suggest it. If you like, he does not realize that "patriotism is not enough."[37] Perhaps his estimate of the moral case against his action is faulty. Or he realizes that he should not be acting in light of the pertinent polity-constituting joint commitments, all things considered, but gives in to an excessive desire to comply with them—an excess, as one might say, of patriotic zeal. Or he realizes that all things considered he should not do this, but coolly acts on behalf of his country nonetheless. Perhaps this is something he makes it a rule to do.

Is it a problem for the simple account that it would count Ed's act as patriotic in each scenario? I think not. Intuitively, Ed's action is patriotic in each case.

Assuming that the simple account—as represented by P1—is on the right lines, the following positive and negative points about the intuitive concept of a patriotic act now suggest themselves. Positively: that concept is geared, in part at least, to emphasize the trumping quality, from a rational point of view, of joint commitments over contrary inclinations and self-interested considerations as such. More precisely, it is geared to pick out actions that respect that trumping quality, and which are therefore rational to that degree. Negatively: the intuitive concept of a patriotic act is not geared to discriminate between cases in which one respects the requirements of rationality *all things considered,* and those in which one does not. Thus it allows that Ed acts patriotically in all of the scenarios envisaged. For the sake of a label I call this *the trumping hypothesis.* I return to it later.

I now turn to the question whether the conditions posited by the simple account are *necessary* for a patriotic action, as the account proposes. In this context it is important to recall that according to the construal with which I am working here one acts from the basic patriotic motive when one acts in light of one or more of the joint commitments that constitute one's polity, so as to conform to it. Not all of the actions that *conform* to such a commitment, in the sense defined earlier, are acts of *compliance* such that one *must* perform them in order not to run afoul of the commitment. Thus some actions are in the spirit of the commitment, while being *supererogatory* with respect to it.

The simple account of a patriotic action is couched in terms of conformity as opposed to compliance. Thus if Frank signs up to join the army because the polity-constituting joint commitments to which he is a party require this, his act

---

[37] The quoted phrase is attributed to the British nurse Edith Cavell prior to her execution by the Germans after she admitted helping British servicemen and others to escape from German-occupied land during the First World War. Its broader context is: "...this I would say, standing as I do in view of God and eternity: I realize that patriotism is not enough. I must have no hatred or bitterness towards anyone" (quoted in Gilbert [Martin] 2004, pp. 202–203).

is patriotic on the simple account. And so is Gina's deliberately refraining from taking perfectly legal steps to avoid estate taxes in light of the polity-constituting joint commitments in her case, though this action is plausibly regarded as supererogatory with respect to them. The simple account thus covers a relatively broad range of actions even in the case of the minimal polity—the core of a polity as such. In so doing it allows for a plausible distinction between acts that fulfill one's "political obligations" and potentially patriotic acts even in this case.[38]

In the minimal polity, the polity-constituting joint commitments are joint commitments to support and uphold particular political institutions. For present purposes, for the sake of a label, I shall refer to such joint commitments as political. Suppose, then, that we allow that a given person's *"political obligations"* are coextensive with those actions *he is required to perform by virtue of those political joint commitments to which he is a party.* The class of *patriotic actions* that are open to him will then be broader than the class of actions that fulfill his political obligations: They will include actions that are supererogatory in relation to a given political joint commitment. If one goes beyond the minimal polity, the class of patriotic actions will be even broader, on the simple account, since they may relate to polity-constituting joint commitments other than the political.

In spite of the relatively broad range of actions recognized as patriotic by the simple account one may yet have the following worry about it. If the basic patriotic motive is necessary for an act to be patriotic, it seems that one who does something in order to benefit his country may not have performed a patriotic act. He will not have done so if he is not at the same time acting in light of one or more polity-constituting joint commitments to which he is a party, in order to conform to them.

It is not clear that this result should be worrying. To say that an act is not specifically patriotic is not to say that it is bad. Nor is it to say that it is *un*patriotic.[39]

An action of the type being considered here may of course be quite admirable. And, as intended, it may be beneficial for the country concerned. That does not make it patriotic, intuitively.

Perhaps it will help to firm up the point to make it clear that someone may intend to benefit his country without, intuitively, acting *on its behalf.* Suppose, for instance, that Hilda, a wealthy business owner, sets up an educational foundation with the intention of helping the young people of her country more actively to participate in the political life of that country. From this description one might be inclined to judge that Hilda's action is a patriotic one. Yet surely we need to consider the motives that underlie it.

---

[38] My discussion of this point was prompted by a query from Primoratz.

[39] I say more about unpatriotic acts below.

Suppose her aim in life is to better the world wherever she can, whether by benefiting her own country, or another. She may have chosen to benefit her own country on the grounds that this is her best chance to make a difference in the world for the good. Her interest in benefiting her country may not be so impersonal. She may simply want to live somewhere with a more vibrant political culture. In none of these cases does she act specifically on behalf of her country. Nor, as far as her story has been told so far, is her act patriotic intuitively.

That said, there are several ways in which an act intended to benefit one's country will count as patriotic both intuitively and on the simple account. Intuitively, as noted earlier, to act on behalf of one's country is always to some extent to act in favor of it—or in behalf of it. And when someone acts in behalf of his country in this way, then all else being equal his act is patriotic on the simple account. His action may be mandated by the pertinent joint commitments, or it may be supererogatory. The case of Gina, above, fits the latter description—she fails to take perfectly legal steps to avoid estate taxes in order to support the political institutions of her polity, over and above the call of her political obligations. Such supererogatory acts may most clearly suggest benevolent intent. It seems wrong, however, to say that only such acts are patriotic intuitively.

Those seeking to benefit a polity by altering or abolishing some of its existing institutions, or adding to them, may be acting patriotically both intuitively and according to the simple account. They would be so acting if, for instance, they act in light of what they take to be a fundamental political value of their society that, in their opinion, requires the institutional change in question. In this way the actions of those who advocate reform and even relatively radical revolution may be patriotic.

In this context it is worth noting that explicitly *personal* protests against existing political institutions in favor of what the protestor personally conceives of as the good do not in and of themselves constitute a *failure* to conform to a joint commitment to support and uphold those institutions. Thus suppose we are jointly committed to uphold as a body a particular set of political institutions. If I say of one of our institutions, "I personally think it is unconscionable," I emphasize that I speak in my own name, as an individual, rather than as a party to the commitment. So I do not fail to conform to it.[40]

One is likely to feel more comfortable, however, if one is able to protest in the name of a relatively fundamental polity-constituting joint commitment. An important aspect of a protest of this kind is that it allows the protestor to align himself with his fellow-citizens and to minimize overt reliance on his personal judgment. One may think here of the title of Lysander Spooner's *The Unconstitutionality of Slavery*, and debates around its implicit claim.[41]

---

[40] See Gilbert (2006) for further discussion.
[41] Spooner (1845).

In concluding this section I recur to a question set aside earlier: how might one characterize an unpatriotic act in light of the foregoing discussion? In considering this question I start by considering two cases. In the first case, Ike deliberately fails to pay the taxes he should pay according to the laws of his country, consciously flouting polity-constituting joint commitments to which he is a party. He makes his decision not to pay these taxes without reference to any moral considerations, but as a matter of simple self-interest. Indeed, he thinks that these taxes are perfectly fair and otherwise unexceptionable. I take his action to be unpatriotic.

In the second case, Jürgen is considering an order to go out to fight in a particular war. As it happens, the moral character of this particular war is such that he ought not to fight in it though his doing so is required by the polity-constituting joint commitments to which he is a party. Jürgen realizes this, and on that basis refuses to obey the order. I would say that Jürgen's refusal is neither unpatriotic nor patriotic.

Consonant with the idea that it is *not unpatriotic* is the following consideration. Though there are issues about how legal systems should handle conscientious objection, both general and selective, such objection is not generally understood to undermine one's patriotism.

In judging Jürgen's refusal *not to be patriotic*—though not unpatriotic either— I have assumed that it was prompted by purely moral considerations. I would agree that someone's refusal to fight *was* intuitively patriotic if, for instance, it stems from his sincere belief that the war in question and his fighting in it falls foul of joint commitments that lie at the foundation of his polity—in spite of what the properly elected authorities have ordered. This judgment, of course, accords with the simple account of a patriotic act.

I take it that, should Jürgen decide to take whatever punishment his country metes out to him when he refuses to fight, and to do so on his country's behalf, his submission to this punishment would be patriotic. The same goes for Ike, with relevant changes. The laws of Athens suggest something like this in Plato's *Crito*, in which Socrates is urged by his friend Crito to flee Athens to avoid the death penalty, and the laws of Athens are imagined to respond with a variety of arguments against such flight (Plato 1978). The intuitive judgments in question here, also, accord with the simple account of a patriotic act.

I turn now to a third case, one that is significantly different from both of the previous ones. Consider Kai, who has gone into battle in his country's army when ordered to do so by the authorities. Overcome by panic born of fear, he flees from the battlefield, all the while berating himself for acting as he does, since he believes that all things considered flight is unwarranted for him in his position as a citizen. Though Kai's flight in panic is not a patriotic action, it is not clearly unpatriotic either.

For one thing, one might wonder if Kai's flight is truly an action. Certainly there is nothing deliberate about it. He has not coolly decided to leave the field. Indeed, he berates himself for his flight. There is clearly a tension within him and part of that tension, expressed in his self-castigation, is his understanding that he ought to stay and fight—to serve his country. The other part of that tension is contributed by his fearful state of panic, something he would prefer not to be in and that—we may assume—is beyond his current control.

Kai's case recalls the poem by Horace that includes the famous line *"dulce et decorum est, pro patria mori."* In rough translation, it immediately goes on: "Death also pursues the man who flees…".[42] Taken together the lines suggest the following: all else being equal, at least, standing and fighting on behalf of one's country is *more appropriate than fleeing the field of battle*—and is "sweet" insofar as one understands that one is indeed doing the appropriate thing. This is a thought that Kai endorses.[43]

How might one represent the gist of these three judgments on cases in characterizing an unpatriotic action? How might one rule in Ike's case while ruling out Jürgen's high-minded refusal and Kai's fearful flight? Something like the following ideal-typical account suggests itself:

> (U)One's act is *unpatriotic* if and only if, in performing it one intentionally fails to comply with the polity-constituting joint commitments to which one is a party, on grounds solely of personal inclination or self-interest, as such.

Note that one who is unpatriotic in the sense that (U) articulates acts contrary to the requirements of rationality. This, I take it, gives the concept of the unpatriotic an inherently negative aspect.

I have so far left out of consideration a case like Ike's but where the stakes are higher. This case deserves special attention.

Consider Larry: reflecting that that he is not prepared to risk death for his country, he ignores a letter ordering him to join the army to fight in an ongoing war and disappears into the countryside. Moral considerations play no role in his reasoning. He does not argue, for instance, that it would be morally wrong for anyone to lose his life in this war. Nor does he have any moral qualms about this war, bloody as it is. He acts purely on grounds of self-interest. Is his refusal to fight unpatriotic?

---

[42] In Latin: *"Mors et fugacem persequitur virum."*

[43] A different perspective, also reflected in Kai's case, is found in the poem *"Dulce et decorum est,"* written in the years 1917–1918 by British war poet Wilfrid Owen, who chronicles the horrors of life in the trenches in the First World War and ends with the line partially quoted in its title, which it introduces as "the old Lie" (Owen 1988, p. 50).

One who participates in a given set of polity-constituting joint commitments is faced with a consideration that trumps his self-interest, as such, in every case. Of course a given joint commitment may be hedged with provisos.[44] Assuming, then, that there are no pertinent provisos in the case in point, (U) would deem Larry unpatriotic.

This result accords with a nuanced discussion in which Michael Walzer allows that in a certain context one is obligated to risk one's life in war, and, if it comes to that, to "die for the state."[45] The context in question sounds very like that of participation in a polity-constituting joint commitment as I have characterized it here. Thus Walzer writes "up to some point in the history of his actions, he might have changed his mind. After that, he had 'spoken', and egotism was no longer his right." The egotism at issue here is that of one who chooses not to risk his life for his country.

I shall not attempt to say more about this case here. Suffice it to say that one who thinks that in a very high-stakes case such as that of Larry we cannot say that the person in question is unpatriotic could amend (U) accordingly.

Suppose, as seems plausible, that (U) or something like the variant just contemplated is more or less correct. The following hypothesis then suggests itself: the contrast between patriotic and unpatriotic acts is geared to distinguish between acts that appropriately rank one's polity-constituting joint commitments against one's inclinations and self-interest, as such, and acts that do not. This suggestion accords with the trumping hypothesis, mooted earlier, in relation to the concept of a patriotic act.

According to the trumping hypothesis, the intuitive concept of a patriotic act is geared in part at least to emphasize the trumping quality, from a rational point of view, of joint commitments over contrary inclinations and self-interested considerations as such. It now seems that can also be said of the intuitive concept of an unpatriotic act. Thus the patriotic act is one that respects the trumping power of polity-constituting joint commitments over contrary personal inclinations and self-interest as such; the unpatriotic act does the opposite, at least within certain limits.

If this is right, then once someone appeals to moral considerations and acts on the resulting all things considered judgment, we leave the territory divided between the concepts of the patriotic and the unpatriotic. The same is true when one's action involves no *intentional* subordination of inclinations and self-interest to the commitments or vice versa. Thus the concept of the unpatriotic makes a clear judgment on Ike the tax-evader's case, but does not claim for itself Jürgen's

---

[44] See Gilbert (2006, pp. 284f). for some further discussion.
[45] Walzer (1970, Chap. 4). The quotation in the text below is at p. 98.

high-minded refusal and Kai's fearful flight. The concept of the patriotic act, meanwhile, claims none of these.

Patriotic Persons

In light of the foregoing, how might one characterize a patriotic person or, for short, a patriot? My discussion of that question here will start with the following rough ideal-typical account of someone I shall refer to as the "rational" patriot.

> (RP)One is a *rational patriot* in relation to one's country C, if and only if one acts, or is disposed to act, in order to comply with the joint commitments constitutive of C, insofar as, in one's own sincere judgment, one is rationally required to do so, all things considered.[46]

In this section I show how several different kinds of patriot may be characterized in relation to the rational patriot.

First, some clarificatory notes on the account of a rational patriot are in order. It speaks not of a patriotic person, period, but of a person who is patriotic in relation to a given country. In principle, one may call two different countries one's own—consider the case of the dual citizen. In principle, at least, one could be patriotic in relation to one of these countries and fail to be patriotic in relation to the other. Indeed, if there is an enduring conflict between the countries one may regularly be forced to act on behalf of one rather than the other, making what may seem to be an invidious choice. For the sake of simplicity, in the discussion that follows, I shall suppose that a given person has just one country he may call his own, and that the question whether he is patriotic or not concerns his patriotism in relation to that country.

Second, the rational patriot is assumed to understand that one's joint commitments generally trump one's personal inclinations and self-interest, as such, from the point of view of what rationality requires one to do, though it may be that all things considered one ought not to conform to a given joint commitment. Further, the sincere judgments of such a patriot on what he ought to do in the situations he is in conforms to that understanding, and he is disposed to act as he then understands is rationally required of him.

In the rest of this section I explain how several different kinds of patriot may be characterized in relation to the rational patriot.

---

[46] It would not be unreasonable to define a "good citizen" in the same way. I think, though, that "good citizen" may often implicitly be defined differently. For instance, this phrase may be defined in terms of *actual conformity* to laws and so on, rather than by reference to *motive*. Here I respond to Primoratz (personal communication, 2008).

John Quincy Adams might have approved of the patriotism of the rational patriot in terms of its moral soundness. For he wrote: "I disclaim as unsound all patriotism incompatible with the principles of eternal justice."[47] Possibly, however, he would have had his qualms about the account because of its emphasis on subjective factors.

Suppose one refuses to fight on behalf of one's country in a particular war because one believes that moral considerations are such that all things considered one should not fight in that war. What if one's all things considered judgment is wrong? What if one's "weighing" of the considerations involved is in fact self-serving?

The reference to *sincere* judgment in the account of a rational patriot is intended to rule out self-serving judgments. Meanwhile, one can usefully distinguish between what I shall call *wise* rational patriots and *unwise* rational patriots. To give an account of the former:

> (WRP) One is a *wise* rational patriot if and only if one is a rational patriot whose pertinent sincere all things considered judgments are correct.

Though few may satisfy the conditions of this ideal-typical account, many will do so to some extent.

Someone might wonder how many rational patriots there are. Though one's actions may regularly be required given the set of polity-constituting joint commitments to which one is a party, it seems possible that these commitments rarely figure in one's reasoning about what to do. One may regularly pay one's taxes out of habit, for instance. Or one may have in the forefront of one's mind that one does not wish to lay oneself open to a spell locked up in jail. Such things may be true of many of those actions that conform to a given agent's polity-constituting joint commitments.[48]

Mere conformity to such commitments is not, I would judge, enough to make a person patriotic. In cases such as those described, however, it may be that one would retrieve the fact of one's joint commitments, were one moved to act contrary to them, and then would act as would any rational patriot. Thus the person paying his taxes with the thought that he does not want to go to jail, when apprised of the fact that he is most unlikely to be caught, may reflect that

[47] J. Quincy Adams, letter to his father, quoted in Allison (2005, p. 184). Adams is said to be responding to U.S. Commodore Stephen Decatur's famous (or infamous) toast in 1816 that begins "Our country..." and includes the words "right or wrong." I have been unable to find an indubitably accurate quotation of this toast, which is reported differently in different locations that I have checked. It is often quoted as "My country, right or wrong!" but, apart from the substitution of 'My" for "Our" this is not clearly correct.

[48] The discussion in this paragraph is indebted to Barry Shreiar.

he cannot in any case refrain from paying his taxes, in spite of the personal cost of not doing so, since "These are our laws after all."

This type of person, it might be said, is as much of a rational patriot as he needs to be, for practical purposes. In light of this judgment one might want to amend the account of a rational patriot accordingly. Or one can simply note that the account given is ideal-typical, and that some people whom one would reasonably count as patriotic approximate its conditions in the way just indicated.

By definition, to be a rational patriot one need not act above and beyond what he sees as *required* by the pertinent joint commitments, all else being equal. A given person may act or be disposed to act in ways he sees as either required or supererogatory with respect to such commitments, insofar as, in his own sincere judgment, he is rationally permitted to do so. One might label such a person a rational *super-patriot*.

I now consider some further cases in which it is likely to seem that we are faced with patriots of a kind. The first can appositely be introduced with some famous words from Thomas Paine in 1776: "These are the times that try men's souls. The summer soldier and the sunshine patriot will, in this crisis, shrink from the service of his country; but he that stands it now deserves the thanks of every man and woman."[49] What is it to be a "sunshine" patriot? Whatever precisely Paine had in mind I focus here on Alex, who understands that, all else being equal, he ought to act as required by the polity-constituting joint commitments to which he is a party, where his contrary inclinations or self-interest do not alter the situation, and he frequently performs patriotic acts. Whenever he personally faces a less than trivial loss, however, he fails to act as required by the joint commitments. As Paine puts it, he "shrinks" from the service of his country.

Is Alex a patriot? I do not mean to press the case either way for his status as a patriot of sorts. Certainly if he is a patriot, his is a distinctively flawed type. He is an exaggerated version of Kai, the soldier who flees from the battlefield all the while berating himself. We can assume, indeed, that Alex is inclined to berate himself for his shrinking, since he understands the irrationality of the pertinent actions. One might refer to him, then, as an *akratic* patriot.

Someone who surely is a patriot, though of another distinctively flawed kind, is one who is not only disposed to act as required by the polity-constituting joint commitments to which he is a party, whether or not such action conflicts with his inclinations and self-interest as such, but is also disposed to act as so required *even when all things considered he ought to act otherwise.*

As my discussion of patriotic acts indicated, this description subsumes more than one type of case. Here I focus on the case of Belle, who makes it a rule to comply with any pertinent polity-constituting joint commitments whatever else

[49] Paine (2004, p. 3).

is true. She therefore fails to act appropriately when the moral situation is such that all things considered she should not act on a given polity-constituting joint commitment. Belle and those like her are a species of *blinkered* patriot.

It is worth emphasizing here that though rationality requires one to honor one's joint commitments *all else being equal,* it does not require one to honor them *whatever else is true.* One may be *committed* through such a commitment to do what the designated authorities tell one to do; one may *owe* it to them or to one's fellow citizens to do so, in the sense of "owe" most closely pertinent to joint commitments, yet—taking morality into account—rationality may require one not to do so, all things considered.[50] Thus blinkered patriots of Belle's type are also *irrational* patriots.

As is clear from this brief discussion, those who may be deemed patriots of a kind come in a variety of guises. In concluding this section I focus on the rational patriots. When they are wise, they will do no more than fulfill those obligations, political and otherwise, that are imposed upon them by the polity-constituting joint commitments to which they are parties, when all else is equal. Yet doing "no more than" this may be doing a great deal *pro patria.* They and those who approximate them—along with any wise and rational super-patriots in their midst—surely are the mainstay of a good polity.

What of their contribution to a bad polity? The wise rational patriot will only support and uphold a given polity-constituting joint commitment if he ought to, all things considered. The considerations for and against such support, meanwhile, are likely to be complex. For instance, the only alternative to a particular, bad set of political institutions in a given context may be something far worse. In the imperfect world we have, then, bad and relatively bad political societies may often be supported by the actions of their wise patriots, acting as they should, all things considered.

Patriotism and Pride

Before concluding, I relate what I have said so far to the connection that is often made between patriotism and pride. It seems often to be supposed that a patriotic person will be proud of his country. I take this to be close, but not equivalent to, the idea that he will ascribe to his country one or more virtues or achievements.

I take it not to be *equivalent* for the following reason. One might ascribe virtues to a country not one's own, as one might in some sense of the term love another

---

[50] Cf. Oldenquist (2002, p. 34), discussing the "loyalty patriot:" "To a loyalist, the thought, 'P is my country,' though it counts for something, need not outweigh moral arguments against reprisal or military intervention."

country. Thus one encounters United States citizens who are self-confessed "anglo-philes"—persons, according to one dictionary, who are fond of or greatly admire England and things English. It is not clear indeed, that there are any conceptual restrictions on who or even what one can think well of or in some sense love. Pride is different in this respect. If I witness a neighbor's daughter executing a perfect dive, I would need to explain why I commented: "I am so proud of her." There would be no such need to explain if the young woman were my own daughter.

Intuitively, if a country is my country then surely no conceptual barrier is stepped over when I say that I am proud of it or of some of its deeds. One might see this as predictable since after all the country is "mine." Nonetheless it makes sense to ask how it can be that pride is a proper response on my part to my country's stellar achievements—to elaborate my relationship to the country that I am entitled to call mine—and "ours." Even Astrid, an invalid who stayed at home while her country's army won an important battle against an aggressor, is apparently in a position to say, with pride, that "we" won the battle, including herself in the referent of "we."

The joint commitment account of a country that I have sketched here offers a way of understanding the propriety of Astrid's pride in this connection. Astrid can be included in the "we" because and insofar as she is a party to the joint commitments that are constitutive of the country in question. To that extent she is, in J.-J. Rousseau's terms, an "indivisible part of the whole."[51]

Quite generally, it seems that if I am in a position to say that "we" have done, realized, judged, valued, sought—and so on—something, I am in a position to feel pride over this doing, realizing and so on. The joint commitment account of such assertions offers a way to explain this.

There are, I think, good reasons for not insisting that, by definition, a *patriot* is proud of his country. For one thing, someone may not be given to pride, on his own account or on account of anything. Perhaps pride would be appropriate in his own case or in another case, perhaps that of his country. He simply does not feel pride in these cases. If he otherwise passes the bar as a patriot, it would seem wrong to deny him that label on account of his lack of pride in his country, however, fine it is.

More to the point, perhaps, one's country may be such that pride is not an appropriate attitude toward it, given its attributes and actions. It may not be evil, corrupt, or degenerate, it may simply be so-so—or good enough. It may have its merits, but it may have significant flaws. Depending on its actions, what it does may merit not pride but shame, guilt, or remorse, or, simply, lack of pride.[52]

---

[51] Rousseau (1983), p. 23 (Book I, Chap. 6, "On the Social Compact").

[52] On feeling guilt over what one's group, including one's country, has done, see Gilbert (1997). On feeling remorse, see Gilbert (2000).

Understanding that "something is rotten in the state of Denmark," Hamlet may be disappointed, angry, yet still be disposed to action on behalf of his country, when the occasion arises, if that is how he ought to act all things considered.[53] This, he understands, is his country—whether or not it is a proper object of pride at this moment, or ever has been. I propose that his not being proud of his country has no tendency to justify refusal to call him a patriot.

Concluding Remarks

Many people are inclined to understand patriotism in terms of love or pride, or the ascription of virtue to one's country. That said, there is dispute as to precisely what patriotism is and whether or not it is a good thing.

I have outlined a perspective on patriotic acts and persons that makes no definitional appeal to love, pride, or ascriptions of virtue. It is grounded in a particular, precise account of what it is for a country to be one's own. On this account, several forms of patriotism are possible. In some forms, patriotism does not recommend itself from a rational point of view and is hardly a good thing. In other forms it is.

Acknowledgments

Warm thanks to Cruz Cervantes, Angela Conyers, Mark Fiocco, Cara Gillis, Sean Greenberg, Casey Hall, Elizabeth Hirst, Aaron James, Nicholas Jolley, David Malament and Alice Silverberg for discussion, to Angelo Corlett, Simon Keller and Barry Shreiar for written comments on a draft of the chapter, and to Chad Kidd for research assistance. Thanks also to Igor Primoratz for his invitation to contribute to the issue of *The Journal of Ethics,* in which this chapter first appeared, and for helpful comments on a late draft. This is the first time I have approached the rich topic of patriotism. I have focused on sketching a perspective that is suggested by my prior work on the related topics of social groups in general, political obligation, and collective moral responsibility.

[53] The quotation is from *Hamlet,* Act I, Scene 4, line 90 (Shakespeare 1998, p. 84). The speaker is Marcellus. Hamlet has the same sense of things.

References

Allison, Robert J. 2005. *Stephen Decatur: American naval hero, 1779–1820.* Boston: University of Massachusetts Press.

Broome, John. 1992. Are intentions reasons? And how should we cope with incommensurable values? In *Practical rationality and preference: Essays for David Gauthier,* ed. C.W. Morris, and A. Ripstein. Cambridge: Cambridge University Press, 98–120.

Feinberg, Joel. 1970. The nature and value of rights. *Journal of Value Inquiry* 4: 243–257.

Gilbert, Margaret. 1989. *On social facts.* Princeton: Princeton University Press.

Gilbert, Margaret. 1996. *Living together: Rationality, sociality, and obligation.* Lanham: Rowman and Littlefield.

Gilbert, Margaret. 1997. Group wrongs and guilt feelings. *The Journal of Ethics* 1: 65–84.

Gilbert, Margaret. 2000. *Sociality and responsibility: New essays in plural subject theory.* Lanham: Rowman and Littlefield.

Gilbert, Margaret. 2003. The structure of the social atom. In *Socializing Metaphysics,* ed. F. Schmitt. Lanham: Rowman and Littlefield, 39–64.

Gilbert, Margaret. 2004. Scanlon on promissory obligation: The problem of promisees' rights. *The Journal of Philosophy* 101: 83–109. [Chapter 12, this volume.]

Gilbert, Margaret. 2006. *A theory of political obligation: Membership, commitment, and the bonds of society.* Oxford: Clarendon Press.

Gilbert, Margaret. 2007. Searle on collective intentions. In *Intentional acts and institutional facts: Essays on John Searle's social ontology,* ed. Savas Tsohatzidis. Dordrecht: Springer, pp. 31–48

Gilbert, Martin. 2004. *The first world war: A complete history.* New York: Macmillan.

Habermas, Jürgen. 1992. Citizenship and national identity: Some reflections on the future of Europe. *Praxis International* 12: 1–19.

Hart, H.L.A. 1955. Are there any natural rights? *The Philosophical Review* 64: 175–191.

Horace (Quintus Horatius Flaccus). 1901. *Odes and epodes.* Boston and Chicago: Allyn and Bacon.

Ingram, Attracta. 2002. Constitutional patriotism. In *Patriotism,* ed. Igor Primoratz, Amherst-Humanities Books, 217–232.

Keller, Simon. 2005. Patriotism as bad faith. *Ethics* 115: 563–592.

Lewis, David K. 1969. *Convention. A philosophical study.* Oxford: Basil Blackwell.

Nash, Ogden. 1938. *I'm a stranger here myself.* New York: Little Brown and Co.

Oldenquist, Andrew. 2002. Loyalties. In *Patriotism,* ed. Igor Primoratz. Amherst: Humanities Books, 26–42.

Owen, Wilfred. 1988. Dulce et decorum est. In *Wilfrid Owen Selected Poetry and Prose,* ed. Jennifer Breen, New York: Routledge, 50.

Paine, Thomas. 2004. *The American crisis.* Whitefish, Montana: Kessinger Publications.

Plato. 1974. *Republic* (trans: Grube, G.M.E.). Indianapolis: Hackett.

Plato. 1978. Crito. In *The collected dialogues of Plato,* ed. E. Hamilton and H. Cairns. Princeton: Princeton University Press.

Primoratz, Igor. 2002a. Introduction. In *Patriotism,* ed. Igor Primoratz. Amherst: Humanities Books, 9–24.

Primoratz, Igor. 2002b. Patriotism: Morally allowed, required, or valuable? In *Patriotism,* ed. Igor Primoratz. Amherst: Humanities Books, 187–200.

Rousseau, Jean-Jacques. 1983. *The social contract and discourses* (trans: Cress, D.A.). Indianapolis: Hackett.

Searle, John. 1990. Collective intentions and actions. In *Intentions and communication,* ed. P.R. Cohen, J. Morgan, and M.E. Pollack. Cambridge: MIT Press, 401–415.

Shakespeare, William. 1900. *The life of King Henry the Fifth.* Oxford: Clarendon Press.

Shakespeare, William. 1998. *Hamlet.* New York: Oxford University Press.

Spooner, Lysander. 1845. *The unconstitutionality of slavery.* Boston: Bela Marsh.

Sreenivasan, Gopal. 2005. A hybrid theory of claim rights. *Oxford Journal of Legal Studies* 25: 257–274.

Verbeek, Bruno. 2008. Rational self-commitment. In *Rationality and commitment*, ed. Fabienne Peter and Hans-Bernard Schmid. Oxford: Oxford University Press., 150–174.

Walzer, Michael. 1970. *Obligations: Essays on disobedience, war, and citizenship*. Cambridge: Harvard University Press.

Walzer, Michael. 2002. Civility and civic virtue in contemporary America. In *Patriotism*, ed. Igor Primoratz. Amherst: Humanities Books, 259–272.

17

De-Moralizing Political Obligation[1]

Introduction

The *problem of political obligation* goes back at least as far as Plato's *Crito*. It is generally put in the form of a question. It is commonly understood that the *problem* is this: though many people incline toward a positive answer, it is hard to find grounds for such an answer.[2]

Here is the version on which I shall focus:

Does one have an obligation to support the political institutions of one's own country in particular—and if so, what precisely is the ground of this obligation?[3] In short, are there *political obligations*?[4]

[1] This chapter draws on Margaret Gilbert, *A Theory of Political Obligation: Membership, Commitment and the Bonds of Society* (Oxford: Oxford University Press, 2006), reprinted in paperback in 2008 with some revisions, and can serve as an introduction to the argument of that book. It focuses on the kind of *obligation* invoked in the book's account of political obligation, comparing and contrasting it with the kind of obligation commonly invoked in discussions of the topic. The first version was discussed at a panel on political obligation at the 2007 Annual Meeting of the American Political Science Association in Chicago, the other panelists being George Klosko, Mara Marin, and Jeremy Waldron. Later versions were discussed at a seminar on political theory at Nuffield College, Oxford, in 2009 and a political science colloquium at Stanford University in 2010. The comments received on these occasions were much appreciated. Thanks to Maura Priest for comments on a late draft. Responses to some extended comments can be found in Margaret Gilbert, "A Theory of Political Obligation: Responses to Horton, Jeske, Narveson and Stoutland", forthcoming in *Jurisprudence: An International Journal of Legal and Political Thought*. This chapter contains explicit or implicit responses to some other commentators, including David Miller and David Lefkowitz.

[2] "Many people incline...." See Gilbert, *Political Obligation*: 6; also, on the significance of this, Margaret Gilbert, "Group Membership and Political Obligation," *Monist* 76, (1993), reprinted in Margaret Gilbert, *Living Together: Rationality, Sociality, and Obligation*, (Latham, MD: Rowman and Littlefield, 1996), citing A. John Simmons, *Moral Principles and Political Obligations* (Princeton, NJ: Princeton University Press, 1979).

[3] This question is open to more precise specification at a number of points. I indicate a number of places where such specification is in order in the course of my discussion.

[4] I should emphasize that I mean here to introduce the sense of the phrase "political obligations" *as I shall understand it in this chapter.* As will emerge, others tend to interpret it more narrowly in their writings.

I have intentionally left the qualifier "moral" out of this formulation. The existence and nature of political obligations of *any* sort should be of interest.

In saying this I assume that, having an *obligation*, one has—at a minimum—sufficient reason to fulfill it. As I intend the phrase, one has *sufficient reason* to do something if from a rational point of view one must do it, at least if there are no considerations on the other side. "Rational" and related terms are here used in a broad, intuitive sense—not in the sense of game-theory or the theory of "rational choice."

I speak here of what one might call *genuine* as opposed to imputed obligations. *Imputed* obligations as I understand these are obligations stipulated within a system of rules, such as a legal system. A system of rules as such is an abstract object. The practical relevance of imputed obligations to a given person depends on that person's relation to the system of rules in question. In other words, given only that a certain obligation is imputed to me by a certain system of rules, it is not yet clear that I have sufficient reason to fulfill that obligation.[5]

Some may think that moral obligation is the only kind of genuine obligation. That depends, of course, on what moral obligation is. Assuming a standard construal of "moral obligation"—to be discussed below—I believe that *there is a central kind of obligation other than moral obligation such that if one is so obligated, one has sufficient reason to fulfill the obligation.* In other words, I believe that there are genuine obligations other than moral obligations.

In focusing on a "de-moralized" problem of political obligation, I do not mean to downplay the importance of the following version:

> Does one have a moral obligation to support the political institutions of one's own country in particular—and if so, what precisely is the ground of such obligation?

This, or something like it, is the way the problem of political obligation is generally put.[6] In particular, it is generally couched in terms of moral obligations. I hope to show that much is lost if the *only* version of the problem considered is moralized in this way.

In what follows I first distinguish two significantly different kinds of obligation or, if you like, different senses of the term "obligation." I then focus on the second kind of obligation and briefly outline my positive theory of political obligation, which invokes it.[7] Finally, I explain how the theory handles the situation in which the political institutions in question are morally bad.

---

[5] On imputed obligations see Gilbert, *Political Obligation*. A variety of considerations may of course give one reason to conform to imputed obligations in a given case.

[6] See Gilbert, *Political Obligation*, 18–25 for discussion of four different ways of delimiting the problem. As noted there, it is generally addressed as a moral question.

[7] Gilbert, *Political Obligation*, offers an extended development of this theory that includes replies to various objections to the theory as previously expounded including those of A. J. Simmons in

Two kinds of obligation

When people speak of "obligations" they may have one of two very different things in mind.

i. Obligation as moral requirement

Suppose a political philosopher says:

(1) "One has an obligation to support just political institutions."

He might alternatively use the word "duty" instead of "obligation." I focus on obligations in this chapter but the points made about them carry over, *mutatis mutandis*, to duties.

The speaker may well be ready to preface "obligation" here with the adjective "moral." Let us assume this is so. Indeed, he may well be ready to rephrase the point in terms of *moral requirement*, as follows:

(1a) "One is morally required to support just political institutions."

To be more precise (though in a vague manner) he might preface this with "all else being equal." That is, he may not wish to argue that *whatever the circumstances* one is morally required to support just institutions.

I do not have a theory of moral requirements to offer, but will make two points I take partially to characterize such requirements as it is common to understand them, and as I shall understand them here.

First, that I am morally required to do something is a fact about me as opposed to me and some other person or persons. In other terms, I am the one upon whom the burden of this requirement falls. Of course, someone else may figure in the *content* of the requirement, as when I am required *to benefit you* in some way. Indeed, some may think such "other-relatedness" is an essential aspect of a specifically *moral* requirement. That particular issue is beside the present point.

Second, though people may sometimes say it is obvious that a particular moral requirement exists, it is common to argue on behalf of such a requirement by invoking some value that will be promoted by conformity to it. For example, Thomas Scanlon has defended a particular moral principle of fidelity

"Associative Political Obligations," *Ethics* 106 (1996). Precursors to that book-length treatment include Margaret Gilbert, *On Social Facts* (London: Routledge and Kegan Paul, 1989): 415–416; Gilbert, "Group Membership"; Margaret Gilbert, "Reconsidering the 'Actual Contract' Theory of Political Obligation," *Ethics* 109 (1999).

by reference to the value of "assurance."[8] The values in question will themselves fall within a limited range—hence people distinguish between moral values and, say, aesthetic values. Precisely how that distinction is to be articulated is not pertinent here.

ii. Obligation as owing

Moral philosophers commonly allow that:

> (2) All else being equal, at least, one who makes a promise (for short, a *promisor*), has an obligation to do what he (or she) promised to do.

It is common to allow that this can be expanded as follows:

> (2a) All things being equal, at least, a promisor has an obligation to the person to whom he made the promise (his *promisee*) to do what he promised to do.

The obligation in question is an obligation "to" or "toward" someone. In this case, it is an obligation to the promisee. "Obligations to" particular people, or to people in general are often referred to as "directed obligations," and I shall sometimes follow this practice.

It is common to allow that the following statement is equivalent in meaning to (2a):

> (2a*) All things being equal, at least, a promisor owes his promisee his (i.e. the promisor's) performance of the promised act.

And that equivalent to (2a*) (and (2a) of course) is this:

> (2a**) All things being equal, at least, a promisee has a (claim-) right against his promisor to the promisor's performance of the promised act.[9]

I return now to (2a*): All things being equal, at least, a promisor owes his promisee performance of the promised act. My general focus in what follows is

---

[8] Thomas Scanlon, *What We Owe to Each Other* (Cambridge, MA: Harvard, 1998) and elsewhere.

[9] In a famous essay, H.L.A. Hart relates owing to (directed) obligation, on the one hand, and to rights against others, on the other. See H. L. A. Hart, "Are There any Natural Rights?" *Philosophical Review* 64 (1955). All of the relevant terms are susceptible of different interpretations—and have received them in the literature. In the next section of the text, below, I address the interpretation of "owing."

on *owing* in the sense in which a promisor, all things being equal, at least, owes his promisee performance of the act he has promised. I refer to owing *in this sense* in order to help pin down the sense of "owing" in question, since as it is used at this point in time the term "owing" is ambiguous.[10]

A word should be added about the prefatory "All things being equal, at least" in (2) through (2a*). There has been debate over whether *all* promisors owe their promisees the promised act. The present point is not affected if one allows that this may not be so in some circumstances, as these formulations are intended to do.[11]

The first thing to note about owing—in the sense now in question—is that, contrary to what may generally be supposed, *it not obviously a matter of moral requirement*. This point can be elaborated slightly as follows.

My being morally required to do something is a fact about me, as opposed to a fact about me and some other person or persons. In contrast, I cannot simply "owe" the performance of some action. I must owe its performance to someone. Owing, in other terms, is a matter of relationship. In what I take to be the central case, on which I shall focus, my owing is a fact about me and some other person—you, for instance.[12] Possibly this fact about me and you can be built up out of a moral requirement on me plus some further facts, including facts about you, but that it can is not obvious on the face of it.

Again, the way to argue that I owe you an action is not obviously the same as the way one would argue that I am morally required to perform that action. In the case where I promised you that action, you would most likely say, simply: "You promised", and this would suffice. Your statement does not seem to appeal to any value, explicitly or implicitly. Meanwhile, as we have seen, a standard way to argue for the existence of a given moral requirement is by reference to a particular value or values that it promotes.

It is true that when they offer explanations of promissory obligation philosophers often cite some value that is promoted by promise-keeping, or some interest that is well and appropriately served by it. That they do this does not show that any such appeal is necessary in order to explain that the promisor owes fulfillment of the promise to the promisee.

The primary aim of these philosophers, I take it, is to justify the claim that—all else being equal, at least—one is morally required to act as promised. They may see this as a way of showing that one owes fulfillment of the promise to

---

[10] Cf. Frances Kamm "Owing, Justifying, Rejecting," *Mind* 111 (2002) on Scanlon's use of "owe" in *What We Owe*. Kamm takes this not to be the sense that connotes a correlative right.

[11] See chapter 13, this volume, for discussion of the point that every promisor is obligated to perform his promise.

[12] The contrast to what I take to be the central case is "owing to oneself." Cf. Gilbert, *Political Obligation*: 153–155 (the paperback version, 2008, revises this passage slightly).

the promisee. Whether it is a way of showing this or not is the question now at issue.[13]

There are, then, at least the following *differences* between the two kinds of obligation at issue—my being *morally required* to perform a certain action and my *owing* another person that action. My being morally required is a fact about me as opposed to me and some specified other person, and it is typically argued for by appeal to some value or values—an appeal that is, I shall assume, called for. My owing is a fact about me and the other person in question, and there seems to be no need to appeal to values in justifying its existence.

At the same time, my being morally required and my owing have at least the following important things *in common*. In the case of *both* moral requirement *and* owing one has sufficient reason to do a certain thing: what one is morally required to do, in the first case; and what one owes another, in the second case. Someone might suggest that your owing him an action only gives you sufficient reason to do it because owing is a matter of moral requirement. That is at best not clear. What is clear is that my owing him an action does, intuitively, give me sufficient reason to perform that action, while my being morally required to perform that action has the same effect. Whether the first point is true because the second is true remains to be seen.

In both cases an obligation of the kind in question may run counter to one's personal inclinations or self-interest, and be decisive with respect to what one is rationally required to do. If in a given instance one is morally required, all things considered, to act in ways that are contrary to one's inclinations, that is presumably decisive with respect to what one is rationally required to do. One's owing someone an action contrary to one's inclinations is not an "all things considered" matter. It does not take one's inclinations "into account". At the same time by virtue of what it is, it surely trumps one's inclinations, as such, in terms of what one is rationally required to do.

Importantly, the fact that I owe someone an action may be conjoined with the fact that I am morally required—all things considered—*not* to give that person what I owe him. Plato made this possibility clear at the beginning of the *Republic*, with his example of the man who demands the return of the weapon he left in someone's safe-keeping before he went mad.[14] Assuming, as we may, that the person who has the weapon owes its return to the man who is mad, morality requires him not to return it. I return to this point in the last section of this chapter.

---

[13] This paragraph and the preceding one added in response to a comment from Maura Priest.
[14] Plato, *Republic*, Book I.

Two problems of political obligation

I have argued that there are at least two radically different kinds of obligation to which allusions are made in our discourse. I have referred to them as moral requirement, on the one hand, and owing, on the other. They allow for at least two radically different versions of the problem of political obligation mooted at the outset of this chapter. These problems are:

(1) Is one morally required to support the political institutions of one's own country in particular? If so, what grounds this moral requirement?

(2) Does one owe it to any (other) person or persons to support the political institutions of one's own country in particular? If so, what grounds one's owing such support to this person or these persons?

In both cases, one may think that the answer will depend on the answers to various further questions such as, in the case of (1): Are the institutions just? In the case of (2): Has one done something to bring it about that one owes it to someone to support these institutions? Has one made a pertinent promise, for instance?

It is possible, however, that in the case of (1) or (2), or both, the question itself contains the material for an answer. In particular, it may be that *the fact that a country is one's own* is argument enough for the moral requirement or the owing in question.

This opens the question, "What is it for a country to be one's own?" Surprisingly, this question has received scant attention in the contemporary literature on political obligation. Having developed an answer to it, I have argued elsewhere for a positive solution to the problem of political obligation as originally posed, in the form of a positive answer to problem (2), above. Among the important consequences of this argument is, most likely, a qualified positive answer to problem (1).

En route to briefly setting out my argument and considering some of its consequences, below, I say more about my understanding of owing and its provenance.

Owing

As I indicated earlier, it is common to see all of the following as equivalent in terms of their meaning:

(1)   X owes Y his (X's) phi-ing;

(2)   X is obligated to Y to phi;

(3)   Y has a (claim-) right against X to X's phi-ing.

One might think, then, that rights theory, and in particular the theory of claim-rights, is the place to look in order to learn what it is for one person to owe another an action, in the sense of "owing" at issue. As far as the currently prevailing theories are concerned, however, this is not the case. I shall not attempt to argue this at length here, but make a few pertinent points.[15]

Rights theorists generally see claim-rights as divided exhaustively into legal or other institutional rights and moral rights. Since it appears to be the most relevant here, I focus on the moral part of the discussion. Here theorists tend to start with the obligation side of things, understanding directed obligation in terms of moral requirement. More precisely, for me to have a certain directed obligation is a matter of my being subject to a particular moral requirement, all else being equal, plus whatever bells and whistles a particular theorist adds to the picture.[16]

A given theorist may or may not be concerned with the sense of "owe" at issue here. In any case, I believe that the existing moral requirement accounts fail to capture that sense, and that there is reason to think that all such accounts will fail in this way.[17]

My general problem with such accounts—in connection with the pertinent concept of owing—can be made more precise in terms of a further explication of that concept. To anticipate: I do not see how moral requirement accounts of claim-rights can account for an important aspect of the matter.

The further explication is this: to say that I owe you an action of mine that I have yet to perform is to say that you have the standing to *demand* of me that I perform it, should it appear that I am not going to do so. You are also in a

---

[15] There is a lengthy discussion in a monograph on rights that I am currently preparing to be published by Oxford University Press. For some related discussion see Margaret Gilbert "Giving Claim-Rights Their Due" in *Rights: Concepts and Contexts*, eds. B. Bix and H. Spector, (Ashgate: Farnham, Surrey, 2012).

[16] The dominant contemporary theories or types of theory, in this connection, are "benefit" or "interest" theories and "will" or "choice" theories. See e.g. Gilbert, "Claim-Rights".

[17] See Margaret Gilbert, "Scanlon on promissory obligation: the problem of promisees' rights," *Journal of Philosophy* 101 (2004) [chapter 12, this volume].This criticizes in particular two different moral requirement accounts: Raz's interest theory of rights, and the theory implicit in Scanlon's account of promissory obligation (a moral requirement on the promisor is conditional on the putative right-holder's failure to "consent" to non-performance). M. Thomson, "What Is it to Wrong Someone? A Puzzle About Justice" in R. Wallace, P. Pettit, S. Scheffler and M. Smith (eds), *Reason and Value: Themes from the Philosophy of Joseph Raz*, (Oxford: Clarendon Press, 2004), criticizes Raz's theory from a somewhat different angle, while his criticism appears to be more tentative than my own.

position to *rebuke* me for non-performance, a rebuke being understood here as an after-the-fact demand.

Here, clearly, I am concerned with a sense of the term "demand" such that it is not the case that everyone is in a position to address any demand he likes to any other person, the same going for the pertinent sense of the term" rebuke." One needs a special standing or authority in order to issue demands or rebukes in these senses. Such standing or authority, again, is not a matter of *justification* moral or otherwise. It has to do with whether or not one is *in a position* to issue a demand or rebuke—whether or not such demanding or rebuking would be justified.

In order further to explicate the concept of owing at issue here I now add the following equivalent to the list beginning with "X owes Y his (X's) phi-ing."

(4) Y has the standing to demand of X that he phi—and to rebuke X for not phi-ing

Are there other equivalences that will further help to explicate our understanding of owing? Without emphasizing the point, Joel Feinberg has suggested that for someone to demand an action one has a right to is him to demand that action as *his*.[18] Clearly, in order to be helpful in the further explanation of owing, one cannot explain "demanding as his" as "demanding as what he has a right to." Clearly, too, one cannot explain "his" as "an action he will perform."

For now I set aside this possible line of development of the idea of owing. I return to it briefly later.

Joint commitment as a source of owing, rights, directed obligation

It can be argued that a future action of mine is owed to you if we are parties to a given *joint commitment*. There follows a brief account of joint commitment with special reference to matters pertinent to the present topic.[19]

I start with an example of a non-joint commitment.[20] One who makes a personal decision, for instance, thereby *commits himself* to a certain course of action, thus creating (I shall say) a *personal* commitment. This commitment may aptly be referred to as a *commitment of the will*. It is "of the will" in two senses.

---

[18] Joel Feinberg, "The Nature and Value of Rights," *Journal of Value Inquiry* 4 (1970): 251.

[19] For a longer treatment see, e.g. Gilbert, *Political Obligation*, 127f, Margaret Gilbert, "Considerations on Joint Commitment", in Georg Meggle ed. *Social Facts and Collective Intentionality*, (Frankfurt: Hansel-Hohenhausen, 2002) [chapter 2, this volume.].

[20] For a longer treatment see, e.g. Gilbert, *Political Obligation*, 127f.

A personal decision is in some sense *an act of the will* of the person in question, and it has the effect of *binding* that person's will, at least in the sense that his will is no longer free from the point of view of what rationality requires. For, by deciding, I give myself sufficient reason—in the sense articulated earlier—to act in the way I decided to act. I have the option of changing my mind, but unless and until I do so, the points just made stand.[21]

By deciding, then, I achieve some measure of control over my future, given that I am sensitive to the demands of reason. Precisely how I do this is an important question whose answer depends on precisely what a decision is. I set this question aside here.

I turn now to joint commitment. I focus on what I call the basic case and, within that class, on cases where there are no special background understandings.[22]

A joint commitment is also a commitment of the will, in this case of two or more wills. A joint commitment is jointly created by two or more people. *All commit all.* Similarly, all must participate in the rescission of the joint commitment.

Each of those who are jointly committed is himself committed: as far as the commitment side of things goes, once the joint commitment has been made, his situation is much like that of one who has made a personal decision. The difference, with respect to this side of things, is that no one can unilaterally free himself from the constraints of commitment. One may, of course, act contrary to the commitment, assuming one has the physical power to do so. If one does, however, he is open to criticism in more ways than one, as I discuss below.

People *form* joint commitments by expressing to one another their readiness jointly to commit one another in the relevant way, these expressions being common knowledge among the people concerned. For present purposes "It is common knowledge that p between persons X and Y, or among the so-and-so" can be construed, roughly, as "It is entirely out in the open between X and Y, or among the so-and-so, that p."[23] As all understand, the offering of these expressions, in conditions of common knowledge suffices for the joint commitment in question to be established.

I take it that *making an explicit agreement* is one way of forming a joint commitment, but it is not the only way: all that is necessary (and sufficient) is that

[21] I convey here my own sense of the matter. I do not say that by deciding to do something I make doing that thing more desirable in itself, or in the consequences that flow from its being what it is. I say only that a decision, *in and of itself*, has the normative force suggested.

[22] In a non-basic case, a basic joint commitment has put some person or body in a position to create new joint commitments for the parties, possibly without the knowledge of the parties. See, e.g., Gilbert, *Political Obligation*.

[23] For a relatively fine-grained discussion of "common knowledge" in the context of joint commitment formation see Gilbert, *Social Facts*.

the conditions just noted be fulfilled. There are other ways of doing this than by making an explicit agreement.

Indeed, the establishment of a given joint commitment may be considerably extended in time, as expressions are made by different people and, as necessary, disambiguated by reference to context or explicit avowals. Nor need the parties be able to point to a moment in time when it was finally established. That does not mean that they cannot be perfectly clear that it is in place. Similar points may be made about the termination of a joint commitment.[24]

Another point that is particularly relevant in the context of this chapter is that the parties to a given joint commitment may be many and they may be spread over large tracts of land. Each may know few of the other parties personally or even *know of* them as individuals—as one may know of someone by reputation while not knowing him personally. In other words, there may be common knowledge among many far-flung persons who do not generally know of one another other as individuals that they have all expressed their readiness to be jointly committed with the others in a certain way. For instance, it may be common knowledge among the numerous inhabitants of a large island, or among those on the island who have reached a certain age, that all of their number have made such expressions.

Briefly to indicate how this may happen: it may be common knowledge among these people that island-dwellers frequently travel to different parts of the island and talk about how things are in the regions they have left. Just as they have gathered from travelers visiting them that people everywhere else on the island have expressed their readiness for a certain joint commitment of the island-dwellers, they can be sure that people everywhere else will have gathered that they have expressed such readiness also. In some such way it may come to be common knowledge among the island-dwellers that they have all expressed their readiness jointly to commit one another in the way in question: in which case they are, indeed, jointly committed.[25]

A related point is that in certain circumstances someone may, in effect, *sign on* to a given joint commitment after it has first been formed. An example of a situation of this kind would be when a newcomer comes to the island in the previous example after the joint commitment in question has been established. He is greeted by an official representative of the island-dwellers and told about the established joint commitment in a manner apt to solicit his endorsement. He responds "I'm on board with that." He is now in a position to act as can any co-creator of the commitment. In what follows, for brevity's sake, I shall refer

---

[24] On different ways of creating and terminating a joint commitment see Gilbert, *Political Obligation*, ch. 7.

[25] For further discussion of this and related topics see Gilbert, *Political Obligation*, 173–181.

both to those who created and those who signed on to a given joint commitment as one of its *creators*.

A further pertinent point is that the process of joint commitment formation and maintenance need not involve a strong form of voluntariness. As long as the parties mean to express their readiness for joint commitment—and are indeed ready for it—that is enough. One may mean to do this, and be so ready, in a context in which someone else is forcefully pressuring one to do so, or where one has little real choice in the matter.

For instance, one's being born into situation where there is an established joint commitment of the kind in question does not prevent one from, in effect, signing on to it one when reaches the age to understand what one is doing. The fact that one has little choice in the matter does not mean that one cannot be ready to sign on: on the contrary, it makes it more likely.[26]

The *content* of any joint commitment can be represented as follows:

The parties jointly commit *to phi as a body.*

Here "phi" stands for a verb such as "endorse," "accept," "believe," "aim at," "prefer," and so on.

What is it to jointly commit to phi *as a body,* for whatever instance of phi? Consider the case of a joint commitment to *support as a body a given political system.* I take it that this can be understood as a joint commitment to *emulate, as far as is possible, a single body or person which supports this system,* by virtue of the actions of each. In other terms, they are to support this system *together.* Analogous things can be said of joint commitments with other contents.

I am to argue that joint commitment is a source of owing. Any source of owing is important from a practical point of view. But a source that is a widespread element in human life is particularly important, whether or not it is the only such source. As I have argued elsewhere, joint commitment underlies a host of central social phenomena in the human realm, including social rules and conventions, acting together, and more.[27]

Once the idea of joint commitment has been clarified, one may find it obvious that the parties to any such commitment owe each other actions that accord with it. More precisely, one may find it obvious that they owe each other such

---

[26] For further discussion on these points see, e.g. Margaret Gilbert, "Agreements, Coercion, and Obligation," *Ethics* 103, reprinted in *Living Together*; also Gilbert, *Political Obligation*: ch. 10.

[27] On social rules see Margaret Gilbert "Social Rules: Some Problems with Hart's Account, and an Alternative Proposal," *Law and Philosophy* 18: 1999, reprinted in Gilbert, *Sociality and Responsibility: New Essays in Plural Subject Theory* (Lanham, MD: Rowman and Littlefield, 2000). On social convention see chapter 9 this volume. On acting together see chapter 1 this volume; for an extended treatment see Gilbert *Political Obligation* chs. 6 and 7.

actions in their capacity as parties to the joint commitment. One way of articulating this sense of things is as follows.

Someone who is owed a given action has the standing to demand it of the one who owes it. Now suppose one party proposes willfully not to act in conformity with a given joint commitment. It is hard to deny that another party has the standing to demand that the first act otherwise, in the name of their joint commitment. He can say, in effect, "Hey, our *commitment* doesn't permit you to do that!"

He might amplify: "In having me join with you in *committing* us both, you put me in a position to *call you to order*, should you propose not to act accordingly. Similarly, just as—in the case of a personal commitment—you are in a position to berate yourself for failing to do what you committed yourself to do, all of those who are parties with you to a given *joint* commitment are in a position to berate you for failing to act according to that joint commitment. They are in that position qua *co-creators* of the commitment."

What of the suggestion noted earlier, that someone's standing to demand an action is the standing to demand it *as his?* This idea fits the context of joint commitment quite well.

When we create a given joint commitment—*by jointly committing* ourselves—*we directly make it the case that each of us has sufficient reason to perform conforming actions.* I say that we have done this *directly* because, in conditions of common knowledge, our mutual expressions of readiness jointly to commit us all, and these alone, sufficed for the purpose.[28] That each has *sufficient reason* to perform means that, if rational, and presuming all else is equal, he *will* perform. Further, that will be so unless the commitment is terminated with the concurrence of each. In this relatively strong way, *we have bound each of us to perform the actions* in question when the appropriate time comes. In this sense at least these conforming actions are *ours.*

Given that our jointly committing ourselves sufficed to make the conforming actions ours in the sense indicated, it would make sense to say that each has made these actions his, *qua one of us.* He is thus in a position to demand such actions as his, qua one of us, where "his" is understood in this fashion.[29]

Before leaving the topic of joint commitment it is worth pointing out the following. What each is committed to, through the joint commitment, is to do his part—in conjunction with the others—in emulating as far as possible a single

---

[28] I do not say that in jointly committing ourselves we have somehow willed *the fact that we are capable, by willing, of determining what each is rationally required to do, all else being equal.* Rather, given our jointly committing ourselves, there is no question that this determination has taken place: *our willing in and of itself is normative for us.* This, I take it, is true a priori.

[29] In other places I have made this argument in different terms. This way of making it eschews metaphor.

body that phi-s, for some instance of phi. Thus what he must do, in the event, is co-ordinate his own actions with whatever actions others put forth so that they emulate as far as possible a single body that phi-s.

In some cases there may be several distinct and, indeed, disjoint combinations of actions of the parties that will count as conforming to the commitment. So each is, in effect, jointly committed to contribute to this combination of actions, *or* that combination of actions, *or* this third combination of actions, for instance, depending on which action of his will, in the event, best contribute to conformity to the commitment. Indeed, the set of actions in question may be *open-ended* in the sense that there is no limit in principle on the number of ways that conformity with the commitment could be achieved.

To be precise, then, each must do whatever fits best with whichever of the possible conforming combinations of actions the others are doing their part in, if any, and owes such actions to the others.

The main gist of this section is this: one case in which you *owe* me an action is when you and I are parties to a joint commitment. You then owe me actions conforming to the joint commitment. These actions are owed solely by virtue of the existence of the joint commitment and, in particular, by virtue of the fact of its joint imposition.[30]

The plural subject theory of political obligation

Assume that, as I have argued, one case in which you owe me an action is when you and I are parties to a joint commitment. Suppose now that the members of a large population are jointly committed to support as a body the maintenance of a particular political system among them.[31]

In short, they are jointly committed to support as a body that particular political system. Then each member of the population is obligated to each to support, together with the rest, the system in question. Equivalently, each owes every other actions supportive of that political system.

All that remains to constitute this as a solution to the problem of political obligation with which I started is to construe one's country as a political society of which one is a member, and to allow that the members of a given population constitute a political society if and only if they are jointly committed to support as a body the maintenance of a particular political system among them, a political system being constituted by one or more political institutions.[32]

---

[30] A stronger claim would be that participation in a pertinent joint commitment is the *only* way in which one person can owe another an action. For brief discussion see Gilbert, "Claim-Rights," 317–321. For present purposes I need only work with the weaker claim.

[31] As indicated earlier, this could come about in a variety of ways.

[32] For more on the scope of "political" institutions see Gilbert, *Political Obligation*, ch. 9.

I do not argue that the pertinent construals of "country" and "political soci-ety" are the only current or plausible ones. Surely they are not. The first has some currency, however, and the second fits well with another idea with some currency: the idea that a society is a social group in a certain somewhat narrow intuitive sense. For it can be argued that any population of jointly committed persons constitutes a social group in this sense.[33] Thus the proposed solution to the problem of political obligation accommodates in intuitive ways what seems to be a common intuitive judgment: that one is obligated to support the political institutions of one's own country in particular.[34]

I have given the label "plural subject" to any group of jointly committed persons. People constitute a plural subject, by definition, if and only if they are jointly committed with one another in some way. Hence, I refer to the above solution to the problem of political obligation as *the plural subject theory of politi-cal obligation*.

According to this theory, in sum, if one construes the relevant terms in quite plausible ways, one is indeed *obligated* to support the political institutions of *one's own country*, that obligation being a matter of owing one's compatriots such support on the basis of one's participation in a pertinent joint commitment.

Those with political obligations of this type have sufficient reason to fulfill them—a situation they are not in a position to change by an act of their own will, absent special background understandings. Their compatriots are empowered to enforce these obligations at least to the extent of making authoritative demands for compliance and rebuking those who are non-compliant. Insofar as their com-pliance is owed to their compatriots, it would seem that their own contrary incli-nations and narrow self-interest are not enough to justify non-compliance. All in all, then, whatever we call them, political obligations of this type are forces to be reckoned with.

Political obligation, morally bad political institutions, and content-independence

The following question may now be raised: what if the political institutions in question are morally bad—to whatever degree? Is one still obligated to support them, all else being equal? This question deserves a longer treatment than I shall give it here. In offering a brief answer, I start by backing away from plural subject theory for a moment.

---

[33] See Gilbert, *Political Obligation*, ch. 6. See also Gilbert, *Social Facts*, ch. 4

[34] Among many other sources see Simmons, *Political Obligations*, opening discussion.

Suppose one considers the following development of the first part of the non-moralized problem of political obligation with which this chapter began, namely:

(N) Is one obligated to support the political institutions of one's own country in particular, *including any such institutions as are morally bad?*[35]

Many would automatically give this question an interpretation in terms of moral requirement. So let us first consider the following moralized version of it:

(M1) Is one morally required to support the political institutions of one's own country in particular, *including any such institutions as are morally bad?*

The question clearly suggests that there can be morally bad political institutions. That is, the concept of a political institution is not itself moralized so as to rule out the possibility of morally bad political institutions. I shall proceed on this assumption.[36]

If the answer to this moralized question were positive, then whatever person or body is in a position to create or change a particular set of laws, say, would have enormous *moral power*, by which I mean the power to control the behavior of those responsive to moral requirements. For, in effect, they would have the power arbitrarily to impose *new moral requirements* on members of the relevant political society, requirements which would hold, *whatever the required actions were*, though perhaps not irrespective of other circumstances.

Most writers on political obligation would agree, I think, that the answer to the moralized question (M1) is negative. The nature of the political institutions of one's country—the content of a law, for instance—can make a difference to what one is morally required to do with respect to them. This plausible judgment may stand without further discussion for present purposes.

Note that the question that has just received a negative answer is distinct from the following question:

---

[35] The words "including…?" have now been added to the formulation given earlier.

[36] Though this may seem obvious, there has been some tendency historically and in contemporary writings to think differently about *law*. I take it that laws are political institutions par excellence, and that there is a viable non-moralized conception of law. Many social concepts are, evidently, susceptible of moralization; and there is probably always a tendency toward it. The concept of a "community" is another pertinent example.

(M2) Is one morally required to support the political institutions of one's own country in particular, *absent any considerations on the other side, including considerations relating to the moral quality of these institutions?*

It is perfectly possible that this question receive a positive answer though the previous question (M1) receives a negative one.

Indeed, the plural subject theory of political obligation may well support a positive answer to (M2). This will be the case if one is morally as well as rationally required to give people what one owes them, absent any considerations on the other side. Whether or not that is so is a question for moral judgment. I set it aside here.

Theorists often assume that one's political obligations, if they exist, will be in some sense independent of the content of the political institutions in question. For instance, they are independent of the content of particular laws. Different interpretations of such *content-independence* are possible. Consider again question (N) above:

Is one obligated to support the political institutions of one's own country in particular, including any such institutions as are morally bad?

This contemplates a strong kind of content-independence, envisaging that there may be political obligations to support the political institutions of one's country however bad they are.

I am assuming that this strong kind of content-independence is not available for political obligations conceived of as moral requirements. That does not mean that there are no political obligations with this kind of content-independence.

Indeed, the plural subject theory of political obligation seems to support a positive answer to question (N). I say that it seems to support a positive answer. It does support one on the face of it, and I have no argument to hand that counters this argument. Here is the argument in favor of a positive answer.

First, according to the theory, with its specific interpretations of the pertinent terms, one owes one's compatriots one's support of the political institutions of one's country by virtue of one's joint commitment with them to support as a body those institutions. Their being the political institutions *of one's country* just *is* one's being party to this commitment with these others. Thus one is obligated *to these others* to support the institutions in question. This directed obligation is a function of the joint commitment. *Given the joint commitment, the obligation exists.*

Second, it seems that some of the institutions in question may be morally bad—they may, for instance, be unjust, or unduly harsh, or possess some other vice of political institutions. They need not involve injustice, harshness, and so on toward compatriots; they could involve overweening, oppressive attitudes to outsiders, enemies, or transients, for example.

Where the institutions in question are morally bad, it seems that those who entered the joint commitment may not have understood that this was so. Or they may have been willing to commit themselves in spite of it. Perhaps they acted culpably in doing so. Perhaps they did not: they may have had no real choice. Be all that as it may, they entered the joint commitment and thereby obligated themselves. That is, they put themselves in the position of owing their conformity to the commitment to the other parties.

Suppose this is so. One can allow that these people may well be morally required not to support the institutions in question, in spite of the joint commitment; in other terms, they are morally required not to give the others what they owe them. And it may well be that this is what rationality requires them to do, all things, including all moral things, considered. This does not take away from the fact that they owe the others their conformity to the commitment—indeed it presupposes that fact.

Political obligations of joint commitment, then, appear to have the following strong kind of content-independence: they are grounded in something independent of the content of the institutions in question, and they hold irrespective of that content. They hold as long as the joint commitment that grounds them lasts—and no longer.

Some practical implications of the foregoing

Why would it matter that I owe my compatriots compliance with a particular morally bad law, say, if I am morally and rationally required not to comply with this law, all things considered?[37] There are several pertinent points to be made here, including the following.

If I see things clearly, and act appropriately in terms of my compliance with this law, I will realize that I am not giving my compatriots what I owe them. This could affect my behavior in various ways.

I may feel that I should explain myself to my compatriots. Should I give them such an explanation, my doing so could have important effects: possibly I will convince them not to comply with the law or to make efforts to change it.

---

[37] Cf. David Lefkowitz, review of *Political Obligation*, in *Notre Dame Philosophical Reviews* 6 (2007).

Again, I may be aware that I owe my compatriots conformity to the law, and not see that the law is morally bad. Perhaps I do not consider the question of its goodness or badness. Then my perception of my obligation may be what moves me to act: from the point of view of my own partially skewed understanding of the situation I will indeed be acting appropriately—I will be respecting specific rights of my compatriots.[38]

Alternatively, I may not be sure how things come out in terms of what I ought to do, all things considered, though I am aware both that I owe conformity to the law to my compatriots and that it is a morally bad law. I may honestly judge that giving my compatriots what I owe them is the thing to do in this situation, and hence conform to the law.

As the last two points indicate, people who understand that they are obligated to others, and do not see anything else in the situation that allows or prescribes that they default on their obligation, may fulfill their obligation because, *as they correctly discern*, they are obligated. Sometime they will then be doing the right thing; sometimes not.

Even if I understand that I am morally and rationally required not to conform to a given law, though I owe such conformity to others, I may be swayed by the realization that these others have the standing to demand my conformity. Perhaps they should not do this all things considered. After all, given that I am rationally required not to comply, should they not hold off on these demands? Perhaps they should hold off, as I realize, but they may not, as I also realize, and this may give me pause.

It is not pleasant to be faced with the demands and after-the-fact rebukes of others. Anticipation of them may still the voice of morality in me, particularly if it fails to speak to me through others. I may proceed to comply with the morally bad law.

My compatriots' demands may not be merely potential. They may focus on the fact that I owe them conformity, and demand compliance. Again, the voice of morality may be stilled in me.

In short, obligations of joint commitment may be *motivationally significant* even in situations where all things considered rationality requires that one not support a particular political institution or set of institutions, either because of their moral badness or because of other factors. To deny that obligations can exist in such situations is liable to be puzzling rather than helpful if one is trying

---

[38] Chapter 18, this volume has a related theme. See also chapter 16, this volume.

to advise someone about what to do in the context of morally bad political institutions, or to explain behavior supportive of such institutions.

This, then, is what I propose: failure to recognize the de-moralized problem—and concept—of political obligation stands significantly to hamper the
understanding of political scientists and activists as well as philosophers.

Commands and Their Practical Import

The issue of command authority

Suppose Alan says to Jake "Leave town immediately!" He is not play-acting or joking. The imperative he addresses to Jake is seriously intended. Suppose, indeed, that it is an authoritative command.

It would generally be assumed that, in that case, there is a sense in which Jake now has a duty to leave town immediately. It would also generally be assumed that this is not just a matter of Alan's say-so. Rather, Alan's say-so sufficed to make it the case, given whatever background conditions were also required.

Under what conditions does one accrue the ability to create duties in others simply by uttering an appropriate imperative? Are there any restrictions relating to the moral quality of the act enjoined? Some seem to think there are none.

People often obey unconscionable commands—commands to do very bad things. They sometimes attempt to defend themselves by saying that they were only *following orders*, or only *doing their duty*.

Others often judge that this is not a sufficient defense. These people should have disobeyed the orders in question, given their content. That is the correct practical judgment, all things considered.

Is there a duty of obedience to authoritative commands, irrespective of the morality of their content? If so, what is the relationship of this duty to what one ought to do, all things considered? Does it clinch the matter? If not, what is its practical import? These are the questions this chapter explores. Two well-known cases make vivid their importance.

Two cases

In Hitler's Germany, Adolph Eichmann's work as an administrator was instrumental in sending numerous innocent people to their deaths in concentration camps. At his trial in 1961 he gave as a justification for his role in this slaughter the fact that he was following orders. As he put it at one point,

> The guilt for the mass murder is solely with the political leaders...I was held fast in those dark duties.[1]

Eichmann thought or purported to think that "I was following orders" was an adequate justification for doing what he did, in the circumstances. In other terms, he thought or purported to think he did what he ought to have done all things considered.[2]

Eichmann's self-exculpatory discourse has echoes in the thought and behavior of many less notorious individuals. Around the time of Eichmann's trial, moved by the "slaughter on command" to which Eichmann contributed, psychologist Stanley Milgram conducted now famous experiments on deference to authority.[3]

In the best known of these experiments, the subjects were told they were participating in a scientific study on learning techniques. A confederate of the experimenter, the "learner" was strapped into a chair. Each subject was instructed as follows. From an adjoining room, he was to administer electric shocks of increasing intensity to the learner, as and when the learner gave the wrong answer to a question.

In fact no real shocks were given. The subject heard an actor's gasps, pleas, and shrieks, as increasingly intense shocks were administered. Contrary to the expectations of the experimenters, as many as 62% of the subjects went as far as they were commanded to go. Some questioned the experimenter at certain points, but in spite of thinking that *the shocks were so bad they might well kill the learner*, they went ahead and did what they were told to do.

Milgram commented:

> With numbing regularity good people were seen to knuckle under to the demands of authority and perform actions that were callous and severe.[4]

---

[1] Taken from Eichmann's statement after he was sentenced to death. See www.pbs.org/eichmann. Along the same lines Eichmann said: "I accuse the leaders of abusing my obedience." Perhaps he also meant to place the blame (largely) on others when he said "Obedience is commended as a virtue."

[2] Elsewhere he suggests that a countervailing consideration might be equally adequate in the face of an order; there would then be an impasse practically speaking: "I never carried out killings...If I had received the order to carry out those killings, I would not have escaped using a trumped up pretext...Since because of *the compulsion exerted by an order*, I would have put a bullet through my brain in order to solve the conflict between conscience and duty" (emphasis mine).

[3] The quoted phrase is from Stanley Milgram, *Obedience to Authority: An Experimental View* (New York: Harper and Row, 1974), 1. I take my descriptions of the experiments from this text.

[4] Milgram, *Obedience*, 123.

Eichmann's self-exculpatory discourse and Milgram's experiments vividly raise the question of the proper relationship of orders or commands to action. Is there a duty to obey? If so, what kind of duty is it? And what bearing does it have on what one ought to do, all things considered?[5]

Robert Wolff on commands

A good place to start a discussion of commands is Robert Wolff's classic work *In Defense of Anarchism.*[6] Wolff argues for *the non-existence of authoritative commands* in the human realm.[7] His claim is not empirical. He offers an a priori argument to the effect that authoritative commands are *impossible.*

Here is something Wolff and I agree on: to speak of an "authoritative command" is pleonastic. In order for Jones to *command* (or *order* or *instruct*) Smith to do something, he needs the *authority* to do so.[8] Thus Wolff's thesis can be couched more briefly as follows: in the human realm *there can be no commands.*

One can hold this while allowing that people often *purport* to command others to do things without having the necessary authority. One can also allow that people sometimes talk of "commands," simply, when what is at issue is a purported command. They may be using the term "command" in Wolff's and my relatively rich sense, but with implicit scare quotes around it; or they may be using it in an attenuated sense. Such attenuated senses of richer terms are common.[9]

In what follows I shall assume that in order to *command* someone to do something one needs the authority to do so, as a matter of logic. In other terms, one needs a particular type of *standing.* My use of the term "command" in this discussion should be understood accordingly.

Wolff thinks there are often good reasons for *acting in accordance with* a *purported* command. What he denies is that any purported commands are issued with the requisite authority—hence there are no *genuine* commands. There is then nothing to *obey.* For obedience presupposes authority in the one who is obeyed. Without

---

[5] I do not invoke a fine-grained theory of "oughts" here. Rather I make use of judgments that I take to be intuitive, and to which any such fine-grained theory should be to some extent answerable.

[6] Robert Paul Wolff, *In Defense of Anarchism* (New York: Harper Torchbooks), 1970.

[7] Wolff is not concerned with commands supposed to be divine. Given what he says, it looks as if he would need to deny the possibility of authoritative commands to any human being whoever the putative commander might be. Since I incline to doubt his argument for the human to human case, there is no need to consider the plausibility of this implication here.

[8] Cf. Wolff, *Anarchism*, 4: "Authority is the right to command." I do not say that he and I agree on what the requisite authority amounts to.

[9] See Margaret Gilbert, *A Theory of Political Obligation: Membership, Commitment, and the Bonds of Society* (Oxford: Oxford University Press) 2006, opening discussion. The nature of authority in general and political authority in particular receives attention in chapter 11 of that book.

the requisite authority, then, there is neither command nor obedience, though there may be action that, for good reasons, accords with a purported command.

A tension in Wolff's discussion

Wolff's argument for the non-existence of commands has been widely criticized, and rightly so. It will be helpful, nonetheless, to consider some central aspects of it here. One way of representing Wolff's argument is in terms of the following seven steps.

(1) A human being has a primary, overriding obligation to be as autonomous—as self-governing—as possible, with respect to other human beings.
(2) *Were* Jones to command Smith to do something, Smith would be *obligated* to do that thing, or, as Wolff sometimes puts it without noting a distinction, Smith would have a *duty* to do it.[10] Indeed, there could not *be* a command without such an obligation on the part of the commanded.
(3) Were there such an obligation, it would be an obligation of the same kind as the primary obligation to be maximally autonomous.
(4) Were both obligations to exist, however, they would be in conflict.
(5) One cannot have conflicting obligations of the kind in question at one and the same time.
(6) In the case under consideration, the primary obligation to be autonomous—precisely as primary—would preclude an obligation to obey a given command.

Therefore,

(7) There can be no such thing as a human-to-human command.

I shall focus on step (3): were there an obligation associated with commands, it would be of the same kind as the obligation to be maximally autonomous. It can be argued that this point is in tension with other points Wolff makes about commands in the course of his writings. I have in mind in particular the following:

> my duty to obey is a duty *owed* to them [that is, those who command me to do something][11]

---

[10] Some authors distinguish between "duties" and "obligations" as referring to different things but many do not, using them as equivalent in meaning. I shall proceed here in the latter way, though I shall endorse an important difference between one class of obligations/duties and another. I thus endorse the distinction Hart wanted to mark by the use of different terms.

[11] Wolff, *Anarchism*, 6.

I take it that Wolff's point can be rephrased as follows: my duty to obey is a matter of *owing* obedience to those who command me to do something.[12]

This rephrasing makes it clear that neither the word "duty" nor the word "obligation" is needed to describe the situation. The word "owing" suffices.

That said, following a common practice, I shall sometimes say that I am obligated *to* (or *toward*) someone to obey him, or that I have such a duty *to* him, as alternatives to saying that I owe him obedience, alternatives I take to be its equivalents. Following another common practice, I shall refer to an *obligation* (or *duty*) "to" someone as a *directed* or *relational* obligation.[13]

Here is the tension among Wolff's points, put now in terms of obligation. On the face of it, the obligation to be maximally autonomous, if it exists, is *not* a matter of *directed* obligation. One way of making the point, consonant with Wolff's discussion, is to say that the obligation to be maximally autonomous is a moral requirement and, at least on the face of it, requirements as such lack direction.

Suppose, then, that Wolff is right in saying that were I in receipt of a command, *I would owe my obedience to the one who commanded me or (in other terms) I would be obligated to that person to obey him.* It is not clear that the obligation here is of the same kind as the supposed obligation to maximize one's autonomy. Though there are surely reasons why the word "obligation" has been used in both cases, the differences between these cases may be so significant that it may be seriously confusing to subsume both under the same label.

Wolff's idea that there is a primary obligation to be maximally autonomous can be questioned as to both its meaning and validity. My point is that *whatever the outcome of such questioning, the possibility of commands may not be impugned.* In particular, the following is possible: commands give rise to directed obligations that are capable of co-existing with a primary moral requirement to be maximally autonomous, and—one might add—with any moral requirements that both conflict with and override them.[14]

---

[12] Though the phrase "owing a duty" is common in some philosophical discussions, and goes back a long way in the vernacular, I confess to finding it rebarbative. In particular, I find "owing obedience" fine and "owing a duty of obedience" awkward. I proceed, therefore, in the terms I find most comfortable.

[13] The directionality of duties is not always interpreted in terms of owing; indeed, it has occasioned long-standing disputes among its interpreters. On the pertinent dispute between the two groups of rights theorists often referred to as the will and interest theorists see Margaret Gilbert (2012) "Giving Claim-Rights Their Due", in *Rights: Concepts and Contexts*, eds. B. Bix and H. Spector, Farnham, Surrey: Ashgate, 302-304.

[14] In saying that these obligations are "overridden" I mean that they remain—one still has them — but all things considered one ought to not to act in accordance with them, but rather accord with the moral requirement in question.

Can directed obligations co-exist with moral requirements that override them?[15] Clearly, this depends on what directed obligation, or *owing*, amounts to. With Wolff in at least some of his moods, I regard that as highly relevant to the nature of commands.

Prototypical commands—the owing account

Before considering the nature of owing, I offer a rough account of what I shall call *prototypical commands*. In calling these commands "prototypical," I mean to allow for derivative cases of other types, such as those dependent on collective stipulations of command authority.[16] I limit my discussion in this chapter to prototypical commands. When I refer to "commands" in what follows, then, I mean "prototypical commands." The account accords with part of Wolff's discussion, and several other discussions also.[17] It has two stages. First, one who commands needs the authority or standing to do so, so the first stage of the account runs roughly as follows:

[1] X *has the authority to command Y to perform a particular action @ if and only if, if X addresses an imperative to Y to the effect that Y is to do @, then, by virtue of this address, Y owes it to X to do @.*[18]

This does not attempt to explain *how X may come by* the authority to command Y, or, in other words, how it may come to be that if X addresses an imperative to Y to the effect that Y is to do @, Y owes it to X to do @. It says rather that for X

---

[15] If they could, one might wonder, why would that matter? After all, they would be superseded by the moral requirements in question. I say more about this toward the end of this chapter.

[16] See e.g. Gilbert, *Political Obligation*, 207-212.

[17] Several writers on authority have connected commanding with a *right* to be obeyed, e.g. G. E. M. Anscombe, "On the source of the authority of the state" in *The Collected Philosophical Papers of G. E. M. Anscombe, Volume Three: Ethics, Religion and Politics* (Blackwell: Oxford, 1981), 132. In *The Morality of Freedom* (Oxford: Oxford University Press, 1986), 23, Joseph Raz refers to the idea that "authority over persons" centrally involves a "right to rule, where that is...correlated with an obliga-tion to obey" as common, giving several citations. See the text below on the relationship between Y's owing X some action and X's right to Y's performance of that action.

[18] I thank Gary Ebbs for pointing out that if the analysans is construed as a material conditional that would have the unwelcome consequence that if X does not actually address any imperatives to Y, then X has the authority to command Y to do @ (personal communication, October 2011). The account is, indeed, rough, and Ebbs' observation makes it clear that it needs to be further clarified or amended. Ebbs himself suggested rewriting [1] "as a schematic condition, as follows: (1*) Y has the authority to command Y to do @ if and only if, by virtue of a condition C (X,Y) that holds for X and Y, X and Y are each committed to accepting that if X addresses an imperative to Y to the effect that Y is to do @, then, by virtue of this address, Y owes it to X to do @." Ebbs observed that one can accept (1*) without committing oneself to a filling-in of C(X,Y) that is irreducibly relational.

to *have* this authority is for it to be the case that if X addresses an imperative to Y...etc. I say more about the genesis of command authority in due course.

The second stage of the account runs as follows:

[2] X *commands* Y to do @ if and only if (1) X has the authority to command Y to do @ (per the account in [1], above) and (2) X has addressed an imperative to Y to the effect that Y is to do @.

For the sake of a label I shall call this *the owing account* of commands.

In practice a given person usually has the authority to command a given other to do anything that falls within a certain range of actions. At the same time, this range is unlikely to include all possible actions. And it may be limited to a single action.[19] In addition, one's authority may be limited to certain contexts. Thus Alice's student Josh may owe Alice his compliance with the imperative "Stand here!" when she issues it to him in class, but not if she issues it to him in the supermarket.

The owing account of commands is open to revision in light of such observations as those above. For present purposes it can be left in its current form. I explore it further shortly. First, I compare and contrast it with an account of a type that is well-entrenched in the literature.

The owing account compared with a popular form of account

Perhaps the most popular type of account of commands in the literature has its origins in suggestions of H. L. A. Hart and Joseph Raz. I shall focus on a version derived from Jean Hampton, and will refer to it as the *standard* account.[20]

Because the difference between the owing account and the standard account lies there, I restrict myself to the first stage of the standard account, which I label [1A]:

[1A] X has the authority to command Y to perform action @ if and only if, if X addresses an imperative to Y to the effect that Y is to do @, then, by virtue of this address:

    (i) Y has a reason to do @, *regardless of what @ is.* Or, in standard technical terms, Y has a *content-independent reason* to do @.

---

[19] On the last point see Leslie Green, *The Authority of the State* (Oxford: Oxford University Press, 1988), 50 for an example.

[20] Jean Hampton, *Political Philosophy* (Boulder, CO: Westview Press, 1997), 5. See also Green, *Authority*, 41–2.

(ii) In deciding whether to comply Y is rationally required *not to consider* at least some of kinds of consideration in favor of not doing @. In Raz's terms, the reason Y has to do @ is an *exclusionary reason*.[21]

If X has the authority to command Y to do @ according to the owing account, then it would seem that X also has such authority according to the standard account. The reverse, on the other hand, seems not to be true.

As to the last point: Suppose (by hypothesis) that Ynez has been commanded by Zack to do whatever Xandra says Ynez is to do. According to the standard account, it is now the case that *Xandra has the authority to command Ynez to do @*. For if Xandra now says that Ynez is to do @, Ynez will have then have a content-independent reason for complying with Xandra's imperative, a reason that excludes at least some other reasons from consideration. I take it, however, that it is not the case that Ynez now *owes it to Xandra* to do @. Rather, she owes it to Zack.

I turn now to this point: if X has the authority to command Y to do @ according to the owing account of commands, then X also has such authority according to the standard account. Without further elaboration of the nature of owing, the following points seem to be correct, intuitively. First, if Y owes it to X to do @, then—on account of this owing relationship—Y has a reason to do @, regardless of what @ is. Second, Y's owing it to X to do @ excludes at least some of Y's reasons for not doing @.

Among the considerations that seem to be overruled by the fact that one owes a certain action to another is one's own inclination not to perform it and one's desire not to perform it. If I owe you a certain action, in any intuitive sense of the term, it does not seem to be a sufficient excuse for not doing it, that I don't feel like doing it. The same goes for my wanting to do it.

Purely self-interested considerations, also, may be excluded. Certainly, saying "It would be a nuisance for me to have to do it" does not seem to be a sufficient excuse for refusing to perform an action you owe someone.

I propose that in understanding commands we do better to focus on *owing* than on those *consequences* of owing highlighted in the standard account. Owing has other significant consequences, and to stay with the standard account is to ignore them. It is now time to say more about owing.

---

[21] Green says that Y has a content-independent reason that excludes "some" of Y's reasons for not doing @. Hampton says it excludes "all (or almost all)" of Y's reasons. Joseph Raz seems closer to Hampton when he writes "if he was ordered to commit an atrocity, he should refuse. But his is an ordinary case, he thinks, and the order should prevail" and goes on to suggest that "he" is right about "the nature of authority." Joseph Raz, *Practical Reason and Norms* (Princeton: Princeton University Press, 1975), 38.

Owing—and a pertinent question

The term "owe" is currently used in more than one sense. I now say something about the central, intuitive sense in which I am using the term.

I have in mind a sense of "owe" such that if Jones owes Smith a specific action, there is an important sense in which Smith has a *right* against Jones to Jones's performance of that action.[22] Indeed, Smith's having such a right against Jones to Jones's action *is* Jones's owing Smith his action viewed from Smith's perspective.

Though this point is firm it is not of great help without a satisfactory account of rights of the kind in question.[23] For now, I focus on one point that bears on this question. If Jones owes Smith a specific action, Smith has the standing to *demand* it of Jones, and to *rebuke* Jones for not performing it. Indeed, if Smith has this standing, then the action in question must be one that Jones owes to Smith.[24]

Clearly, "demand" here means more than "issue a seriously intended imperative." To demand in the present sense—which I take to be central—requires a certain standing or authority. One is not *in a position to* demand that someone do something unless one has this standing. In this way *demanding* and *commanding* are similar.[25]

I take a *rebuke* to be an after-the-fact demand. It, too, would then require a special standing or authority—as I think is intuitively the case.

Where I speak of *having standing* I mean sharply to distinguish this from *being justified*, and in particular from being justified all things considered. I may have the standing to demand that you do something though you are so frail that you will collapse if I make this demand. In the circumstances that may well entail that I would not be justified all things considered in making the demand.

In connection with demands there is a further point that I take from Joel Feinberg. I take it to be intuitive, though it is clearly in need of further elaboration. The point is this: A person, X, has the standing to demand an action of a

---

[22] Cf. H. L. A. Hart. "Are There Any Natural Rights?" *Philosophical Review* 64 (1955), 180.

[23] The most prominent contemporary rights theories do not seem to provide such an account. I discuss this in detail in a book to be published by Oxford University Press, and more briefly in Gilbert, "Claim-Rights." See also ch. 12 this volume, with special reference to Raz's interest theory of rights.

[24] I do not say that it must be owed to Smith qua Smith, i.e. that very person.

[25] One *difference* between demanding and commanding can be put in terms of rights. In order to be in a position to demand that you perform a certain action, I need *already to have a right to that action*. I may be in a position to command that you do such-and-such, *without* already having a right to that action. It is true that once I *have* commanded you to do it, I will then be in a position to demand of you that you do it. At that point I will, indeed, have a right to it. Before, though, I may not have.

person Y if and only if that action is in a particular sense already X's.[26] Putting this together with the foregoing points we would then have the following: in the pertinent sense of "owe," if I owe you an action, it is in an as yet unspecified sense *yours* already. You are therefore in a position to demand it of me *as yours*.

Agreements and commands: the agreement proposal

One way to explore the relationship of owing further is to start from the observation that one paradigmatic *context* for it is an everyday agreement. Thus if Smith and Jones agree that they will both take the 5pm train, then by virtue of this agreement, Smith now owes Jones his, Smith's, taking the 5pm train, and, likewise, Jones owes Smith his taking the 5pm train.

Someone may wonder if there are not some exceptions by virtue of the content of the agreement or the circumstances in which it was made. Let us focus on agreements that are unproblematic in these respects.

Given that agreements are a paradigmatic context for owing, we can ask what it is about them that makes this so. In this section, before sketching an answer to that question, I note that there is an important relationship between agreements and commands.

One can create a situation in which a command is issued by making an agreement. Thus suppose that Fay and Jack agree that she will bring him any book that he tells her to get from the library. Jack then says "Get me *The Brothers Karamazov*!" Fay now owes Jack her bringing him *The Brothers Karamazov* by virtue of their agreement. At the same time it is surely apt to say that Jack commanded, ordered, or, perhaps better in this case, *instructed* or *told* Fay to get the book in question.[27]

Recall now the roughly sketched owing account of commands:

[1] X *has the authority to command Y to perform a particular action @ if and only if,* if X addresses an imperative to Y to the effect that Y is to do @, then, by virtue of this, Y owes it to X to do @.

Assuming [1], and given the previous points about agreements, the following "agreement proposal" suggests itself:

X has the authority to command Y to do @ if X and Y have agreed that Y will do @ if X says he is to do so.

---

[26] Cf. Joel Feinberg, "The Nature and Value of Rights," *Journal of Value Inquiry* 4(1970): 251.

[27] Evidently there are several words akin to "command," including "order," "instruct," and "tell (someone to do something)," Apparently context dictates which one is most appropriate. For present purposes the differences between them are not significant.

The agreement proposal only claims to state a sufficient condition for one's having the authority to command, not a necessary one. In addition, though it tells us one way to produce a command it does not give us any insight into the relevant mechanism.

Agreements, owing, and joint commitment

How precisely do agreements create the owing relationship?

There has been much discussion of promises and, to a lesser extent, agreements, in philosophy. The focus has been on how promises and agreements *obligate* those who make them. The standard contemporary approaches to this question see the obligation in question as a matter of a moral requirement grounded in a general moral principle such as Thomas Scanlon's *Principle F* (for fidelity).[28] Such principles tell a person what he is morally required to do, having entered a promise or agreement. The central problem with these accounts for present purposes is that they do not show that the parties to an agreement, as such, owe each other performance—in the pertinent sense of "owe."[29]

In exploring this question further it would be good to start with some understanding of what an agreement is. My proposal in that regard—discussed at some length elsewhere—has been that the making of an agreement involves the creation of what I refer to as a *joint commitment.*[30]

I say something about joint commitment shortly. I first explain how I think a joint commitment is involved in an agreement.

Roughly, if we enter an agreement, on my proposed account, we jointly commit to endorse a certain *plan* as a body. What this means as far as each individual is concerned is roughly this: he is to do what he can together with the others to emulate a single endorser of the plan in question: they must seem to be "of one mind" in the relevant respect. I take it that the content of any joint commitment can be expressed in terms of doing something *as a body,* similarly understood.

---

[28] See e.g. Thomas Scanlon, *What We Owe to Each Other* (Cambridge, MA: Harvard University Press, 1998). *Principle F* is quoted in chapter 12, this volume, at p. 281. Though there are important divisions among contemporary theorists they generally see the obligation in question as a matter of moral requirement.

[29] For discussion see Margaret Gilbert. "Scanlon on Promissory Obligation: The Problem of Promisees' Rights," *Journal of Philosophy* 101, 2004 [chapter 12, this volume].

[30] I argue against the common "exchange of promises" account of agreements in Margaret Gilbert "Is an Agreement an Exchange of Promises?" *Journal of Philosophy* 54 (1993). There is a briefer treatment of this account in Margaret Gilbert, "Three Dogmas about Promising" in *Understanding Promises and Agreements* (2011) ed. H. Sheinman, Oxford University Press: New York [chapter 13, this volume].

Joint commitment and owing

I now say something about joint commitment, and relate it to owing. A joint commitment falls into a general class of commitments I call *commitments of the will*.[31] To
introduce this class of commitments I start with the example of a personal decision.

Suppose I have decided to have lunch at Sam's cafe, and have not changed my
mind. Suppose further, that at lunchtime I set out in the direction of another
establishment. I take it that a failure on my part to go to Sam's for lunch need
not be a bad thing in and of itself. There may be equally good places to go to for
lunch, in the other direction. Nor need my not going to Sam's, in and of itself,
be likely to have worse consequences than some alternative courses of action. In
short, I need not have failed to respect one or more *good reasons* for acting in the
way my decision dictates.

That said, if I have decided to lunch at Sam's and have not changed my mind,
then, if all else is equal, I am not responding appropriately to the considerations
bearing on my situation if I fail to go to Sam's for lunch. In other terms, as I interpret the emphasized phrase, I am not doing what is *rationally required*, all else
being equal. Without prejudice to whether *reasons* are involved, I shall say that if
one is rationally required to do something, all else being equal, one has *sufficient
reason* to do it. I understand one to be *committed* to do @, if and only if one has
sufficient reason to @.[32]

A personal decision creates what I call a *personal* commitment of the will. In
this case the person who is committed unilaterally commits himself and he is
in a position unilaterally to rescind it. Personal intentions also create personal
commitments.

Two or more people create a *joint* commitment when, roughly, each has
openly expressed to the other that he is ready *together with the others to commit
them all* to doing something as a body, in a broad sense of "do."[33] In other terms,
each is ready to *co-author* a given commitment of them all. They understand that
once this has happened the commitment in question has been co-authored. At
this point they are *jointly committed* in some way.

The interchange between Fay and Jack described earlier can be construed
along these lines: each has openly expressed his or her personal readiness jointly
to commit them to uphold as a body the plan that Fay will get whatever book
Jack says she is to get from the library.

---

[31] On commitment more generally see e.g. Margaret Gilbert "Commitment" in *The International
Encyclopedia of Ethics*, ed. Hugh LaFollette (Hoboken, NJ: Wiley-Blackwell, 2013).

[32] That this is a broad notion of commitment is not an issue for present purposes. For further
discussion in favor of the idea that personal decisions, in and of themselves, commit a person in the
sense at issue here, see Gilbert, "Commitment."

[33] Here "doing" is broadly construed so as to include believing and other cognitive attitudes.

A joint commitment cannot be rescinded unilaterally by just one of the parties, absent special background understandings. The need for its co-rescission parallels the need for its co-creation.

Evidently a joint commitment of two people is not a conjunction of two personal commitments, as would occur when two people made two corresponding personal decisions. I take it, however, that when they have jointly committed themselves each of the individuals in question is committed to do what he can to achieve the satisfaction of the joint commitment in conjunction with the actions of the other. That is, each now has sufficient reason to do this. That, as I shall argue, they *owe* each other such action adds a further consideration in favor of it.

One can argue in various ways that owing is part and parcel of every joint commitment. Though more can be said, I take it that the following observation suffices to make the point.

Intuitively, the parties to a joint commitment have the standing to demand conforming actions of the others and to rebuke them for not conforming to the commitment. If asked by virtue of what Jack has the standing to demand that Fay produce a certain library book he could convincingly invoke their joint commitment. (In practice, of course, he would speak of their agreement.) Assuming that each does have the standing to demand conformity of every other and rebuke every other for non-conformity, then each owes every other conformity.

I proposed earlier that A person, X, has the standing to demand an action of a person Y if and only if that action is in a particular—as yet unspecified—sense X's. Is each party to a joint commitment in a position to demand conforming actions as *his*—in any sense? It would take me too far afield to discuss this in detail here. Suffice it to say that it would be plausible for a party to a joint commitment, as such, to say something like this: "We have made conforming actions *ours* in the sense that *we have together directly determined that they will be performed by the person in question, all else being equal.*[34] More fully, they will be performed by him insofar as he has sufficient reason to perform them, and is disposed to act as rationality requires. Those actions, then, are *mine* in my capacity as a party to the joint commitment in question."

Owing and joint commitment: a side note

I have argued that joint commitment is a source of the owing relationship. Is it the only such source? That is too large a question to enter here. One strand in favor of a positive answer, however, may briefly be mentioned.

---

[34] He can say that they have *directly* determined this insofar as this determination depended on nothing more than the exercise of their wills (in conditions of common knowledge).

We have tracked down one sense in which someone may see another's action as his. This is the sense exemplified in the case of any joint commitment. It is hard to see how an action can be his in *this* sense outside the realm of joint commitment. And a *unitary, relatively narrow* sense of "his" is reasonably conjectured to be at issue in all cases of owing—in the sense at issue here.

I refer to a "relatively narrow sense" for the following reason. Someone may point out that "his" could relate to a broad but still unitary sense that subsumes not only the situation that is pertinent to the parties to a joint commitment but other situations as well. That may be doubted, on the grounds that if owing is a relatively precise idea, as it seems to be, the sense of "his" in question will not be so broad as to skate over significantly different types of situation. In short, a single, relatively narrow sense of "his" might reasonably be conjectured to be at issue in all cases of owing.

I cannot pursue this line of discussion further here.[35] It is important to note, however, that if joint commitment is the sole source of owing it follows that it is the only source of authoritative commands.

The practical import of commands: reflections on "the story so far"

The owing account of commands has now been given a partial articulation in terms of an agreement-constituting joint commitment. Here is an example of how it plays out in a particular case.

Officer Old and private Pert are party to an agreement-constituting joint commitment to the effect that Pert is to do whatever Old tells him to do within certain limits. Old now says to Pert "Stand to attention!" Old's purported command having fallen within the limits in question, Pert now owes his standing to attention to Old. In short, Old has *commanded* Pert to do something. If Pert stands to attention in recognition of this, Pert has *obeyed* Old and not merely done what Old said he was to do. Instead of saying that Pert owes Old conformity to his command one can also say that Pert has an *obligation* or a *duty toward* Old, according to the terminology I have adopted.

I have not argued that the case of Old and Pert as just outlined represents the whole story of commands or even prototypical commands. Nor do I believe that it does. Surely an *agreement-constituting* joint commitment is *not* necessary to ground a command. As suggested in the last section, joint commitment of *some* kind may well be.

---

[35] There is related discussion in Gilbert, "Claim-Rights". The matter is taken up more fully in a monograph in progress that focuses on rights of the sort in question here.

If it is, that would to some extent support the longstanding idea that one person's authority over another is always matter of the second person's "consent"—though there are features associated with consent as normally conceived of that are not necessary features of participation in a joint commitment. In particular, such participation can have its usual effects without being voluntary in any strong sense.[36]

I want now to ask some questions and draw some conclusions about the story so far. That is, I want to assume for the sake of argument that the story of Old and Pert *represents the whole story*. Insofar as the whole story, like theirs, is a joint commitment story, the conclusions made here will be generally applicable.

What, if anything, does this story have to do with morality? I am inclined to say that Pert's *owing* Old conformity, in and of itself, is not a moral matter. The *argument* for it was not, as far as I can see, a moral one.[37]

More important than whether or not the argument for Pert's owing Old conformity is a moral one—which depends on the question of the boundaries of the moral realm—are the implications of this owing from the point of view of practical reasoning. I focus on two pertinent points here.

First, I see no reason to think that the directed obligations or duties, the owing that is associated with Old's command, is such that rationality requires one to "give" what is owed in every conceivable circumstance. Indeed, on occasion, it may require one not to give what is owed. This accords with judgments about owing that go at least as far back as Plato's *Republic*.[38] It does not contravene the suggestion made earlier that the fact that I owe someone an action excludes some possible factors in the situation from consideration.

Second, as the way I have put the first point suggests, the directed duties in question are what one might call *intransigent*. That is, though one is in a given case rationally required to act contrary to them, all things considered, *they are still there*—prior to their fulfillment—unless and until the pertinent joint commitment has been rescinded.

This is not to say that, when one is rationally required to act contrary to a directed duty, its *source* remains though *it* disappears. It is present whenever its source is. That is, the owing relationship obtains whenever a joint commitment obtains.[39]

---

[36] See Gilbert, *Political Obligation*, ch.10, for further discussion. The appeal to consent often goes along with moral judgments of a kind that have played no role in my discussion here.

[37] It may be, of course, that one can mount an argument to the effect that all else being equal people are morally required to perform those actions owed through their joint commitments.

[38] I have in mind Socrates' counterexample to Cephalus's view of justice in Plato, *Republic* Book 1: it is not always just to give someone what you owe him.

[39] Here there is a contrast with obligations in the sense of moral requirements at least as I understand these. See e.g. the discussion in Gilbert, *Political Obligation*, 159–61.

Relatedly, these are not "prima facie" duties in Ross's sense, such that it is only when all else is equal that one with a given prima facie duty has a "duty proper."[40] Indeed, Ross's duties, whether prima facie or proper, are—on the face of it—not directed duties. That is, they are not a matter of owing.

Going back now to the first point, it seems that there is more than one type of case in which one may be rationally required to act contrary to a command. In one type of case, there is nothing objectionable about the command in itself, but one should not obey it in the circumstances. Thus if Jack instructs Fay to bring him a particular book from the library, and she finds that this book has been reserved for another patron, she should not attempt somehow to take it from the library nonetheless—not just on account of Jack's instruction. Or so I assume.

In another type of case the command is to do something bad enough morally speaking that all else being equal one ought not to fulfill it. Let us call such a command *immoral*.

Can there *be* immoral commands? That is, pleonastically, can there be an *authoritative* command of this nature? Looking at this from within the joint commitment framework the situation seems to be this.

In particular cases, there could be background understandings or explicit conditions that rule such commands out, restricting what the parties are jointly committed to. For instance, Maria says to John "I'll do anything you say, as long as it is not illegal or immoral." He accepts this, and the pertinent joint commitment is established. John then tells Maria to do something that is clearly immoral. Maria does not owe John her doing this, given the content of their joint commitment.

Possibly there is a refined and convincing philosophical argument to the effect that such a proviso is always implicit when relevant joint commitments are made.[41] I do not have such an argument in hand. I shall therefore work with the assumption that, as it seems, immoral commands are possible.

One reason for thinking that they are is that people—Milgram's subjects, or some of them, for instance—may understand the enormity of what they are being instructed to do, yet still believe that they have indeed been *instructed* to do them. Their situation then compares with that of two characters in Shakespeare's tragedy *The Life and Death of Richard the Third*:

Second murderer: The urging of that word judgment hath bred a kind of remorse in me.
First murderer: What, art thou afraid?

[40] W. D. Ross, *The Right and the Good* (Oxford: Oxford University Press, 1930), 19ff. Ross carefully explains that this is what it is to be a "prima facie" duty in his sense.

[41] The existence of an implicit proviso within every joint commitment would be different, I take it, from the existence of a free-standing joint commitment to e.g. respect standard moral norms as a

Second murderer: Not to kill him, having a warrant for it; but to be damned
   for killing him, from the which no warrant can defend me.[42]

Given that unconscionable commands are possible, the target of such a
command will be obligated to the commander to obey it He will be obligated
through the joint commitment that gives the commander his authority. In other
terms he will *owe* his commander obedience. In other terms again, it will be his
duty—to his commander—to do what he says. At the same time it may be morally wrong for him to fulfill this duty.

This prompts a return to the cases with which I began

Understanding the duties associated with such commands as directed duties
grounded in a joint commitment, one can now see one way in which some of
those involved in Milgram's experiments could have been misled by the nature of
the situation into giving electric shocks past the point of human tolerance when
commanded to do so. And one can see how some people could hold themselves
to be *held fast* in their *dark duties* as Eichmann maintained that he was.

They will indeed have been held fast insofar as *they could not, of their own voli-
tion, destroy the duties in question*—even though those duties were duties to do
awful things. Looking only to the duties with which they were shackled, they
may have thought they were *therefore* rationally required to comply. Even *given*
the existence of these dark duties, however, this was a mistake. Logic allows for
this to be true: *all things considered, they should not have done what was indeed
their duty.*

The morality of obedience

I return, finally, to Robert Wolff's discussion. Suppose—most likely contrary-to-
fact—Robert Paul Wolff is correct in supposing that one is morally required
never to act on the basis of another's orders, and that this moral requirement
supersedes all others. It would not follow that there were no commands. On
the contrary, there could be commands, and the person commanded would, as
usual, owe his obedience to his "commander." For this owing is not a matter of
moral requirement.

Someone might say: in the circumstance envisaged, how could that matter?
As we have seen, it could matter a great deal, if only because of the possibility of a

body. In the second case, the existence of immoral joint commitments would not be ruled out, even
assuming that the free-standing joint commitment could be argued to take precedence over them
from a practical point of view.

   [42] William Shakespeare, *The Life and Death of Richard the Third*, Act 1, scene 4.

narrow focus, by commander and commanded alike, on the real directed duties involved. That is one reason it is important to think hard about *the morality of obedience,* by which I mean the question when it is morally required that one obey a command and do one's duty by one's commander, and when it is morally permitted or even required not to do this duty.[43]

[43] Versions of this chapter have been presented as talks at West Point United States Military Academy (2004), the University of Miami, Coral Gables, and Columbia University (2005), as the *Warren Steinkraus Memorial Lecture* at SUNY Oswego (2006), at the York University political science workshop, and as part of the Reading University impartiality and partiality series (2007), as a plenary lecture at the collective intentionality conference, Berkeley (2008), at the ANCO seminar in Paris (2009), as one of three lectures at the University of Palermo (2010), as the *Norton Lecture* at the University of Newark, Delaware, at the USC workshop on authority, and at the University of Indiana, Bloomington (2011), and at Tom Christiano's seminar on authority at the University of Arizona, Tucson (2012). I am grateful for the stimulating comments I have received. Special thanks to Gary Ebbs for constructive written comments.

BIBLIOGRAPHY OF THE AUTHOR'S PUBLICATIONS IN THE PHILOSOPHY OF SOCIAL PHENOMENA

Abbreviations in parentheses refer to location of a given article, if any, in a specified collection of the author's works. The present work is not listed in the bibliography but is referenced as [JC] for that purpose.

Monographs

On Social Facts (1989), Routledge: New York. Reprinted 1992, Princeton University Press: Princeton.
A Theory of Political Obligation: Membership, Commitment, and the Bonds of Society (2006), Oxford University Press: Oxford.

Essay Collections

Living Together: Rationality, Sociality, and Obligation (1996) Rowman and Littlefield: Lanham, MD. [LT]
Sociality and Responsibility: New Essays in Plural Subject Theory (2000), Rowman and Littlefield: Lanham, MD. [SR]
Marcher Ensemble: Essais sur les Foncements des Phenomenes Collectif (in French) (2003), Presses Universitaires de France: Paris, France. [ME]

Articles

'About Conventions,' *Second-Order* (1974) vol. 3, no. 2, pp. 71–89.
'On An Argument for the Impossibility of Prediction in the Social Sciences' (with Fred R. Berger) (1975) *American Philosophical Quarterly*, Monograph 9, Basil Blackwell: Oxford, pp. 99–111.
'On Being Characterized in the Speech of Others' (1976) in *Life Sentences: Aspects of the Social Role of Language*, ed. Rom Harré, John Wiley and Sons: New York, pp. 10–20.
'Game Theory and Convention' (1981) *Synthese*, vol. 44, no. 1, pp. 41–93. [LT]

'Agreements, Conventions, and Language' (1983) *Synthese*, vol. 54, no. 3, pp. 375–407. [LT]

'Notes on the Concept of a Social Convention' (1983) *New Literary History*, vol. 14, pp. 225–251.

'On the Question Whether Language Has a Social Nature: Some Aspects of Winch and Others on Wittgenstein' (1983) *Synthese*, vol. 56, no. 3, pp. 301–318.

'Coordination Problems and the Evolution of Behavior' (1984) *Behavioral and Brain Sciences*, vol. 7, no. 1, 106–107.

'Modeling Collective Belief' (1987) *Synthese*, vol. 73, pp. 185–204. [LT]

'Rationality and Salience' (1989) *Philosophical Studies*, vol. 55, pp. 223–239. [LT]

'Folk Psychology Takes Sociality Seriously' (1989) *Behavioral and Brain Sciences*, vol. 12, pp. 707–708.

'Fusion: Sketch of a Contractual Model' (1990) in *Perspectives on the Family*, ed. R.C.L. Moffat, J. Grcic, and M. Bayles, Edwin Mellen Press; Lewiston, pp. 65–78. [LT] [JC]

'Rationality, Coordination, and Convention' (1990) *Synthese*, vol. 84, p. 1–21. [LT] [ME]

'Walking Together: a Paradigmatic Social Phenomenon' (1990) *Midwest Studies in Philosophy*, vol. XV, *The Philosophy of the Human Sciences*, ed. P.A. French, T.E. Uehling, Jr., and H.K. Wettstein, University of Notre Dame Press: Notre Dame, pp. 1–14. [LT] [ME]

'Wittgenstein and the Philosophy of Sociology' (1990) in *Ludwig Wittgenstein: A Symposium on the Centennial of His Birth*, ed. S. Teghrarian, A. Serafini, and E. M. Cook, Longwood Academic: Wakefield, N.H., pp. 19–29.

'More on Social Facts: Reply to Greenwood' (1991) *Social Epistemology*, vol. 5, pp. 233–344.

'Collective Belief' (1992) in *A Companion to Epistemology*, ed. J. Dancy and E. Sosa. Basil Blackwell: Oxford, pp. 70–71.

'Group Membership and Political Obligation' (1993) *The Monist*, vol. 6, no. 1, pp. 119–133. [LT]

'Agreements, Coercion, and Obligation' (1993) *Ethics*, vol. 103, no. 4, pp. 679–706. [LT]

'Is an Agreement an Exchange of Promises?' (1993) *The Journal of Philosophy*, vol. 54, no. 12, pp. 627–649. [LT]

'Norms' (1994) in *Blackwell Dictionary of Twentieth Century Social Thought*, ed. W. Outhwaite and T. Bottomore, Blackwell: Oxford, pp. 425–427.

'Durkheim and Social Facts' (1994) in *Debating Durkheim*, ed. H. Martins and W. Pickering, Routledge: London, pp. 86–109.

'Remarks on Collective Belief' (1994) in *Socializing Epistemology: The Social Dimensions of Knowledge*, ed. Frederick F. Schmitt, Rowman and Littlefield: Lanham, MD, pp. 235–253. [LT]

'Sociality as a Philosophically Significant Category' (1994) *Journal of Social Philosophy*, vol. 25, no. 3, pp. 5–25.

'Me, You, and Us: Distinguishing Egoism, Altruism, and Groupism' (1994) *Behavioral and Brain Sciences*, vol. 17, pp. 621–622.

'Social Epistemology and Family Therapy' (1995) [English original published in Italian translation], in *Esperienza e Conoscenza*, ed. Gianguido Piazza, Milan: Citta Studi, pp. 247–248.

'Group wrongs and guilt feelings' (1997) *Journal of Ethics*, vol. 1, no. 1, pp. 65–84.

'Concerning Sociality: The Plural Subject as Paradigm' (1997) in *The Mark of the Social*, ed. John Greenwood, Rowman and Littlefield: Lanham, MD, pp. 17–35.

'What Is It for *Us* to Intend?' (1997) in *Contemporary Action Theory*, ed. G. Holmstrom-Hintikka and R. Tuomela, vol. 2, Dordrecht: D. Reidel, pp. 65–85. [SR]

'Credenze Collettive e Mutamento Scientifico' (1998) (English original 'Collective Belief and Scientific Change' tr. into Italian by G. Piazza), *Fenomenologia e Societa*, vol 21, no. 1, 32–45.

'Social Norms' (1998) *Routledge Encyclopedia of Philosophy*, Routledge: New York, vol. 8, pp. 834–836.

'In Search of Sociality' (1998) *Philosophical Explorations*, vol.1, no.3, pp. 233–241.

'Reconsidering the 'Actual Contract' Theory of Political Obligation' (1999) *Ethics*, vol. 109, pp. 226–260. [SR] [ME]

'Obligation and Joint Commitment' (1999) *Utilitas*, vol. 11, pp. 143–163. [SR]

'Social Rules: Some Problems for Hart's Account, and An Alternative Proposal' (1999) *Law and Philosophy*, vol. 18, pp. 141–171 [SR]

'Sociality, Unity, Objectivity' (2000) *Proceedings of the 1998 World Congress of Philosophy: Invited papers*, pp. 153–160.

'Joint Action' (2001) *Elsevier Encyclopedia of the Social and Behavioral Sciences*, ed. N. J. Smelser and P. J. Baltes, Elsevier: Amsterdam. vol. 12, pp. 7987–7992.

'Collective Remorse' (2001) in *War Crimes and Collective Wrongdoing: A Reader*, ed. A. Jokic, Basil Blackwell: Oxford, pp. 216–235. [SR]

'Considerations on Collective Guilt' (2001) *From History to Justice: Essays in Honor of Burleigh Wilkins*, ed. A. Jokic, Peter Lang: New York, pp. 239–249.

'Collective Preferences, Obligations, and Rational Choice' (2001) *Economics and Philosophy*, vol. 17, pp. 109–119.

'Philosophy and the Social Sciences' (2002) in *The Scope of Logic, Methodology and Philosophy of Science*, ed. P. Gardenfors, J. Wolenski and K. Kijania-Placek, Kluwer Academic Publishers: Dordrecht., pp. 439–449. [ME]

'Belief and Acceptance as Features of Groups' (2002) *Protosociology*, vol. 16, pp. 35–69 (online journal: www.protosociology.de). [JC]

'Collective Guilt and Collective Guilt Feelings' (2002) *Journal of Ethics*, vol. 6, pp. 115–143. [JC]

'Acting Together' (2002) in *Social Facts and Collective Intentionality*, ed. Georg Meggle, Frankfurt: Hansel-Hohenhausen, pp. 53–72.

'Considerations on Joint Commitment: Responses to various comments' (2002) in *Social Facts and Collective Intentionality*, ed. Georg Meggle, Frankfurt: Hansel-Hohenhausen, pp. 73–102. [JC]

'Collective Wrongdoing: Moral and Legal Responses' (2002) *Social Theory and Practice*, vol. 28, no. 1, pp. 167–187.

'The Structure of the Social Atom: Joint Commitment as the Foundation of Human Social Behavior' (2003) in *Social Metaphysics: The Nature of Social Reality*, ed. F. Schmitt, Rowman and Littlefield: Lanham, MD, pp. 39–64.

'Scanlon on Promissory Obligation: the Problem of Promisees' Rights' (2004) *Journal of Philosophy*, vol. 101, pp. 83–109. [JC]

'Collective Epistemology' (2004) *Episteme*, vol. 1, no. 2, pp. 95–97. [JC]

'A Theoretical Framework for the Understanding of Teams' (2004) *Teamwork: Multidisciplinary Perspectives*, ed. Natalie Gold, Palgrave-MacMillan: New York, pp. 22-32.

'On the Nature and Normativity of Intentions and Decisions: Towards an Understanding of Commitments of the Will' (2005) in *Patterns of Value II*, ed. Wlodek Rabinowicz and Toni Ronnow-Rasmussen, Lund University: Lund, pp. 180–189.

'Shared Values, Social Unity and Liberty' (2005) *Public Affairs Quarterly*, vol. 19, no. 1, pp. 25–49. [JC]

'Corporate Misbehavior and Collective Values' (2005) *Brooklyn Law Review*, vol. 70, no. 4, pp. 1369–1380.

'Shared Values and Social Unity' (2005) *Experience and Analysis: Proceedings of the Austrian Wittgenstein Society*, pp. 373–376.

'Rationality in Collective Action' (2006) *Philosophy of the Social Sciences*, vol. 36, no. 1, pp. 3–17. [JC]

'Can a Wise Society Be a Free One?' (2006) *Southern Journal of Philosophy*, vol. 44, pp. 1–17.

'Croyances Collectives' (2005) in *Le Dictionnaire des Sciences Humaines*, Presses Universitaires de France: Paris, pp. 225–225.

'Acting Together, Joint Commitment, and Obligation' (2006) in *Facets of Sociality*, ed. Nikos Psarros and Katinka Schulte-Ostermann, Ontos Verlag: Frankfurt, pp. 153–168. [JC]

'Who's to Blame? Collective Moral Responsibility and Its Implications for Group Members'
(2006), *Midwest Studies in Philosophy*, ed. Peter French, vol. 30, pp. 94–114. [JC]

'Mutual Recognition, Common Knowledge and Joint Attention' (2007) in *Hommage à Wlodek.
Philosophical Papers Dedicated to Wlodek Rabinowicz*, ed. T. Rønnow-Rasmussen, B.
Petersson, J. Josefsson and D. Egonsson, www.fil.lu.se/hommageawlodek.

'Searle on Collective Intentions' (2007) in *Intentional Acts and Social Facts*, ed. Savas Tsohatzidis,
Dordrecht: Springer, pp. 31–48.

'Collective Intentions, Commitment, and Collective Action Problems' (2007) in *Rationality
and Commitment*, ed. Fabienne Peter and Hans-Bernard Schmid, Oxford University
Press: Oxford, [pp. 258–280.

'La Responsabilite Collective Et Ses Implications' (2008), *Review Francaise de Science Politique*, vol.
92 no. 2, pp. 268–285

'Social Convention Revisited' (2008) in *Topoi*, special issue on convention, vol. 27, pp. 5–16. [JC]

Interview (2008) in *Philosophy of the Social Sciences: Five Questions*, ed. Diego Rios and Christoph
Schmidt-Petri, Automatic Press: Copenhagen. pp. 47–55.

'Two Approaches to Shared Intention: An Essay in the Philosophy of Social Phenomena' (2008)
in a special anniversary issue of *Analyse u. Kritik*, vol. 30, pp. 483–514. [JC]

'A Real Unity of Them All?' (2009) *The Monist*, special issue on Europe, vol. 92, no. 2, pp.
268–285. [JC]

'Shared Intention and Personal Intentions' (2009) *Philosophical Studies*, vol. 144, pp. 167–187.

'Pro Patria: An Essay on Patriotism' (2010), *Journal of Ethics*, vol. 13, special issue ed. I. Primoratz,
pp. 319–340. [JC]

'Culture as Collective Construction' (2010), published with a commentary by Annette Schnabel
and the author's response in *Kolner Zeitschrift for Sociologie und Sozialpsychologie*, pp.
384–410.

'Joint or Collective Intention' (2010) in *Encyclopedia of the Mind*, Sage Publications:

'Collective Action' (2010) in *A Companion to the Philosophy of Action*, Wiley-Blackwell: Thousand
Oaks: CA.

'Three Dogmas About Promising' (2011) in *Understanding Promises and Agreements* ed. H.
Sheinman, Oxford University Press: New York, pp. 80–108. [JC]

'Mutual Recognition and Some Related Phenomena' in *Recognition and Social Ontology*, ed. H.
Ikaheimo and A. Laitinen, Brill: Leiden, pp. 270–286. [JC]

'Foundations and Consequences of Collective Moral Responsibility' (2011) in *Teoria e Critica
Della Regolazione Sociale*, Quaderno 1: http://www.lex.unict.it/tcrs.

'Giving Claim-Rights Their Due' (2012) in *Rights: Concepts and Contexts*, ed. Brian Bix and
Horacio Spector, Ashgate: Farnham, Surrey, pp. 301-323.

'Commitment' (2013) *The International Encyclopedia of Ethics*, ed. Hugh LaFollette, Hoboken,
NJ: Wiley-Blackwell.

'Conversation and Collective Belief' (2013) (with Maura Priest) *Perspectives on Pragmatics and
Philosophy*, ed. A. Capone, F. Lo Piparo, and M. Carapezza, Springer: Dordrecht.

'Social Rules' (2013) (with Maura Priest) in *Encyclopedia of the Social Sciences*, ed. Byron Kaldis,
pp. 931–933.

'The Nature of Agreements: A Solution to Some Puzzles About Claim-Rights and Joint Intention'
(forthcoming) in *Rational and Social Agency*, ed. Manuel Vargas and Gideon Yaffe,
New York: Oxford University Press.

"A Theory of Political Obligation: Responses to Horton, Jeske, Narveson and Stoutland" (2013)
in *Jurisprudence: An International Journal of Legal and Political Thought* vol 4.

"Responses to Some Questions on Social Convention and Related Matters" (2013) in *Convenzioni*,
Post n. 4, Mimesis: Milano-Udine.

'How We Feel" (in press) to appear in *Collective Emotions* ed. Mikko Salmela et al., to be published
by New York: Oxford University Press.

'Individual versus Collective Epistemology' (with Daniel Pilchman) (in preparation) to appear in
Essays in Collective Epistemology, ed. J. Lackey, to be published by Oxford University Press.

Book Reviews:

Review of W. Wallace, *Principles of Scientific Sociology*, in *Ethics*, 1987, pp. 180–181.

Review of M. Robins, *Promising, Intending and Moral Autonomy*, in *Philosophical Review*, 1991, pp. 315–317.

Review of L. May and S. Hoffman, eds., *Collective Responsibility: Five Decades of Debate in Theoretical and Applied Ethics*, in *Canadian Philosophical Reviews*, 1993, pp. 165–170.

Review of P. Pettit, *The Common Mind*, in *Mind*, 1994, pp. 560–563.

Review of C. Bicchieri, *Rationality and Coordination*, in *Philosophical Review*, 1996, pp. 105–108.

Review of R. Hardin, *One For All*, in *Philosophical Review*, 1998, pp. 135–137.

Review of A. Baier, *The Commons of the Mind*, in *Ethics*, 1999, pp. 894–897.

Review of J. Elster, *Ulysses Unbound*, *Mind*, vol. 111, no. 444, 2002, pp. 339–403.

Review of C. Kutz, *Complicity: Ethics and Law for a Collective Age*, in *Philosophy and Phenomenological Research*, vol. 67, no. 1, 2003, pp. 233–235.

Review of K. Graham, *Practical Reasoning in a Social World*, in *Philosophical Review*, vol. 113, no. 1, 2004, pp. 130–132.

SUBJECT INDEX

Technical terms of the author's are in boldface type, as are pages that define/introduce the term

acceptance
  related to belief, 132–3, 141
  collective, 83n4, 134, 152n48, 159
  conceptions of, 134, 158, 160
  contextual, 146
  exemplified, 134
  by individuals, 158–9
  joint, 40n9
  proposal for, 159
  rejectionism and, **13, 133**, 134
  subject of, 156
  and truth, 146n34
  as voluntary, 155
  See also belief; collective belief
accountability, 229–230
  See also answerability; blaming,
    blameworthiness
acting together, collectively
  agreements and, 10–11, 23, 26–8, 29
  the agreement hypothesis, 26
  antagonistic participants, 27, 28
  and collective agents, 82
  and collective goals or intentions, 11, 12, 30,
    34, 69–70, 82–3, 88, 238, 240
  and collective moral responsibility 11, 74,
    237–40
  and collectives, 63
  concluding, 54
  costs and benefits, 55
  distinctions among, 28n12
  everyday concept of, 96
  examples of, 23, 24, 27, 28, 53
  and excuses, 53
  and expressions of readiness, willingness,
    29, 33n21
  feelings of guilt over, 255–6
  few or many participants, 12

  foundation for, 30
  freedom of, 72–4, 241–2
  and freedom of participants, 11, 55, 73
  genesis of, 26–9, 33
  and helping behavior, 122n64
  idea of, 3
  intentional base of, 237
  and interfering behavior, demands, rebukes,
    8–9, 53, 71
  interrupted, 81
  and joint commitment, 11n31, 34, 69–71,
    88–9, 240, 336
  not known to group members, 75
  and morality, 35
  and obligations, rights, 10–11, 23, 24–6, 34–5,
    52–4
  observations on, 23, 24–6, 26–8
  organicist conception of, 229–30
  organization of, 29
  and permission-seeking, 54
  rationality in, 89–92
  rudeness while, 54
  and structure of human sociality, 23
  "together" not spatial, 24, 53n60
  and theorists, theory of, 13, 53, 95–6
  two-person case, 24
  without preamble, 27, 28
  worries about, 82, 91
  See also collective goals; moral responsibility,
    collective; rebuke(s)
action, of one person
  alone, 30, 33
  blameworthiness of, 61
  in context of collective action, 75–80, 240,
    244–6
  coordinating with another, 8, 211, 402
  erroneous, 6, 7, 31, 347

action, of one person (*Cont.*)
  freedom, autonomy of, 61–2
  goals of, 30, 32–4
  impact on *us*, 7
  inaction as, 115
  intentional, 62, 69
  pressures on, 76
  speech as, 115
  "tangential", 76
  See also coordination; decisions, personal
aggregate(s),
  versus collectives, social groups, 59, 199, 200,
    204, 237, 344, 345
  with common features, 200, 237
  and discrimination, 200n38
  and forming a body, 116
  responsibility of, 60
  and summative accounts, 190
  and unity, lack of, 167, 181, 200, 346
agreement(s)
  and acting together, 10, 26–28, 29, 33, 89
  bilateral executory, 46n33
  and commands, 418–9
  versus contract, legal, 86
  and decisions, personal, 87
  and "fusion", interpersonal, 261
  implicit, 27
  being in, 106
  and intentions, personal, 102–4
  and joint commitment, 16, 49, 35, 65, 219,
    263, 398
  joint decision account of, **29**, 49, 89, 117,
    221, **316–7**, 419
  morally neutral, 35
  give obligations, directed, 5, 203, 314, 419–10
  obligations of, interdependent and
    simultaneous, 315–6
  as "ours", 345
  and promise-exchanges, 28, 46n33, 314–6
  premeditative quality of, 27
  rescission of, 65
  give rights, 23, 26, 28
  and shared intention, 89, 98–9, 104
  side-, 112
  signing on to, 66n24
  and social conventions, 209, 213
  standard approaches to, 28, 89, 314–5
  on terms, 104
  See also promise(s)
animals, non-human, 143n28, 163
anomie, 201
answerability
  to oneself, 38
  betrayal and, 38n5
  and joint commitment, 40, 48, 50, 88,
    175, 198
  See also obligation, directed
apology, 53, 86–7, 213, 229, 253

arbitrariness, 220
  See also rebuke(s)
atrocities, 15, 76, 416n21
attitudes, 13, 184
  See also collective belief, sharing values
"as a body"
  phrase not essential, 33, 138, 370
  See also joint commitment, to act **as a body**
authority, authorities, 352
  See also command(s); rule, ruling
authorization, 40, 67–8, 218n47
autonomy, 411–2
  See also command(s)

belief
  and acceptance, 132–3
  and collective belief statements, 144
  criteria for an account, 142–3
  in epistemology, 14
  in a capacity, 140
  and collective belief*, 14
  mind-to-world direction of fit, 146
  and truth, 134
  about value, 182–4
  relation to will, 134, 194
  See also acceptance, collective belief
betrayal, 38n5
binding, being bound, bonds
  as bondage, 183, 205
  by decisions, intentions, 84–5, 309, 398
  Devlin on societal, 182–3
  by common morality, 183, 205
  by common thought, 183, 205, 350
  by joint commitment, 87–8, 206
  one another, 347
  oneself, 296
  and promises, 296, 298, 309
  Rawls on societal, 182, 183
  and sharing values, 183, 199, 206
  and social unity, 183, 205, 206, 352
  people together, 205, 206, 347
  of will(s), 84
  willed, 313
  wish to avoid, 55
  See also commitment(s), generally; obligation
    (duty); social unity, union
blaming, blameworthiness, 61–2
  and guilt, owing payment, 41
  See also moral responsibility
body, as a. *See* "**as a body**"
body, collective, 118–9, 332

care, concern, 259, 262, 334–5
change
  in collective values, 205
  in laws, institutions, 364, 377, 403, 404, 406
  in membership, 67, 69
  of mind, personal, 6, 31, 38, 84, 102

in preferences, 4
progressive, 152n48, 205
scientific, 152n48
See also decisions, personal; protest
citizens, citizenship
benefits to, 345
body of, 254
dual, 381
and Europe, 343
good, 381
and joint commitment, 254, 354, 365
as legal status, 345, 363
and love of a country, 385
of minimal polity, 372
misrepresented, 353
moral requirements on, 17
nature of, 4, 17, 355, 378, 363
passive, 371
protest by, 377
and owing, 17–8, 384
and social contract, 345
See also patriotism; political obligation(s)
claim-rights, claims. *See* rights
coercion, duress
of collective, 74
internal to a group, 242
and joint commitment, 47, 66, 242, 400
and political obligation, 78n43
and "readiness", 33n21
and rights, 277
See also punishment
cognitive states, 134
See also acceptance, belief
collectives, 59–60
versus **aggregates, 59**
See also social group(s)
collective acceptance. *See* acceptance, collective
collective action
as action of collective, 63, 72–4
and collective agents, 82
inclinations and, 12, 92–3
problems, 12, 92–3
in rational choice theory, 12, 81
rationality in, 89–92
See also acting together, collectively
collective attitudes, 12–5
See also collective belief; collective values;
    collective emotions; sharing values
collective belief
versus collective acceptance, 159
accounts of, 184n13
and analytic philosophers, 132
authority of, 132
basic cases of, 136
behavioral requirements of, 176, 192–4
coercive power of, 131, 160
without collective consciousness, 9
and collective knowledge, 71

and context, 146–7, 176–7
and conversation, 15n28
Devlin on, 185, 186
different types of, 131n1
the distributive condition, 137
and diverse believers, 135–6
Durkheim and, 131–2
and evidence, 72, 147–51
as "joint acceptance", 141
joint commitment in, 140, 176
individuals as bedrock of, 135
literature on, 72n35
negative points, 13, 137
and offending against, 137
plural subject account of, 71, 132, 137–40,
    141, 172–7
without personal beliefs, 9–11
and **rejectionism, 13, 132–3, 160**
in science, 13
and social epistemology, 132
and standing to rebuke, 171–2
statements, 131, 133, 136, 142
summative accounts of, 14, 168–171, 172
and truth, 145–7, 151–2, 152–3
and the will, 153–7
See also acceptance, collective; **collective
    belief***; collective epistemology; sharing
    values
collective belief*, 133, **137–8**
collective blameworthiness. *See* moral
    responsibility, collective
"collective commitment", 50n52
See also "joint commitment"
collective or group consciousness, 9
collective emotions, 15, 73, 231
See also collective guilt feelings
collective epistemology, 14, 165–6, 179, 180
See also acceptance, collective; collective
    belief
collective goals
and acting together, 11, 12, 34
and collective belief, 155–6
joint commitment account of, 30, 32–33
See also acting together; shared (joint,
    collective) intention
collective guilt feelings
benefits of, 15, 230–1
and collective moral guilt, 235–6, 237–42
collective subject of, 255
everyday attributions of, 231, 255
and feelings of individuals, 255–6
and feelings of personal guilt, 242–6, 255
and feelings of membership guilt,
    246–51, 255
genesis of, 252–4
pangs of, 254–5
plural subject account of, 252, 255–6
possibility of, 230, 232–5

collective guilt feelings (*Cont.*)
  See also collective emotions; guilt, feelings of;
    membership guilt, feelings of
collective intentions
  and acting together, 11n11, 12, 69–70
  joint commitment account of, 12,
    69–70, 83
  See also collective goals; intentions, personal;
    shared (joint, collective) intention
collective moral responsibility. *See* moral
  responsibility, collective
collective reasoning, 72
collective values. *See* sharing values
command(s)
  agreement proposal for, 418–9
  and standing, authority, 210n16, 306n26,
    411, 414
  commitments of will as, 174
  versus demands, 417n25
  divine, 411n7
  excuses invoking, 409–10, 411
  and group action, 246
  immoral, 18, 122n63, 245, 424–5
  and joint commitment, 18, 67–8, 422
  Milgram's experiments on, 410
  and morality, 409
  non-moralized account of, 18
  for one's own, 288
  owing account of, 414–5, 422
  popular account of, 415–6
  practical import of, 422–5
  of promisee, 278
  prototypical, 414–6, 422
  purported, 411
  to do right, 204n48
  and rights, 18, 277n23, 414n17
  self-directed, 174
  with stipulated authority, 67–8
  ubiquitous, 18
  Wolff on, 411–3
commitment(s), generally
  give **sufficient reason**, **64**, 401, 420
  grades of, 85
  as incentives, 83
  and morality, sociality, 31, 39, 192
  See also commitment(s) of the will
commitment(s), of the will, **64**, **72–4**
  decisions and intentions, and, 420
  and moral considerations, 222n62
  personal and joint 31–2, 193
  and reasons, 192, 198
  as reason-providing, 31, 39, 199, 222
  rescindable, 6
  subject of a, 7
  trump inclinations, 198, 222n64
  varieties of, 64
  See also joint commitment(s);
    commitment(s), personal

commitment(s), personal, 31–33, **38**–9, **63**,
  138, **192**
  and answerability, 38
  sole authority over, 138
  and change of mind, 6, 31, 38
  and decision, personal, 6, 38, 63, 192, 420
  and personal intention, 62–4, 420
  and joint commitment, 45n31
  may be lightly made, 192–3
  process and product, 6
  and self-chiding, 38
  singularist concept, 6
  unilateral rescission, 6, 38
  unilateral creation, 39
  See also commitment(s), of the will
common knowledge
  accounts of, **29**, **43**, **51**, 65, 211, 239, 267n2
  Balzer on, 43n22, 51
  and collective attitudes, 222, 251
  how connects parties, 191
  in coordination problems, 92
  of co-presence, 324, **325**–**6**, 335, 337
  discussions of, 29n15, 51n54, 89n11,
    95n3, 324
  and distanced populations, 51
  early focus on, 95n4
  effect of, 313
  of expressions of readiness for collective
    action, 29, 51
  in family, marriage, 78, 251
  individual, 211
  individualist, singularist notion, 95, 166n5
  joint attention goes beyond, 336, 337n32
  in joint commitment formation, 32, 46, 65,
    66, 86, 87, 115, 117, 119, 139, 174, 196,
    219, 239, 311, 316, 321, 329, 366–7,
    398, 401
  in large populations 51, 66, 196, 239, 399
  Lewis invokes, 211
  and mutual recognition, 324
  and openness*, etc., 43, 46
  or "out in the open", 14, 29, 65, 267n20
  of personal intentions, decisions, feelings,
    principles 43, 92, 251, 284
  population, 211
  possession of concept of, 333
  of reasons-responsiveness, 225, 226
  and summative accounts of social phenomena,
    172, 190, 191
  Taylor on, 94–5, 165–6, 326–8
  two kinds of, 211
  See also joint attention; open*, openness*;
    mutual recognition
communication
  common knowledge without, 325
  and conforming to a joint commitment, 330
  forms of, 43
  in joint commitment formation, 311

as transmission, 327
See also conversation
concept(s), everyday
analysis of, 3
across cultures, 3
graspable without analysis, 9
human actions informed by, 2
joint commitment as, 9, 30
and social science, interpretive and
descriptive, 2–3
conditional personal commitments
assumption (CPC), 42–5
See also conditional personal intentions
conditional personal intentions,
externally conditional, 43
internally conditional, 43
and joint commitment, 42–5
matching, 43
not in *On Social Facts*, 46–7
puzzles about, 44
See also joint commitment(s); intentions
personal
contracts. *See* agreement(s)
content-independence, of obligations, 314,
402–6, 415–6
conventions. *See* social convention(s)
conversation
as acting together, collective action, 28, 81
and collective belief, 13n28, 159,
266n19
and fusion, 266
interrupted, 81, 92
philosophical, 96
in *On Social Facts*, 13n28
social phenomenon, 4
involving strangers, 266
writer and reader, 327n8
coordination
and joint commitment, 55n71, 92
problems of, 3, 55n71, 92, 207n1, 211,
220n54, 226
and shared sub-plans, 123n66
and social convention, 211, 214
co-presence, 325
country, one's own
acting on behalf of, 357
joint commitment account of, 17, 362, 365,
371, 402
love of, 17, 358n4, 360–2, 363
and membership guilt feelings,
246–51, 255
pride and shame regarding, 247
"right or wrong", 382n47
See also membership guilt, feelings of;
patriotism; political society
culture(s), 3, 181, 215, 266, 333, 337
See also sharing values; social convention(s)
custom, account of, 220

decisions, joint. *See* agreement(s)
decisions, personal
versus acting, 29n15
acting against, 31, 420
and agreements, 87
binding, persists how long, 64, 89, 114,
115n45, 347
and change of mind, 6, 31, 38, 64, 84, 102–3
coerced, 66
give commitments, personal, 6, 7, 31, 115
to decide, 39
forgetting, 347
versus joint commitment, 42, 92–3
versus intentions personal, 64, 102–3
normativity of, 31, 64, 84, 92, 114, 115
and promissory obligation, 309
and reasons, 115, 309n30
rescission. *See* change of mind
as self-addressed command, 196
give sufficient reason, 114
without weighty reasons, 3, 84
and the will, 7
See also commitment(s), generally; intentions,
personal
demanding, with standing
authoritative pressure, as, 277
collective judgment and, 185, 186
Devlin and, 185–6
versus commanding, 417
disapproval, personal, insufficient for, 185
and joint commitment, 8, 120, 175, 198,
222–3, 313n39, 369, 401, 421
not justification, 111, 202–4, 417
and meta-interventions, 199
and moral norms, 187, 217, 308
one's own, 8n16, 110, 216–7, 278, 307, 312–4,
397, 401
and owing, 110, 216, 395–7, 401
and promises, 282, 306
versus purporting to demand, 306
and rights, 395–7
and the standing to rebuke, 110, 189, 216,
278, 307
versus urging, 55
See also joint commitment(s); rebuke(s)
deontic logic, 34, 50, 275n16
derivative, individual commitment. *See* **joint**
commitment(s)
disapproval, personal 185, 191
distanced populations, 51
dyad, two-person group, 11–12

ego(s), 259, 261, 268
emotions, feelings
collective, possibility of, 234–5
feelings of membership guilt, 246–50
feelings of personal guilt, 243, 247–8
and fusion joint commitment, 265

emotions, feelings (*Cont.*)
  guilt feelings, conditions on, 242–4
  methodological concerns, 234
  phenomenological aspects, 232–3, 247–8, 254–5
  precipitating joint actions, 27
  See also care, concern; collective emotions;
    collective guilt feelings; love; patriotism
enforcement. *See* punishment
entre nous, 327, 331
epistemology, traditional
  and belief, 14, 144, 145–6
  and belief-acceptance distinction, 132
  and common knowledge, 166n5
  focus on individual case, 141–2, 163
  methodology of, 14, 134, 141–4
  neglect of collective case, 132
  standard points in, 145–6
  See also collective epistemology, social
    epistemology
etiquette, 54
  See also social convention(s)
European Union, 17, 181, 341, 343, 351–5
exchanging, 28n13

family, families, 78, 79, 190, 201, 229, 231, 261
  therapy, 260
  See also fusion, of persons; marriage(s);
    parents, parental influence
freedom, liberty
  and acting together, 11
  of action of a collective, 72–4
  and blameworthiness, 61
  degrees of, 62
  and fusion, 261
  gaining another's, 55
  Mill on, 202, 203
  preference for, 55
  in relation to collective values, 201–3
  of a society, 203
  as voluntariness, 61
  See also punishment
friendships, 4, 189
fusion, of persons
  and agreements, 261
  benefits of, 16, 259
  bodily, 260
  and care, concern, 259, 265
  clinical psychologists on, 260
  of egos, souls, 257, 259
  and loss of freedom, self, 261, 264
  in marital relationships, 4, 265–8
  plural subject account, 264
  and positive feelings, 259, 267, 269
  a sense of, 260
  when salient, 16
  types of, 267–9
  See also marriage

game-theory
  and convention, 4, 211, 214, 218, 220n54,
    226
  coordination problems, 3, 4, 15, 55n71, 92,
    100n25, 226
  Hi-Lo game, 101n25
  Prisoner's Dilemma, 12, 92, 93, 226n71
  and structures of inclination, 92–3, 226
groups. *See* social groups
group languages, 19, 37
group minds, 135
government(s), 242, 253
  See also rule, ruling
guilt. *See* guilt, feeling of; blameworthiness
guilt, feeling of
  and feeling-sensations, pangs, 232–4, 254
  three kinds of, 255–6
  personal, over what I did, 243, 255
  personal, over what we did, 246–51, 255
  and remorse, 231
  utility of, 231
  and victims' feelings, 231
  See also collective guilt feelings

holism, holistic
  of joint commitment, 39, 40, 46, 135,
    207, 312
  pernicious kind 9
  talk about groups, 229–30

"I" perspective, 94
  See also individualism
identification, 249–50, 262, 342, 343, 354
individualism
  in accounts of sharing values, 182, 191
  in analytic philosophy, 94
  of Hart and Lewis, 94, 207
  and *On Social Facts*, 135n13
  versus "supra-individualism", 9
  See also **singularism;** holism, holistic
intentions, personal
  conditional, 42–5
  contributory, 103
  correlative, 105
  versus decisions, personal, 64, 102–3
  versus joint commitment, 42
  may fade away, 64
  normative force of, 64
  two kinds of, 70
  how rescindable, 102–3, 107–8
  and shared intention, 4, 12, 101–2, 103, 105,
    107–8
  See also commitment(s), of the will;
    conditional personal intentions; decisions,
    personal; shared (joint, collective)
    intention
interfering, 71

interventions, 185
"intuitive," "intuitively", 208, 303

joint action. *See* acting together
joint attention, 16, 335–7
joint commitment(s)
   to act **as a body,** 7, 32–3, 41, **64,** 86, 116–8,
      138, 141, **192–4,** 252, 311–2, 370
   all parties commit all, 219, 347
   and **aggregates,** 67
   authorizing, 40, 67–8, 218n47
   basic case, 7, 32, 46, **47, 48, 86, 115,** 139n52,
      218, 311, 347, 352, 367, 398
   and collective level of existence, 311
   are commitments of the will, 6
   commitments, personal, not sum of, 7, 31, 64,
      65, 115, 138
   complex web of, 15
   concomitant, 48
   concurrence of thoughts, more than, 196
   and conditional personal commitments,
      42–5, 115
   conforming actions, possibly disjunctive set
      of, 402
   conformity to, what involved, 7, 194, 195,
      311, 330
   content, 41
   and context, 176, 194
   and decisions, personal, 196, 329
   demise of, 65–6, 87, 225
   derived, non-basic, case, 218n47, 311n32,
      352–3, 398n22
   duration, 15, 68–9
   and duress, voluntariness, 47, 66
   effects of, 195
   explanations of, **5–10, 31–3, 40–1, 64–7,**
      85–8, 115–9, 138–40, 172–7, 192–6,
      311–2, 329, **397–400,** 420–1
   expressed condition, 46
   expression condition, 46
   expressions of readiness for, 47–8
   formation of, 7, 32, 40, 42–9, 51–2, 65,
      66, 86–7, 115, 117, 139–40, 196, 219,
      367, 398
   and general features, 367, 399
   general form of, 7, 86, 138. *See also* to act as
      a body
   of group members as such, 139
   helpful behavior and, 70, 71, 265
   and identification, 249
   versus inclination, 93, 380
   of individuals as such, 139
   and interventions, meta-interventions, 199
   joining an established, 66–7
   of large populations, 17, 51–2, 66, 68, 78, 79,
      97n16, 98n18, 196, 204, 219, 239, 250, 351,
      354, 399

and morality, 8, 75, 334
and mutual recognition, 48
nested, 351
normativity of, 7, 75, 86, 367–8, 380. *See also*
   obligations of,
object of, 45n30
gives obligations and rights. *See* joint
   commitment, parties to a
and offense, 198
in *On Social Facts,* 1
as "ours", 198
overridable, 91, 368, 369, 423
and owing, 400–1
parts, has no, 32, 138
persistence of, 87–8
and **personal commitments assumption, 45**
and political obligation, 402
constitute plural subjects, 9, 37, 63, 116, 176,
   197, 320, 331
as process and product, 6, 7, 46–8
relationship, matter of, 331
rescission of, 40, 65, 118
as self-addressed edict, 174, 196
signing on to, 348, 399
source of command authority, 18
gives standing to demand, rebuke, etc. 8, 34,
   70, 71, 120, 175, 198, 199, 263, 312, 369,
   397, 400–1, 402, 421
as the "structure of the social atom", 18
subject of, 7
trumping quality of, 224, 334, 368, 380
of two or more people, 31, 64, 174, 310
two-person case, 24, 40, 41, 54, 260
types of, 87–8
violation, 32, 193, 195, 198, 225, 398
variety of contents, 64
voidable, 40n11
and one's own will, 48
and willful nonconformity, 225
See also commitment(s), generally;
   commitment(s), personal; joint
   commitment, concept of; joint
   commitment, parties to a; **plural**
   subject(s)
joint commitment, concept of
   explanatory power of, 195
   is fundamental everyday concept, 1, 30, 67,
      85, 118
   and "holism", 9, 39, 40, 46, 227
   metaphysically innocuous, 119, 217–8
   not singular st, 6
   See also joint commitment(s)
joint commitment, parties to a
   answerable to other parties, 40, 48, 50, 88,
      175, 198
   are co-creators of the commitment, 401
   have concept of joint commitment, 46

joint commitment, parties to a (*Cont.*)
  can demand explanation, 198
  have dependent commitments, 7–8, 32, 41
  dependent commitments interdependent, 41
  dependent commitments not personal, 41
  dependent commitments simultaneous, 41,
    138, 263, 316
  and emulation of a single phi-er, 7, 194, 195
  may not know of it, 46
  obligations content- and context-
    independent, 313, 405
  obligations of, 8, 34–5, 49–50, 120–2, 312–3,
    368–9, 407–8
  organized by it, 12, 124
  owe each other conformity, 400–1, 420–2
  pleasures of, 55n71
  rights of, 335. *See also* obligations of
  safeguards of, 334
  unified, 67, 197–8, 331, 346–7, 350, 353
  See also joint commitment(s); right(s)
"joint commitment" (phrase), 30, 32, 37, 50
  See also joint commitment(s)
joint readiness, 47n38

knowledge, 52, 72
  See also belief; common knowledge; collective
    belief
knowledge requirement, for
  blameworthiness, 62

language
  and convention, 207–8, 222
  group, 19, 118, 197, 337
  and mutual recognition, 333
  power of, 327
  sociality of, 38n3
large groups, populations. *See* joint commitment,
  large populations
law(s), legal
  and agreement, 345
  of agreements, contracts, 298
  versus collective values, 204
  of complicity and conspiracy, 229
  and convention, 209
  of one's country, 378
  criminal, 199n35, 204, 248n36, 275
  in the *Crito*, 345, 378
  enforcement of, 186n20
  and joint commitment, 372
  and morality, 404
  morally bad, 405, 406, 407
  obedience to, 372,373, 381n46, 383, 407
  obligatio in Roman, 276n18
  of nature, 339
  owing conformity to, 406–7
  as political institution, 404
  and political obligation, 405

  punishment, 277n22
  reasons of, 298
  and stipulated rights, 295
  writers on, 275, 287
  See also political society; punishment; rules,
    social
liberty. *See* freedom, liberty
living together, 17, 18, 23, 189
love
  of country, 360–1
  and duty, 360
  and "fusion", "merging", union, 15, 259,
    260, 269
  and lovers, 259–60
  unclear meaning of term, 269, 360
  in definitions of patriotism, 17, 360, 361, 362
  and valuing, 358n4
  See also care, concern; fusion, of persons;
    marriage; patriotism

marriage(s)
  caring behavior, 264
  and collective beliefs, values, etc., 15, 257
  and "fusion", 259, 261
  long-lasting, 261
  and the self, 259, 260, 263, 268
  and singularism, 4
  and values, having the same, 189
  unity in, 257
  See also fusion, of persons; love; social unity
member, membership
  blameworthiness, 79n45
  speaking as a, 194
  See also membership guilt, feelings of; social
    group(s)
membership guilt, feelings of, 247
  intelligibility of, 248–50
  Jaspers puzzles over, 250
  relation to collective guilt feelings, 250–1
  See also collective guilt feelings
mentality, collective, 134–5
"moral" matters, various
  arguments, concerns, judgments, 8, 80,
    190–1
  collective judgments, 182n9, 197
  community, 188n21
  judgments, personal,186–8
  philosophers, on promising, 5, 272–3, 296,
    299–302
  police, 202
  power, 404
  principles, norms, 5, 187, 217, 271–8, 404
  "ought", 214
  residual notions of, 222
  See also moral requirement(s); moral
    responsibility; sharing values
moral requirement(s)

characterized, 391–2
dogma regarding, 299, 305, 307, 321
and promises, agreements, 5, 299
as promoting some value, 391
as obligation, 391
and other types of obligation, 8, 304, 321, 392–4
in Scanlon's work on promises, 16, 278–81, 391–2
versus requirements of reason, 64
See also obligation (duty)
moral responsibility
rough account of, 62
backward-looking, 58–9
and causation, 58
forward-looking, 58
freedom and, 61–2
for ignorance, 205
and intention, 62
and knowledge requirement, 62
See also moral responsibility, collective; obligation (duty)
moral responsibility, collective
articulated model of, 60–74, 238–42
and collectives, 59–60, 74, 205, 230
for collective wrongdoing, 60–74, 237–42
different ideas of, 60
in populations of all sizes, 11–12
intelligibility of, 55–6, 236
and joint commitment, 55–6, 75, 238
for past acts, 11, 55–6
and personal responsibility of members, 11, 58, 59, 60, 74–80, 242
responding to, 80
moral wrongdoing
and standing to rebuke, demand, 186–8
See also moral responsibility; obligation (duty)
moralism 5, 8
mutual recognition, 329, 332
and care, concern, respect, 334–5
and co-presence, 324
as collective, 329n13
and social conventions, norms, 333
and the entre nous, 331
example of, 329
and joint attention, 337
in joint commitment formation, 16, 43, 48
important, 48
presupposes, 332–4
process and state, 329n13
and public actions, 330
pure and mixed cases, 332–3

nations
accused of wrongdoing, 229, 235–6
beliefs of, 235
and guilt feelings, 231, 247, 253

and identification, 247
joint commitments within, 353
and unity, 17, 345
See also citizens, citizenship; collective guilt feelings; moral responsibility, collective
"none of my business", 185

obedience, morality of, 411–4
See also command(s)
obligation (duty)
ambiguity of terms, 50, 391
and answerability, 50
associated with agreements, promises, 5, 49, 242–4, 278–81, 298, 299–310, 314–6, 319–20
and content-independence, 314, 402–6, 415–6
genuine versus imputed, 390
of joint commitment, 34–5, 50
as moral requirement, 271, 278, 299, 391–2
non-moral, to do wrong, 35, 121–2, 295, 390
and rights, 34
and social phenomena, 5
types of 34–5, 291, 391–4
See also commitment(s), generally; obligation, directed; moral requirement(s); owing; right(s)
obligation, directed
and agreements, 5, 203, 314, 419
and joint commitment, 34–5, 49–50, 120–1, 312–3, 316–7
and living together, 8
logical correlate of, 34, 50, 109, 275
and owing, 8, 109–11, 276–8, 368, 392
matter of relationship, 8
and moral values, 9
and rights, 8, 34, 50, 109, 275
and social phenomena, science 5, 9
and the standing to demand, rebuke, 5, 8, 34, 108
three elements, 34
two-stage interpretation, 368
See also agreement(s); obligation (duty); owing; rebuke(s); right(s)
Ockham's razor 1, 4
offending against, 216–7
officials, emissaries, 72–4, 252–4
On Social Facts
and important social phenomena, 37, 197
and individualism/holism, 135n13
interprets Durkheim, 132n3
and joint commitment, 1, 11, 37
on mutual recognition, 329n13
on readiness quasi- and joint, 47n39
on social groups as plural subjects, 199, 331
topics included in, 10, 13, 23, 37

open*, openness*, 43
  expressions **made openly***, **46**
  in large populations, 51–2
  See also common knowledge
owing
  account of commands, 414–7, 422
  different senses of term, 110, 417
  a duty, 412, 413
  interpreted, 110, 216, 392–4, 395–7, 417–8
  and joint commitment, 88, 90–1, 400–2, 421
  obedience, 413
  obligation as, 8, 88, 111, 276-8, 368, 392
  overridden, potentially, 413
  payment, 41
  philosophers on, 217n39
  sources of, 421–2
  and the standing to demand, 110, 120, 396–7
  See also demanding, with standing; obligation,
    directed; right(s)

parents, parental influence, 78, 79, 201, 242,
    335–7, 351
patriotism
  and bad polity, 384, 386
  and **basic patriotic motive**, 17, **357**, 360–1,
    362, **365**, 366–70
  and benefits to one's country, 362, 376–7
  dual citizenship and, 381
  and dying for one's country, 372, 379–80
  acts expressive of, 372–81
  and humanitarian concerns, 17
  and love of country, 358, 360–2
  moral status of, 17
  and lack of patriotism, 376, 379, 380
  and one's country, polity, 362–5
  personal protests and, 377
  and pride or its lack, 17, 384
  revolutionaries and, 377
  and **the trumping hypothesis**, **375**, 380
  types of, 360, 381–4
  See also political society
philosophy of social phenomena, social
    ontology, 1
plural subject(s), **9**, **63**, **139**, **331**
  account of collective belief, 139
  and collective form of moral responsibility,
    55–6
  concept of, not singularist, 10
  concerns, misunderstandings about, 9,
    331n18
  general theory of social phenomena, 37, 197
  and melding of parties, 15
  not "over and above" participating individuals,
    9–10
  persistence over generations, 11, 68–9
  versus **singular subjects**, **119**
  and subjectivity, consciousness, 9
  theory of, 37, 57

unitary, indivisible, 56
  vary in character, 63n15
  and "we", 110, 331n18
  See also joint commitment(s), "we"
political institutions, 363
political leaders, 201
  See also rule, ruling
political life, 16
Political Obligation, A Theory of, 11n23, 12n24,
    64n17, 64n23, 66n24, 78n3, 389n1, 390n4,
    390n5, 397n19, 398n22
political obligation(s)
  actual contract theories of, 66n24
  and demands, rebukes, 17, 403
  content-independence of, 18, 402–6
  de-moralized problem of, 389, 390
  Horton's theory of, 343
  obligations, genuine, 390
  and owing, rights, 17, 395–7, 406–8
  and justice, 395
  and morally bad institutions, 390, 402–6
  and moral requirement, 391–2, 395
  plural subject theory of, 402–3
  problem(s) of, 298n5, 389, 395
  interpretations of, 376, 389
  and a political society, nature of, 402
  See also patriotism; *Political Obligation,
    A Theory of*
political philosophy
  association problem in, 261, 341, 345
  and evaluation of patriotism, 357
  and evaluation of political societies, 17
  and moralization of issues, 17
  and philosophy of social phenomena,
    1, 96
  and problem of political obligation, 389
  and shared values, 181, 206, 350
political society
  account of, 362–5, 402
  emissaries of, 72–4, 252–4
  Hobbes on, 16, 18, 67n27, 271, 341
  See also country, one's own; moral
    responsibility, collective; political
    obligation(s)
population, 59–60
pride. *See* patriotism
Principle F, Scanlon's
  consent clause of, 281–2, 284–5, 308
  and moral requirement, 300, 419
  and owing, 308
  and promisees' rights, 282–6, 308
  and promisors' obligations, 291–2
  and a "right to rely", 285–6
  and shared intention, 113, 121
  stated, 281, 300
  and supplementary principles, 289–91
  See also promise(s)
Prisoner's Dilemma, 12, 92, 93, 226n71

promise(s)
acceptance of a, 318
and agreements, close cousins, 271, 297,
     314, 317
and authority of promisee, 276
as **joint decision**, 319
central contemporary approaches, 16
conditional, 42
versus contracts in law, 298
give obligations to the promisee, 318
give rights, 16, 271, 282, 274–8, 290,
     294n38
and the **immoral promises dogma,
     301**, 302–5, 321
versus intention or decision, 297
intuitive points on, 16, 302–3
and "I promise", 296–7
mutual, exchanged, 314–5
and the **moral requirement dogma,
     299**, 305, 307, 321
and the **no willing dogma, 300**, 305, 321
plural subject account of, 16, 42, 46n33
     296, 310–20
and release, promisee's power of, 319
and self-binding, 296
with single promisee, 274n14
and standing to demand, insist, rebuke, 271
three dogmas about, 16, 296
See also agreement(s); promisor, the
     obligation of a
promisor, the obligation of a
and content-independence, 305, 314
is directed, relational, 278, 305–7
and expectations of promisee, 273, 274, 280,
     281, 293
Hume on, 273n11, 294, 300
and immoral promises, 301–2, 302–5
intrinsic to the promise, 319
as joint commitment obligation, 16, 319
and moral requirements, principles, 16, 293,
     299–300
neither moral nor legal, 294–5
owing, a matter of, 278
and personal intentions, 292–3
Prichard's point about, 302–5, 314, 319,
     320, 322
primary, 219
primary and secondary, 291
the problem of, 298
release from, 278
and correlative right of promisee, 275, 278
     290, 291
Scanlon on, 16, 271, 272, 273, 278–87,
     289–93, 299–30, 321
social practice accounts of, 272–4, 294
theorists on, 298
and two senses of "obligation", 298
and standing to insist, rebuke, 278, 282

and the will, 272, 300–1
     See also owing; Principle F; promise(s)
protest, 77, 377
punishment
fear of, 201
informal, 201, 202, 204
and joint commitment, 203
justification of, 202n42
legal, 171n19, 199n35, 202
by "moral police", 202–3
morality of, 202–4
by parents, teachers, etc, 201
and patriotism, 171n19
and personal freedom, 204
philosophical literature on, 202n42
predictable, 172, 201
purported, 171
rebukes as, 171, 199, 202, 277n23
requires standing, 171, 202n42, 210n16

quarreling as a joint action, 27
quasi-readiness, 47n39
questioning someone, 43

racism, 201
rational choice theory, 12, 81, 82, 390
reason, reasoning, reasons
and sense of "bound", 64
human, 82
and **reasons, 3**, 84, **115**
requirement of, 31, 64, 84, 114, 174, 390
sufficient, 64, 114, 390, 401, 420
See also commitment(s) generally; obligations
rebuke(s)
and acting together, 52–4
as after-the-fact demand, 110, 189, 216, 307
and coercive power, 177, 277
and collective belief, 171–2
"entitlement" to issue, 25n8
joint commitment, basis for, 8, 120, 175, 198,
     222–3, 263, 369, 421
for morally right action, 369
and social conventions, 210, 216
and moral norms, principles, 9, 187, 188, 217
and **the no standing claim, 187–8**
and personal moral judgment, 186–8
as punitive, 171, 199, 202, 277n23
and Scanlon's Principle F, 282–6
and sharing values, 188, 198
and shared intention, 108, 111
and obligation, 108. *See also* and rights
purported, 210n16
proper standing required for, 25, 216, 278,
     307, 397
and reason to, 199, 203–4
and rights, 8–9, 25, 52–4, 110, 271, 277
between strangers, 187–8
     See also demanding, with standing

reify, reification, 230
  See also holism, holistic
rejectionism, 132–3
  See also collective belief
reparative action, 15
requirement(s). *See* moral requirement(s);
  reason, reasoning, reasons
right(s)
  in acting together, 24–26, 34–5
  and agreements, promises, 34, 271, 274–8,
    288
  or claims, 109, 275
  to do wrong, 186n20
  and their equivalents, 287–8, 305, 396–7
  Hart's points, 25n7, 274–6, 277
  function of, 286n31
  and interests, 287–8
  joint commitment source of, 35, 222–223,
    294n38, 312–3, 401, 402
  legal, institutional, 295, 396
  liberty-, 109
  moral, 295
  and moral requirements, 396
  to be obeyed, or to rule, 414n17
  and obligations (or duties), directed, 34, 275,
    288, 396
  and owing, 109–10, 276, 306, 396, 400–1
  "to rely", 285–6
  rudeness and, 54
  and shared intention, 109
  sources of, 295, 400
  special versus general, 276
  and standing to demand, rebuke, 25, 34, 110,
    111, 271, 277–8
  technical senses of term, 287, 288
  theories of, 109, 286, 287–8, 295
  and use of force, 277
  valuable possessions, 295
  waiving, 275, 288
  See also obligation, directed; promise(s);
    rebuke(s)
rudeness, 54
rule, ruling
  establishing, 67–8
  of person or body, 67
  personal 363, 367
  See also command(s)
rules, social,
  and agreements, social acceptance, 274, 290
  versus collective values, 204–5
  conventions as, 220, 333n21
  Hart on, 94
  and joint commitment, 33, 118, 347
  regarding promising, 289
  and rights, 54, 68, 54n66, 54n68, 290
  rule, of governance, constitutional rule,
    351, **363**, 367
  See also social convention(s)

self, **ego,** 259, **261**
  See also fusion, of persons
shared (joint, collective) intention, 12–13
  and agreements, 89, 98–9, 104, 112
  agreement, without, 99, 113
  Bratman's account, 4, 12, 101–2, 106, 113
  changing, rescinding a, 107–8
  and coercion, 112
  concurrence criterion, 12, 106–7, 120, 126
  core conditions for, 111
  disjunction criterion, 12, 102–6, 120, 126
  future-directed, 12, 98
  immoral, 113, 121–2
  joint commitment approach, 12, 69–70, 83,
    181
  obligation criterion, 12, 108–113, 120–1,
    126
  and participatory intentions, 230
  personal intentions perspective, 12, 101,
    105, 107, 108, 112–3
  plural subject account of, 114–20, 121,
    122–6
  puzzle about, 99–101
  and rights, 109–11, 112
  sentences, 97–8, 100
  singularist accounts, 4, 101
  and standing to demand, rebuke, 109–11
  and sub-plans, personal and joint, 122–4
  target for an account, 100, 105
  See also **singularist intentions**
sharing values
  reduces *anomie,* 201
  as a collective act, 182n9
  and collective belief, 184n13
  as **collective sharing, 200**
  and common knowledge of personal values,
    190–1
  complex summative account of, 191
  effects of, 205
  different conceptions of, 182, 183, 184–5
  frames choices, 201
  genesis of, 196
  and harm to others, 203
  joint commitment, plural subject account,
    182, 191, 192, 197
  liberty, diminishes 14, 201, 202–3
  morality of enforcement, 202–4
  and norm permitting "rebukes", 192n23
  and "our" values, 197
  and personal values, 195
  or just one value, 200
  singularist, individualist accounts of, 182, 191,
    192n23
  and social unity, bonds, 14, 181, 184n13, 185,
    186, 189–90, 197, 199
  social unity question, 182, 200
  and standing to intervene, 185–6, 188, 191,
    201

summative account of, **184**–6, 188–190
  and valuing, 183
  See also collective belief, social unity
singularism 2–**4, 45, 182**
  in accounts of sharing values, 182, 191
  beyond, 4, 6, 10, 191–2
  aka **individualism**, 207
  and personal commitments, 45
  problems with, 4, 5
  Weber as singularist 18
  See also **individualism; singularist intentions**
singularist intentions, 99–100, 115n46
  in account of shared intention, 101–2
  versus personal intentions, 99–100
  shared intention without, 119–20
  See also **singularist assumption**
singularist assumption, 99–**100**
social concepts, central, 30
social convention(s)
  may be started by agreement, 209, 333
  and arbitrariness, 220–1
  the **collectivity criterion, 215**
  consequential, 14
  and "conventional means", 215n35
  and coordination problems, personal
    preferences, 15
  criteria of adequacy for an account, 14, 210,
    214, 215, 220–1, 225
  "cutting across" societies, 215–6
  evaluating accounts of, 227
  examples of, 209–10
  immoral, 14, 225
  as jointly accepted fiat, 218
  joint commitment and, 218–9
  versus (social) moral principle, 220
  and mutual recognition, 333
  normativity of, 214
  and offense against parties, 210
  the **offense criterion, 210,** 216–7
  the **appropriate "ought" criterion, 214**
  as "our" convention, 4, 209
  and owing conformity, 216–7
  procedural, 54
  realism of accounts, 226
  as social rules, 220
  and special rights, 217
  and specific protections, 209–10
  and standing to demand, rebuke, 216–7
  starting points on, 209–10
  See also social convention, Lewis on; social
    conventions, the joint acceptance account
social convention, the joint acceptance account
  and accepting a fiat, 219
  and appropriate-"ought" criterion, 222–5
  and arbitrariness of convention, 220–221
  and collectivity criterion, 221–2
  and "coming to an understanding", 222

  and conformity, expectations, 218, 225
  and conventions from agreements, 221
  not game-theoretic, 218
  holist, non-individualist, 217, 225–6
  and immoral conventions, 225
  "joint acceptance" in, 218
  invokes joint commitment, 14, 217–9
  and Lewis's account, 225–7
  and offence criterion, 222–3
  parties not "moralized", 225n69
  and social rules, 220
  See also social convention(s)
social convention, Lewis on, 3, 24
  and adoption by agreement, 213, 221
  and arbitrariness, 220n54
  and collectivities, 215–6
  and coordination problems, 211, 213
  critics of, 212n24
  and established concept, 207, 208
  and expectation, 213
  individualism of, 207
  Lewis's account, 211–2
  and Lewisian accounts, 207n1
  and the "ought" of convention, 214
  and "preferences", 212
  problems for, 212–3
  and putative counterexamples, 208n13
  and qualifier "social", 207–8
  and rebukes, demands, 216
  describes self-perpetuating system, 4
  and "recurrence", 212
  and "regularities", 211–2
  and word meanings, language, 207–8, 222
  See also social convention(s)
social epistemology, 132, 165
social group(s)
  and affectivity, 230
  versus aggregates, 59
  as body of persons, 119n56
  change in features, members, 67
  characterless, 332
  co-extensive, 170–7
  constituted by social groups, 352
  cross-time identity of, 80
  examples of, 59, 181–2, 229
  freedom of action of, 72–4
  fundamental kind of, 332
  hierarchy in, 67
  improving, 231
  and individuals, 67, 143
  and joint commitment, 17, 67, 199–200, 349
  both large and small, 17
  large and complex, 181–2
  and mutual recognition, 324, 332
  as plural subjects. *See* and joint commitment
  population, species of, 60, 165, 237
  positive aspects of, 61
  pressure on members of, 74

social group(s) (*Cont.*)
  richly textured, 67
  societies as, 181, 403
  "teams" as, 59n3
  victims of, 231, 256
  pleasures of, 55n71
  and "we", 165n2
  See also aggregate(s); joint commitment(s);
    social unity; society, societies
social, human sciences, 3, 335–6
  interpretive versus descriptive, 2–3, 4, 227
social unity, union
  agglomerations of nation-states and, 17, 181,
    341
  appeals to a contract, 17, 345–6
  authors on, 182–3, 342–5
  binding people together, 183
  classic texts on, 67n27, 341, 345
  and a common morality, 182–3
  coordination and, 4
  explaining, 5–6, 17
  identical values and, 188–9
  joint commitment and, 17, 67, 197–8,
    346–53
  on large scale, 4
  objectivist stance, 344
  and qualitative identity, 189, 190
  shared values and, 181–3, 190, 197
  singularism and, 4
  and societies, social groups, 181–2
  stable, solid kind, 189, 200
  and standing to intervene,188–9
  subjective conceptions of, 17, 342–4
  substantial, 190
  superficial kind of, 189
  Taylor on, 182n9
  See also sharing values; we
social relationships. *See* social group(s), social
  unity
social rules. *See* rules, social
social world, the, 4
sociality, 324
society, societies,
  free, 203
  and loss of freedom, 202
  See also political society, social group(s)
strangers, 186, 187–8
sufficient reason, having, 114, **214**
suicide, 201n40
supra-individualism, holism, 9

telling someone off. *See* rebuke(s), etc.
"They did it", 79n46. *See also* "we"
tradition, account of, 220

trust, 267

unity. *See* social unity

walking together, i.e. going for a walk together,
  10, 24–5, 54
  See also acting together
war
  and group action, 246
  just, theory of, 241
  and patriotism, 372–3, 379–80
  personal innocence in, 245
  pressure to participate in, 242
  responsibility for, 235–6
"we"
  and view of agreements, 315
  believe, intend, value, and so on, 4, 65, 70, 77,
    136, 197, 264, 331
  collective uses of, 331n18
  distributive use of, 21
  emphasized, 94–5
  and emotions (pride, guilt), 343, 385.
  exclusive versus inclusive, 89n46
  formation, 264, 341–2
  and fusion, merging, 262
  and groups, 169n2, 249, 265
  and Hi-Lo game, 101n25
  includes self, 77, 79
  initiatory, tendentious uses, 219, 353
  and intentions, 100
  ignored, 94
  and joint commitment, 89, 110, 264, 331n18,
    385
  part of a, 262
  and past misdeeds of group, 21, 79–80
  and "plural subject", 110
  richly textured, 266
  semantics of, 21, 262n13, 328
  See also "I" perspective; plural subject(s);
    social group(s)
will, human
  can be capricious, 35
  "conditional commitment" of, 46–7
  commitment, source of, 6, 7, 12, 35, 64,
    83, 420
  and expressing willingness, readiness,
    33n21, 47, 48
  lien on, 198
  and obligation, 273n11, 294, 300–1, 305, 321
  of parties to a joint commitment, 35
  See also commitment(s), of the will, joint
    commitment(s)

Index prepared with the help of Philip Walsh

NAME INDEX

Adams, John Quincy, 382
Adenauer, Konrad, 236n14
Altham, J., 301n14, 304n20
Anderson, Benedict, 51n53
Anscombe, Elizabeth, 70, 297n2, 301n14, 303n18, 304n20 414n17
Arneson, Richard, 287n33,
Austin, J.L., 297

Bach, Kent, 28n13, 43n20, 315n46
Bacharach, Michael, 59, 96n11
Balibar, Etienne, 341n1
Baltzer, Ulrich, 43n22, 51–2
Bardsley, Nicholas, 101n25
Barnum, Priscilla, 169n14
Baron-Cohen, Simon, 335n27
Bittner, Rudiger, 30n17, 53–5
Bentham, Jeremy, 287n32
Beran, Harry, 303n16
Bloch, Maurice, 178n40
Bouvier, Alban, 72n35, 166n7
Bowen, Murray, 260
Brandt, Richard, 185, 275n17
Bratman, Michael, 4, 12–3, 24n5, 53n62, 53n64, 71n34, 81, 89, 95, 97, 98n19, 100n20, 100n22, 101–2, 104–5, 107n32, 109n34, 112–3, 119n57, 121n61, 122–5, 132, 142n27, 192n23, 230n4, 236
Brink, David, 289n34
Broome, John, 174n26, 366n19

Cavell, Edith, 375n37
Clark, Austen, 144n29
Cohen, Gerald, A. 140n23
Cohen, Jonathan, 132, 133n7
Cook, Michael, 204n48
Corlett, Angelo, 166n7

Darwall, Stephen, 217n40
Dennett, Daniel, 144n29

Devlin, Lord Patrick, 182–3, 185–6, 188, 197–8, 199–200, 203n47, 205–6, 350
Dickens, Charles, 21
Doestoevsky, Fyodor, 129
Durkheim, Emile, 18, 67n27, 95n4, 131–2, 157, 160, 166, 167n9, 171, 177, 201, 209n15

Ebbs, Gary, 414n18
Eichmann, Adolph, 409–11, 425
Eliot, George, 209
Engel, Pascal, 142n27, 158

Feinberg, Joel, 61, 109–10, 244n30, 279n24, 303n16, 306, 335n26, 368n29, 397, 417, 418n26
Frank, Robert, 83
Fuller, Lon, 269n23

Galston, William, 283n27
Gaylin, Willard, 259–60, 261n10
Green, Leslie, 415n19, 416n21

Hampton, Jean, 415, 416n21
Hart, H.L.A., 25n7, 54n66, 94, 109, 171n19, 182n9, 202n42, 203n47, 220n52, 222n62, 271n4, 274–7, 279n24, 287, 306, 333n21, 350n26, 368n28, 392n9, 400n27, 412n10, 415, 417n22
Hegel, Georg, 324
Hennig, Boris, 55, 56n72
Hobbes, Thomas, 16, 18, 67n27, 89, 341
Hofstadter, Douglas, 257
Hohfeld, Wesley N., 109n36, 275, 276n18, 295
Hollis, Martin, 82, 89
Horace, (Quintus Horatius Flaccus), 357, 379
Horton, John, 343, 344n10
Hume, David, 4, 189, 272–3, 294, 297n2, 300–1, 305n22,

Ingram, Attracta, 362n11

Jacobs, Dirk, 341, 343
Jamieson, Dale, 212n24
Jaspers, Karl, 58n1, 61n6, 76, 247–50

Kamm, Frances, 285n30, 393n10
Keller, Simon, 358n4, 361n9
Kenny, Anthony, 174n27
Korsgaard, Christine, 90
Kripke, Saul, 327n8
Kutz, Christopher, 102n28, 229–30, 232, 236–7, 243
Kymlicka, Will, 181n1, 182, 184, 185n14, 190

Laitinen, Arto, 324n1, 325n3, 330n15, 330n16
Lawrence, D.H., 259–60
Lefkowitz, David, 389n1, 406n37
Lehrer, Keith, 132
Lenman, James, 192n23
Lewis, David, 2–4, 29n15, 51n54, 52n57, 81, 86n11, 94, 95n3, 96n9, 139n21, 166n5, 191, 207–9, 210n17, 211–22, 225–27, 284n29, 325n4, 348n19.
Lewis, H. D., 61n6
Lindgren, Ralph, 259n4, 269n23
Little, Maggie, 318
Locke, John, 339

MacCormick, D.N., 287n32, 300n10
MacMahon, Christopher, 72n35, 102n28, 166n7, 179n43
Maier, Robert, 341, 343
Marmor, Andrei, 212n24, 215, 216n36, 220n52, 221n54
Maslow, A.H., 259–60
May, Larry, 229n2, 248n36, 250n37
McCullers, Carson, 268
McInnes, Mairi, 169n14
Meijers, Anthonie, 72n35, 133n8, 134n11, 142n27, 145–8, 150–5, 158, 166n7, 178n41
Milgram, Stanley, 410–11, 424–5
Mill, John S., 186n20, 202–4
Miller, David, 389n1
Miller, Kaarlo, 49n44, 49n47, 95, 100n20, 101n25
Miller, Seumas, 53n62, 212n24, 230n4, 237
Millikan, Ruth, 160n63, 212n24, 221n56
Morris, Herbert, 231n6, 247

Nussbaum, Martha, 233, 234n12

Oldenquist, Andrew, 369n43, 384n50
Owen, Wilfred, 357n1, 379n43
Owens, David, 299n9

Paine, Thomas, 383
Peacocke, Christopher, 337n32
Pettit, Phillip, 166n7

Piazza, Gianguido, 166n7
Plath, Sylvia, 168
Plato, 92, 143, 259, 260n6, 268, 345, 369, 378, 389, 394, 423
Pratt, Michael, 292n37
Preyer, Gerhard, 166n7
Primoratz, Igor, 357n2, 358n4, 360, 362n10, 376n38, 381n46
Prichard, H.A., 272, 274n12, 292n37, 303–5, 309–10, 314, 319–20, 322

Quine, W.V.O., 220n54
Quinton, Anthony, 136n15, 168n12, 184n13

Rawls, John, 182–3, 300n10
Raz, Joseph, 271n4, 272n5, 287–8, 297n2, 299n6, 300n10, 301n12, 301n14, 303n17, 306n23, 396n17, 414n17, 415–6, 417n23
Robins, Michael, 4n8, 42, 44, 46, 49, 212n24, 225n68, 272n4, 273n10, 274n12, 292n37, 294n38, 306n23, 309n30
Rosenberg, Jay, 95n6
Ross, W. D., 424
Roth, Abraham, 37n1, 102n28, 115n47, 166n7, 179n43
Rousseau, Jean-Jacques, 18, 19n35, 89, 181n3, 250, 341, 345, 385

Scanlon, Thomas, 16, 71n34, 89n16, 113, 121, 216n38, 217n39, 271–4, 277n23, 278–83, 285–6, 288–94, 299–300, 308, 321, 391, 392n8, 393n10, 396n17, 419
Schelling, Thomas, 3, 207n1
Schiffer, Stephen, 29n15, 51n54, 52n57, 139n21, 166n5, 212n24, 325n4
Schmitt, Fredrick, 72n35, 150n42, 166n7
Schutz, Alfred, 81
Searle, John, 24n5, 53n64, 71n34, 81, 89, 95, 99, 100n20, 101n25, 115n46, 119n57, 230n4, 289n35, 299n6, 303n16, 342–3, 351n28, 362n11
Sellars, Wilfrid, 95, 99, 100n20, 101n25, 230n4, 343n6
Shaffer, Jerome, 233n10, 234n12
Shakespeare, William, 359n5, 386n53, 424, 425n42
Shiffrin, Seana, 299
Sillari, Giacomo, 95n3, 211n19, 325n4
Simmel, Georg, 18, 95n4
Simmons, A. John, 186n20, 202n42, 344n10, 389n2, 390n7, 403n34
Smith, Thomas, 118n55
Socrates, 345, 369, 378, 423n38
Sorokin, Pitirim, 259, 261–2, 265n18
Spooner, Lysander, 377
Stalnaker, Robert, 132, 133n6, 134n11, 146n34

Stein, Gertrude, 194
Sugden, Robert, 82, 89, 96n11, 101n25

Taylor, Charles, 94, 165, 166n5, 182n9, 183n9, 185n14, 324–8, 331–2
Taylor, Gabriele, 243
Thomson, Judith, 300n10, 307n27
Thomson, Michael, 396n17
Tollefsen, Deborah, 72n35, 165n4, 166n7, 179n43
Tomasello, Michael, 335–6
Tummolini, Luca, 221n55
Tuomela, Raimo, 42n14, 49n44, 50n51, 72n35, 89n15, 95, 100n20, 101n25, 102n28, 133n8, 153n49, 166n7

Upton, Hugh, 276n18

Vanderschraaf, Peter, 95n3, 211n19, 225n4
Van Fraassen, Bas, 132

Velleman, David, 42, 43n25, 45n33, 89n15, 101n24
Verbeek, Bruno, 114n44, 309n30, 366n19
Vitek, William, 23n14, 280n25, 319n50

Waldron, Jeremy, 186, 283n27, 389n1
Wallace, Jay R., 244, 300n10
Walzer Michael, 181n1, 241n24, 371, 380
Weber, Max, 2, 18, 95n4, 96, 227, 265n18, 351, 363
Wertheimer, Roger 186n20
Wilkins, Burleigh, 74n38, 236n14
Williams, Bernard, 143n28, 145, 146n34, 153, 155
Winch, Peter, 95n4
Wittgenstein, Ludwig, 38n3, 260
Wolff Robert, 411–4, 425
Wray, K. Brad, 72n35, 133, 134n11, 148n38, 150n44, 151n47, 166n7

Names index compiled with the help of Maura Priest and Philip Walsh